Accent ANTHOLOGY

Accent

ANTHOLOGY

Selections from *Accent,*
A Quarterly of New
Literature, 1940-1945

Edited by

KERKER QUINN *and*

CHARLES SHATTUCK

Essay Index Reprint Series

BOOKS FOR LIBRARIES PRESS
FREEPORT, NEW YORK

indexed in SSI

INTERNATIONAL STANDARD BOOK NUMBER:
0-8369-2302-2

LIBRARY OF CONGRESS CATALOG CARD NUMBER:
70-156601

PRINTED IN THE UNITED STATES OF AMERICA

EDITORS' NOTE

Pleased as we are to have this opportunity to give a fuller and more lasting circulation to writing that was threatened with eclipse by the exhaustion of our supply of back issues of ACCENT, we regret the impracticability of making the anthology larger than it is. And we must, in fairness to contributors whose work is partly or wholly omitted, comment on our procedure in cutting down the first five volumes of the quarterly to approximately 40 per cent of their original bulk.

Aside from customary editorial considerations—the abiding interest, the length, and the variety of contributions—certain arbitrary principles of selection have been set up and followed as faithfully as possible. For instance, our decision to limit each contributor of prose to a single story or essay has been enforced with but one exception, despite the difficulty of determining which of three articles by Kenneth Burke to use, which of three stories by Walter Van Tilburg Clark, which of two sketches by Katherine Anne Porter, and so on. The rationing of poetry, though not based on the single-selection rule, has often necessitated our reprinting but a fraction of a poet's available work.

No writer has been admitted to more than one of the three sections of the anthology, although Richard Eberhart, W. Y. Tindall, R. P. Blackmur, Brewster Ghiselin, Ankey Larrabee, Horace Gregory, Nicholas Moore, and others were eligible for inclusion under more than one heading.

Several authors—such as Thomas Mann, William March, John Dos Passos, and John Crowe Ransom—are not represented here at all because their contributions have since been embodied in popular books of their own. And our failure to make room for more than a handful of book reviews has resulted in the omission of criticism by Marianne Moore, Haakon M. Chevalier, Robert

Penn Warren, Eliseo Vivas, Stanley Edgar Hyman, Winfield T. Scott, Lincoln Kirstein, Allen Tate, John V. Kelleher, Austin Warren, S. I. Hayakawa, Herbert J. Muller, and a score of others whose judgments have given substance to individual issues of ACCENT and would have been welcomed by readers of the anthology.

Most of all we regret the impossibility of representing *every one* of the younger writers, many appearing in print for the first time, whose work imparts to ACCENT, as to all literary magazines, the freshness and balance which are essential to its health.

For generous participation in the labors and pleasures of publishing the quarterly we are indebted to Kenneth Andrews, W. R. Moses, W. McNeil Lowry, Robert Bauer, Arthur J. Carr, Marion Carr, Donald Hill, Helen Hill, Allan Holaday, John Schacht, Keith Huntress, Thomas Bledsoe, the late Earl Oliver, Kay Peer, Paul Proehl, Verne Purcell, Lura Williams, Sally Jauch, Peggy Bachman, Morton Moskov, Carl Hartman, and Glen Park. And we make grateful acknowledgment to the authors for permission to reprint their work. The responsibility for compiling this anthology lies with the undersigned.

KERKER QUINN
CHARLES SHATTUCK

Urbana, Illinois

CONTENTS

II. POETRY

III. CRITICAL PROSE

I

NARRATIVE PROSE

SIDNEY ALEXANDER:

THE WHITE BOAT

ELLIE MAE ironed the last wrinkle out of the last shirt and sighed. Done, thank the Lord, the long day dusted and washed and folded away. She kicked the legs from under the ironing board and stood it in the closet. The late afternoon sun was slanting almost level through the windows, glowed red on the waxed mahogany desk, burst into green flowers on the broad-loom.

Ellie hurried to the hall closet and slipped out of her smock. Five-thirty; now if she could only get out of the house before Mrs. Raymond returned. How that woman could talk! And the obligation of polite interest, the murmured acknowledgments, the yes ma'am, yes ma'am. Oh she wouldn't bother with the zipper, it never worked anyway. She grabbed the paper bag with the hand-me-down-shoes and started for the door. Then she remembered. She rushed back to the living room and snatched the two folded bills from under the baboon paper-weight. She was just reaching for the doorknob when Mrs. Raymond walked in.

"Hello Ellie!" she said, glancing quickly around. "My you're fast today."

"Yes ma'am."

"Sit down a minute." She went into her bedroom and the voice continued. "I meant to phone but I was stuck there under the dryer. You know, these hairdressers, they putter so. Anyway, I met Mrs. Meyers . . ." The disk was interrupted by the splash of water. Ellie sat at the edge of the chair still clutching the paper-bag. Lord, lord, the electric clock showed twenty-two of six . . .

3

". . . so there I was with the whole affair dumped in my lap. Calling me at the last minute like that. Some people simply have no consideration."

She was coming in now: the white terry robe swollen with the figure, the sandy-gray hair rhythmically set. She grimaced at her teeth in the mirror.

"Four would be the best, I think. I'll have the dinner ready then, and you can start serving at once."

"What, ma'am?" Ellie said with a start. She had been staring at the clock.

"Good Heavens, Ellie! Don't you *ever* listen? My Mah-Jongg club'll be here again tomorrow. It's not really *my* turn but Mrs. Meyers said *her* girl is sick and no one else could take it. So what could I do?" She smiled benevolently. "Anyway, you'll make some extra money."

"Thank you, Mizz Raymond," Ellie murmured and got up to leave, "but I'm afraid I cain't do it."

"You what?"

"I cain't do it . . . I made other 'rangements fo' tomorrow."

"Good heavens, Ellie!" She plumped down on the sofa, petulant as a child. "Now what am I to do? Where am I to get a girl?"

"I'll get someone fo' you . . ." Ellie began.

"Well, I never . . ." She flounced her shoulder impatiently, and then, slowly, the incongruous pout melted away. "I suppose it *is* rather at the last minute, Ellie. But I'd rather have *you* than an outsider. After all, you've been with me for years. You know best how we want things."

"I appreciates that, ma'am, but . . ."

"Oh break your date, whoever he is!"

"It ain't a he, ma'am," Ellie said, glancing at the clock in horror. "I really got to go now . . . I . . . I'll send another girl. Don't you worry. G'night, Mizz Ray."

"Ellie . . ." the voice scratched and clung like a claw.

"Yes ma'am?"

"I see you've got the shoes."

She turned slowly around.

"Yes ma'am. Ain't they fo' me?"

"Of course," Mrs. Raymond laughed. "I merely wondered if they'd fit all right."

"Oh they do fine, thanks, they don't need much fixin'."

Mrs. Raymond looked at the paper bag. "I wish you'd change your mind about tomorrow."

"That's impossible." If she don't stop, I'll throw the shoes in her face, Ellie thought, I swear to God I will. What she tryin' to do?

"My, I've never seen you in such a hurry."

"Well ma'am, I got to be uptown by six-thirty. I got somethin' special . . ."

"You know, my dear, extra money doesn't grow on trees."

"I know that, ma'am."

"After all, I *did* take you off relief," the woman went on with exasperating deliberation. "I think I've been good enough to you. I haven't been a nag. And now, when I ask you for a special favor, just once, you can't do it. Really, Ellie, I'm surprised. I . . . I feel just a little hurt."

Behind the impassive brown face, the cords of anger tightened. She stood in the foyer by the door, saying nothing, the paper bag clasped to the cheap gingham dress.

"What's all this about tomorrow, anyway?"

"A pers'nal matter," Ellie said abruptly. She could tell her but why should she? What business was it of hers? I've got my own life to lead, she thought.

She reached out for the door knob, and added softly: "Please, Mizz Raymond. I don't want to lose my job. I cain't afford that. Any other time I be glad to work extra. But tomorrow I just cain't. Don't worry 'bout the party. I'll get someone experience'. I know lots o' girls . . ."

She looks like a pot ready to boil, Ellie thought, as she stepped cautiously out the door.

The Odd Fellows Hall was crowded as a subway station when she got there. They were milling around the cashier's window and the perspiring clerk was shouting: "No, they's all gone!

Now will y'all *please* get out!" Ellie shoved her way to the window and waved a dollar bill frantically in Charlie Walker's face. He spotted her and reached into the drawer.

"Lucky fo' you," he said, sliding the tickets under the grill. "Ah could've sold 'em ten times ovah. Ah said to myself, ef she don' show up in five mo' minutes, Ah sells 'em—reserve or no reserve. *Man*, looks like ev'body's goin' on this yere ride!"

She grinned triumphantly and slipped the tickets in her purse. As she was shouldering her way out, several men shouted: "How much y'askin' foh 'em sistuh? . . . Ah gives yuh two-fifty, what d'yuh say? . . ."

She shrank away from their smiling familiarity and, with her lips set primly, broke through the crowd and out into Lenox Avenue. It had been a stifling day but now the sun had gone down and the street lay in the shade like a swimmer under water. The gray monotonous barracks of the tenements had emptied out, and before every hallway and store little groups were clustered. Ellie heard their voices—talking about the weather and the ballgames, relief and rent and war and the Brown Bomber and the price of butter. She liked to walk on Lenox Avenue; it was a dancing happy street, and now it just suited her mood. The voices all about her were soft and comforting as a familiar bed. She sank back into her own, and suddenly the thought of Mrs. Raymond came to her, like a spur.

She turned west on 137th street, hurrying with the task to be done. As she had expected, Clara's father was sitting on the camp chair on the stoop, his crutches up against the building wall. He was chatting with the janitor.

"Hello, Ellie Mae!" the old man greeted her.

"Hello, Mist' Adams. How y'all feelin' today?"

"Purty good thank yuh. This hot weathuh's good fo' th' arthritis."

"Yeah . . ." She glanced around the street. "Daughter Clara round?"

"Naw. She be back fo' suppuh. Ain't no fit company, anyhow. She's boilin' mad. Waited all mohnin' over t' Odd Fellows 'n then told they was no mo' tickets."

"I've got mine," Ellie couldn't help announcing.

"Me too," the janitor put in, grinning so widely that his spotted gums showed.

"Y' all's lucky." He sighed and shook his old head. "She wanted to go real bad. She sick'n tired hanging round. Gits on a young gal's nerves. *Ah* don't care, Ah cain't go anyway. Not with these laigs," he added, patting his thighs.

"They's some kinda rumor floatin' round," the janitor said, " 'bout phony tickets bein' sold."

"I don't know nothin' 'bout that," Ellie said grimly. "I paid good American money fo' mine."

"Well, phony or no phony," the janitor went on, "ain't *nobody* gonna keep me offa that boat. No *suh!* I ain't been on a ride fo' years. Ef the ticket is phony, that's *their* lookout."

He went down the cellar steps and as he disappeared, the old man turned to her with a pleading expression: "Ellie Mae, kin yuh spare a coupla dollahs? Clara spent our last relief fo' duh food stamps, 'n now they done turn out duh gas. We gets our nex' check duh fifteenth. We kin pay yuh then."

"I'm sorry," Ellie explained gently, putting her hand on his shoulder. She could feel his sharp bone through the shirt. "I've been puttin' a little aside each week fo' the tickets. That's how come I got 'em. Only paid the last installment just now. But I tell you what," she added quickly as he frowned. "That's why I came over. I got a job fo' Clara fo' tomorrow. That is, if she's free . . ."

"Oh she's free all right. She's boilin' mad because she's so free."

"Well, here's the address," Ellie said, writing it on the back of an envelope. "Tell her to be there promptly at fo'. She's a crab, this Mizz Raymond, but she pays good."

He took the envelope and nodded.

"So long, Mist' Adams."

"So long, Ellie Mae."

"Have a good time!" he shouted after her, waving his crutch. "What? . . . Yeah, Ah tells her . . . promptly at fo' . . ."

✦

She was humming a little tune as she approached the house, her mind clean and ordered now as the apartment she had toiled in all day. Tonight she and Ruby would make sandwiches and wrap them in wax paper. Hard boiled eggs and fried chicken and tuna. Yeah, the kids better get to bed by nine, she thought. Then they could all get down to the pier bright and early. The best seats were at the bow. No wind. Port and aft, she thought, I wonder what it means. Port like wine. Oh it would be fun all right: her legs stretched out on the deck chair, sun on her face and the green land sliding by . . .

The brakes squealed like a woman in pain and she spun around and saw a cluster of skinny brown legs scattering in all directions. The truck driver's red face was stuck out of the cab and he was shouting: "Yuh goddam kids! Why don't yuh watch what yer doin'?" From stoops and hallways came jeers and whistles. Ellie Mae saw a small boy leaping like a monkey on the brownstone stoop, taunting the truck driver. She walked over and slapped the boy's face.

"Aw ma, what'sa big idea?"

"G'wan upstairs!" she said. "I told you not to play with these hoodlums."

More whistles and hoots, this time directed at her. "Roy, Roy, th' momma's boy! Yaaah! Yaah!" A rotten potato whistled past her head.

"Now git away from here, yuh no-good niggers," she shouted, "or I'll slap the bottoms of every one of yuh!" She pushed Roy ahead of her, into the house.

"Where's yo' cousins?" she asked.

"I don't know," Roy said angrily.

"What yuh mean yuh don't know? Weren't they home when you came back from school?"

"Aw, I don't know where they is."

"How many times I tell yuh to play in the playground, not in the street?"

"Playground's too far."

The wooden steps creaked and in the blackness of the hall they felt the sullen anger shrouding them, keeping them apart. Ellie heard the boy sniffling. She felt around for the lock, pushed open the door and switched on the light. Roy went over to the open dumb waiter shaft and started fiddling with the ropes.

"Keep away from there!" she said sharply. "You wanna fall down and break yo' neck!"

"Aw, jeez, I cain't do *nothin'* round here."

She looked at his face and suddenly felt sorry at this bitter homecoming. She put her arm around his shoulder and added gently: "Tain't that, son. I don't want you to get hurt, that's all. That's why I don't want you to play in the street. That's why I want you to stay with Ronnie 'n Lucy."

"What I gonna do with girls?" he replied, roughly pulling his shoulder out of her embrace. "What you want me to do? Play dolls till you'n Aunt Ruby come back? 'Sides," he added maliciously, "they don't stay home either."

"What do you mean?"

"Aw nothin'. Ast them."

"Well, never mind. Go in an' wash yo' face."

What they up to now? she thought angrily as she was setting the table. Slidin' down the same hill as they mother? It's easy enough fo' the men. Have a good time an' leave. Leave you with the misery . . . She remembered Abram, the way he used to laugh. Yeah, an' what I got now? Never sent a dime fo' the boy. If I ever find him . . . An' that no-count bum of Ruby's. They all alike. I got to talk to Ruby 'bout the girls. What good that do, though? Ruby ain' got no sense, never did have.

Now, where's the butter at? You'd think those girls be grown up enough to help a little. Looka the place. Didn't even make the beds. Lord, what I suppose to do—work all day cleanin' other people's houses 'n then come home 'n clean my own?

She heard them stomping up the stairs in unison. Hip hip, HOP, hip hip, HOP. They came bursting in the door giggling, their little budlike breasts shaking in the middy blouses.

"Lo, Aunt Ellie," Veronica said, kissing her on the cheek. Lucy was strutting back and forth before the boy lifting her knees high like a drum majorette, singing a march tune.

"Where you two been?"

"Oh auntie, don' be mad. They was a tryout over t' school for cheerleaders. Lucy's goin' to be a major drum. Lookit 'er strut! BOOM BOOM BOOM! . . ."

"Good Lord, stop that racket! You wake up the dead! An' how many times I tell you to stay with Roy till we gets home? He mos' got killed 'count o' you."

Lucy looked at the boy and said: "He don' look dead to me. Hey Roy, you dead?" she added, tickling the back of his neck.

"Aw lemme alone!"

"Stop it, Lucy. Go in an' clean yo' room. An' you cut the bread. Yo' momma'll be home in a minute." She looked at the girls busy at their tasks, and relaxed. The boy was just bein' mean, that's all. They good girls. Cain't expect 'em to watch the boy every afternoon. They got young blood. Still, that truck . . .

She glanced at the girl working beside her at the table; the shining bronze-black hair, the warm flush of skin, the serious expression as she wielded the knife. She's pretty, Ellie thought, she looks like her mother, thank God, not like him. Ronnie started to whistle.

"Yo' mother know you got lipstick on?"

"She should know," the girl laughed. "She give it to me. Oh Auntie Ellie, you so old fashioned." She hugged her tightly. "Mmmm! We gonna have a time tomorrow!"

"Yeah . . . Lucy use it too?"

"What? Lipstick? Naw . . ." She flung her hair back. "She ain't fifteen yet."

The door opened and Ruby slouched in, her hips working under the tight cheap coat. "Hy! Ellie Mae. Lo, Ronnie."

"Lo, momma," the girl said coolly and went on helping her aunt.

"Jeez, what a day," Ruby said, slipping off her hat and touching up her hair with a weary automatic gesture. "Damn subway." She flopped into a chair, stretched both legs out, examined their shape a moment, unhooked the wide copper-studded belt and took the jangling brass spirals off her ears. "Stick they elbows eve'y which way. Cain't hardly breathe. Sweat all day in a laundry. Sweat home in a subway. Gawd . . . Lo, Lucy," she added, breaking out in a bright smile.

"Well, go git washed," Ellie said. "Supper's ready."

And now they all sat around their evening meal, dipping bread into the deep plates of reheated stew, and they talked about the small events that made up each one's day. Only Roy sat glumly until he heard his mother mention the boat-ride tickets, then suddenly he was jumping up and down in his chair . . .

"Whoo! Whoo! I'm comin' round the bend!"

"You gonna git bend right over my knee if you don't finish that stew."

Ruby laughed in her heavy way. "You ain't got no fun in yo' soul, Ellie. I sometimes wonder how you got him at all."

Ellie glared at her.

"I don't think it's fun to talk that way in front of children."

The two girls were hurriedly sopping up the stew. They glanced at each other over the spoons.

"You don't think *nothin's* fun."

A lot she knows, Ellie thought as she cleared away the dishes, she don't care 'bout nothin' but galavantin'. If it wasn't for the kids, I'd take a sleep-in job. But who I gonna leave 'em with, *her?*

"Coupla new fellahs at our place," Ruby said. "They really solid." She lit a cigarette and slowly exhaled the smoke through her nostrils. Lucy watched her with fascination. All her movements flowed as if there were only roundnesses in her life and no sharp edges.

"They both comin'," Ruby added shyly. "I dated one of 'em fo' you. He gotta good job so yo' betta be nice."

"Yeah, that's all I'm worryin' about," Ellie said, managing a laugh. She was always arguing with her sister, but tonight . . . tonight was different, she could even be tolerant of Ruby tonight. It was like the night before Christmas, or the night Abram marched in—all triumphant and smiles—and announced his new job on the docks. It was a prelude-night, the eve of intercession, the promise of a holiday.

"Is it a big boat, momma?" the boy asked suddenly. He had constructed a paper craft out of Ruby's newspaper, and he was steering it in and out of the dangerous shoals of plates and glasses, hoo-hooing at his cousins to get out of the way, he was coming, he was an ocean liner, he was a captain, he was a whale . . . And then the reality struck him and the toy boat was forgotten, teetering at the edge of a white waterfall.

"Yeah," Ellie said indulgently.

"How big?"

"Oh maybe a block."

"Maybe two," Lucy said.

"Big enough to cross the ocean?"

"Two oceans maybe," Lucy said. "It's bigger'n Noah's ark."

Ruby laughed and stroked the boy's cheek. "Uh huh. They's two of each kind on it an' some left ovah." She winked at her sister. Lucy giggled.

"Anyways," Ellie said calmly as she gave Ronnie the waxed sheets and started to prepare the sandwiches, "it ain't as big as some people's mouths . . . Now let's get fixin' on the lunch. Y'all gotta be to bed by nine." And Lucy put on the eggs to boil, and Ronnie measured out the sheets and the boy retrieved his paper boat and was the sea captain again under the table. Ruby yawned and strolled into the bedroom. Ronnie watched her, suddenly serious, and when she had gone . . .

"Aunt Ellie. Why do you an' momma fight?"

"Who? Us? What you talkin' about? We don' fight." She handed her another slab of chicken and added less sharply: "I guess we tired, that's all, just plain tired."

The girl was silent for a while.

"Aunty."

"Yeah?"

"You ever been on a boat ride?"

A flush of memory broke through the clouds on the weary brown face. She half-smiled. "Yeah . . . A long time ago."

"I ain't never been."

"I know."

"I bet it's lots o' fun."

"Yeah, it's fun. Now go wrap yo' sneakers 'n middy blouse."

The girls were busy in the corner and now Ruby was in the

room again, and when she looked up at her, she remembered the hurt note in Ronnie's voice, and she spoke gently: "Goin' out?"

"Uh huh. Got a date." She reddened her lips, clipped on the earrings, buckled the tight coat.

"I thought maybe you might help with the sandwiches," Ellie commented softly.

"Oh they ain't much," Ruby said. "You don't mind, do you honey? It's the fellah I told you about."

"You gonna see him tomorrow, ain't you?"

"Uh huh." The teeth flashed brightly under the fresh-rouged lips. "But that's *tomorrow*."

Yeah, that's tomorrow, Ellie thought when her sister had gone. I'm always waitin' fo' tomorrow and she . . . she takes it when it comes. I don't know, maybe she's right. Most tomorrows are the same . . . But no, she thought . . . and the thought rose up and warmed her and dissolved the dank mist of her mood—some tomorrows are different . . . some tomorrows she would sail . . . yeah . . . some . . . yes . . .

"C'mon," Ronnie whispered to her sister. "You cut 'n I'll wrap. Aunty's fell asleep in her chair."

It was only a quarter to seven, but already there was a small crowd on the pier.

"You see," Ruby complained sleepily, "other people got the same idea."

"That's all right," Ellie said brightly. "They ain't many. Now let's get up front."

"Hey, lookit the boat, momma!" Roy shouted. "Lookit the big boat!" He broke away and raced to the wooden gate, peering through the slats like a prisoner at the sight of freedom.

"You better keep yo' eyes on him," Ellie instructed the girls, "or he's gonna fall in the river."

The pier was open at the sides without rails or guards. Over by one of the stanchions, a boy with a wide flat cap was swinging his bat at an imaginary ball. His girl applauded, her big yellow bonnet flapping like the sun-bathed wings of the gulls. People were trickling onto the pier, at first in twos and threes and then in larger groups until by seven the pier was almost half filled.

It was a typical excursion crowd, bright with many-colored garments in the morning, rippling with expectant laughter. And yet there was about it the special air of rarity, the eager festival-hunger in the eyes of chamber-maids and porters, the happiness grasped and gulped without measure. Everywhere they set their lunch boxes and thermos jugs, everywhere they pinched and danced, helloed, waved, dropped stones into the water. It was the day of furlough, of leave, in the lives of work-soldiers. The August sun was hot even at this hour, but the air was clear and the river lay in the early light like a slate-blue cape sparkling with rhinestones.

Ellie breathed deeply. She was content. The promise of the day ahead sparkled like the riverpath. Over on the Jersey shore she could see the roller coaster of the Palisades Amusement Park, and the apartment houses perched up on the cliffs, and the shimmering drops of sun that were cars climbing there. She piled her packages against the wooden railing, and through the slats looked at the white steamer slowly breathing on the water.

"What time they lettin' us on?" she asked a woman waiting beside her.

"Not till quarter of eight."

"Thanks." She mopped her forehead. It was getting very hot.

"Oh there they are!" Ruby suddenly exclaimed, and began to wave her arm. She had been watching all the newcomers. Two men spotted her and came dog-trotting up.

"Lo honey," she greeted the younger-looking of the two. He squeezed her hand and held it a moment.

"Ellie," she said happily, "this here's Randy Jackson. An' . . ."

"Charles McKenna," the other man announced in a deep plush voice. He extended his hand. "Glad to meet you, Miss Porter." He was very assured, very dignified, and her quick resentment was somehow mute against his manners. He certainly wasn't like his friend, Ellie thought, looking at the two of them laughing uproariously at some private joke; at least he acted like a gentleman. Even the boy seemed to take a shine to him and soon was clamoring to be lifted on his shoulders that he might look over the gate. And when Ellie saw the firm arms clasp her son and lift him, and the way the boy clung to McKenna's neck, she softened, and vague ideas like shadows on the river went floating through her mind. Yeah, everything was different today, even this man was not what she'd expected.

The crowd was filling in very rapidly now and people were pressing up behind them and against each other. The dock swarmed like a beehive in the holiday sun—the rainbow clusters, the package heaps, the happy voices, the metallic squeals of children weaving in and out. A young fellow had perched himself upon a stanchion and was strumming on his guitar:

> Honey, you the
> Spangle an . . .
> the dingdong oh!

And the crowd was pressing against her again—it was a great impatient beast—and Ellie didn't even mind when her friend suggested that he take her arm and shield her somewhat with his shoulders. There was comfort there, and sanctuary, and she found herself dreaming along paths she had rejected; and the paths were sure, not overgrown with brambles and treacherous thorns, and before she realized it she was leaning hard against him and the path led to a meadow overgrown with flowers, and she tried to back away, suddenly angry at her impulse . . . It was soon time now and cries were heard: "It's gettin' late. Hey, open up the gate!" A group of boys took it up in unison: clapping their hands in rhythm like an impatient audience in a theatre.

Ellie heard an angry murmur behind her and then a sudden burst of laughter.

"What's happenin'?" she asked McKenna. They were packed in so, she couldn't twist around to see.

"Oh it's nothin'," he said craning his neck and looking back over the crowd. He sure tall, Ellie thought, bigger'n Abram even. "Some committeeman tryin' to get through," McKenna explained. He smiled broadly. "Uh uh . . . a kid's stolen his badge. He's mad all right. He's goin' back fo' a cop."

"Oh where's Roy?" she cried out, suddenly apprehensive. "Roy!"

"He's here, don't worry," Ronnie's voice came from somewhere.

"Well hold onto him. We goin' on soon."

"Yes *suh!*" Randy Jackson said.

Ellie could just make out her sister's salmon-colored turban bobbing in the molten mass at her left.

"Mm . . . what a day!"

"Hey! quit yo' shovin' . . ."

"Who's shovin'?"

Something hard pressed against her back. A policeman shouldered by. He was nudging ahead with his night stick, clearing a path for two very excited committeemen: their collars sweaty, their faces angry and worried. They announced something to the crowd but Ellie couldn't make it out in the babble of voices, and then the committeemen had passed and everyone was falling in behind them and shoving toward the gate. Voices screamed from the pier's edge: "Hey watch out! . . . You nearly pushed someone ina water!" Those at the edge were pressing toward the center of the dock, and those behind were pressing forward, and soon Ellie was gasping in the cross-current.

"Mist' McKenna!" she panted, clutching his arm. "What's goin' on? I cain't hardly breathe!"

"I don't know," he said seriously. "Everybody's gone crazy 'bout somethin'. Better hang onto me."

She was suddenly jolted forward. The crowd was boiling like a whirlpool around her. She heard a frenzied outcry and Randy Jackson's head bobbed up. He was flailing away at somebody and yelling, "Who the hell you think you kickin'?"

"Lemme go!" the man cried hysterically. "I gonter get on the boat! Nobody gonna rob me!"

"Aw, pipe down man."

"Hey, break it up."

"What's the matter, Randy?" McKenna asked, shouldering his way to the fight.

"Aw, this guy start kickin'. 'Fraid he wouldn't get on. Seems like some phony tickets been sold. They gonna examine all the tickets."

"Hey! They gonna examine all the tickets!"

"Somebody's out o' luck."

"Well, it ain't gonna be *me!*"

"Me neither . . ."

"Yeah . . ."

Frantically, Ellie clawed open her handbag and felt for the tickets. Oh, they were there all right, and they were good, she told herself, they must be good, they were *her* tickets, she had slaved for them, sweated for them, they were her magic pass for one day of freedom. She looked around hysterically as the word spread among the people, spread like a prairie fire feeding on the dry stalks of their lives, their denial, their anger.

And as she surged forward in the flame she heard within herself a confused voice shouting like the madness without: "Who they think they is? Who they think they is?" And she was not clear whom the "they" referred to, but it was there, it was always there, that overhanging "they," that threat that would deprive her of her holiday. Frenzied, she kicked and scrambled toward the magic gate but when she got there a policeman was braced against it, his badge glittering coldly in the sun, his arms outstretched against the crowd:

"Now take it easy everybody! Stand back! We're just gonna check the tickets, that's all! Everybody with legitimate tickets will get on!"

He turned his lobster-red face to a committeeman, and Ellie saw that it was Charlie Walker, the sweat streaming down his cheeks, his shoulders moving grotesquely as he kept jerking away from the many-handed crowd.

"Mist' Walker! Mist' Walker!" Ellie shouted, edging forward and thrusting her tickets in his face. "You sold me these tickets! They's good, ain't they? You sold 'em to me!"

"Wait a minute!" he said. "We gotta take 'em one at a time!" Another committeeman came up and whispered in his ear. Walker nodded his head, went through the gate, and started running up the landing to the boat. Helplessly, Ellie looked at him until he

had disappeared and then she turned pleadingly to the other committeeman but he was too busy checking the tickets. The policeman shoved her back into line. And then from nowhere she heard
Roy screaming, "Momma! Momma!" and she turned around to
get at him but didn't know where to look. Everywhere children
were being trampled under their elders' feet. She could just make
out the heads of Ruby and the girls tossing at her left like corks
in a storm. "Roy!" she screamed in anguish, "Rooooooooy!"

"Take it easy," McKenna's rich voice sounded behind her.
"I've got the kid." Roy was perched like a frog on his shoulders,
the tears streaming down his cheeks. He saw his mother and
began to wail even louder.

"It's all right, son," Ellie said, soothingly. "We all be on the
boat soon."

Several more had been passed by the committeeman and Ellie
could see them running on the landing beyond as if they had
escaped from a stampede. And now the committeeman was looking at her tickets too, and he was shaking his head and saying:

"Sorry, Miss. These here's phonies."

"They cain't be!" Ellie shouted, "I bought 'em myself only
yesterday at the lodge. Mist' Walker sold 'em to me himself!"

He looked at her uncomprehendingly.

"Ah don' know nothin' 'bout that," he said. "They was tickets
sold all over Harlem. We can't get 'em *all* on this boat."

"But Mist' Walker . . ."

"Well, he ain't here now, lady. So you just have to stand ovah
there an' wait. Nex'."

Ellie stared at him dumbly. Her hair had fallen over her eyes.
She stood there swaying, breathing hard, bracing herself against
the gatepost. She felt the huge anonymous pressure urging behind
her. And then a string snapped and she grabbed the committeeman by the lapel, and she was screaming: "Yuh dirty rotten
crook! Y'ain' gonna keep my kids offa this boat! Nobody's gonna
keep us off what we're entitled to!"

"Take yo' hands off me!" the committeeman said, shaking himself loose. "We not keepin' you off. Yo' jus' gotta wait here a
little while till Walker gits back."

"Well, I ain't gonna wait!" Ellie cried. "All my life I been waitin'. I ain't gonna wait no mo'. We're goin' on that boat right now!"

"Stand back!" the policeman yelled, but now the crowd had exploded into a thousand angry shouts: "Quit holdin' her up! . . . Let her on! . . . Let ev'body on! . . . C'mon, damn yuh, open it up!" . . . The policeman saw their faces and he pulled his gun and shot it into the air. From a distance came the wail of a siren.

"Yuh better open up that gate or somebody get hurt," Mc-Kenna shouted.

"Don't tell me what to do, yuh goddam nigger bastard!" the cop replied. And then the fight began. Fruit flying in all directions. People slipping on bananas and tomato skins. A woman's hysterical laughter. Boys shinnying over the fence. The policeman's whistle over and over again. And Ronnie tugging at her sleeve and crying, "Aunty! Aunty! What we gonna do?"

Oh what happened to her lovely day? The white boat floated ironically in the sunshine. Now it was seen and now again lost as the fury milled about her and drove her from the gate. And Ellie Mae forgot the boy, forgot McKenna and the green shoots of promise, oh she only knew that she must get on that boat, and with her arms stretched before her she moved through the pandemonium like a sleepwalker following a vision. Now she had come to the policeman again and he yelled at her to stop but she did not hear him, and darkest night and a thousand shrieking stars crashed into the citadel of her skull, and the white boat abruptly disappeared as she fell to the dock, the blood spurting from her mouth, the black tide swirling on and over the silent dreamless head.

PAUL BARTLETT:

GRILLED WINDOWS

IT's GETTING dark and I've had my second hypodermic and I feel warm and my pillow feels warm and I feel safe and the house is still. I liked the story about the woman who took dope; what adventures she had, six months in Harbin, six months. . . . I see a sort of dream and my child's back again; I'm back in Colima and it's hot and the sun's on the slopes of the volcano. . . . It doesn't seem to me I was born there. Doesn't seem like I used to look out the windows at the volcano and think about its lavender top and all the big fields around the town . . . sugarcane and orange and lime groves and that old bridge with the stone benches on it and the palms leaning over the hot streets. It's all so plain and yet I wasn't ever there; maybe I was.

The house was on Carranza Street, numero 18, big rooms, grilled windows. There was the patio inside and the corral in back of that, with wooden doors between the grilled windows on the street side, toward the volcano, toward the people that walked on the street, back and forth. The wooden door was so old Cortez might have knocked on it. Papa . . . the kind of colonel who spends most of his time at home, locked in his room, laughing, gambling. Women and gambling.

He'd have been better off if he'd stayed peasant like mother, just sleepy peasant, brain full of sueños, brain that 'said: sure, you do it; Maria bring this, Carlota bring that . . . niña take Chula out to the jardin. That was the first nana; there was another nana; I remember scars on her throat, terrible things, gold on her teeth, big earring in one ear, rebozo always dirty . . . fed me sweet potatoes and sugarcane and dirty meat. That buzzing sound—those are the flies on my legs and hands and neck and face.

Go on, get back in your room, that's a good bed in there, papa would roar. Wooden planks, with straw pallet over them, sheet to throw over me. Lie in bed while he had another party and the mariachis killed the air, seven years old, lie in bed, nothing to ask, or kneel by the bed and say . . .

All of them slept in the same room with me: Arturo, Carlos, Raoul. They said they were my brothers. Ate out of tin plates. Orange trees in the patio, banana trees leaning against the wall where the bougainvillea burned. Pigs in the corral. Papa came home drunk. Here's a parrot for you. And Carlos brought me the armadillo. Smart.

Why did I try to be smart? I'd better have played out my games with the parrot and the armadillo; sit in the sand, wait. They told me all the dirt, the human kind. Carlos with his girls, Arturo with his Jesuit "friend"—just to have him come into our room was to think pigs were better.

Verde, the parrot, had a rasping croak . . . I hear him so plainly and I can smell the orange blossoms and see the snow on top of the volcano and feel the heat as we walked over the bridge. Every day was alike and heat was volcanic and it riddled you and you lay down anywhere and the flies came. It was as if somebody gave you injections of flies and heat. . . .

I'd like to go back, get warm, get really warm. Like to go to school again, over the hot cobbles, with the nana, with the heat on the wall where the Presidencia was, with the heat in the long fronds of the palms, heat dancing in the air in front of us, between us and the volcano. Sweat runs down my arms and back and legs. And there's Coco, standing at the corner with his terrible old bicycle and there's Concepcion going in her store. . . .

When I was eight papa said: if you speak to a stranger I'll beat you. When I was nine my brothers took me to a Sunday promenade in the plaza. When I was ten I said adios to a stranger. When I was twelve they sent me off to school in Guadalajara.

I was scared when I went away. I was afraid to stay home any longer and I was afraid to go, and I went away fearing my father and his drunken parties, remembering crumbs of nice things: the snow of the pico de fuego, the smell of orange trees over garden walls, the sound of doves calling, the water bubbling under the bridge with the palms hanging low over the sides of the stream, palms hanging over sun-bright walls; I remembered the faces seen through grilled windows; I remembered my parrot and armadillo and there were other crumbs; there were dirty things about sex and women and the parties (parties I never saw); there was something about high mass and candles and the sound of rain, the jerking of an earthquake; there were glimpses of mama's face . . . how strange, to see, to hear, to feel. . . . I feel safe and warm—the house is still.

Guadalajara made me want to become a nun. Maybe it was the town's bigness that got into me, maybe I just wanted to become a nun . . . there were so many faces and skirts in the school: faces and skirts; I'd never seen so many kinds, not close, not all around me, not making a noise, not . . . I wanted to run off and I dreamed of running off. I was pretty then. I thought some man might like to keep me until I was old enough to love. I remember the way my eyebrows curved.

Skirts and faces made me shyer. I tried to play their games but I never liked to. Didn't want to stand there and be yelled at, didn't want to yell back. Somebody hit me on the head with a baseball and I fell and they left me on the field. They said: come on, leave her there, she's a baby. And the blood ran out of my head and then somebody saw the pool and ran for help. My heart began to bother me after that.

God, how plainly I see the school, its ramshackle rooms, windows with glass knocked out, broken steps, two patios, clock that never kept time, picture of Hidalgo, patio trees dry and twisted, like the brains of the sisters that ran the place. Just one nice thing, that was the red bougainvillea that sprawled across a big wall. Same color as the one at home.

I see him now, I see him clearly and he sees me and he's coming, he's coming closer and closer; he's smiling at me. Yes, little Gabriel, climb on my bed and smile at me. You don't look like you'd been dead. Are you dead? You've come back because tomorrow is the dia de los muertos. I'll buy you a sugar skull to-morrow, a thirty centavo skull, and I'll have your name put on it: Gabriel—in gold letters. De veras! Won't you like that?

Gabriel, go away. I want to forget you. . . .

Don't come back.

I must sleep.

We used to write notes and hang them over a wall at school. Boys fastened replies to the strings and we spent hours fishing, giggling, whispering, listening, lying on the dead leaves, smiling . . . there was the French girl; she liked me. There was Trini. She could sing and she and Sister Ana sang for us sometimes.

Not hot, not cold, days when we sat in the sun to study our French and Sister Agatha would sit beside me and I could smell her and hear her beads and there was a silver cross she liked to play with and there was that strange loneliness that would come over me when she sat by me a long time; I wanted to talk to her and put my face in her lap. I wonder how old she was. I wanted to say: take me to town this afternoon, let me see something besides these walls and the hideous dry trees. And she would smile and I would smile. She taught me about the Virgin and taught me prayers and taught me to jump over bad cracks in the floor if I wanted special good luck. But I got better grades when I counted cricket chirps; I got so I could tell by the way the sisters crossed themselves whether I'd be lucky all day.

Papa died. I was fifteen. There were no more checks for the fees at the collegio and it was back to Colima, to the patio and the parrot . . . the armadillo was dead . . . it was hot and the heat was waiting for me at the bridge; there was no Carlos, no Arturo; Arturo was married; Carlos had a job at La Fortuna. Raoul. . . .

Cobbles got hotter and hotter every day and a cloud hung over the top of the pico de fuego and I sat on the ledge of the window in my room and looked out—there wasn't any rain. I walked the patio, went back to the corral: my mind was walking, walking everywhere, with sex, god, hate, hope. I used to climb up the patio wall when it was hot in the late afternoon; I'd get a little better air up there. I went there day after day.

An old woman lived next door, wrinkled, white-headed, bent with arthritis. She got so she called up to me and we got so we'd talk. She asked me down to visit her and I scrambled down and she gave me wine and dulces and I saw her shabby rooms and listened to her. She had potted azaleas, roses and hibiscus in the patio; the patio tiles were cracked; she had two clarins and we'd sit among the potted things and talk and the birds would sing. She told me about love and two men—rivals—god, how fiercely she told the story. About a killing, stolen money . . . she shut herself up because he betrayed her. Never went out. He was dead. She never went out.

Strange I've never loved Alberto. I've tried. Can't. I don't know why. . . . He isn't good-looking but it's not that; it's not his silly laugh; he's thin but it's not that. I liked him when he came to the house. Mother liked him. He would come early, maybe at nine. I'd sit in the room, hold his hands through the grilled window; we'd kiss, our faces against the bars. Mama said: he'll make a wonderful doctor.

He's not.

I'm just as much alone as when I was back there. My mind goes away; it walks away and there's the clock and the picture of Hidalgo and there's Sister Agatha sitting by me and there's Gabriel and he's eating the baby food and getting ready to die.

I hate him; I hate time; I hate the way it's gone. Why should I be thirty-three, my face wrinkled, my skin yellow? I look at my hands. I think, what's going to happen to my heart? I could become a nun; I guess it's not too late. But the woman who took dope never became a nun.

It might have been better if I'd never gone away again. It wasn't like going to the ocean for a while, coming back on the train with coconuts and zapotes and bananas and oranges. There's never anything like the ocean and the sand and the sound. There's the palmero with the parrots and canaries; there's the mist beating up into the light, drenching you, keeping the hot sun off. There are the shells, the long ones shaped like horns, the ones that are colored green and blue and white. At Cuyutlan we'd pick up the oval shells, the thin ones, the ones with the palm tree in the center

—just as though it was a real palm. How easily they broke, only a touch and they were shattered, only a touch and the tree was broken.

We ate on the veranda one year. . . . I guess it was the Madrid Hotel, near the beach, near the ola verde; sleeping there was like sleeping in someone's hands, the waves I mean. Charles was French. He'd come down from Mexico City, he liked the shells, the mist, the beach that curved to a white cliff. He talked differently, mouth different, eyes different; he touched my hands. He said, I work in a bank. There were palms close to the beach on the wet sand, the out-running tide flats, changes, his eyes different because of the changes. He told me how old he was; I told him. A star was over the water, as if it were the light on a ship; then mama called.

I lost the shells we picked up together, lost them when we moved away, I guess it was then. I'd like to have gone back and picked up some more shells, let them break in my hands. I wasn't wearing black clothes then. Mama, in her black, so empty, stiff, saying don't do that now, don't do that. Of course I'll wear black things, till I die. It's only right that I should. The church knows best, she shouted.

Queretaro is dry and full of the bleached eyes of looking; the sky is paler; the wind blows oftener. I met them, the Ochoas, the Uribes, the Martinezes, the Gonzalezes. Sr. Uribe had a patio that had a figure of the Virgin, carved in San Luis Potosi. Sra. Ochoa had a boy named Alberto. The trolley ran past our house; there were jacaranda trees; there was a store across the street named Corona. Bad, mama said, bad to move at my age, bad to get away from the old friends. What awful panaderias they've got here. Ah, the servants, and Raoul never gets home until late every night. He shouldn't be working like that. You must do something.

I thought of the empty hot heat in Colima and shook her by the shoulder but she only cried.

I'm lonely.

It's my turn now.

Gabriel—I miss you. You were so sweet and nice and good and clever and you were my first. First. Why are you dead? But maybe it's that way, la vida, sad, life of loneliness, sad. I'm always in this house, and I don't know why; I'm shut in and the clock and the picture, they're ticking together. No cine, wear black, mustn't eat out, wear black all your life, no radio, no dances, no . . .

What's that shaking the room, a truck on Avenida Juarez?

It's like the trembling of the ground in Colima. The walls would shake; the caged birds would flutter and try to get out.

I should have been a nun. I could kneel and pray and ask god to take care of my heart when it hurts. I could ask god to make me a place for myself in myself. I wouldn't lie.

But I've always lied. There was all that deception about my family, grandpa being Spanish, papa an haciendado. There was all that stuff to cover up the things that Carlos did. There were all those lies about the woman he should have married. I've told everybody it wasn't my fault that Gabriel died. I've told everybody that I love Alberto. . .

When it's dark and Alberto's away and the maid's gone out that man comes and sneaks up the back stair. He always wears black and has that dirty black scarf around his mouth. I hope I never see his face. Maybe he hasn't any mouth. He hasn't come back for more than a week. Such a strange sound, scuffing his feet on the concrete, hitting the toes of his shoes against each step. Tomorrow, I'll put your pictures on the mantelpiece, Gabriel. I'll get out all the best snapshots of you, the ones I took of you a few days before you died, the ones we took of you as you lay there in your casket. You were pretty, Gabriel. You didn't look like you were dead.

I don't know why I wasn't careful about the food I gave you. I don't know why it's so still.

No wind in the trees outside, no trucks rumbling along the street, no trolley, no cars, no people walking. . . .

Strange, to feel this way, to be floating and there are the orange blossoms and there's papa: if you speak to a stranger I'll beat you. There's mama. She's asleep. She's sent Clotilda out for pulque. There's the rain on our roof and the heat near the bridge and there's a wind in the long fronds that hang over the walls. Voices. Voices are moving through me and they wet me with cold tongues; I want to scream.

DORIS BENARDETE:

THE GOLDEN HARP

THE MEN in the saloon looked different from the refined, high-toned men Irene used to stare at every Sunday as she sat outside the shut door of the saloon with her friend Betty Benelli, listening to Betty talk about her surveyor, and watching for the cop on the beat. These men, walking indifferently past the darkened saloon up from the Ferry below, shone like polished glass. They looked clean and, Betty would say, rich and decent. They looked as if they lived in houses with real white bath tubs, as if they never had to go with towel and soap and clean underwear to the public baths around the corner. They wouldn't do wrong by a girl, Betty would say, not men like my surveyor. The man she had been admiring for about two weeks now she called her surveyor because it must be so nice to be a surveyor. My surveyor now would just hold me in his arms and hug me close and then kiss me softly on the lips. Kiss me, my honey, kiss me, she crooned, and say you miss me, my honey, do. Irene was surprised to find that when she discovered Betty's surveyor worked in the large dairy on the next block Betty refused to go see for herself. She went on calling him her surveyor just the same. Surely, she insisted, Irene must be mistaken. My surveyor now, said Betty, and Irene said, Well, now, how about Connie Sullivan? He's handsome if he'd shave, and he'd look all right if he dressed decent. Too many ifs, sniffed Betty. My surveyor now don't drink. Yes, Irene admitted, that's the trouble with Connie. If he only didn't. But gee, how he can sing.

The block they lived on was broad all right, but it had no trees.

The street was paved with cobblestones, and trolley cars ran down the middle, some to the Ferry below and some turning at the corner with a screech. Massive sombre trucks on monstrous wheels rumbled by. The houses for night watchmen, storekeepers, peddlers, longshoremen, laundrywomen, machinists, streetcleaners, plumbers, looked wobbly and decayed like drunken bums. On the two sides of that one block were nine saloons. Nights when not so many cars and trucks went past, you could hear more clearly the voices of men and women. You goddam bloody bastard, I'll knock the guts out of you. Who the hell you think you are to be shovin me round like this? Take your filthy paws offa me or, by God, Jesus, I'll knock the daylights out of your damned eyes. A drunken man might be hit across the head with an umbrella or a stick by some irate woman. Irene had seen one drunk ferociously dragged out of the Dennis' saloon one Saturday night and knocked down in front of the store, his skull split open and his dark hot blood staining the sidewalk.

How those drunks smelled! But not so thick or sweet as the women, who had a special stink that comes out of a woman who never washes outside or in. If one of them sat in the backroom of the saloon any length of time and then left, you could feel her stink coming straight out at you from the sticky walls. It was that strong.

In that backroom Minnie Halloran used to sit by the hour with her waist partly open, her skirt lopsided and twisted, her hair straggling in a ratty tangle out of her hat, smelling of stale beer and dried sweat. There were blood clots in Minnie's eyes, big puffs underneath, long blonde hairs on her upper lip. Sometimes a man—but never Connie Sullivan—would walk in to give Minnie a treat, and then she would smile. You forgot her brown jagged teeth then and saw only her eyes glowing and her dimples flickering.

What're you doin with yourself, Minnie, these days? the man would say.

Oh, just keepin goin, keepin goin, as you can see for yourself, George me lad.

How about joinin me in a cup for old times' sake?

I don't mind if I do, she'd say, and then he'd pay for some whiskies for Minnie Halloran. And then Minnie would get up and adjust her waist, make feeble attempts at pushing her ratty hairstrings under her misshapen hat with the dirty daisies, and walk out, somewhat proudly though unevenly, moving her broad backside up and down, up and down, knowing that George was watching her. After awhile George would get up and lurch after her to a room over one of Mike O'Neil's stables on Hancock Street. You could never find Connie Sullivan there.

Not that she didn't fancy Connie. Connie me lad, she had said to him more than once, why don't you come and sit with me awhile?

Minnie, he'd say, I can't.

But why? Tell me that, Connie, why? Ain't I good enough for the likes of you?

Too good, he'd say. Too good for me, Minnie. You're a saint next to the likes of me. You work. And he always shuffled off and away from Minnie Halloran.

Some Sundays Connie would take Irene's place in front of the saloon watching for the cop on the beat. Not that I like being watchdog, he'd say with a grin, but Jesus, you kids ought to get away from this hell-hole once in awhile. Sometimes he'd be waiting till they got back. Once he said, Jesus, you girls look happy. I wish to Christ I could look so happy.

Irene would say, sing us a song, Connie.

But Connie always shook his head, Naw, some other day, not now, not here, some other time, some other place.

Irene and Betty used to sit on the shed warm days when the skylight of the saloon was open, and they'd peek down and see the men all listening to Connie tell stories or sing songs.

> The harp that once through Tara's halls
> The soul of music shed
> Now hangs as mute on Tara's walls
> As if that soul were dead.
> So sleeps the pride of former days,
> So glory's thrill is o'er,
> And hearts that once beat high for praise,
> Now feel that pulse no more.

Irene's heart would pump so hard she'd be afraid she was going to cry in front of Betty. Connie's full voice sprang from his heart, which must be bleeding, she'd think to herself, for him to sing with such sobs in his voice. Gee, how he could sing.

And the stories he could tell of the old country, about leprechauns and banshees, her father's country, and young men fighting for a new Ireland with its own old Gaelic tongue and its own Hibernian dances and its own old flag with the golden harp on it.

Once when she was sitting outside the saloon alone, he came along and started teasing her about wearing the cross around her neck. And you a Jew's daughter, he said.

No, not me. My father was Irish, and they say I look like him. If he'd a lived I'd a been brought up right.

That's what you think, snarled Connie. It was your father stuck your mother in this dirty dump and then up and died. Your mother's not to blame, kid, she's a good woman if she is a Jew, and he was—but never mind me, Irene, I'm a drunken bum. I'm just lettin off steam. But I can tell you this much, he was no true Hibernian.

On days when Connie watched for the cop, the girls would go out to Greenwood Cemetery where Julia Benelli, Betty's sister, was buried. Betty's real name was Elizabeth Benelli, but nobody ever called her Elizabeth. Her mother called her Lizzie, which went through her like a knife. Her father called her Lisabetta, which she liked but wouldn't say she did because she hated him. Then the girls would walk to Prospect Park, all dressed up in tweed suits with belts and box-pleated skirts and gloves. They would walk like two refined ladies, talking in quiet tones, and then Betty would tell Irene the story she had just finished reading and how she felt she was just like the girl in the book, and so would Irene please call her Japonette? It wouldn't harm anybody, would it? Betty was Japonette for a pretty long time. She liked even more to be called Jane Eyre. She always carried a small leather notebook or a dark library book so as to look intelligent. She had a clever way of doing things. For instance, she always managed to have the cover of the

library book match her suit or coat. Irene could never understand why she had never finished the 8 B.

Near the park was a place Betty had discovered where you
could get a cherry smash for a nickel. If they walked home they
could have the cherry smash. Vanilla ice cream soda with crushed
cherries and cherry syrup and loads of whipped cream. Over
their cherry smashes Irene and Betty would smile in a genteel
manner at each other and speak in soft tones. My surveyor now,
Betty would say, would love this.

The beersaloon was a filthy place. All the customers were men,
standing around, mumbling, drinking, chewing tobacco, and
spitting all over the place, the sawdust on the floor forming
clumps with their brown spit. They cursed and scratched and
twitched and spat endlessly. When Irene came in to ask her
mother for some money they'd stop. They'd say, Sh-h, a lady.
Only Connie Sullivan was different.

But one night before closing time Connie, who usually enter-
tained the men with songs and tales of how he managed to get
money, was put out for making a pest of himself with his grip-
ing. Irene's Uncle Richard put him out. Get the hell out of here,
you drunken bum, and don't come back till you can behave
decent. You ain't got a red cent to spend here and you expect
us to give you the goddam stuff for nothin.

Connie was sore. All right, you sheeny, keep your shirt on.

Connie was sore at Richard, sore at everybody, sore at the
whole goddam stinkin world. He would get even, and by God
he'd get even tonight, so help him Jesus. He walked a few blocks
till the cold night air of spring, nipping his nose, made him
sniffle. He kept wiping his nose with his sleeve, and he kept
getting colder and colder. Finally he came to the block where
the Long Island College Hospital was. A respectable block with
brownstone houses, not as swell as Columbia Heights, but swell
enough for Connie Sullivan. On the lowest step of one of these
quiet houses he sat down, hunching forward as if in torment.
Then he began to shout, O, Jesus, O, Jesus, won't you do some-

thing for me? Jesus, O, Jesus, he yelled, and he hollered till he got hoarse. He sounded mighty sick.

It wasn't long before a gentleman came by who said, Can I help you, my good man? What's troubling you?

Connie made out at first he couldn't hear. He kept shrieking, Jesus, O, Jesus. Look down this once on me.

The man put his hand on Connie's shoulder. Are you in pain? he said gently.

Connie looked up with the eyes of a saint. Pain's not the word for it, sir. It's me tooth.

The man helped him up and took him to the open door of the emergency ward of the hospital.

Just trust yourself to me, my good man, said the gentleman, I'll take care of you.

In the hospital Connie heard a nurse say, Good evening, Dr. Samson, I thought you had finished for the day.

Dr. Samson put Connie in the charge of an interne and a nurse. Hello, Dr. Kelly, here's a man you can help. As one Irishman for another, you ought to do something for him. Before leaving, he put a dollar bill into Connie's hand.

Told to open his mouth so they could examine his tooth, Connie pretended at first he couldn't (thinking they'd think he had lockjaw), but after awhile he thought better of it, opened his mouth wide as hell, and breathed out on them hard as he could such a hot mixture that both nurse and doctor were stunned. Standing at a distance, the nurse swished some strong antiseptic from a syringe into Connie's mouth, and then the interne said, Come back tomorrow morning. We'll try to do something for you then. Meanwhile this'll help you sleep. And he gave him a few pyramidon tablets.

Then Connie took his biggest chance. Jesus Christ, he cried aloud, you tell me to go home and sleep when I ain't got no home. He began to cry. Lemme stay here.

The nurse looked at the doctor, the doctor looked at the nurse. No, sorry, no provisions for cases like yours, but here's something that may help you. He handed Connie a dollar bill, saying, You're no good this way. Why don't you stop? Brace up. Brace up. Dr. Kelly looked at the wreck the man was, and him hardly thirty. Why don't you stop? You're no good this way. He looked fondly into the warm Irish eyes with the laugh and the cry in them. Brace up, man.

The nurse meanwhile had gone away and come back with several other nurses who, on seeing poor sick Connie, contributed to his fund.

He got three dollars and a half that night, and what did he do then? Why, he carried the banner all the rest of the night, but carried it with pride. All that night he remembered the young red-haired interne's words, You're no good this way. Stop. Brace up. No good this way. No good this way. Stop. Brace up. The deep pity in the interne's eyes made him shiver more than the brisk air. What the hell did he give me the money for? he grumbled to himself. I can't use it. I can't. Four o'clock the next morning when Irene's mother opened her saloon, Connie was waiting, the first one to come that day for his free ball. Top o' the morning to you, Ma Dennis, he said. After his free ball he shuffled off with a brief s'long, and wasn't seen for weeks.

One Sunday he came around in the afternoon. The girls saw him coming all dressed up like Astor's pet horse. Betty nudged Irene. Look who's here.

Irene said, Hello, Connie.

Hello, Irene. Hello, Betty. Say, kids, I got a proposition to make. Look, I got money, and it's burnin a hole in me pocket. How about takin a ride with me? What do you say?

Irene said, Gee, I'd love it. Do you think it's all right? I mean my going away like this?

Sure, said Connie, if your friend'll come along.

All right, I'll go, said Betty. Where'll it be?

Well, said Connie, I was thinkin maybe it'd be nice if you'd take me where you go those Sundays I sit here for you.

That'd be grand, said Irene.

They loved the idea of not having to pay for their cherry smashes and not having to walk for them. They watched him swallow two glasses of cold water before pulling the long spoon

out of the creamy concoction. He eyed it like a suspicious sparrow, and then stuck the spoon in his mouth. The cold whipped
cream soothed him. He dug his spoon in again and again, but
he couldn't finish the thing. It's too much like heaven, he said,
with a grin, and I'm not fit like you kids.

Now you've shown me your good time, I'll show you mine.
What do you say?

We should worry, they said with a giggle.

For awhile they were disappointed because they were definitely heading for home again. But when they got to their corner
Connie made them stay on the car till they reached the Ferry
below. They went across to the Battery, and then where did he
take them but to the Staten Island ferry boat. So much riding
the girls had never had in all their lives. The water leaping up
to the sides of the boat and swishing around the huge ferry
wheels. The seagulls dipping into the water and rising up to the
sky. The bits of cloud. The sun coming out every so often. The
boat whistles. The people. Such a lot of people. And all so
refined.

They didn't feel out of place. They forgot to feel ashamed of
Connie. They were listening to him tell stories of how he used
to think he'd be a priest and then he got to reading and to thinking, and then he couldn't stand the gaff any more.

Sing us a song, Irene whispered. You said you would some
time.

He sang to them when they got off at Staten Island and away
from the crowds. A choir boy's voice. Jesus, O, Jesus, he sang,
forgive us our sins, kind Jesus. Irene and Betty forgot the time.
They felt warm all over.

I'll race you, he said, and they started to run through the unfamiliar roads, the girls obliged to follow him. They stopped
when they were out of breath and sat down on some stones by
the side of the road. Connie sang again. The Harp That Once
Through Tara's Halls, and then Ave Maria, and then The Last
Rose of Summer. And Irene and Betty felt like crying. The
impish face of Connie crinkled into quiet smiles. Aw, come on,
kids, cheer up, the worst is yet to come.

Sing us a funny song, said Betty.

Connie said, To tell the God's honest truth, I don't know any.

Sing us another song, said Irene, and he sang Lead, Kindly Light.

The two girls felt sad and happy, warm and cold, lonely and together. In the unfamiliar country quiet of Staten Island, Connie's voice sounded to them like some angel's voice, far away and holy. His eyes were glowing like street lamps at night.

Of a sudden Connie said, I see a star. Let's make a wish. I see the first star, the first star sees me, God bless the first star, God bless me. Then he said, Look, girls, you made me happy today, and I want to give you a present. They ran and ran to catch the boat. They were out of breath and bursting with warm laughter when they got on. This was adventure. After they were on the boat, he gave each of them a shiny half-dollar. Here's to you. Now I'm going to see the captain. He's an old friend of mine. Excuse me if I don't stay with you. I'll be back.

We should worry, said the girls with a giggle.

My surveyor now, said Betty, would never a left us alone like this. Irene said nothing. She felt Connie's full voice still singing inside her.

> No more to chiefs and ladies bright
> The harp of Tara swells;
> The chord alone that breaks at night,
> Its tale of ruin tells.
> Thus Freedom now so seldom wakes,
> The only throb she gives
> Is when some heart, indignant, breaks,
> To show that still she lives!

Now there weren't so many people. But there were more stars. The white caps of the water swished against their boat. My surveyor now, said Betty, would a put his arms around us when we were running, or anyway he'd a kissed us good-bye.

Connie is good, said Irene.

The air smelled different from any air they had ever smelled before. Cold and salty. They began to feel cold. And they took deep, deep breaths of the air. And suddenly Irene smelled not cold saltiness but the stale sour smell of home. And there was Connie beside her, soused as a herring, and messy.

My surveyor now don't drink, said Betty.

Yes, Irene whispered, that's the trouble with Connie. But gee, how he can sing.

CHRISTOPHER BLOOM:

SEVENTEEN PICTURES FROM EMILY'S LIFE

I

S HE STOOD at the window, holding back the ruffled curtain with one hand. She was looking down at the carriage, at the sunlight edging the neck of the horse. It was noon. Everything shone still and calm; the white picket fence diminished down the other side of the road, the apricots hung among green leaves. A white cat languidly licked its tail, looking like an intense white spot on the brown of the road. From downstairs she heard the gruff voice of her father raised in anger against the high, whining voice of another man. He's at it again, she thought, twitching the curtain back in place and flinging herself into a horsehair chair; always thinking he's right. Thank God I'll be going away to college in the fall.

II

One candle burned at her mother's head. The flame threw spiral wavering shadows on the deathwhite face. This is what she saw and heard when she opened the door: the hand of her mother moving slightly, her mother's mouth mothwhispering her name. She thrust down an impulse to scream, glided to her mother's side, fell over the body, cried. Now, she thought, now I can't go to college.

III

She flung down the book and began to cry. From the kitchen drifted steamy odors of cabbage and rice. She heard her father's feet shuffling in his room.

IV

The rain poured down. The road splashed muddily, spotting her shoes and dress. She heard a noise behind her, then a churning, a choking. She turned to see a young man perched in a horseless carriage. He was wearing goggles and a black and white checkered cap, which he raised. "Want a ride, lady?" he said. "You'll be in the rain but you'll get there a lot quicker."

V

She twirled her wedding bouquet between her fingers, picked the petals off a forget-me-not. When she heard the flushing of the toilet and his footsteps growing in the hallway, she flung the bouquet away, blew her nose, and wiped the tears out of her eyes with the back of one hand. She tried to smile. He was at the door and at the same time she heard her father battering around in the next room, muttering curses to himself. She fell on the bed and sobbed into the pillow.

VI

When she stood for the first time in the living room of their new house, white birds began rushing upward in her stomach. She knelt in the middle of the floor, scooped a pile of shavings into her hands, threw them in the air. They showered over her, some catching in her hair, some on her dress. In the elongated rectangle of light they looked like yellow flowers. She pressed them against her mouth and nose, drinking their new wood fragrance. They were flowers of freedom. She made a garland and placed it on her head. Her husband's figure filled the doorway, shutting away the light that had blurred the shavings to yellow flowers. She held a handful out to him, their curls jiggling between her fingers. She smiled at him. "Look!" she said. "Smell them. They smell so good." But he scowled. He took the garland from her head, jerked her to her feet, and began talking about the fireplace.

VII

It looks like him, she thought. She had wanted a girl. It was a little pink squirming boy, the ugliest baby she had seen. Its head was lopsided; its ears seemed to be glued to the sides of its head. When her husband came tiptoeing in she turned to the wall and pretended to be asleep.

VIII

The metronome ticked on top of the piano. She sat on the bench, her fingers laboriously following the notes of the simplest Chopin Etude. She was going over the difficult part again and again. Her eyes were beginning to fill with tears when she knew that her boy was standing and watching. "That's not right, Mama," he said. "That sounds awful."

IX

She was walking along the boardwalk at the seashore with the baby and the boy when she saw a crowd of people by the fishing pier. A pink dot emerged from the crowd, bobbing forward between two dark dots. She heard tinkling laughter and low voices. The pink dot and the dark dots gradually expanded into an old girl friend and two unknown men. The crowd in the background began to disperse. The pink came running forward, laughing and holding out her hands, the bow on her head dancing in the sunlight. The girl in pink opened her painted mouth. "Emily!" she cried. Emily smiled, shifted the baby to her other arm and put out her hand. "I haven't seen you for a long time," said Emily. "What have you been doing?" The girl in pink threw back her head and laughed, her curls leaping up and down like things of joy. "I just escaped from that crowd—everyone wanted my autograph." The girl made an indifferent backward gesture with one hand. "Haven't you *heard*, Emily? After I was through college I sang on the stage for eight years, and I've just signed with the *opera!*"

X

She opened the drawer and found everything tumbled and tossed together in a heap. Reaching under the pile she drew out a rectangle of cardboard and saw that it was torn, the gold seal in the corner wrinkled and the blue ribbon smeared with a fingerprint. Oh those children! Those children! And she began to cry, pressing her high school diploma against her breast.

XI

The girl shoved some papers in her hands. "I drew these of you, Mama, because you're so beautiful."

XII

"We don't have the money to send her to art school I tell you," he said, standing very masculine in the doorway. She stopped beating the eggs, looked at her husband, pursed her mouth. "She's willing to work for part of it." She twirled the beater furiously. She was beating her father and her husband, she was beating everyone who had been cruel to her and had kept her from becoming an artist like the pink girl with a painted mouth she had seen on the beach a long time ago. She was beating her husband because he was going to ruin the life of her daughter. "Besides," he said, shifting his clumsy weight to the other foot, folding his hairy arms. "No girl cf mine is going to waste my money learning any such foolishness. She should be learning how to cook." Emily straightened up. She heard the joints snapping along her spine; she heard the hissing of the gas burners, the popping of steak in the broiler, her husband's breathing and the ticking of the clock. "If you don't send her to school I'll kill myself," she said.

XIII

"It is beautiful," said Emily, standing in front of the delicate plaster figure of a man. Her daughter stood beside her, arms akimbo. Sunlight streamed through the window in the roof. The figure was alive; its contours flowed; its nakedness was her own; she had created the woman who had created this figure. "I always wanted to do something like that," she said, turning to her daughter. The girl hugged her, rubbing the plaster smudge on her face across Emily's cheek. "You could have, Mother," she said, "if you'd had a chance."

XIV

It was not until after the funeral, in her old room in her father's house, that she began to cry. She had seen them lower the casket into the grave, had seen them shovel the dirt, had heard them singing the hymn, all without emotion. She had stood staring at the white mausoleum, wishing she had money enough to bury him in one of the cool corridors with a bronze plaque screwed on a marble slab. It was not until she lay across her old bed, smelling the musty odor of the long shut room and hearing the voices of people downstairs, her father's rasping ancient voice rising above them all in a tone of dogmatic despotism, that she began to cry.

XV

"Papa," she said, "you eat those potatoes. I spent all morning getting them ready." The old man banged his fork on the table. A swinging gossamer of spittle dropped from his mouth to the napkin, snapped, made a spot. "Goddamn it!" he cried. "You've got brains enough to know I like my potatoes mashed!"

XVI

For the sixth time that morning she reached in the mailbox. Her fingers touched the edge of an envelope. Trembling, expectant, the white birds rushing upward in her stomach, she pulled the letter out. But instead of her daughter's name, the return address in the corner read: BELL TELEPHONE COMPANY.

XVII

When she came into the room and saw the miniature figure her daughter had given her smashed on the floor, she wanted to take up the letter-knife and run after her father or her son, one of whom she knew in his clumsiness had swept the figure off the table. She felt as if the figure had been herself, that she had been demolished, and she wanted only revenge. She wanted to slash their faces and their hands, to jab the knife in their eyes. But instead she sat down on the floor and began picking up the pieces one by one.

KAY BOYLE:

CAIRO STREET

T HEY looked out of place in this section of Paris, perhaps
members of a motion-picture company who had lost their
stars and wandered in out of the sudden springtime heat for a
glass of beer while they waited for time or circumstances to ab-
solve them; the one who wore neat dark blue and a hat with a
shape to it the director's secretary, it might be, and the big soft
man in the checked wool jacket the director himself, thick-
shouldered, bald, art-bitten, his heavy thighs clasped fast by chest-
nut-colored velvet trousers, the sallow oriental hand holding the
glass, and the loose dark underlip funnelling beneath the rim as
he drank. The one dressed up like an English soldier, sitting with
his chair tipped back into the corner of the café-tabac and a
cigarette on his lip, might have been the young embittered author
of the piece. His hair was crisp and wavy under the khaki cap,
his brows faun-like, his cheeks hollow, and he might have been
twenty-three-or-four but something like weariness or bitterness
had marked him prematurely. Either he was soured by what they
had done to his story in the filming or else too many nights of
too hard drinking had given him the look of worn and desiccated
melancholy he bore. His long thin legs in their battle-dress were
stretched out under the marble-topped table on which the glasses
of beer stood, and near his boots was the camera, or what looked
as though it might be one, with the strap to sling it onto the
shoulder hanging, and a case for carrying films beside it.

The first one, the little secretary, or clerk, or caterer to the
great, was obviously French, but he spoke the language to them
with a slight uneasiness in the voice and eyes (perhaps because

44

the men he had sat down with were foreigners he had met only a quarter of an hour before, or perhaps because he was too small in stature ever to be at ease with men at all). He was saying:

"In the first six months of experimentation we exhausted war. I was with Tricolore Radio then and we went through the whole chromatic scale: first Madrid bombed, then Helsinki, ships foundering, submarine sucking to the bottom, whine of shells, scream of ambulances—all through the ear." He gave them a fleeting, uneasy smile before he said: "You people who work with the stage or the screen, it's all made simple for you, but on the air you have only the one organ of reception. Everything we deal with has to be reduced to its verbal delivery, sermon, peroration, locution—"

It was early afternoon and the café-tabac was empty of clients except for the three men sitting there with the glasses of beer before them, but because of the lorry traffic outside in Cairo Street it seemed a crowded, violently-animated place. From the boulevard Sebastopol came the big city noises, and here in the narrow one-way street the trucks braked, roared, backfired, crowding enormously and intimately past.

"All kinds of weathers were used up," the little Frenchman said, leaning closer across the table. His quick, cocky hand went out as if he were going to pick up his glass and drink, but instead he adjusted his cuff and went on talking. "Gales at sea, fog-horns, rockets of distress, high winds, blizzards, they've been done over and over. And take an aeroplane—aeroplanes are completely finished. You can't use a triple-motor throb now and hope to hold your public any more than you can get them on the edge of their seats with the sound of a galloping horse." He raised his voice above the increasing tumult of the lorries returning thicker and faster to their own district now to load up for the evening's getaway. "Put a mine-disaster on the stage and you can add to your effect by smell—burn something in the wings. Or volumes of smoke pouring across the screen, but we're tied up tight, we can't rely on anything like that. We have to reach the ear," he said, "the blind, dumb, untutored ear, the universal and completely unaided ear—"

"What the devil do you think Ornstein can do about it?" the young man dressed as an English soldier said. He tipped his chair further back on its two legs in the corner, and lit another cigarette and threw the match away. He spoke French with an accent, his lip contorted with the shape and taste of the words as an Anglo-Saxon's is likely to be. Then he brought his chair forward on its four legs with a crack. "If you're trying to sell him something, it's no good. He's American. He has a radio already," he said.

He picked up his glass and drank, irritation sucking his cheeks thinner, the faun's brows twitching, the girlish, delicately-skinned throat swallowing the beer.

"Let him talk, O'Corey," said the big man, speaking English or any other language with soft-tongued, oriental inaccuracy. He leaned one arm in the brown-and-white-checked sleeve on the marble and looked heavily, lingeringly at the little Frenchman's face, and then without turning his head away and without lifting his hand to his mouth he yawned. On one vulnerable wrist he wore a silver-linked bracelet. Sometime before he had taken his necktie off because of the heat and opened his yellow linen shirt at the neck. "Just let him go on," he said. "He's not so stupid." He looked at the clock over the door and yawned again. "We got three-quarters of an hour to kill. We might as well listen to him as sit doing nothing."

"I'm presenting the difficulties like this to give you an idea," the Frenchman went on, having understood nothing, not the words, nor the yawn across the beer, nor the impatience in the soldier's face. "I'm giving you the technical side of it," he said, "leaving the question of propaganda aside. We can give anti-German, anti-Russian, anti-Japanese propaganda until the time when television comes under international control. Then if Japanese bankers, for instance, have a big share of the stock, the propaganda will alter. Last month I did 'Uncle Tome's Cabin' for Radio Moderne," he said, "and that struck a new note because of the dialect. We played up the blacks moaning in chorus and worked up to the climax of that scene where the dogs go after Uncle Tome across the ice."

"Eliza," said the young man called O'Corey. The lorry coming up Cairo Street braked loudly at the intersection, then shifted gears to take the climb. "It was Eliza they were after," O'Corey said, snarling it across the beer.

"No, Uncle Tome," said the Frenchman, smiling. Ornstein was leaning heavily, slumbrously on the table, his mouth open, looking without wonder, almost without interest at the Frenchman's face. "It had a certain novelty," he was saying, "but it didn't get us past the limits in dimension I was speaking of before. According to the results of our inquiry, sixty-three per cent of our known audience switched off when the horses came up the drive. You can't do horses' hoofs any more. People have had enough. That, and the kind of incident that took place a few months back when a whole crew went out one night in the woods to pick up the troating of a rutting stag, that's all a part of radio's past. We were six hours out there in the moonlight with the apparatus set up and the announcer telling thousands of listeners all over Europe that in another five minutes we were sure to get it. The police had thrown a cordon around the woods in a two-mile radius. The amplifiers were hanging in the branches of the trees, but those Don Juans didn't open their mouths all evening." He started to laugh, but meeting O'Corey's eyes he changed his mind. He waited until the three monstrous trucks had passed the corner, and then he went on saying: "That's why I consider this assignment a step backward as far as radio history is concerned. I'm to hop to Marseilles on a lorry tonight, eat in the Routiers' Restaurants with the drivers, get all the sounds right, and pick out my leading broadcaster on the way. If you tune in on Radio Moderne at 8:35 next Saturday night you'll get the sound-record of the trip I'm going to take this evening. But what I'm interested in," he said, leaning towards the man called Ornstein, "is something else. I'd like to give a sound-projection of an exhibition of paintings, for instance, striking a means between speech and vision that would communicate the painter's intention in the same way the original work of art does."

"O'Corey, he's not so bad," said Ornstein, and he took the folded silk handkerchief out of the top pocket of his checked jacket and wiped the moisture off his face and brow. "He's fecund, you know, he's fecund," he said, and he put his arms down on the table again and leaned on them, looking indolently at the little Frenchman on the other side. "He won't live long, he can't live long," said Ornstein, dreamily. "Somebody'll have to rub him out." He sat there looking at him as if at a specimen caught wild somewhere and put into a curved container, on view to mortals as he climbed up the sloping side, climbed up it over and over again and each time did not quite make the edge but fell back to the center; watching him lift himself again and start climbing up the side again, clinging to absolutely nothing with his puny hands.

"As long as television belongs to the highest bidder and the bidding isn't closed yet," the Frenchman said, "I can't go in for that. But there's talk at the studio of a scale, perhaps in color or perhaps in a new musical notation, which is still to be perfected. If television were liberated, as it should be, like helium, we'd none of us have to pay entrance fees to museums, but until it is I'm looking for the way to broadcast the essence of a classical nativity by sound, and another to project to the ear a Dali paint-ing, for instance—"

"It's half past three," said O'Corey, taking his cap off and flinging it down on the marble. "How long is this going to go on?"

Outside, in the other street, a brewery-lorry came to a halt by the curb, and the driver, bare-armed and wearing a leather apron over his shirt and trousers, came in through the open door. He jerked his billed cap to the back of his head and said bon jour to the waiter standing behind the zinc and the three men at the table. Three lorries mounted the incline of Cairo Street, bearing their companies' names and their destinations printed on them, and on one the route mapped out with Paris at one end of the broad fair indicated avenue and Marseilles at the other, as single and simple as if no towns or landscapes lay between the two. The Frenchman's voice was lost in their thunder a moment, and the brewery-truck driver came and went; went carrying the empty kegs easily out from behind the counter, and came with his tough bare arms stretched down to the weight, carrying in the full. When he came for the fourth time through the door, O'Corey leaned back in his chair and raised his hands to his mouth and called out through the traffic's tumult.

"Your beer's rotten. Anybody ever told you that?"

The bit of dead cigarette on the truck driver's lip moved with his grin.

"German talk-water!" he called back across the café to the table, and O'Corey suddenly began laughing, the eye swift, eager as a bird's, and the thin belly jerking under his belt as he laughed.

"It isn't that television isn't perfected," the little Frenchman was saying. "It has to be tied up by patents before they can let it go. They say it's even possible for death to be directed by it. For example, by bringing into the vision of an ill or aged person, possibly a victim of a heart ailment, a speeding locomotive. There was a case I knew of in the same line of reasoning," he said, looking only at Ornstein now. "A man driving in a car with a friend, a nervous man who had been under treatment in a psychopathic clinic, and the car approached a railway crossing where the barriers were raised and it was clearly quite safe to cross. The driver of the car did not hesitate, drove onto the tracks, and there the nervous passenger gave a loud scream and seized his arm. 'The train's coming, the train's coming!' he shouted out, and he collapsed on the seat. There was no train visible, and when they were clear of the crossing the driver stopped the car to revive his friend, and discovered he was dead. But here comes the interesting part," the Frenchman said, pausing for the effect. "The doctors later pronounced that he had not died of heart-failure but from bodily injuries—contusions and a broken back—"

The brewery-lorry driver was going out again with an empty keg hanging at arm's length before him, the yoked wood of the barrel riding against his apron's leather as he walked. His cap was on the back of his head off his sweat-matted hair, and his face was turned to look at O'Corey, his mouth laughing but no sound coming from it because of the clamor of trucks filing past.

When he came back in again his hands were empty and he wiped his face with a dark blue rag and leaned on the zinc.

"Beer thins the blood, bloats the stomach, weakens the arteries, wears out the privy," he called across the café, and he picked up the glass of red wine the waiter had set beside him on the bar. He glanced at the window and door an instant, and then he raised his hand in a closed fist and shook it towards the three men in the corner in salutation before he drank. O'Corey brought his chair down hard on its four feet, and then he stood up, tall, slender, a little stooping in his khaki, and with one hand in his trouser's pocket he slouched across the café to the bar.

"Not mobilized?" he said, with his accent, standing beside the lorry driver, and the other man lifted the fingers of one hand and shook his head.

"Five children," he said. He stood drinking his wine and looking at the young man in the English uniform, looking at him over the glass with black, clear, merry eyes. O'Corey's narrow, haggard face was delicate as a woman's and his eyebrows twitched as he spoke.

"I'm leaving for Norway in twenty minutes," he said. "Have a drink on me before I go."

ERNEST BRACE:

THREE MEN OF FIFTY

O'BRIEN had been the first of the three to enter the hospital. His was a serious cardiac case and for three days he fought for breath under an oxygen tent. Mr. Handley with pneumonia was brought in the next morning. And finally, Henry Weilen relaxed limply on the third cot and gave up his long struggle to keep on working in spite of stomach ulcers. None of the three had ever even heard of either of the others, and it was many days before their proximity assumed any greater significance than the chance of a common subway ride.

O'Brien's personality was the first to emerge from its suffocating weight of physical misery. Propped high on his cot he discovered one morning that for an hour or more he had forgotten all about breathing. The cot creaked under his two hundred and fifty pounds as he turned to look at Mr. Handley.

"How ya feelin', Jack?" he asked.

Mr. Handley's frail, bony head turned very slowly. As he saw the pale blue eyes watching him, he understood, as he had feared, that he was being called "Jack." He wanted not to answer at all and to look away coldly, but he did not quite dare. There was no telling how long they might be neighbors, and even for a sick man in a hospital ward, he supposed wearily, there were social obligations.

"Comfortable, thank you," he replied and looked away.

The blue eyes hardened. O'Brien's nose, already rosy, became scarlet.

"Yeah?" he said. "Well me, I got an awful pain in the neck." He rolled over so that his back was toward Mr. Handley.

51

Mr. Handley turned over on his right side so that he faced away from Mr. O'Brien. And then he wished he'd remained on his back. He looked abruptly into the lustreless eyes of Henry Weilen, and he was conscious of the necessity to smile or say good-morning or offer some friendly gesture. But before he could even twitch his features into a hint of greeting, the eyes closed. Mr. Handley frowned irritably. He was mildly ashamed of himself and his timid dignity, but more than that he resented the necessity which had exposed him to being addressed as "Jack" and to seeing the hopelessness of dull eyes. He sighed and stretched out on his back.

He dozed for a while and was awakened by the pressure of a hand on his shoulder. He blinked into the annoyingly sardonic smile of Dr. Janey, senior interne. He sat up.

"Well, how goes it today?"

"I feel better."

"You'll be all right in a few days. Your temperature's normal. Let's have a look at your back."

The doctor adjusted the ear pieces of his stethoscope and listened with weary concentration while Mr. Handley breathed and reiterated a quick, nervous "one, two." He thumped the bony back a bit and with a final slap moved away from the bed.

"You can sit up fifteen minutes this afternoon," he said.

Mr. Handley watched the nurse make a note in her book.

"I'm awfully weak. I hope I won't catch more cold."

"You'll be all right if you keep wrapped up. The longer you stay in bed the weaker you'll get." He yawned and walked away, saying something to the nurse which made her laugh.

Mr. Handley settled back against the pillows. Why, he wondered, didn't the news that he was enough better to sit up make him happy? It wouldn't be long now before he'd be out of the hospital and back home. He ought to be glad. He ought to be smiling. But instead he was filled with fears and resentment and disappointment in himself.

He was not going to die, after all. And yet he was more afraid now than he had been when he had been fighting desperately for every breath. He would be able to go home again. He would climb slowly back up the stairs, cross the dim landings, smell the odors of cooking food, hear the sound of radios, of people's voices. He would sit again in the green chair by the window and look up toward the corner at the drug store and the traffic light, and stare at the black, lustrous pavement on rainy nights. And he would hear Helen moving about in the kitchen, busy with the long unnoticed but now vivid routine of getting dinner.

It wasn't, of course, until one was snatched away from such hum-drum intimacies that they became important or even desirable. But now they were the dim, familiar background against which moved the ghostly shadows of his fear. The life to which he would return had become surprisingly precarious. From the warm protection of his cot he could see only bleak vistas of illness, poverty, and hunger. Had he really wanted to die and get it over with?

If he had been able to afford a private room it wouldn't have been so bad. At times, even when he had been very sick, the presence of so many anonymous bodies in the same room with him had seemed even more stifling than the congestion of his lungs. And now his convalescence was making him more and more aware of the other fevered, struggling bodies. He was conscious of the fragile unimportance of his own personality. He was merely "Jack." Nothing that happened to him could have any meaning to anyone but himself. Now, for the first time, he understood how frantically he had struggled all his life to build up his little tower of dignity, and he knew too that, as with all fortifications, the reason for his tower was fear. But what specifically was he afraid of? He did not know. He could not choose from his welter of potential threats any one that seemed more menacing than the others. He feared poverty and yet, of all the people in the hospital, he had the least reason perhaps for such a fear. His civil service job was as certain to keep him fed and to end in a pension as it was never to make him rich. No, the fear was not the result of any immediate threat. It was a part of his living, like hunger. Dimly he perceived that his safe little job was the result of his apprehensions, not the reason for them. Above all else in life he needed safety and protection. That was the reason he hated the hospital ward. There was no protection, no safe retreat from the world.

At precisely two-thirty that afternoon the visiting hour began with the entrance into the ward of Mr. Handley's wife. O'Brien leaned out toward the bed on the other side and whispered, "I tell you he's got her trained, all right." He laughed.

As usual Mrs. Handley kissed her husband on the forehead, placed a newspaper and a magazine and a bag of fruit on his table, and sat down.

"Well, how are you today? You look well."

He smiled faintly. Her remark was meaningless, for she had told him he looked well when his fever was highest. He did not want to tell her he was going to sit up that afternoon. Somehow his improving health seemed to put him in the wrong, to discount all his complaints. He would tell her later, perhaps.

"I'm fairly well," he said. "But I'm terribly weak."

"What do you expect?" She patted his shoulder efficiently. "You'll be all right, if you'd only stop worrying and fretting so. They tell me you're going to sit up today."

He nodded almost guiltily.

"Well, you might look more pleased. Anybody'd think they'd told you you had to have an operation. My goodness, I can't understand you."

Mr. Handley said nothing. He felt hurt. Not even Helen seemed capable of understanding his feelings. He watched her quick, interested eyes look along the row of beds. Nearly thirty years of living together could not quite overcome the self-conscious embarrassment of their strange situation. Here they felt they must talk and there was nothing to say. Helen was far off in a strange world. She seemed to lack all comprehension and fear of this one.

"In a way I should think it would be more interesting here where there's so much going on than if you were shut off by yourself in a little room," she said, turning back to him.

"Maybe you'd like it better. Women always seem to be interested in other people's diseases."

"Don't you ever talk to any of the other patients?"

"Not any more than I can help."

"But why? I—"

"Because I don't want to," he interrupted bitterly. "Because I hate them the way I hate people who push against me in the subway."

Her surprised glance slid away from his sharp eyes. For the remainder of the hour they found it more difficult than ever to talk.

When she had gone Mr. Handley felt unaccountably sad. The spurt of his venom seemed to have left him weak, almost nauseated. He did hate the other patients. Why should he be ashamed of that? He couldn't help it. And yet he was, though not exactly ashamed of his outburst, distrustful of his emotion and afraid of it too, as if it were the first swift symptom of some dread disease.

A little later as the nurse helped him out of bed he was more conscious of the many eyes watching him than he was of his flabbily tottering legs. But as he subsided into the protection of his chair he realized that he used to climb the four flights at home with far less exhaustion than he felt now. He drew the blanket tightly around his thin shoulders and blinked up into the sunlight streaming through the window.

"Jees, I wish I was you."

Mr. Handley looked up startled into O'Brien's sombre eyes.

"Why?" he asked.

"Sittin' up like that. You'll be gettin' out of here soon now."

"Not very soon, I'm afraid," Mr. Handley mumbled politely. "I'm still pretty weak."

"Yeah, but you get over that quick. I been here three times now. Once you're on your feet it don't take long to learn how to use 'em again. Christ knows if I'll ever use mine again. And a hell of a lot of good it'll do me anyway. You don't get cured of a heart like mine."

Mr. Handley stared out the window. He ought to express sympathy, but what was the use? In a way, he was sorry for O'Brien, but without quite knowing it he was more sorry for himself. Whoever came near you in here began immediately to unload his troubles on you. He didn't go around complaining to the others. Why couldn't they let him alone?

"Friendly bastard, ain't you?"

Mr. Handley moistened his lips nervously and looked up at O'Brien. He hadn't expected a direct attack and he couldn't think of anything to say. O'Brien's eyes were clear and immovable.

"I—I have enough troubles of my own and I try to forget about them."

"Yeah? Well, someday I hope you have a bad heart and no job and then you'll get some idea of what trouble is." O'Brien turned away.

Mr. Handley moistened his lips again. He was not angry now. A feeling of guilt stifled every other emotion. He vaguely understood that there was only one way to free himself: that was to attempt explaining his feelings to O'Brien. But there was nothing to explain. All he wanted was to be let alone. Yet in spite of all reason Mr. Handley spent most of his fifteen minutes out of bed in formulating excuses he might express to O'Brien.

He was exhausted when he got back into bed. Some other time he would say something pleasant. He was too tired now. He closed his eyes and dozed.

When he woke up he had a bewildered feeling that something had happened. He blinked and closed his eyes. Was it a vanishing dream? Or had there really been some excitement while he slept? He opened his eyes wide and raised his head. An orderly was wheeling a screen back from O'Brien's bed. The bed was moving. They were pushing it out into the aisle. A sheet covered O'Brien's head.

Mr. Handley lay perfectly still with his eyes closed. He was seeing O'Brien's puff-ball face and the radish-nose balanced on top of it. "How ya feelin', Jack?" The words seemed as permanent in Mr. Handley's thoughts as a carved epitaph. The resentment they had first roused was as dead as O'Brien himself. They had become sombre and dignified with pity.

Mr. Handley tried to squirm away from his own thoughts, but he could not avoid them. He understood now that he had a great deal in common with O'Brien. The man's living and straining

and groaning and greedy breathing had become now more significant than his hard, brittle eyes or his blatant voice. It seemed
to him that O'Brien would have had a great many interesting
things to say, things that Mr. Handley wanted very much to
know. He could not even imagine what they might be, but he
could sense the stirring emotion of hearing them.

He turned over on his side, facing away from the empty bed.
His back seemed physically aware of emptiness, as if the blanket
were pulled away. Without seeing it at first, he stared at the
high bald forehead of Henry Weilen. Gradually the face emerged
into Mr. Handley's consciousness, the sunken waxy cheeks, the
thin nose, the pallid taut-drawn lips. Henry Weilen was asleep.
His breathing seemed to cause no perceptible movement of the
covers drawn up under his bony chin. Mr. Handley stared at
them breathlessly. Yes, from time to time there was a flicker of
movement. Breathing seemed such a precarious, difficult business;
no single inhalation gave promise of a succeeding one. He turned
over on his back and tried to forget the morbidity that had assailed him. His thoughts seemed to have no other function than
the dredging out of great chasms of fear.

A little later he realized that he was turning his head regularly
to reassure himself that Henry Weilen really was breathing. More
fervently than ever he longed for seclusion. A private room
would have removed him from the contagion of all this afternoon's distress. But why should he think himself more sensitive
than other men? Whence came his necessity to hold himself
aloof?

He did not know that he had dozed until he woke with a start.
There was a screen around the next bed. He could see a doctor
and a nurse behind it. He raised upon his elbow and, rubbing
the sleep from his eyes, watched anxiously. He did not want
Mr. Weilen to die. Henry Weilen's dying would mean something very personal to Mr. Handley. Although he knew even
less about Weilen than he had about O'Brien, he had a feeling
that the man's death would leave him more lonely than he had
ever been in his life. And it would not be a passing loneliness;
it would sink deeper and deeper into his consciousness. No one

would know it was there, but he would never be able to forget it. He sighed with deep relief as he caught a glimpse of Henry Weilen's eyes. At least the man was still alive and conscious.

Mr. Handley lay back against his pillows. He glanced over at the empty bed where O'Brien had been. Poor O'Brien. He could still sense his revulsion against O'Brien's grunting, lumpy body, still imagine that it had a fetid odor, and yet the emotion epitomized by "Poor O'Brien" was pervasively sincere. He thought then of home but with no nostalgia. Home was another, an alien existence. It had nothing to do with the life here, with the business of laboring and suffering and dying. It was a refuge—safe, almost unreal. But first there was something he must accomplish here. He could not decide exactly what it was, but at least the sense of necessity was very real and clear.

They moved the screen away from Mr. Weilen's bed. The doctor and the nurse left the ward. Mr. Weilen looked pale and tired.

Mr. Handley had to clear his throat twice before he could speak. "How are you feeling?" he asked. He knew that he had quite failed to give any warmth to his question. He hoped only that Henry Weilen would not perceive the tremendous effort behind it.

The long, heavy-jowled head turned slowly. Henry Weilen looked at Mr. Handley in pallid surprise.

"Awful."

"I'm sorry to hear that."

The tired eyes surveyed Mr. Handley with mild scepticism.

"Well, at least you're in a place where they have every facility for taking good care of you," Mr. Handley added.

"I wish they wouldn't bother. I wish they'd let me die and get it over with."

"Oh, you mustn't let yourself feel that way. You mustn't get discouraged."

"Why not?"

"Well, it doesn't pay to—"

"I know it doesn't pay. Nothing pays. If it paid to be cheerful I'd be singing and laughing twenty-four hours a day. It won't pay them to fix me up and get me out of here, either. And it won't pay the undertaker to bury me. They know how to patch you up so you can give an imitation of somebody still alive, but they can't tell you how to live. Suppose they do fix my stomach up so it can digest food again? What I want to know is what I'm going to use my stomach for when I get out of here? And nobody can tell me that."

Mr. Handley swallowed nervously. He realized that the stock conventional phrases that had got him into this unpleasant realism were not adequate to see him through it. Any bland assurance that something might turn up would be merely insulting. What *did* people do under such circumstances? What would he do himself?

"If it was just dying or being sick, I wouldn't worry. Everyone has to do that. What scares me is living."

"But you'll certainly get help somewhere. After all, they don't just let people starve."

"Don't they?"

The matter-of-fact question both annoyed and frightened Mr. Handley. "Haven't you any family or relatives?" he asked.

"No. My wife died ten years ago. We didn't have any children. I lost track of all my relatives. Anyway, they were the kind who need help, not give it. Oh, I know there are ways to get useless bodies taken care of, but you have to give up first, and that's hard."

The man sagged back wearily into silence and lay staring up at the ceiling. Mr. Handley watched the tears form in the corners of Henry Weilen's eyes and roll jerkily down his cheek. Finally Mr. Handley closed his own eyes.

The next morning he woke up with the feeling that there was something special he had to do that day. He remembered Henry Weilen and glanced over at his bed. Their eyes met and they said good-morning. Weilen seemed more cheerful than he had the day before, but somehow his smile held more tragedy than his tears. Certainly his problems could not have been solved during the night. Actually it was impossible that they could ever reach a solution. What did people like that do? What could they do? What could they do, not just with their bodies but with their thoughts and their hopes? Mr. Handley thought guiltily of his own job and its certain pension. Even with such assurance he feared the future. He desired nothing so much as complete protection from the world. And here at last he lay in a public ward, exposed to—well, to what? What precisely was it that he feared and shrank from?

When he got up that afternoon Mr. Handley sat in the chair on the other side of his bed, next to Henry Weilen. He felt a little embarrassed when the nurse had gone and he glanced up to find Weilen looking at him curiously.

"I thought I'd sit over here," he said, "so I could talk to you, but if you're too tired, or'd rather keep quiet I can read."

"Oh, no. I almost go crazy lying here thinking. But I had the idea that you didn't like to talk."

"Well, I suppose I don't—most of the time. It's always been hard for me to talk to most people."

"I've spent my life talking to them—all sorts. I was a floorwalker. I got so I hated people, but I'd go crazy alone."

"I should think you'd like to get away from their silly questions for a while, even if it's in a hospital."

"Oh, it wasn't the questions so much. It's the way they fight and push and claw and lie to get what they want. That's one thing that makes me feel so helpless now. I know about how much you can expect from people. There are only two kinds, really—the greedy and the ones who are poor because they aren't greedy enough."

"Won't the store where you were working do something for you when you get out of here?"

Henry Weilen's face wrinkled crookedly. "The store's greedier than the people who come to buy. But don't worry about me. I'll be able to get along somehow. I didn't mean to get so excited yesterday, but I was feeling pretty low. The worst part's knowing you won't ever be able to do anything with your life again, that you've got to look around and find a place to wait till it's over."

"I know. It's terrible."

"Well, one thing, nowadays there's lots of others like me. Wherever I go I won't be alone."

"But there shouldn't be anybody in that position. It isn't right."

"Sure. It isn't right my stomach should be no good either, but there's not much anybody can do about it."

"But can't the doctors help you?"

"Not much. I waited too long and I've had attacks like this before, only this is worse."

"But if you're careful—"

"Sure, if I live on special foods and don't eat a lot of restaurant grease and things like that I might be all right for quite a while, but when you're poor or live on charity you eat what you can get, not what's good for you."

Mr. Handley stared silently out the window, feeling he ought to say something hopeful but knowing no hope. What could there be for a man in that predicament? What would there be for himself? Peace, security. He felt his fragile body suddenly flag with fear. It was scarcely a day since O'Brien had died, and his memory held only a fast-fading tinge of emotion. As Weilen had said, it was living, not death, that was disheartening. In a few days now he would go back home, climb up the stairs, through the noises, through the smell of living. And after a few more days he would be saying to himself: What was that fellow's name? Weiley? Bailey? . . . He wouldn't be able to remember . . . I wonder what ever happened to him? And then there would be johnnycake for dinner and he would forget all about him. That was the peace of living, the peace that led one stealthily by pleasant by-paths to death. A little more money and he would have been able to guard his privacy against all this.

"Maybe I'll be able to think of some way to help you," he was saying suddenly, without having planned to speak. "I want to give you my address. I want you to let me know when you get out of the hospital. Something might turn up. I might hear about something." His ideas of what it might be were even more vague than his words.

"Listen, Mr. Handley, I wasn't asking you to—"

"I know you weren't. I probably won't be able to do anything, but I'd like to see you again, anyway."

There could be no doubt of Mr. Handley's earnestness. Henry Weilen seemed almost embarrassed by it. He stared at the slip of paper Mr. Handley gave him. "It's funny," he said at length; "I thought you were different."

They were silent and awkward for a long time, and when they began talking again it was of the weather.

Of course Mr. Handley regretted his impulsiveness, particularly since any hope he had aroused in Weilen was pure deception. What would Helen say when she heard about it? But that was not the point. Why had he made such a childish and meaningless gesture? It hadn't been just because he felt sorry for Weilen. There was some necessity in himself to accept a challenge. At least he had wrenched his attention loose from the jangling merry-go-round of his former thinking. People seemed less like hungry dogs yapping at his dignity.

He awoke the next morning with a sense of heavy responsibility. As he remembered Weilen he closed his eyes and tried to go back to sleep. A thin tremor of dread assured him that he was irrevocably awake. What a fool he had been yesterday. He shrank from the prospect of even bidding Weilen good-morning. He was both embarrassed and annoyed. Had he hoped to right the world's injustices by becoming a busybody? If he were really in a position to do anything it might be different, but he had merely added a futility to his worries. What would Helen say? There was no explanation for a thing he could not himself understand. With petulant desperation he turned to look at Weilen. The bed was empty.

A week later Mr. Handley went home. In the taxi he could almost believe for a few minutes that he was escaping from the dark cavern where he had briefly seen the gray shadows that were O'Brien and Weilen. But later, as he was climbing with slow effort to his home, up through the intimate noises and the alien smells, he knew that there was a third shadow and that it was his own. At dusk he sat in the green chair by the window and looked up toward the traffic light at the corner and the bright drugstore window. Though his chair was close to the hot radiator he shivered. He felt tired and very very lonely. He wished there were someone he could talk to, someone who was tired and afraid as he was tired and afraid. "How ya feeling, Jack?" he muttered. It didn't sound right. He tried again. "How ya feeling—"

WALTER VAN TILBURG CLARK:
THE INDIAN WELL

I N THIS dead land the only allegiance was to sun. Even night
was not strong enough to resist; earth stretched gratefully
when night came, but had no hope that day would not return.
Such living things as hoarded a little juice at their cores were
secret about it, and only the most ephemeral existences, the air
at dawn and sunset, the amethyst shadows in the mountains, had
any freedom. The Indian Well alone, of lesser creations, was in
constant revolt. Sooner or later all minor breathing rebels came
to its stone basin under the spring in the cliff, and from its overflow grew a tiny meadow delta and two columns of willows
and aspens, holding a tiny front against the valley. The pictograph of a starving, ancient journey, cut in rock above the basin,
a sun-warped shack on the south wing of the canyon, and an
abandoned mine above it, were the only tokens of man's participation in the well's cycles, each of which was an epitome of
centuries, and perhaps of the wars of the universe.

The day before Jim Suttler came up, in the early spring, to
take his part in one cycle, was a busy day. The sun was merely
lucid after four days of broken showers, and, under the separate
cloud shadows sliding down the mountain and into the valley,
the canyon was alive. A rattler emerged partially from a hole
in the mound on which the cabin stood, and having gorged in
the darkness, rested with his head on a stone. A road-runner,
stepping long and always about to sprint, came down the morning side of the mound, and his eye, quick to perceive the difference between the live and the inanimate of the same color, discovered the coffin shaped head on the stone. At once he broke

into a reaching sprint, his neck and tail stretched level, his beak agape with expectation. But his shadow arrived a step before him. The rattler recoiled, his head scarred by the sharp beak but his eye intact. The road-runner said nothing, but peered warily into the hole without stretching his neck, then walked off stiffly, leaning forward again as if about to run. When he had gone twenty feet he turned, balanced for an instant, and charged back, checking abruptly just short of the hole. The snake remained withdrawn. The road-runner paraded briefly before the hole, talking to himself, and then ran angrily up to the spring, where he drank at the overflow, sipping and stretching his neck, lifting his feet one at a time, ready to go into immediate action. The road-runner lived a dangerous and exciting life.

In the upper canyon the cliff swallows, making short harp notes, dipped and shot between the new mud under the aspens and their high community on the forehead of the cliff. Electrical bluebirds appeared to dart the length of the canyon at each low flight, turned up tilting. Lizards made unexpected flights and stops on the rocks, and when they stopped did rapid push-ups, like men exercising on a floor. They were variably pugnacious and timid.

Two of them arrived simultaneously upon a rock below the road-runner. One of them immediately skittered to a rock two feet off, and they faced each other, exercising. A small hawk coming down over the mountain, but shadowless under a cloud, saw the lizards. Having overfled the difficult target, he dropped to the canyon mouth swiftly and banked back into the wind. His trajectory was cleared of swallows, but one of them, fluttering hastily up, dropped a pellet of mud between the lizards. The one who had retreated disappeared. The other flattened for an instant, then sprang and charged. The road-runner was on him as he struck the pellet, and galloped down the canyon in great, tense strides, on his toes, the lizard lashing the air from his beak. The hawk stooped at the road-runner, thought better of it, and rose against the wind to the head of the canyon, where he turned back and coasted over the desert, his shadow a little behind him and farther and farther below.

The swallows became the voice of the canyon again, but in moments when they were all silent, the lovely smaller sounds emerged, their own feathering, the liquid overflow, the snapping and clicking of insects, a touch of wind in the new aspens. Under these lay still more delicate tones, erasing, in the most silent seconds, the difference between eye and ear, a white cloud shadow passing under the water of the well, a dark cloud shadow on the cliff, the aspen patterns on the stones. Silentest of all were the rocks, the lost on the canyon floor, and the strong, thinking cliffs. The swallows began again.

At noon a red and white cow with one new calf, shining and curled, came slowly up from the desert, stopping often to let the calf rest. At each stop the calf would try vigorously to feed, but the cow would go on. When they reached the well the cow drank slowly for a long time; then she continued to wrinkle the water with her muzzle, drinking a little and blowing, as if she found it hard to leave. The calf worked under her with spasmodic nudgings. When she was done playing with the water, she nosed and licked him out from under her and up to the well. He shied from the surprising coolness and she put him back. When he stayed, she drank again. He put his nose into the water too, and bucked up as if bitten. He returned, got water up his nostrils and took three jumps away. The cow was content and moved off towards the canyon wall, tonguing grass tufts from among the rocks. Against the cliff she rubbed gently and continuously with a mild voluptuous look, occasionally lapping her nose with a serpent tongue. The loose winter shag came off in tufts on the rock. The calf lost her, became panicked and made desperate noises which stopped prematurely, and when he discovered her, complicated her toilet. Finally she led him down to the meadow where, moving slowly, they both fed until he was full and went to sleep in a ball in the sun. At sunset they returned to the well, where the cow drank again and gave him a second lesson. After this they went back into the brush and northward into the dusk. The cow's size and relative immunity to sudden death left an aftermath of peace, rendered gently humorous by the calf.

Also at sunset, there was a resurgence of life among the swallows. The thin golden air at the cliff tops, in which there were now no clouds so that the eastern mountains and the valley were flooded with unbroken light, was full of their cries and quick maneuvres among a dancing myriad of insects. The direct sun gave them, when they perched in rows upon the cliff, a dramatic significance like that of men upon an immensely higher promontory. As dusk rose out of the canyon, while the eastern peaks were still lighted, the swallows gradually became silent. At twilight, the air was full of velvet, swooping bats.

In the night jack-rabbits multiplied spontaneously out of the brush of the valley, drank in the rivulet, their noses and great ears continuously searching the dark, electrical air, and played in fits and starts on the meadow, the many young ones hopping like rubber, or made thumping love among the aspens and the willows.

A coyote came down canyon on his belly and lay in the brush with his nose between his paws. He took a young rabbit in a quiet spring and snap, and went into the brush again to eat it. At the slight rending of his meal the meadow cleared of leaping shadows and lay empty in the starlight. The rabbits, however, encouraged by new-comers, returned soon, and the coyote killed again and went off heavily, the jack's great hind legs dragging.

In the dry-wash below the meadow an old coyote, without family, profited by the second panic, which came over him. He ate what his loose teeth could tear, leaving the open remnant in the sand, drank at the basin and, carefully circling the meadow, disappeared into the dry wilderness.

Shortly before dawn, when the stars had lost lustre and there was no sound in the canyon but the rivulet and the faint, separate clickings of mice in the gravel, nine antelope in loose file, with three silently flagging fawns, came on trigger toe up the meadow and drank at the well, heads often up, muzzles dripping, broad ears turning. In the meadow they grazed and the fawns nursed. When there was as much gray as darkness in the air, and new wind in the canyon, they departed, the file weaving into the brush, merging into the desert, to nothing, and the swallows resumed the talkative day shift.

Jim Suttler and his burro came up into the meadow a little after noon, very slowly, though there was only a spring-fever warmth. Suttler walked pigeon-toed, like an old climber, but carefully and stiffly, not with the loose walk natural to such a long-legged man. He stopped in the middle of the meadow, took off his old black sombrero, and stared up at the veil of water shining over the edge of the basin.

"We're none too early, Jenny," he said to the burro.

The burro had felt water for miles, but could show no excitement. She stood with her head down and her four legs spread unnaturally, as if to postpone a collapse. Her pack reared higher than Suttler's head, and was hung with casks, pans, canteens, a pick, two shovels, a crowbar, and a rifle in a sheath. Suttler had the cautious uncertainty of his trade. His other burro had died two days before in the mountains east of Beatty, and Jenny and he bore its load.

Suttler shifted his old six-shooter from his rump to his thigh, and studied the well, the meadow, the cabin and the mouth of the mine as if he might choose not to stay. He was not a cinema prospector. If he looked like one of the probably mistaken conceptions of Christ, with his red beard and red hair to his shoulders, it was because he had been away from barbers and without spare water for shaving. He was unlike Christ in some other ways.

"It's kinda run down," he told Jenny, "but we'll take it."

He put his sombrero back on, let his pack fall slowly to the ground, showing the sweat patch in his bleached brown shirt, and began to unload Jenny carefully, like a collector handling rare vases, and put everything into one neat pile.

"Now," he said, "we'll have a drink." His tongue and lips were so swollen that the words were unclear, but he spoke casually, like a club-man sealing a minor deal. One learns to do business slowly with deserts and mountains. He picked up a bucket and started for the well. At the upper edge of the meadow he looked back. Jenny was still standing with her head down and her legs apart. He did not particularly notice her extreme thinness, for he had seen it coming on gradually. He was thinner himself, and tall, and so round-shouldered that when he stood his straightest he seemed to be peering ahead with his chin out.

"Come on, you old fool," he said. "It's off you now."

Jenny came, stumbling in the rocks above the meadow, and stopping often as if to decide why this annoyance recurred. When she became interested, Suttler would not let her get to the basin, but for ten minutes gave her water from his cupped hands, a few licks at a time. Then he drove her off and she stood in the shade of the canyon wall watching him. He began on his thirst in the same way, a gulp at a time, resting between gulps. After ten gulps he sat on a rock by the spring and looked up at the meadow and the big desert, and might have been considering the courses of the water through his body, but noticed also the antelope tracks in the mud.

After a time he drank another half dozen gulps, gave Jenny half a pail full, and drove her down to the meadow, where he spread a dirty blanket in the striped sun and shadow under the willows. He sat on the edge of the blanket, rolled a cigarette and smoked it while he watched Jenny. When she began to graze with her rump to the canyon, he flicked his cigarette onto the grass, rolled over with his back to the sun and slept until it became chilly after sunset. Then he woke, ate a can of beans, threw the can into the willows and led Jenny up to the well, where they drank together from the basin for a long time. While she resumed her grazing, he took another blanket and his rifle from the pile, removed his heel-worn boots, stood his rifle against a fork, and rolling up in both blankets, slept again.

In the night many rabbits played in the meadow in spite of the strong sweat and tobacco smell of Jim Suttler lying under the willows, but the antelope, when they came in the dead dark before dawn, were nervous, drank less, and did not graze but minced quickly back across the meadow and began to run at the head of the dry wash. Jenny slept with her head hanging, and did not hear them come or go.

Suttler woke lazy and still red-eyed, and spent the morning

drinking at the well, eating and dozing on his blanket. In the afternoon, slowly, a few things at a time, he carried his pile to the cabin. He had a bachelor's obsession with order, though he did not mind dirt, and puttered until sundown, making a brush bed and arranging his gear. Much of this time, however, was spent studying the records on the cabin walls of the recent human life of the well. He had to be careful, because among the still legible names and dates, after Frank Davis, 1893, Willard Harbinger, 1893, London, England, John Mason, June 13, 1887, Bucksport, Maine, Mathew Kenling, from Glasgow, 1891, Penelope and Martin Reave, God Guide Us, 1885, was written Frank Hayward, 1492, feeling my age. There were other wits too. John Barr had written, Giv it back to the injuns, and Kenneth Thatcher, two years later, had written under that, Pity the noble redskin, while another man, whose second name was Evans, had written what was already a familiar libel, since it was not strictly true, Fifty miles from water, a hundred miles from wood, a million miles from God, three feet from hell. Someone unnamed had felt differently, saying, God is kind. We may make it now. Shot an antelope here July 10, 188— and the last number blurred. Arthur Smith, 1881, had recorded, Here berried my beloved wife Semantha, age 22, and my soul. God let me keep the child. J. M. said cryptically, Good luck, John, and Bill said, Ralph, if you come this way, am trying to get to Los Angeles. B. Westover said he had recovered from his wound there in 1884, and Galt said, enigmatically and without date, Bart and Miller burned to death in the Yellow Jacket. I don't care now. There were poets too, of both parties. What could still be read of Byron Cotter's verses, written in 1902, said,

> . . . . here alone
> Each shining dawn I greet,
> The Lord's wind on my forehead
> And where he set his feet
> One mark of heel remaining
> Each day filled up anew,
> To keep my soul from burning,
> With clear, celestial dew.
> Here in His Grace abiding

The mortal years and few
I shall . . .

but you can't tell what he intended, while J. A. had printed,

My brother came out in '49
I came in '51
At first we thought we liked it fine
But now, by God, we're done.

Suttler studied these records without smiling, like someone reading a funny paper, and finally, with a heavy blue pencil, registered, Jim and Jenny Suttler, damn dried out, March—and paused, but had no way of discovering the day—1940.

In the evening he sat on the steps watching the swallows in the golden upper canyon turn bats in the dusk, and thought about the antelope. He had seen the new tracks also, and it alarmed him a little that the antelope could have passed twice in the dark without waking him.

Before false dawn he was lying in the willows with his carbine at ready. Rabbits ran from the meadow when he came down, and after that there was no movement. He wanted to smoke. When he did see them at the lower edge of the meadow, he was startled, yet made no quick movement, but slowly pivoted to cover them. They made poor targets in that light and backed by the pale desert, appearing and disappearing before his eyes. He couldn't keep any one of them steadily visible, and decided to wait until they made contrast against the meadow. But his presence was strong. One of the antelope advanced onto the green, but then threw its head up, spun, and ran back past the flank of the herd, which swung after him. Suttler rose quickly and raised the rifle, but let it down without firing. He could hear the light rattle of their flight in the wash, but had only a belief that he could see them. He had few cartridges, and the ponderous echo under the cliffs would scare them off for weeks.

His energies, however, were awakened by the frustrated hunt. While there was still more light than heat in the canyon, he climbed to the abandoned mine tunnel at the top of the alluvial wing of the cliff. He looked at the broken rock in the dump, kicked up its pack with a boot toe, and went into the tunnel, peering closely at its sides, in places black with old smoke smudges. At the back he struck two matches and looked at the jagged dead end and the fragments on the floor, then returned to the shallow beginning of a side tunnel. At the second match here he knelt quickly, scrutinized a portion of the rock, and when the match went out at once lit another. He lit six matches, and pulled at the rock with his hand. It was firm.

"The poor chump," he said aloud.

He got a loose rock from the tunnel and hammered at the projection with it. It came finally, and he carried it into the sun on the dump.

"Yessir," he said aloud, after a minute.

He knocked his sample into three pieces and examined each minutely.

"Yessir, yessir," he said with malicious glee, and, grinning at the tunnel, "the poor chump."

Then he looked again at the dump, like the mound before a gigantic gopher hole. "Still, that's a lot of digging," he said.

He put sample chips into his shirt pocket, keeping a small black, heavy one that had fallen neatly from a hole like a borer's, to play with in his hand. After trouble he found the claim pile on the side hill south of the tunnel, its top rocks tumbled into the shale. Under the remaining rocks he found what he wanted, a ragged piece of yellowed paper between two boards. The writing was in pencil, and not diplomatic. "I hearby clame this hole damn side hill as far as I can dig in. I am a good shot. Keep off. John Barr, April 11, 1897."

Jim Suttler grinned. "Tough guy, eh?" he said.

He made a small ceremony of burning the paper upon a stone from the cairn. The black tinsel of ash blew off and broke into flakes.

"O.K., John Barr?" he asked.

"O.K., Suttler," he answered himself.

In blue pencil, on soiled paper from his pocket, he slowly printed, "Becus of the lamented desease of the late clamant, John Barr, I now clame these diggins for myself and partner Jenny.

I can shoot too." And wrote, rather than printed, "James T. Suttler, March—" and paused.

"Make it an even month," he said, and wrote, "11, 1940." Underneath he wrote, "Jenny Suttler, her mark," and drew a skull with long ears.

"There," he said, and folded the paper, put it between the two boards, and rebuilt the cairn into a neat pyramid above it.

In high spirit he was driven to cleanliness. With scissors, soap, and razor he climbed to the spring. Jenny was there, drinking.

"When you're done," he said, and lifted her head, pulled her ears and scratched her.

"Maybe we've got something here, Jenny," he said.

Jenny observed him soberly and returned to the meadow.

"She doesn't believe me," he said, and began to perfect himself. He sheared off his red tresses in long hanks, then cut closer, and went over yet a third time, until there remained a brush, of varying density, of stiff red bristles, through which his scalp shone whitely. He sheared the beard likewise, then knelt to the well for mirror and shaved painfully. He also shaved his neck and about his ears. He arose younger and less impressive, with jaws as pale as his scalp, so that his sunburn was a red domino. He burned tresses and beard ceremoniously upon a sage bush, and announced, "It is spring."

He began to empty the pockets of his shirt and breeches onto a flat stone, yelling, "In the spring a young man's fancy," to a kind of tune, and paused, struck by the facts.

"Oh yeah?" he said. "Fat chance."

"Fat," he repeated with obscene consideration. "Oh, well," he said, and finished piling upon the rock notebooks, pencil stubs, cartridges, tobacco, knife, stump pipe, matches, chalk, samples, and three wrinkled photographs. One of the photographs he observed at length before weighting it down with a .45 cartridge. It showed a round, blonde girl with a big smile on a stupid face, in a patterned calico house dress in front of a blossoming rhododendron bush.

He added to this deposit his belt and holster with the big .45. Then he stripped himself, washed and rinsed his garments in the spring, and spread them upon stones and brush, and carefully arranged four flat stones into a platform beside the trough. Standing there he scooped water over himself, gasping, made it a lather, and at last, face and copper bristles also foaming, gropingly entered the basin and submerged, flooding the water over in a thin and soapy sheet. His head emerged at once. "My God," he whispered. He remained under, however, till he was soapless, and goose pimpled as a file, he climbed out cautiously onto the rock platform and performed a dance of small, revolving patterns with a great deal of up and down.

At one point in his dance he observed the pictograph journey upon the cliff, and danced nearer to examine it.

"Ignorant," he pronounced. "Like a little kid," he said.

He was intrigued, however, by some more recent records, names smoked and cut upon the lower rock. One of these, in script, like a gigantic handwriting deeply cut, said ALVAREZ BLANCO DE TOLEDO, Anno Di 1624. A very neat, upright cross was chiselled beneath it.

Suttler grinned. "Oh yeah?" he asked, with his head upon one side. "Nuts," he said, looking at it squarely.

But it inspired him, and with his jack-knife he began scraping beneath the possibly Spanish inscription. His knife, however, made scratches, not incisions. He completed a bad Jim and Jenny and quit, saying, "I should kill myself over a phoney wap."

Thereafter, for weeks, while the canyon became increasingly like a furnace in the daytime and the rocks stayed warm at night, he drove his tunnel farther into the gully, making a heap of ore to be worked, and occasionally adding a peculiarly heavy pebble to the others in his small leather bag with a draw string. He and Jenny thrived upon this fixed and well-watered life. The hollows disappeared from his face and he became less stringy, while Jenny grew round, her battle-ship gray pelt even lustrous and its black markings distinct and ornamental. The burro found time from her grazing to come to the cabin door in the evenings and attend solemnly to Suttler playing with his samples and explaining their future.

"Then, old lady," Suttler said, "you will carry only small children, one at a time, for never more than half an hour. You will have a bedroom with French windows and a mattress, and I will paint your feet gold.

"The children," he said, "will probably be red-headed, but maybe blonde. Anyway, they will be beautiful.

"After we've had a holiday, of course," he added. "For one hundred and thirty-three nights," he said dreamily. "Also," he said, "just one hundred and thirty-three quarts. I'm no drunken bum.

"For you, though," he said, "for one hundred and thirty-three nights a quiet hotel with other old ladies. I should drag my own mother in the gutter." He pulled her head down by the ears and kissed her loudly upon the nose. They were very happy together.

Nor did they greatly alter most of the life of the canyon. The antelope did not return, it is true, the rabbits were fewer and less playful because he sometimes snared them for meat, the little, clean mice and desert rats avoided the cabin they had used, and the road-runner did not come in daylight after Suttler, for fun, narrowly missed him with a piece of ore from the tunnel mouth. Suttler's violence was disproportionate perhaps, when he used his .45 to blow apart a creamy rat who did invade the cabin, but the loss was insignificant to the pattern of the well, and more than compensated when he one day caught the rattler extended at the foot of the dump in a drunken stupor from rare young rabbit, and before it could recoil held it aloft by the tail and snapped its head off, leaving the heavy body to turn slowly for a long time among the rocks. The dominant voices went undisturbed, save when he sang badly at his work or said beautiful things to Jenny in a loud voice.

There were, however, two more noticeable changes, one of which, at least, was important to Suttler himself. The first was the execution of the range cow's calf in the late fall, when he began to suggest a bull. Suttler felt a little guilty about this because the calf might have belonged to somebody, because the cow remained near the meadow bawling for two nights, and because the calf had come to meet the gun with more curiosity than challenge. But when he had the flayed carcass hung in the mine tunnel in a wet canvas, the sensation of providence overcame any qualms.

The other change was more serious. It occurred at the beginning of such winter as the well had, when there was sometimes a light rime on the rocks at dawn, and the aspens held only a few yellow leaves. Suttler thought often of leaving. The nights were cold, the fresh meat was eaten, his hopes had diminished as he still found only occasional nuggets, and his dreams of women, if less violent, were more nostalgic. The canyon held him with a feeling he would have called lonesome but at home, yet he probably would have gone except for this second change.

In the higher mountains to the west, where there was already snow, and at dawn a green winter sky, hunger stirred a buried memory in a cougar. He had twice killed antelope at the well, and felt there had been time enough again. He came down from the dwarfed trees and crossed the narrow valley under the stars, sometimes stopping abruptly to stare intently about, like a housecat in a strange room. After each stop he would at once resume a quick, noiseless trot. From the top of the mountain above the spring he came down very slowly on his belly, but there was nothing at the well. He relaxed, and leaning on the rim of the basin, drank, listening between laps. His nose was clean with fasting, and he knew of the man in the cabin and Jenny in the meadow, but they were strange, not what he remembered about the place. But neither had his past made him fearful. It was only his habitual hunting caution which made him go down into the willows carefully, and lie there head up, watching Jenny, but still waiting for antelope, which he had killed before near dawn. The strange smells were confusing and therefore irritating. After an hour he rose and went silently to the cabin, from which the strangest smell came strongly, a carnivorous smell which did not arouse appetite, but made him bristle nervously. The tobacco in it was like pins in his nostrils. He circled the cabin, stopping frequently. At the open door the scent was violent. He stood with his front paws up on the step, moving his head in serpent motions, the end of his heavy tail furling and unfurling constantly. In a dream Suttler turned over without waking, and muttered. The cougar crouched, his eyes intent, his ruff lifting. Then he swung away from the door again and lay in the willows, but where he could watch the cabin also.

When the sky was alarmingly pale and the antelope had not come, he crawled a few feet at a time, behind the willows, to a point nearer Jenny. There he crouched, working his hind legs slowly under him until he was set, and sprang, raced the three or four jumps to the drowsy burro, and struck. The beginning of her mortal scream was severed, but having made an imperfect leap, and from no height, the cat did not at once break her neck, but drove her to earth, where her small hooves churned futilely in the sod, and chewed and worried until she lay still.

Jim Suttler was nearly awakened by the fragment of scream, but heard nothing after it, and sank again.

The cat wrestled Jenny's body into the willows, fed with uncertain relish, drank long at the well, and went slowly over the crest, stopping often to look back. In spite of the light and the beginning talk of the swallows, the old coyote also fed and was gone before Suttler woke.

When Suttler found Jenny, many double columns of regimented ants were already at work, streaming in and out of the interior and mounting like bridge workers upon the ribs. Suttler stood and looked down. He desired to hold the small muzzle in the hollow of his hand, feeling that this familiar gesture would get through to Jenny, but couldn't bring himself to it because of what had happened to that side of her head. He squatted and lifted one hoof on its stiff leg and held that. Ants emerged hurriedly from the fetlock, their lines of communication broken. Two of them made disorganized excursions on the back of his hand. He rose, shook them off, and stood staring again. He didn't say anything because he spoke easily only when cheerful or excited, but a determination was beginning in him. He followed the drag to the spot torn by the small hoofs. Among the willows again, he found the tracks of both the cougar and the coyote, and the cat's tracks again at the well and by the cabin doorstep. He left Jenny in the willows with a canvas over her during the day, and did not eat.

At sunset he sat on the doorstep, cleaning his rifle and oiling it until he could spring the lever almost without sound. He filled the clip, pressed it home, and sat with the gun across his knees until dark, when he put on his sheepskin, stuffed a scarf into the pocket, and went down to Jenny. He removed the canvas from her, rolled it up and held it under his arm.

"I'm sorry, old woman," he said. "Just tonight."

There was a little cold wind in the willows. It rattled the upper branches lightly.

Suttler selected a spot thirty yards down wind, from which he could see Jenny, spread the canvas and lay down upon it, facing towards her. After an hour he was afraid of falling asleep and sat up against a willow clump. He sat there all night. A little after midnight the old coyote came into the dry-wash below him. At the top of the wash he sat down, and when the mingled scents gave him a clear picture of the strategy, let his tongue loll out, looked at the stars for a moment with his mouth silently open, rose and trotted into the desert.

At the beginning of daylight the younger coyote trotted in from the north, and turned up towards the spring, but saw Jenny. He sat down and looked at her for a long time. Then he moved to the west and sat down again. In the wind was only winter, and the water, and faintly the acrid bat dung in the cliffs. He completed the circle, but not widely enough, walking slowly through the willows, down the edge of the meadow and in again not ten yards in front of the following muzzle of the carbine. Like Jenny, he felt his danger too late. The heavy slug caught him at che base of the skull in the middle of the first jump, so that it was amazingly accelerated for a fraction of a second. The coyote began it alive, and ended it quite dead, but with a tense muscular movement conceived which resulted in a grotesque final leap and twist of the hind-quarters alone, leaving them propped high against a willow clump while the head was half buried in the sand, red welling up along the lips of the distended jaws. The cottony underpelt of the tail and rump stirred gleefully in the wind.

When Suttler kicked the body and it did not move, he suddenly dropped his gun, grasped it by the upright hind legs, and hurled it out into the sage-brush. His face appeared slightly insane with fury for that instant. Then he picked up his gun and went back to the cabin, where he ate, and drank half of one of his last three bottles of whiskey.

In the middle of the morning he came down with his pick and shovel, dragged Jenny's much-lightened body down into the dry-wash, and dug in the rock and sand for two hours. When she was covered, he erected a small cairn of stone, like the claim post, above her.

"If it takes a year," he said, and licked the salt sweat on his lips.

That day he finished the half bottle and drank all of a second one, and became very drunk, so that he fell asleep during his vigil in the willows, sprawled wide on the dry turf and snoring. He was not disturbed. There was a difference in his smell after that day which prevented even the rabbits from coming into the meadow. He waited five nights in the willows. Then he transferred his watch to a niche in the cliff, across from and just below the spring.

All winter, while the day wind blew long veils of dust across the desert, regularly repeated, like waves or the smoke of line artillery fire, and the rocks shrank under the cold glitter of night, he did not miss a watch. He learned to go to sleep at sundown, wake within a few minutes of midnight, go up to his post, and become at once clear headed and watchful. He talked to himself in the mine and the cabin, but never in the niche. His supplies ran low, and he ate less, but would not risk a startling shot. He rationed his tobacco, and when it was gone worked up to a vomiting sickness every three days for nine days, but did not miss a night in the niche. All winter he did not remove his clothes, bathe, shave, cut his hair or sing. He worked the dead mine only to be busy, and became thin again, with sunken eyes which yet were not the eyes he had come with the spring before. It was April, his food almost gone, when he got his chance.

There was a half moon that night, which made the canyon walls black, and occasionally gleamed on wrinkles of the overflow. The cat came down so quietly that Suttler did not see him until he was beside the basin. The animal was suspicious. He took the wind, and twice started to drink, and didn't, but crouched. On Suttler's face there was a set grin which exposed his teeth.

"Not even a drink, you bastard," he thought.

The cat drank a little though, and dropped again, softly, trying to get the scent from the meadow. Suttler drew slowly upon his soul in the trigger. When it gave, the report was magnified impressively in the canyon. The cougar sprang straight into the air and screamed outrageously. The back of Suttler's neck was cold and his hand trembled, but he shucked the lever and fired again. This shot ricocheted from the basin and whined away thinly. The first, however, had struck near enough. The cat began to scramble rapidly on the loose stone, at first without voice, then screaming repeatedly. It doubled upon itself, snarling and chewing in a small furious circle, fell and began to throw itself in short, leaping spasms upon the stones, struck across the rim of the tank and lay half in the water, its head and shoulders raised in one corner and resting against the cliff. Suttler could hear it breathing hoarsely and snarling very faintly. The soprano chorus of swallows gradually became silent.

Suttler had risen to fire again, but lowered the carbine and advanced, stopping at every step to peer intently and listen for the hoarse breathing, which continued. Even when he was within five feet of the tank the cougar did not move, except to gasp so that the water again splashed from the basin. Suttler was calmed by the certainty of accomplishment. He drew the heavy revolver from his holster, aimed carefully at the rattling head, and fired again. The canyon boomed, and the east responded faintly and a little behind, but Suttler did not hear them, for the cat thrashed heavily in the tank, splashing him as with a bucket, and then lay still on its side over the edge, its muzzle and forepaws hanging. The water was settling quietly in the tank, but Suttler stirred it again, shooting five more times with great deliberation into the heavy body, which did not move except at the impact of the slugs.

The rest of the night, even after the moon was gone, he worked fiercely, slitting and tearing with his knife. In the morning, under the swallows, he dragged the marbled carcass, still bleeding a little in places, onto the rocks on the side away from the spring, and dropped it. Dragging the ragged hide by the neck, he went unsteadily down the canyon to the cabin, where he slept like a drunkard, although his whiskey had been gone for two months.

In the afternoon, with dreaming eyes, he bore the pelt to Jenny's grave, took down the stones with his hands, shoveled the earth from her, covered her with the skin, and again with earth and the cairn.

He looked at this monument. "There," he said.

That night, for the first time since her death, he slept through.

In the morning, at the well, he repeated the cleansing ritual of a year before, save that they were rags he stretched to dry, even to the dance upon the rock platform while drying. Squatting naked and clean, shaven and clipped, he looked for a long time at the grinning countenance, now very dirty, of the plump girl in front of the blossoming rhododendrons, and in the resumption of his dance he made singing noises accompanied by the words, "Spring, spring, beautiful spring." He was a starved but revived and volatile spirit. An hour later he went south, his boot soles held on by canvas strips, and did not once look back.

The disturbed life of the spring resumed. In the second night the rabbits loved in the willows, and at the end of the week the rats played in the cabin again. The old coyote and a vulture cleaned the cougar, and his bones fell apart in the shale. The road-runner came up one day, tentatively, and in front of the tunnel snatched up a horned toad and ran with it around the corner, but no farther. After a month the antelope returned. The well brimmed, and in the gentle sunlight the new aspen leaves made a tiny music of shadows.

JAMES T. FARRELL:

A SHORT STORY

H E READ the newspapers in the reading room of the public
library. He took a keen interest in the columns and columns of print, telling him of faro games, broads, millionaires,
mergers, conferences, fires, dead generals, live generals photo-
graphed with a chest full of medals, accidents, deaths, and broads.
There were many others in the crowded room reading newspapers for the same reason that he was. Outside it was beginning
to get dark, and the room was warm and friendly with its
humanity, its electric lights, and the forgetfulness in the dead
columns of yesterday's and yesteryear's newsprint. He read on.
An international conference, farmers going berserk and raiding
stores for food, strikes, appeals for charity that made him laugh,
mergers, broads getting married while other broads were getting
divorced, broads in bathing suits snapped on the sands of California, murders, ministers, accidents, steamships, prize fighters,
and broads, broads, broads.

Reading on, seeing the pictures of women in the paper, and
scratching himself, feeling the dirt ingrained into his own body,
he could not make himself believe that he actually belonged to
the same species as these women whose pictures were in the
papers. He had to force conviction on himself to believe that,
yes, after all, these dames whose mugs and chassis were in the
paper, they were only human too. He went on reading until he
began imagining that he, himself, was a big shot, and able to
associate with broads just like these dames in the newspapers.
He read on. Columns of print, columns that he read trance-like
until he couldn't read any more because of his hunger. Then he

concentrated on the food advertisements, trying to make himself believe that he had been fed. Then, back again to the society news to see what was going on in that realm. More columns of print . . .

It was going to be pretty chilly walking all the way over to the Munie for a free flop. Right now if he had sixty cents in his jeans to spare, he could live like an aristocrat and take a room for the night at the Mills Hotel at Thirty-sixth Street and Seventh Avenue. But that was paradise. That was the flop house where there was no delousing. And to think of the life of some of these big shots whose names were in the papers. Press one button for a meal. Two buttons for a drink. Three button; for a dame. The bastards, their life was almost that simple. Six months ago, he'd got himself fixed up to look almost human, and he'd gone to the Lonely Hearts Club, and danced with a dame. Jesus, what hadn't that done to him! And, Jesus, to be with one when she was naked. Right now he'd rather think of having a dame naked and willing in a room with him than of anything else, even food. No, it was a toss-up between the two pleasures. And since he could think of both of them, why be stingy with his thoughts?

He was damned hungry. You'd think there was an ocean storm in his guts. And if he only had a cigarette. Now that would be kingdom come.

He got up and left the reading room, leaving the newspaper file on the table. He went outside and walked around to the Fifth Avenue steps. He stood there shivering, watching the passing panorama. It was getting late in the afternoon of a gray January day. There were noises, busses and automobiles, people, people who belonged to the human race. And there must be a lot of rich dames in the crowd walking by on the sidewalk. He was seeing all kinds of fur coats. He tried to visualize how some of these dames in the fur coats would look naked. But he had business to attend to, some little conferences here and there. He gazed about him with the shifty, beggary-eyed expression of the stiff. He was looking for someone to hustle. He turned up his coat collar, stuck his hands in his trouser pockets, and stood there, still shivering. He tried to hustle a well-dressed, sappy-looking young fellow who had an armful of books, but it was no soap. He descended the steps and picked out a clean-shaven bird with a pearl gray hat. He started giving the fellow a long hard-luck story about how he had just come in from Chicago where things were right fierce, and he was busted and wanted a flop, a chance to get a clean shirt out of the laundry, a good meal, a chance to spruce up and see if he couldn't rustle himself a job because he'd come all the way from the west coast since last fall and things were bad all over the country and he guessed it was best to try his luck in New York. He got a quarter and a half pack of Camels and, in giving obsequious thanks, he asked God to bless his benefactor. He hustled another dime, and then he walked around to Forty-second Street, and over toward Broadway.

At Broadway he had more luck, unusual luck, and he stopped hustling for the day with the sum of one dollar in his pocket. Tonight he could sleep at the Mills Hotel in paradise. But first of all, he was going to stow away some grub. He ate in a Coffee Pot over on Ninth Avenue, and while he was putting away some hamburgers he thought back to his flight from home at seventeen, his wanderings back and forth across the face of America, warm nights in the jungles, cold nights in cities, the time that he'd got a dose from a two-bit whore that he'd picked up on West Madison Street in Chicago, an idyllic summer that he'd spent on a farm. But he guessed that he was just one of those guys who was born to have it jammed up his can, and that was all. He kept remembering and remembering.

After eating, he went out and bought some cheap moonshine. The first drink warmed him, and he didn't mind its bitter taste. He'd drunk much worse. The second swig was even more warming. The third made his head a trifle light. He walked along the crowded streets of New York with a new-born confidence. He thought of movie actresses, society dames, chorus girls, rich broads, all of them parading before him. He held dialogues with himself, addressing obscene words to the images of motion picture actresses that he held in his mind.

Baby, there's many the broads better than you that I tossed out of bed. See! But just for the sake of sweet, sweet, sweet charity, and because I feel pretty good and at the top of my form tonight after cleanin' up on the street, and because I'm warm-hearted and soft and don't like to disappoint the gals, well, come on, kid! You can sleep with me this time.

He smiled. He disappeared in a dark entranceway for another drink. He reappeared on the sidewalk, smiling again with all his new-born drunken assurance.

He held more dialogues with the visions of naked women.

You, you're a bitch! I say you're a bitch! See! And there's only one way for a bitch like you to get tamed!

He saw himself with a naked movie star cowering before him while he advanced on her with a horsewhip. She shivered, drew back, screamed, crouched in a corner. He drove her from corner to corner, lashing her bare back and buttocks, horsewhipping her until her lovely back was welted and oozing blood.

He laughed raucously, and strangers stopped to look at him, all of them perplexed, some of them frightened.

He staggered on. The world became soft, friendly, and it made him so happy that he sang. He stopped several times for a drink, no longer bothering to go into corners or dark entranceways, but stopping in the center of the sidewalk, pulling out his bottle, and swigging. He walked on, singing drunkenly, happier than he had been since Christ knows when. The world became happier and happier, less and less hostile. He became one real guy all right. His belly was warm. He didn't feel any chill. He didn't need an overcoat now.

He zigzagged up and down streets and, reaching Third Avenue, he told the elevator girders that his name was Mr. Christ. In Tompkins Square, he kissed the bare trees and told them that they were lovely girls. He flopped down on a bench in the deserted square, pulled out his bottle, and had another drink. He felt the quarter in his pocket.

He got up and staggered on. A couple of trees seemed to punch him in the mouth. He called them dirty sons of bachelors and laughed. The world became full of blackness. It rocked, twirled, wheeled, spun, jigged under his feet. He swayed and another tree seemed to punch him in the face, and then a white streak seemed to jab through a cosmic darkness. He fell down and whirled on the earth like one spun on a rapidly moving wheel. He labored to his feet and staggered along until he fell in a doorway on Third Avenue and lay there, as if dead. The wind whistled and snow started falling.

BEN FIELD:

AN ANSWER FOR MY UNCLE

After his arrival from Chicago, Uncle Meyer moved in with us. As we had our own house then, there was plenty of room for both families, and the children could play in the garden around the rose bushes and the hydrangeas which looked as though Mother had washed and blued them.

Uncle assured us that the moment he found a job he would go out and rent a lovely house. The moment stretched into months, the months ran into years. Mother was not the kind of a woman who considered it burdensome to help others. What was hard for her was Jack's behavior.

Jack would limp into the house after his day at the shop and he would fall into a rage to see her tending to the needs of both families. Mother had nursed Jack day and night after the accident which had crippled him, and his gratitude to her and his sense of duty made him resent her carrying most of the burden of Uncle's family, particularly since he insisted that Meyer was lazy.

Jack wasn't altogether fair to Uncle Meyer. Uncle was not lazy. He just could not hold on to a job for any length of time no matter how much he tried.

Father saw that clearly. Once he said, "You've had as many jobs as the Kings had women. Tell me, Meyer, what would happen if you were to lie with one job for a full year?"

Uncle cracked his prominent knuckles, which sounded like empty nuts. "Brother, if those murderers had clubbed you, strong as you are, you would be running around in a clouded world. You, too, would find it hard to put a hand to something."

"Right, a thousand times right," was the soothing answer. Father was a high-strung man, but he never lost his patience with his younger brother.

Aunty, always at her sewing machine, forgot that I was in the next room at my school work. "Always the eggs bother you men!" A tall harassed woman, every spring during her stay with us she spent a month in bed, went to a mysterious doctor in the city, returned looking as white as a corpse, and for days we would find spots like half-dollars in the bathroom.

"How these women cackle," chuckled Father. "You are just threads and ribbons. Look at my mother, may she rest in peace. At forty a widow, she married again, giving birth to me, Meyer, Isaiah, and the girls."

"True," said Mother in her breathless way, "but you yourself have said that the children died like flies."

"Some did not die. They were murdered by those beastly Christians," cried Meyer. "I can see it like it is today. The peasants must make sure he is Jewish. They tear off his clothes. He is as old as my dear nephew." He pointed in my direction. "Like him like two drops of milk."

Aunty stopped her sewing. She said dully, "We know, husband, we know."

He ignored her as usual. "A band of young Jews got together. No more are we going to be weaklings to let them twist us like Purim tops. We arm ourselves."

In the midst of his story in came the children from the garden, pushing the baby carriage. Judah was wearing the conductor's cap on his swollen head. He pulled a string, which served the purpose of a bellcord, and kept ringing an old alarm clock. Uncle had been a street car conductor. A passenger had called him a sheeny Jew when he had forgotten to ring a stop. He had given up the job after that incident. "Next stop Cooney Island," sang Judah.

"They attack us with clubs and knives and the forks of the field. We pay them back a thousand fold." He plunged his fist above his head. "Isaiah, brother of mine, we have not forgotten you!"

His shout made the baby pop into tears, and the twins, Bessie and Tessie, who were pushing the carriage, began whimpering.

Mother had a way with children. She took the baby into her arms. "Sister, go on with your sewing. I'll take care of the little ones."

Although three years old, the chicken-chested baby could neither talk nor walk. Something appeared to be the matter with each one of the children. Mother hinted that marriages of first cousins were not right. Father swore that the pogroms with the murdering hooligans were at the root of the trouble.

With the baby in her arms, Mother prepared supper. Both families sat down to the table. Little Judah, his blue conductor's hat on his head, stopped ringing his bell and calling out Coney Island long enough to eat. The two girls sucked chicken bones and smiled through their tears at him.

The door was kicked open. In limped Jack in his greasy overalls. He washed his hands at the kitchen sink and ate his supper glumly. After supper, still silent, he packed his military pipe with the china bowl covered with German verses about the soldier who would rather go to his girl than stand guard.

Stealthily, Mother started clearing away the dishes.

And then the storm broke: "Again this cleaning? Now I'll have to pay more doctor's bills. Let Uncle clean. He ain't put his fist to anything so long it'll drop off soon. Let him do a bit of work. It'll give him the muscles Jews ought to develop to get along in the world."

Uncle's face grew white.

With a throaty exclamation, though she was not feeling well, Aunty seized a pan and started scouring it.

"Again talking like you come from the high windows," cried Father. He slapped his hand on the table. "Not another word from you!"

Quickly Mother caught hold of Jack's neck and drew him upstairs to the parlor. I retreated to my room, but I could not finish my lessons. Fear and anxiety were working like twin screws in my brain.

Late that night we were awakened by the wailing of the baby.

Bessie and Tessie started peeping. Judah crept around in his conductor's cap. "Next stop, Cooney."

Uncle got out of his bed. He had to tell us about his hideous
dream. "The peasants are dancing around me like a band of
Tartars. They fall on me, rip off my head. Out comes blood
green as gall and bitter as worm cabbage."

"Don't think twice of it," said Father. "In a dream you knock
out whatever gives you heartache during the day. It pays to have
dreams."

The children refused to go back to bed. They crawled into
our room. Uncle and Father continued discussing dreams.

Jack had to be up at four in the morning to get to his shop
on time. He could not sleep. He rose, limped from one end of
the room to the other, and lit his pipe which glared like the
Cyclops' eye. "He won't work, he won't let others sleep. To
hell with it!"

Uncle fluttered his crumpled hands. "Where are our belong-
ings?" He went down to the basement and clattered back with
his broken wicker trunk. "If not for those beasts, I could make
a good expressman." He stuffed pillows into the trunk.

"Meyer, what are you doing?" Mother went to him, put her
hands on his shoulders, and shook him.

"I am not wanted. Every piece of bread is counted. A nephew
to be that way, your own flesh and blood to blow up like a
turkey with a straw on its nose. I will not stand for insults.
Jews will not stand—"

"Let them sit!" shouted Jack.

"You lout," cried Father, "once and for all, this is still my
house. You will get out of here before any of these small fowl,
piece of filth you."

Jack took his hat and coat and left.

Mother had one of her dizzy spells. We had to help her to
her bed where she lay flattened out as under a press. Uncle put
the trunk back and sat near her with a lowered head. After she
had calmed the terrified children, Aunty wept, saying that everything must be done to right this great wrong. "It is a hard working young man. Is it so easy to earn a crust of bread in the

world? He must sleep, rest. We are to blame. You crept with a sound head into a sick bed when you asked us to stay with you. You had no right, brother-in-law."

Father threw up his hands, and fled from her remonstrances.

There was no question but we would have to do something about Uncle Meyer immediately. Peace would be ours only if Uncle worked. We must do all within our power to put him on his feet again.

It would be wrong to ask Jack to help. He was earning good wages, but even if he were willing, every cent he could spare was being put away to start his own machine shop. Father's dry goods store wasn't doing well. Feeling that setting up Uncle in the most modest way would be the first right step, Mother gave him the money she had been saving for a coat, to which I added what I had scraped together for books and a microscope.

Uncle kissed her, crushed me to his bony chest, and prepared to become a business man in a realistic fashion. He rented a push-cart with the declaration that it was high time he slipped the yoke of no-work off his neck and made our eyes blink with wonder. He bought cartons of balloons, toy canaries that whis-tled, little boys who made water when their rubber hats were squeezed.

On my way from school I would stop off at his cart to find him singing his wares. With a wink at me, he trotted after a stout woman with children clinging to her skirt, took her by the hand and rattled Russian at her until she turned and yielded. Red from his exertions, he cried, "In the old country you take baths in a bathhouse, and you have a little besom to beat yourself with. I said her children were sticking to her behind like leaves from the besoms. Jews can say anything to one another. Ach, children, what a happy world it would be if they let us live." He sighed and started singing a song for the other peddlers about the Germans with the long whips. "Die Deutschen mit die lange Beitchen."

Uncle worked with a will. Business was good. But when win-ter came, the world seemed to lose interest in toys. Mother's ill-ness and the last ugly quarrel had taught him a lesson. The day after he had disposed of his last bit of stock, he hired out as a bottle-washer in a junkshop. Here he worked in a steam-choked cellar, his skin rubbed raw from the tin tubs, his breath going like an asthmatic's. This job lasted until spring when he found a place in a delicatessen shop where he prepared papers of mustard, made salads and sandwiches, and during the rush hours served at the tables.

"It is the best job I have had in years. Twenty-five dollars with tips makes me feel like Baron Rothschild. But look, here is a boss, a redheaded one like a bedbug. I slice the corned beef too thick. I give customers too much bread on the plates. Don't they pay for it? Is business a robbery? But, he, just because he hired Christians who are lazy, must he treat me that way? And his wife! A tongue long as our exile, a real Empress Catherine."

"What has Catherine to do with it?" asked Jack, who was on friendlier terms with him now that he was working.

"You don't know Catherine the Czarina?"

"Never had the pleasure."

"Jews should know their friends and their enemies. They should know their history. Once they found a Jewish soldier, strong as an ox, blood and milk, another Maccabee. They brought him to her, that dissolute woman."

"So?"

"He was a good Jew, and Potemkin, her lover, he hated us also."

Jack yawned. "They brought her a horse once. That's why there are so many horses in Russia."

Uncle did not dare to complain again although his boss was a heartless man. He docked him for breaking a plate, docked him when a customer palmed off on him a counterfeit dollar bill, and during rush hours, he terrorized him as well as the Irish dishwasher. And when Meyer gashed his hand, he called him a fool and discharged him.

Uncle could not look for work until his hand had healed. To make himself useful, he helped Father in the store, shopped for Mother, and assisted with the gardening. He accompanied me to the park to identify birds and trees and visit the zoo, which was part of my biology work.

The waddling geese cried, "Huncle, huncle," a loose rooster cocked his head, the wapiti stalked up with velvet on their horns to give us the once over.

"There's Ivan the thief," cried Uncle. He squinted at the Russian bear, and his face lit up tenderly at meeting such an old friend. In the monkey house, he said: "What little people they are. Tell me, my nephew, why are they happy while we sit in tears?"

I was dumbfounded at the question.

"You are a smart youngster. Come, tell your stupid uncle."

I gazed up at the pale, screwed-up face. "They, too, have their sufferings, Uncle."

He scratched his chin doubtfully. "Have they? They aren't Jews. They don't have to go into a hard world for bread."

We sat down in the grass together.

"I will tell you. Maybe you can learn from Uncle," he said humbly. "In Russia there was no place for us. This you know. I went to England after the war and couldn't earn enough bread to make a blessing over. I came to Canada. I worked in a mine of stones, quarry they call it. The bosses acted like Pharaohs. I spoke up, and when that did not help, I ran away. They shot after me because I broke my contract. I walked at night and hid during the day from the gunmen. I cross over to America and work in Chicago in the seltzer business with your aunt's brother. Soon mankind loses its taste for seltzer and dies for soda water. I come here, and again it is the old story. . . . All I want is my wife and children should not go hungry. For myself a piece of hard bread can be a feast if the soul is at peace. But no, they won't let us live!"

"Who, Uncle?"

"The goyim."

We sit and argue. I try to convince him he is wrong, that there are Irish and Italian boys in school with whom I am on excellent terms, that the faculty adviser of our chess club has warmly praised the Jewish players even though he is a Christian.

"Oh, they must say we have the best brains. There is no head like a Jewish head. That is the reason they hate us. Grow up and you will see. You can't teach them. Teach a wolf, and he will run back to the forest." He blew his nose between his fingers. "Look how fat he is, like a rich man with a goitre." He smiled at the pigeon strutting in the grass, and for a moment the age-old sorrow was forgotten.

Before Meyer's hand could heal, Aunty became sick. This time, the doctors warned her, she would have to go through with it. Despite their warning, she took hot mustard baths, dosed herself with quinine, and Mother found her late one night jumping off the steps into the cellar.

The women wept in each other's arms.

"It is a Jewish child," said Mother. "A dear little life. Another Jew. You must bring it into the world."

She had a severe confinement. The whole night she walked the floor. Early in the morning Uncle burst into our room. His eyes were burning. "Born in a shirt. A little Messiah born in a shirt!"

The man's joy knew no bounds. The neighbors, the merchants on the block, all who cared to listen were told again and again that a child born in a shirt signifies the greatest of all good fortune. "Let one Jew be happy, and all Jews rejoice with him. Let one Jew fall, and all Jews limp. The world will turn into a Jerusalem, not a Russia. Do you know what Russia did to us?"

He drew a deep breath. "A nobleman took the Jewish girls from a village, shamed them all, and when they were about to have babies, he put them into a tree, yes, a tree like birds or pigeons, then he took his fowling gun and shot them down."

A groan broke from him. "Thank the Lord, my nephew, that you will never know what it is to have their spittle on your bread. Thank the Lord God you live in our great America."

The baby was sickly. Its wailing penetrated every corner of the house. Doctor's bills mounted. But we were fortunate. Before a violent explosion could wreck everything, Uncle came to us with a plan which promised us permanent peace—he must be allowed to go to Palestine.

During his hunt for work, he had met a Jew who had owned a poultry farm in the Mountains, and was now looking for a partner to buy an orange grove near Jaffa. Palestine was the homeland of the Jews, and Jews should live there. Did not the good Jew say after holy services, "If I forget thee, O Jerusalem, let my right hand forget her cunning and the tongue cleave to my mouth"? And the dead, have they not the soil of the Land of our Forefathers put into their coffins?

He bought a chromo of Theodor Herzl, hung it up in his bedroom on the eastern wall, and before retiring and on rising studied the imposing figure of the Zionist with the heart-shaped brow and the rich black beard so like Father's. Palestine was on Uncle's lips day and night. To be under his own tree with his three girls and the two circumcised ones! What a dolt he had been not to have understood that the gates of freedom lay there in Jerusalem.

Jack should have realized that this was our salvation. He had scant sympathy for the plan, however. Somewhat spitefully he countered, "Don't Palestine belong to the Arabs?"

"That's a lie!" shrieked Meyer.

Fortunately Father was away in the synagogue. Mother ran into the room.

"What difference does it make what they put on you—earth from Palestine or horse droppings? You're dead when you're dead."

The tears started in Uncle's eyes. He sobbed out loud.

Gruffly Jack answered Mother's reproaches, loaded his pipe, and walked morosely in the garden.

Though Uncle was shaken by this cruel blast, within a week he brought up once more the subject of Palestine. Father examined his insurance policy and arranged to borrow on it. The loan society of his synagogue let him have several hundred dollars. He wrote to the relatives in Chicago and pried a considerable sum out of them. Taking on a new lease on life, Uncle scurried around and found various odd jobs. At the end of the year we had gotten together enough for steamship tickets and for the partnership.

It was a clear mild day when we went to see them off. The girls were dressed in new clothes, the baby was sleeping peacefully, and Judah sported the conductor's cap with the visor polished.

The bell clanged. The liner rang like a giant harmonica. Uncle kissed me for the last time. "You have grown like a dog since your stupid uncle came into your life." He pressed my head against his bony chest. "You will not forget this Jew, this wanderer, will you? And your prayers, your tphilin?"

I felt my nose pinch, my eyes blur.

"Good-bye, Cooney, Cooney Island."

The tiny tugs puffed and huffed, the liner edged away slowly, the three of us kept waving from the pier (Jack had said the hell he'd come, but he had bought the children gifts) and then the dear faces seemed to be swept up in one huge fist and crushed into tears and smoke.

After the departure we were heavy-hearted. The house was like a tomb. But the first news from the travelers wiped out our anxiety. It was a card postmarked Naples. "Day and night my heart beats louder than this wonderful ship. It is a miracle what is happening to us. Your aunt's pains have all vanished as if in the deep sea. The children are growing in the length and the breadth. You should see the little one. He is a hero. He will grow up and ride a white horse for us . . ."

After the arrival in Palestine, we received a thick letter with photographs of the family as well as of the hatchet-faced partner and his wife; the faces were touched up so that it seemed as if grown-ups and children had been eating jam as they sat for the photographer. "The land is so rich, put a stick in the ground, and it blooms. We go around smochkin oranges. My nephew, I will send you a little rooster and his wife. They will eat bugs off your flowers and raise a large family . . ."

Conscientiously Uncle kept sending us weekly letters. He went into rhapsodies about the sweet-scented groves, the communes with the great fields and hills. In ecstasy he discussed agriculture, machinery, irrigation, described the pipes like fifes through which the "Jewish rain" sang. "I could go on with these wonders a thousand and one nights. Ach, what is America? At last, the Jew rests. The wanderer has found his home."

I sit in our tiny bedroom trying to answer Uncle Meyer's last letter. It seems centuries ago that he left us, and misfortune after misfortune has dogged his steps. The first season rains rotted the oranges. The partners lost their grove. They joined a settlement where a family had to sleep in one room, and the meals were at best a bowl of stew. Then they went north to the dairy country. Here the land was poor. The partners had to separate, and Uncle got a job as a hodcarrier in Haifa.

When unrest broke out among the Arabs once more, we were without news from him for a year. Mother became ill worrying about the children. Finally, a rambling, incoherent letter arrived to tell us about Jews bombed in their quarters, slaughtered in the streets, mutilated on the country roads. "The young man, I knew him well. Two drops of milk, like our Isaiah. They took him off the truck, those Arab bandits. This in our own Holy Land!"

As I sit in my room wondering how to answer Uncle's letter, Jack comes in from work. Wearily he flings himself in his greasy clothes on the bed, stuffs the strong tobacco into the pipe which still declares to an indifferent world that the soldier had rather go to his girl than stand guard.

I pretend I am reading to myself: " 'Yes, my nephew, I miss you, my old philosoph. The Jew has no home, not even a stone for a pillow. Tell me why the flowers, the trees, the birds, why the bugs of the earth and all creatures have homes, but we Jews—' "

"Sh—!" cries Jack. "Why did he run off and start up with those Arabs? He don't belong there any more than I do. Running from one country to the other, his pants on fire, yelling about the goyim. Is Palestine the only place where a Jew can be happy? Why in hell didn't he stay put in the country where he was born? Was he afraid he'd have to work? America ain't all roses, but catch me running off like a damned fool!"

Jack has become terribly hard and embittered. His plans for

a shop have come to nothing. We have lost the house with the garden, and every week through all sorts of subterfuges, a little is taken out of the shrinking pay envelope to send to Palestine.

The key clicks in the door. Father comes in from the synagogue. His beard has turned gray. He shuffles into the kitchen with his evening greetings, and Mother rises from her corner and feebly spreads the tablecloth.

The faces of my dear people hover before my eyes. I see the little children, their harassed mother, and my poor uncle. And it seems to me that the venture in Palestine was no solution. The old problem has been flung back into our laps, and our struggles and sufferings have only just begun.

I push the books to one side on my table. I pick up my pen. The sounds of the city soften as it grows darker. I sit for a long time without stirring and wonder what I can say at last to my Uncle Meyer.

JAMES HANLEY:

FANCY FREE

J<small>UST</small> docked off a ship, and I'm in a pub called The Mare's Nest, and I'm fancy free. All on my own, shipmate. I've ordered a pint of real ale and now I can stand here drinking it; no need to hurry about it, no need to think of anything save a new ship, dream about a special kind of ship a sailor wants and never gets. I sup at my ale and I think about this dream ship.

Everything fine and shining here; talk about music, hear them singing back there, and that man with the accordion, and Susie's one large smile. This pub's shaped like a horseshoe, always come to the same place everytime I dock. It's that girl, Susie. I wouldn't mind marrying her, shipmate. I'm always teasing away at her, aiming to get her to do some unfreezing, but she won't bite. No, sir. Nice and warm here, too, all that stuff shining in bottles, and this broad counter full of glasses and everybody's happy, drinking away there, you wouldn't think there was a war on at all. Everybody talking, and always that music back there. Aim some feller's just got home from a long trip and is celebrating, maybe Australia.

That swing door's opening, people going in and out, no end to their coming and going. I drain my glass, reckon I'll fill it again, so I gets my eye on Susie. We've had many a chat, Susie'n me, yes sir, many a chat you might call exclusive, had her on my own. Well, I've got her on my own now. So first thing I say is, "Hey there, Susie, fill her up again." Over she comes. Lord! She's fat, but jolly with it.

"Hello," she says.

"Hello you," I say, my eye on all her buxomness, that face like a light, all smile, and pretty teeth.

"And how are you?" she says.

"Me! I'm fine, how's yourself?" and all the time I'm getting her measure, height and weight and looks; what a weight, sailor.

"My! You're growing into a fine big girl, Susie," I say. "Your ma must be well pleased with you."

Hands me my beer, talk about a smile being broad, you can't beat this one, I gamble you never saw one like it in your life, sort of smile can swallow you up. Oh she's a big girl all right, and she could give a sailor a fine time, too, but she's odd. That's what's wrong with Susie, she's odd because she doesn't like sailors, and she tells me so. Course I just laugh.

"What's wrong with a sailorman, Susie?"

"What isn't?" she says, impish to the hilt.

"How about you and me going off to the Pavilion. Flash Dan and Gertie are on this week. Say yes."

"I never go to theatres."

"You should. A theatre's a damn fine place if there's good turns on."

"No," she says. "I wouldn't go, even then, *really*," and she means this, and you know she means it.

"Well, will you come for a walk, how about a nice walk, or a ride on a tram into the country?"

"Into the country. In the middle of January?"

"Sorry," I say, "my rotten geography, all to hell these days. Well, a walk then, just an ordinary kind of walk, and I'll buy you a box of chocolates, and what's more I'll take you home. There's fair for you, and I don't mind meeting your ma."

"But I don't want to go for a walk," she says.

And I know why. That's what's odd about Susie. She hates sailors, and that's tough on many a man who could give her a good time. I'd even marry her, if she'd marry me. But nothing doing. She's no one for sailors.

"Listen, Su, you answer me a fair question. Why'd you hate sailors? No different to any other men 'cept they're more often away than at home, have a habit of getting lit up now and again, sprawling themselves about." I keep looking at her, holding her own look. And I am thinking.

Take a sailor off a ship, unleash him, let him go, and what happens? Goes and gets lost.

"You're a fine big girl, Susie, and a credit to your mother, not forgetting your da, and I aim to marry you if you'll only give me a chance."

See her face go Turkey red. I'm the hundredth man who's said that.

"I'd never marry any sailor," she says.

"Ah, Susie, you're so used to being asked to marry a sailor that you forget that one might be genuine."

Hear her laugh then, just like a tumble of bells.

"Suppose that man's you," she says.

"Yes sir. That's correct. That man's me. What about it, Susie?"

She goes away and refills my glass.

"I'm not joking," I say. "I *mean* what I say."

"You sailors make me ill," she says, bubbling up with laughter; everybody's looking at us, but I don't mind.

"Stop teasin' a man, Susie."

"Not teasin'. I mean what I say, just like you do, Mr. Sailor."

Mr. Sailor. There's something new. Calling a man Mr. Sailor.

"Oh, all right, you won't marry me, and that's that. Good-bye, Susie."

I pick up my drink and I walk off into the snug. First chap I meet up with is Saxeby, haven't seen him for two years. Nearly shakes my arm off.

"What are you having?" he says.

"Mild and bitter for me."

"What! Plain beer. No siree," and he calls for whiskies.

He calls for five Jamesons, which show he has company. In comes Susie.

There's a red face for you, blush on blush coming to it, so, aiming to set it on fire, I calls out, "Well, shipmates, meet Susie, a fine big girl who's going to marry me and become Mrs. Johnson. Here's your health, Susie," I say, raising my glass.

How she scuffs out! Think of a mouse scuffling into a corner and that's just how she is.

"All the best, sir. Here's to the next trip."

"Half a minute," Saxeby growls; "*here's* to the next trip. Why, I'm only just home."

Susie goes off and I watch her go. Before I leave Saxeby I have three more Jamesons, two shandies, even a glass of port to top up with. Then I go back to the bar. Susie is all on her own washing the glasses.

"How about it, Susie, I really mean it," I say.

Leaning up against the counter I can see her smiling to herself; she has her back to me.

"Oh, be off with you; I tell you I'd never marry a sailor."

"O. K. I'll take you at your word," and I do—finish off my beer and decide to go.

Off you go, man, off you go; you've as much as you can carry now without making yourself a nuisance in this town where you don't know nobody, and don't give a damn anyhow, save for a pretty girl who could melt the ice in a man. Hug yourself to yourself, sailor, then get out. And don't *sprawl*. Keep your head up. So at last I'm out, and Susie's still filling up the glasses.

Turn your coat collar up, draughty in these streets, folk hurrying by, and nothing much to see of their faces, terribly hurried they are, except a woman or two, how they sidle along. Plenty of time on their hands it seems. Sidle and lurk, could turn themselves into shadows if they wanted to. Catch you coming round a corner, coming out through a pub door, calling two a crowd and saying "Sorry," touching you, as though they were trying to crush through a crowd and there's no crowd at all, just you and her. O. K. You hear her say she's sorry, and while she's saying it you get a nostril full of stuff they have about their persons, smells good.

"Hello there! How's things?"

"Hello sailor!"

"Cold isn't it?"

"Isn't it just?"

Right you are, shipmate; away you go. And away we go, me

and her, right to the pub where Susie works, aim on making her jealous. Here we are. I call out for two drinks, she likes port, all those kind of Janes have a palate for port, and while I'm calling for it, I'm dead up against a whippersnapper, a fish-flesh shrimp of a man, a sniff and snoop of a man, reckon he never walked proper in all his life, hopped and lurked about maybe from the time he was born. See his kind behind walls, in corners, passing through any place where the lights are just going out. Up hard against him, since this pub's crowded, and that counter full.

"Scuse me," I say, aiming to get our drinks from the crowded counter.

He moves back, fish-eye wide open on this Jane who's with me. Is this sniffer and snooper married, I ask myself.

"Here you are, kid," and I hand this Jane her drink.

That shrimp of a man can't keep his eye off my Jane at all. Out of the corner of my eye I watch him, and then I wink at him.

"All the best, sister."

"All the best, sailor," she says, and hang it, I know she's said the very same thing to many another sailor; machine touch to her way of saying it. Eyes sparkling and cheeks shining, teeth laughing up at you, nothing new to these, not exclusive to you, sailor, any goddam sailor who's got the shivers and wants to stop being an iceberg. See her smile. That port sure warms you up, I'm thinking, but I don't say it to her, got more sense, tie those silly words into knots and fling them through that door, meaning nothing, like acting in a play, say it a hundred times over, and she'll say back her piece. But Susie's different. She won't cotton on to a sailor-man, and now I'm thinking it's that what makes me like her so much. A fine girl, all right, but tough on sailors. Some women are like that.

O. K. shipmate. Forget her, that's what they call romance for Jolly Jack the Sailor. O. K. sister, look my way, you who I met just now holding up that street corner. I say look my way, sister. You've a way with you, you're four-square; you know what I want, and I know what I want. Right! Fair's fair, shipmate, now we know where we are.

"Have another port, kid?"

"That's fine," she says.

I say, "It's cold tonight. I was asking Susie there if she'd come for a walk with me into the country, but she doesn't like that place in the middle of January, and it's just tough that I'll be on a grey ocean just when the place is beginning to look green. That's tough on her as well, eh Susie," and again I call out her name; this makes her blush all over again. I like that; to see her blushing is like watching all kinds of bright colours.

"Hey, there, Susie, bring another drink, will you?"

"D'you mind saying exactly what you want?" she says, cocking her head up.

"Same as before."

This Jane's jammed up close to me now, and so is this shrimp-shank man; he wears a grey suit. Can't keep his eyes off my girl at all. I don't mind though, so long as it sticks to just looks. This bird's all stranger to me, and he looks dry. All right, sailor, give him a drink, too. The whole world's shining here, and everybody's gay; give this fish-eyed feller a drink; he looks as if he could do with one. Let him guzzle it down, then you can get off about your business. Time's flying.

Have a good look at this Jane you met up with, have a good look while she's trying her port. I do, and watch her head nodding. She has her eye on me; I see her little gloved finger pointing towards that door, and that look and that finger say, "Time to go, sailor," and so it is, but first let me get this queer man his drink.

All on his own here, now what's he look like, *really?* Well what? Take a good squint. Ha ha! Sometime or other this man was pressed down, some large hand on his head, pressing him down, because that was his place in this city, sailor, being pressed down and fated to wear a grey suit for ever. Take another look. So I take another look.

"*D'you* want this drink or not?" and this makes me look up. Why, it's Susie with the drink!

"Course I want the drink, it's for this pal of mine."

Straightaway I hand him this drink, take a bit of a sniff as I do, bad manners of course, but just curious, no more than curious. There must be a reason why a man drinks gin neat.

"Good luck to you, sir," he says.

To *me!* Hang it, it's made me grow at least ten foot high. Good luck, sir. Ah! He can take his stuff, too. That gin's clean gone, well gone. Something to this little man, after all, fidgeting about under my shoulder.

"Have another." And up goes his hand, then he's shaking his head.

"Oh, come on, have another," I say, and suddenly this Jane's pinching my arm and nudging me, but I'm not noticing, just thinking about how this feller would look if he got really drunk.

"Two gins there, Susie."

And two she brings. "Thank *you.*"

"Here you are, all the best to you. Not my kind of drink, shipmate, but try everything once; that's the kind of a person I am."

I look at this Jane.

"Hold hard, sister." I'm saying to myself, "Hold hard there!" This nudging, this pinching at my arm's getting fair irritating, so I say out loud, "Hold hard, sister, I'm coming in half a tick."

"Come now," she says, "come right now, can't wait all bloody night for you."

There's language for you, sailor. That gets me proper. So I say, "O. K. You clear out right now and find another mug; I'm aiming to get warmed up on nothing else but gin tonight. But if it's a cup of tea or coffee, or a pair of silk stockings, sister, well, I'm not a begrudging man, so here you are."

Watch her smile, money for nothing, that's what her expression says, and off she goes. Don't know whether I'm sorry or glad, can't make up my mind about it. I look at this grey-suited man.

"Look here, shipmate, why not let's go round into the snug? Up against a counter a sailor's bound to be free and easy, and so's any Jane who likes to come in for a glass of port. I aimed at getting the ice melted out of me tonight, but now I've changed my mind."

The little chap looks at me now. Ah, there's a bird face for you, sir, keeps looking hard at me.

"Melting the ice out of you," he says.

"Yes, getting unfroze," I say. "What's the matter with that?"

No answer. He's dumb. I aim he don't understand my language. Let's go round to the snug, shipmate. Round we go. That snug's cleared out, there's a fire just for us two. We sit down on a dark wood settle. In comes Susie with more stuff.

"All the best, shipmate," I say, and he nods his little head.

"And the same to you, sir."

Sir again. I'm tickled to death. Now I can get a good look at him.

A sniff of grey whisker over a weak chin, and a pinched-looking gob. "I say, shipmate," I say, "something tells me I've seen you somewhere before."

At once he says, "And I've seen you. I know you, all your tribe."

Tribe! This is a new one on me. Tribe!

"Oh, and what tribe do I belong to?" I ask him.

He pauses, licks round his whisker, drops of anything must be precious to him. Look at his hands. White, long and dry sort of look about them, too. Like they were always aiming to clutch on to something warm, something that lasts. What's this mean, shipmate? Why, that this bird is lonely. Now I 'know. Yes sir. So I start talking to him about all manner of things that'll interest a man, and he talks, too. Blast my eyes! This fish is warming to it, slow, but warming to it all the same. Those Jamesons have come in and we're drinking hard now, and liking it. Looks as if we'll be here until throw-out.

"So I belong to a tribe, eh," I say, smiling at him. Then I shout, giving him a clout on the back at the same time, "Have another, come on, drink that one up and have another. Winter's begun."

"Never knew it ended," he says.

Now that's odd, I think, queer to say a thing like that.

Susie comes in with two more drinks. Damn! How I enjoy looking at this girl.

"I say, Susie, look here, I want to talk to you, hang it, you're as fine as fine," but she's gone and the swish of a skirt is all I hear for reply.

Already this man's had four Jamesons, two gins, a shandy as cleaner-up, and now two more Jamesons are coming in.

"All the best, sir."

Sir again. Been sirring me half the evening.

"I've seen you *somewhere* before," I say. "Damn certain I have. If I'm not being too curious, what's your name?"

"Ranke," he says. "Ranke. Fred Ranke."

Ranke! Have you met anybody name of Ranke, sailor, I ask myself. No, you haven't. Then where've you seen this man before?

"Work in this town?"

That gets him. Yes, he works in this town.

"What makes you look so grey?"

Figures, he says.

"What kind of figures?"

"Oh, just figures."

"Where do you work?"

"Take a turning to the right from here and when you get to the bottom of the street, another sharp turn left, then across a road, and up an alley, this brings you into a wide street, look up, and there you are. That's where I work. Follow me?"

"Half a minute," I say. My mind's working fast, taking right and left turns, then across that road, down the alley, here I am in the wide street, look up as he said. Hell's bells, why, I know this place. Heck of a size, *huge* place.

"That's where I work," he says.

I sit back. I watch him. His face's changed, now it looks just like I seen it look when he's working. Got him. Now I know.

"Pass down between great walls, marvellous walls these, might be walls leading into Paradise, and doors everywhere, all shining, and clink and clank of office machines, and ringing of telephones, and they're not the only bells that ring. Go far down this corridor, always keeping to the port side, sorry shipmate, I mean the left-hand side, and we come to a hole in the wall, iron grille there. You're behind that. Am I right, shipmate?"

"You're quite right, sir," he says, "that's where you've seen me before."

I'm not surprised by sir any more. This man's so used to being in a world full of them, so I accept sirs by the dozen, and never get tired of him addressing me in the same way.

"Isn't that right?" I say. "You're behind a grille. You pay out coin to sailors' women, you have your hands dug into mountains of money; it might be sand or sugar or rubbish to you, so used to having your hand in it. Isn't that right?"

A mere nod of the head from him.

"This grille's finely woven, you might be a priest behind your confessional, you can't see anybody or anything except the face that's sort of flowed up to you. Another thing, you never look up. That's right, isn't it."

Another nod from him, he knows damned well I'm right.

"O. K.," I say. "Now, if you pushed your head through this grille, which you never do, and might be frightened to do, if you did, you'd see a fair long line of sailors' women, all drib and drab and shuffling up to your hole, and leaning about on walls and whispering, and never talking too loud, and edging up to your grille for their money, oh, so slowly edging up, by the mere inch, and one at a time they come to your grille. You don't move, do you? Your hands move, you say 'Name,' and then you take a look at the paper she hands in, and then from sheer habit you say 'Ship?' and she says that ship, and you dive into the mass of money and hand some out, never say good day, never say thanks, say nothing at all. That's you, now isn't it?

"Sun might be pouring in all over that place, still you say nothing. O. K. Saying nothing's a duty to do, and you do your duty, but now suppose you once or twice glanced up when a name was named, and a ship's name called out to you, why, you might have happened on my own sister who draws my monthly money. But you haven't happened on anybody. Two words circle your mind all morning. Name and Ship. And you dig your hands into money. That's why the grille's there, though believe me, shipmate, no sailor's woman would ever take more than was rightly hers, though you might not believe in that, since you believe in nothing except figures, your head's full of them, full of nothing else, shipmate. How break away from them at day's end. I don't know, and God knows that you push yourself around all evening, crushing into this and that pub, all the time aiming to get away from your Figures, dancing in your head I'll bet, following you around everywhere. Isn't that so?"

"Maybe," he says, "maybe."

"I watched that Jane watch you," I say. "I could have had her for a mere nod of the head, but I can be an independent man, sir. But you couldn't, because you've lost the knack of looking at women in the right way. You'd scare them stiff. That's tough on you, but blame the grille, shipmate."

First time in all that evening I see this man smile. I can't believe it at first. He really smiles. And now his glass is empty.

"Have another, shipmate, have another."

In comes Susie.

"Hello, Susie. Well, have you changed your mind yet?"

"What about?" she says.

"Why, marrying me, of course."

She tosses her head. "It's time, we're closing, better go out by the back way, and watch you don't bump your head in the dark."

"I won't bump in any dark, don't you worry," I say. "Besides, this shipmate of mine knows how to get through dark places, don't you shipmate?"

Susie's sizing him up, smiling at his whisker and his gray suit. She looks hard at him, and then he gets up, sort of vanishes, anyhow he's gone, vanished just like he was shadow and not man.

"Who's that?" Susie says.

"Some poor rat," I say, "lived in this town all his life and grey from counting figures. But never mind him now. How about a date for tomorrow night, Susie, girl, you know I love you, truly I do."

I'm just beginning to feel fine, though I daren't put my hand in my pocket just yet, I don't want any shocks. "I love you, Susie," I say again.

All smiling, my, she's got pretty teeth, comes right up to me, gets hold of my arm.

"Why'd you tell lies?" she says. "I'd marry you if you didn't tell lies."

"What? *Me!* I never tell lies."

She squeezes my arm, that makes me feel good, but only for a moment, time for having a shiver, sailor, she doesn't mean what she says, kidding you up, though she likes saying it.

There! I got her now. Right round the waist.

"Give us a kiss, Susie," I say.

What a fine big girl she is, and such rosy cheeks, and what a back she has.

"I'll bet you could haul away on any weight of rope, Susie," I say.

"Time, gentlemen, time please."

There you are, sailor, you know that voice. That's the boss of this place. And there he is looking at the two of us, he's been watching us all the while, talk about being sly.

"Now then, you two," he says, rather sharply, but he doesn't mean it of course, for Susie's the one who brings him all his business here. Besides, everybody knows she's promised to marry half a dozen men already. Having them on. That's part of the business, too.

"I say, look here, Susie, it's your night off tomorrow, and Flash Dan and Gertie'll still be on at the Pavilion. Say yes, there's a dear. I'll take you to the best seats, too, that's in the pit. I'll give you a whale of a time, honest I will. I mean it."

There she goes. Laughing again, ring a bells, sailor, Lord! I love listening to Susie laugh. And she *can* laugh, and shake with it, carrying all that weight like she does.

"Come on, kid, give's another kiss, won't you?"

That's just how I'm feeling now, shipmate, nice and rosy.

"Only one," she says.

Fine, fine! And I give her a kiss, hold on hard. Hell's bells, this girl could unfreeze a whole cargo of sailormen.

"How old are you, Susie? Nineteen and a half. Fine big girl for nineteen. Your ma must think a pile about you, Susie, not forgetting your da of course, who made a miracle happen."

Here we are, both laughing, and old Finch the licensee watching us all the time, but he knows me, I'm not dangerous and never was. But my, she's got a waist like a fisherman.

"You're the nicest girl I ever met in this town," I say.

"Oh, you liar," she says, giving me such a dig in the ribs, her voice rising. What does anything matter, anyhow, she's liking it and so am I. Not every night a sailor feels as gay.

"You *will* come to the Pavilion with me tomorrow night then. It's quite a respectable place, you know. Once saw our skipper sitting in a box there, that shows how good it is. Do come, Susie."

"I'll think about it," she says.

"No, don't think at all, just say yes, Susie," and I'm still holding on to her.

"Time, gents, time," Mr. Finch cries out. "Time, gents, time." What a fog-horn of a voice the man has, to be sure.

Every sailor's gone except me, oh yes, this is a sailors' pub, sir. Yes, they've all gone now, back by quays to many a ship tied up, and some hard fast for their homes, and some away to get warmed up somewhere else, if you can get warmed up in this town, and they say there's places you can, by giving three soft taps on certain doors. Many another place these men have gone off to, up this and that street, and down that long, greasy-looking road, bit of a fog about tonight. If I go off down that road I'll happen up against a sailor hard bound and dry with it. I once met up with a sailor like that. Mightn't think it, but there are quite a few barnacled sailors about, barren of a ship's warmth and a sea smell.

Well, a shipmate just home knows how to warm up such men, yes sir, and I say that without boasting.

There, she's gone. Wriggled out of my grasp while I was doing a bit of thinking. Ah well! But I hate letting her go. Am I dreaming, shipmate, has she really gone? Yes, she's gone. Let her go, sailor, and bang, your whole world's gone, how deeply fallen away to nothing, like breathing bubbles, all gone. Just then Mr. Finch comes in.

"Time, sailor," he says. "Everybody's away. You're the very last. Off you go."

"Waiting to take Susie home," I say.

"You run off and get ready then, Susie," he tells her.

I can't believe it. She's actually letting me see her home this evening. In two minutes she's back, ready to go. I grab her arm.

"Night, Mr. Finch," I say.

"Night, shipmate. Best of luck," and he gives me a wink. Off we go. We walk slowly that dark road.

"Look here, Susie, do marry me. I mean every word I say."

"I told you I'll never marry a sailor, *never*."

That's done it, that's finished it. You are dreaming, sailor, really dreaming. I see her to the house where she lives. I give her a squeeze.

"I mean what I say," she says.

O. K. You won't marry a sailor; all right, Susie. Go and marry that shrimp of a man I met up with tonight, gutless under his grey suit, marry him. There's a man pressed all his life by some large kind of hand, I reckon. Marry him, Susie, and press him to death. You hate sailors. All right then, go on hating them. Here's where you live, go in to your ma and da, tell them what a good girl you've been, tell them a sailor tried to get warmed up but that you just weren't biting. Tell them that. Night, Susie. I mean good-bye, Susie. You were fine for what you are. O. K. Here's where I turn. Down this street, and down another one, darker than dark is, then across to that dock. Up the gangway, along for'ard to your bunk, that's your place. O. K. Watch me give her a kiss and then I'm gone. That was all fine while it lasted, and any amount of singing and gay colours in The Mare's Nest this evening, and I'd all of Susie inside me, dreaming away there like there was nothing else to do in this life but dream. And I enjoyed every minute of it. Off you go, sailor. She could fix everything up, she could make a whole world shine for a sailorman, but she's not biting, because she just doesn't like sailors. O. K. Susie. Good-bye.

And away I go back towards my ship.

"Don't sprawl about, sailor," I tell myself, "for heaven's sake don't sprawl about. People'll think you're lost. Pull your coat collar up and get along. February's a cold month, hug yourself to yourself.

"One of these days I'll meet up with a decent Jane who'll marry me," I tell myself, "and all will be well then, yes, all will be well then, sailor."

JACK JONES:
THE MUGGING

JUDY FORGANG:

THE END faded in on the screen and Jimmie squeezed my hand and we got up and tripped over people going out. In the lobby we sat down on the plush couch and held hands.

You're more beautiful than Lana Turner, Jimmie said.

You're more handsome than Clark Gable, I said and laughed.

No, I mean it, said Jimmie. He did, too.

I looked at him, a little embarrassed. When a boy's that sweet on you, it makes you less sure sometimes. It's as if you were afraid he'd had a shot of dope that might wear off too soon.

Let's go walk in the Park, said Jimmie. It's only nine-thirty.

No, let's not.

Why?

It's too dark.

I'll be there.

That's the trouble. Remember what you almost did last time?

Please. I won't do anything. I promise.

You promised last time too.

Oh Judy! he said like a baby wanting candy.

All right but only until ten o'clock.

We won't get over there till fifteen of.

Fifteen past ten, then, I said.

We walked out of the 102nd Street Theater and started west. It was late in May and a lovely Saturday night, not too warm but warm enough so that you didn't have to wear a coat.

Did you register? I asked him.

I'm going to, Jimmie said, there's plenty of time.

You'll really like it at City College, I said. I've only been one year and I'm crazy about it. You only missed one year and you're not twenty yet.

OK, Jimmie said impatiently.

I'm not going this summer so you'll catch up with me. We'll be in some classes together.

Jimmie looked sulky and for a minute I was afraid.

You're not in any trouble, Jimmie? I asked. Three years ago he'd got sucked into a gang that broke into store windows at night. He'd been caught and given a three-month suspended sentence.

Hell, no, said Jimmie.

I could see that he was telling the truth and smiled at him.

I wish you'd read more instead of shooting pool, I said.

Listen, said Jimmie, let's forget about it. I'm going to register next week and haven't we anything better to talk about?

All right, I said.

We walked into the Park and plunged down a southern-bound path. The dim-out made it pretty dark but the moon and stars were out. The night air was fresh and clean. We went slowly, arm in arm.

Let's sit down for a minute, Jimmie said.

Now don't start, I said.

What's the matter, Judy? Jimmie asked.

All right, for a minute, I said. Then we'll have to go home.

We sat down on a bench. There was no one in sight.

Jimmie tried to kiss me and I let him. Then I started to get up but he wouldn't let me go.

Jimmie, let me go, I said.

Kiss me again.

I kissed him again. We held it for a long time. I could feel the flush in my cheeks.

Please let me go, I said.

Jimmie did but I felt weak and couldn't get up. Jimmie kissed me again.

Don't, I said, that's what you did last time.

Don't you want to? Jimmie asked.

I couldn't lie to him. Yes, I said.

Let's.

No.

Yes.

I didn't say anything. Jimmie got up and pulled me up and we started walking. About a hundred yards deeper into the park Jimmie lifted me over a railing and vaulted over himself. We climbed a short hill and went another hundred yards before we found a place—a valley between two brief hills whose ends were screened by pine clumps.

John T. Lucas:

I'd just been to see Maxwell Blake, the Negro writer. That's how I happened to be up in Harlem. *Progressive Fiction* couldn't afford to pay more than a cent a word but I'd thought perhaps Blake had some old manuscripts around that he'd like to get rid of. So I called up. He said sure, to come up and poke around.

I bought three stories, all excellent, and he promised me his future stories he couldn't get rid of to the commercial press.

I left Blake's place and walked west to 2nd Avenue and 114th, then started south. I'd gone about halfway to the Lexington Avenue subway when I had a sudden impulse and crossed 2nd Avenue and went toward 3rd instead of waiting until I'd got level with the Lexington station and *then* crossing.

I didn't like the looks of the street I was on much; and I hadn't seen anybody since I left Blake. But then, it was pretty late—eleven-thirty. I started to walk faster.

I was never so startled in my life when suddenly I heard someone just behind me, walking faster. I suppose he'd been crouching in one of those sunken stone porches. I stopped dead and turned around.

I only caught a glimpse of his face but I saw that he was a Negro and his left cheek was twitching. He crowded up and pushed me down the stairs into a porch.

My God, what do you want?

He hit me in the mouth with a gun-butt and I fell to one knee. I shouted. A broken tooth choked my throat and I had to stop to cough it out. The Negro was holding what looked like a raincoat in his left hand and his right was under it. I couldn't see the gun. I didn't dare shout again but it was too late. He was crazy.

Don't kill me! I whispered. Don't kill me!

There was a sound like an airgun popping and a streak of hot light sped through

TOMMY NORSHELL:

What's the matter? I asked. You look kind of dopey.

Nothing, Jimmie said.

You look like somebody on the roof dropped a mailbox on your bean, I said.

Why don't you shut up? asked Jimmie.

We went over to Jack's poolroom. Jack let us have a table at the back for two bits and we got up a poker game with two other colored guys. We had the window there open and the spring air flowed in. It was Sunday night.

I got a new pack from Jack and we chipped in for it. I split the seal with my thumbnail. Everybody was feeling swell and we were going to have a hell of a time.

Jimmie was counting the chips.

Half-penny ante? I asked, shuffling the cards.

Yeah.

OK.

OK.

I started dealing. We were playing straight poker, but about the twelfth hand Jimmie, who hadn't even been able to open yet, said, How about deuces wild?

No, one of the other guys said.

Cut for it? asked Jimmie.

They did and Jimmie won.

Sure enough, right after that he started raking it in. We played fast and furious until eleven o'clock. Then Jimmie started losing.

Deal me out on this one, said Jimmie. I'm gonna take a leak.

We were too hot over the game to notice him. He was back in ten-fifteen minutes.

All the time I was dealing the next hand I could feel there was somebody just come up behind my chair watching. I finished dealing, gathered in my hand and tossed back my head. It was Kickie Brown.

My God, Kickie, I said. Whereinhell you been?

Plenty places, Kickie said grinning.

Hello Jimmie.

Hi, Jimmie said.

My eyes went to Kickie's left cheek. That twitching tic was still there.

Well, said Jimmie, whyn't they got you in the Army?

They ain't caught this nigger yet, said Kickie.

Everybody laughed. The other two guys, who didn't know Kickie, thought it was a joke. We got back to the game.

I didn't turn my head again but I was thinking of Kickie. He got that name in P. S. 57 because he always fought with his feet. He was the first guy who ever kicked me in the balls.

What're you doing, Kickie? Jimmie asked. Him and Kickie used to be pals, but Jimmie's girl broke that up three years ago.

Layin around, said Kickie.

Jimmie looked at the clock. Christ, he said.

I looked at it. He had a job in a Queens war plant and had to get up at six.

One more hand, said a guy.

OK.

We played it and Jimmie got his coat and we went outside with Kickie.

Just then a police radio car came helling down between the elevated pillars, siren blasting. It turned off into a side street a couple of blocks up. We let it go. Nuts to it.

Where you goin? Kickie said. He was breathing kind of fast.

Home, I said.

Look, Jimmie, said Kickie, do me a favor?

What?

Get rid of this, Kickie said. He shoved something I couldn't see into Jimmie's hand and ran down the street to the el stairway and pounded up.

Christ, said Jimmie, staring at his hand. What'll I do with this goddam thing?

It was a heavy steel-blue gun.

I looked around quickly. No one watching.

I don't want it, said Jimmie. He looked for some place to ditch it.

You want it? Jimmie asked.

Hell, no.

There was a guy walking toward us. Jimmie shoved the gun under his coat until the guy went by, then started walking. I followed him down the block around the corner into an alley where there were some ashcans. Jimmie dropped the gun in one can that was half-full, so it didn't make any noise.

Jimmie and I came out of the alley. There was no one around.

The crazy bastard, Jimmie said. He was pretty mad.

Yeah, I said. Well, so long, Jimmie.

Two days later I heard Jimmie had been arrested.

LEE STEWART:

The headlines were coming swell today. I thought of a beaut for the story of the Volunteer Land Army girl just up from New York: CITY GIRL COWED, SPENDS NIGHT IN TREE. I looked up grinning and saw Maxie walking quietly toward me across the city room floor. When Maxie was quiet he was boiling mad. I didn't know what the hell it was but I couldn't help getting scared.

Stewart, Maxie said, you write this headline?

Yeah, I said, what's wrong with it?

I looked it over breathing through my mouth. MAN SLAIN, ROBBED ON UPPER THIRD AVENUE.

What's the matter? I said.

You know goddam well what's the mater, Maxie said. You get paid for writing headlines, not obits.

I let my pan freeze slow and shut up.

You headline stories like that this way, said Maxie. He wrote HARLEM MUGGERS SLAY, ROB CITIZEN.

What's the point? I asked again, but I knew this time.

You better catch on, said Maxie.

HARRY PANZER:

We found the gun Monday afternoon.

For Christ sake, I said to the Sanitation Department guy on the phone, don't touch it!

I got down there fast in a radio car and grabbed the gun. It was in an ash can about three blocks down from the killing. I took it to H. Q. It was the right gun, all right, Ballistics said. Fingerprints too. The killer sure was careless, though probably his prints weren't on file.

The guy that was killed, Lucas, had had his pockets cleaned out and we got a description of what was in them from his wife, so if the killer took a notion to pawn anything we might get him. But it was a tough case. Muggings always are, for usually there aren't any clues. In this one there was the old raincoat we found near the body that the killer used to muffle his gun. But that was no good. It'd been stolen from a City Councilman last year in a 42nd Street Automat. I guess the killer was pretty scared, to ditch the gun. Or maybe he was afraid he'd get caught with it on him.

The Fingerprint Classification Division called up before midnight. We had him! The prints on the gun checked with the ones on file of a Negro boy named Jimmie Conroy who'd got a suspended N.

I went down with five men and arrested him.

SAM SILVERSTEIN:

George was bringing in that pretty nigger girl to visit Conroy. I guess George was feeling kind of peppy today and wanted to have some fun, but anyway, as soon as he brought her into the bullpen he started right in.

Madam, he says like she was the Queen of India, this is what is popularly known as the bullpen.

The nigger girl knew right away what he was up to, but she didn't say anything. She'd been to City College, I read in the papers, and I guess she wanted to be treated same's a white girl. I've always thought they shouldn't let any niggers go to college, because they always get ideas like that from the Red literature they let them read.

Actually, says George, as we very well know, its correct name is the detention room.

I understood, the nigger girl said very proud, that I was to be allowed to see Mr. Conroy.

Well, this was going too far of course, and George took her down a peg.

What do you mean Mr. Conroy? he said. There's no Mr. Conroy in this jail.

Yes there is, said the nigger girl.

No, there ain't, said George. If you came to see a Mister Conroy you better go back home.

The nigger girl got it all right. George could have kept her out too, if he'd wanted.

I came to see Jimmie Conroy, the nigger girl said.

Oh! says George like he'd just caught on. You mean that nigger Conroy coming up for trial tomorrow?

The nigger girl hesitated. Yes, she said.

George walked her over to me.

This is what is popularly known as a keeper, George says to the nigger girl. Actually, as we very well know, his title is Correction Officer.

A cop in the corner of the bullpen snickered. I cracked a smile.

The nigger girl looked like she couldn't stand much more, so George said, OK Sam, escort the lady to our honeymoon suite.

I took the girl's arm and we started through the door.

Watch them close all the time, says George. Or we'll have a batch of pickaninnies on our hands before we can get her out of here.

The nigger girl started to cry, but I had to laugh.

Louie Martinelli:

Q: What time was it?

A: About eleven-thirty.

Q: Can't you be more exact?

A: No, sir.

Q: Very well. You said that the defendant then began to lose heavily. What happened?

A: He said—he said he had to leave the room.

Q: In the poolroom where you and the defendant were playing, where is the lavatory located?

A: Downstairs in the hall.

Q: Then it would be an easy matter for the defendant to have left and reentered the building unobserved?

Mr. Rednick: Objection!

The Court: Sustained.

Q: I apologize. (To the witness) Now, as a rule, are there people loitering in the downstairs hall?

A: I guess not. Most guys go upstairs right away.

Q: When you came upstairs that night, was there anyone in the hall?

A: No, sir.

Q: When you left?

A: No, sir.

Q: Very good. What—

Mr. Rednick: I object to the prosecutor's lauding the witness whenever the prosecutor thinks he has made a point.

The Court: Denied.

Q: When did the defendant return?

A: About fifteen of twelve.

Q: Can't you be more exact?

A: No, sir.

Q: Very well. What did the defendant do next?

A: Well, we went on playing and pretty soon a guy they called Kickie came up and threw the bull around—

Q: Omit extraneous material.

A: Sir?

Q: We are not interested in Kickie.

Mr. Rednick: I object strongly to the prosecutor's attempting to stifle the witness' testimony. We are prepared to—

The Court: Objection denied. You will have an opportunity to cross-examine. Continue.

Q: What happened then?

MARGIE GLADE:

Q: You thought nothing of it?

A: That's right. But when I heard about the murder I guessed I'd better tell the police.

Q: Quite correct. You're certain of the time?

A: Yes.

Q: What makes you certain?

A: I'd just looked at my clock. It was exactly eleven-forty.

Q: Then what did you do?

A: I heard a sharp noise and looked out the window. Across the street a man came up the steps of one of those cellar things. He looked up and down like he was afraid—

Mr. Rednick: Objection.

The Court: Sustained. Strike out the last sentence of the witness as a conclusion of the witness.

Q: You saw the man, describe his actions.

A: He walked quickly down the street and turned the corner. My window's on the opposite corner and I could see him go down the street. He went into Jack's poolroom two blocks down.

Q: How do you know it was Jack's poolroom?

A: Because there was the poolroom sign above the place he turned off. I see that sign every day and I'd know it in the dark.

Q: What did the man look like?

A: I saw he was a colored man and kind of tall, but that's all I could see.

ROBERT PEARSON:

The ballot was ten to two for conviction.

We talked it over for half an hour and voted again. Ten to two.

Now none of that, I said. As foreman of this jury, I want to know who the guilty pair are.

I was careful to smile. It never does any good to antagonize the minority.

They owned up a little awkwardly. Jurors 2 and 12, Mr. White and Mrs. Stein.

We'll have to convince you, I said. What is it about the prosecutor's case that doesn't satisfy?

I don't think there was enough evidence, said Mr. White.

It seems to me they jumped on that boy because he was the first Negro they could get anything on, Mrs. Stein said. She was the sentimental type, very nice, but not the kind of person that should be on a jury.

We worked on them for three hours. Finally Mr. White conceded that maybe there *was* enough evidence, since we all seemed to think so. But Mrs. Stein wouldn't give up.

Did you hear the prosecutor harping on the Norshel boy's color when he testified for Conroy? she asked. It looked to me as if he didn't think he'd get to first base any other way.

It was a blazing afternoon and we were all tired. The others were beginning to get annoyed, but I cut in before anyone said something that'd only make Mrs. Stein more stubborn.

Now, Mrs. Stein, I said, you know we all have the highest respect for your fairness. But don't you think that perhaps you're letting your sympathy for the Negro race run away with you?

I don't think he had a fair trial, she said.

I didn't let her get me angry.

Mrs. Stein, I went on, I seem to recall that you testified that you were a member of some racial relations organization. Now you were the twelfth juror selected, and the prosecutor had used up all his peremptory challenges or you would have been excused. The judge refused a challenge for cause when you said you would try the case impartially. We others all testified to having no prejudice against members of the Negro race. In fact, you were the only one whose impartiality was in doubt —except the prospective jurors who were excused. Confess, I

smiled,—we won't tell on you—aren't you just the least bit preju-
diced *for* the defendant?

I don't think so, said Mrs. Stein.

But I knew we had her. The next vote was twelve to nothing
for conviction.

WALTER GREENFIELD:

You are a disgrace to your race, I concluded.

I sentence you to death by electrocution at the legally desig-
nated place of execution of the State of New York on the twenty-
sixth day of July nineteen forty-three.

KICKIE BROWN:

I saw it inna morning blatt. Jesus, but it took the truck off
my ass!

NEGRO KILLER TO DIE IN
CHAIR FOR FATAL MUGGING

Oh boy, oh boy.
Watzit? Sissie asked, flippin over a card.
Nuttin.
But, Jesus, I thought, I sure am sitting pretty, when they jerk
that switch. Supposin they ever find out. So what? They can't
do anythin without lettin everybody know they burned Jimmie
for nuttin.

DAVID CASWELL TODD:

Editorial

With the murder of John T. Lucas *Progressive Fiction* lost
one of its most valued and respected editors. Two days ago a
Negro boy was sentenced to die in the electric chair for that
murder. Judge Greenfield, in passing sentence, declared to him:
"You are a disgrace to your race."

In the name of John T. Lucas, who would have written this editorial if he could, we protest.

The conventions of a fair trial have, to be sure, been respected. But it is clear that the evidence which resulted in conviction was flimsy: Jimmie Conroy's fingerprints were on the gun—no more. The testimony of Tommy Norshel that he was with Conroy during the evening falls just short of establishing an alibi—just short because Conroy left the room for a few minutes at about the time of the murder; but Norshel's story of how Conroy got the gun, it being thrust into his hands on the street by "Kickie" Brown, was contemptuously ignored by police and court.

The prosecutor succeeded in diverting attention from this testimony by magnifying out of all proportion Conroy's adolescent brushes with the police, rhetorical dexterity transforming his petty offenses of apple-stealing and window-breaking into major crimes of gangsterism: and by labelling "incredible" Conroy's failure to turn in the gun to the police (as if any Negro with a police record could possibly turn in a hot gun without implicating himself in whatever crime had been committed!) His calculated brutality in dragging from Conroy's girl-friend the details of their love-relationship, implying that Conroy's motive for the crime was his need of "quick cash" for a "hurry-up marriage" was shocking and his final descension to open appeal to race prejudice, e.g. his remark to the jury: "Oh, those Negroes all stick together," worse.

The police do not trouble to conceal that they have made little effort to find Kickie Brown. They were more interested in rushing through a conviction of their first catch, and clearing their books of an unsolved crime, than in introducing another complication, Brown, into the case. "It's the defendant's worry." In the simple majesty of this principle the police rest content.

Of the jury it is only necessary to point out that Negroes were excluded from it.

We believe that the judge is a sincere man. But the essence of his attitude is illustrated by the remark quoted: he would never castigate a convicted white man in terms of race.

It is our impression that Jimmie Conroy is innocent. Time is needed to extract the facts which will confirm that impression.

But he *may* be guilty. If so?

Death for Jimmie Conroy means that the victim, not the culprit, will be destroyed. The culprit is the environment that guided his life like a corridor of steel. It is not too much to say that if the murderer had not been Jimmie Conroy (supposing that it was), it would have been another product of the environmental corridor. It is useless to destroy products; we must strike at what produces them. Until we do, legal killing like that about to be applied to Jimmie Conroy is frequently no more than inaccurate revenge. Therefore, *Progressive Fiction* requests Governor Thomas Dewey to commute his sentence to life imprisonment.

D.C.T.

DANIEL SOUTH:

The execution was set for tonight at eleven.

Conroy's lawyer was still trying to get the Governor's stay. I'd ordered a direct phone line kept open to Dewey's office. *The Daily Worker* was claiming he'd been framed, as they always do whenever a Negro is convicted of a crime.

The Negro boy was quiet and taking it pretty well. At ten-thirty the Reverend told me that he always says he's innocent.

Well, what do you think?

Warden, the Reverend said, I stopped thinking about ten executions ago.

There are some pretty smooth liars, Reverend, I warned him.

What he told me wasn't smooth at all.

I looked at my wrist watch. Very little time. I have fought capital punishment all my life, I thought, and tonight, in fifteen minutes, I shall order my twenty-fourth execution. And next week my twenty-fifth. Will it ever stop? I thought, feeling a little tired.

At five of eleven I called Joe and Pete and we walked to the death house. We passed the outer guards and went down the long barred-window corridor.

Jimmie was in the special section, the fourth cell. Right ahead, about twenty yards down the blank corridor, was the execution room.

Jimmie was sitting on his iron cot with his head between his palms. He looked up as I came near and then closed his eyes and sat there waiting, his face perfectly blank.

Well, Jimmie, I said, I guess we have to go.

JIMMIE CONROY:

The sound did not die away.

Louder. Approaching feet. My heart exploded. I can't stand it. No. I can't.

I know what I'll do I'll shut my eyes and won't open till it's all over and just think Judy Judy Judy. The tall warden and the guards walked into sight. They stood outside my cell and looked in I shut my eyes. I heard the warden say something I didn't listen.

JUDY JUDY JUDY JUDY JUDY [1] JUDY JUDY JUDY JUDY JUDY JUDY JUDY JUDY JUDY JUDY JUDY JUDY [2] JUDY JUDY JUDY JUDY JUDY JUDY [3] JUDY JUDY [4] JUDY JUDY JUDY JUDY JUDY [5] JUDY JUDY JUDY [6] JUDY JUDY JUDY JUDY [7] JUDY [8] JUDY JUDY JUDY JUDY JUDY JUDY JUDY JU [9]

---

[1] The guards are taking his arms. He moves forward.
[2] The raw light of the execution room warns his eyelids.
[3] They have pushed him down into the metal chair.
[4] They have started to strap him in.
[5] The wet electrocution plate chills his leg.
[6] The rigid skullcap settles.
[7] The hood brushes his face.
[8] Have you anything to say.
[9] The executioner sees the warden nod.

JULES LAFORGUE:
TWO PIGEONS

Translated by HARRY LEVIN

TRANSLATOR'S NOTE. This story is the only unpublished piece of prose that Laforgue left completed at his death. In many ways, in its sudden transitions from grandiloquence to inconsequence, from self-conscious sentimentality to hard-boiled irony, it is a specimen of his ripest and most characteristic work. For its theme, it glances back to a fable of LaFontaine about the misadventures of a pigeon who left its mate, with a moral imploring lovers to live in their affections toward each other and not in the external world. For its psychological tone and elaborated style, it looks ahead to the novel of Proust.

YOU REALLY mean it? Then it isn't a mere melodramatic test you've been trying to impose on your poor, well-meaning Gaspard?"

"No. That would upset the good intentions of all the Gaspards in the world."

"Nonsense, Juliette. Your little heart is too light for such a heavy-handed joke, a joke which I should call elephantastic!" These quibbles were one of his two or three vices.

"That's where you make a man's mistake. My little heart is quite heavy, I assure you."

"Well?"

"I'm going to give it some exercise. I've already told you, I've been telling you for the past two days."

"And am I supposed to stand here and watch the boat pull out, and then go home? The least you can do for me is to suggest an attitude, my capricious Juliette."

"The attitude of a civilized person toward one of his equals."

"But supposing that civilized person is—as they say—out for revenge."

"Let him be. I'm not worried about your kind of devotion."

"You might at least say, 'Gaspard, I'm leaving you because you won't kill me when I leave you. You definitely would have in the early stages of our love, and hence you no longer love me as you did.' But you leave me just to be leaving."

"Why don't you kill me then?"

"Because I'd rather know what I was doing."

"If you loved me, you could find out by looking in my eyes."

In moments of leave-taking, our throats are muffled by the very vastness of the space into which we are being precipitated. Lovers would be smothered, if they did not grit their teeth and confine their conversation to cut-and-dried patter.

Besides, Gaspard and Juliette had exhausted indoors their last and latest farewells.

Along the pier they continued to pace out their suspense.

Boys and girls were playing hide-and-seek among the piles of barrels, and getting cursed by gangs of roustabouts with blue blouses and tiny golden rings in their ears; but the curses were only a formality, for roustabouts ordinarily make good husbands and kind fathers.

Those August twilights! An exaggerated full moon, with the glitter of dull gold. A whole settlement of swallows ranging, skimming the warm water, reeling with incessant twitterings, trying to sketch their daytime patterns against the twilight as if —heaven help us!—there would never be another opportunity. Always those twilights in unfrequented harbors! A dog barking at the smell of stew aboard a moored tender, lanterns hoisted aloft to celebrate some sort of mass to the Virgin of the Waters, and masting and rigging everywhere disentangling the day in a reluctant good-bye. (It must be a strange experience, for a tree from the forest, to become a mast and go sailing away. . . .)

High above the confusion of passengers and packages, the white-cabined boat chafed at her tow-lines and fretted at the uproar. The two large smokestacks were idle, but two little funnels that ran alongside them were angrily blending their screams in a jet of pure white mist.

Just then, from the other side of the village, a bell conscientiously tolled the Angelus. It was an honest and rather stupid bell, and it seemed to be hinting: "Do as we do, my sisters and myself. Look at this village of some three hundred hearths, with a church for the blessed Lord and a little cemetery for the blessed dead. Isn't that everything? And my voice never changes, and I am well-preserved. Do as I do, children of a prodigal century, resign yourselves to the provincialism of never being anywhere else."

Gaspard, fists clenched, waited until the officious bell was through, before venturing his final plea (which was so lofty that I hesitate to offend delicate sensibilities with an expression like "clinching the argument").

"Juliette, listen. Juliette, you're all alone in the world."

"Excuse me, no more than ever."

"You won't leave like this?"

"You think it will be like yesterday? I was coward enough to let myself be argued out of it by your last-minute manoeuvres, and my baggage left without me. You've gained nothing by that. This time you'll lose everything."

"But won't I have anything left?"

"Yes, hope, like everyone else."

A few villas were already aglow with domestic lamps, and these motionless pendants of light, under the renewed spell of that remarkable golden moon, had the effect of unpretentious jewelry, family heirlooms perhaps, or old-fashioned trinkets from the days of Queen Bertha and her spindle.

"How well these evenings suit your beauty, Juliette! And who will tell you so better than I? Juliette, in the name of the love you have sworn to me so often on these occasions—"

"I swore once for all."

"That's right, don't get excited. As I was saying, what will become of me now?"

"That depends on your plans."

Gaspard had taken a knife out of his pocket, and was using his nail to open it.

"Look here. Ask me to gash my wrists or forehead, or wound myself seriously, to prove that the sight of you has always disturbed and provoked my blood!"

"You see, you can't even open it."

"Just a minute, you'll see."

"Gaspard, drop that knife, unless you want the crowd on this pier to see me have a nervous breakdown."

"I disgust you—that's the incontrovertible truth!"

"No, it's only that I'm being reasonable."

"Reasonable is a funny word for any of the sickly, sophomoric reasons I've succeeded in wringing out of you. You can't even repeat them without laughing."

Glancing away into some fictitious seventh heaven, she repeated: "This year a peculiar phase has come over my feelings, a mad impulse to put in an appearance at the little town where I was brought up, and leave someone behind me—"

"Always there."

"Someone who has understood me—so far, at least—and who will preserve an artist's awareness of that curious creature whose life crossed his, and wonder, on evenings like this, 'Where in the wide world is she now?'"

"But it's the fable of the two pigeons all over again!"

"Not at all. Your reading misleads you."

"It's my fault for letting your imagination lie fallow, so that these rank weeds could take root in it."

"No, it's life, my feelings, my dear little native town. Oh, if only I don't die tomorrow!"

"There's enough trouble for today, Juliette. Let's go back. You can tell me everything at tea, and I promise to start living tomorrow on a new and improved plan."

"Tea, here, this evening?" She choked on the absurdity of that little *genre* painting. "When I tell you it's a matter of life and death to me!"

"Where shall I write?" Gaspard asked, after an oblique silence.

"There. Nowhere yet."

"Will you write me then?"

"Perhaps."

"Do you think you'll come back?"

"That's just it. With a past that will keep you continually mean and jealous."

"All right. I'll wait for you, my poor Juliette. You know the way."

He paused, smiling as wanly as the moon, lit a cigarette, twisted his moustache moonwards, and remarked in the tone of a connoisseur:

"Ah, charming nights are for romantic souls. Look, poetry! Are you warm enough? I fear you have forgotten your bottle of salts."

"Of course. What a shame! How foolish of me!"

"Here it is," said Gaspard, drawing it coolly out of his watch-pocket.

"How nice! Thank you. I wonder if I remembered to put a dozen photographs in my bag?"

Gaspard inspected her from breasts to knees. "Yes, and you can hand them out to advertise the beautiful freak! Good-bye."

And he turned his back and walked off, disappearing behind the customs-house in the direction of the villas. Juliette followed him with her eyes, until the fragments of her anguish were released in an expansive sigh.

In the direction of the villas, for which it was the final sound of the day, the ship's bell began to chime. Juliette hurried.

"Your ticket is for yesterday, madam. It must be stamped again, over on the other side."

On the way back, before she could cross the gangplank, she came upon Gaspard waiting beside an embracing group.

"Let me embrace you too," he exclaimed, good-bye in his heart.

"Good-bye, my dear," she said, in a discreet voice, which did not exclude a considerable residue of friendship.

He clasped her pitifully, and their mouths interpenetrated without reservation.

"Wave your handkerchief, won't you?" he concluded jauntily.

The uproar had subsided, the boat was no longer fretful, coils of dripping rope were being hauled aboard, and first wildly, then regularly, the blades of the propeller began to spank the pleasantly innocuous water, which suddenly rushed up into the evening. . . .

Juliette watched the vulgar pier recede into the lovely evening . . .

"Well! Why didn't you wave?"

She turned around; it was Gaspard; he had embarked too. Fondly he was knotting his scarf and feigning an interest in the pair of little red signal-lights at half-mast.

"Such weakness!" she said. "Cheap buffoon! But you had better behave yourself. You're only another passenger here, and I'm a respectable woman."

She went down into the lounge. He followed at a distance and sat down in the entrance. She walked around the room and went upstairs again. He went upstairs again.

On the rear deck she settled down into a steamer-rug with the elegant unconcern of a woman of the world, already seasoned to the gaze of fellow-travellers, apparently anxious for nothing but a cozy niche in which to think about her private affairs, in full view of a moon and a sea that were public property.

Leaning against a rail not far away from her, Gaspard lit his stubby, old-fashioned pipe and waited, never losing sight of that dear, departing profile, outlined for the moment by the moon.

"This is mild insanity," he thought. "Is she really there? And am I really here, a stranger, waiting for some kind of pretext to introduce myself? On this extraordinary boat, in this improbable moonlight. An odd episode! Undoubtedly the crisis of her twenty-fifth year, if women have such things as crises in their twenty-fifth year. Never mind, she's a charming creature. And after all, I'm madly in love with her."

The thought came in puffs out of Gaspard's pipe. He knew everything—philosophy, history, moral sciences, and paradoxes—and he managed to fuse it all into a comfortable set of ideals. That was what had originally attracted Juliette, perhaps in a mood of unhappily romantic languor. Actually the serene and lovely evening, the unlooked-for departure were casting upon his imagination all the romantic spell of an elopement which prudence would never have sanctioned. And he gradually forgot the volley of harsh retorts, yes, insults with which she had dismissed his whole-hearted appeals during the past two days. He forgot the rather serious scene that had just taken place.

"Three more hours on shipboard," he mused, "and then, in some hopeless little hotel room, I shall crush her adroitly to my bosom. Poor, wild, migratory bird! And wipe away her tears of gratitude and pardon. She does her hair so nicely!"

Juliette had always worn her hair short, with little curls at the back of her neck. And just as on previous occasions when, from the depths of his chair in a familiar drawing-room, wondering obscurely about love, he had watched her behavior among her delightful friends, so now Gaspard repeated to himself again:

"Would it not be possible to brush aside, to untangle those little curls with intimate and trembling hand? Oh, I'm not speaking for myself, but for someone! Brightly and softly looking up at you, she would accept it as the most natural thing in the world; and then she would place her head upon your shoulder, and so on."

And he remembered that, whenever he had rehearsed that outrageous obsession as to the possibility of caressing her curls, he used to cheer himself up by thinking: "After all, she's just a little animal, a charming little mammal who will grow old like the rest, etc., etc." He remembered too, that the fantasy would habitually reach a climax: "Oh, to be alone in a room rented for the occasion! She would be crying like a Magdalene, because—she would say—I had hurt her, and would never understand her. And on the verge of further tears, she would roll her little handkerchief into a ball, and press it against her mouth to keep from crying out, etc., etc."

At this moment Gaspard looked up. In the moonlight, silent tears were glittering against the outline of Juliette's profile. "I can't stand it!"

He repressed his desire to comfort her, not through fear that she might raise a scandal (he was no longer mindful of her grim warning), but in a sudden burst of voluptuous hopes that caused him to whisper: "Soon enough, soon enough the time will come."

To sustain his patience and adjust his mood, he tried to conjure up extraordinary mirages out of the pastoral moonlight. A bit of copper deflecting a beam of this particular light, likewise deflected his reverie; it became the reflection of the lamp in the samovar that stood in the little apartment where they had spent such contented evenings. Tonight, with the house deserted and dark, there would be no tea, no lamp, no drawings, no games of checkers. The window would be closed to the coolness of the miniature garden, and the crickets would have to sing to themselves, if their hearts (their little, dark crickets' hearts) bade them.

But what could our universally admired Juliette have to cry about?

For three days, a newspaper item announcing a fatal illness had been awakening in her the poignant image of a smile of long ago, a masculine smile behind waxed moustaches; hardly an irresistible smile, the world being what it is; but the smile which had been responsible for the earliest sleepless nights of Juliette's womanhood. For three days that hypnotic smile, sinking into death somewhere across the sea, had been luring her and prompting her to embark immediately, her sight submerged in the thankless, sleepless nights of long ago. Luckily, there happened to be one of those perfectly matter-of-fact boats, which are regularly, winter or summer, at the disposal of romantic souls.

Whenever she had dreamed of imaginary affairs, they would all lead to the same situation: she dying in solitude, and the door opening at the last moment, and he—the man with the perpetual smile—coming to kneel at her bedside, telling her how she had always looked exquisite with her short curls, and imploring infinite and posthumous pardon for his inexcusable conduct on the ninth of September, 1877. And now it was she (would she get there in time?) who was going to ring at his gate in a quiet side-street, go in, cross his study, open the door of his room, kneel at the bedside of the dying man, who would be amazed by so much greatness of soul in such a frail envelope, and tell him how she had always lived for his disdainful smile, and pardon him for his venial conduct on the ninth of September, 1877! After that, she would cheerfully retrace her steps to Gaspard's villa, and tell the whole story, just as it had happened, to Gaspard.

This is what any novelist could have read between the lines of the ticket that Juliette had put into her imitation Russian leather purse.

A lunar chill descended to the deck. Forward, a chorus of emigrants was singing with an evident lack of enthusiasm.

Suddenly Juliette got up, pushed aside her deck-chair, wiped her pretty eyes, and came over to sit down next to Gaspard. "Excuse me."

"You poor thing!" With groping hands he fondly knotted his own scarf about her throat. "When we get there you can tell me everything. Tomorrow we'll take the first boat back. Or, if you prefer, we'll go on a little vacation."

She grasped his helping hand feverishly.

"Look. I have no secrets from you. But if you have any regard for me, let me go through with this. Try to understand! If you and I are in love, it's because we're the sort of people who are commonly called romantic, who without notice would go to incredible extremes to satisfy an unconventional whim, who derive their morality here." Twice she pointed, presumably at her heart.

"I see your point. You have nothing more to say?"

"No. You will know everything when I come back."

"When you come back?"

"In a month. Don't be stingy, Gaspard. Supposing you were given only a month to create a masterpiece."

"A masterpiece! That doesn't reassure me. I want to know if you'll be safe."

"Of course. It will do me no more harm than a novel I might be reading, one that you—who are so well-read—might give me to read."

"Am I as well-read as that?"

"As nature herself."

Gaspard could only indicate, in a gesture of boundless confidence, the cities on the other side.

"You expect to spend the night alone on the express? And am I expected to spend it in the next hotel?"

"Don't worry me any further! My errand is enough of a strain. I should have left yesterday."

"All right, I'll obliterate myself. I'll wait. Really, I must be in love with you!"

They definitely seemed to have exhausted everything, but they continued to sit there in the cold. Over his heart he held her still adolescent head, so full of its portentous secret, a secret as disconcerting as a masterpiece.

The emigrants were no longer singing. At rhythmic intervals the horizon was decorated with lights. The ship's bell began to tinkle in subdued gaiety, evidently as insensitive to arrivals as to departures.

There was the station. The baggage that had gone on ahead was collected and ready for the customs. Still an hour and a quarter to waste scrutinizing announcements of boats that you have no intention of taking, etc., etc. Gaspard installed his fugitive in a ladies' compartment, and sealed with an indelible kiss those pretty lips of a child suffering from too much fiction.

Six o'clock in the morning. A cheerful red brick station at the edge of a forest of firs. The express would take twenty minutes for coffee and then leave. Already its whistle pierced the fresh solitude of the morning.

Juliette, dropping into a chair before the lunch counter, the morning paper frozen to her knees, fixed a sombre eye directly upon the ground, where they bury people. Someone was watching her, and when she showed no sign of getting on the train again he got off, muttering: "She said she would go at least as far as Orleans, and she gets off here! An unheard-of station, with no connexions for—"

It was still that absurd, obtuse Gaspard! The evening before, having sealed Juliette's lips with a definitive kiss, he had jumped aboard the same train at the last moment, despite the pledge he had voiced with such infinite resignation, because it seemed to

him that the departing whistle of the express had a suspicious
sound. But in his determination to dispel his doubts and to remain
incognito to the bitter end, he had not yet made himself known
to Juliette.

"What is she waiting for here?" he wondered, detouring
around her to avoid the exit. The southern courtesy of an attend-
ant intercepted his manoeuvre, and he found himself forced out
into the open.

She glanced up at him, at this vague intruder, and turned away
haughtily. Then, as the train began to move, she rushed in front
of the locomotive. There was a second of agonizing hesitation,
and then she reappeared on the other side, escaping across the
flats.

Gaspard, who had dashed over to push her off the track,
had to wait until the train had passed. Two attendants held him
back while a second interminable train went by. Five minutes
later, when the track was clear, and he had crossed it in spite of
the efforts of an overconscientious bureaucracy, and was making
his way across the flats, Juliette was nowhere to be seen.

"This thicket of firs probably conceals her from me. She
must be over there—"

He ran holding his elbows to his sides, still gasping at the
suicidal apparition of a few moments before.

Plunging into the thicket, he could only guess, from a glimpse
of water between the freshly disturbed ferns, that there was a
ditch to jump over.

"How could she have jumped over it?" he asked.

Then he jumped. A cry went up when he fell heavily into
the second ditch, which was dry and covered by ferns, sprawling upon a soft, slight body, and quickly overcome by the twing-
ing vertigo of a complete sprain.

He realized, before he fainted of the pain, that it was Juliette
who lay beside him, turning her bloody and mangled face to
his, and finally fainting too.

The hours of a radiant morning, as unique in its own way
as the previous twilight, passed over their two bodies in that

deserted pit on the flats, interrupted only by the murmur of hornets in the fretwork of ferns.

At eight o'clock they were brought back to the town in a carriage belonging to some resin-gatherers, whose curiosity had been aroused at finding a couple in that condition.

Thus Juliette and Gaspard found themselves together in a hotel room.

It took Gaspard an indefinite amount of time to recover. And Juliette was disfigured forever, her cheek badly patched up and her lovely aquiline nose now turned up. The demure angel of yesterday has become a hard-featured hag, although her complexion is still that of a peach. Such is life!

Gaspard loves his Juliette as much as ever. He keeps up appearances so well that it looks like twice as much as ever.

But Juliette knows that fundamentally Gaspard lives only for beauty, that the pursuit of beauty is his only vocation. She knows that she is demoralizing and degrading him by the spectacle of her shattered mask.

She will not commit downright suicide, but she will kill herself in little doses. It will take several months. Every day she becomes more transparent, more mechanical, as she improves her leisure by knitting thick veils.

Ah, a veil for a shroud will soon go down in the ledger . . .

It will take several weeks.

And Gaspard will unhesitatingly survive her.

MEYER LIBEN:

THE CALLER

FORMERLY a sound sleeper, and sleeping regular hours, he began to wake up every morning at 4 a. m. He had tried the experiment, on a few evenings, of setting his alarm for 3:30, then waking and listening for a sound. But there was no sound between 3:30 and 4 a. m., and he was unable to understand what it was that woke him every morning at the same time.

He did not wake with a start, rather he found himself with his eyes open, speedily awake, looking out the window, and with a feeling of light-headedness which enabled him to see clearly the most indisputable and necessitous facts.

Mainly the death and disappearance of all most intimately connected with him, the inevitable death and disappearance seen clearly and with mounting sense of anxiety.

This early morning experience was the recurrence of a childhood experience of the same sort, where the sense of extinction involved the whole planet, and incidentally its inhabitants.

But now the planet remained, only certain individuals disappeared from it, off the face of it and under the ground of it. Moreover, where the child, visualizing total extinction, fell asleep shortly afterwards, now the young man, with a less apocalyptic, if more intimate view of disaster, was unable to fall asleep, but grew more awake, more and more light-headed, and more and more anxious.

Out of this state developed his relation to the telephone company. Wide awake and lonely, wide awake and anxious, he dialed for the correct time, and listened for minutes on end to the impersonal rhythms of that announcer.

Or dialed the Weather Exchange, and listened to the imper-sonal and unchanging pronouncements of that operator. She never varied her announcement, she never varied the tone of her voice, announcing alike storm, calm, and meteorological freaks.

He waited for a break in that voice, never with success, and took to questioning that voice, but never with success; merely the infuriating, evenly-timed announcements, and never a break in the voice, come question or demand, or the hoarse shrieking which he sometimes adopted.

If only because the time of the day changes, the voice of *that* announcer seemed more personal; if, from quarter minute to quarter minute, it could change its pronouncements, couldn't it also break out of that ring of time, and answer a simple query of his?

It could not, it never did, he was never able to detect a personal rise or fall in that voice, wheedle or scream as he would.

Apart from his loneliness and anxiety, he was overcome by a childhood feeling of the personal relation between the subscriber and the operator. "Hello Central Hello." At that time young men were supposed to make dates with the operators.

But here was this impersonal voice, the wax voice, which de-fied all interruption to continue on its even course, this voice which told over and over the time of the day and the state of the weather.

With a sudden inspiration he dialed the Operator!

That personal voice asked him once, twice, what he wanted, but he was too surprised to answer, and further, wanted nothing but to talk to her.

"Is this the operator? Well, there is something wrong with my phone. Could you, do you think someone could come up to repair it?"

He made up the most fantastic pretexts to converse with that personal voice, and listened with the greatest interest to her technical retorts.

His requests were not unreasonable—neither in conversation with the Operator, nor with Long Distance, nor with Information, nor with the Repair Department (to which, on the above occasion, the operator referred him).

With Information he could carry on long conversations about the numbers of non-existent people such as dead or removed friends, at existent-enough addresses.

"Well," he'd say, "perhaps it's spelled with an *e*," or "I'm not quite sure what the initial is," and he'd wait for her reply, and then added information, changed spelling in an effort to capture forever that personal voice.

But that could not be. "Sorry, we have no such listing." And the same result with Long Distance, who hung up after giving him the rates to Chicago, San Francisco, and Detroit.

All this was better than the impersonality of the Weather and the Time, but by no means satisfying, for he was never able to depart from the business at hand—the least attempt at a remark apart from the business at hand left him with a dead receiver after a curt "Sorry, sir," or a dead receiver with nothing said at all.

This was far from the "Hello Central Hello" of his childhood, and returning to bed, wide-awake, he could only gaze at the night breaking up, and as the grey light spread out, he was able to fall asleep, exhausted, for the few hours before his working day started.

Only to begin again the following a. m., or the one after (for occasionally he slept through like a log, slept past his waking hour) to face that clear recognition of intimate doom. This was unbearable, so he went to the phone.

He was through with the official calls, and dialed a stray number. A sleepy irritated voice answered. The caller listened and apologized, then listened to the abuse which followed the apology.

Or he dialed and an anxious, pain-stricken, wide-awake voice answered; the caller hung up quietly.

Or a business-like voice answered, giving the name of the firm, asking him to state his business. He almost became involved in a commercial transaction, though the product was unfamiliar to him.

One morning he dialed a sympathetic voice, a voice almost the echo of his own. Here he detected the same sleeplessness, the same anxiety.

"Yes, yes," said that voice, "I simply cannot sleep, I am filled with foreboding. I see very clearly the end of all my dear ones, there is nothing I can do to stop this. But when I begin working, I transfer this anxiety to my tasks, and am therefore known as the most conscientious worker in my shop.

"But this anxiety, spread over these trivial tasks, takes revenge on me by awakening me every morning and forcing me to face the anxiety. Confronted with this burden, I am lost, I can only stare out and await my release with the beginning of the working day."

And the voice proceeded to disclose in detail tribulations and methods of escape, and to delineate, in the sharpest manner, the mood of anxiety and yearning.

It was only later in the day, and with a sinking feeling, that our friend realized that he did not know the name, or more important, the number of that voice.

Such an oversight! He was planning to communicate nightly with that voice. He tried to remember the number, that was impossible. He scribbled a few numbers down, and that morning he dialed them, unsuccessfully.

One number was no number at all, and another number brought on a little girl's voice, which babbled incoherently and endlessly.

So he lost that sympathetic, echo voice, and was never able to find it again.

But he jumped from his bed a few nights later, tripped all over himself, and reached the ringing telephone on the fourth ring. It was about 3:30 in the morning, the only time he was ever awakened at such an hour by the telephone.

"Dr. Jones, you must come over immediately. Frank has had another attack."

He interrupted the party to tell her that this was the wrong number.

What a let-down, after being sure that this was the sympathetic voice, that the voice had somehow tracked him down, eager to continue the conversation which had started so auspiciously.

Then he began to call acquaintances and friends. This was a risky business. Generally he'd sit there and say nothing, listening to the familiar voice. In this way, distracted as he was, he learned a good deal. Some of his friends grew frantic as they asked for the identity of the caller and got no reply. Others cursed, a few hung up without a word. In general, they behaved no differently than they did in the normal social intercourse.

But on some occasions, simply to draw out conversation, he disguised his voice, gave the effect of having a wrong number, etc., and listened with some interest to the reaction on the other side. At least this was something to do, it kept him away from the bed and from the slowly approaching dawn; when the light began to spread, he felt most uneasy.

One call, however, almost cost him his anonymity—he so far forgot himself as to use a typical expression, and the very use of that expression had the effect of bringing his voice back to its natural tone. There was a short pause, then the friend said:

"Who is that?"

The caller gave a fictitious name.

"Who is that?" asked the friend again. "Is it . . . ?" and he mentioned the caller's name.

The latter was panic-stricken and cut off the call immediately afterwards. When the two met a few nights later, the friend looked at him with a curious expression, started to ask a question, but decided against it.

One evening, at about seven o'clock, our caller was leaving his little apartment. There was a knock on the door, and an elderly man entered.

"I am a representative of the telephone company," he said, and flashed a card with a mounted picture which could have been a representation of the Duke of York, so panic-stricken did our friend become at the sight of this stranger.

"I've tried to get you a couple of times," said the stranger, "but haven't had much luck."

"Is it the bill?" asked our friend, putting on a bold face and making for the door. "I'll take care of that tomorrow."

"I'll walk over to your office during lunch hour," he added.

"It's not the bill," said the stranger.

"Not the bill," repeated our friend, in a tone which indicated the utter impossibility of anyone coming to see him on business unconnected with the paying of an overdue telephone bill.

"It's not the bill," said the stranger, looking around the room (his eyes settled on the telephone). "It's something else."

"In that case," said our friend, foolishly, "I'll be going along."

"Look," said the stranger, "we've been getting some complaints about you, and I'm here to check on them. Are you in the habit of using your phone in the early hours of the morning?"

"What do you mean by the early hours of the morning?" asked our friend, in a question which began on a tone of shrewdness and ended up in a barely suppressed fit of hysterical laughter.

"By early hours of the morning," said the stranger, "I mean the hours between four and six."

"What a crazy thing," said our friend. "The only time I use the phone at those hours is when I'm planning a hike for Sunday morning and might phone Weather in order to find out if the weather conditions are favorable."

"So you're an outdoor man," said the stranger, and his eyes, roaming the room, seemed to be looking for some tangible evidence of outdoor life, such as a knapsack or a pair of snowshoes. Obviously disappointed in his search, he went on:

"Just the Weather, eh?"

"Oh, and the Time also," said our friend, "if my watch has stopped and I've got to make a train."

"The Time, the Weather," mused the stranger, and he began to shuffle through some papers. "Well, that part is all right, but how come you make telephone calls to all kinds of strangers at all kinds of hours?"

He said this without looking up from his papers, a kind of lightning thrust which was supposed to unbalance the suspect.

"What do you mean by all kinds of strangers?" asked our friend, too much off balance to be disturbed by such a thrust.

"By all kinds of strangers," replied the investigator, "I mean all kinds of people that you don't know and that you have no business calling at any time, much less five o'clock in the morning. By all kinds of strangers I mean the following."

And he proceeded to detail, with dates, and sometimes the subjects of conversation, a list of names.

As our friend listened to this long recital, he suddenly remembered that sympathetic voice, and waited for a clue that might enable him to track down that voice.

The investigator came to the end. There was a pause.

"Look," said our friend, somewhat excitedly, "there was one man, I mean he understood this whole business perfectly, he was not the kind of man to complain, but still, it's possible, it was a local call . . ."

His voice trailed off.

The investigator looked at him coldly.

"Do you think I'm going to act as a spy for you? You have admitted your guilt. You are definitely a nuisance."

(As he said this, he looked exactly the part of a minor field functionary in the Public Nuisance branch of the Psycho-Neurotic division of a giant utility corporation.)

Our friend seized the agent by the arm. "Do you sleep well at night? How do you do it?" he asked.

"From the time that I was eighteen years old," said the investigator, "I have gone to bed every night at eleven o'clock, and woke up every following morning at seven o'clock (that includes Saturdays, Sundays, and holidays) and furthermore, have slept like a log for those eight hours, and woke up refreshed.

"Dreams," he said, "rarely disturb me."

"You mean," inquired our friend, "that you never get up about four in the morning and feel anxious, even a little responsible?"

"Look," said the agent, "my responsibility ends when my day's work is done (*you* must own your own business) and I don't have much time to be anxious, and if I were anxious, I would never get up at four in the morning to prove it.

"My advice to you," went on the agent, "is to go home, forget about it and then go about your business without losing any sleep over it."

He chuckled at his joke.

"How?" asked our friend, like a fool.

The agent looked irritated.

"I am going to help you gain mastery over yourself," he said.

He moved swiftly to the door and opened it. A lanky repair man entered. He gave the agent a knowing look; the later nodded.

Without a word, the repair man went over to the telephone, started to unscrew the box from the wall.

"Here," cried our friend, "you can't do that."

He rushed to a spot between the repair man and the box. The repair man shrugged his shoulders and waited.

"Can't I?" inquired the agent, and he flourished a document, waved it about.

"This," he said, "is an order, which gives me the right to remove this telephone."

He did not specify whether it was a court order, or a company order, but our friend stepped back at this sudden show of authority. The repair man stepped forward to continue his work.

"Don't take it so hard," reasoned the victorious old agent. "This is the best thing that could have happened to you. Now you'll get up at your crazy hour and go back to sleep again, for lack of anything to do."

"Suppose," asked our friend, "I decide to go out to the railroad terminal around the corner and call from there?"

"You won't do that," said the company man, "you won't have the energy. Furthermore, the activity will lose all its charm in a public place.

"But should you try it," he went on severely, "you won't get off so easy. We'll be watching you."

"They'll hound you," said the repair man, casually, going on with his work.

Our friend turned to this possible ally in some excitement.

"You must find this type of work very distasteful," he said.

"I'm a technician," replied the repair man. "I disassociate myself from the intent of the job."

This answer was a disappointment to our friend, who nevertheless persisted.

"You are trying to be neutral," he said, "but you don't always succeed. Nor would it be any credit to you if you achieved such a disassociation from your job."

"I keep my ideas to myself," said the repair man, but the tempo of his work increased.

"This is getting very tiresome," said the veteran agent. "It's a peculiar thing," he went on, turning to our friend, "but we get into such a discussion every time we're out on a case of this sort."

Our friend felt humiliated at being included in a *category*.

The telephone rang. The repair man pulled the box from the wall, the ring was cut off.

"What's the idea?" cried our friend. "You cut off a call."

"You are no longer a subscriber," said the agent, rather grimly. "You are no longer entitled to incoming calls."

He shook hands with the ex-subscriber, and then, in a stray gesture, with the repair man. The latter scooped up the telephone directories.

Without a telephone, without telephone directories, without the agent and the repair man, our friend was really cut off.

He walked to the window and vacantly watched the agent and repair man get into a car and drive away.

"Tomorrow I'll move," he decided. "I'll change my name and subscribe again."

AGNES W. MACDONALD:

REUNION IN AMERICA

MR. STERLING was on his way to the St. Paul Union Station.
He looked out of the streetcar window and realized for
some dozenth time that day that it was August again—the sixth
August—since he had gone to Euston Station in London and met
—No, he didn't meet her; he missed her, in spite of his faultless
preparation. And it wasn't this Miss Dalton that he had gone to
meet. Miss Dalton was not the kind of woman you missed.
Indeed was she one you could escape? Anyway, he didn't want
to miss her today because whereas six years ago Miss Jeannie
Knowles had led him to her, today—he hoped—Miss Dalton was
to lead him to Jeannie Knowles. Just to meet and then—he could
perceive no opposition, except that his furlough was not so long
as his holiday had been. He didn't anticipate beginning at the
beginning again; he would see her in her own home and not as
a guest in Miss Dalton's flat; and—he was wearing the uniform
of His Majesty's officer, a new uniform too. He smoothed its
lapels and sat back. Annie, his sister, whom he had come to
visit, had called it "graund" reverting to her old-country combination of pride and accent.

He had always been fond of Annie, and he really had meant
during all those years of engineering in London to come over
here to Minnesota at least once to visit her. Since the war had
brought him to Canada, she had been urging him to come on
furlough. Last month she had foresightedly written to engage
him for an American Thanksgiving. He had replied with his usual
caution that if he could get away that soon he would come.
And then—suddenly—two weeks ago, after that undreamed-of

summons from Miss Dalton, he had sent a letter—sent it express —saying he had arranged a week and she had replied in their native idiom, "Haste ye on."

Now he was here. And if he did see Jeannie the way he hoped, he would forget the past inconveniences of Miss Dalton's pursuit. Was she really flexible and kind after all? Perhaps he was through her being allotted another trial with Jeannie.

At the moment there was just one drawback: he needed sleep. His furlough had followed a month of unremitting duty; his journey from Winnipeg had been sleepless and Annie and her husband had kept him talking until the small hours of the morning. He himself would have let all the talk wait for a day or two; as soon as he had learned the approximate route to Mrs. Knowles's home and heard that Annie continued to be friendly with the family (though she never saw them now) he was ready to get to bed.

This morning Annie had remembered seeing in the paper that both Mr. and Mrs. Knowles had gone to some camp in Texas to see their sons but she didn't know about the two girls—oh, of course they must be at home if they were having this woman from London.

"So they stayed in her flat in London?" she had asked suddenly in the midst of her remembering. "It's a braw feast o' memories you'll be enjoyin'. And is it the London person or one of Mrs. Knowles's daughters you'd be interested in seein' most? Jeannie was a fair lass six years ago—and she will be yet. I mind hearing something about her not so long ago—I just can't remember what."

He was sure Annie would have remembered a wedding. Mrs. Knowles had befriended her years ago when she came a bride from Edinburgh and it was to repay some of that kindness that she had written to him to do something nice for the two daughters when they visited London . . .

He would never forget that fortnight. The weather . . . this fine, soft afternoon was so like it. It was just around this time of day too that he had set out for Euston Station to meet the Flying Scotsman. This train that Miss Dalton was coming on today was due—? He took out her letter, flattening it out into one stiff sheet. Her writing was too individual, but he could always read it more easily and without perplexity when she wrote in a hurry on this thick paper. That tissuey stuff he connected with her reminiscent-prophetic mood at its most dangerous stage. He could not always follow her.

It seemed that simultaneously with writing this present letter, she had been reading a message from someone in the Knowles family telling her *of course* to come on down to St. Paul (she was in Toronto for the duration) and They trusted They could recognize her after the six-year intermission. His eyesight had become promptly inadequate at that sentence. He couldn't figure out whether that was *Mary* or *They* that she had scrawled. She used capitals so unreasonably. He couldn't possibly make it into Jeannie, and after due consideration he could not really trust it to be *Mary*, for he believed that Miss Dalton, in spite of her avowed conversion to utter democracy, would still use the Victorian "Miss" Mary . . . She was tired of the digs where she had been installed by the English family whose children she had been guiding for ten months without respite. They were all off on a fortnight's holiday and she had decided to "accept" the invitation of long standing issued by the Scottish aunt of "those two American girls I had in London That summer—when You and I first Met. Their dear aunt in Scotland once told me that I ought to experience their hospitality some day. So I applied for a Sample, and my Letter has been so very graciously answered . . ." She did not say who answered it . . . he thought of another handwriting . . . "I am to reach St. Paul—" Yes, he had the time right, 5:19. It was only three o'clock now. Of course he believed in getting to places early, but this was prodigal. He would spend the interim watching for one of the—well, watching.

At the Union Station he found a bank-holiday swarm, against an ironic background of wartime. Undiverted, he noted the key spots of his terrain and then found a point of vantage for observation. At 4:15 he was "prepared." An hour on a station bench was but a wink of time against the continuous cinema of wartime life. The station congregations chasséd. The warm air needed refreshing . . . You could get a bit dizzy amid these sway-operatic crowds. Who were leaving? Who arriving? Another troop train came in . . . A spontaneous young woman, synonymous in slacks and flour-sack headcloth with any number of others clotting the exits and entrances, had got off her job to meet *her* guy she was telling someone yards away, and she had missed him she was betting all she had. She looked frantically from exit to concourse, again and again. Then, spying some uniformed figure like scores of other, she yelled toward her confidante off in the concourse, "Oh, here he comes back, Rita. He's here! There! (pointing with staccato stabs toward the exit) Good-bye." She met her guy as unreservedly as she had dramatized her dilemma. Mr. Sterling recrossed his legs tolerantly and looked away from all motion and waited, remembering.

II

In August, 1938, in London, Mr. Sterling was a mild-appearing, deliberative man in the middle thirties. It seemed as if he never felt anything so very keenly and as if it would take a revolution to alter his routine. His manner was such that whether he was mingling in a crowd or going by himself he never seemed hurried or uncertain. If taken unawares he no doubt could think on the spot, but in what one might by a stretch of meaning have called his domestic and social life, he never needed to jump to a conclusion or act impulsively. He simply went into everything directly but not hastily. One couldn't help thinking that habitual preparedness like his must preclude from life the spice of excitement.

His clothes were as inconspicuous and as permanent in style as his manner. Bowler hat, dark brown suit with white shirt, black or brown shoes with squarish toes, the kind that have a big smooth, hard-looking bump over the great toe. He did vary his ties occasionally because he didn't buy all of them himself. Sometimes he got a bright one for Christmas from "one of the boys"—who were the three other men who also lived in digs at

Mrs. Matters' place; and sometimes Mrs. Matters gave him a tie.

He was short, for a man, and sturdy. His hands were like that too, with the fingers inclined to be stubby. But they could manipulate dexterously delicate bits of things like tiny parts of machinery or pieces of a jig-saw puzzle or the fastener of Mrs. Matters' pearl necklace.

His hair was short too. He kept it that way because he was used to it and without excessive attention it became freakish at a normal manly length. It was too curly, he thought. He was right about the curliness; it fuzzed comically just after he'd had a haircut. He didn't think much about his appearance any more —about its possibilities, that is. He just followed his pattern of ten years or so, and no one tried to revise him.

Now, as he hastened out of Euston, he looked as if he had been taken unawares. He glanced over the crowds still waiting to fill up the approaching train of big London buses that were swinging around near the exits, and without deliberating he hailed a cab.

There had been such an unexpected exodus from the Flying Scotsman that he had developed a jumpiness over the possibility of missing the young lady he had come to meet. He had come, calmly prepared to spot her the minute she passed through the platform gates where he stood watching closely for a young woman obviously alone and American; and when no more travelers came by he peered re-searchingly after the crowds spreading fan-like in the street beyond the station exits.

He was certain about the train, for he had made a special note of it when he received her letter. He felt his left breast distrustfully for a second; yes, he had brought the letters with him. He had thought of how well the time of her arrival and the period of her stay in London fitted in with his own program. He had the habit of planning his weeks more than his days because he was an engineer who took on contracts running a week or a fortnight or six weeks or maybe months, and between jobs he could take a holiday when and if he wanted to. He had remembered that he was to finish with Judson and Rye on Wednesday and she had said Friday, August 19, for two

weeks. Being so methodical and devoted to detailed preparedness, he had even made a note of her telephone number on her
envelope. He always did this kind of thing. It was the cause
really of his usual unhurried, mild manner.

Puzzled as he was by the young woman's failure to appear,
without realizing that he had not considered at all what kind of
person might answer his call, he had telephoned to her address
at once and asked whether Miss Jeannie Knowles was there. She
was there—answering the phone herself—apparently all ready to
speak to him.

"Is this Mr. Sterling?" she had asked before he had recovered
enough to say hello or how do you do. Her voice made him
feel light and relieved and quite welcome. She had a lovely voice.

"I was hoping you would call soon. Can you come out, Mr.
Sterling? I came two days early—quite unexpectedly. I hope
you'll come out. Come now."

He was not used to talking with young women who were
pretty, as she was sure to be with a voice like that. It put the
logical questions to ask out of his mind.

Of course he would go out though. He had planned to take
her out there in a cab. But oh she had never expected him to
meet her train. She would explain why she had come early.

"Do come out now, Mr. Sterling," she repeated.

So he had decided on the cab for himself.

About eighteen minutes to St. Mark's Road, he figured quickly.
And No. 1 Pelfield Gardens would be one street beyond that.
He possessed a vast fund of detailed knowledge of urban and
suburban London. He had not just heard of places; he knew
how to get to them.

In the cab he could check things in those letters; you never
knew how a bus would incommode you.

"1 Pelfield Gardens," he told the cab driver. "It's out Kensing-
ton—one street beyond St. Mark's Road."

"Righto, sir," said the man.

Mr. Sterling sorted out from papers in his vest pocket two
letters. He opened the one from Annie, his sister in America,

who had written purposely to tell him about Mrs. Knowles's
daughters. "It's their first time across and they are going to London of course. They are going to visit an aunt in Glasgow . . .
Be nice to them and show them London . . . Their mother was
very kind to me when I came over here . . . I have told them
you know London like a book and I gave them your address
. . . Show them some of the places in old books. They like
books."

"They like books"—that was not just specific but somehow
that had made him think Miss Knowles would be quiet and genteel like the people Annie would be sure to make friends with.

He scanned the rest of the letter again. No; he was sure of it.
It didn't say how old the daughters were or anything like that.
Annie never wrote more than she thought essential. This was a
long letter for her. But he wished she'd written more. She had
a very affectionate nature, and he had always been fond of her.
She was always going to write oftener but didn't get around to
it. She had not written for months before; so she must like the
girls' mother a lot.

Well, he had been surprised when he got the letter from Miss
Knowles because you never could tell whether people would
write to the addresses other people gave them or not. He thought
maybe she was lonesome, but her handwriting didn't look like
a lonesome person's.

He read her letter over now. It was on folded paper and written on the pages as they came. She didn't turn the paper in
different directions the way Annie did. It was brief. "Dear Mr.
Sterling." Inexplicably he wished for a passing moment that he
could be reading "Darling Archie" in quick, bright handwriting
like that.

She was coming down to London on the Scotsman on Friday,
August 19, alone, for a fortnight. The Glasgow weather had
been dourly bad, and now her sister had the mumps. So her aunt
was sending her to a one-time traveling acquaintance of hers,
Miss Cassie Dalton, 1 Pelfield Gardens. She would be glad to see
him if he could call. His sister had given her his address. "She says
you know all of London." He had concluded from this part of

her note that she and her friends would appreciate a guide. He had thought too that maybe her aunt got her to write; her letter didn't read the way her voice sounded.

He returned it to his pocket gently and leaned back in the cab. He thought about the places he could take her—and her aunt, or rather this other woman. The usual tours planned for tourists might be best to begin with—Trafalgar Square, The Tower, The British Museum, Buckingham Palace. And maybe she would know some places she'd like to have him find for her. Then he thought of what he'd like to do. He was so fond of music; he even played an accordion. Of course he wouldn't play his accordion for her, but he would like to take her to some of the musical plays. There was one with pretty music and lots of dancing, at the Alhambra. He wondered whether she liked music and dancing. He used to like dancing, but he had not danced for about a decade—not since he went into digs. He hadn't had a girl in all that time. Reggie was the only one of the quartet at Mrs. Matters' who had a girl. He went out with her often and was going to marry her before long. Mr. Sterling would miss Reggie, who used to ask Archie to go with him and his girl and said they would get him a girl, but he never went. He was always too busy with some job. They all enjoyed Reggie's romancing, but Mrs. Matters never encouraged any of her other three. She would say they were past that now. They didn't like her to say it at first, but they got used to it after a few years of repetition.

Mr. Sterling was nice to Mrs. Matters, took her in things—like what he might have taken to his girl; but with other women—especially the light, easy, pretty ones—he felt shy. He didn't especially care for Mrs. Matters' type; it was too much the managing kind—to have for a girl, that is—but it was the only kind he met any more. None of them had voices like Miss Knowles.

No. 1 Pelfield Gardens looked a nice, three-story flat building on the corner. Reading the names of the residents posted beside the front door, Mr. Sterling learned that Miss Cassandra Dalton occupied the top flat. So he opened the door and went into a paneled hall painted gray, that had several closed doors in it and a steep stairway going up one side. It was the kind of hall that nobody did anything to make attractive because all tenants used it. When he had gone up the first flight of stairs he could not see the front door any more.

The next flight curved slightly and had soft rubber corduroy pads on them. As he was rounding the curve, he heard one of those noticeably cultured voices calling, "Come right on, up here. I won't come down. I've been off my feet all day. It's just awe-ful! To be surprised this way when one is without a dependable servant. I got one today at last. But Miss Jean did not mention you until after you had phoned. Oh, dear."

The voice was, of course, Miss Dalton's.

She was a little, dark, squatty woman with bright eyes, and she had on a hardy-looking plain blue dress that resembled a coat and was badly in need of pressing. She limped conspicuously as she preceded him into the flat, toward a divan where she had evidently been ensconced. While she returned to it and frankly prepared to rearrange herself with one flannel-bound leg raised on it, he looked about for Miss Knowles and saw close to the divan a small table on which were a kind of miniature chest —containing, he could just discern by the economical light, dingy jewelry—several bracelets, rings, necklaces, and earrings—and several letters that were very obviously not of current age. Was this woman re-reading her past correspondence? And where was she keeping Miss Knowles? He only noticed that it was some kind of big shawl Miss Dalton was spreading over her thickish legs, but she evidently took his preoccupation for unspoken question, for she explained in an answering tone that it was a real India shawl, that she had grown up in India where her father was an army officer and she had never really got used to being without servants galore. When Mr. Sterling stated that he had spent a year or two in India and knew the place, she seemed to imbibe a little vitality with his statements, but he didn't hear her when she begged to know whether he had ever had any contact with

Sir Stanley Addison there, because a distant noise drew his immediate attention.

"Oh, that's dear Miss Jean," said Miss Dalton. "I sent her for
my other glasses and she is probably looking in the wrong places.
The servant problem is awe-ful. I promised to read her letters
I've had again and again from foreign girls I've taken into my
flat or guided over Europe. So now you'll hear them too. Oh,
you did find them, Miss Jean, while I have been looking after
Mr. Sterling. It was him like you thought."

Mr. Sterling appeared unusually mild as he watched and listened to Miss Jean Knowles, but inside he was deeply disquieted.
In this dim room she was like a light. Everything about her was
light and free and easy. Her hair matched her voice—soft and
airy and golden. She smiled often; whenever she talked her face
was animated. She talked to him freely and informally. He supposed it was the American way. You might think a girl acting
like this showed a partiality for you. Mr. Sterling would like
to have known how much there was to that idea. His first surprise when he heard her voice over the telephone was turning
into wonder.

But he kept his feet on the ground. And it was Miss Dalton
who helped him to, though she could never have guessed it.
To him, at first, she seemed only a sterner version of Mrs. Matters. He found it quite easy to talk with her, though he did not
especially want to.

"Tell me," she croaked from the divan, "did you go to the
station *before* phoning?"

She got the preliminaries of this meeting straightened out step
by step. Through numerous "tell me's" she learned also the essentials of Mr. Sterling's background, the one of particular interest
being that he had lived for a few years in India.

The mention again of that land reminded her of the harassing
servant problem. She had had a week's supply of cutlery and
dishes piled in her kitchen when Miss Jean arrived because, trying
to wipe around her own place she had slipped on those awe-ful
stairs without a railing and twisted her ankle. Mr. Sterling probably noticed those new rubber pads. She had phoned the land-

lord and insisted on some kind of protection. And, deprived of a servant and the use of her ankle, she was doomed to uncleanliness until Miss Jean came: she had only a few coppers and anyway she could not climb up to drop coins into the gas meter—and so—

"Tell me," said Miss Dalton suddenly as if deciding to let someone else have a turn, "do you have this problem in America?"

Mr. Sterling had been arranging a new confidence within himself as he listened to Miss Dalton and watched Miss Jean.

"I don't think the problem's quite this bad," said Jean. Only her blue eyes laughed; and they laughed naturally.

Miss Dalton was slightly disconcerted. She worked her ankle under the India shawl as if it were a puppet. Then she reached out to the tipsy pile of opened letters on the little table, saying, "I must read you some of these—and show you some. I've had scores of them."

She read flattering passages from letters composed by foreign girls whom she had harbored and instructed in London.

"If you know French, my dear, but—" and she folded that one up.

"Here's one in Italian." This one she handed over.

Jean smiled and glanced at the writing. "It's Greek to me."

One a dear, dear German girl had written in English. Miss Dalton passed her that one.

"I've studied German, a little," said Jean. But evidently a little was not enough; the bi-lingual style seemed to bewilder her, for she returned the pages with an enigmatic glow toward Mr. Sterling.

"Well, everyone expresses some particular gratitude, you see," concluded Miss Dalton gathering untidily the pile of soiled letters. She replaced the collection of dingy jewelry in the chest and pressed the letters in on top and clamped down the lid. Carefully, she lowered one leg down from the divan, mourning, "This leg has tied me down awe-fully—though we were beginning to talk about starting out tomorrow in a taxi—Remember, my dear?"

"That was on Wednesday—remember?" Miss Knowles answered. But she did not permit Miss Dalton long to remember back that far; she took advantage of this lag in the quizzing. "You won't need to hurry your ankle—if Mr. Sterling," she smiled at him questioningly. "Are you quite free to take a holiday, Mr. Sterling? You see I came early with some friends of my aunt's and I've been waiting—"

"Yours for a fortnight," said Mr. Sterling, promptly. It didn't sound like himself answering.

"No more marking time for mumps and sprained ankles then."

"But, my dear young lady, I said we would star—"

"Oh, yes; I know," Jean assured her. "I just mean I can't be sure that something isn't going to happen to Mr. Sterling now —his glands or his business or—something."

Mr. Sterling could speak positively now. And he did. He was a man who made plans and persisted in them. So it was arranged that he should call for Miss Knowles in the morning and take her to begin London.

He went away feeling suddenly developed, delightfully astonished. He never would have imagined meeting a young lady like this one through his sister Annie. For a fortnight he would have a new interest in life, away from contracts. He pictured himself actually sharing the company of a feminine lady. He would show her London. He thought it was all right that Miss Dalton had turned her ankle.

The next ten days were different from any in the last ten years of Mr. Sterling's life. Reggie and the other boys pulled his leg a lot while Mrs. Matters pouted with an awkward coyness about being neglected. None of them knew just what Mr. Sterling was doing except that he was showing an American lady around London and that he was wearing a new flat type of sport shoe and the red tie Reggie had given him one Christmas—and was forgetting to have his regular haircut.

"I saw you in Portman Square about 5:30," said Henry. "With a proper dark-haired woman on your arm. She likes you I don't doubt. But she's no American lady."

"No; she's not the one."

"The one, is it?" chipped in big Joe.

Mrs. Matters was silent. Her attitude then was somewhere between sulkiness and rebellion.

The truth was that after three days of nursing her ankle on the divan and waiting for the return of Miss Jean and Mr. Sterling, Miss Dalton had decided to join them as the legitimate duenna of the girl and as the contemporary of the engineer. She required no invitation. She simply got ready and announced that she was going too. Of course she slowed up the tempo of the outings. Miss Jean stepped lightly and lively, and Mr. Sterling was learning her pace. They hopped on and off buses, swung along parkway or embankment, climbed mountains of stairs nimbly, poked or flew through curio shops, caught the subway or excursion train at a gasp. Miss Dalton put the brakes on. First, she required a cab for every appreciable distance—and Mr. Sterling's help getting in and out. Then, she relaxed somewhat on the cabs but leaned more on Mr. Sterling's arm. Jean got to going on ahead.

"You're like a child, my dear. Go on, if you like. We'll make up on you. I like to see you stepping on ahead."

Mr. Sterling didn't like it so well—indeed he didn't like it at all, but he was a polite man and sympathetic, and he didn't see how he could help letting Miss Jean go on. He thought about her all the time now, even when he appeared attentive to Miss Dalton by his side.

"Tell me, didn't you really ever know Sir Stanley Addison in India?" that solid lady asked as they moved along slowly through Madame Tussaud's Waxworks, one of which resembled Sir Addison. She referred often to the fact that she and Mr. Sterling both had lived in India. She worked it into a genuine tie between them. He was trying at that moment to keep an eye on Miss Jean. Was she talking with a stranger? Or was that —yes, it was just that figure. He was out of his wonder by now and in a state of disquiet again.

It was not just Miss Dalton's weight of body and speech that distressed him. It was more Miss Jean's bland acceptance of this interruption in their idyllic companionship. She had got him in-

terested in her—and in himself: he looked at himself in the mirror now when he got home at night. She had asked if his hair
was naturally curly and chided him for not giving it a chance
to wave. She moved her fingers quickly and lightly over his
head to show him. "Like that," she said, making waves. She took
hold of his hand when they crossed a crowded street; he liked
that. It made him feel young too. The feeling of her soft fingers
made him realize how firm his own hands were. Now he was
anchored to Miss Dalton.

Jean would fall back to them occasionally with laughing eyes
and a light quip and she would now and then ask Miss Dalton
sweetly whether she wanted a cup of tea and she would sometimes ask him a question about location. But she never tried to
say anything trivial expressly to him because he had acquired a
special understanding and intimacy. He was really disappointed.

When they would get back to the flat for dinner and the
newest maid usually was not ready, Miss Dalton sent Mr. Sterling
down to buy ices from the man who carried them in the street
below. Once he came back with a bunch of zinnias he bought
from the flower cart on the corner because he thought they
were so bright and gay and he hoped Miss Jean would open the
door as she had the other times he had gone down for the ices.
But she wasn't at the door or in the parlor even. Only Miss
Dalton reaching out possessively for ices and flowers and crying,
"Oh, you thoughtful man!"

They sat down to eat and Miss Dalton gushed over the zinnias
again. "Aren't they awe-fully sweet," she declared.

"They make the brightest spots in Indian summer at home,"
said Jean serenely. "We call them old maids."

Mr. Sterling wondered whether she meant anything by that.

Miss Dalton went on dividing the cold salmon.

At first Miss Dalton had told dear Miss Jean to skip down like
a fairy for the ices, and the next time Mr. Sterling insisted on
following her, and then they had gone together and taken their
time and he had helped her up the stairs and she had laughed
saying he must think she was Miss Dalton, which made him feel
embarrassed, and Miss Dalton accused them of taking too long

and forgetting about her waiting to cut into the meat pie or something else, and so she had something different for Miss Jean to do while kind Mr. Sterling hurried down to get the ices and then she began to have pudding instead of ices.

Mr. Sterling was happy and yet he was growing less happy instead of more so. The fortnight was flying past and Miss Mary in Glasgow was recovering from the mumps and was coming soon and he wasn't ever seeing Miss Jean alone now—and she didn't appear to mind. Once she even excused herself from sitting with him and Miss Dalton, who was begging him to tell her about the building of the Crystal Palace, while she wrote a note to somebody. When she came back into the dim room and sat on a hassock quite near him, he felt relieved and pleased and knew that his own voice lilted noticeably to himself. She just listened till he stopped and then she said, "I'd like to have a glass house."

And Miss Dalton said, "You Americans want such funny things, my dear. Now we'd never think of anything so frivolous over here, would we?" She was bound to strengthen the bond of taste between them.

This time he only answered, "I'm afraid I couldn't have thought of it or I would have."

The next morning when he came he had a little china house that you took the roof off to fill it with marmalade or jam.

"It's not glass—but we may pick up a glass one," he said.

Jean had it in her hands admiring it and saying it was a charming little thing and many thanks if it was meant for her.

It was, he said, just for her.

Miss Dalton was not quite ready that morning. She was still winding a flannel bandage around her ankle in case it was too soon to trust to her own strength.

And in another day or two Mr. Sterling appeared to be losing more of his natural mildness and sympathy and to be thinking a great deal more than one should on a fortnight's holiday. Besides, he seemed a little impatient without reason: Miss Jean was as fair and as bright and as free and easy as ever; Miss Dalton managed their itineraries adroitly and was improving in looks and temper; only he seemed inharmonious.

One night he wrote for tickets to "Waltzes from Vienna" at the Alhambra—the musical show he had told Miss Jean about on their first excursion before the adoption of Miss Dalton. She had said she'd love it—going to see the Waltzes. And he had said they'd go. Now he did a bold and unsympathetic thing and he did it without letting himself deliberate and turn unselfish. He wrote for two tickets. And he resolved to act—on the spur of the moment when they came. The tickets were for Friday of the second week.

That morning Mrs. Matters had trouble with her electric washer and he tried to fix it for her in a hurry, which was not according to his custom; he found he couldn't hurry, that it would require an hour or two for repair; he phoned the flat to explain his delay.

The maid had said, "I think it's the gentleman."

And so Miss Dalton had claimed the phone and sympathized and advised and insisted that he could come just as well after lunch, which he did.

And when he arrived he found that Miss Jean had received a message from her sister saying that she was traveling suddenly and alone because their aunt's maid now had the mumps and their aunt was going to stay by her through the first of them.

"It's just a chapter of accidents or a comedy of errors," said Miss Dalton smoothing her ankle and twisting it testily. "I sent Miss Jean in on the bus. We depend so much on you, Mr. Sterling, and we don't want to impose on you to that extent. I told Miss Jean we don't do that with our men over here." She smiled the remnant of a coaxing smile. He tried to imagine their conference, but his vision of Miss Jean was elusive.

He spent the afternoon in the dimmer than usual parlor of the flat—it had become cavernous. Miss Dalton served tea when he came and was looking her own very best and brightest and she really found a great deal for them to talk about, but Mr. Sterling could keep up only his naturally mild appearance of interest until she began to talk about Americans and their curious ways and then this particular young lady American that they both took around with them. She divined that Miss Jean had a sweetheart. She got mail every day—from somewhere. She always ran to take in the mail.

"From her aunt about the mumps," said Mr. Sterling.

"Something more than that, I foresee," spouted his hostess. "She's always so light and happy—but so silent about why."

"Maybe that's her nature. She was that way the first night I came." He did not want any sweetheart—but of course Miss Dalton might be trying to tell him something if he was not too obtuse to get it.

By dinner time he felt miserable because of the conversation and because Miss Jean and her sister did not come—and because he had those tickets and there were only two.

"They should be here," he said.

"Maybe they are looking around; Miss Jean knows the business sections now." Miss Dalton looked over the dinner table. "Just go down for ices for us two," she said, and Mr. Sterling started down the rubber-padded stairs slowly.

Someone was down below on the first flight. He felt his heart leap up oddly, and his face he knew was betraying his revival. He waited a moment.

"Set the bag down a minute, Jean. There. Is Archie here now?"

"I don't call him Archie, I tell you. You—! He's not goodlooking, Mary, but he could be, and he was awe-fully swell to me when I was ready to explode here, and he's kind and sympathetic to Miss Dalton—and I think—well, he's sort of—nice and thinks of things—not kiddish. But I think maybe now he likes *her*. She gets so excited about him, and I can't do that. I feel sorry for her anyway—the witch. Besides, he never makes a point of seeing me alone."

"And you like him. You think he's sort of—"

"Well—oh, I don't know. Come on up anyway."

"There's someone coming down. I th—"

"Miss Dalton probably sending the maid down for an ice."

Dinner proceeded quite brightly, with Miss Dalton often apologizing to Mary for their easy ways. It was later than usual when she said, "Now tonight we just have ices. We occasionally have ices in this warm weather, Miss Mary. But Mr. Sterling will need to go after two more. He got his and mine up just before you came."

"Oh, but I didn't get them up. Jean and her sister were here before I could get started, you know." He defended his neglect, looking directly at Miss Dalton.

Miss Mary said that was right. He thought her advent into this situation very timely.

"I'll go down right now," he said. "Vanilla, two chocolates, and—Mary?" (She had called him Archie on the stairs.) "Chocolate too, Oke." Such boldness made him feel chipper.

"It may be too late. The man is usually passed by this time," complained Miss Dalton.

But Mr. Sterling went on down and wandered light-headedly about. When he did return, he had three bunches of flowers.

"Did you get them?" called Miss Dalton from the parlor.

"What?—oh, no; I didn't. He was gone, but I brought these instead." He held out the flowers: zinnias he handed to Miss Dalton who exclaimed with delight, "Again!" Pansies he extended to Mary, whose eyes spoke. Little roses to Jean, who just became more charming.

"Now, we'll need three vases," said Miss Dalton. "Let me see." She started haltingly out to the kitchen and in a minute they heard her calling, "Mr. Sterling, will you come please? It's just too high. Mr. Sterling! Will you—?"

"I guess she wants something lifted down," said Mary. "I'll help her. You just go right ahead, Mr. Sterling."

Thus directed, he went right over to Jean and said, "I have our tickets for the show, Jean, for the Waltzes. Two tickets—just for you and me."

And he sat on the arm of the stuffy old chair to show them to her and she looked at the tickets and smiled up at him with the added allure of surprise, which made him exceedingly bold so that he put his arm around her shoulders and kissed her tenderly. And then he thought she seemed to be the shy one. They whispered understandingly and were so quiet that they could easily hear Miss Dalton coming with the vases. Then he moved off the arm of Jean's chair and Mary came back ahead of Miss

Dalton, chanting, "The vas-es are com-ing now." She communicated a new optimism to him.

But Miss Dalton, counting over her zinnias, seemed to sense something more than the fragrance of flowers in the air.

And that afternoon was the peak of the brief romance. (Miss Dalton had insisted on two more tickets—so that Miss Mary could go too.) Even with Mary's silent support he had not contrived more than minutes with Jean unsupervised before Judson and Rye demanded his full-time services down in Dorking; and Miss Dalton, as erstwhile manager, engineered all correspondence with him . . . until there had come that multiple-folding picture postcard sent down to him by Jean from some highland village. The printed title called it Souvenir of Bonnie Scotland and the outside card showed a blooming lass wearing a typical plaid shawl inviting him to "look under my plaidie." But then when he lifted the shawl, only a lot of diminutive pictures came trailing down before him. Written on the last card of the accordion-like series, was a final word of thanks for his part in that happy fortnight, an invitation—if he ever did get to America—and the announcement of both their ship and their sailing-date. Mrs. Matters had not considered the souvenir worth sending on to him; she knew he'd seen plenty of Scotland. So it waited until his return to London and by then Jean and Mary had left for America. By then, too, in his busy engineer's routine, Jean had become his favorite though disturbing phantom. It was between jobs that he knew he had never fully forgiven Mrs. Matters for her error in judgment. And because of his mistrust he had not been sorry when the war forced him to move from her house . . .

Having allowed him not quite enough time to forget her, Miss Dalton wrote a letter which from a polite man required an answer. A series of such enforced letters, then meetings, might have stirred a more imaginative man to suspect some eventual fate in their contacts. But Mr. Sterling never thought of himself but as a free man.

III

Startled and chagrined, Mr. Sterling stood up suddenly feeling that someone should have called him. 5:26! You couldn't tell when the train you were waiting for came. There was always something coming in. Suppose he had lost a chance to see Jean alone or with Mary, if they had come to meet Miss Dalton. He stopped after a few steps toward the concourse to examine all he could of the crowds coming through. A Euston exodus was a trickle compared to this. There were four double doors here where an unbroken passage would have been better. He concentrated on a quickly summoned vision of Miss Dalton, keeping his eyes on the row of doors. Nobody coming by now seemed to be alone. Maybe she had gone through, but he couldn't be sure yet . . . Everybody began to look alike.

Feeling disquietingly inadequate and in need of contact with something more stable than wartime trains and identical-looking travelers, he went into a phone booth and called Annie.

As soon as she heard his voice, she cut in, "You're at the Knowles's now then; are you?"

"Where? I'm still—"

"Oh—Jeannie phoned here for you. There was a last-minute change."

Could it be that Jeannie had come instead of Miss Dalton? Ach, how daft he could turn in one second!

"Are you there, Archie? Archie, are you listening?"

"I'm here. Go on about Jeannie."

It was a relief to get everything so direct from Annie: Mary had got word in the nick of time that her sister was coming on furlough and would expect to be met in Minneapolis; so she had picked the London lady from her train over there and the two had waited for Jean. And the London lady had fretted Mary incessantly; and so Jean had phoned; and she *was* still the vivacious young girl, so like her mother.

"She said for you to go right out. That was an hour ago or more. You better take a cab."

And he did go and take a cab, thinking that it was now going to be just like six years ago when that same message had directed him: "Come out. Come now." But this time he was wholly prepared—he thought.

The ride out gave him a chance for a preview.

The cab stopped before a comfortable-looking white house whose deep screened-porch darkened its front and his vision. He repeated the house number as he paid the driver.

"That's right," said the man, and he added, "Okay," slamming himself in and leaving Mr. Sterling alone on the sidewalk.

He could gradually discern a form on the porch. But it was Miss Dalton's. She pushed the door open for him and stood both chiding and consoling him distinctly as he went up to her. Before leading him into the square hall ahead where he could see, by the light of a spreading lamp on a carpeted table, a wide staircase, she lowered her voice intimately to let him know that she suspected some "friend" had been the reason for Miss Jean's coming home; she and Miss Mary emanated a suspicious good-humor. She couldn't say more now—

Mary called from the living-room at his right to come in and he was so welcome. She began approaching—in some sort of rosy slack suit—and saying what a shame and repeating to come right in and she hoped he did not mind the wait too much— Of course, if he had only let her know that he was to be in the picture . . . Anyway, what a reunion this was going to be! She directed him to take a chàir at which she nudged, calling it her dad's favorite, while she went back to leave his cap on the hall table.

Though but dimly lighted from a large white lamp on a heavy round table under two windows he faced at the end of the room, the room, he could see, had a lived-in look. Miss Dalton arranged herself in the center of a divan-sort-of-thing between two book-cases and facing the empty brick fireplace, so that in her uprightness she almost fitted into a picture he did not recognize; (It was the Sibyl of Cumae.) he noticed a nebulous similarity between Miss Dalton and the figure of the prophetess. He could

observe only that much in detail before Mary was passing between him and Miss Dalton to another chair across the hearth
from him. She moved into the right spot a big square needle-
point covered stool and sank into the chair behind it, picked up
some gray knitting from the stool, looked closely at it for a
moment, and said, "Four more rows of this same. My tenth pair
in two months—in spite of heat. I suppose you knit too, Miss
Dalton?"

Miss Dalton didn't—yet. But if she had not begun to knit, she
had known sacrifice.

"My dear, have you ever stopped to think how lucky you are
to have your living-room on the first floor like this? Oh, my
poor wee flat in London— We know all about shambles and
wrecks of homes, don't we, Captain Archibald?" she asked significantly.

"Yes," he agreed. He was watching Mary and wondering
where Jean was.

"Tell me, my dear, how old is a place like *this?*" The London
lady moved her up-turned palm around as if she were indicating
an extensive farm.

"Too old for us—and too big too now." It was Jean answering
and coming down the stairs into the hall behind him.

She stopped at Mr. Sterling and shook hands and without per-
mitting an interruption explained again how she had come home
—got a furlough to spend with Mary while their parents were
away with the boys. When she stopped speaking, he felt that
he had to stop watching her face and holding her hand though
he didn't want to do either.

"I didn't know you were in service" was all he could say at
once. He felt semi-blinded by something about her; yet she had
not turned upon him that intimate smile that he had hoped for.
It helped his memory that she wore a dress and when she went
over and opened higher the windows beyond the lamp he thought
she hadn't altered in six years; he perceived traces of winning
mannerisms he had never noticed about anyone else.

"If I'd known Miss Dalton was to be here with Mary, I would
not have needed to come—could have taken my furlough later."

Miss Dalton looked at him significantly but he did not notice. "I'm jolly glad you didn't know," he said boldly.

"Well, that's nice. It's great having you surprise us like this too—"

"I'm so pleased that you changed, Miss Jean," interrupted Miss Dalton vaguely with a drawn-out sort of look that one associates with fond reminiscences. "Women in uniform is all one ever sees in Canada today. They're ever so trig and patriotic too of course, but they are awe-fully monotonous."

"Jeannie looks swell in hers," said Mary across to Mr. Sterling. "I want to get into one. I'd wear it all the time."

"Jeannie would look swell in anything," stated Mr. Sterling with upsetting daring. He was determined to go on from where he had left off six years ago. But no one appeared to hear him. Maybe he was not being so forceful as he imagined.

"I hope you won't need to wear one at all," said Miss Dalton generously.

"Oh, she will," said Jean. "We know things are far from over."

"That's the way over here; even the young people know everything. I have noticed it in Canada too. I'm getting to like it better." Miss Dalton was too genial.

"People being well-informed, you mean?" asked Mary, keeping a stitch waiting while she looked over at her for confirmation.

"Ye-s-s, that too." (She had meant living in Canada.) "And knowing what they want and going ahead to get it. It's a good way."

"Government by the people," Mr. Sterling put in.

"Well, I didn't mean that—but that's it too." She smiled cryptically. "I've told Captain Archibald, of course. He knows my views. In our correspondence I told you we kept up." And he could not guess at what relationship between them she had insinuated before he came. "I am afraid I want England to be different when we return to her—if we ever should."

Mr. Sterling wished Mary's curiosity would impel her to ask what Miss Dalton meant by *we*, but both the American girls seemed content to respect her right to vague references like that.

Mary did follow up her first enthusiasm for reunion: "Where are we going to begin tomorrow?" she asked. "We want to show Miss Dalton our Twin Cities. In time of peace we might show her the state but not now with gas measured by the drop."

Miss Dalton said, "You kind Americans! I knew you would be charming like this."

Jean got right up and found a long pad and moved over a little table in front of Mr. Sterling and pulled her seat over beside him and said he could write down all the places they named.

Harmony was here—for a moment.

"Just five days this time!" Jean exclaimed to him; and Miss Dalton called out, "That's all."

"Well, I suppose. We did London in a fortnight. Remember?" Jean bent forward to hug her knees.

"London is past," tolled Miss Dalton. "And it is much too late, my dear, to begin anything tonight. Mary says it has been awe-fully warm here during the day. I'm sending Captain Archibald right off—now—like that." She made a sliding cut-slap with her right hand across her left; she might have been some vicious Atropos dramatizing from her throne.

And in spite of his resolve to be masterly, Mr. Sterling left.

The next day, which began by being very warm, when Mr. Sterling arrived is not-too-hopeful a state of mind, he found Miss Dalton alone on the porch stretched out on a long wicker settee reading large magazines. On a round wicker table within her easy reach was a thermos jug which she explained held iced-lemonade.

"I fancy you miss our charged waters too," she said sympathetically as she pushed up into a more solid bank at her back the pillows surrounding her.

"I don't seem to mind the heat," he said. "It's only 88. Where are the girls?"

Jean had gone into town to the blood bank and Mary had

phoning to do. She presumed a tour would be out, because she had had little sleep in the heat and the girls thought a day on the porch like this should refresh her.

"And what about tomorrow?"

"We'll see. All this is refreshing. I shall enjoy a fortnight of it."

Mr. Sterling wondered whether the daughters of the house shared their guest's contentment. He himself was far from content this morning. In fact, he was bewildered. He could not be persuaded to stay for lunch with Miss Dalton, though she got up to look for Mary to add her entreaties.

"I know they expect you to lunch with me, Captain Archie. Wait. I'll just speak to Mary."

But she could not locate her hostess, and Mr. Sterling went away.

"You phone in the morning, before coming," she instructed him.

The next day, a day of Indian heat, he did not phone until after noon and then Miss Dalton told him not to come: "We sit in the dark quite unclothed. I have important letters to answer —in spite of this awe-ful heat—and, by the way, *later on*, after this holiday, I'll be seeing you. The girls are doing everything to make me comfortable. So there's nothing you need to come for."

The next day he phoned very early; yet, Miss Dalton's throaty "Yes" blunted the little spear of hope in his breast. She advised him to come after luncheon. When he did appear—late—a mood of desperation had preceded him and settled especially on Mary. Jean's attitude seemed sprinkled with flippancy.

In the evening while they were sitting on the porch with Miss Dalton while she took an indefinite period to cool off after the exertion of dinner, a young lieutenant in the air service who was home on leave dropped in with an assured familiarity. Somewhat formally, he addressed questions about Canada, jointly to Captain Sterling and Miss Dalton, sometimes saying "you-two."

At length, Jean straightened him out: "Miss Dalton and Mr. Sterling are not together in Canada. See?" She turned a comically instructive eye upon him.

He said he was able to, and at once began to emphasize humorously the separateness of his remarks. This revision amused everyone except Miss Dalton, who mentioned having important correspondents in Winnipeg and complained of an increasing sultriness. At that the visitor said it was getting dark and he'd better glance over their victory garden before it got too dark and when Mary began to get up to accompany him, Jean insisted that she knew enough about the garden and he said she would do all right and they laughed and he said good night—with especial ceremony toward Miss Dalton—and went through the house with Jean. And it did seem unquestionably darker to Mr. Sterling then.

Mary said Tom was a good kid—a remark not enlightening. It didn't help either to have Jean return; she came in the front way quietly and sat off by the door, and then said the night was nearly perfect and she would like to sleep out on the grass in Highland Park. Though Miss Dalton gasped audibly at this desire, Jean ignored that reaction and silently slipped away and only called down good night to them all.

On his dismal way home Mr. Sterling could but conclude that the furlough, judged by his first objective in arranging it, seemed to be fated to failure.

On the fourth day he left early with Annie's husband for a war plant inspection, where he lost that incipient sense of injustice and whence he returned without having consciously resolved anything but knowing he would take a step of initiative toward seeing Jean. The determination inspired by Mars would aid Cupid.

But a revolution had commenced without his interference.

"Too bad you didn't come back at noon," said Annie. "You said you would."

"I did that, but the plant's a bigger place than I realized . . . and the war bigger still."

"Jeannie phoned and wanted you. It may not be too late. I promised you'd call back. I'm sorry if you've missed something with her."

He would be worse than sorry.

Not without that eternal hope, he dialed, waited—then felt Miss Dalton respire into the phone before she spoke. She cautioned him against coming now. Jean had *phoned* him? Well! But now—she had a visitor; he was in the garden with her. He and two others had been there for dinner. But it had been so hot. She herself was keeping strictly to the porch. However, he must come tomorrow—early—before the heat. *She* had news.

Mr. Sterling did not wait for tomorrow.

With the cooperation of Annie he presently looked in the mirror at the most determined example of His Majesty's officer that he had up to this time achieved.

"I wouldn't let any fine London person put me off about Jeannie Knowles," Annie said. "I wouldn't that. And it's not too late either. The heat's just letting up nice."

From a distance the house inside looked black, but obliquely on its front fell light from somewhere across the street. He could gradually hear one husky voice waving through some agreeable excursion that ended on an upgrade; then, no response but stillness. As he turned in toward the house, Mary's voice broke up the dour quiet on the porch, saying, "Why, *here's* Mr. Sterling. Welcome, stranger." And she held the screen door wide open for him. (It was like the glad relief of a person waiting for the doctor to get there and take over a tiresome patient.)

Quickly he saw Miss Dalton was still at length on the wicker couch, a huge fan within reach, which she began to use vigorously. Jean came out in a moment (to bias the diagnosis?) and openly regretted that he had not come much earlier—then said with the charm no ordeal can quite stifle maybe his sister had *just* told him that she had phoned?

Enlivened by her own initiative, she slipped through to a chair in a remote corner of the porch and continued, "*We've* scarcely even seen you, you know, and now Miss Dalton has been gloating that she will—" She was speaking in a new, querulous key.

Hitherto her appeal for him had seemed accidental on her part. Never before had she manifested this preference—sounding the personal note. Now she was pointing to his duty to deal and judge fairly . . . he wasn't keeping up with what she was saying so fast.

Apparently, at any rate, Miss Dalton had not reported his call. She was not going to allow him to report it either. As if she had fanned herself into sufficient strength, she raised her body sideways as you do the lid of a grand piano to gain volume, and she chimed out—with a sweetness that hinted she felt guilty of a discordant sulking and to make amends was slyly and generously ready to announce something. (She aimed her voice at Jean.)

"Your boy-friend, Jean, is a cheery chap. I am awe-fully sorry he had to leave. And the other two—though I didn't just fall for their—" she laughed jumpily like one more than literally feeling her way in the dark. Her laughter sounded like an amateur at a mitrailleuse.

"Boy-friend!" snorted Mary, dropping courtesy for justice. "We never saw any of them before today, and we'll probably never see them again. They're all C. R. A. F. boys from Texas passing through town, and they brought greetings from our brothers. Just good old American hospitality. Does that surprise *you?*"

Miss Dalton settled back slowly into a sibylline silence. She swung the skirt of her housecoat over her extended legs—forgetting the heat.

Jean, shifting and stirring like a beflustered nymph, started out of her distant retreat. "I'm going out to the garden."

"Mosquitoes are bad, Jeannie," Mary reminded her.

Her immediate though ambiguous rejection of that warning reassured Mr. Sterling of Jeannie's earthliness: "I can stand them."

Miss Dalton lifted herself again and spoke: "*I* never could. The heat and mosquitoes together, Captain Sterling and I simply cannot take."

This was—well—it had a threatening flavor—

"They've never bothered me," said His Majesty's officer to Mary, and rising to prove it continued, "Long ago in India I became immune to heat and flies and—" whatever creature his reckless impulse tempted him to add his innate politeness would not permit his tongue to name. "I'll keep anything off Jeannie."

"If you don't, she'll get terribly bitten," said Mary.

On gallant step he was starting straight into the dark deep hall when Miss Dalton's voice commanded, "Wait! Stop, Captain Sterling!" (She was actually on her feet.) "Can you *hear* me?" (But she must not follow him.)

He turned and beheld her, a stiff untidy blotch, framed within the screen door, obscuring the very light she needed. Mary had moved into a wing; he could see her shoulder. Plainly, Miss Dalton, peering forward into the blank darkness, could not discern his distance. No sound offering her a clue, with two unskillful yet dramatic movements she swathed her legs tightly in the long skirt of the housecoat, raised her bosom, rasped her throat preparatorily, and gathered all her vocal volume for some magnetic parabasis. In her haste, she neglected her honeyed bait! Her voice was bitter.

"You are to come back at once, Captain Sterling. I intend to announce my news I told you about . . . Are you coming back here, Captain Sterling?"

He did not like to hear women shout like this, and he was the cause of this shouting . . . one oath would probably—but of course he could not use oaths on women . . . he let a long moment of silence intervene . . . if she resumed, he would reply . . . he was replying, hushedly, yet unequivocally, like one at last confronted openly by his enemy: "Whoo-isht, woman! Keep quiet! And I am *not* going back."

It was the inevitable stab, but even if she continued the act, he would not go on. He felt impatient to be after Jeannie; he opened a door; yet he waited, to be sure it was condemnation he had evoked.

"Bothersome fraud! You can't count on *him*, not on his word —I warn you! After all I've been through arranging this—"

It was enough. Her pitch was levelled for Mary; she believed he was gone . . . and Mary was shoving something near to receive her dispirited form . . .

✦

He found Jeannie in shrubbery—trilling some wordless tune defiantly. When he came very close, she stopped and whispered, "I was wrong last night. 'You-two' needn't be apart in Canada; she's not going back to Toronto. She's going to governess in Winnipeg."

"*Is* she?" He turned, listening, toward the house; but he could hear nothing.

"It'll just be farther back to London for her," he prophesied.

ROGER MARTIN DU GARD:

CONFIDENCE AFRICAINE

Translated by JOHN JAMIESON

TRANSLATOR'S NOTE. *Confidence Africaine* was first published in France in 1931. Although it is little longer than the average short story, it carried enough weight to justify the French publishers' decision to issue it as a separate small volume. It is one of the classic French *nouvelles*, perhaps superior to anything done in this form since the time of Flaubert and Merimée, and to anyone who is familiar with French fiction of the 1920's and 1930's it also offers a subtle commentary on the literary theories and practice of some of M. Martin du Gard's fellow novelists.

The story is presented as a personal confession, a form that has always attracted French novelists—from Diderot and Benjamin Constant down to Gide and Mauriac. When the confession framework is used, the essential narrative stands at one remove from the reader. The author tells us what the narrator was like, how he made his acquaintance, etc.; then he repeats what the narrator told him; and at the end he describes how the narrator now appears to him in the light of this revelation. In *Confidence Africaine*, as a further complication, the author appends to his character's narrative, which he has been copying out of an old diary of his own, a few sentences purporting to indicate the alterations he had thought of making both in the narrative and in his introduction to it, should he ever decide to use the confession as literary material. I have dwelt on this arrangement of the framework, with its calculated shifts in point of view, because I think it is largely responsible for the story's richness in overtones; the style itself, especially in the central narrative, is simple almost to baldness.

The irony of the story is directed first at the romantic theory of illicit love. The two chief characters have loved passionately and sinfully; but far from having been set apart from ordinary humanity by their sin, they are shown in their later years as perfectly commonplace, just like anybody else. It is implied that the gloomy and sinister sinners of Mauriac, Julian Green, *et al.*, are nothing but a literary convention and have very little in common with real human beings. This point is emphasized—perhaps a little overemphasized—in the "literary notes" with which the story ends. For the peaceful, prosaic ending something more dramatic must be substituted; the fat, slovenly, unappealing woman of forty must be suppressed entirely: a woman who has loved and sinned must not look like this—in a book.

At the same time the story is an answer to the critics who deplore the sexual episodes of *Les Thibaults*. They are *not* untrue to life, the author insists, and herewith he offers more and even stronger material of the same sort.

Underlying these is another and more vital theme: the impotence of even the most passionate love against such powerful agents as time, separation, and custom; *usus*, not *amor*, *vincit omnia*. The lover is represented as having accepted this fact with calm Latin realism. To modern readers nurtured in the romantic traditions of the last hundred and fifty years this must seem the culmination of all the irony in the story. We can't help regarding a tragic or unhappy ending—the lover's unavailing refusal to accept the changes that mere time and habit have wrought—as inevitable in a story with this theme; witness the final chapters of Fitzgerald's *The Great Gatsby*. Martin du Gard implies that such an ending is by no means inevitable—that this too is only a literary tradition.

May, 1930

My dear friend:

You have urged me very flatteringly to give you "something" for your readers. I was about to reply once more that everything that I have to say passes automatically into my *Thibaults*, when it occurred to me that I might copy out for you some pages from an old diary of mine. The subject is a conversation —a confidence, rather. It was told to me last summer on the steamer coming back from Africa. My companion spoke without any regard for literary or moral considerations and I set down his story exactly as I heard it. Perhaps you will not find it as interesting as it seemed to me then. I wonder, too, whether you will see fit to offer your readers a narrative which I admit is likely to shock some good people. Whatever may become of these pages, I shall have given you proof of my good will and constant sympathy.

But as I begin to copy them I see that they will hardly be intelligible without a few words of introduction.

Three years ago, in the course of an automobile trip in the Midi, I was obliged to make a detour and stop at Font-Romeu, where little Frantz H. was finishing his cure. I decided to speak to his physician and find out on the spot if my pupil was really well and if he could safely return to Paris to continue his studies.

I was pleased to find Frantz in excellent condition. He was waiting impatiently for the day of his departure, and I arranged to spend a fortnight with him in order to take him on some excursions in the surrounding region—one of the most beautiful in all France.

There were not many guests at the *Pension des Roches*. Frantz introduced me to a youngish, dark-skinned man—an Italian—with a cordial expression and mild, absent-minded eyes. His name was —for your readers, I shall call him Leandro Barbazano. He had been there for six months, at the bedside of his nephew—let us call him Michele Luzzati—a lad of sixteen who could no longer get up at all, so near was the end: indeed, he died before the end of my stay. Frantz spent a few minutes every morning and evening in Michele's room; he was the only person the doctor allowed to visit him. I myself had only one glimpse of Michele alive. I remember him better as he lay in death—no more than a skeleton, but with the beauty of a Persian prince. The window curtains were closed; no crucifix, no candles; not even flowers: nothing that pertains to a funeral. In the dusk of the room, his profile was outlined on the white pillow with a chiseled perfection that would have seemed unearthly but for the smooth and gleaming skin of the face, in which there still remained an indefinable appearance of life and youth. The mute, animal intensity of the uncle's grief was agonizing to see. It surprised the professional attendants, who had been anticipating every day for five or six weeks the inevitable death of the boy.

Frantz's friendship with the nephew had brought me into daily contact with the uncle. People become acquainted quickly in health resorts. I liked Barbazano's simple and straightforward character at once. He was the son of a bookseller in a large city of Northern Africa which I shall designate only by the letter *Y* (Oran, Algiers, Constantine, or Tunis, as you choose), and he was continuing his father's business in partnership with his brother-in-law Luzzati, the father of Michele. The Barbazano-Luzzati firm, he told me, was the leading book store of Y. Leandro himself was a little crude, being of common origin, but he had a sufficiently cultivated mind, thanks to his reading and travels. He had served his apprenticeship in book stores in France, Switzerland and Italy; he spoke several languages and was familiar with the main currents of European literature. This formed the subject of our first conversations. Later he began to talk to me about himself and his nephew. I had been touched from the first by the maternal attentions which he lavished on Michele. I learned that he had left his home and his business three years before to attempt this rescue; he knew every little sanatorium in the Alps, the Jura, the Vosges; all treatments, all climates had been tried—in vain. Although all the doctors agreed that the boy had been tuberculous to the marrow from infancy and could never have been cured, Barbazano reproached himself for not having attempted to save Michele's health sooner, and this unjustified remorse was frequently the subject of frank talks between us, which did more to bring us together than all our literary discussions.

I was with Leandro during the slow passing of Michele. Those three days of waiting created a temporary but active bond of friendship between us. When the boy died I put my car at Barbazano's service for the necessary errands and formalities. Contrary to our expectations, Michele's body was not taken back to Africa: the Luzzatis wired Leandro to have their son buried in the little cemetery of Font-Romeu. I was struck by one detail: Barbazano had the watch, fountain pen, cuff links and other trinkets that had belonged to his nephew put into the coffin with him; then he had his linen and all his clothes burned in the incinerator of the pension. He was capable of tenderness, but he was not sentimental.

Frantz and I accompanied Barbazano in the funeral procession as if we had been his oldest friends. The burial was soon over: the passage from the hotel to the cemetery was brief, and there was no religious service. The next day we took Leandro to the station at Perpignan and, touched to the heart, saw him leave for Marseilles with only a tourist's suitcase in his hand and not a single souvenir of the child he was leaving behind him.

I resumed my trip north a few days later.

Barbazano wrote to me as soon as he had arrived in Africa.

We exchanged two or three letters and a few cards; then our chance connection began to lapse. However, I had word from him the next year. He reminded me of a conversation we had had about the Fascist regime, repeated his wish to become a French citizen, and asked for my assistance. I did what I could for him, and a few months later he informed me that he had been naturalized.

Last summer when circumstances brought me to North Africa and to Y itself, I immediately thought of Barbazano. I let him know that I was coming. He met me at the wharf and greeted me in his usual fashion—undemonstratively, but with a masculine cordiality that was altogether authentic. He scarcely resembled the bowed, feverish, care-worn man from whom I had parted three years earlier at Perpignan. His pure Roman face, precisely modeled in spite of a slight fleshiness, had a serene and happy expression. On seeing him again I was struck with his resemblance to the death mask of little Michele, the extraordinary nobility of which, I believe, will always remain in my memory.

During the six weeks I spent at Y, Leandro Barbazano put himself out in a thousand ways to remove all difficulties from my path and make my visit enjoyable. I even had a little trouble in declining some of his proposals. He wanted to introduce me to the various groups of local writers and even had the notion of having me give a lecture in the municipal theater. When I assured him that I was incapable of speaking in public and that I had absolutely no message to give to the people he wanted to assemble in my honor, I remember that he shrugged his shoulders and replied with a disarmingly authoritative air: "Come, now! You will do as your colleagues do. All the authors who come here give a lecture. The historians on history, the poets on poetry, the novelists on the novel. They talk about themselves, their works, their method of writing, their hobbies, their diet. And no matter how well they have taken care to stock the stores with their books, everything is sold out inside of a week." I nearly had to lose my temper and scowl at him for several days in order to escape this ritual exhibition.

But I am digressing. I will only add a word about the Barbazano-Luzzati book store. It was evidently one of the best in the
city. Situated on one of the busiest corners, it was filled with
customers all day long. At noon and at seven o'clock in the
evening, a clerk lowered the iron shutter across the front of
the store, leaving only a low, empty doorway: the store then
ceased to be a bookshop and became a little gathering-place
where men of letters, teachers, journalists, and students met
when their work was over; there for an hour the latest minor
publications from Paris were passed religiously from hand to
hand. I too should have come willingly to the room behind the
store for a daily chat with Leandro; but he always wanted
me to stay for lunch or dinner, and rather than share those
noisy and overabundant family meals I preferred to eat at the
cook-shops I chanced upon while strolling through the native
quarter. For Leandro lived with his brother-in-law and his sister.
He did not appear to mind it in the least, and this surprised me,
for they seemed very different from him.

Ignazio Luzzati was a very old man, with round shoulders
and a puffy Levantine face; but behind his steel-rimmed glasses
gleamed a pair of steady, determined, and very watchful eyes.
He sat all day, like a buddha, on a dais at the back of the shop;
too fat to climb the ladder or even come and go through the
galleries of books, he had erected this overseer's platform from
which he conducted all sales by himself, calling out remarkably
exact orders to the young Jewish and Italian clerks, who had
been trained to obey him like hunting dogs.

The sister of Leandro had such a gracious name that I cannot bring myself to change it—all the more as it was her sole
adornment. She was called Amalia. Although much younger
than her husband (indeed, he seemed more like her father), she
too had a decidedly oriental corpulence. Certainly she wasn't
beautiful: I should even say that her creased turtle-like eyes, her
fat face, her oily complexion and her pear-shaped body, flabby
and distorted from pregnancies and nursing, were calculated to
make her a sovereign remedy against concupiscence. I understood her appearance better after seeing her gorge herself with a

compote of figs steeped in fresh cream and honey. In addition to the platefuls of macaroni which she consumed at meal times, she munched sweets from morning to night, and nearly always talked with her mouth full. Her cash drawer was full of stuffed pistachios, dates, loukoums, and the change was always sticky. In justice I must add that there was something passionate and imperious about her gluttony that took away most of its repugnance. This voracity seemed to be the outlet, the last resort, of all a woman's ardor; it was almost pathetic.

About her swarmed a half-dozen little Luzzatis of both sexes, from fifteen years old down to two, all fat and dumpy, with chubby cheeks and round bottoms, and flabby as frogs; they were afflicted with hoarse voices and thick mops of hair and were all unspeakably vulgar. The thought that they were the brothers and sisters of the admirable Michele did not at first enter my mind; but when it finally dawned on me, the effect was stupefying.

When I was first introduced to the Luzzatis I thought it proper to say a word about the son whom I had virtually seen die three years before. "He had long been doomed," sighed Mme. Luzzati. I was disagreeably impressed by this conventional expression of sorrow. "Adipose tissue," I reflected, "retards all activities and even paralyzes the most natural feelings." The mother's indifference surprised me all the more when I turned to old Luzzati and saw that he was in tears. Thereafter I avoided mentioning Michele's name. But two or three times, perhaps, in the course of my visits and the meals I was obliged to take with the Luzzatis, Leandro or I referred to our meeting at Font-Romeu, and each time the eyes of Papa Luzzati silently filled with tears. There could be no doubt that Michele had been his father's favorite child.

I was recalled to France without having had an opportunity to go farther south. In any case, the season (it was the beginning of August) was unfavorable. To compensate for this, Barbazano offered to show me some of the sites along the coast. We devoted the last week of my stay to this excursion. Leandro was a well-informed guide, a sensible and congenial companion. I like these simple and candid people who are what they are and have no false pretensions. Leandro had a practical mind, trained by experience, direct and adaptable and free of all mysticism. His natural good sense reminded me of a mountain stream, cold, a little rough, but clear and lively. He was not obsessed by general ideas and he talked undogmatically, as a sincere man who had often had to change his opinions; but on most questions he had sound views, formed by contact with facts rather than by thumbing books. His conversation—and he spoke only when he actually had something to say—was always refreshing. His presence counted for a great deal in the happy memory which I have of that tour along the African shore.

Consequently, I was glad to learn on our return to Y that he had to go to Marseilles for a few days on business and that if I chose to wait for a later boat we could go together.

The crossing was ideal. Only a few passengers. Not a breath of wind, not an eddy in the water. When night fell, it was so mild and balmy that we did not have the heart to go below and sleep in our cabin but decided to wait for sunrise on deck, stretched out side by side in our canvas chairs.

It was there in that incomparable isolation, that Leandro spoke to me for the first time about his past, in words which I have scrupulously preserved and which I now copy down for you.

August 24

—Arrived at Marseilles yesterday morning. Said good-bye to Leandro after a last dinner together at the Vieux-Port. I, rather moved at leaving him. He, not at all: cordial, natural, as always, and perfectly matter-of-fact.

Shall be in Paris this evening, but shan't reach Beleme until Friday. Should like to take advantage of this railroad trip to set down the story Leandro told me on deck that fine evening of the 21st.

Had exchanged desultory remarks about modern literature— the timid progress of psychology in the contemporary French novel, the boldness of certain German and English novelists, etc.

He mentioned the article in the *Revue des deux Mondes* in which I was criticized for having dealt with "questionable" subjects in my book—subjects that were deemed utterly "unlikely." He then made a vague remark, something like this, but in an unexpectedly irritated tone: "I don't know how people are made, Monsieur du Gard! Everything always seems unlikely to them. Isn't life made up almost entirely of unusual details?" The conversation dropped. Then he said, rather abruptly: "Look, Monsieur du Gard, this is the first time I've ever felt like telling this to anyone . . . You have seen our life at the store—Amalia, old Luzzati, their swarm of children. At first sight what could be less unusual, you think. Well, who ever knows? . . . If I were sure I wouldn't spoil this fine evening for you with my talk . . ."

My only response was to draw my deck chair up to his.

Now that I have decided (he said), I will tell you the whole thing crudely, just as it happened. But I must go back twenty years. And even farther, for the beginning. To our childhood.

We were brought up by our father—my sister and I. My mother died when I was three: I don't remember her. Amalia, who is four years older than I, was seven then. My father was extremely harsh and domineering. We didn't love him. You see —I warned you that I would be frank. He was the son of an Italian who had kept a newspaper stall. He himself had long since taken over this little business. He made money little by little and then opened this book store. He was almost illiterate. He had had a hard life. When he was married for the second time, to our mother, he was already aging. My sister and I never knew him except as an old man with a white goatee and decayed teeth and a hard skin that had gradually become lined with creases—just like a piece of wet parchment, you know, that has been left to shrivel in the sun. We never kissed him.

Very well. A little while after my mother died we moved to an old building at the entrance to the Jewish quarter. I must describe it to you because of what came later. It was at the corner of two streets. The book store on the ground floor was in a good location for selling. Behind it there was a back room and then a big kitchen that opened on a court. From the back room you went up by a little winding staircase—I can see it still—to the room on the second floor. It was fairly large but it was only one room. For several years all three of us lived there. I remember only a little about that time. I slept in my father's bed and my sister on a mattress in a corner. Amalia was probably eight or nine years old. She took her role of big sister seriously. She looked after me—got me up in the morning, washed my face, took me to paddle in the gutter in the court, and I believe she used to slap me, with permission.

A little later—I was beginning to go to school, I was about eight and Amalia twelve—there was a considerable change in our lives. We stopped sleeping in the room on the second floor. Our father said that he had attacks of asthma at night and was waking us up. I believe this was true. But Amalia later pointed out to me that this recurrence of asthma had coincided with the arrival of a serving woman who had been hired to do the cooking and gradually began to keep house for us. Not that it matters. Business was not going badly. Father had money. He rented a room for my sister and me on the fourth floor, on the same level as the terrace. We reached it by the main stairway for tenants. It was bright and cool enough, with white marble flagstones and glazed tile on the lower walls. It was quite deep, for Father had been able to divide the back part of the room with a sort of low partition made out of planks and old packing-cases. This gave each of us a long, narrow cell shut off by a curtain: just enough room for a bed, a night table, and a chair. The washstand was in front of the window, in the undivided part of the room; my sister and I took turns using it.

It was there that we grew up. We were very free, you understand. There was no one to oversee us on our top floor. But we did not abuse this freedom. The difference in our ages seemed to fade away year by year. We got along with each other perfectly. All the more because we had to endure Father's ill-temper together, storming from morning to night down on the first floor.

That period passed quickly. I was twelve—fourteen—sixteen. When I think of it, it must seem strange to you, a girl of twenty sharing her bedroom with a brother of sixteen. But I assure you, Monsieur du Gard, it surprised no one there. In the first place we had always shared the same room. And then that low partition between us gave us each a little nook of his own. And besides, in those days, families used to be crowded together any which way in those old tenements. Promiscuity like ours was quite commonplace.

Very well. Like all girls of her age, Amalia had a sweetheart. She was pretty enough, God knows. Her sweetheart was a boy of the neighborhood, an Italian like us, the son of a grain dealer. They would meet for five minutes at nightfall, at the corner of the alley behind the house, whenever my sister could find an excuse to go on an errand. Often too, thanks to me, they would meet on Sundays at the soccer match, when my sister was allowed to go with me. Amalia had no secrets from me. In our room in the evening, while we were undressing and long after we had gone to bed, we would talk endlessly about ourselves through the wooden partition. She would tell me about her handsome Stefano and how she was going to marry him as soon as he had done his army service. For my part, I didn't hesitate to enlighten her on my first schoolboy sprees and my little affairs with the girls of the neighborhood. We were really like two sworn friends. Don't imagine that I am telling you all this simply to rehearse old memories. It is necessary for a full understanding. Anyway, I am now coming to what I wanted to tell you.

Very well. I was seventeen years old. I had just taken my degree. That rather impressed my father. Nevertheless, he refused to let me continue my studies. He had put me to work in the store. But he did allow me to take a few courses at the University, so that I had more freedom than an ordinary clerk. I made good use of it. I was a healthy young fellow and God knows I was interested in women. I had a lot of little adventures in the neighborhood; but momentary adventures—love affairs of twenty minutes, without an aftermath. Sometimes on Saturdays when Amalia went upstairs to bed, she found the water jar placed in a certain way which meant: "Don't worry, I won't be in till midnight." But this didn't happen very often.

Then, that year at Easter, or perhaps Pentecost, the daughter of one of our neighbors, a tenant on the third floor, came home for a vacation. Her name was Ernestina. She was a swarthy little Italian, thin and wiry, a real alley-cat. She was two years younger than Amalia and so two years older than I. She had been our playmate in the old days and even as a child had drawn me into corners to kiss. But we hadn't seen her for several years; her mother had sent her away to work for an uncle who had an export business in the south. I realized on our first meeting that Ernestina had learned other things down there besides book-keeping. The very day after her arrival she let me take her up to the terrace of our house. There was a little wooden shed there to pile the laundry in when it was dry. All told, it made a very satisfactory nook for a boy of seventeen and a girl of nineteen bent on having a good time together. Ernestina was evidently determined to make the most of her vacation and to have me make the most of it with her. The only idea in our heads was to be together as much as possible. We had to invent ruses. Her mother kept her in in the evenings. Several times, when Amalia was at the cashier's desk in the store, I was able to take Ernestina to our room. But that wasn't enough. We were becoming more and more avid. We dreamed of having a whole night in each other's arms. It was she who found the way: the last day, I don't know how, she managed to make a false departure, and while her mother thought she was on the way to the train, she came in and hid in my room in order to spend the night there with me. I was to take her to the station at dawn.

Naturally we had to tell my sister, and that seemed perfectly simple to Ernestina. I remember saying to her: "Since you think it's so simple, settle it with Amalia yourself; I don't want to talk to her about it." My sister had known about our affair from the beginning. Just the same, I must admit it embarrassed me to bring my mistress to the room where my sister was sleeping and make love a few feet away from her. But we had talked freely about such things for years. Besides, I didn't know for sure what experience she herself had had; Ernestina said that Amalia knew as much as she did. And then, there was that famous partition. And above all, the desire I had for Ernestina did not leave much room for scruples . . . You see, I am telling you all this without embellishment.

To tell the truth, Amalia did not fall in with the scheme very gladly. I wasn't present when they discussed it, and Ernestina would tell me nothing; but all that day I could see from my sister's attitude that she was annoyed. Perhaps without entirely knowing why herself. I suppose that if she could have spent the night elsewhere she would have done so. I suppose. I am not absolutely sure; she may have been a little curious too.

It had been terribly hot that day. Ernestina had been in the room on the fourth floor since six o'clock in the evening, and I had gone up several times to kiss her and bring her something to eat. After dinner my father and Lucia sat out in front of the shop, as they often did, for a breath of air. Lucia was the housekeeper, who now lived with us. I sat down beside them so as not to give the impression of slipping away too soon. I wondered what had become of Amalia. Had she gone upstairs already? At dinner she had said she had a headache. By nine o'clock I was so impatient that I said good night and had the audacity to go off and leave the closing of the shutters to my father, contrary to all our habits. My father did not take such matters lightly.

Very well. I expected to find the two girls gossiping upstairs. Not at all. It was dark as night in the room and completely silent. I groped my way to my bed. Ernestina was there. She whispered to me: "Don't make any noise, Amalia is sleeping. She has a headache." Her breathing could be heard on the other side of the partition; she appeared to be asleep. But it was hardly nine o'clock, and her falling off to sleep seemed unnatural, after a day like that.

I admit I had something else to think of than Amalia's sleep, and that both of us very soon forgot that she was so near us. At the end of a few minutes we had abandoned even the most elementary discretion. It was quite a night, Monsieur du Gard, and Ernestina had no reason to regret missing her train. . . .

It was necessary for her to leave the first thing in the morning. As soon as it was dawn we had to dress hastily and slip out of the house. Amalia was still asleep. Ernestina did not say goodbye to her.

She was still asleep, or pretending to be, when I returned from the station. It wasn't more than five o'clock. I was tired and went back to bed. Then I got up again as usual at seven. A little later Amalia also got up as usual. I heard her putting on her shoes behind the curtain as I washed myself. She said good morning as if nothing had happened. But when she came out of her alcove I could see from her appearance that she hadn't slept a wink. I had finished washing. As usual, I made room for her and then went down to open the shop. Not a word about Ernestina.

We didn't get along very well the next few days. There were spats over trifles; and instead of laughing in a moment, as we used to do, we would remain hostile and sulk at each other the rest of the day.

Amalia seemed determined to be disagreeable to me. She trumped up all sorts of grievances. Thus, she took it into her head to get up as soon as she heard me getting out of bed and monopolize the washstand before me. She said: "Turn about's fair play—I'm tired of pouring out your dirty water." It was absurd. There was no need for her to be downstairs before eight o'clock; whereas I had to have opened the shutters of the store by then and got the milk and bought the morning paper, if I didn't want to have a row with Father. He always had me read the paper aloud to him at breakfast. The first time, I let her have her way and went downstairs without washing. Very well. But the next day, when she started to do it again, I lost my temper. She was already in front of the basin, in her slip and petticoat. When she saw me coming, she splashed water at me. I am purposely telling you this in detail. Sometimes we used to scuffle in fun, but this time I was in no mood for fooling. I caught her from behind, lifted her up on my knee and carried her to her bed. She was heavy and kicked about like a fiend. I had my hands on her breast, and her buttocks were squirming against me. All this is very clear in my memory: I have often relived that ridiculous scene; moreover, it was that morning, that moment, in that transit from washstand to bed, that it first dawned on me that my sister was a woman made like other women, and even that she was infinitely more desirable than Ernestina. I threw her on her bed, cursing as if I were still furious with her. I remember that she suddenly ceased to struggle: I strode haughtily back to the washstand. I washed and dressed. When I left the room, she was still lying across the bed in the same position.

Very well. Let me go on. I had the habit of reading rather late at night. Amalia had never made any objection. Anyway, the partition separating us kept my little candle-end from bothering her. But she seemed absolutely bent on upsetting my ways. Now she got the notion of making me put out the light, on the pretext she was tired and I was keeping her awake. Naturally, I refused. Then she climbed up very quietly on her chair and blew out the light by waving a petticoat over the partition with her outstretched arm. I relighted it immediately. She began again. I can still see her over the partition, her hair tumbling down and a look of malice in her eyes. I am sure that she hated me that night and sincerely wished me ill. Decidedly, Ernestina's vacation had spoiled a number of things.

The next evening I had taken care to protect the flame, and when I saw her ineffectually shaking her petticoat over the partition, I burst out laughing without interrupting my reading. I heard her lie down again. I thought that that childish prank was over. But not at all! I was reading peacefully: suddenly I saw her leap towards me and upset the candlestick with her hand. Then it all happened in a minute. I lost my head completely. In two seconds I was on my feet and had her around the waist. Just what did happen? I am trying to remember everything as distinctly as I can. It was dark. I was wild with fury. So was she. She was a husky girl. I tried to overcome her, to throw her on the floor, with the fixed intention of thrashing any desire for further tricks out of her. We were pressed together in the dark, both in our nightgowns, and struggling like two madmen. Finally I lifted her off her feet. She clutched the back of my neck with her fingernails. I inhaled that scent of flesh still warm from the bed—the same odor that I had breathed all one night on the body of Ernestina. With a sudden movement, I bent her over backwards on my mattress. In the same instant I found myself caught between her two bare legs, which she closed behind me. I swayed. I fell on her. There wasn't much left of my anger, I confess—just enough to sharpen my desire. I sought her lips, furiously. I believe that she was awkwardly holding them out. . . .

And there you are.

You see how naturally things like that can happen. It's very simple even, when you think about it and trace everything back step by step.

Well, it went on for four years. Four years. Even a little longer. And I am not ashamed to tell you, Monsieur du Gard: they were the four happiest years—the only really happy years—of my life!

Amalia was a virgin when I took her. But she was—what shall I say—passionately inexperienced. I was seventeen, and except for Ernestina I had had only lucky escapades, often enough without even a bed—between two doors, in the corner of a cellar, beneath the trees in a park, in the fields. I didn't know what a continuous, daily union was. It is incredible how much love is augmented by the habits that grow up between two bodies. And then, of course, we were both ardent and quite insatiable, as one is at that age. This wasn't all. Looking back, I believe I can distinguish still another thing. When a man and wife are on good terms and have lived together a long time and become utterly used to each other's nearness, they are united by a very deep feeling, a wordless, internal understanding of which they are scarcely aware and which is quite indescribable. It is this that makes them a couple. Young people have no idea what it is like. Well, thanks to our seventeen years together, our intimacy of brother and sister, and to our having the same blood in our veins, we gained immediately that kind of secret understanding that settled couples have . . . But you will analyze all this much better than I can, Monsieur du Gard.

The strangest part is that no one around us ever suspected a thing. To be sure, we were careful to ward off suspicion. From time to time, on Saturday nights, I would ask my father for a little money to go and "shoot pool"; and the next day Amalia would tease me openly at the table for looking tired. For her part she broke off with the grain dealer's son and let herself be courted publicly by one of our neighbors, a rather stupid fellow who was satisfied to meet her occasionally in the street— just what was needed to create a little neighborhood gossip.

Well, it went on for four years. And no doubt it would have gone on still longer. But two things intervened about which we could do nothing.

The first was the approach of my military service. I had already taken a medical examination at the Italian consulate. At the end of the year I was to join a Sicilian regiment and spend two years in Italy. No way of getting out of it. I swear many a time I thought of deserting! If it hadn't been for my father, I might have done it. What a stupid trick that would have been!

The other thing came from my father. He was nearly seventy, and he had decided that Amalia should marry. Some time before, to better the business, he had hired a former bookseller from Naples, a hard worker, with age and experience, who was beginning to make our store one of the best places in the city. You have met him: it was Luzzati, my brother-in-law. He was about fifty years old then. He had saved up a pretty little nest-egg. And he had a passion for my sister, silent but stubborn and intense, like himself. Father thought it an excellent match: at one stroke he would assure his own future and that of his children. Luzzati was going to purchase half of the business and get the daughter of the house into the bargain; and he promised to accept me as partner when my term of service was over. Thanks to this arrangement, my father, who was getting old

and more and more asthmatic, could retire and live on his in-
come without waiting until I was old enough to manage the
store.

There was only one obstacle: the attitude of Amalia. Oh, she
did not dare say no to Father. But she was evasive and kept putting off her reply to gain time. From the day Luzzati entered
the household she had taken a dislike to him. Between ourselves
she always called him "the old pig." She found him obsequious,
repulsive. She heaped insults on him. She said to me: "I would
rather kill myself."

Looking back, I have an unhappy memory of that year. It
was the first time Father had encountered such opposition in
his own family. You could see that he was boiling with suppressed anger. But I believe he would have turned his daughter
out into the streets sooner than give up his plan. The months
passed. Amalia held firm. In our room we forgot all that. Our
passion was only intensified by those threats and by my approaching service. I was to embark at the beginning of October.
Father's rage became terrible. He scarcely spoke at all to Amalia.

In the mountains towards the south, about a hundred kilo-
meters away, there was a well-known vocational school in a sort
of convent. It was managed by nuns; young girls were sent there
for two or three years to learn all sorts of manual trades. Sometimes Father would speak of it significantly at the table while
looking at Luzzati, who took his noon meal with us. One Sunday evening as Amalia started up to bed he followed her to the
staircase and said, looking her full in the eyes: "If you don't
consent by next Sunday I will take you to the vocational school,
and you shall stay there as long as necessary." We knew very
well that he would do as he said. You may object that Amalia
was of age. But that was our way of life, Monsieur du Gard,
and it never occurred to us that we could throw off our father's
authority, no matter how old we were.

Amalia cried for several days. I did not know what to say to
her. The thought of her marrying "the old pig" was as unbearable to me as it was to her. But the idea that we might be deprived of the three months we had left before my departure,

was still more horrible. That was what decided her. She was heroic. She consented, but on the condition that the marriage should not take place before the end of the year and that until then Luzzati should not treat her as his fiancée or say a word to her about it. Father was beside himself. But Luzzati accepted; he even seemed happy. Amalia told me: "It's all the same to me, I will kill myself as soon as you are gone." And she was capable of it, Monsieur du Gard. It made me sweat to think of it. Finally I overcame my repugnance and told her: "Accept him. I shall be back in two years, and we will go to France together." She didn't even answer me. I am sure I would never have convinced her. But suddenly she had an idea of her own. An entirely unexpected idea. "Yes, I will marry him; but only if you will arrange to make me pregnant before then." You see? Since there was no way out, she consented to sleep with Luzzati and to be his wife for two years, if she was sure of having a child by me and of not having one by him. Very well. We "arranged" matters, and sure enough two months later we knew what we wanted. I was satisfied. I knew now that Amalia would not commit suicide and that she would wait for me.

I am reaching the end of my story—or nearly. But what I have left to say is not very cheerful.

I left for Sicily in October and they were married.

Seven months later Amalia had a child. A boy. As you have already guessed, it was Michele. He was only just alive, as if he really had been born prematurely: in the first year alone they nearly lost him a dozen times.

During all that year Amalia wrote ardent letters to me in secret. In every one she talked about my coming home and our running away together. I thought of nothing else myself, but naturally I could only write to her about trivialities. And then, little by little . . . the tone of her letters changed. One day she announced that she was pregnant again. Only that. I was more surprised than jealous. Frankly, I was beginning to think less about her myself. You will understand that: to enter into a new life at twenty is an intoxicating experience; and besides, there were pretty girls in Sicily. Then her letters became fewer. Finally I had a telegram announcing my father's death. In a word, when my service was over and I came home, I found Amalia heavier and full of her own life, with her two children— Michele always pale and sickly, and Giustina, that fat girl you've seen, who never made any difficulties about living and already appeared to be the elder. The first few days Amalia avoided being alone with me, I believe. Before her husband she did not seem at all embarrassed to see me. I was the one who looked like a fool. Did she consider the past mere childishness? Or had she simply forgotten how she felt then? You will believe this or not, as you choose, Monsieur du Gard, but *there was never anything between us again.*

Anyway, I stayed with them only a short while that time. The store was doing very well. I wasn't needed there. I persuaded my brother-in-law that it would be a good thing to let me go and study the book trade in France. And so I left. I served a stage of apprenticeship in Marseilles, another in Lyon, another in Geneva, and a fourth in Paris. I was there when the war broke out.

I returned to Italy. I worked for another stage in a book store in Rome. But not long. The Italian mobilization compelled me to rejoin my regiment. Ten months later I was a second lieutenant. I went through a lot. I don't say that to boast, I did no more than many another. But it helps to explain what happened afterwards.

When I found myself at home again in 1919, safe and sound, and home with them all at the Barbazano-Luzzati store—well, in spite of everything, Monsieur du Gard, life seemed pretty wonderful! My brother-in-law, who was feeling his age, gave me the heartiest welcome. Amalia, mother of a family now, seemed happy. I can see her as she was then. I can see the four children, sturdy and noisy and tumbling over each other from morning to night, around Michele's armchair. He would smile at them gently . . . Poor little fellow . . . Monsieur du Gard, telling this to you now, I should like to be able to say that it was solely because of him that I stayed there and settled down with them. And it is certainly true that I adored the child. But no, it wasn't because of him that I accepted their family life so easily. It was congenial to me. The past was far off and had no effect on me. The war had made a great break. My sister, Luzzati's wife, always pregnant or nursing a baby, with her fat little children ɩnd her old husband never reminded me—*has never since reminded me*—of the Amalia of my youth. That is the absolute truth.

And then, that store of ours had an attraction for me that no other bookshop could possibly have. Luzzati has always treated me as his employer. You have seen him there: he keeps the selling end, all the dull routine work, for himself. He has let me do a little publishing. I started that review. I built up those collections I showed you. I felt that I was happy. I was.

There was only one dark spot in that life—Michele's health. Even about that I deceived myself for a long time. He was never really sick. I would say to myself: "It's the heat, the climate . . ." or else: "It's only a phase—he'll grow out of it." I didn't see how he was fading away. I was hurt, though, to see that Amalia obviously cared more for his brothers and sisters. Oh, quite without thinking: it was simply that only the healthy ones were her true children. You imagine perhaps that Michele was a sort of living remorse for her, for the two of us? No. It might have been so. But it wasn't. I must confess one thing to you: it wasn't until very late that I myself realized my guilt in the matter. Very late: at Font-Romeu, and a little before . . . Suddenly I told myself that I was responsible, after all, for that birth, that sickness, that martyrdom. And yet— Responsible? How can one know? As for my sister, I will swear she never thought of it. For her—without her realizing it, of course— Michele's death was a relief. Yes. And at bottom, Monsieur du Gard, it was for me too. In spite of the grief I felt, I am happy now. I am even more happy, more tranquil, than before. We are all happy. All of us together.

That is the way it happened, and nothing can change it.

✦

He stopped. And it all seemed so simple to me that night that I had nothing to say.

(Here followed some notes of a professional nature, in case I might want to use this story some time as literary material. I shall not copy them all for you, my dear friend. I shall only set down these few lines in closing.)

. . . It would be necessary also to change the ending, as from the return from Sicily; and above all not breathe a word of my recollections of the obese Amalia of forty, enthroned behind the cashier's desk in the midst of her brats—or gobbling her honeyed figs—or letting her imposing breast flow out of her jacket to humor her last-born, a fat-cheeked urchin nearly two years old and still unweaned, who ate at the table with us and then at the end of the meal greedily scrambled up into his mother's lap to suck a few gulps of stale milk by way of dessert.

VENARD McLAUGHLIN:

THE SOLDIERS

T HE TWO mud-covered men sat side by side in a gully at
the edge of what had recently been heavily timbered land.
Now the trees were blasted and broken. Many white-torn
branches littered the ground, some of them still bearing green
leaves.

A few hundred yards away beyond sterile broken ground a
road roared with tanks and trucks and marching men. The roar
was dull under a low sky still heavy with rain.

One of the men bandaged the other's arm. He himself wore
a dirty cap of bandage wound low over his forehead. He squinted
past a smoking cigarette stub as he worked while the other looked
on calmly.

"That was very bad while it lasted," said the bandager. "We
are fortunate to be still alive."

"That is true," said the other. "But it stopped so suddenly.
Are those our men or the enemy in the road?"

"Hold still, if you please, until I've finished this . . . I can't
say for sure. Everything is so splattered with mud."

"The wise thing for us, then, is to stay here until we learn
what has happened."

"That is unquestionably the wise thing."

"It is also the desirable thing. Here, we can rest. Here, we can
see and not be seen."

"That also is true," said the bandager. He finished his task and
leaned back sighing, looking about. "I dislike such destruction.
Before we came here this was a beautiful forest. Now you can
see for yourself what it is. I should never have become a soldier."

"Nor I," said the other. "At home I was a school master. I prefer schoolmastering greatly."

"Is that a fact? Or is that a manner of speaking?"

The school master looked up puzzled. "I beg your pardon?"

"For instance, take my case. I was a chemist. But that was a manner of speaking. Like most men I needed to earn a living. For that purpose I was a chemist." He stared thoughtfully at his mud-caked hands. "Actually, the point of my life was to draw a wolf."

The school master frowned. "As a hunter, may I ask, or as an artist?"

"As I have said, I was merely a chemist. My life was simply centered on the drawing of a wolf."

The school master looked carefully at his companion. "Perhaps," he said gently, "it would be better for you to lie down and rest a bit. Is the wound painful?"

"A bare scratch, I assure you. No, I am not confused. I am merely clumsy in my way of putting it. Perhaps, since that road may contain either friend or enemy and we are forced to remain here in hiding for a time, perhaps it would not bore you to hear of my wolf."

"I am very curious," said the other.

The chemist drew tobacco and papers from a pocket and the two men rolled cigarettes. A small fighting plane dropped suddenly from the clouds over the road with cackling machine guns raking the men and machines below. The school master raised his head cautiously to peer over the edge of the gully. He sat again lighting his cigarette.

"It is too murky to make out the markings. That plane may belong to us or the enemy; and we still do not know who marches in the road."

"In that case," said the chemist, "we are very wise to remain here. Now, if my wolf will not bore you—"

"By no means."

"Very well. But I must tell you that my father was, during his life, a very wealthy and successful man. It was because of his wide-spread business interests, as a matter of fact, that this thing of the wolf came about. My father had become very wealthy at the time of the last war trading not only with our own people and the government, but with the enemy as well—a thing which, of course, could not happen in this war which is a struggle between Good and Evil—"

"Assuredly not," said the school master. "Such a thing is today unthinkable."

"—and for some months at the war's close my father and I were in Russia where he had reason to fear the loss of great investments. It was there the wolf thing happened."

The school master waited a moment in silence for the other to go on. "Yes?"

"I scarcely know how to say it," the chemist said. "You must know, also, that my father was a great, bearded man with the long dark eyes of our people. His voice could be thunder or soft as a woman's. He was an intensely vital man, strong and arrogant. He was never much troubled over little matters of ethics. You will think I am disloyal to his memory."

"Not at all," said the school master.

"You must, of course, see how he was to understand. A wholly objective observer would possibly sum up his habit of mind as predatory. I shall not say that."

"Of course not."

"But at any rate the Russians are a stupid people and my father had, in spite of their internal disorders at that time, arranged things satisfactorily and we entrained for home. Now, if you remember, there were difficulties at that time. Our train was stopped, the crew shot at once, and the rest of us herded out on a flat snow-covered plain. In the moonlight the whole affair was full of shadow and confusion. I was very young and although badly frightened I was intensely excited and wide-eyed as well. My father kept me close at his side and when they had searched us and were lining us up to be shot he suddenly leaped forward, struck down several men, seized one of those hard little Russian horses, and sent him galloping with us across the plain."

"My word!"

"Yes indeed. That was my father. They fired two volleys
after us, but for some reason no one followed. At the second
volley my father sagged forward against me, but he straightened
almost at once and we made for some low craggy hills not far
distant where we found a small cave and sent the horse on
with a slap on its rump. In that cave my father died. He had
been hit badly in that second volley."

The school master clucked sympathetically.

"Now, what follows is really the important part," said the
chemist. "You must know that this cave we came to was, to the
eye, scarcely more than an indentation under an eyebrow of
rock. In the inside darkness there was every indication that it
was no more than this. Now, imagine for yourself how it was
when, with my father's head in my arms, with his last breath
still sounding in my ears, a magnificent wolf stalked from the
blank wall at my back, passed me and loped gracefully down
the hill to the plain. You will understand how I dropped my
father's head and ran to the cave mouth, staring after that beast.
You can understand my thoughts. Where had he come from?
In the darkness had we mistaken space for rock wall? Why had
the beast not attacked? You can see I was young and highly
excited. Without weighing consequences I ran after the wolf
fascinated by the beauty of him in the moonlight. I have never
before nor since seen anything so wholly beautiful. When he
disappeared I turned to go back to the cave, and I could not find
it. I searched until dawn, becoming hopelessly confused and bewildered. I never again saw that cave."

The school master cleared his throat and stared thoughtfully
down at his bandaged arm. The chemist sighed and continued.

"It would be irrelevant to relate how finally I came to my
home. The point is that ever since that night I have tried in
vain to capture in some manner the beauty of that black running
animal. It has become the purpose and center of my life. You
will appreciate, of course, that as I grew up I realized the reason
for the staggering impression of that night." The chemist raised

his eyes to the shattered trees overhead. "I need scarcely point out that the beast was in reality the soul of my father."

The school master straightened. "I have heard of such things."

"And I have seen it. Thus the centering of my life upon this problem is not really esthetic. It is also a search to know myself. For in the lines of that beast was the essence of all that my father was. When I finally draw it I shall know my father, and since I am his son I shall know something of myself. I hope you can see how everything else in my life is subordinate to drawing the wolf?"

"Perfectly," said the other. "I am grateful to you for revealing this thing to me. For I can see that I, too, am only what I am as a manner of speaking. I can see that almost unconsciously my life has been centered, as has yours, on something to which all else is secondary. At the risk of boring you—"

"Please," said the chemist. "Don't think of that." He raised his head to stare at the road still full of machinery and men. "It is an excellent way to pass the time." He lighted another cigarette and lay back comfortably. "Think of it. Here we are exposing our souls to each other, in a manner of speaking, yet had we not been wounded in defending this forest and crawled into this gully we might never have known of each other's existence."

The school master's head jerked up and he stared at the other. "Pardon," he said at last. "For a moment I thought you said *defending* this forest."

"And so I did," said the chemist, "but whether we did or did not do it is beyond me."

Under its caking of mud the school master's face became tense and his eyes darkened. "But we were *attacking*. Surely you remember how we crawled on our bellies over this barren stretch under the enemy's merciless fire."

"No! You are confused," said the chemist. But now he looked again at his companion. "We lay in the wood, *defending*—"

"No, no! It is you who are confused. As I know anything, we attacked!"

"And I know beyond possible doubt that we were defending!"

The two men confronted each other. The school master moistened his lips.

"Can—can it be?"

"It seems utterly inconceivable," said the chemist.

"Yet, you were defending?"

"Yes."

"And we were attacking. Then—"

"Then," said the chemist, "we must be enemies."

"I—I doubt our sanity. Look, is not your uniform of this material?" He scraped dried mud from his tunic.

The chemist did likewise. They looked at the cloth and then at each other.

"We are enemies, then," said the school master.

The chemist drew a long breath. "In that case we have a duty."

"We have indeed. We must kill each other."

"Unquestionably. Personal preferences in a war such as this of Good and Evil—" The chemist broke off in embarrassment.

"It is truly a war of Good and Evil," said the school master, "but we are gentlemen. We will not discuss which is which."

"We will not indeed. But the duty remains."

"Beyond doubt."

"Still," said the chemist, "we are not yet aware whose people march in yonder road."

"That is true."

"Therefore, if we fire our rifles at each other the marchers will undoubtedly hear the shots and come to investigate. Then, if one of us survives he may fall into enemy hands and be himself killed."

"Yes," said the school master. "It is a needless and foolish risk."

"That is my thought. I therefore propose that you relate your story to me while the army passes by. Then, when it has gone, we may kill each other in comparative safety."

"That seems very wise," said the school master. "Here, then, is what your story of the wolf showed me of myself. As I have said it has become a conscious centering of my life only during the past few minutes. But I can now see how my whole life has been built around it. As a matter of fact—" The school master paused in confusion. "These things are hard to say in words, are they not? It is like stepping naked into a public street."

"Exactly. But please go on."

"Well, then," said the school master, "I will say it. From earliest childhood it has been my ambition to make a plum skin stand alone. Many people, in fact all the people I have ever known, eat plums whole, skin and all. I have never been able to do that. From infancy I have peeled plums and I have never peeled one without either trying or wishing to try to have the skin stand, bloated with air, as though the thing were still whole." He rubbed his nose and flakes of dried mud fell over his chest. "So stated, it seems ridiculous. Particularly by one, like myself, who holds doctorates from the world's leading universities."

"Not at all, not at all," said the chemist. "Have you ever succeeded?"

"Never. But I have never given up."

"Nor I. I have never drawn the wolf, but I too have never given up."

The clanking of tanks and march of feet grew fainter.

"But tell me," said the school master hurriedly and a little loudly, "during this war have you had occasion to continue your drawing?"

"As a matter of fact, I haven't. In war there is room for nothing but war."

"I have also found it that way. Not once, until today, have I thought of my life-long ambition."

"War makes many things unnecessary," said the chemist. "Perhaps that is why it has been so long and universally popular."

"Perhaps," said the school master. "Do you notice? It has become very quiet."

"Yes. The army has gone."

The school master sighed. "We must then kill each other, I presume."

"We are enemies," said the chemist. "We have that duty."

The two men moved slightly apart and then raised their rifles.

"Pardon me," said the school master apologetically. "But with this injured arm—. Would you be good enough to adjust my sight? It is at present set high. That would, I am afraid, be incompatible with the instant circumstance."

"Allow me," said the chemist. He adjusted the sight and handed back the weapon. Then he sat up very straight. "By the way. Doesn't it strike you as being abnormally quiet?" Both men lifted their heads, listening. "A thought comes to me. Suppose an armistice has been declared? Suppose the fighting has stopped?"

The school master lowered his rifle. "An armistice!"

"Then we should be murderers!"

"We should, certainly! It has become very quiet!"

"Very," said the chemist. "I have no desire to become a murderer."

"Nor I. It is quite possible an armistice has been declared."

"Quite."

The two men looked thoughtfully at each other.

"In that case," said the chemist, "our duty seems clear. We must try to find our respective armies."

"That is the only thing left to do."

"Then we will know exactly our position."

"Exactly."

Both men stood up and saluted. After a few steps the school master turned.

"I suppose if the war is over you will return to the center of your life and continue trying to draw the wolf?"

The chemist paused and nodded. "And you will attempt to make plum skins stand alone?"

"Yes."

"Of course," said the chemist, "if the war is not over—" he shrugged, smiling. "I shall be too absorbed."

"And I, too," said the school master. "Good day."

"And to you also a good day," said the chemist.

GILBERT NEIMAN:

KERMESS

THEY had been having a big time with the jaripeo in the afternoon, lassoing the bulls, hogtying them, and riding them. The bulls were not brave, however. They had been brought in from the fields. They were bulls for work, not for sport, and they all ran back for the pen after their first charge out. They were very bad bulls. There was one good one, but no one wanted to ride him. There must have been about thirty charros on horses with ropes, and they were all bored; they scattered in surprise, trying to get out of the way, when he came out. The charros had been acting very vain and haughty at the lack of good bulls, and when the good one came out it was so unexpected that they had all they could do to keep out of its way. One man finally got a front hoof, throwing his lasso from a respectable distance, and threw him. No one offered to ride him after they got him tied. It took them twenty minutes to tie him. They finally opened the gate to the pen and slapped hard with their palms on the inside of the corral fence, calling "Toro," and making ah-ha noises in their throats like bleating sheep. The bull eventually calmed down and hobbled in to rejoin the tame ones from the fields, but it took a lot of time and persuasion to make him.

In the evening there was a kermess. All kinds of booths were up for eating and drinking. There were two gambling tables of *pares o nones* and three or four of cards and blocks. You laid your money on a card, the blocks were upset, and if one of the blocks finished rolling down the incline with a card matching yours face up, you were paid off five to one. Most of the Indians bet only pennies, except on *pares o nones,* where they would sometimes risk as much as a twenty-cent piece.

The young unmarried girls were dancing beneath a level tarpaulin hung low over the space between the two long rows of booths. There was an occasional married couple among them. The couples shuffled down one side of the center poles and up the other, raising a fine, powdery dust which was not visible in the dim electric light but which tickled your nose. Every once in a while, you would hear someone sneeze and someone else yell "Salud!" The families were lined up along the sides to watch the dancers. Some had brought chairs on which the mothers and elder daughters sat, fathers and brothers standing over them. In the aisles between the families and the booths were constantly roving the loose males, some of them tall and lean with the hungry stare of the young dissipated Indian who is feeling the need of a woman. There were a great many rouged girls from the cantinas interspersed among the pairs dancing. It was easy to single them out by the way they danced. Some of the Indian girls from respectable families danced closely, but not that way.

Right in front of a center booth, when a haupango was over, a lithe, undissipated Indian with dignified eyes returned a young, light brown girl with plaits to the vacant chair beside her mother. She smiled bashfully at her mother as she sat. He nodded his head gravely and walked through the couples that strolled in a circle between pieces to his original post on the opposite side of onlookers. They had not exchanged a word. He had asked her father if he could have the dance, and those were the only words she had heard him speak. Her eyes were on his back as he made his way through the couples, but when he reached the other side and turned to look at her, her eyes were following the passing couples. Her father was massively built and looked as if he had killed enough men in the revolution. He towered over the two chairs, swaying on his feet a little. He swayed steadily.

A squat, stocky mestizo with grease on his chin and a smear of red chili sauce on his shirt left the center booth where he had been eating and watching to tap the father on the back and ask permission to dance with the girl. The burly, swaying parent looked uninterestedly down at the insignificantly little fellow and did not condescend to reply in words. He was feeling a warm, assenting mood, however, so he made a complying gesture with his hand and stared back at the dancers. After all, the main purpose of these dances should be to get daughters respectably married off before they reached an age when they would do something less respectable on their own. Every man, tall or short, thin or fat, was a prospect. The mestizo walked around the chairs and, planting himself before the girl, stuck out an arm, as if he were going to yank her up. She was seated passively in her chair, enjoying the dancing, which had just started. His being squarely in front of her did not seem to spoil her view or annoy her in the least. She simply watched the dancers to one side of him.

"Come on, nina. Let's dance."

She did not hear him; she was serenely intent on the sight of the circulating, shuffling couples. She was looking down at the end, where the circle went from one lane to another.

"Come on and dance. Your father said yes." He stiffened his arm, hand ready to grasp.

The girl gave him a glance of distant curiosity, and shook her head as if she were shaking off a fly. He jerked his hand down to his side, and glared at her with the red hot eyes of an angry bull.

"Your father told me yes."

She did not see him any more. He was not there any more as far as she was concerned; she was placidly pleased with the spectacle of the dancers. He looked up with hot eyes at her father, who did not see him either. He was moving back and forth, seemingly hypnotized by the rhythm of the dancers, but really heeding the hot ebb and flow in his stomach. The mestizo shrugged his shoulders and went to the center booth behind the family and ordered a beer.

A skinny Indian, as young but not as handsome as the first one, pushed through the dancers from the other side, and, standing where the mestizo had stood, caught the father's attention and received a nod. The girl arose and he put a long arm about her, keeping his distance. They danced smoothly together. He could not do a huapango as well as the first boy, but when the band went into a danzon he did that very well. The medley lasted ten minutes and he returned the girl to her seat just as the mestizo was buying his third beer.

It was several minutes before the orchestra commenced the next dance, which was a jarana about Vera Cruz. No one came up to ask for the girl this time. The mestizo drained his beer bottle and walked to one side of her chair, tapping her on the shoulder and pointing to the dancers. She turned sidewise on her chair, so that her back was to him. He stared at the tightly woven plaits down her wide back, looking them up and down. Then he shrugged his shoulders again and returned to the same booth, where he paid for a taco and demanded that they put more sauce on it. His eyes were fiery red; the extra sauce brought tears which he blinked back. He watched the father, who was swaying less rhythmically on his feet, having lost the ebb and flow sensation by thinking too much about the girls he saw dancing. The tall parent walked to a different booth and ordered a bottled lemonade, resting his broad hands on the counter for support. He had been drinking pulque since the day before.

The stubby mestizo wiped the fresh sauce from his chin and streaked his dirty white pants with it. He went over to the girl and stood directly in front of her as he had done the first time, stretching out his left hand, placing his right one on the belt under his jacket.

"Come on and dance this one," he said.

The girl stared at him fully in the eye and said no, her voice unexpectedly strong and deep. He flushed for a moment, as if she had called him a bad name; then biting his upper lip in, he pulled his right hand out from under his leather jacket, and before you could say or do anything she was lying doubled up and moaning on the ground, her nose in the fine upper layer of powdery dust. After he did it, the mestizo dropped both hands to his side and stood gaping down at her, his mouth wide open, looking as if he had just hit her very hard with his fist and taken her wind out. Two men, who had been dancing, grabbed his arms, and he did not resist. All along that line of onlookers the word ran, and three soldiers in faded khaki came trotting down the aisle between the families and the booths to the place where the thing had happened. The two Indian dancers gripped him firmly, although his arms were limp. One of the soldiers stooped, rolled over the girl's body, and pulled out the knife. When the knife came out it was dripping bright blood. The man commenced bucking.

A third Indian reached his throat from behind and stopped his bucking against them. When the hold on his throat was released, he slumped his head down on his chest and stared at the girl dully. The soldier who had removed the knife felt her wrist and then put his hand gently inside her dress, feeling low under her left breast. His fingers came out red and he looked up glumly at the two Indians gripping the runt of a mestizo, who was starting to buck again. Another pressure on his throat, and he quickly stopped.

The father, who had been out vomiting behind the booth, came into the group and attempted to talk to the soldiers, asking foolish questions, too sick to believe his eyes. The soldiers did not answer, but some men in the gathering crowd patted him consolingly on the back, and said the pendejo would be shot the next day. That was, of course, a lie, because it was well known that the mestizo's brother was a ministro in the town Court House, and nothing ever happened to brothers of ministros. It made no difference, though, because the father did not hear a word of what they said, and asked over and over again if that could be his daughter lying there on the ground. The music had stopped, and the musicians who could leave their instruments joined the enlarging circle. Some more soldiers in less faded khaki came up, and finally a sub-lieutenant with a pistol.

The sub-lieutenant was all efficiency, preening himself with the chance of showing his authority. He snapped questions at the soldiers and looked professionally at the girl and at the criminal. Someone had spat on the little mestizo and the saliva was running down his forehead; he could not rub it off because the Indians would not release his arms. Way was cleared, and three soldiers in front and two behind with the sub-lieutenant and his

drawn pistol, marched him off. The Indians holding his arms
were allowed the pleasure of dragging him, his toes drawing
parallel lines in the dust. He would not take a step and they
dragged him along twenty yards. Then the lieutenant booted
him. The mestizo gave a grunt and started walking.

It was an hour after the knifing that two young men came
from the hospital in an old Ford to pick up the body. A group
of men had taken the father away, no one knew where. The
old woman was left sitting there alone, staring at her daughter.
She did not cry. She was furious at everybody, but she did not
strike or scratch anyone, because she could still see her girl's
body. No one dared to speak to her. She followed the hospital
attendants and refused to be helped into the back seat of the
Ford. She sat down there with the girl lying in front of her on
the stretcher that the young men had balanced across the two
doors of the back seat. The attendants from the hospital got in
front and drove off down the deep-pitted road, the dead girl's
body jolting heavily up and down on the blood-stained, sagging,
half-rotten canvas.

ROSEMARY PARIS:

REHEARSAL FOR INVASION

THERE are two islands in the Atlantic which form between them a long narrow bay, with a channel at either end where the rip tide froths the water. There were once hotels here and whaling boats and carriages jogging along the sandy roads. But that was long ago and now the wind over the plain meets only grass and bayberry bushes. Between blue sky and bluer water quick white gulls wheel and dive for fish. They make the only sound besides the placid lapping of the waves along the shore and the far-away drumming of ocean breakers.

But one day, quite suddenly, the silence was shattered. A covey of landing barges nosed into the bay with a roar of motors that reverberated from shore to shore. When they neared a narrow spit of land that made a shallow inner bay within its curve, they gathered off shore in a worried cluster, all comings and goings and angry mutters of motors revved up and then allowed to subside into under-water grumblings and puffs of smoke. Finally, somehow reassured, they took turns approaching the shore in trios, confident now and speeding ahead in a tossing of foam until they breasted the sand. There the front lip of the barges lowered so that the troops inside could disembark.

The men lumbered across the beach, scuffing the sand with their heavy boots, to plump their packs down on grass and bayberry bushes. Some were in khaki and others in blue fatigues, but they were all monstrously swollen by helmets and life-jackets, and they moved stiffly as if they were not accustomed to walking. The empty barges backed away to be replaced by others.

In spite of the din of barge motors and the confusion of new arrivals, there were immediately little centers of correlated activity. Tent poles appeared from nowhere and were hammered into the ground. The canvas tents flapped restlessly as they were being hoisted, and even after they were securely tied there were shivers of wind across them. One of the bigger barges disgorged a jeep that began at once to dash spasmodically here and there among the men. A single file of men trickled out over the plain to chop down the scattering of stunted pines. As they walked back to the cook tent only the branched trees could be seen moving, as if each had legs of its own.

Then from farther along the bay beyond the point came a new sound. Here were other troops beached for landing practice. In sharp silhouette against the horizon, dwarfed by the distance, they bunched and scattered unaccountably. The wind brought their voices in brief crescendos, like the noise of a crowd at a football game. Overhead the gulls slid into the wind's current and screeched protestingly.

Among the earlier arrivals there were three men sitting alone and to one side, not far from where others were digging a foxhole with a flurry of spades and sand. One of the three lay on his back, lifting his head now and again above the thick finebladed grass. The other two sat side by side with their helmets in their laps. They might have been quite alone on the flat plain, sitting with the heels of their boots dug into the sand. They might even have been bathers taking the sun before a swim. But before long an empty barge came to shore and without a word they stood up, bending under their packs and flinging over their shoulders as well the dangling rolls of pup tent, clothing and blanket. They trudged with heads down across the sand and into the boat. The lip snapped to behind them and the barge stirred up a tangle of seaweed as it backed away and swivelled its blunt nose to the west.

It was the last barge to leave and its roar drifted gradually away. The sun was setting now. The ebbing tide left delicate tufts of flame-colored seaweed to gleam among wet stones. The men beyond the point disappeared as suddenly as they had come, as if they had been snatched into the sea. In the dying wind the cook-tent smoke rose straighter and straighter into the air, smudging the tent's orange flank.

The men were quieter now, their work done, and they clustered near the cook tent with metal plates in their hands. A crowded jeep nosed into the road to town and disappeared in a smothering of dust. One or two of the men with their trousers rolled up stood like children in the shallow water or skipped pebbles across it. The pale sky to the west turned gold and pink and lavender.

When night settled there were no lights in the camp. But in the hush of darkness there was a restless stirring, a murmur of voices, an occasional excited laughter.

The respite was brief, for with the early dawn the barges grumbled back down the bay. On shore the tents were packed, the poles uprooted, the breakfast fires smothered with sand. When the barges reached the shore the patient lines of men filed aboard. As the barges backed away the troops sitting deep in the hold looked like ninepins. Only the helmsman was human, swinging his unwieldly barge with a flick of his wrist, and standing with legs braced as it sped away.

When the last echo of the barges had faded, the gulls swooped down to rock lazily on the waves off shore as if something in the churned up water and floating seaweed demanded their attention. It was very still. The sky was low and the water grey and sullen.

Over the sand and the trampled grass of the camp site were the usual leavings: cans, papers, corn cobs. There were several upheavals where well-meaning efforts had been made to bury refuse and fill in fox-holes. A large, partially filled hole was only too obviously what it was because the nearby bushes were festooned with toilet paper.

Here and there were other scraps of paper. "Dear Joe, I've just been down to B'klyn . . ." and a little farther on, typed in red ink: "Have a ceegar Mr. Clements."

At the spot where the three soldiers had sat alone there were three comfortable imprints in the sand. These three could see from there to the pale shore opposite with its peaceful abandoned farmhouses, and down along the bay to the white line of foam where the breakers rolled in over the sand-bar at the channel's mouth. They saw what the summer people and the whalers used to see. There was little change. As the three men had looked at these things their companions had hurried about around them.

The tide was in again now and had lopped off a generous slice of beach, but the strip left was pock-marked with footprints. There were layers of footprints: booted and bare, quick and emphatic. Most of them were pointed toward the bay and there was about them an air of urgency, of something that must be done, that could not wait.

Slowly the waves licked up the beach, and as they receded the sand was wet and smooth. In a day or so the footprints would be gone, quietly, without urgency, and for good.

KATHERINE ANNE PORTER:
AFFECTATION
OF PRAEHIMININCIES

M ARIA MATHER bore many children, some of them afflicted, and she accepted all her griefs and theirs with formal resignation. Not so much with this first child, Cotton. She spent on him the freshness of her maternal passion as if there would never be another. Stray glimpses of her, caught through a web of small-chronicle, show her praying and fasting for his sake, careful that his first words should be a prayer. Cotton seemed sound enough after the first precarious months of his life: in his second year he was undeniably frail, and when he formed his first pious words, his parents were horrified to discover that he stammered. There was no defect in the organ of speech, it was a nervous condition, and he could not utter a word without a painful struggle.

Dedicated as he was to the church, family pride, family reputation, family vocation were all at stake and in a fair way to be lost. It was obvious to the young parents that the devil had made an immediate assault upon an enemy he had reason to fear even in the cradle. They communicated their dismay to the child. The fate of his soul and the success of his career in the world were identified in earliest impressions with the necessity for loosening the catch in his speech. With precocious understanding he sat in his oak high chair, brought from England by grandfather Mather, and prayed to be cured of his stammer.

When he was three years old, he could read and spell, and his serious education began in the free school of Mr. Benjamin

Thompson. Family legend contends that he was an apostle from the first, and stammer or no, he began at once to lead his school-mates in prayer. At playtime he preached little sermons to them. The feebler wits of the school listened and were impressed, but sturdier spirits made fun of him, poked him and pinched him when the master was not by, and gave him the joy of suffering for his principles. Increase Mather liked to believe that his child was a saint at three years, and resented the treatment he received. He encouraged him in his unutterable priggishness, and soothed his vanity by explaining that persecution was the fate of good souls in a wicked world. He also cautioned the schoolmaster to be gentle with his child. The Mathers were all tender parents in an epoch of systematic brutality towards the young. Richard Mather had been so dreadfully flogged and kicked by his school-master that his childhood was embittered. Much as he longed for an education, he had begged his father to take him from school. His father sympathized and persuaded him to endure for the sake of learning. Richard overlived the experience, but not the effects of it, nor the memory, and all his life he spoke against the popular cruelties against children, and was tender with his own. Increase was even more indulgent: he was almost unique in his age because he did not beat his young, but rather erred to the opposite extreme.

The special consideration he received in school gave Cotton a certain advantage over his playmates. He found himself sup-ported in his apostolic attitude not only at home, but by public opinion, and this early became confused in his mind with the voice of God. The primer lessons were composed of moral maxims, and he learned that "The Butterfly, in gaudy Dress, the worthless Coxcomb doth express." He was offered such fallacies of natural history as "The Crocodile, with watery eyes, O'er man and every creature cries." Infant religiosity was praised in such bold rhyme-schemes as "Young Obadias, David, Josias, All were pious."

These infantile studies could not detain him long. He swal-lowed the primer and the horn-book, moved into the next grade, added Greek, Latin and arithmetic to his list, and proceeded upward without pause. "Zerxes the Great did die, and so must you and I . . ." was the primer lesson that stuck fast in his mind and urged him to a feverish speed. Death was at his shoulder, he might be stricken at any moment, he had no time to lose, he must hurry!

In his fifth year he resolved to be great. "He expected it, and therefore he bore and did many things, and disregarded all difficulties." This is Cotton's son Samuel, writing a long generation later, in the Mather fashion presenting with minute filial care a selected phase of his parent's career.

This inflated self-importance of the infant Cotton was a reflection of the family feeling. He was surrounded by every possible attitude of moral grandeur, a tallness and solemnity of manner utterly unrelieved by any sense of proportion. He "played saint" in imitation of his elders. And saintliness carried a certain social prestige. He went to services in a meeting house where the pews were carefully allotted according to social position, and he could not help seeing that he sat with his mother in the very front pew while his father occupied the pulpit. In his dangerous precocity, he absorbed everything without discrimination, and began to imitate the methods of his elders. He soon mastered the technique of exacerbating his sensibilities in prayer, and could burst into a flood of nervous tears at the crisis of a petition, precisely as his father and mother did, and as sometimes the whole congregation did, bowing in shaken rows while their anguished groans ascended to heaven.

He believed that New England was the most important country in the world, and Boston the greatest city, and his family the most distinguished of all families, and this belief remained almost unmodified into his middle age. To a natural personal arrogance the Mathers added theological pride, and a jealous vanity that showed an alarming tendency to resent slights real or apparent. People were continually uncomfortable in the presence of Increase Mather for fear they might do or say something damaging to his feelings. Respect for the clergy had been an article of faith in the early colony. The outward observances of this respect survived, but the spirit was weakening, and

Increase was sensitive to the slightest breeze of change in this regard.

Cotton adored his father, and his grandfather Mather he revered as a solemn presence stalking through his infant days giving reproof and admonition in his overpowering voice. But to his grandfather John Cotton went his secret hero worship. He was dead, but mother and grandmother conspired to keep his memory alive in a romantic aura of all that was courtly, superb, learned and charming in this world. The city of Boston itself was his breathing monument, and Sarah Mather could not praise him enough.[1] It was natural that the admired husband who had called her tender names should somewhat overshadow the living one with whom she shared the chilly pieties of old age. It was true that a miracle had saved Richard Mather for New England. The ship that brought him almost sank in the harbor, everyone agreed there was no natural cause why it should have remained afloat, but God spared all for the sake of bringing Richard Mather safely to shore. This was a miracle clearly, but insignificant compared to the blazing comet that hovered above Boston during Grandfather Cotton's last sickness, disappearing on the day of his death.

A godless innkeeper had been made uncomfortable by John Cotton's presence as a guest, professing himself unable to curse and damn with that saint under his roof. Once John Cotton had prayed for the dying child of his bitter enemy, Pastor Wilson, and the child had recovered at once. The man who had sworn to John Cotton's non-conformity before the High Commission had fulfilled prophecy by dying of the plague under a hedge; Mr. Leverett, who swore to a lie in defense of John Cotton and Christ's kingdom, was even now in New England, safe with

[1] In Boston, England, John Cotton married, as his second wife, a young widow, Sarah Story. He used to call her his "dear sweetheart and comfortable yokefellow."

Years later, Richard Mather married, as his second wife, John Cotton's widow, Sarah. In the meantime, John and Sarah Cotton's daughter, Maria, had married Increase, eldest son of Richard Mather. They were the parents of Cotton Mather.

honor. His reward had been certain, visible and negotiable, the just end of virtue.

Little Cotton imbibed these stories and the system of ethics they were designed to illustrate, as revealed truth. The more marvelous the tale, the more farfetched the moral, the easier for him to believe. Daily proofs of the family greatness were shown to him. He saw his father, when involved in a doctrinal dispute, turn to Richard Mather for consultation. When Richard wished to clench an argument, he turned to the writings of John Cotton, and the disputants were silenced.

Before his milk-teeth were loosened, the child assumed the task of outpraying and outdoing these spiritual giants. His stammer grew worse, and his parents kept days of humiliation for his relief. The house was filled with lamentations of suffering souls engaged in begging off from the cruelties of an implacable, invisible Presence that hourly threatened them with fresh calamities. Cotton had thought at first it was the Devil who had tied his tongue. Now it appeared that the visitation might be from God, enraged at some mysterious failure of holiness in Cotton's soul. Appalled, much confused, he wept and implored with the others, not without some pardonable pride in his elevated situation at the very center of a divine mystery.

Cotton had been absorbing knowledge from Mr. Thompson, from his father, and from the thousand odd books on his father's shelves. It was already the finest collection in the colony, where every family of any pretension prided itself on the possession and at least a quoting knowledge of good literature. It was socially correct to be known as a great reader: respect for the learning implicit in books increased, as times passed, into a nostalgia for the world of urbane European culture, and every ship brought fresh consignments of the latest works, not all of them theological or moralistic, to adorn the homes and minds of New Englanders who leaned with undiscriminating confidence on the printed word. Increase Mather had the foundations of true learning, and he read for love, even for amusement at times; the young Cotton had the desire to be learned and above all to be called learned, and he read voraciously everything he could lay hands upon. His memory was photographic, and at six years his little head was a mere rubbish heap of printed matter. He was then turned over to the famous pedagogue, Mr. Ezekiel Cheever, to be prepared for Harvard. Cheever was pious and a master of languages, and his unpleasant fondness for beating small boys caused him to enjoy a notable reputation as a disciplinarian. But he did not apply the ferule to Increase Mather's prodigious child. Even he was not so bold as that. All Boston was familiar with the father's sensitiveness about his son who was born a genius and a saint besides. Cotton pursued his apostolic labors among his classmates and devoured knowledge with an inhuman persistency that would be quite incredible if all the records of his later life did not bear witness to his unwearying pursuit of a single idea. This idea took on monstrous shapes and sizes, it sprouted in a thousand variations, but it remained essentially unaltered: the single aspiration of Cotton Mather to identify publicly and unmistakably his personal interests and ambitions with the will of God.

Harvard had lived up to the expectations of its founders and was the pride of New England, considered a cultural center equal to anything England could show. It was now an affront to local self-esteem to send promising young men to Europe for their degrees. Harvard was more than a university: it was a political hostage. Its rights, its very existence, were bound up with the first charter, and anything that menaced the charter menaced Harvard. It was the stamping ground of the clerical party: the whole death struggle of the theocratic state was to be enacted here, and the times were ripening for it. The destructive third generation was rising, critical of its grandfathers, cheerfully casual about the rather musty notions of its fathers. Harvard held firmly to its original aim of fitting the sons of ministers for the ministry, but many of them thus prepared fell away from their vocation and entered other professions, or even went into trade. Merchants' sons who had no intention of entering the church were now admitted, a little grudgingly. It was necessary to admit them, for otherwise they would go to England for their education and return with minds expanded beyond the permissible limits of provincial life: or worse, they might not come back at all. This had happened often enough.

A thirteenth-century schoolman would have approved the curriculum, with its heavy emphasis on logic, rhetoric and syntax, its geometry and arithmetic and astronomy, but alas, no music. A smattering of physics, a long list of dead languages, Greek, Syriac, Chaldee, Hebrew: and Latin, now on the point of dying out as the peculiar language of scholars. The students read the Bible exhaustively in all languages. In addition, and this was most important, the "scholar must understand that the end of his life was to know good, and Jesus Christ which is eternal good," and to attain this they read the scriptures and prayed publicly twice a day. Blasphemy was first among the seven major offenses, and its variations were minutely classified. The sinner was punished by a flogging, attended by prayer.

Into this ample lap of learning the great Ezekiel Cheever literally kicked his pupils, having first prepared them thoroughly in Greek, Latin, and the fear of God. At twelve years Cotton Mather had absorbed all that Cheever could teach. On June 22, 1675, Increase Mather wrote in his diary that Cotton had gone to live at the College. "The God of all Grace be with him, and never leave nor forsake him, but bless him and make him a blessing wherever he shall be, amen!"

The president and the instructors were prepared to treat the young genius very handsomely, granting him the same privileges and exemptions he had enjoyed under Cheever. The students were not so complacent. An unpleasant episode occurred almost at once. On the following 11th of July, Increase received dark news from his son. His cousin, John Cotton III, son of John Cotton II of Plymouth, brother of Maria, had joined with some older lads and hazed the newcomer severely. Also they made him run errands for them, and there were hints of harsher things. No doubt they were a set of young savages, but no doubt either that young Cotton Mather was supremely irritating in his assumptions of superiority, not only to the students but to the instructors. He complained with tears to his father.

Increase visited his brother-in-law at Plymouth, and commanded him to discipline his son, who was even now getting a reputation for wildness. He then called the overseers together, and laid his grievances before them. Many differences had been smouldering for a great while between Mr. Mather and the other fellows of the Corporation, and from this entirely legitimate pretext began a quarrel that brought numberless hidden grudges to light. His colleagues promised the enraged father to abolish the student custom of forcing the freshmen to act as fags for the older youths. In the matter of hazing, carried on secretly and with remarkable solidarity, they confessed themselves helpless. They would do what they could. This was merely a surface abuse, said Increase Mather. The trouble lay deeper. He was not interested in the custom itself. He merely demanded that his own son be protected from the brutalities of his classmates. This they could not promise.

Ten days afterward, the father was still seething. He rode again to Cambridge and held a long conference with acting President Orian Oakes and Mr. Thomas Danforth, a corporation member. He threatened to take Cotton from Harvard if they could not insure him respectful treatment from the students, regardless of seniority. Mr. Oakes pleaded that this would be a great mistake, very harmful to Cotton's future, and asked that he be left where he was. He assured the injured father it was nothing like so serious as Cotton seemed to think, but could give no acceptable reason why the students were mistreating him. Increase felt sure—and he was right—that the persecution was no mere boyish prank, but the material result of a true jealous animosity. The boy was at a painful age, and was mentally overgrown and bodily small and fragile. He had a beautiful face and very careful manners, and was absolutely skinless in his contact with strangers. The effort to overcome his stammer kept him in a continual nervous tension: his desire to make a perfect impression caused him to assume a fantastic preciosity of address. All his life he had been shielded, flattered and adored by his family and friends, and, except for his very first school days, he had suffered not one rumor of a world of physical shocks and psychic cruelties. His schoolmates had in them merely the very human desire to hurt and wound a creature who had rather too easy a time of it: the perfectly savage and natural impulse to destroy what they could not understand or sympathize with. Cotton's state was pitiable, all the more so because he had nothing within himself to combat the disaster. He suffered blindly and appealed to his father: and his father, dismayed to the soul at the predicament of his adored child, could only storm and rage and provoke fresh disturbances. He left Cotton at the College and went away angry.

At the August commencement Cotton had new woes to confide. Among other things, the Fellows of the Corporation had called the students into a special meeting and had remonstrated with them severely for tattling of College affairs to the outside world. Cotton felt this was aimed at him for the crime of confiding in his parent. Increase wondered what they meant by the outside world. Was he not a member of the Corporation? Cotton said the students were whispering among themselves that Increase Mather wanted to be president of Harvard, and this was the reason for his highly critical attitude towards everything that was done there.

This was a real blow. He did wish to be president, it was the dearest ambition of his life, and it galled him that a set of upstart boys had divined and spoken lightly of his closely guarded secret. At the next corporation meeting, Mather took the aggressive in earnest and provoked an open quarrel. He threatened to resign his fellowship. The Fellows and the President, he charged, had abused him in allowing his son to be abused, and they had wronged him in allowing the students to slander him by saying he wished to be president.

Mr. President Oakes was astounded and embarrassed at this frankness. He protested he had never heard of such a thing. With a great show of diplomacy he attempted to reassure Mr. Mather, and probably wished the mischief-making Cotton far away. He thought it would be a great pity if Mr. Mather resigned from his place; as Mr. Mather thought so too, and was merely waiting for an invitation to relent, that part of the business passed over swiftly. The scandal about his ambitions was more difficult. Mr. Oakes said something about this, too, but with less effect. He declared that nobody believed, or had even hinted, that Mr. Mather desired to be president. That Mr. Mather *should* some day be made president, no one had much doubt: and if there was any uneasiness in connection with this, it was simply the fear that Mr. Mather might in such an event remove the College to Boston. His prejudice against Cambridge was a matter of common knowledge.

After being driven to the wall by further arguments from the still unpacified Mr. Mather, Mr. President Oakes owned with some desperation that there were persons who thought that Mr. Mather was not always so plain and outright about things as he might be, but begged him not to let this trouble him. No doubt jealousy was at the bottom of it, for the interests of Harvard touched everyone keenly, and as for himself, he wished nothing better than to see Mr. Mather settled in the president's chair at Cambridge.

Further than this magnanimity no man could be asked to go. But Mr. Mather retorted that if he should ever be persuaded to accept the presidency of Harvard, it would be at the cost of great self-denial, and sacrifice of his personal welfare. The Mathers father and son were never to lose an occasion to repeat that every step of their lives for the public good had been accomplished at the expense of their private interests.

Mr. Oakes was tremendously impressed by this, assented to everything, and promised Mr. Mather that he should be treated with more respect in the future. The discussion had shifted so subtly from its prime base that Cotton was for the moment no longer the center of attention. Mr. Thatcher and Mr. Danforth, two Fellows of somewhat progressive, or anti-Mather, tendencies, were not so agreeable, and refused point-blank to humor the whims of one that they persisted in regarding as a mere corporation member like themselves. As nothing less than complete victory would satisfy Increase Mather, he again took horse and rode to see the governor.

Leverett must have shuddered to see him coming. Mather was

a gadfly to the governor and the magistrates as well as to Oakes and the Fellows. He harried their flanks in the matter of political and social reforms, as he pursued the faculty of the College with warnings about heresies and apostasies. Mather visited the magistrates in turn, admonishing them of their duties, criticizing their conduct of public affairs and laying fresh programs before them. When his advice was disregarded, as it was all too often, he fell into a fever of resentment and prayed against the enemies of God and New England and Increase Mather.

On his visit, the governor was tactful and sympathetic. He promised to intervene in the college trouble, and everything should be righted at once. Mr. Mather was to rest easy about his son. The situation simmered down a little, but nothing had been resolved. Mather kept a day of humiliation because all his labors seemed so fruitless. "I do but cumber the ground," he groaned. In this episode he perceived that the whole country was in a perilous state. The College seemed doomed to go down under its present woeful management. Moreover the Indians were again rising in force, and the English were not receiving the customary aid from God. The abomination of witchcraft seemed about to devour a people lost in atheisms. The powers of darkness appeared to be getting a firm grip on New England. He wrote to country ministers and asked them to send him particularized and authenticated instances of diabolic possessions and enchantments such as might have come to their attention. The country ministers were delighted with the idea, and highly curious documents began to come in to the North Street parsonage. Mather was much heartened by the unexpected results of his request. He decided to make a book of them, a book that should be a solemn warning and a horrid example.

Cotton had committed an indiscretion in the belief that his father was all-powerful. His father's failure to revenge Cotton's personal wrongs gave a severe check to his faith, and threw him into a new phase of doubts and inner searchings. He saw himself for the first time in direct relation to a world existing outside of himself, grossly self-sufficient, powerful, intractable, immersed in affairs utterly strange to him, entrenched in a point of view not his, and, above all, personally hostile to him. Hitherto he had cultivated a self-doubt, spiritual humiliation, as a rite. In his conflicts with God, with Evil, with his own soul, he emerged finally triumphant, always. In his first encounter with the world, the monster he was born to control and to win for God, he was defeated, bruised, and left prostrate.

Moreover, in his anxiety to uphold his own prestige at college, he had brought on a premature crisis in his father's affairs, embarrassed his cause, and thrown the whole orderly procession off the track. It was a symptomatic episode: he had begun his dual career of assistant and obstructionist to his father. The long struggle between filial piety and ambitious self-interest was on. He had meant to be a spiritual lord of life in college, and he had simply precipitated a rather nasty row involving his father in a series of undignified gestures. He fell into gloom, for if he dimmed the radiance of his father, he darkened all his own prospects. No Mather was ever lacking in self-esteem, and all of them believed, in their more exalted moments, that the world was in substantial agreement with their estimate of themselves. For Cotton, this encounter with a group of lads carefully selected from his own caste, but never quite his equals, for that was impossible, dedicated like himself to a life of holiness in the sacred vocation, gave him a problem in realism very hard to reconcile with his stubborn fantasy of personal grandeur.

He bore it badly. He fell into a deep self-pity and wept in a chagrin that he tried vainly to metamorphose into a state of penitence and purification. It was quite hopeless: he was lost, rejected of God and man, there was no refuge from his inner demon. He suddenly began to stammer again, and all the careful work of his childhood was swept away. The fear of death took hold of him: no literary invention this time, no planned invitation to pleasant horror, no fixed contemplation of the King of Terrors until the imagination was lashed into a foam. Perfect cold inexorable fear crept into his flesh and along his nerves: death became a reality to him. This brought on a long course of afflictions; he feared he had sinned away his day of grace, as the hopeless

Calvinistic phrase would have it. He was driving himself unmercifully at his studies, because now above all times he must stand at the head of his classes. He quarreled quietly and bitterly with his cousin John Cotton: and afterwards spent long hours examining his conscience, appalled at what he found there. Night after night he lay sweating and sleepless, clenched upon himself, waiting for the stroke of death, with his soul in disorder and unable to prepare itself for eternity. The foulness of his thoughts and the abominable behavior of his body disconcerted utterly that portion of his mind dedicated to the intellectual pursuit of sainthood. Until now his sins had been mostly rhetorical, he accused himself in general of all the enormities, not knowing what they might be, but in his blithe vanity assuming that he was the chief of sinners. Now in his adolescent upheavals, his pains and monstrous dreams and nervous shudderings, his uncontrollable mental and physical states, he recognized the precise, full nature of sin, and his moral collapse threatened to become complete. He believed his shocking experiences to be unique in the world, and shameful beyond words, and he went with a sense of guilt within, and, what was always terrifying to him, a fear of losing his reputation if anyone should suspect his infamous state.

At home, his brothers Samuel and Nathaniel were violently ill. They had worms, the plague of children in that day. Nathaniel and then Samuel almost yielded up the ghost in prolonged vomiting attacks. Cotton went home and Maria clasped again this most beloved of her children, and they spent a long dark day of tears together, praying for the sick. Increase was almost afraid to pray, for the cause seemed lost: "Now I thought it might be some discouragement to Cotton in case he should see his poor sinful father's prayers were not heard; yet I humbly pleaded it with God."

Salad oil and a clyster were also invoked, and ipecac, and the poor little wretches were dragged through to life. In this moment of relief, Cotton confided the state of his soul, more burdened than any flesh could be, to his father.

He found comfort. His father was not horrified. On the contrary, he was much encouraged at these signs of the death struggle of the Old Adversary in his son. He explained it all so clearly: that these agonies were the first signs of true conversion: and they spent the evenings praying and reading and talking together in the quiet study, among the friendly books, far from the bitter distractions of the world. These hours were very calming to them both, for Cotton was tranquilized to learn that his bodily rebellions were not new in the history of the soul's adventures, and Increase felt growing up by his side a confidant and disciple. Their companionship grew towards equality, and Increase began to confide somewhat of his interests and his problems with his ungrateful and sinful congregation, and those obdurate, hard-hearted fellows of the Corporation who were undoubtedly ruining Harvard.

Increase Mather was very quietly doing a dangerous and subversive thing in a political way. Two of the regicides, Whalley and his son-in-law, Goffe, were mouldering in perpetual exile in Connecticut. Increase was one of their agents, and he protected them well, sending and receiving their letters for them, and managing their affairs so adroitly that they were never apprehended. Cotton learned with awe that his admirable father could defy the King of England for reasons of conscience: that New England was a separate country owing no loyalty to any power but the Congregationalist church: and of all the factions within this sacred edifice, the faction headed and controlled by his father was in the right. His spirits revived, their joint defeat at the College seemed less important.

Though one single Synod had refuted eighty-two heresies, thus outstripping Arius by two, yet new ones cropped up like wild grass, and Increase was kept busy quoting his father and his father-in-law at the heretics, with added doctrine of his own. By now they had almost forgotten Calvin, only his tremendous idea, borrowed from Zwingli, remained: and the struggle set up in the ordinary mind by the doctrine of predestination had resolved itself into a mere Manichean warfare between the almost equally matched, separate and authoritative powers of good and evil. Increase Mather was a scourge to the provincial theologians, rising at them in this fashion:

"As for your errors respecting discipline, sacraments, their covenants, etc., I can bear with them yea, and these Arminian heterodoxia respecting Christ's dying for these reprobates doth not much trouble me. But your denying the meritorious obedience of Christ is such desperate heresy as no man that liveth with Jesus Christ in the Christian religion can in sincerity . . . bear with. Nevertheless, I still desire to respect you, and earnestly beseech Christ to let you see your error."

After receiving a letter or two of this kind, the startled rural prophet would ordinarily sink into a permanent silence.

On such examples Cotton formed his style and his point of view. He improved on them both with stouter language and even denser stubbornness. His character was now definitely formed, his mind at fourteen had reached the limit of its growth: all else afterward was mere expansion in the sense of things observed and memorized, a collected mass of information, but the actual capacity of his mind was measured finally at adolescence. He was a typical wonder-child.

Now his personality exhibited strange contradictions. He laughed and wept easily, and though tears were comprehensible to those about him, his tendency to merriment was very disconcerting. He lacked the sober caustic humor and hard cruel wit which appertained to the character of the English Puritan: possibly to all Puritans of all races and epochs. His gayety was spontaneous if somewhat nervous, and because he believed it sprang from an unworthy levity in his nature he tried to suppress it. This in turn led him to attempt an impressive dignity and profundity of manner, which degenerated into sheer youthful pomposity, and caused him to suffer some ridicule in other places than Harvard. This was the beginning of his hysteria and habit of making frightful puns. At first he made them as jests, hoping to amuse his hearers. Later the habit became automatic, and he played on words in contexts that shocked his hearers: that do, indeed, startle the reader even today. (John Cotton, for suavity and gentleness, he described outright as a "soft bag of

Cotton," and he lamented that the stone from which Richard
Mather suffered proved to be his tombstone.) He was bemused
by the mysteries of his physical being and hoped to conquer
himself by systematic discipline. He prayed intensively by rule,
and began to increase his days of fasting in secret, and to read
erudite treatises on the mechanics of meditation. Thus early he
was an expert technician, and was forever inventing exercises
calculated to advance his cause in Heaven, and on earth. After a
fast he always felt more authoritatively spiritual, and this would
call to mind the lost state of his little brothers and sisters. They
had their own schemes for personal piety, and they could seldom
be persuaded to follow his lead in devotion. It was the Mather
pride. They would do their own praying. Nathaniel was especially individualistic. He ended by influencing Cotton.

For some years it was nip and tuck between Cotton and his
brother Nathaniel for the family laurels of sainthood. "It may
be truly written on his grave that study killed him," Cotton
wrote long afterward. "His candle would burn until after midnight, until, as his own phrase has it, he thought his very bones
would fall asunder." Nathaniel's bones were troublesome at best.
He was so frail he could not walk until far past the time for
walking. Horrible pains in his joints crippled him recurrently
for long periods: he suffered an epileptic stroke that affected his
tongue, and for several years he stammered worse than his
brother. Even in this state, and handicapped by six years junior-
ity, he threatened to outpace Cotton not only in piety but in
learning.

The Mather pride afflicted him to a degree, and he awakened
the conscience of Cotton, who, being proud with a difference,
might have gone all his life mistaking this dark voice for a virtue,
except for Nathaniel who overlooked nothing. When Nathaniel
abased himself for whittling a stick on Sunday, and, for fear of
being seen, hid himself behind a door while he whittled, Cotton
could do no less than search himself for misdeeds even more
subtle: they called themselves atheists, and admitted with mutual
tears that they deserved hell. They supplemented each other
admirably: while Cotton assisted Nathaniel in languages and

mathematics, Nathaniel assisted Cotton in the finer points of moral self-torture. All of the children ate, drank, and breathed despair of God's mercy, and their sufferings began even in babyhood. Later, when he was editing his private papers, Cotton destroyed his own records until his eighteenth year, but preserved Nathaniel's long monotonous plaints of mental and bodily disease. He perceived that Nathaniel had a literary style worth his study. In keeping his own diary afterwards, he selected from his brother's papers many passages that he felt were equally pertinent to his state, and copied them in as his own entries. "O make my tongue a Tree of Life," sang poor Nathaniel, and the phrase seemed such a happy one it reappears regularly through all the years of Cotton's own petitions.

Nathaniel wrote: "What shall I do? *What shall I do to be saved?* Without a Christ, I am *undone, undone* forevermore! O for a Christ! O for a Christ! Lord give me a Christ or I die!" These are the unpleasant rhythms of a misplaced emphasis: and to increase the confusion, both brothers were confused about their sexual status. Both of them sought their God in the role of vestal virgins. Nathaniel at this time, and Cotton much later, employed a curious symbolism. "Oh, Lord Jesus, I come to thee! Who am I that I should be married to the King of Glory? I do accept Thee for my head and husband."

The family interests and interior distractions did not prevent Cotton from achieving the highest record for scholarship at Harvard. He mastered Hebrew beyond the requirements, and began to compile his own systems of physics and logic. His vacations were spent in his father's library, where he read himself into headaches, and cudgelled his brains to think up new religious exercises.

Daily he rose from the family table, an abundant board where he enjoyed himself sinfully, and repaired to his study, there to invite an attack of indigestion by instructing himself in doctrine and meditation on the state of his soul. The house was not large, and Maria Mather had almost completed her work of bringing ten children into the world. Slaves, bonded servants, and visiting

relations were stowed away somehow, and by excellent management father and eldest son were comfortably secluded in separate studies. Cotton, pacing measuredly back and forth, would
select a theme. Doctrinally he posed himself a question. He then
considered the causes, the effects, the adjuncts, as well as the
opposites and resemblances of his theme. As his theme was invariably himself, his sinfulness, the question how best he might
repent and stand well in the sight of God, he arrived logically
at a general examination of his conscience, which resolved inevitably into a minute consideration of concrete sins; in the
course of events there followed a severe expostulation with himself, and at last a resolution, increasing in imaginative momentum,
to repent on the strength of the grace offered with the new
Covenant.

The results were monotonously the same. Terror would strike
through his carefully contrived defenses, the true and awful
meaning of these words and ceremonies would suddenly become
clear, shattered he would fall to the floor weeping and imploring
to be saved from eternal damnation. All his uncertainties and dis-
appointments would rush upon him, and he would sob dolefully
with his forehead on the floor. Later he would rise, make himself tidy, for he was fastidious in his dress, and, seated at his desk,
he would record his crisis in detail, with pride and self-congratu-
lation in his achievement.

At home everything was quite perfect. No one disturbed or
criticized him, friends and parents admired him fondly, and even
in far-away England Uncle Nathaniel was aware of his nephew's
importance. He thought Cotton a remarkable child and sent him
a "Brachygraphic fitted to the Latin tongue," and insisted that
he learn it at once and teach it to his brothers and sisters. Himself, he had not time nor patience for it, it looked very difficult,
but shorthand was a branch of learning he desired to see in the
family. It had the prestige of novelty and exclusiveness: "Brachygraphic is not known nor practised anywhere in Europe but
in England." The gift and the advice went unregarded, and he
wrote anxiously about his character-book, saying he had been

unable to find another. Cotton Mather depended on longhand to the end of his days.

In this same year there are other glimpses of Cotton seen outside the official biographical records of his youth. Uncle John Cotton, minister at Plymouth, was head of a household reasonably afflicted, reasonably pious and somehow cheerful. As a small-town pastor he was aware that his family lacked the advantages of the metropolis. Also he seemed to have forgotten the little incident of his son helping to terrorize Cotton at Harvard two years before. He was continually writing to his sister Maria, enclosing a few shillings and wanting in return a piece of sealing wax, or several yards of good black cotton ribbon or a modest length of green galloon. At times he wished his sister to buy these things on credit at the same shop where she had bought his wife's cloak and he would pay for all in the spring. He sent an occasional barrel of good salt beef for their winter use, and in turn he hoped they would take his son John under their roof for counsel and prayer. No denying, the contrast between young John and his cousin Cotton was so marked that even John's father must admit and deplore it. He would make up all expense by sending tubs of butter and other necessities.

Increase was in no particular haste to grant this request, for later still another inducement was offered: John Cotton was training a little Negro slave for his dear brother in Christ Increase. The child was only seven but would be very useful for cutting wood and drawing water. He was being properly prepared for these duties, for even now he could answer the question, Who made him?

Then he wrote suggesting an alternative: "Concerning your son Cotton, that he may live here with me this winter: God hath given him grace, and his learning is above what those of his standing have usually attained to, whence he is able to do good to others: and you know it is recorded as the honour of your blessed father that at fifteen years he was called to be a schoolmaster; and why may not his grandson have it put into the records of his life, that before that age he was accounted worthy to be so employed?"

The third John Cotton was hopelessly in arrears with his studies, and his lately persecuted cousin was being haled to the rescue. Cotton was to have comfortable board free of charge. He would return to Boston in the spring with five pounds of silver in his pocket, besides what money other Plymouth families would be happy to pay him for private tutoring. He should have the tenderest treatment, and, as a final argument, it was suggested that the change of air might save Cotton from the smallpox, for Boston was in the midst of one of its frequent plagues.

Cotton could not be tempted by anything. The trouble with his uncles on both sides of the family was that they could not comprehend the altitude of his destiny. Shorthand! What had he to do with that? Tutoring! He did not in the least desire to compete with his grandfather Mather on these grounds, and the money was no inducement. He was perfectly comfortable at home. He remained at Harvard and near his father. Into the records of his life went a very grand letter to his Uncle John: "I know your candour will not charge me with idleness. Your courtesy will not implead me for forgetfulness, and most of all, you will not without reason accuse me of unwillingness to serve you in what I may, even *usque ad aras*, and if possible, there." He then pleaded delicate health, and "uncertainty of conveyance, and that again seconded by other evocations." He was in fact a busy and important young man, and his Plymouth relations quite evidently needed to be reminded of it. Yet he was not without his generous will to helpfulness. He called upon his muddied shoes to testify how unweariedly he sought the Plymouth boat, "who," (the shoes) "in this time when Boston is become another Lutetia (q. *luto sata*) do proclaim they wanted a pair of goloshooes when travelling near the dock-head." He declared he would fling salt upon the tail of time, or persuade the wind and tide to be favorable to his design if he had the power: but he had not. In short he labored to prove his scholarship and let his uncle know he had no intention of burying himself in Plymouth during the winter season of study.

Then he turned to a subject made for his pen. "Never was it such a time in Boston. Boston burying places never filled so fast.

It is easy to tell the time when we did not use to have the bells tolling for burials on a Sabbath day by sunrise: to have seven buried on a Sabbath night after meeting. To have coffins crossing each other as they have been carried in the street:—to have, I know not how many corpses following each other close at their heels—to have thirty-eight die in one week." Still, smallpox or no, he would not come to Plymouth. Providence had been tender in his own family. He had been touched slightly. Brother Nathaniel and sister Sarah also, but sister Maria went out of her head for several days and they feared to lose her. His father's prayers had been responsible undoubtedly for the mildness of this affliction, yet he assured his uncle he was even now preparing himself for the worst, in case Providence should suffer a change of mood.

This air of royal condescension towards his Plymouth relations was a faithful reflection of his father's attitude. The family correspondence was a little one-sided. John Cotton was always affectionately respectful, a little apologetic. He was the poorer of the two, but was always offering small tributes. He was always pressed for money and trying to explain it: he was after all unable to send the little Negro because there were no clothes in the house fit to send him in. The Mathers replied seldom, in the tone of those who held the deciding vote. The near relations were often mystified by the inexplicable remoteness of their distinguished kinsmen. Time and again they forgot themselves and treated the Mathers quite simply. They were soon recalled to a sense of their impropriety.

RICHARD POSNER:

THE GRAVE

O NE DAY, not very long ago, I was out on one of my customary hikes. What I usually do is get to the depot about five
a. m., take any bus that happens to come along, and ride until
the sun's bright and the scenery seems worth exploring.

Part of the fun is not knowing where you're going. Naturally,
sometimes I'm in for a disappointment, but nine out of ten times
it's as exciting a way to start the week-end as anything I know.
Especially in the spring or fall. Not enough people, I'm afraid,
know what a bird, or a strangely shaped tree, can do to a man's
blood pressure. And for someone who spends nine or ten hours
a day, five days a week, in an office, there's nothing in the world
more wonderful than to inhale all the country air and follow a
stream of water wherever she'll take you. Maybe through a
woods, or behind a farmer's barn. You don't know where you're
going . . . you just watch the current pushing pebbles to one
side and carrying sand along until, tired of its burden, the stream
makes a sudden turn, and leaves the tiny particles behind.

On and on . . . building and tearing down again. Always
moving. I wonder if a stream's really got a mind of her own?

I just kept on walking that day, never once worried about the
time. You know how it is— On that kind of a day I love to swing
my arms and take long, slow steps. I follow a road for a while
and then I go through a field searching for a stream again. Well,
that day passed, just like most of the others—filled with the tiny
excitements that can't be fingered. Just moments to tuck away
until . . . well, the air was so soft and clean and fresh that I
walked without any thought of time. I just walked and walked.

Then I remember kneeling to catch some tadpoles. After that I must have dozed off, because when I finally woke I was hungry and the stars were out bright and strong. I picked myself up and took inventory. I thought I saw a town about two miles off. By those lights in the distance I figured it didn't have more than a few thousand population. But it was really so late that I didn't realize that most of the folks were already fast asleep. I started to walk toward the lights. It was chilly and I had to flex my fingers to get the cramp out. The moon was distant and cold. Certainly everything seemed different from the afternoon. I hurried, since nature was fast losing her usual evening charm.

About ten minutes after I reached the outskirts of town I passed a yard in which someone was shoveling something or digging a hole. I thought maybe someone was digging for worms. I climbed over the fence. I really think I was hoping a man was digging worms for fishing, someone friendly enough to let me join him—that is, after I got a bite to eat. The moon was behind the clouds, so I just followed the sound. It was a steady and rhythmic sound, yet so calculated and definite that if I had given it some forethought—as I do such things during a business day—I might have become frightened. Pretty soon I thought I heard talking. I groped along, stubbed my toe and finally saw a man's silhouette against the sky.

He was mumbling to himself. His shovel was almost as tall as he—and he wasn't a short man by any means, though on nights like that, with a man outlined against the sky, I'll admit it's hard to judge.

Before I could say hello, he looked up, said "Howdy," and continued to dig. "Guess you've come to hear about Edie and me. Make yourself comfortable. That stump'll do."

Partly out of curiosity, mostly out of obedience, I sat down.

"I might just as well start from the beginning," he said without once looking up. "That's if a man can ever find a beginning. Well, I'm forty-three, and my wife's four years younger. We married eight years ago last April.

"I wasn't ever the mushy sort. My courting was usually done with two pound boxes of chocolates or a picture show. Edith liked milk chocolates and could put up with my taste for movies with sad endings. So, as I was saying, without much to-do we were married eight years ago last April.

"That first year—most nearly every Sunday in spring—we used to take the bus to the Johnson City botanical gardens and walk among the cherry trees. I don't know if that's what newlyweds are supposed to do, but we did it. Sometimes I'd kiss her when no one was looking. She used to say that that made me feel foolish and that's why I did it. She always said that I was just like some spoiled kid. Well, I'd kiss her, and then we'd both walk along casual-like. It wasn't at all like being married, if you know what I mean.

"Well, after a while it was only natural that both of us should want a family. I preferred a boy. And Edie never really said so, but I know that she was kind of hankering for a boy too. We both decided not to be too particular, however, so we never really talked about it being a boy or girl. We'd have been happy with either one. So a boy was born, only dead. The doctor said it was too bad, but he didn't think Edie would have any children any more.

"Do you think my wishing for a boy could have anything to do with it?

"You should have seen us that winter! Edie came back from the hospital and wanted to take everything in from one end of town to the other. We ate dinner out all the time. Even went to shows and the night club. She never drank anything hard, though. 'Might kill the child,' she used to say.

"I kind of felt it would hurt her too much to remind her that she wasn't still carrying the kid, so I just never said anything. She soon tired of the night life and we settled down again to meals at home. She's a mighty good cook. Her steaks are really something. Lord, what a flavor. But I'm off the track again. It makes me so warm to talk, and my hands and feet are just about numb. Been here a good few hours digging this hole.

"Well, after we settled down that winter, everything went along pretty much as usual. Her cooking got better and better, and we kept the nursery door closed so as not to remind us.

Everything went along pretty well, as I said, except for one thing. Edie kept complaining about a pain in her right side. Every time I'd mention a doctor either she'd make believe she didn't hear me, or else say that the pain would go away pretty soon. I was sure it was appendicitis. One night the pain came so strong she let me call the doctor—only it wasn't old Doc Lempkin, because she made me call this young Doctor Howard. He's a good-looking young fellow. I guess she figured Lempkin was so gnarled and ugly that looking up into his face would scare the pain out of anyone. Yes, you heard me right. I said, scare the pain out of anyone. You see, the doctor told me afterward that my wife just didn't want to lose the pain, and it was just something she imagined anyway. He gave me some pills for her nerves and told me not to say anything to her about what he just told me. He came back every afternoon for a week and used to rub her side where she said she had the pain. I don't know why he used to rub her side if there really wasn't any appendix trouble, but that's what he did. He was so gentle it was a pleasure to watch. Well, after that week she never complained of the pain again.

"It was about eight or nine months after that appendix business that something kind of strange happened. She bought light blue yarn and all the other knitting paraphernalia and took sewing lessons. She wanted to make baby clothes. At first I thought it was for a friend. Lord, she went about it with loads of pep. I haven't ever seen anything else quite like it in her. One night I asked her whose baby she was knitting for. She looked up at me surprised and hurt, answering, 'Ours, of course.'

"She didn't get any further than the first sleeve, however, before she pulled it apart. I didn't want to question her about it, since, after all, knitting's a woman's business. She never made that sleeve again. But every night, after the dishes were washed, she'd sit opposite me in an easy chair, cross both legs under her and go through the motions of knitting. She'd have the wool right there on her lap, but she'd never use it. Instead, she'd work hour after hour with the empty needles. I became so used to the dull clicking of the needles that I actually began to look forward to that sound. It became so warm. You should have seen her sitting there so intent with the lamp dropping its light across her shoulder. I used to put my paper down and just sit and watch her expression. I loved the lines moving up the base of her nose, and the way she'd twist her mouth after whispering to someone, 'dropped one.'

"When she finished a night's work she'd carefully put the ball of wool away in a small cloth bag. She never put the needles in the same bag, but always placed them alongside the bag. She was mighty careful with those needles.

"I must seem foolish now, standing here with a shovel near a hole in the ground, but you'll understand. Anyway, being here gives me a chance to talk. The night helps too.

"I told you about her steaks, didn't I? I can taste one now, they're that good.

"Let's see. Oh yes, well, any fool could see what was ailing Edie. So we decided to adopt a child. It didn't matter, as I said before, whether it would be a boy or a girl, just so long as it belonged to us and we could love it.

"Everything was just wonderful that day we went out together to the home for adopting children. Oh, you could just touch the clear fall air. I even opened my mouth so I could drink it in. 'Watch out,' Edie joked, 'or you'll catch a mosquito.' I don't think I would have minded a mosquito in my mouth.

"But everything went wrong. We were both given blank cards to fill out. Where it asked how many children we had I wrote, 'none,' but Edie wrote, 'six.' There it was, plain as day, 'six.' I tried to say it was a mistake, but Edie stuck to her story. 'He knows I have six children,' she insisted. I took her home. She didn't say a word to me on the bus. Just sat with her hands folded, and looked straight ahead. When we reached the house she broke down and started to cry. Thank God. I think that was the first time I'd seen her cry since our trouble began. I cried a little too.

"Something had to be done. But she wouldn't see a doctor. And I was afraid that if I started to explain a few funny things, they wouldn't understand. All she needed was a baby, or something she could really put her mind to. That's how I came to think of a dog. Funny, isn't it, that it should have come to me sudden-like, that maybe what we needed was a dog. And you don't have to sign a lot of answers to get a dog either.

"But before I get to the dog I've got to tell you something else about those knitting needles. You see, one day I was putting some things on my bedroom table and, sure as Sunday, I stuck my finger on one of those damn needles. Guess I lost my temper and cursed a bit, too. Well, anyway, without thinking, I put them away in another drawer. What happens, but that evening Edie comes in the living room as usual and sits in a soft chair opposite me, crossing her legs. Then I hear some low crying. Poor Edie, she didn't want to disturb me. She was crying because she couldn't find her knitting needles. 'I'll get them,' I said. But I guess there was something in my voice that she kind of felt was asking her what my voice couldn't. She knew I wanted to ask why she always needed those needles. So, just as I'm leaving the room, she stops crying and says real kind and gentle-like, 'You see, I need them to pull out the stitches from my operation. It won't heal, dear, unless I pull out the stitches.' That's what Edie said, and I went and got the needles.

"Well, we got a dog. But not until after I had to hear a lot of complaining from Edie. She insisted that she wouldn't have a dog in the house and what a mess they are and how she was really afraid of them anyhow. Honest, it was wonderful to hear her put up a fight that way. She'd actually stick out her chest at me and say, 'Look here, there'll be no dog in my house.' She'd wave her finger, too, and get all flushed. God, it was just like the old Edie. 'No dog in my house, mister. It's either me or the dog, mister,' and I'd just smile at my old Edie and pick her right up in the air. She'd protest and kick her feet, and then lean her warm face against my shoulder. Gee, it was good. I used to feel like saying, 'Edie, why can't you be like this all the time?' But I didn't dare.

"You see, I knew that in a few minutes she'd be herself again, her hands hanging stiff and dead at her sides, her body the stem of some dry weed. God, it was the fingers I hated to see. Her long, wonderful fingers just hanging there, not saying anything.

"On certain days the color used to come back to Edie. Not often, mind you, but on one of those rare days she'd come alive again. Those were the days that tortured me. Let a person be dead or alive, I say, but not both. Well, on one of those days when she lost her waxiness, she came over to me—it was a Saturday afternoon—and said, 'Well, let's get going to look for a dog. Mind you, no females. I don't want a hundred puppies sprawled all over my house.'

"I remember putting on my new suit for the occasion. Sounds funny, doesn't it? But a man's got to wear his best suit sometime. Walking over to the bus that afternoon reminded me of the afternoons we used to go to the botanical gardens.

" 'Want some chocolates, Edie?' I asked, but she didn't answer.

"Well, there were some awfully cute cockers in two pet shops. But I had my heart set on something that grew up bigger. I wanted something real strong. I felt that that was more what Edie needed. There were also dachshunds, but, well, who wants anything so close to the floor, if you know what I mean. Anyway, I finally decided to take a look around at the dog pound. I didn't even know where to find the place, but we got there. Edie wouldn't go down the cellar with me to where they kept the dogs. The howls kind of scared her, I guess.

"What a noise they made by the time I reached the bottom of those steps! The keeper laughed and said they smelled my flesh.

"He walked around the place with me and I kept getting more disappointed every second. There were all kinds and shapes, but mostly females. They sure fussed over me . . . But I was ready to give up. There was only one cage left. 'Any males?' I asked. 'Yep,' the keeper answered. Lord, what a filthy lot they were. And they sure were hard to tell one from the other. But there was one thing I noticed. When I came up to the cage the whole lot, except one, ran towards me and yelped to beat the band. Standing apart from the others was this black and white animal. He looked pathetic. He seemed so out of place. Those two sad eyes attracted me beyond the whole wolf-pack. Yes, he had me caught and wouldn't let go. He wouldn't bark like the other dogs, either. Even the long tail remained absolutely motionless.

"Meanwhile the other animals tired of their positions against the fence. They left, not one by one, but all together. It was then that this black and white statue took a deep breath—I'm sure he must have taken a deep breath—and slowly walked over to the fence. He was an aristocrat for one moment longer and then he turned his profile against the wiring and with this one motion begged all the affection there remained in me to give. Yes, he was my dog—Boy.

"How is it, you ask, that we came to call him 'Boy'? Well, that's not a very long story. But first let me tell you something else. We tied a clothesline to an old leather collar around his neck, and so doing, the keeper patted him saying, 'You've got a thoroughbred English Pointer there. He's young and mighty strong too.' Could he have understood? At the word 'strong' his muscles tensed and he pulled us up the stairs after him. It scared me. I didn't know how I'd hold onto the rope. Out in the street I kept calling, 'who-a boy, easy fellow, easy boy,' and poor Edie, not knowing whether to be happy or sad, trailed behind me laughing. Yes, Edie seemed better already.

"How well I remember the first time I washed him—the way he pulled back every time I raised the soapy washcloth, and how he would crawl so reluctantly forward again, allow a moment's rubbing, then retreat again. He was wet and bedraggled. I pitied him; someone once washed me behind the ears too. I was all for giving up and decided it might be better to get out the grime and dirt at several sittings, but Edie was stubborn. 'That thing doesn't come in my house unless it's clean,' she said. 'Well, boy,' I said, looking down at his dripping whiskers, 'that means you get the works.'

"The way Edie stood over us I think she wanted his very soul purified.

"You should have seen him—all wrapped in a big bath towel. And when I took it off even Edie laughed at the way he'd shake himself like a rolling barrel. Those long ears flapped so fast for a minute I'd have sworn it was a propeller tuning up. Yes sir,

every motion, every quiver of his wet, black snoot, or his husky
fanny, was exciting.—What would he do next? When would
he bark? Can he bark? Will he sleep on the scatter-rug near the
stove? Is he happy? That first night we watched every movement, each reluctant tail-wag for some sign. Hungry as he must
have been, that first night, he was particular over his tin of liver,
chicken broth, and carrots. 'Carrots are good for you, boy,'
Edie pleaded, 'carrots are good for you. Make you grow big
and strong. Carrots are good for you.'

" 'Lord, Edie,' I joshed, 'how much bigger do you want him
to grow?' She just stared at me that peculiar way of hers and
turned back to the dog as if to say, 'Don't listen to him.' She
turned around and bent over him again saying, 'Eat your carrots, boy.'

"Well, at first we took him out all the time on a leash like
the dog book said to, but soon he seemed to like us pretty well,
so I'd take it off whenever we'd go to the small park near here.
He'd romp and gallop just like a horse and sometimes push his
black snoot right into the piles of leaves as he ran. Yes, for the
first time in a long while I was noticing the seasons. Autumn,
with all the red and dirty-gold leaves. Nope, I'm not afraid to
say I loved them with their crunch underfoot. They were pre-
serving something inside of me I thought was dead.

"I leaned against one of the thick, tall maples and threw a
stick over Boy's head and shouted, 'Get it, boy; get it, boy.'

"And when he came running back with the piece of wood—
so fast I thought he would surely crash into me—we both laughed.
Yep, that was the first time I saw Boy with the soft black flesh
of his under jaw pulled back into his mouth so's his big white
tooth stuck out on one side and made him look like a silly fool.

"Yes, we were both happy that day. And walking home with
him alongside me, both of us slushing through those leaves, I
thought how nice everything could be. Then I saw a sparrow,
oh, about thirty feet away, and all of a sudden I thought of
robins. I don't know why, but it really wasn't a sparrow I saw,
but a robin. So I picked up a small twig and ran toward it
threatening. Just like a damn fool, I threatened it and yelled

on top of my lungs to get the hell out of here you damn robin sticking out your breast for all the world to see it's spring. Only it wasn't spring and the sparrow flew away.

"I leashed Boy again, and he pulled me off toward home. Yes, I know I promised to tell about his name, only now it seems so unimportant. No, that's not really so. Out here in the cold those are the things that are important. The little things; just the unimportant little things. They're mostly all I remember anyway. The big things are so much harder to hold and touch.

"Well, as soon as we got him, Edie and I tried to think up names. First there was Storm, only he didn't seem too stormy. Then Edie thought she'd like Ernest, but I convinced her that it wouldn't do. Sometimes, though, I'd swear she whispers, 'Ernest.'

"Anyway, Prince, King, Sport, Spot, and Duke seemed much too ordinary. Once we thought of naming him after a Russian hero, but it was too long to shout in the street. So all the time we were thinking about a name to call him, we'd just say, 'Here, boy. Here, boy,' until he answered to Boy so well that we decided it would be easiest to leave it that way. I'm awfully glad it wasn't anything more high-falutin. After all, real kings don't have to be called King all the time, and as I think I said once before, Boy was a pure-blood aristocrat, though I'm not saying it mightn't have been pure street-chance that his folks met and married—and not because of breed but because of the air and the sunshine and the leaves.

"We had him just a little while when a warm Sunday comes around that made Edie think it was just the time to give him a real bath in the cellar tub. You should have seen us down there. Even Edie tried to coax him into the tub, but no go. I had my pockets filled with big biscuits to hold out in front of his nose when the going got tough. He was stubborn as hell. 'Look,' Edie kept saying as she splashed around with the water, 'it's good. Umm, it's so nice and warm and goody. Umm yum-yum.' But he'd slink again on his stomach. Then I'd yell at him and he'd whine short, high-pitched sounds and bounce the tip of his tail up and down against the dirty floor. Then he'd grin nervously for a second. He'd raise one paw from under his chin as if to push me away. 'Oh, you poor, fool dog,' I'd say and get real gentle with him. Then, when that didn't help, I'd try to pull him to the tub. But it didn't help either.

"And not only wouldn't the biscuits bring him any closer to the tub, but when I finally gave him one, he refused to touch it. He was that nerved up. Edie and I finally quarreled—she said I yelled at him too much—and she ran up to the apartment bawling.

"Well, he finally let me give him a sponge bath like I did the first night, and I've never asked him to get in a tub again.

"After I rubbed him dry—he tried to help me by licking the soap off his fur—I decided that he could romp around outside in the sun. I knew that there wouldn't be many more days like that one before the snow would come. He romped and jumped around and seemed to have forgotten all about the bath. And I stood watching him. I stood on the front lawn wich my shirt sleeves rolled up. My bare arms felt so good I wanted to take my shirt off and roll around on the dying grass, just like Boy. But the neighbors would see and think it strange. 'Go ahead, Boy,' I called, 'jump around and have a good time and get yourself dirty.' Our lawn is high above the street. Looking down at everyone walking by all dressed up for church, I felt happy and free.

"When Boy ran across the street toward a small dog, I paid no attention and went in the house, expecting him to come back when he was ready. I expected him to come back on his own accord, the way he'd been doing the day before. The sun was still bright and I knew that he was having a swell time. But at the end of an hour I became fidgety. I grabbed a jacket and walked in front of my house, to the corner, around the block, and all over the neighborhood, calling Boy. The sun started to drop and show its shape, and the air felt much cooler by the time I got back in front of the house. I called a few more times and knew, even if I really couldn't see them, that all the neighbors were listening to me call my dog, and were laughing and making fun of me.

"Well, he didn't come back that night or the next day either. We ran an ad in the paper and I just about gave up hope of ever seeing him again. For two days steady I went out in the street calling after him until I didn't even notice my voice anymore. Edie walked around the house without saying a word. She started carrying her needles around with her. She'd hardly drop them for more than a second, and when she did, they'd always be some place where she could see them. I couldn't go to work because every time I heard a dog bark I'd run out on the porch. The next day the ad ran again. About two that afternoon a neighbor's kid rang the bell and was all excited because he said he saw our dog down the street, heading toward the house.

"And sure enough, a minute later I saw Boy in front of the house, smelling at the steps. I couldn't even say, 'Here, Boy.' I just waited and there he came up the steps with his head low and his body looking like it was all ribs and shoulder blades. He got up to my feet, and without even barking, dropped on the porch exhausted. You should've seen Edie and me chase around for food. The poor thing was starved. I guess we could've killed him with all that food, we were so excited. I've got to hand it to Edie, she had better control than I. She kept singing all the time, while all I did was cry a little. Not much, but enough to know that Edie would be able to make fun of me about it some day.

"Can you blame me now for being cold? I'm so cold inside of me and wanting to be colder still. If only I could fall now on my knees and kiss the earth and hug it until she begged me to let go. I'm pulled together inside, all tight in the stomach, yet not tight enough.

"So we were a family. And we were both good to Boy, and he got to love us and we spoiled him and yelled at him and sometimes wouldn't let him sit on the good couch and then again sometimes would let him sit on the good couch. And I began to feel warm about Edie all over again. It was like having a mother in the house. Now that we had Boy there wasn't hardly ever much reason to go out. So we stayed home.

"I read the papers and Edie cooked and baked late at night for the fun of it. Sometimes she'd make fancy meat dishes for Boy and then again sometimes she'd insist on making apple pies to get him jealous because he couldn't eat any. It was a good happy life in its way, mostly because things were quieter, and Edie hardly ever got excited, and with Boy around, I could kind of forget what I wanted to forget. And after all, how much more can any man ask? As I said, I'm not a youngster, and having passed forty made me figure that maybe I had a rich happy life without even knowing it.

"By now Edie was sort of like any wife who's married a while, I guess. She had her duties and that was something for me to be thankful for. She gave me a clean house and good meals. And there was no use getting excited about how it would be if things had started different.

"But things were so nice, you know what I mean—after all that went on before—things were so nice that I just thought I'd be satisfied if they never changed, but ended up quietly with Edie, Boy, and me all moving or sitting in our own way. But I couldn't feel that way long. Even when I wanted things to stay the same I began to think how nice it would be if Boy was really our son. In the back of my head sometimes, while I read the evening paper and had my feet resting on the stool, I could hear Edie drop casual remarks to Boy about the weather, or the trouble with putting too much cinnamon in apple pie, and I could hear him follow her on the linoleum. And from the back of my head the sounds moved up closer, as if trying to touch behind my eyeballs, and made me drop the paper and dream of what it would be like to really have a son, to have really had that baby that was born dead. It was Edie's fault, I'd think, because every now and then she'd say how nice it would be if Boy were just a little bit more human. Or, maybe it wasn't her fault at all, but his, because as I said before—he wasn't like most dogs and did things with his paws, or the way he'd lie on his underside like the Egyptian sphinx and follow us with his eyes like some wise old man, that made me think that only one degree more would make this animal the thing we wanted. I had all

I could do to convince Edie that hunting dogs don't wear pretty sweaters.

"Then one night, just as I was sitting down for dinner, Edie said, 'You know, Boy can talk.' All I said was that it was nice, and thought to myself that I hope to hell she doesn't start telling me what he said. She didn't say anything more about it. Edie was a smart one. She just waited until I'd hear for myself.

"It happened the next morning, while I was putting on my rubbers. He walked over and kept jabbing at me with one paw as if trying to say something. This wasn't unusual. But when I pushed him away, so I could walk without tripping over him, he started to choke and make sounds as if he were trying to bring up phlegm. I got scared and tried to run for some water to give him when the sounds got loud and awful like an idiot-child trying to say something. I almost screamed, it came so sudden. Then he jumped up on me while I stood there, and still making those sounds, he pushed his face up toward mine, trying to kiss me.

"From that time on it only seemed like days before everything strange began to happen. Maybe it was weeks. First his tail didn't move the way it always used to. It just hung all the time, as if a rag were tied to his body. It got so I wished the damn thing would fall off the rest of his body. If I didn't hate blood so, maybe I'd have cut it off. Anyway I expected it to fall off by itself any second. Then—maybe it was months instead of weeks—all the hair began to fall off his ears. I used to love their silky smoothness. And there they were pink and bare like the skin of a rotted peach.

"I never let him out of the house any more. You see, I still loved him. But what did I really love? Was this thing, this creature of our desire, the result of two bodies? Was he now really half Edie and half me? He was changing every day closer to what I wanted and farther from what I loved.

"I'd let him out of the house only late at night when the streets were deserted. I'd have him on a strong leash. But really, which was the prisoner—Boy pulling the leather from a neck-collar, or me holding the empty end?

"Why did I still love him? Maybe it would have been better to let him roam the streets where all the neighbors could look and scream or laugh. Maybe I would have let that happen. But he was mine now. All mine and Edie's. And they would have taken him away. They wouldn't have understood, they wouldn't have fed and kept him. They would have only destroyed him. They would have no reason. Only I could be allowed to find a reason, because he belonged to me. And, hanging onto that leash, I felt strong and alive again.—Some men part their hair different when they reach forty, but I had nothing to fear, because now I owned as I never owned before. Now I could take him on long walks into the fields and touch the endless umbrellas and reach right through them, and stand straight and yell on the top of my voice and no one could hear. He would yell and I would yell and no one would hear, because we were alone and had our secret. No one ever saw his bare ears, his lifeless tail. I was careful.

"Yet I think I began to detest him. How could I pat his oily skin? But the eyes were still the same. Those pleading eyes refused to change. And Edie? Yes, you can picture Edie. She was on the floor playing with him night and day. 'He's just what I want,' she'd say. Once I came home and found him squirming around in diapers made of sterilized dish cloths. I wanted to kill her. Yet when I saw her standing in the kitchen doorway with lipstick and rouge on her face for the first time in years, all I did was walk up to her, kiss her warm, wrinkled brow and say, 'Good evening, Edie.'

"Well, one day, while I was home, he escaped. It was that fool Edie. She left a window open and somehow he crawled through it. I chased out after him. I was afraid they'd see him.

"I found Boy a few minutes later in the little park near the house. He was crying and it was a job to get him to go back with me. He made one of those awful sounds. He was trying so hard to speak to me. I turned around and asked him if he couldn't understand me, if he didn't know why I had to do this? He waited a moment, licked the palm of my hand, and followed alongside me.

"We walked slowly. I didn't care any more. Let people see. Let the whole world see. 'This is the son of Edie,' I called, 'this is the son of Edie.' But they passed by us. Not one stopped. 'See, he's mine. He's mine and Edie's. He's been living with us,' I shouted. 'Take him,' I begged, 'take him and love him. Love him and kill him.' But they wouldn't listen. They hardly looked at me. I pointed to Boy. I said, 'He's one of you now. He's human.' But no one seemed to notice him. They just looked at me and walked past us. Maybe it's because he wasn't anything they'd ever expect to see, so they just didn't see him. Or maybe they were too busy to see, so they just didn't see him. Or maybe they were too busy with themselves. I don't know. And I don't care anymore."

He shook his head slowly, looked up at the clouds, smiled, and raised his shovel once again. He put every ounce of strength into its downward thrust, and was carried with it over the hole. He leaned with his full weight against the handle, and finally, resting one knee on the ground, started to pry the shovel loose. He couldn't get it out. Then he just shrugged his shoulders, and sat on the ground with his feet hanging over the side of the hole. Suddenly I felt a kind of shaking under me. It was like sitting on a bowl of gelatin. The earth around the hole started to crumble. My companion leaned back for a second and smiled at the moon. Then he bent forward and looked into the hole as if expecting to catch his reflection. He grabbed a handful of the crumbling dirt, waved to me, and slid feet first into his hole.

I heard only the intimate whisper of a relaxed and grateful garden. The moon, still aloof and cool, glanced from behind its cloud and quickly took shelter behind another veil. Water started to flow from the hole. First just enough to be re-absorbed by the earth. But soon it poured forth in a delightful volume that swept away all before it. I was fascinated. It was working its way downward, right in front of me. I stood up. I could hear my own gastric juices blending with the spring. I remember standing on top of the stump so as not to get my feet wet, and

wondering where I could get a steak, or if I should follow this
new stream toward another adventure. Or whether I should run
to the next house and tell them that their neighbor just drowned.
I just stood there that way trying to figure out which course
to follow. It was so pleasant, with the water rushing by . . .

J. F. POWERS:

LIONS, HARTS, LEAPING DOES

THIRTY-NINTH pope. Anastasius, a Roman, appointed that while the Gospel was reading they should stand and not sit. He exempted from the ministry those that were lame, impotent, or diseased persons, and slept with his forefathers in peace, being a confessor.' "

"Anno?"

" 'Anno 404.' "

They sat there in the late afternoon, the two old men grown grey in the brown robes of the Order. Angular winter daylight forsook the small room, almost a cell in the primitive sense, and passed through the window into the outside world. The distant horizon, which it sought to join, was still bright and strong against approaching night. The old Franciscans, one priest, one brother, were left among the shadows in the room.

"Can you see to read one more, Titus?" the priest Didymus asked. "Number fourteen." He did not cease staring out the window at day becoming night on the horizon. The thirty-ninth pope said Titus might not be a priest. Did Titus, reading, understand? He could never really tell about Titus, who said nothing now. There was only silence, then a dry whispering of pages turning. "Number fourteen," Didymus said. "That's Zephyrinus. I always like the old heretic on that one, Titus."

According to one bibliographer, Bishop Bale's *Pageant of Popes Contayninge the Lyves of all the Bishops of Rome, from the Beginninge of them to the Year of Grace 1555*, was a denunciation of every pope from Peter to Paul IV. However inviting to readers that might sound, it was in sober fact a lie. The first popes, persecuted and mostly martyred, wholly escaped the author's remarkable spleen and even enjoyed his crusty approbation. Father Didymus, his aged appetite for biography jaded by the orthodox lives, found the work fascinating. He usually referred to it as "Bishop Bale's funny book" and to the Bishop as a heretic.

Titus squinted at the yellowed page. He snapped a glance at the light hovering at the window. Then he closed his eyes and with great feeling recited:

" 'O how joyous and how delectable is it to see religious men devout and fervent in the love of God, well mannered—' "

"Titus," Didymus interrupted softly.

" '—and well taught in ghostly learning.' "

"Titus, read." Didymus placed the words in their context. The First Book of *The Imitation* and Chapter, if he was not mistaken, XXV. The trick was no longer in finding the source of Titus's quotations; it was putting them in their exact context. It had become an unconfessed contest between them, and it gratified Didymus to think he had been able to place the fragment. Titus knew two books by heart, *The Imitation* and *The Little Flowers of St. Francis*. Lately, unfortunately, he had begun to learn another. He was more and more quoting from Bishop Bale. Didymus reminded himself he must not let Titus read past the point where the martyred popes left off. What Bale had to say about Peter's late successors sounded incongruous—"unmete" in the old heretic's own phrase—coming from a Franciscan brother. Two fathers had already inquired of Didymus concerning Titus. One had noted the antique style of his words and had ventured to wonder if Brother Titus, Christ preserve us, might be slightly possessed. He cited the case of the illiterate Missouri farmer who cursed the Church in a forgotten Aramaic tongue.

"Read, Titus."

Titus squinted at the page once more and read in his fine dead voice.

" 'Fourteenth pope, Zephyrinus. Zephyrinus was a Roman born, a man as writers do testify, more addicted with all endeavor to the service of God than to the cure of any worldly affairs.

Whereas before his time the wine in the celebrating the communion was ministered in a cup of wood, he first did alter that, and instead thereof brought in cups or chalices of glass. And yet he did not this upon any superstition, as thinking wood to be unlawful, or glass to be more holy for that use, but because the one is more comely and seemly, as by experience it appeareth than the other. And yet some wooden dolts do dream that the wooden cups were changed by him because that part of the wine, or as they thought, the royal blood of Christ, did soak into the wood, and so it cannot be in glass. Surely sooner may wine soak into any wood than any wit into those winey heads that thus both deceive themselves and slander this Godly martyr.' "

"Anno?"

Titus squinted at the page again. " 'Anno 222,' " he read.

They were quiet for a moment which ended with the clock in the tower booming once for the half-hour. Didymus got up and stood so close to the window his breath became visible. Noticing it, he inhaled deeply and then, exhaling, he sent a gust of smoke churning against the freezing pane, clouding it. Some old unmelted snow in tree crotches lay dirty and white in the gathering dark.

"It's cold out today," Didymus said.

He stepped away from the window and over to Titus, whose face was relaxed in openeyed sleep. He took Bishop Bale's funny book unnoticed from Titus's hands.

"Thank you, Titus," he said.

Titus blinked his eyes slowly once, then several times quickly. His body gave a shudder, as if coming to life.

"Yes, Father?" he was asking.

"I said thanks for reading. You are a great friend to me."

"Yes, Father."

"I know you'd rather read other authors." Didymus moved to the window, stood there gazing through the tops of trees, their limbs black and bleak against the sky. He rubbed his hands. "I'm going for a walk before vespers. Is it too cold for you, Titus?"

" 'A good religious man that is fervent in his religion taketh all things well, and doth gladly all that he is commanded to do.' "

Didymus, walking across the room, stopped and looked at Titus just in time to see him open his eyes. He was quoting again: *The Imitation* and still in Chapter XXV. Why had he said that? To himself Didymus repeated the words and decided Titus, his mind moving intelligently but so pathetically largo, was documenting the act of reading Bishop Bale when there were other books he preferred.

"I'm going out for a walk," Didymus said.

Titus rose and pulled down the full sleeves of his brown robe in anticipation of the cold.

"I think it is too cold for you, Titus," Didymus said.

Titus faced him undaunted, arms folded and hands muffled in his sleeves, eyes twinkling incredulously. He was ready to go. Didymus got the idea Titus knew himself to be the healthier of the two. Didymus was vaguely annoyed at this manifestation of the truth. *Vanitas.*

"Won't they need you in the kitchen now?" he inquired.

Immediately he regretted having said that. And the way he had said it, with some malice, as though labour *per se* were important and the intention not so. *Vanitas* in a friar, and at his age too. Confronting Titus with a distinction his simple mind could never master and which, if it could, his great soul would never recognize. Titus only knew all that was necessary, that a friar did what he was best at in the community. And no matter the nature of his toil, the variety of the means at hand, the end was the same for all friars. Or indeed for all men, if they cared to know. Titus worked in the kitchen and garden. Was Didymus wrong in teaching geometry out of personal preference and perhaps—if this was so he was—out of pride? Had the spiritual worth of his labor been vitiated because of that? He did not think so, no. No, he taught geometry because it was useful and eternally true, like his theology, and though of a lower order of truth it escaped the common fate of theology and the humanities, perverted through the ages in the mouths of dunderheads and fools. From that point of view, his work came to the same thing as Titus's. The vineyard was everywhere, they were in it, and that was essential.

Didymus, consciously humble, held open the door for Titus. Sandals scraping familiarly, they passed through dark corridors until they came to the stairway. Lights from floors above and below spangled through the carven apertures of the winding stair and fell in confusion upon the worn oaken steps.

At the outside door they were ambushed. An old friar stepped out of the shadows to intercept them. Standing with Didymus and Titus, however, made him appear younger. Or possibly it was the tenseness of him.

"Good evening, Father," he said to Didymus. "And Titus."

Didymus nodded in salutation and Titus said deliberately, as though he were the first one ever to put words in such conjunction:

"Good evening, Father Rector."

The Rector watched Didymus expectantly. Didymus studied the man's face. It told him nothing but curiosity—a luxury which could verge on vice in the cloister. Didymus frowned his incomprehension. He was about to speak. He decided against it, turning to Titus:

"Come on, Titus, we've got a walk to take before vespers."

The Rector was left standing.

They began to circle the monastery grounds. Away from the buildings it was brighter. With a sudden shudder, Didymus felt the freezing air bite into his body all over. Instinctively he drew up his cowl. That was a little better. Not much. It was too cold for him to relax, breathe deeply and stride freely. It had not looked this cold from his window. He fell into Titus's gait. The steps were longer, but there was an illusion of warmth about moving in unison. Bit by bit he found himself duplicating every aspect of Titus in motion. Heads down, eyes just ahead of the next step, undeviating, they seemed peripatetic figures in a Gothic frieze. The stones of the walk were trampled over with frozen footsteps. Titus's feet were grey and bare in their open sandals. Pieces of ice, the thin edges of ruts, cracked off under foot, skittering sharply away. A crystal fragment lit between

Titus's toes and did not melt there. He did not seem to notice it. This made Didymus lift his eyes.

A fine Franciscan! Didymus snorted, causing a flurry of vapors. He had the despicable caution of the comfortable who move mountains, if need be, to stay that way. Here he was, cowl up and heavy woollen socks on, and regretting the weather because it exceeded his anticipations. Painfully he stubbed his toe on purpose and at once accused himself of exhibitionism. Then he damned the expression for its modernity. He asked himself: wherein lay the renunciation of the world, the flesh and the devil, the whole point of following after St. Francis today? Poverty, Chastity, Obedience, the three vows. There was nothing of suffering in the poverty of the friar nowadays: he was penniless, but materially rich compared to—what was the phrase he used to hear?—"one third of the nation." A beggar, a homeless mendicant by very definition, he knew nothing—except as it affected others "less fortunate"—of the miseries of begging in the streets. Verily, it was no heavy cross, this vow of Poverty, so construed and practiced, in the modern world. Begging had become unfashionable. Somewhere along the line the meaning had been lost, they had become too "fortunate." Official agencies, to whom it was a nasty but necessary business, dispensed Charity without mercy or grace. He recalled with wry amusement Frederick Barbarossa's appeal to fellow princes when opposed by the might of the medieval Church: "We have a clean conscience, and it tells us that God is with us. Ever have we striven to bring back priests and, in especial, those of the topmost rank, to the condition of the first Christian Church. In those days the clergy raised their eyes to the angels, shone through miracles, made whole the sick, raised the dead, made Kings and Princes subject to them, not with arms but with their holiness. But now they are smothered in delights. To withdraw from them the harmful riches which burden them to their own undoing is a labor of love in which all Princes should eagerly participate."

And Chastity, what of that? Well, that was all over for him —a battle he had fought and won many years ago. A sin whose temptations had prevailed undiminished through the centuries, but withal for him, an old man, a dead issue, a young man's trial. Only Obedience remained, and that too was no longer difficult for him. There was something—much as he disliked the term—to be said for "conditioning." He had to smile at himself: why should he bristle so at using the word? It was only contemporary slang for a theory the Church had always known. "Psychiatry," so called, and all the ghastly superstition that attended its practice, the deification of its high priests in the secular schools, made him ill. But it would pass. Just look how alchemy had flourished, and where was it today?

Clearly an abecedarian observance of the vows did not promise perfection. Stemmed in divine wisdom, they were branches meant to flower forth, but requiring of the friar the water and sunlight of sacrifice. The letter led nowhere. It was the spirit of the vows which opened the way and revealed to the soul, no matter the flux of circumstance, the means of salvation.

He had picked his way through the welter of familiar factors again—again to the same conclusion. The last time when he received the letter from Seraphin asking him to come to St. Louis, saying his years prohibited unnecessary travel and endowed his request with a certain prerogative, No, he had written back, it's simply impossible—not saying why. God help him, as a natural man, he had an inordinate desire to see his brother again. One of them must die soon. But as a friar, he remembered from Titus: "Unless a man be clearly delivered from the love of all creatures, he may not fully tend to his creator." Therein, the keeping of the vows having become an easy habit for him, was his opportunity. It was plain and there was sacrifice and it was hard. And he had not gone.

The flesh just above his knees felt frozen. They were drawing near the entrance again. His face too felt the same way, like a slab of pasteboard, stiffest at the tip of his nose. When he wrinkled his brow and puffed out his cheeks to blow hot air up to his nose, his skin seemed to crackle like old parchment. His eyes watered from the wind. He pressed a hand, warm from his sleeve, to his exposed neck. Frozen, like his face. It would be chapped tomorrow.

Titus, white hair awry in the wind, looked just the same.

They entered the monastery door. The Rector stopped them. It was almost as before, except that Didymus was occupied with feeling his face and patting it back to life.

"Ah, Didymus! It must be cold indeed!" The Rector smiled at Titus and returned his gaze to Didymus. He made it appear that they were allied in being amused at Didymus' face. Didymus touched his nose tenderly. Assured it would stand the operation, he blew it lustily. He stuffed the handkerchief up his sleeve. The Rector, misinterpreting all this ceremony, obviously was afraid of being ignored.

"The telegram, Didymus. I'm sorry, I thought it might have been important."

"I received no telegram."

They faced each other, waiting, experiencing a hanging moment of uneasiness.

Then, having employed the deductive method, they both looked at Titus. Although he had not been listening, rather had been studying the naked toes in his sandals, he sensed their eyes questioning him.

"Yes, Father Rector?" he answered.

"The telegram for Father Didymus, Titus?" the Rector demanded. "Where is it?" Titus started momentarily out of willingness to be of service, but ended, his mind refusing to click, impassive before them. The Rector shook his head in faint exasperation and reached his hand down into the folds of Titus's cowl. He brought forth two envelopes. One, the telegram, he gave to Didymus. The other, a letter, he handed back to Titus.

"I gave you this letter this morning, Titus. It's for Father Anthony." Intently Titus stared unremembering at the letter. "I wish you would see that Father Anthony gets it right away, Titus. I think it's a bill."

Titus held the envelope tightly to his breast and said: "Father Anthony."

Then his eyes were attracted by the sound of Didymus tearing open the telegram. While Didymus read the telegram, Titus's expression showed he at last understood his failure to deliver it.

He was perturbed, mounting inner distress moving his lips silently.

Didymus looked up from the telegram. He saw the grief in Titus's face and said, astonished, "How did you know, Titus?"

Titus's eyes were both fixed and lowered in sorrow. It seemed to Didymus that Titus knew the meaning of the telegram. Didymus was suddenly weak, as before a miracle. His eyes went to the Rector to see how he was taking it. Then it occurred to him the Rector could not know what had happened.

As though nothing much had, the Rector laid an absolving hand lightly upon Titus's shoulder.

"He can't forgive himself for not delivering the telegram now that he remembers it. That's all."

Didymus was relieved. Seeing the telegram in his hand, he folded it quickly and stuffed it back in the envelope. He handed it to the Rector. Calmly, in a voice quite drained of feeling, he said, "My brother, Father Seraphin, died last night in St. Louis."

"Father Seraphin *from Rome?*"

"Yes," Didymus said, "in St. Louis. He was my brother. Appointed a confessor in Rome, a privilege for a foreigner. He was ninety-two."

"I know that, Didymus, an honor for the Order. I had no idea he was in this country. Ninety-two! God rest his soul!"

"I had a letter from him only recently."

"You did?"

"He wanted me to come to St. Louis. I hadn't seen him for twenty-five years at least."

"Twenty-five years?"

"It was impossible for me to visit him."

"But if he was in this country, Didymus . . ."

The Rector waited for Didymus to explain.

Didymus opened his mouth to speak, heard the clock in the tower sound the quarter-hour, and said nothing, listening, lips parted, to the last of the three strokes die away.

"Why, Didymus, it could easily have been arranged," the Rector persisted.

Didymus turned abruptly to Titus, who, standing in a dream, had been inattentive since the clock struck.

"Come, Titus, we'll be late."

He hastened down the corridor with Titus. "No," he said in agitation, causing Titus to look at him in surprise. "I told him No. It was simply impossible." He was conscious of Titus's attention. "To visit him, Seraphin, who is dead." That had come naturally enough for being the first time in his thoughts that Seraphin was dead. Was there not some merit in his dispassionate acceptance of the fact?

They entered the chapel for vespers and knelt down.

II

The clock struck. One, two . . . two. Two? No, there must have been one or two strokes before. He had gone to sleep. It was three. At least three, probably four. Or five. He waited. It could not be two: he remembered the brothers filing darkly into the chapel at that hour. Disturbing the shadows for matins and lauds. If it was five—he listened for faint noises in the building —it would only be a few minutes. They would come in, the earliest birds, to say their Masses. There were no noises. He looked toward the window on the St. Joseph side of the chapel. He might be able to see a light from a room across the court. That was not certain even if it was five. It would have to come through the stained glass. Was that possible? It was still night. Was there a moon? He looked round the chapel. If there was, it might shine on a window. There was no moon. Or it was overhead. Or powerless against the glass. He yawned. It could not be five. His knees were numb from kneeling. He shifted on them. His back ached. Straightening it, he gasped for breath. He saw the sanctuary light. The only light, red. Then it came back to him. Seraphin was dead. He tried to pray. No words. Why words? Meditation in the Presence. The perfect prayer. He fell asleep . . .

. . . Spiraling brown coil on coil under the golden sun the river slithered across the blue and flowerflecked land. On an eminence they held identical hands over their eyes for visors and mistook it with pleasure for an endless murmuring serpent.

They considered unafraid the prospect of its turning in its course and standing on tail to swallow them gurgling alive. They sensed it was in them to command this also by a wish. Their visor hands vanished before their eyes and became instead the symbol of brotherhood clasped between them. This they wished. Smiling the same smile back and forth they began laughing: "Jonah!" And were walking murkily up and down the brown belly of the river in mock distress. Above them, foolishly triumphant, rippling in contentment, mewed the waves. Below swam an occasional large fish, absorbed in ignoring them, and the mass of crustacea, eagerly seething, too numerous on the bottom to pretend exclusiveness. "Jonah indeed!" the brothers said, surprised to see the bubbles they birthed. They strolled then for hours this way. The novelty wearing off (without regret, else they would have wished themselves elsewhere), they began to talk and say ordinary things. Their mother had died, their father too, and how old did that make them? It was the afternoon of the funerals, which they had managed, transcending time, to have held jointly. She had seemed older and for some reason he otherwise. How, they wondered, should it be with them, *memento mori* clicking simultaneously within them, lackaday. The sound of dirt descending six feet to clatter on the coffins was memorable but unmentionable. Their own lives, well . . . only half curious (something to do) they halted to kick testingly a waterlogged rowboat resting on the bottom, the crustacea complaining and olive green silt rising to speckle the surface with dark stars . . . well, what *had* they been doing? A crayfish pursued them, clad in sable armor, dearly desiring to do battle, brandishing hinged swords. Well, for one thing working for the canonization of Fra Bartolomeo, had got two cardinals interested, was hot after those remaining who were at all possible, a slow business. Yes, one would judge so in the light of past canonizations, though being stationed in Rome had its advantages. Me, the same old grind, teaching, pounding away, giving Pythagoras no rest in his grave . . . They made an irresolute pass at the crayfish, who had caught up with them. More about Fra Bartolomeo, what

else is there? Except, you will laugh or have me excommunicated
for wanton presumption, though it's only faith in a faithless age,
making a vow not to die until he's made a saint, recognized
rather—he is one, convinced of it, Didymus (never can get used
to calling you that) a saint sure as I'm alive, having known him,
no doubt of it, something wrong with your knee? Knees then!
The crayfish, he's got hold of you there, another at your back.
If you like, we'll leave, only I do like it here. Well, go ahead
then, you never did like St. Louis, isn't that what you used to
say? Alone, in pain, he rose to the surface, parting the silt stars.
The sun like molten gold squirted him in the eyes. Numb now,
unable to remember and too blind to refurnish his memory by
observation, he waited for this limbo to clear away . . .

Awake now, he was face to face with a flame, blinding him.
He avoided it. A dead weight bore him down, his aching back.
Slowly, like ink in a blotter, his consciousness spread. The supports beneath him were kneeling limbs, his, the veined hands,
bracing him, pressing flat, his own. His body, it seemed, left off
there; the rest was something else, floor. He raised his head to
the flame again and tried to determine what kept it suspended
even with his face. He shook his head, blinking dumbly, a four-
legged beast. He could see nothing, only his knees and hands,
which he felt rather, and the flame floating unaccountably in the
darkness. That part alone was a mystery. And then there came
a pressure and pull on his shoulders, urging him up. Fingers, a
hand, a rustling related to its action, then the rustling in rhythm
with the folds of a brown curtain, a robe naturally, ergo a friar,
holding a candle, trying to raise him up, Titus. The clock began
striking.

"Put out the candle," Didymus said.

Titus closed his palm slowly around the flame, unflinching,
snuffing it. The odor of burning string. Titus pinched the wick
deliberately. He waited a moment, the clock falling silent, and
said, "Father Rector expects you will say a Mass for the Dead
at five o'clock."

"Yes, I know." He yawned deliciously. "I told him *that*." He
bit his lips at the memory of the disgusting yawn. Titus had

found him asleep. Shame overwhelmed him, and he searched his mind for justification. He found none.

"It is five now," Titus said.

It was maddening. "I don't see anyone else if it's five," he snapped. Immediately he was aware of a light burning in the sacristy. He blushed and grew pale. Had someone besides Titus seen him sleeping? But, listening, he heard nothing. No one else was up yet. He was no longer pale and was only blushing now. He saw it all hopefully. He was saved. Titus had gone to the sacristy to prepare for Mass. He must have come out to light the candles on the main altar. Then he had seen the bereaved keeping vigil on all fours, asleep, snoring even. What did Titus think of that? It withered him to remember, but he was comforted some that the only witness had been Titus. Had the sleeping apostles in Gethsemane been glad it was Christ?

Wrong! Hopelessly wrong! For there had come a noise after all. Someone else was in the sacristy. He stiffened and walked palely toward it. He must go there and get ready to say his Mass. A few steps he took only, his back buckling out, humping, his knees sinking to the floor, his hands last. The floor with fingers smelling of dust and genesis reached up and held him. The fingers were really spikes and they were dusty from holding him this way all his life. For a radiant instant which had something of eternity about it, he saw the justice of his position. Then there was nothing.

III

A little snow had fallen in the night, enough to powder the dead grass and soften the impression the leafless trees etched in the sky. Greyly the sky promised more snow, but now, at the end of the day following his collapse in the chapel, it was melting. Didymus, bundled around by blankets, sat in a wheelchair at the window, unsleepy. Only the landscape wearied him. Dead and unmoving though it must be, of that he was sure, it conspired to make him see everything in it as living, moving, something to be watched, each visible tuft of grass, each cluster of snow. The influence of the snow perhaps? For the ground, ordinarily uniform in texture and drabness, had split up into individual patches. They appeared to be involved in a struggle of some kind, possibly to overlap each other, constantly shifting. But whether it was equally one against one, or one against all, he could not make out. He reminded himself he did not believe it was actually happening. It was confusing and he closed his eyes. After a time this confused and tired him in the same way. The background of darkness became a field of varicolored factions, warring, and, worse than the landscape, things like worms and comets wriggled and exploded before his closed eyes. Finally, as though to orchestrate their motions, they carried with them a bewildering noise or music which grew louder and cacophonous. The effect was cumulative, inevitably unbearable, and Didymus would have to open his eyes again. The intervals of peace became gradually rarer on the landscape. Likewise when he shut his eyes to it the restful darkness dissolved sooner than before into riot.

The door of his room opened, mercifully dispelling his illusions, and that, because no knock, could only be Titus. Unable to move in his chair, Didymus listened to Titus moving about the room at his back. The tinkle of a glass once, the squeak of the bookcase indicating a book taken out or replaced, they were sounds Didymus could recognize. But that first tap-tap and the consequent click of metal on metal, irregular and scarcely audible, was disconcertingly unfamiliar. His curiosity, centering on it, raised it to a delicious mystery. He kept down the urge to shout at Titus. But he attempted to fish from memory the precise character of the corner from which the sound came with harrowing repetition. The sound stopped then, as though to thwart him on the brink of revelation. Titus's footsteps scraped across the room. The door opened and closed. For a few steps, Didymus heard Titus going down the corridor. He asked himself not to be moved by idle curiosity, a thing of the senses. He would not be tempted now.

A moment later the keystone of his good intention crumbled, and the whole edifice of his detachment with it. More shakily than quickly, Didymus moved his hands to the wheels of the chair. He would roll over to the corner and investigate the sound. He would? His hands lay limply on the wheels, ready to propel him to his mind's destination, but weak, white, powerless to grip the wheels or anything. He regarded them with contempt. He had known they would fail him; he had been foolish to give them another chance. Disdainful of his hands, he looked out the window. He could still do that, couldn't he? It was raining some now. The landscape started to move, rearing and reeling crazily, as though drunken with the rain. In horror, Didymus damned his eyes. He realized this trouble was probably going to be chronic. He turned his gaze in despair to the trees, to the branches level with his eyes and nearer than the insane ground. Hesitating warily, fearful the gentle boughs under scrutiny would turn into hideous waving tentacles, he looked. With a thrill, he knew he was seeing clearly.

Gauzily rain descended in a fine spray, hanging in fat berries from the wet black branches where leaves had been and buds would be, cold crystal drops. They fell now and then ripely of their own weight, or shaken by the intermittent wind they spilled before their time. Promptly they appeared again, pendulous.

Watching the raindrops prove gravity, he was grateful for nature's, rather than his, return to reason. Still, though he professed faith in his faculties, he would not look away from the trees and down at the ground, nor close his eyes. Gratefully he savored the cosmic truth in the falling drops and the mildly trembling branches. There was order, he thought, which in justice and science ought to include the treacherous landscape. Risking all, he ventured a glance at the ground. All was still there. He smiled. He was going to close his eyes (to make it universal and conclusive), when the door opened again.

Didymus strained to catch the meaning of Titus's movements. Would the clicking sound begin? Titus did go to that corner of the room again. Then it came, louder than before, but only once this time.

Titus came behind his chair, turned it, and wheeled him over to the corner.

On a hook which Titus had screwed into the wall hung a bird cage covered with black cloth.

"What's all this?" Didymus said.

Titus tapped the covered cage expectantly.

A bird chirped once.

"The bird," Titus explained in excitement, "is inside."

Didymus almost laughed. He sensed in time, however, the necessity of seeming befuddled and severe. Titus expected it.

"I don't believe it," Didymus snapped.

Titus smiled wisely and tapped the cage again.

"There!" he exclaimed when the bird chirped.

Didymus shook his head in mock anger. "You made that beastly noise, Titus, you mountebank!"

Titus, profoundly amused by such scepticism, removed the black cover.

The bird, a canary, flicked its head sidewise in interest, looking them up and down. Then it turned its darting attention to the room. It chirped once in curt acceptance of the new surroundings. Didymus and Titus came under its black dot of an eye once more, this time for closer analysis. The canary chirped twice, perhaps that they were welcome, even pleasing, and stood on one leg to show them what a gay bird it was. It then returned to the business of pecking a piece of apple.

"I see you've given him something to eat," Didymus said, and felt that Titus, though he seemed content to watch the canary, waited for him to say something more. "I am very happy, Titus, to have this canary," he went on. "I suppose he will come in handy now that I must spend my days in this infernal chair."

Titus did not look at him while he said, "He is a good bird, Father. He is one of the Saint's own good birds."

Through the window Didymus watched the days and nights come and go. For the first time, though his life as a friar had been copiously annotated with significant references, he got a good idea of eternity. Monotony, of course, was one word for it, but like all the others, as well as the allegories worked up by the imaginative retreat masters, it was empty beside the experience itself, untranslatable. He would doze and wonder if by some quirk he had been cast out of the world into eternity, but since it was neither heaven nor exactly purgatory or hell, as he understood them, he concluded it must be an uncharted isle subscribing to the mother forms only in the matter of time. And having thought this, he was faintly annoyed at his ponderous whimsy. Titus, like certain of the hours, came periodically. He would read or simply sit with him in silence. The canary was there always, but except as it showed signs of sleepiness at twilight and spirit at dawn, Didymus regarded it as a subtle device, like the days and nights and bells, to give the lie to the vulgar error that time flies. The cage was small and the canary would not sing. Time, hanging in the room like a jealous fog, possessed him and voided everything except it. It seemed impossible each time Titus came that he should be able to escape the room.

" 'After him,' " Titus read from Bishop Bale one day, " 'came Fabius, a Roman born, who (as Eusebius witnesseth) as he was returning home out of the field, and with his countrymen present to elect a new bishop, there was a pigeon seen standing on his head and suddenly he was created pastor of the Church, which he looked not for.' "

They smiled at having the same thought and both looked up at the canary. Since Didymus sat by the window most of the day now, he had asked Titus to put a hook there for the cage. He had to admit to himself he did this to let Titus know he appreciated the canary. Also, as a secondary motive, he reasoned, it enabled the canary to look out the window. What a little yellow bird could see to interest it in the frozen scene was a mystery, but that, Didymus sighed, was a two-edged sword. And he took to watching the canary more.

So far as he was able to detect the moods of the canary he participated in them. In the morning the canary, bright and clownish, flitted back and forth between the two perches in the cage, hanging from the sides and cocking its little tufted head at Didymus querulously. During these acrobatics Didymus would twitch his hands in quick imitation of the canary's stunts. He asked Titus to construct a tiny swing, such as he had seen, which the canary might learn to use, since it appeared to be an intelligent and daring sort. Titus got the swing, the canary did master it, but there seemed to be nothing Didymus could do with his hands that was like swinging. In fact, after watching a while it was as though the canary were fixed to a pendulum, inanimate, a piece of machinery, a yellow blur—ticking, for the swing made a little sound, and Didymus went to sleep and often when he woke the canary was still going, like a clock. Didymus had no idea how long he slept at these times, maybe a minute, maybe hours. Gradually the canary got bored with the swing and used it less and less. In the same way, Didymus suspected, he himself had wearied of looking out the window. The first meagre satisfaction had worn off. The dead trees, the sleeping snow, like the swing for the canary, were sources of diversion which soon grew stale. They were captives, he and the canary, and the only thing they craved was escape. Didymus slowly considered the problem. There was nothing, obviously, for him to do. He could pray, which he did, but he was not sure the only thing wrong with him was the fact he could not walk and that to devote his prayer to that end was justifiable. Inevitably it occurred to him his plight might well be an act of God. Why this punishment, though, he asked himself, and immediately supplied the answer. He had, for one thing, gloried too much in having it in him to turn down Seraphin's request to come to St. Louis. The intention, that was all important, and he, he feared, had done the right thing for the wrong reason. He had noticed something of the fakir in himself before. But it was not clear if he had erred. There was a certain consolation, at bottom dismal, in this doubt. It was true there appeared to be a nice justice in being stricken a cripple if he had been wrong in refusing to travel to see Seraphin, if human love was all he was fitted for, if he was incapable of renunciation for the right reason, if the mystic counsels were too strong for him, if he was still too pedestrian after all these years of prayer and contemplation, if—

The canary was swinging, the first time in several days.

The reality of his position was insupportable. There were two ways of regarding it and he could not make up his mind. Humbly, he wished to get well and to be able to walk. But if this was a punishment, was not prayer to lift it declining to see the divine point? He did wish to get well; that would settle it. Otherwise his predicament could only be resolved through means more serious than he dared cope with. It would be like refusing to see Seraphin all over again. By some mistake, he protested he had at last been placed in a position vital with meaning and precedents inescapably Christian. But was he the man for it? Unsure of himself, he was afraid to go on trial. It would be no minor trial, so construed, but one in which the greatest values were involved, a human soul and the means of its salvation or damnation. Not watered down suburban precautions and routine pious exercises, but Faith such as saints and martyrs had, and Despair such as only they had been tempted by. No, he was not the man for it. He was unworthy. He simply desired to walk and in a few years to die a normal uninspired death. He did not wish to see (what was apparent) the greatest significance in his affliction. He preferred to think in terms of physical betterment. He was so sure he was not a saint that he did not consider this easier road beneath him, though attracted by the higher one. That was the rub. Humbly, then, he wanted to be able to walk, but he wondered if there was not presumption in such humility.

Thus he decided to pray for health and count the divine hand not there. Decided. A clean decision—not distinction—no mean feat in the light of all the moral theology he had swallowed. The canary, all its rocking come to naught once more, slept motionless in the swing. Despite the manifest prudence of the course he had settled upon, Didymus dozed off ill at ease in his wheelchair by the window. Distastefully, the last thing he remembered was that "prudence" is a virtue more celebrated in the modern Church.

At his request in the days following a doctor visited him. The Rector came along too. When Didymus tried to find out the nature of his illness, the doctor looked solemn and pronounced it to be one of those things. Didymus received this with a look of mystification. So the doctor went on to say there was no telling about it. Time alone would tell. Didymus asked the doctor to recommend some books dealing with cases like his. They might have one of them in the monastery library. Titus could read to him in the meantime. For, though he disliked being troublesome, "one of those things" as a diagnosis meant very little to an unscientific beggar like him. The phrase had a philosophic ring to it, but to his knowledge neither the Early Fathers nor the Scholastics seemed to have dealt with it. The Rector smiled. The doctor, annoyed, replied drily:

"Is that a fact?"

Impatiently Didymus said, "I know how old I am, if that's it."

Nothing was lost of the communion he kept with the canary. He still watched its antics and his fingers in his lap followed them clumsily. He did not forget about himself, that he must pray for health, that it was best that way—"prudence" dictated it—but he did think more of the canary's share of their captivity. A canary in a cage, he reasoned, is like a bud which never blooms.

He asked Titus to get a book on canaries, but nothing came of it and he did not mention it again.

Some days later Titus read:

" 'Twenty-ninth pope, Marcellus, a Roman, was pastor of the Church, feeding it with wisdom and doctrine. And (as I may say with the Prophet) a man according to God's heart and full of Christian works. This man admonished Maximianus the Emperor and endeavored to remove him from persecuting the saints—' "

"Stop a moment, Titus," Didymus interrupted.

Steadily since Titus began to read the canary had been jumping from the swing to the bottom of the cage. Now it was quietly standing on one foot in the swing. Suddenly it flew at the side of the cage nearest them and hung there, its ugly little claws, like bent wire, hooked to the slender bars. It observed them intently, first Titus and then Didymus, at whom it continued to stare. Didymus' hands were tense in his lap.

"Go ahead, read," Didymus said, relaxing his hands.

" 'But the Emperor being more hardened, commanded Marcellus to be beaten with cudgels and to be driven out of the city, wherefore he entered into the house of one Lucina, a widow, and there kept the congregation secretly, which the tyrant hearing, made a stable for cattle of the same house and committed the keeping of it to the bishop Marcellus. After that he governed the Church by writing Epistles, without any other kind of teaching, being condemned to such a vile service. And being thus daily tormented with strife and noisomeness, at length gave up the ghost. Anno 308.' "

"Very good, Titus. I wonder how we missed that one before."

The canary, still hanging on the side of the cage, had not moved, its head turned sidewise, its eye as before fixed on Didymus.

"Would you bring me a glass of water, Titus?"

Titus got up and looked in the cage. The canary hung there, as though waiting, not a feather stirring.

"The bird has water here," Titus said, pointing to the small cup fastened to the cage.

"For me, Titus, the water's for me. Don't you think I know you look after the canary? You don't forget us, though I don't see why you don't."

Titus left the room with a glass.

Didymus' hands were tense again. Eyes on the canary's eye, he got up from his wheelchair, his face strained and white with the impossible effort, and, his fingers somehow managing it, he opened the cage. The canary darted out and circled the room chirping. Before it lit, though it seemed about to make its perch triumphantly the top of the cage, Didymus fell over on his face and lay prone on the floor.

In bed that night, unsuffering and barely alive, he saw at will everything revealed in his past. Events long forgotten happened again before his eyes. Clearly, sensitively, he saw Seraphin and himself, just as they had always been—himself, never quite sure. He heard all that he had ever said, and that anyone had said to him. He had talked too much too. The past mingled with the present. In the same moment and scene he made his first Communion, was ordained, and confessed his sins for the last time.

The canary perched in the dark atop the cage, head warm under wing, already, it seemed to Didymus, without memory of its captivity, dreaming of a former freedom, an ancestral summer day with flowers and trees. Outside it was snowing.

The Rector, followed by others, came into the room and administered the last sacrament. Didymus heard them all gathered prayerfully around his bed thinking (they thought) secretly: this sacrament often strengthens the dying, tip-of-the-tongue wisdom indigenous to the priesthood, Henry the Eighth had six wives. He saw the same hackneyed smile, designed to cheer, pass bravely among them, and marvelled at the crudity of it. They went away then, all except Titus, their individual footsteps sounding (for him) the character of each friar. He might have been Francis himself for what he knew then of the little brothers and the cure of souls. He heard them thinking their expectation to be called from bed before daybreak to return to his room and say the office of the dead over his body, become the body, and whispering hopefully to the contrary. Death was now an unwelcome guest in the cloister.

He wanted nothing in the world for himself at last. This may have been the first time he found his will amenable to the Divine. He had never been less himself and more the saint. Yet now, so close to sublimity, or perhaps only tempted to believe so (the Devil is most wily at the deathbed), he was beset by the grossest distractions. They were to be expected, he knew, as indelible in the order of things: the bingo game going on under the Cross for the seamless garment of the Son of Man: everywhere the sign of the contradiction, and always. When would he cease to be surprised by it? Incidents repeated themselves, twined, parted, faded away, came back clear, and would not be prayed out of mind. He watched himself mounting the pulpit of a metropolitan church, heralded by the pastor as the renowned Franciscan father sent by God in His Goodness to preach this novena—like to say a little prayer to test the microphone, Father?—and later reading through the petitions to Our Blessed Mother, cynically tabulating the pleas for a Catholic boy friend, drunkenness banished, the sale of real estate and coming furiously upon one: "that I'm not pregnant." And at the same church on Good Friday carrying the crucifix along the communion rail for the people to kiss, giving them the indulgence, and afterwards in the sacristy wiping the lipstick of the faithful from the image of Christ crucified.

"Take down a book, any book, Titus, and read. Begin anywhere."

Roused by his voice, the canary fluttered, looked sharply about, and buried its head once more in the warmth of its wing.

" 'By the lions,' " Titus read, " 'are understood the acrimonies and impetuosities of the irascible faculty, which faculty is as bold and daring in its acts as are the lions. By the harts and the leaping does is understood the other faculty of the soul, which is the concupiscible—that is—' "

"Skip the exegesis," Didymus broke in weakly. "I can do without that now. Read the verse."

Titus read: " 'Birds of swift wing, lions, harts, leaping does, mountains, valleys, banks, waters, breezes, heats and terrors that keep watch by night, by the pleasant lyres and by the siren's song, I conjure you, cease your wrath and touch not the wall . . .' "

"Turn off the light, Titus."

Titus went over to the switch. There was a brief period of darkness during which Didymus's eyes became accustomed to a different shade, a glow rather, which possessed the room slowly. Then he saw the full moon had let down a ladder of light through the window. He could see the snow, strangely blue, falling outside. So sensitive was his mind and eye (because his body now faint no longer blurred his vision?) he could count the snowflakes, all of them separately, before they drifted, winding, below the sill.

With the same wonderful clarity, he saw what he had made of his life. He saw himself tied down, caged, stunted in his apostolate, seeking the crumbs, the little pleasure, neglecting the source, always knowing death changes nothing, only immortalizes . . . and still ever lukewarm. In trivial attachments, in love of things, was death, no matter the appearance of life. In the highest attachment only, no matter the appearance of death, was life. He had always known this truth, but now he was feeling it. Unable to move his hand, only his lips, and hardly breathing, was it too late to act?

"Open the window, Titus," he whispered.

And suddenly he could pray. *Hail Mary . . . Holy Mary, Mother of God, pray for us sinners now and at the hour of our death . . .* finally the time to say, *pray for* me *now—the hour of* my *death, amen.* Lest he deceive himself at the very end that this was the answer to a lifetime of praying for a happy death, happy because painless, he tried to turn his thoughts from himself, to join them to God, thinking how at last he did—didn't he *now?*—prefer God above all else. But ashamedly not sure he did, perhaps only fearing hell, with an uneasy sense of justice he put himself foremost among the wise in their own generation, the perennials seeking after God when doctor, lawyer, and bank fails. If he wronged himself, he did so out of humility, a holy error. He ended, to make certain he had not fallen under the same old presumption disguised as the face of humility, by flooding his mind with maledictions. He suffered the piercing white voice of Apocalypse to echo in his soul: *But because thou art lukewarm, and neither cold, nor hot, I will begin to vomit thee out of my mouth.* And St. Bernard, fiery-eyed in a white habit, thundered at him from the twelfth century: "Hell is paved with the bald pates of priests!"

There was a soft flutter, the canary flew to the window sill, paused, and tilted into the snow. Titus stepped too late to the window and stood gazing dumbly after it. He raised a trembling old hand, fingers bent in awe and sorrow, to his forehead, and turned stealthily to Didymus.

Didymus closed his eyes. He let a long moment pass before he opened them. Titus, seeing him awake then, fussed with the window latch and held a hand down to feel the draught, nodding anxiously as though it were the only evil abroad in the world, all the time straining his old eyes for a glimpse of the canary somewhere in the trees.

Didymus said nothing, letting Titus keep his secret. With his whole will he tried to lose himself in the sight of God, and failed. He was not in the least transported. Even now he could find no divine sign within himself. He knew he still had to look outside, to Titus. God still chose to manifest Himself most in sanctity.

Titus, nervous under his stare, and to account for staying at the window so long, felt for the draught again, frowned, and kept his eye hunting among the trees.

The thought of being the cause of such elaborate dissimulation in so simple a soul made Didymus want to smile—or cry, he did not know which . . . and could do neither. Titus persisted. How long would it be, Didymus wondered faintly, before Titus ungrievingly gave the canary up for lost in the snowy arms of God? The snowflakes whirled at the window, for a moment for all their bright blue beauty as though struck still by lightning, and Didymus closed his eyes, only to find them there also, but darkly falling.

KATHARINE SHATTUCK:
THE BEAST

S HE HAD been wakened at dawn by the pounding.
She sat up in bed and saw that the child in the next room
was also sitting up, listening.

"What is that noise?" she cried and sank down, but the
woman continued listening.

The horse hoofs had sounded on the stable floor all the previous evening in uneasy tread, but this was different—louder and
more hollow and intermittent.

Light lay in the room in gray drifts, which feathered off, as
she stared at them, into the scarcely discernible outline of chest,
mantel, wall. The windows blurred grayer and grayer, but the
pounding was insistent and at last she crept from the bed, leaving
her husband asleep beneath the sheet.

So as not to disturb the child she went through the hall and
unlocked the front screen, which was the only door they used
in summer. At sight of the locked door she thought as she did
every morning that locking yourself in was stupid since blackness seeped in through crack and keyhole, screen, shutter, and
glass.

On the lawn in the mist the trees like smoke blew up. The
whole visible world streamed in grayness, unfamiliar, though she
saw it each morning, for she was a light sleeper and rose almost
always at dawn.

The horse was in the stall which her husband had made for
him at the rear of the house. At one time, they had discovered,
it had been a large and commodious out-door toilet and housed

the cesspool from the house as well, so that the floor was hollow, built over an excavation sixteen feet deep.

The night before it had seemed so right to have the horse looking out over the swinging doors into the yard, the long face with its white blaze and the unspeaking intelligence. She was afraid of horses as of all animals; yet they seemed chained and sad to her, unspeakably sad like the enchantments laid on princes in the fairy tales. Poor beast, poor horse, and prince or horse to be feared. Shuddering, she crossed herself, like a child exorcising evil.

She walked on the grass in her white gown and bare feet past the two lilac trees, which crumpled gray south of the house.

At the southwest corner of the house she stopped. She held the hard realness of the stone wall in her hand, as if it were talisman against the danger, unknown and impalpable, a hollow sound of pounding, a non-human, non-animal groaning, that lurked in the shadow across the lawn and beneath the row of elm trees rising beyond the stable.

Birds were waking. Roosters crowed on every farm along the valley. The cheering daylight sound did not disperse the shadow here on the hill, or interrupt the pounding, which must have come from the stable, although she could not definitely locate it, or would not, feeling the urgency of her husband's displeasure if she were unable to tell him she had crossed the yard, unbolted the stable doors, removed the iron rod, and, flinging wide the doors, perceived in all its terror or pity or blackness whatever it was making the sound. He expected so much of her, demanding that she be upright and gay, young and old, all things in one; and she was not equal to being these things.

The doors banged out as if with bursting, and she caught one glimpse of the horse's head rearing; enough to tell her the trouble lay in the stable.

She ran back to the house, crouching in a white bundle on the steps of the porch. Her white face stared over the valley, which disappeared completely in the mist as the sun rose and the trees on the hill became solidly trees, green, blowing a little in the morning breeze, filled with the hidden, raucous cry of birds.

The pounding in the back yard continued.

It became now it was daylight the sound of a horse banging against the stable door. In trouble, she thought with sudden compassion and ran into the room where her husband lay, to wake him.

He came out of sleep slowly and sat up, seeing her before him as in a dream—colorless hair, pale face, startling great eyes.

"The horse!" she cried. "Something's happening to the horse."

Still in the envelope of sleep he stumbled into his shoes, tangling the laces until he gave up tying them. He pulled his trousers on and went swiftly through the house past the child, who was rousing now and crying Maggie for her mother.

It was a clear day. The mist was going in the valley. The hard outline of tree, building, shadow was sharp in the sun.

He ran to the stable and unbolting the doors saw what he already knew had happened, what he had known would happen. When he had first planned to put the horse in a stable at the house, Karl, the Bohemian farmer in the valley, had said you put your horse there she break through. The floor he won't hold her. I tell you. But he had gone ahead with his plans. He had been so eager to have the horse where he could ride him every day, where Maggie and the child could ride. But Maggie would be afraid. Unadmitted, it had been another test, another, perhaps the last grasping after the other days when Maggie was not afraid. Impalpable, untouchable, the past was going, going. All this he thought as he unbolted the doors and flung them wide.

With the doors open, the horse lay in the entry.

His body was wet, trembling, dark, his neck outstretched.

"Ginger!" The man knelt beside him.

In one glance he saw what had happened. A rotting plank, worked loose by the animal's tread, had tipped up with his weight. The right rear leg had plunged through the flooring near the wall, dangling clear to the groin in the hollow room beneath. The animal, struggling to stand on his forefeet, pawing the floor, chest and head rearing, struck in vain against the nothingness beneath, struggling. The great eyes strained as if with speech. Sweat streamed on his coat.

"Ginger!" the man cried. He brought him water, petted him. The quivering, terrified animal for one moment lay quiet, and then the forefeet began again the horrible pounding in their struggle to stand, as if the horse dismembered were struggling to walk. The hideous inarticulate animal cry sounded again.

The man stopped at the house to answer his wife when she called to him. The child was in her arms. Her long hair streamed over them both.

"I'll have to get Karl. He told me it would happen. We may have to get the rendering plant truck. They've got a hoist. I don't know. I feel terrible. It's my fault. I should have known."

He was young, almost boyish, almost innocent in his eagerness to make his living real, naive in his believing.

He sped down the hill in his car.

The summer sun, high in freshness, had dried the dew. The outer trees on the knoll beyond the drive were sharply delineated as trees, but within they stood in black and deep shadow. The cows came up past them in a long blond row.

"Karl's milked," he thought matter-of-factly against the strange skein of the day.

Nights now were so bad that any daylight, however filled with danger, was to be desired. To keep day and night separate—that was the thing—clearly marked in divisibility; the one matter-of-fact, safe, ordinary, peaceful, dull even; the other filled with Maggie's crying. The line between light and darkness was sudden. Something indefinable happened. Not a line in geography to be crossed or perceived, it was the same air, the same place, but different.

She had been gay always, the happiest creature he had ever known, the freest. He had counted on her the most, been surest of her. And now, silently, efficiently, she did her daylight tasks in grayness, crying at night. Scene after scene filled his eyes, and now as if some demand too great were being made of her, she was changing under his eyes. He could not understand.

He stopped the car and opened the gray lattice-work gate to

the farm and drove the car through. On either side were flowered banks of daisies, larkspur, horsemint.

Chickens were pecking in the road and fluttering ahead of him, squawking.

The dogs at the farmhouse barked and the farmer came out, chewing the last cud of his breakfast.

"Gee Christ whiz!" he said and wiped his mouth with his hand.

He jumped into the car.

"That horse he'll kill himself," he said. "You get a son beetch hurry."

In the yard again he took charge.

Maggie, in her white gown, still holding the child, whom she had dressed, however, cowered in the background beyond the grass-grown cistern head.

Karl, short, lively, wiry, dark, with coarse leathered skin and a back that had lifted a loaded wagon sunk to its hubs in mud, fluttered around the horse like an angry fly. The animal worn by his frantic and unavailing struggle lay now with stretched neck on the stable floor, steaming sweat, its stench rising in a vapor around him. He was a chestnut, large for a saddle horse, with a handsome beautifully blazed face.

"He'll kill himself." Karl twisted the horse's tail and heaved against the flank, but one man's strength was no match for a horse's weight.

They tore the flooring loose, and, lowering a ladder into the pit beneath the room, they descended into the ammonic stink below to watch the action of the horse's leg in its fight against the vague, the untouchable blackness beneath. Karl, unconvinced that brute force was not the answer, pushed against the hoof; and the horse, with the fearful reaching of the dying after air, struggled to stand, hoofs pounding, head straining, eyes starting.

The futile pounding forelegs gave up and he sank down.

The men scratched their heads, cursed, and tried new tactics. A block and tackle was like a child's idea. They tied a rope around the horse's belly and pulled at the forelegs as if to saw them off, so that the dismembered quarters could then be lifted out at will and be disposed of. The watching woman saw it and with a scream protested. Karl in one of his lightning leaps disappeared to the barn and returned with a huge drag chain, which they fastened to the bumper of the car and to the rope around the horse's middle. Then the man, maneuvering against his will, put the engine into low, reversed, pulled in low again—gasoline engine against horse, a cruelty the woman could not endure and she screamed again. The straining beseeching face of the animal wavered behind the blowing fumes of gasoline.

With five attempts they succeeded in dragging him half over the threshold. But at the moment the hind quarters came free, the foreleg went down into the hole, the momentarily released weight of the board giving like a child's teeter-totter. And then the horse gave up.

"She's a no go." Karl wiped the sweat from his face with the back of his hand and stood panting with the exertion of pushing at the horse. "She's a no go."

"I'll get some more men."

He jumped into the car and disappeared down the hill.

People were going to early mass in the valley. A common Sunday quiet lay on the air. At the foot of the hill he had to wait for a car to pass. People waved to him. He did not recognize them, did not respond. The thing—whatever it was—that was happening on the hill encased him in its shadow. On the edge of it stood Maggie, holding the child. He had not had time, he had not had the heart to go to her and with his arm about her suggest that she dress, leading her toward the house. She with the submissiveness that was so new in her, so frightening, would have gone, would have returned neatly dressed in a shirtwaist and skirt, her hair twisted in its knot behind—a woman and a stranger to him. Only in bed now did he know her. He could not define the change in her, could not discern its meaning. He rubbed the shadow away from his eyes and concentrated on the horse, the men he was to get, this actual thing that was to be done.

He crossed the bridge.

The river, dark brown where it did not reflect the banks,

moved on its sluggish inevitable way to the Mississippi. They had spent hours on the river together, swimming beside their canoe, lying on the cushions, watching the green closed world slide past. Now she was afraid of water and would not go, hating it with a violence out of all proportion to the fear even. He saw the small white face, the glittering eyes, the beating fists: "I will not go, I will not go." Her anger was not against him, he thought. It was some life sickness he could not grasp.

He turned to the left and stopped in the yard of a farmhouse on the edge of the town.

Slim Drummond stood beside his black car in the yard, paring his fingernails. He was dressed in black for church, but turned over the car keys to his eldest daughter when he heard of the accident, and came out in five minutes dressed in blue jeans and shirt. A wide-brimmed Stetson hat, old and greasy, was pushed back on his head. He was tall and as slim as a boy, but with an old man's face and powerful hands.

"Call Jim Roberts," he said. "Tell him to bring his hired man. A horse'll kill himself."

They went up the hill. Karl was working over the horse, which lay exhausted on the floor, in resignation worse than struggle. Karl's broad Bohemian face with its creased leather hide and black eyes recognized Slim's presence, but he did not speak.

The child was running in the yard, pattering, picking flowers, and the man picked her up and handed her to her mother, patting her arm and looking at her gravely.

"I think you'd better go inside, Maggie," he said.

Taking the child's hand she moved toward the house.

Whatever it was happening to the horse in the yard held her and she stopped by the house, identified with the struggle as if the horse by getting free would free her too from terror, this loneness she had stood in since she first knew two people could come no nearer than touch. It wasn't the work; it wasn't the fears even or that living was harder than she had thought. It was that you did it alone.

The men stood over the horse, silently appraising the work to be done.

A car roared on the hill, and Jim Roberts came around the house—a big man, thick of chest and strong, with a good-natured face. He pushed his hat back and scratched his head.

There was a moment of disagreement; Karl favored the block and tackle. But suddenly coordinated, as if the work to be done determined the method, making the many one, they took their places: the man at the head, tugging on the halter; Karl at the shoulder pushing; the other two at the tail, lifting it like a handle.

The great neck lay stretched on the threshold, trembling.

Woman and horse, one, waited an indefinable moment when, lifted in terror, they were not yet free.

In rhythm, in silence, and with tremendous effort, the men heaved the horse out of the stall. Sliding free of the stable, the four legs lay stretched on solid ground, the head lay on the grass. The huge body was motionless, hardly a horse, as if by death disenchanted. Blood like sweat streaked the quivering groin.

"She's a beesiness," Karl panted, squinting at the underside of the horse, his hands on his knees. "He's a big. Get him up. Let him piss. He's a swelled."

The four men stood over the body, breathing. Karl pranced like a matador or an insect. "Get him up. She's a—"

"Let him lie a minute. Let him get his breath. Ginger. So boy." The man rubbed the muzzle and picking some clover gave it to the horse.

The men slapped and beat at the horse, calling the threats men use against animals in command; and at last the horse stood, wavering on its slender legs, crumpling, then solid. Nothing was broken then. The man gave him water to drink.

The woman came along the grass, leading the child by the hand, walking in her white nightgown, her bare feet showing beneath. Her hair, covering her shoulders, hung to her waist. The sun as if caught shone in it. The delicately boned face and great eyes were uplifted, the face was strange. Unhesitating, without fear, she came up to the horse and taking the head in her arms rubbed the muzzle with her face. The man, warmed in gratitude, put his arm on her shoulders.

"Poor Ginger," he said, feeling Maggie's hair against his face.

His eyes stung. Everything was all right, he thought. Everything was going to be all right. He had been imagining fears. The horse's predicament had made him foolish.

She looked into the horse's face and said, "Poor horse, poor beast," and kissed it, rubbing the blaze with her cheek.

Karl seized the halter and led the horse up and down the yard. The legs were stiff. Blood bright red showed on the groin where the animal had been cruelly sawed as he had hung.

The woman, leaving the child, went back to the house.

Now the exertion was over, the return to commonness seemed a little silly. They pushed their hats back, wiped their faces. The man took a cigarette and handed the others each one.

"He's a beesiness," he said and they laughed in relief.

Smoke uptrailed in silly morning incense. A chicken was crowing. It was still morning, the same world. The floor of the stable was shattered and splintered, the grass on the threshold was pounded, hair from the horse's tail lay on the floor, but other sign of disaster there was none, he thought. Shadows lay in their accustomed order. On the clothes line at the edge of the yard a child's bib was blowing.

Karl led the horse down the hill to the barn.

Slim Drummond and Jim Roberts muttered they must be getting on.

The man caught up the child in his arms. He watched them drive away, the black Chrysler car shining in the sun in unmeaningful daylight reality.

The child patted his chin and said: "Your horse will be all right, Daddy. I think your horse will be all right."

A wren flew away from the cistern. The doors in the empty stall were open, banging a little in the wind.

The child in his arms was saying: "Your horse will be all right."

They went into the house.

She was sitting by the table in the kitchen.

He put his hand on her shoulder. "Are you all right, Maggie?" She had knotted her hair behind and put on a blouse and skirt. "Are you all right?"

Table and counters in the kitchen were scrubbed white. There were no shadows in the room. In the neat whiteness of stove, icebox, walls there were no shadows.

"Are you all right?"

She turned. He saw the line of the cheeks he had loved for their roundness, the white plane of forehead beneath the hair.

"I'm all right," she said. She touched his hand with her face, giving him the talisman he wanted, knowing its worth.

IRWIN SHAW:

THE VETERANS REFLECT

THE BELLS were ringing everywhere and the engineer blew the locomotive whistle over and over as they roared up the springtime valley. The hills rolled back from the blue river and the frail green of the young leaves made them look as though pale green velvet cloth, thready and worn, had been thrown as drapery over their winter sides.

Peter Wylie sat at the window staring dreamily out at the Hudson Valley rolling sweetly and familiarly past him. He smiled when a little girl in front of a farmhouse gravely waved an American flag at the speeding train and the engineer gravely saluted her in return with a deep roar of the whistle.

Peter Wylie sat at the window of the speeding train and avoided listening to the booming voice of the gentleman talking to the pretty woman across the aisle. He stretched his legs comfortably and half-closed his eyes as he watched the green, quiet country over which, faintly, between towns, came the pealing of bells, because that morning the war had ended.

". . . Dead two years," the gentleman was saying. "His ship went down off Alaska and that was the last we heard of him. Twenty-one years old. Here's his picture, in uniform."

"He looks so young," the woman said.

"He had a blonde beard. Hardly had to shave. The ship went down in eighteen minutes. . . ."

The bells were ringing, Peter thought, and the graves were full of young men who had hardly had to shave, in uniform. His two cousins on his mother's side, killed in Africa, and Martin, who had been his roommate for three years, killed in India, and all the boys from the squadron . . . The graves on the plains and the mountains, the shallow graves on the hard coral islands, and the long well kept cemetery of the military dead outside the hospital which you looked at through the tall window of your ward as nurses whispered outside in the corridor and the doctors hurried fatefully by on their crepe soles. "Convenient," you said with a slow, remote wave of your hand and with what you hoped was a smile, to the nurse, who seemed always to have come from behind a screen where she wept continuously when not actually needed at a bedside. "Modern design."

"What?" the red-eyed nurse had asked blankly.

You had been too tired to explain and merely closed your eyes with the beautiful rudeness of the dying. But you hadn't died. There was a strange platter-like excavation in your abdomen and you would never really enjoy your food anymore, and you would always have to climb stairs slowly even though you were only twenty-nine now on this day when the bells were ringing, but the cemetery and the military dead were still there and here you were on a train going up the Hudson Valley on your way home to see your wife and child and the guns were quiet and the airplanes idled in the hangars and the pilots sat around and played cards and tried to remember the telephone numbers of the girls in their home towns.

You were on your way home to see your wife and child. For three years, alone at night, sleepless in strange rooms on other continents; on leave, at a bar, sleepless drinking and laughing and the brassy old juke boxes playing songs that cried *far away and long ago, far away and long ago* and all the women being earnest about the war and patriotically anxious to jump into bed with all the pilots, navigators, bombardiers, flight-sergeants, wing-commanders, meteorologists, radio-operators of the air forces of all the United Nations, including the Russian; for three years on the long droning flights across the hundred-mile ripples of the Pacific; for three years, even sometimes at the moment when the bombardier said, "O.K., I'll take it from here," as the plane ducked in over the target and the anti-aircraft fire bloomed roughly about you, the faces of your wife and daughter slid through your mind, the woman's firm-boned jaw, the moody blue eyes, the wide, full mouth, familiar, loving, changing, merry, tragic, tenderly and laughingly mocking in the secret wifely female understanding of the beloved weaknesses of the man of the family—and the child's face, small, unformed, known only from photographs sent across the oceans, looking out at him through the night with sober, infant gravity . . . Three years, he thought, and tomorrow morning the train will pull into the dirty old station at Chicago and there they'll be, standing in the soot and clangor, hand in hand, the quick, delightful woman and the fat child, picking his uniform out among the other uniforms, with three years' waiting and loving and hoping showing in the faces as he strode down the platform. . . .

"Bong-bong!" shouted a little bald man, who was leading two women drunkenly down the aisle toward the diner. "Bong-bong! We did it!"

"Ding-aling! Ring out the wild bells!" the blonde woman right behind the bald man cried out. "Welcome to America!"

"We applied the crusher," the bald man told the crowded car. "The old steel spring technique. Coil back, coil back, coil back, then . . ."

They disappeared around the bend of the car over which the small sign said modestly, "Women."

Across the ocean, in the mountains of another country, a man strode out of a darkened house to the long, armored automobile waiting on the night-deserted road. Two men, bundled in army greatcoats, hurried behind him, their boots sighing softly in the damp earth of the courtyard. The chauffeur had the door open but the man stopped and turned around before he got in and looked at the dark shapes of the mountains rising behind him against the starry sky. He put his hand uncertainly to his collar and pulled at it and took a deep breath. The two men in the greatcoats waited, without looking up, shadows by the slowly fluttering young foliage of the oaks that bordered the path. The man turned and slowly got into the car, carefully, like an old man who has fallen recently and remembers that his bones are brittle and mend slowly. The other two men sprang into the front seat and the chauffeur slammed the rear door and ran around to the front and leaped in and started the motor. The automobile sped quietly down the dark road, the noise of its going making a private and faraway *whoosh* that died on the huge and growing darkness of the mountain-circled Spring night.

In the back of the car, the man sat bolt upright, his eyes narrow and unseeing, staring straight ahead of him. Off in the hills a church bell pealed and pealed again and again, musical and lonely in the echoing darkness. The lips of the man in the back seat curled slightly, bitterly, as the sound of the pealing village-bell wavered on the wind. Germans! he thought. Five million German dead all over the world and the Russians on the road to Berlin and everything worse than 1918 and their leader skulking through the night on backroads towards the Swiss border with a chauffeur and two frightened first-lieutenants and they ring bells as though this was the day after the Fall of France! Germans! Idiots! Imitation suits, imitation rubber, imitation eggs, finally imitation men . . . What was a man expected to do with material like that? And he'd come so close . . . so close . . . The gates of Moscow. But he sat. The statue sat. Everyone else ran, the diplomats, the newspapermen, the government, and Stalin sat there and the people sat . . . Peasant. Sitting there in his burning house with his gun and his plow . . . and somehow the house didn't burn. Storm-troopers, assault-guards, blitzkrieg veterans . . . at the gates of Moscow and they died. A little cold and they dropped like hot-house violets. So close . . . so close . . .

The bell rang more strongly and in other villages other bells answered.

They'd hang him if they caught him. He'd cried at the last Armistice, he'd hang at this. . . . The British use a silk rope when they hang nobility. They wouldn't use silk on him . . . And the bells ringing all around him. . . .

He leaned forward and jabbed the chauffeur fiercely in the back.

"Faster!"

The car spurted forward.

"Production," the booming gentleman across the aisle was say-ing to the pretty woman, who was leaning closer to him, prettily attentive. "It was inevitable. American production won this war."

Peter thought of the graves, of the English and Chinese and Australians and Russians and Serbs and Greeks and Americans who filled them, who had fought bitterly with rifle and cannon and plane across the torn fields and stripped forests where they now quietly lay, under the illusion that if the war was to be won, it was to be won by them, standing there, hot gun in hand, with the shells dropping around them and the scream of the planes overhead and the tanks roaring at them at fifty miles an hour. . . .

"I know," the gentleman was saying. "I was in Washington from 1941 right to the finish and I saw. I'm in machine tools and I had my hand on the pulse of production and I know what I'm talking about. We performed miracles."

"I'm sure," the pretty woman murmured. "I'm absolutely sure." She was not as young as she had looked at first, Peter noticed, and her clothes were much shabbier than he had thought, and she looked pretty and impressed and tired and ready to be invited to dinner.

". . . Plants in seven states," the man was saying. "We ex-panded 400 per cent. The war's over now, I can talk freely. . . ."

The war's over, Peter thought deliciously, settling deeper into his chair, and letting his head rumble pleasantly with the click of the wheels as he leaned back against the cushion, the war's over and machine-tool manufacturers who expanded 400 per cent can talk freely to women in Pullman cars and tomorrow I see my wife and child and I never have to climb into an airplane again. From now on I walk down to the station and buy a ticket when I want to go someplace and I sit down with a magazine and a whiskey and soda and the train clicks along on steel and solid gravel and the only enemy activity will be an occasional small boy throwing a rock hopefully at the bright windows of the diner flashing by. Tomorrow afternoon he would be walking slowly along the lake front in the Spring wind, hand in hand with his wife and child. "And that, darling, is Lake Michigan. Do you know the water you took a bath in this morning? It comes right from here, especially for you. When your father was a boy he used to stand here and watch the red Indians sail by in their war canoes at forty miles an hour, reciting Henry Wadsworth Longfellow at the top of their voices. . . . I can see by the look in your mother's eye that she doesn't believe me and wants an ice cream soda. I can also see by the look in her eye that she doesn't think you should have an ice cream soda so soon after lunch, but I've been thinking about buying you this ice cream soda for three years and the war's over and I don't think she's going to make too much of a fuss. . . ."

And tomorrow night, they would lie, soft on their backs in the soft bed, staring idly up at the dark ceiling, his arm under her head, their voices murmuring and mingling with the distant quiet night sounds of the sleeping city, the clack and rumble from the lakefront railroad yards and the soft whisper of automobiles on the highway . . . "I slept in the same bed in Cairo, Egypt, with a boy from Texas who weighed two hundred and thirty pounds. He wanted to get in the Navy, but he was six feet six inches tall and they said he wouldn't fit on any ship afloat or building. Also he was in love with a girl he met in New York who sold gloves in Saks and he talked about her all night long. She has a 36 inch bust and she lives with four girls from Vassar in Greenwich Village and she has a scar on her right buttock six inches long that she got when she fell down iceskating and a man with racing skates ran over her. This is an improvement over sleeping with a two hundred and thirty pound Texan in the same bed in Cairo, Egypt. Yes, I'll kiss you if you want. . . ."

And her voice, close to his ear, in the gentle, tumbled darkness, alive with the fresh night wind off the lake and the familiar smell of her perfume and the frail dry smell of her hair, remembered all the years deep in his nostrils ". . . And she went to the nursery school in Tucson all day while I was on duty in the hospital and they all liked her very much but she had a habit of hitting the other little boys and girls with her shovel and I had to leave her

with my sister. I knew you'd laugh. Stop laughing or I'll stuff a
pillow in your mouth, Mr. Veteran. You can afford to laugh, out
flying around ten thousand miles away with nothing to worry
about but Japs and Germans. Wait till you're a mother and seven
young mothers descend upon you to tell you your child has
swiped at their children with a wooden shovel every day of the
school term. . . ." And the kiss to stop the laughter and her head
under his chin after that and the slow, diminishing chuckles together for the child sleeping in the next room dreaming of other
children and more wooden shovels.

And again, her hand thrown softly and possessively on his chest
. . . "There's a lot more hair here than I remember."

"War. I always put on a lot of hair on my chest in a war. Any
objections?"

"No. I'm well-known as a woman who's partial to hairy men.
Or is talk like that too vulgar for young soldiers? Am I too fat?
I put on eight pounds since 1942 . . . Have you noticed?"

"I'm noticing now."

"Too fat?"

"Ummmmmmnnn. . . ."

"Tell the truth."

"Ummnnn."

"I'm going to diet. . . ."

"You just wait here and I'll go down and get you a plate of
mashed potatoes. . . ."

"Oh, shut up. Oh, darling, darling, I'm glad you're home. . . ."

Or perhaps they wouldn't talk at all in the beginning. Perhaps
they would just touch each other's hand and weep cheek to cheek
for the three years behind them and the years ahead and cling to
each other desperately through the long cool night and go to his
parents' farm in Wisconsin and walk hand in hand in morning
sunlight slowly over the greening fields, their feet sinking into the
soft loam, content in the first hours with love and silence, until
finally they could sit under the wide peaceful sky, off to themselves, with the rich smell of the newly plowed fields and the
water-melon-cucumber smell of the river in their nostrils, and
then, finally, the words would come . . . The things he had

thought on the long flights, the decisions and doubts of the thousand wartime nights, the deep deep hallelujah of his spirit as the train covered the sweet final miles between the war and home. He would tell her the things he had had to bury deep within him through the noisy, bleeding years . . . The times he had been afraid . . . the first time he had seen an enemy squadron small against the horizon, harmless looking dots, growing nearer and larger with insane speed, and the ridiculous way it made him see, over and over again, for some reason, *Acrobatics*, as it was printed in the March Field Bulletin. And at the time he had been shot, six hours away from base, on a rough day, lying bleeding on his parachute while Dennis pushed the bomber toward home, and he had managed to keep quiet for the first four hours, but had wept for the last two hours, almost mechanically, although he had felt very calm. And because he was certain he was going to die, he had for the first time permitted himself to think about whether the whole thing was worth it or not, as the plane bucked in the cold air. He could tell her how he had thought, in those long six hours, of all the boys who had lightly roared off at four hundred miles an hour and lightly and thoughtlessly, or at least silently died. . . . He would be able to tell her that he had soberly decided, bullet in his belly and sure of death in the roaring plane, that it was worth it, that if he had it to do again he would leave home, wife, child, father, mother, country, and search the German bullet out of the cloud once more, part of the enormous anguish and enormous courage of all the men on sea and beach and mountain locked with him in final struggle against the general enemy. And, then, weeping, on the edge of death, as he thought, he could let himself go . . . and for the first time, in the mist of pain, break down the barrier of reserve that had kept him, even in his most secret thoughts, from admitting even to himself how much he loved all those men behind guns—his friends, boys from the same schools, coolly diving, cannons and machine guns tearing out of their wings, at enemy bombers; the pleasant Englishmen foolishly and desperately confident of their ships, sailing formally and arrogantly into hopeless battle like Englishmen in books; the quilted Chinese rifleman standing forlornly on the brown China earth

against tanks and artillery; and huge, muffled Russians, fighting by
day and night and snow and rain, implacably and ingeniously and
tirelessly killing, oblivious to agony or doubt, intent only on burning and crippling and starving and murdering the enemy. . . . He
could tell her how deep inside him he had loved all those bloody,
weary, cruel, reliable men, how he had felt borne up on that huge
tide of men careless of death, and had felt himself to be a part of
that tide, agonized, stricken, familiar with defeat, often falsely and
frivolously led, but better than the leaders, dangerous, brawling,
indivisible . . . and how he had felt linked with those men for
all their lives and his, closer to them even though he could not
speak their language nor they his, than to his own mother and
father, responsible forever for their comfort and glory as they
were for his. And he could tell her of the sober exhilaration of
these reflections, this deep dredging to his thoughts, this ultimate
examination in the light of pain and exhaustion and terror of himself, who never before this had thought deeply or reflected much
beyond the everyday cares of average life in a small town, seated
at a desk from nine to five, sleeping comfortably in a quiet room
in a warm house, going to the pictures twice a week, playing
tennis on Sunday, worrying about whether the car was good for
another year or not. . . .

The long automobile sped down the winding road among the
hills on its way through the night to the Swiss border. The man
still sat bolt upright on the back seat, his eyes narrow and unseeing, straight ahead of him.

Victories, he thought, how many victories can a man be expected to win? Paris, Rotterdam, Singapore, Athens, Kiev, War-
saw . . . and still they kept coming. . . . There was a certain
limit to the number of victories that were humanly possible.
Napoleon discovered, too . . . Napoleon . . . Napoleon . . .
He was tired of that name. In the last days he had ordered
that it was not to be spoken in his presence. . . . And now
they were all hunting for him, like a world full of blood-
hounds . . . Germans, English, Russians, Americans, French,
Austrians, Poles, Dutch, Bulgarians, Serbs, Italians . . . Well,

they had reason. Fools. For a long time it hadn't been hard. The cities fell like rotten apples. But then America and Russia . . . The timing was not quite exact. In politics everything happened before schedule. In war everything happened behind schedule. . . . So close, so close . . . The Russians. . . . Everything else being equal, the bells would be ringing for another reason tonight if not for the Russians. . . . Just that winter had to be the coldest in fifty years. There has to be a certain element of luck. . . . Well, all things considered, he had had a successful career. He had started out as a nobody, with his father always yelling at him that he'd never amount to anything and he never could hold a job. . . . Today his name was known in every home on the face of the earth, in every jungle. . . . Thirty million people had died earlier than they expected because of him and hundreds of cities were leveled to the ground because of him and the entire wealth of all nations of the earth had been strained by him, mines and factories and farms. . . . All things considered, he had had a successful career. . . . Even his father would have to admit that. Though, to be fair, if he hadn't grabbed first, someone else would have grabbed. . . . The thing would have happened without him. He had to admit that. But he had grabbed first and the name known in every home on the face of the earth was Hitler, not any other name. . . . So close, so close. . . . A little cold and they died . . . Idiots! And now they wanted to hang him. If he could only get across the border, lie low. . . . Until the rest of them got tired of killing the Germans. After all, Napoleon came back off Elba. A hundred days. With a little luck he could have stuck. . . . Napoleon . . . the name was not to be mentioned. They were going to start worrying about the Russians very soon . . . The Russians, the Russians . . . the armies had been cut up, they had died by the millions . . . and yet, today they were on the road to Berlin. They were going to need someone to stop the Russians and if he could only lie low for a few months, his name would be mentioned. . . . And once he got back, there'd be no more mistakes. . . . With a little luck . . .

The man on the rear seat relaxed against the cushions and a little smile played around the raw mouth.

"I was interviewed by the Washington *Post*," the booming gentleman was saying, his voice cutting into Peter's reverie. "Right before I left. And I told them straight up and down—production must not stop." Peter looked absently at the booming gentleman. He was a tall fat man with a bald head, but somehow he reminded Peter of all the teacher's pets who had ever been in his classes in grammar school . . . pink, fat face, small, round, pink, satisfied mouth, always impressing everyone with how much he knew and how much in favor he was. Peter closed his eyes and imagined the tall, fat man in an Eton collar with a bow tie and grinned. "Stop a machine for a day," the man was saying, "and industrial obsolescence comes a month nearer. Whether we like it or not we are geared to wartime production."

"You're so right," the pretty woman murmured. Peter looked at her closely for the first time. Her clothes were shabby and she had the same wornout, rundown look that the whole country seemed to have, as though the war had rubbed people and things down to the grain, as though the war had kept the whole continent up too many nights, working too hard. . . . Teacher's pet was bright and shining, as though he had stepped out of 1941 into a world many years older. . . .

"Nobody ever had too many guns. I told them right to their faces."

"You're so right," the pretty woman murmured.

"My son was sunk off Alaska. . . ." Peter tightened as he recognized the note of boasting in the voice, as though the man were saying he had been elected to an exclusive club. "My son was sunk off Alaska and I produced machine tools twenty-four hours a day, seven days a week and I have a right to talk. We got it on our hands, I told them, and we have to face the problem fair and square, what are we going to do with them. . . ."

"Yes," murmured the pretty woman, hoping for dinner, over the rumble of the wheels.

He would walk slowly, Peter thought, in the evening, after

dinner in the big farm kitchen, with the smells of cooking rich and fragrant in the warm kitchen air and his mother red-faced and aproned and his father tall and scrubbed and quiet, smoking his nickel cigar. . . . He would walk slowly along the rutted wagon road with Laura beside him in the bright twilight, full of the warm knowledge that he was in no hurry to get any place, that he could leisurely regard the small hills, accepting the night, and leisurely listen to the last evening concert of the birds, leisurely scuff his shoes in the light country dust of the road over which armored tread had never passed, which had never known blood. . . . He could tell Laura finally that of all the good things that had happened to him in this savage, ecstatic century, the best had happened in the moment when he had walked toward her on a train platform in Chicago the day after the war was over. . . . He could tell her finally how tired he was, how tired he had been when bone and blood and nerve had collapsed, when no effort had ever seemed possible again, when his body had given up all knowledge of victory or defeat. . . . And when somehow planes had to be flown and guns manned and swift, deadly action taken by that sodden bone and blood and nerve . . . and some-how the action taken because of the feeling deep within him that on other fields and in other skies, wearier and more desperate men were still manning guns for him and flying more dangerous skies. . . . And the promise he made to himself that when it was over and he was home, surrounded by care and love, he was never going to hurry again, never knowingly perform a violent act, never even raise his voice except in laughter and song, never argue with anyone about anything. . . . He wasn't going back to his job. Nine to five in a bank at a desk was no way to crown a career of bloodshed 30,000 feet over three continents. Perhaps Laura would be able to suggest something for him to do, some-thing quiet and unhurried and thoughtless. . . . But first he was going to do nothing. Just wander around the farm and teach the baby how to spell and listen to his father explain his particular reasons for rotating his crops in his own particular way. . . . Maybe two, three, five months, a year of that, as long as it took to drain off the blood and weariness, as long as it took for his crippled spirit to open the door of its wartime hospital and step out firmly . . . as long as it took . . .

"The job's just begun," the booming gentleman was saying. "Let them ring the bells. It amuses them. But tomorrow morning . . ."

"Yes," said the pretty woman, eager to agree with everything.

"We've got to face the facts. A businessman faces the facts. What are the facts? The Russians are near Berlin. Right?"

"Yes," said the woman, "of course."

"Berlin. Fine. Unavoidable. The Russians are sitting on Europe. . . ."

Peter tried to close his eyes, close his ears, go back to the dear dream of the twilight country road and his wife's hand in his and the dust that had never known blood. But the man's voice tore through and he couldn't help but listen.

"As a businessman I tell you it's an impossible situation." The man's voice grew louder. "Intolerable. And the sooner we realize it, the better. The truth is, maybe it's a good thing this war was fought. Dramatizes the real problem. Makes the American people see what the real danger is. And what's the answer? Production! Guns and more guns! I don't care what those Communists in Washington say, I say the war has just begun."

Peter stood up wearily and went over to the booming gentleman. "Get out of here," he said as quietly as he could. "Get out of here and keep quiet or I'll kill you."

The booming gentleman looked up at him, his face still with surprise. His little red mouth opened twice and closed silently. His pale eyes stared harshly and searchingly at Peter's worn, bitter face. Then he shrugged, stood up, put out his arm for the lady.

"Come," he said, "we might as well eat."

The pretty woman stood up and started hesitantly, frightenedly toward the door.

"If it weren't for your uniform," the booming man said loudly, "I'd have you arrested. Armistice or no Armistice."

"Get out of here," Peter said.

The booming gentleman turned and walked swiftly after the woman and they disappeared toward the diner. Peter sat down, conscious of every eye in the car on him, regretting that he had found his next years' work placed so soon before him and crying so urgently to be done. Well, he comforted himself, at least I don't have to travel for this one.

The engineer blew his whistle on a ten mile stretch of clear track because the war was over and as the hoarse triumphant sound floated back, Peter closed his eyes and tried to think of his wife and child waiting in the noisy station in Chicago. . . .

RICHARD SULLIVAN:

THE WOMEN

MAYBE night is the time when women come into their power.
Men are strong in the bright sun, but darkness is for women. Barnaby thought of this afterward, when he was going to
sleep. When he was putting Julie to bed, early, he first realized
that he was the only man in the house; and he felt a sudden
unexpected excitement even then in thinking about the three
women, his daughter, his wife, and his mother: he thought of
his relations to each of them, of how some way, with a kind of
bewildering rightness, just by the fact of existing himself, he
had made these three into a unity which had some sort of strange
meaning, some significance so deep and involved that at last it
merged into mystery.

He had been disappointed that his father wasn't home. His
mother had run out onto the side porch when they drove in the
driveway. "Hello!" she cried, "hello! hello! Oh, *honey!*" He had
stopped the car by this time and Julie had scrambled out over all
the bags and packages in the back seat, and now his mother was
rocking her tall body sideways hugging Julie on the bottom porch
step. "Oh, *honey!*" she cried. "How *are* you? My, how *big* you're
getting!" She tried to get free of clinging Julie, who was squealing, "Gramma, Gramma, where's Shep? Is my Shep here? I want
my doggie!" It was just dusk and he was struck with how joyous
and familiar his mother looked in the sunless air, trying to get
past their squealing little girl to them. "My, *my!*" she cried. "You
look *good!*" She hugged Nell, who was out of the car ahead of
him. "How're you feeling, Nell?" she asked anxiously. "You
stand the drive all right? You didn't get any *bouncing*, did you

—Oh, *Tommy!*" she cried, as he seized her and whirled her around in a full circle. "You let me *down!* What way is that to treat your own ma! Come on, come *on* in the house! Oh, I'm so *glad* to see you, I was beginning to get *worried.* Your letter didn't say what time, Tom. I didn't know what time you'd get here. I kind of figured for supper, but earlier than this, *earlier.* We're going to have chicken and it's all *brown* now, but you'll have to eat it anyhow. Come on, come *on!* We'll talk while we eat. I've got a girl in to help me."

The old collie Shep was prancing in slow circles, whining with Julie hanging on his neck, and Barnaby was unpacking bags from the car, and his mother was running on as she always did, her excitement spilling out in a chattering flow of words, and Nell was standing there waiting, looking tired, calling to Julie to be careful of the dog, "He hasn't seen you for a long time now. Don't tease him!" and in the dark trees you could hear the birds against all the open quiet, and out on the road the distant putter of a car. Then, "Dad isn't here," he heard his mother saying. "They wanted him out in the country, I don't know what it is out there, he tried to get the other agent to go, but his wife's expecting any minute, she's further along than you, Nell! and he had to go, there was no getting out of it but he felt so bad, said I should tell you how bad he felt and to give Julie a great big squeeze for him, and he'll be back by noon tomorrow sure, he said, whatever's wrong out there!"

He had expected his father to be here. During the hot afternoon, driving through sun-haze on the flat cement, he had looked forward to sitting on the side porch at dusk with his father; they used to sit out there half an hour before supper, talking, watching the sun go down, drinking beer slowly out of bottles icy-wet from the old brown icebox in the back hall. But then this afternoon there had been three detours, and he knew they'd be lucky to get home before dark; and now they were here but his father was gone.

He was disappointed, but it wasn't until later that he had begun to think about his father's absence as somehow emphasizing the women's presence. During supper Julie, who was over-tired, fussed and whimpered and then right at the end of the meal upset the glass of milk she had refused to drink. He nervously slapped her fingers; he didn't mean to punish her for what was really an accident but all this talking and the knowledge that Nell was worn-out made him nervous. Nell got up. "I'll get her ready for bed," she said. "She's out on her feet."

He stood up too. "Tom," his mother said in a low voice, "I wonder, Greta's out there in the kitchen. Dad always drives her home at night. They live on the Green Bay road, you don't know the family, I guess. Johnsons? No, they moved there since you went away."

"You want me to drive her over?" He glanced quickly at Nell; sometimes she liked him to help with Julie at night.

"Would you?" his mother said. "It's over a mile, I don't like to have her walk. It's kind of late, I thought I'd tell her to stack the dishes, she can do them in the morning. I don't usually keep her this late."

He had met Greta when first they came in, his mother proudly introducing them all; she was a big girl in a washed-out billowing dress; he had heard her moving around out in the kitchen while they were eating.

When she came out to him waiting in the car he was disturbed. She had changed her dress; she was wearing a dark skirt now and a fresh white blouse with a sailor collar. As she stood on the porch outside nodding to what his mother inside the doorway was saying, he, in the car, saw her as for the first time: saw the flaring skirt, the good long legs, the big stateliness of the girl; then realized uneasily, almost with alarm, that she was not really a girl, that that was just his mother's word; she was not adolescent at all, but grown, mature. Turning his head he stared at the tiny darting insects whirling in the white brilliance of the car's headlights; over the low pulse of the motor he could hear the leaves moving in the night wind. You got to a certain age and you thought maybe now thank God the fever and sensitivity were gone, or at least focussed, you were old enough certainly, and then a strange woman is going to get in the car with you for a mile-ride home and it all starts again, with the crazy bugs in the headlights and the soft stir of the wind and the low steady motor. If she'd been a girl, a kid, it'd be nothing; he was old enough so young girls couldn't trouble him. But this woman—

He opened the car door for her. "Now you'll have to tell me the way, Greta. It's been a long time since I travelled the side-roads around here." In the light from the dashboard he noticed the blue stars on her white collar, the rounding blue braid encircling her bare firm arm at the sleeve edge. He moved far to his side of the front seat and lit a new cigarette from the butt of his old one. I'm a married man, he said to himself, what's the matter with me—

They drove through the darkness; the fields were sweet beside the road; they passed a low place where frogs croaked; it was a thick night, no stars, the air heavy and tremulous as before rain. Her voice was clear, polite, distant; she told him where to turn; it was only a little way; soon they were there. "Well, thank you very much, Mr. Barnaby." She had long brown lashes and her face was plain and pale. Twisting the door handle she leaned momentarily toward him; he caught the faint sharp fragrance of sachet, so feminine, so familiar; then with a little movement she was out of the car. "Goodnight, Greta!" He watched her running swiftly over the grass to the small lighted house.

Backing the car around he felt relieved, then exultant. It hadn't been anything. You worried and were nervous and then it was nothing. Attraction, that was all, the instant automatic tug; it didn't have to mean anything; you just ignored it. He had her placed in his mind now, as the trees by the roadside here were placed, known marks against the night landscape, always to be recognized; not strange any more, but known and scrupulously to be admired, at a distance, though, at a distance. He let his arm hang out the car window, feeling the soft pressure of heavy darkness splitting and flowing around him. It was good to be home.

Nell called from upstairs as he came into the house, "Tom!" His mother was in the kitchen washing the dishes she had said she'd leave stacked for Greta in the morning. "Hi!" he called to her. "See you in a minute!" And he went up to Nell in the dark bedroom.

She was lying across the foot of their bed, her legs stretched out to Julie's cot: the smooth quicksilver flow of light on silk— "Daddy! Daddy!" cried Julie, bouncing on her pillow. "You have to tell me a story!" He bent over Nell; she did not move; in the light from the hall he could see the moist brown hair curling loosely at her temple—it always waved in the damp weather; he could not see her eyes looking up at him; but the shadows on her face changed when she spoke: "I'm so tired, Tom. I just couldn't tell her a story."

"You feel sick?"

"Tired."

"Sure? Anything wrong?—Be *quiet*, Julie!—The drive too much for you?"

"No."

He put one hand out toward her: her slim and delicate knees, he thought, this lovely line of bone and rounding flesh. But she quickly sat up. "No, don't. I've got to help your mother do dishes."

"You *don't* have to!" he told her angrily. "Go to bed if you're tired!"

"I want to help her." She stood up, brushed slowly, provocatively past him in the narrow space between cot and big bed; then she stood in the doorway, watching him look at her, outlined in profile against the hall light, small, fragile, very trim in her coarse green linen but swelling in the faint and beautiful curve of early pregnancy; the light caught the clean straight line of her nose, her vivid lips; she turned slightly and it marked one breast and shoulder.

"Did you have a nice ride?" she asked mockingly.

Nodding he said: "It's getting ready to rain."

"Have a good talk with Greta?"

"She told me where to turn," he said. "I wish you'd go to bed."

He sat on the cot beside Julie, who was beating her heels savagely on the mattress. "Daddy!—Please!" He turned to her.

"Shhhh!" When Nell spoke again he was surprised; he thought she had gone.

"Well, she was certainly excited about getting a ride from *you*," Nell said. "The way she talked to your mother anyhow!" Slowly as he watched she shifted her weight from one hip to the other, and the pattern of light on her dress changed. She laughed lightly, intimately. "Are you glad to be home, Tom?"

"Yes, I'm glad."

"As glad as you thought you'd be?"

"I don't know," he said. "Yes, I guess so. Why?"

"I just wondered." She laughed again with the same light intimate suggestion of being in on a secret. Laughing she went down the hall.

"*Daddy!*"

He looked out of the dark room into the empty bright doorway where Nell had stood.

"All right, honey. Once upon a time," he said vaguely, and stopped.

"*Dad-dy!*"

"Once upon a time there was a little girl named Esmerelda."

"Not that one! I-didn't-want-that-one!"

She was spiteful and tired. He looked down at her for the first time since Nell had gone. She lay angrily staring up at him, her arms coming out of the puffy sleeves of her nightgown in sturdy right angles, out and up, dark on the pillow, like a frame for her head. As he bent over her she grabbed his face with both her hands. "I-want-the-island!" she hissed at him. Under the bedcover she thrashed her legs furiously and squirmed. Head down, he smiled. The terrific femininity of the child! Her small fingers were digging into his cheeks; with complete and angry confidence she was demanding things of him, prepared to be sweet if he was obliging, ready to weep if he refused. My God, he thought, slipping his arm under her, someday she'll get married, some little squirt of a boy so high now will grow up and marry her; I suppose it's all right, there's nothing I can do. Hugging her, he rocked back and forth with her, remembering his mother hugging her on the bottom porch steps when they came, rocking with her. She was warm, talcum-fragrant, and tiny; she had Nell's fragility. Now she twisted in his arms. "All right, all right," he murmured, hugging her, "I'll tell you the island." She settled back and he sat up. "Once upon a time in the middle of the ocean there was a little island, and in the centre of the island there was a high hill . . ."

He spoke the familiar words of the story without really thinking of them, yet hearing them, like someone else's words, a kind of slow murmurous background beyond his thoughts. He thought of the three women, his mother, his wife, and his daughter; he thought of mirrors, a hall of mirrors, down which reflections went glancing in light. Out of my mother's womb, he thought, and felt a little embarrassed;—and then in my wife's contemporary womb I perpetuate my parents. Julie wriggled beneath the covers: bone, he thought, and flesh—and he wondered if the child Nell was carrying would be a girl or a boy. He spoke the words of the story to his daughter, and thought of Greta Johnson: she was in another continuity, outside this house; here there was only mother and wife and child together with him, and everyone else was far off, even his father. He finished the story and glanced at Julie. She lay quiet with closed eyes. He sat there beside her: reflections glancing in a long hall of mirrors, he thought; and, puzzled, he groped in his memory for some faint tantalizing clue, and suddenly remembered looking as a boy, in this very room or maybe in the kitchen, at a magazine cover on which was a man looking at the cover of the very same magazine on which was a tiny man looking at the tinier cover of the very same magazine on which— It was like that now, yes, overwhelming and elusive. He felt a little giddy, yet was pleased at recapturing the memory. It was good to be home, curious to be remembering what in this very same room or maybe in the kitchen—

Softly he stood up. Julie sighed deeply in her sleep. He waited, crouching over the cot-head. Then slowly he backed away. At the door he stopped, glancing at the open window across the room, then went back and gently drew the cover up closer around Julie's neck.

Then he went out of the bedroom and downstairs to Nell and his mother.

They had finished the dishes and were sitting at the kitchen table talking. Bright light glittered on the porcelain table top, but out of the back hall and the pantry spilled the brown gloom he remembered there; and the scalloped edge of oilcloth on the pantry shelves thrust its old design out at him with a sudden urgency: once he had pulled a chair over to stand on to get something from one of those scalloped shelves, the chair had tipped, he had bruised his head or his hand, his mother had rocked him—

Both women looked at him as he came toward the table, his mother sitting angularly back in a straight chair with her hands in her lap, Nell leaning forward.

"Now look, good ladies," he said, "I don't want to cut in on you, but you're going to have the next twelve days for talking. It's nine o'clock now and *you*"—he pointed to Nell—"are going to bed!"

His mother took off her glasses. "Can't he leave us alone?" she said to Nell.

"Quiet! Quiet!"

"Is he always so bossy?"

"Always," said Nell. But she stood up.

"I'd run away from him," said his mother. "I'd leave him. I'd get another man."

Nell laughed. "Tomorrow," she said. "I'll do it tomorrow. But right now I'll humor him and go to bed. I am tired."

"What he needs is a talking to and I'm his ma. Come here, Tom Barnaby!"

He pushed Nell toward the door. "Go on!" he said. "I've got to argue with my mamma."

Nell slipped away from him and kissed his mother goodnight.

"I'll be up to see you in a minute," he called to her as she went out.

He sat down at the table; his mother laughed with gladness. "You oppus!" she said.

"How're you feeling, Mother?"

"Good."

"I mean honestly now."

"Sure, honestly—good."

"Have you had any more trouble?"

"No-o-o!" she snorted contemptuously.

"I'll find out from Dad anyhow. You might as well tell me."

"Stop doubting your mother!—Oh, I'm *glad* you're home, Tommy!"

"Well, I'm glad to be home."

"I wish Dad was here. He felt so bad going away when you were coming. Honestly he just did everything to get out of it, but that other agent, I don't know whether you know him, he's a new one, Eberhardt his name is, and I guess I told you his wife is—"

"Wait, Mother," he told her, getting up. "I'll be back in a minute. I want to hurry Nell along up there."

Before she could answer he hurried from the kitchen. Nell was up in the bedroom undressing in the dark. From the doorway he watched her swift pale movements. "I'm getting *big*," she whispered.

"Good reason."

Mincingly she came close to him, on tiptoe, her bare feet and the flowing ankle-length gown making her seem very tiny. "You don't really like me this way," she murmured.

"Oh yes."

"Well, you seemed pretty much interested in giving that girl a ride home!"

He laughed. "She's in another continuity, Nell."

"*What?*"

"She's in another continuity."

"Well, I don't like her," Nell said, "and I never will. She better keep away from you while we're here!"

"What's the matter with you?" He tried to hold her but she twisted away; he caught the fresh bright fragrance of her perfume.

"She's a big dumb blonde," said Nell; she waited; he said nothing. "Do *you* think she's good-looking?" she said.

"No-o-o!"

"She's big as a house. I'd hate to see her if *she* got pregnant."

He laughed. "Look," he said, "why don't you go to bed?"

Slowly she sidled up to him, very small, very yielding when he seized her. But she pressed him back after a moment. He tried to hold her, his face in her hair. "What's that you've got on?" he murmured breathing in deep.

"Do I smell good?"

"Umm."

"I swiped some of your cologne." Laughing softly she slid out of his arms and ran on tiptoe to the bed, her gown full and floating. He was after her at once, but she lay primly under the sheet, smiling up at him. "No, Tom, don't. I *am* tired."

"Yes," he said, standing over her, "you're tired. Why don't you let me alone if you're so tired?"

"I'm a disturber of the peace," she said. "When are you coming to bed?"

"Oh, in a little while. I'll talk to Mother for a while now."

"Well, of course, if you'd rather do that—"

"Don't," he said.

"You'd better come soon," she said.

He kissed her. "You're no good," he whispered. "I'm going over to see Greta."

"What did you say about her before? About a continuity?"

"She's not in our continuity," he repeated.

"Oh," said Nell.

"But she's our contemporary," he added.

"Oh, yes!" said Nell. "Goodnight now."

He looked over at Julie in the cot, remembering again with uneasiness that one day she would probably be taken away from him by one of her contemporaries, and there was nothing to do about it. At the door he waved to Nell. Then, shutting it quietly behind him, he went downstairs to his mother.

✦

She was in the front room in the old big chair beside the dimly humming radio. The newspaper was in her lap, and the light beside her was bright; at the window beyond her he heard a pinching bug bump the screen once and then sluggishly buzz. But it was not till he was directly in front of her that he saw she was not reading. Her head was tilted forward and her eyes were closed. At that moment she looked her age, a gaunt stringy grey woman; from her he got his big loose bones, his ranginess; he looked at her hand lying limp on the chair arm, her blunt large-knuckled fingers with the wiry sinews stretching across sunken freckled flesh. Then instantly her hand quickened; her eyes opened and smiled at him; and at once her whole body was revitalized; energy came from her with an almost electrical urgency.

"Ha!" she said. "Taking my nap."

"Did you take your nap this afternoon?"

"No."

"You wrote me you were supposed to take one every day."

"A-a-h!" she cried, waving her hand at him. "That was a month ago!"

He laughed at the excited contemptuous face she was making.

"Nell all right?" she demanded, leaning toward him.

"Sure. She was tired, that's all. It was awfully hot driving."

"How's she been?"

"Well . . . pretty sick for a while there. I wrote you. She's all right now."

"I hope it's a boy," she said, grinning suddenly.

"Yes, we hope so too. But you can't do much about that."

She brooded. "Nell drinking much milk?" she demanded.

"What the doctor told her," he said. "I forget just what it is. Milk and orange juice."

"She ought to have a lot of milk and vegetables. All kinds of vegetables, raw if she can take 'em that way. I remember with you, all I wanted was milk and carrots. *Raw* carrots. I used to scrape them and soak them in cold water. Dad thought I was crazy, but it was the best thing I could have eaten. Old Dr. Adamson told me afterward I couldn't have—"

"It's not that it really matters about its being a boy," he interrupted. "I mean we really don't care."

"Oh, no!" she said emphatically. "No, *of course!* But still with Julie now it'd be nice if this time—"

"You and Nell," he said, "you both want boys. So does Julie, she wants a brother. Me, I'll stick to girls. I don't care."

"You always did like the girls, didn't you, Tom?" she grinned.

"Sure!"

"I *wish* Dad was here," she said, as if this was what they had been talking about all along, or was so intimately connected with the subject as not to make any real break. "You know that other agent, that Eberhardt, I think he shoves off all the *hard* work on Dad. I can't say anything, you know how Dad is. But now you take last month, it was just like this, Eberhardt was supposed to go out to Silver Lake . . ."

Her voice went on in its strong old familiar rhythm; he found himself listening to its sound, not its words. Then he realized that it was like his own voice earlier this night, a background to his thoughts, an unobtrusive steady flow of sound beyond him; he could listen to it or not, as he liked; and even without listening he could be aware of it without any distraction to the stream of his own thoughts. With Julie he could do this same thing, hear her and yet not hear her. But not with Nell; her voice was never a background; you had to listen when Nell talked. Maybe it was something in the blood, the way the blood flowed, the same blood in his mother and him and his daughter. And thinking of blood he let himself listen again; his mother was almost whispering now; she was leaning toward him, her eyes intent, her glasses upraised in one hand. ". . . and so Dad says, 'Well, if the doctor wants it that way why don't you get that Greta Johnson to do the real hard work for you, she's real nice and she's had experience, she can even stay with you while I'm out on trips.' But of course after I'd heard about her I didn't know what to do. Still, I had to get somebody."

"How long have you had her, Mother?"

"About four months. Since Easter. I wrote you when I got her but of course I didn't want to put things like this in a letter. You see nobody knows if she was ever married to this man, her mother says they were married and then separated, but she never says anything herself, not a word has that girl said since she's been in this house about that man or her having the baby—"

"This is Greta you're talking about?"

"Sure, Greta. You'd never think, would you? But I *must* say, if all girls were as good workers as she is, and so *nice* to talk to—"

"How long ago was all this? I mean—"

"Oh, the boy's two years old now. I kind of wish she'd mention him sometime to me, I'd like to send him something. *You* know—"

"Does he live with her, at her folks?"

"Sure. And the best looking little boy, Dad says. He sees him sometimes when he drives Greta home at night. I've never seen him. You didn't see him tonight, did you?"

"No . . ."

Just then Julie cried in the bedroom.

"Well, it was late tonight, maybe his grandma put him to bed."

Julie cried again. Barnaby got up and ran on tiptoe to the foot of the stairs. He stood there a few seconds listening. Another continuity, he thought, she certainly is in another continuity. My contemporary—

His mother clicked off the almost inaudible radio. "Julie *sick?*" she whispered tensely.

He shook his head, waited an instant more at the stairs, then crossed the room to her. "She wakes up that way," he explained, softly. "I don't know what it is, dreams or indigestion or what. She goes right back to sleep, though."

His mother stood up. "We better go to sleep too," she whispered. "We disturb her, jabbering this way."

"Well, I'll lock up and put the lights out," he told her. "We'll jabber some more tomorrow."

She started toward the stairs, then checked herself contemptuously. "Every *night!*" she cried. "*Every* night I start climbing those stairs. Can't remember I sleep down here now!"

When she had gone out of the room he started snapping lights; he latched the front door; then, unbuttoning his shirt, went out on the side porch and stood looking up at the sky. There were no stars, only a kind of faint low-hanging luminosity. A damp wind blew. He was tired. Sometimes too much happened. He felt secure. Glad to be home. All mixed up and good. Tomorrow have to sort out his thoughts. About his mother and wife and daughter and Greta, yes, Greta. Thoughts about everything, mirrors and continuities. Tomorrow Julie will marry and my father will come home, tomorrow. He shut his eyes and the wind blew on his face.

Inside the house he heard his mother call him. She wants my father home and the baby a boy. "Here I am," he called, and went in.

She wore a flannelette gown; her hair hung in two sparse braids. He put his arm around her and led her to her bedroom. She smelled faintly of camphor or menthol.

"Go to bed now," she told him as he tucked her in.

In the darkness he could not see her face, but he bent down and her groping hand found him and patted his cheek.

He kissed her. "Good night, Mamma."

"Good night, Tommy!"

He shut the door quietly.

Then Julie cried again upstairs and undressing as he went he hurried to her.

It was warm and black in the bedroom, warm and black, and he stumbled toward Julie's cot. "What is it, honey?"

She wailed something wordless; he stretched out his arms to find her in the black room. "It's all right, honey, it's all right," he whispered. "We don't want to wake Mamma, honey."

"Story," said Julie, and sat up mumbling. "Story," she said.

He pressed her gently back on the pillow. "Once there was a little girl named Esmerelda," he murmured, "and she asked her daddy to tell her a story. 'All right,' he said, 'I'll tell you a story. Once there was a little girl named Esmerelda and she asked her daddy to tell her a story. "All right," he said, "I'll tell you a story. Once there was a little girl—"'"

He slowed up and stopped. She lay quiet. Hurriedly he pulled off the rest of his clothes in the darkness.

In the big bed Nell sat slowly up. "Wha's a matter?" she whispered sleepily.

"Nothing. It's all right." He climbed into bed.

Very low and rich and intimate her laughter came in the secret darkness. "Silly story," she murmured. "Esmerelda."

She rolled away from him, her sleep-warm fragrance filling all the darkness. Faraway, faraway he heard the wind, and on the roof now slow black rain dropped quietly. Home, he thought, and secret darkness. Then she laughed again. "Silly," she explained drowsily, "same old thing, goes on an' on."

He felt sleep in the dark room hover over him, soft and compelling. "That's right," he murmured to her, "goes on and on." And beside him in the darkness Nell laughed with rich and sleepy delight.

HYMAN SWETZOFF:
THE TRIP

CHARLES hadn't slept a great deal on the train; he had been too excited. Now his small face, long and pale, assumed the look of the feeling of fear that had come suddenly out.

He had been to Boston before. It seemed to him, alone, to take on a crackling newness. The marble pillars hid something. Uncertainty made him pause and go across the marble where his loneliness increased because of the glassy look of things; he felt he was being stared at through the case it formed around him.

His mother had always approached a taxi madly. The driver seemed to know where she was going. Charles started to run, duplicating his mother's rush, but he felt the driver knew this and he stopped. The driver opened the door and Charles stumbled in.

It was too dark to see where he was going but the city seemed to have the same feeling as New York; after coughing out this information to himself, he fell asleep.

After he had been prodded awake and carried upstairs, kissed by an old lady slightly taller than himself and put to bed, he could remember only the kiss and the rich aroma between his lips and hers.

He accepted the experience of waking in his own pajamas, in a large room, entirely soft-carpeted, with the large windows partially covered with heavy drapes, as he did any experience his mother had given or shown him. The bed was warm and comfortable and he stayed in it as he would have been allowed to had he been at home. His mother ofter stayed in bed for a long time. She recognized this instinct in her son as hereditary and, since it came from her, let him lie. In his home he was always quiet, a little jar half-filled with a liquid that rarely slapped against its sides.

Even now he moved a soft slender white foot from the bed as though he were afraid he might spill something. He discovered on looking out that he was in the gambrelled third story of a house that looked like all the other houses around it, staring out to a peaceful iron-rimmed park.

After Charles had washed and dressed he opened the door to go downstairs. Outside, a small candle burned on a table, the darkness surrounding the light with jagged edges. The floor, the bannister, the doors continued down the corridor and disappeared. The floors were carpeted here, too.

Quickly Charles shut the door behind him and ran down the stairs, down another long hall and down more stairs where the small woman stood waiting for him.

The wrinkles of her face lifted in surprise . . . What is the matter? . . . in a light voice held down with a heavy accent.

Charles blushed . . . I . . . was afraid.

Her face did not have to go far to resume its natural expression—a larger wrinkle, in the center of her face, curved.

He sat at breakfast as he did at luncheon, with three women. His mother's "friend" (he could not discover how or when and therefore could not see his mother choosing this woman as a friend—she would not be one of his) and another woman still smaller than his mother's friend. Her mother. He could not quite understand what they said, they were so strange. The other woman, to his left, had her hat on and talked generously, and on her he put a name because she reminded him of someone he knew. Then, promptly, he tried to forget them all.

The dining room was lit even in the early morning from a green-shaded lamp suspended low over the table. The light was never bright and from where he sat on a low chair he could see one small bulb shining.

Wandering from the room through a spacious high foyer into a sitting room, Charles found the atmosphere the same. It was like the bottom of a deep well. He might have been living continually with memories caught between two leaded panes of glass.

His mother's friend came in some time after and suggested he take the air, putting in her voice the line of demarcation between his sex and hers. Charles looked out of the window. Obediently he slipped from the chair.

The texture and color of the day hadn't changed. He had never seen the house from the outside and his eyes followed the brownstone façade up and down until his attention was caught by a small sign in the first story window. He grimaced a little and read: *Rooms for Rent.*

He walked around the park as he would have walked around himself. He felt among the trees the same serenity he felt when he was alone. And now he was even more serene: he knew everything. There was no doubt about this woman's relationship with his mother, and he thought of it with a certain fastidiousness.

Entering the house was like passing through all the shades of black.

During lunch he became slightly nettled when the loquacious one began to give off a feeling of being vexed and saying so in so many words (though she said nothing about her vexation). Now and then she muttered under her breath.

The landlady was pouring wine from a tall dark glass decanter. Embarrassed, one movement seeming the cause of the other, Charles lowered his eyes to his plate, perfectly aware when he raised them that the glass had been emptied and was going to be filled again. He lowered his eyes again to the plate. His mother had never approved of women's drinking, and he remembered this with the touch of glass on glass, and the gurble of liquid as it spilled, it seemed, into the cavity of his ear. As she sat, the landlady stiffened in her chair and swayed through the meal. The loquacious one talked, oblivious of the fact that she was not answered.

Grateful to be able to leave, he finished his milk, excused himself, and went into the sitting room, pushing one of the armchairs near the window. By degrees he lowered himself out of sight into a book. The other armchair creaked and sighed; there was a faint rustling of silk, the rasp of paper on wood, and a slight wind from the turning pages of a magazine. The woman with the hat had come in. Charles tried to look at her with the top part of his eyes, but she was staring at him and he had time only to notice that now she wore no hat and that her chair was nearer to him than it had been.

He read hastily, disturbed to tenseness from being watched, disturbed because a faint hum was taking the place of the letters on paper. He looked up. It was as though she had snapped down the lid of a box.

I want to put you next to something . . . Casually she rose and moved to the sliding doors of the parlor. After closing them she sat down again.

Don't let her . . . she shrugged her shoulders, shifting her eyes to the closed doors . . . make you do things. She's like all landladies. Give them a finger and they take the whole hand . . .

And you know how foreigners are, always keeping wine in the house . . .

Charles stared at her red middle-aged face and boyishly cut hair.

She has barrels of it, barrels. She drinks all the time . . . She waved her hand. The same hand straightened the jacket of her suit.

She'll do anything to get you to do something for nothing. For instance, when I first moved in . . .

Charles was pleased at the idea of a story.

. . . I asked her to clean my room and she said she would. That's simple, isn't it? . . . without waiting for an answer . . . I moved into the next room. I waited, of course, but she did it so slowly I decided to help. I wanted to get settled . . . Do you know what she did? . . . The woman stared at Charles, who shook his head . . . No sooner did I start to help than she walked right out of the door and didn't come back . . . I . . . she closed her eyes with indignation . . . I cleaned the room myself . . .

But wait . . . Charles stopped moving . . . She said she would get a boy to help me. He was no boy. He was a man . . . Her voice stopped high and came down . . . He was drunk. She gets him drunk. She gives him all the liquor he wants . . . Her voice lowered and became low with hatred and disgust . . . And you can see *he* has all the earmarks of a gentleman . . .

Charles stared. He couldn't understand, but in him a gaseous vapor of fear began to form. He had been listening so intently that with her he began to form a hate that distended the landlady to a vague but horrible meaning.

You are not feeling well. You had better go home . . . her voice softened. Charles came to himself with a start. But she hadn't been talking to him . . . So I sent him home . . . Then, no sooner finished . . . It's good you are not staying long. This house is a morgue.

She talked on, telling him about her life, asking him polite questions, become unusually formal after the first outflow of confidence. The constant vacillating between being a grown man and a small boy tired Charles. He wished she would go.

It was almost dark when she left the room. Charles waited until he thought he heard her climbing the stairs and then he too left. He seemed to hear voices behind him and he hurried into the lighted dining room, shivering. The house was a morgue, he thought.

The door leading from the dining room into the kitchen was open. He heard movement there, and as he stepped forward curiously, a man's voice came to him, gentle, precise. He did not move. The house had fallen into a deeper silence, entering him, making him as sensitive as a tuning fork. A masculine voice said . . . Thank you . . . and a woman's voice answered it, coquettishly. That was the landlady's voice. And the other was the gentleman's—with all the earmarks, Charles thought, fascinated. His mind leaped like a satyr from thought to thought. This was the man . . . who . . . His mind would not stay still. All the half-formed words that were spoken and held at the same time when he was in the room, all the glances, long, slippery, directed sometimes toward him and sometimes toward other things—they all came back. He could not stop them.

At supper Charles looked as little as possible at anything but his food. After it was finished, the immense fear of the emptiness and the gloom almost prevented him from going upstairs. Now he was really afraid to go up, but more afraid to stay down and listen. He didn't want to hear anything.

While he had been thinking, he had come up the stairs into his room. He undressed quickly and slid into bed, and was no sooner covered than the landlady came in. She seemed to know when he was getting up and when he was going to bed, and she came in so quietly that she made of her entrance something full of tact. Charles could appreciate it now.

Are you all right?

The words fell down on him as she bent over. Charles stiffened, rejecting the slight winy touch of the lips to his rigid cheek. The whole afternoon flooded to him. He could not understand why his mother had sent him here except for him to learn these things that were so formless and yet filled him with unspeakable fears and thoughts.

Outside, the stairs creaked as though two people and not one were descending. She had switched off the light beside his bed, but he put it on again, aware of the darkness that enclosed him, of the flickering candle outside the door. His feet were cold against the sheets; he wanted to cry. He thought he heard something, someone walk up the stairs, and when a door closed he started to cry.

Someone had been in his room and put off the light. Startled, he realized that he had fallen asleep and that someone had entered his room. His door wasn't locked and he didn't dare turn the key. Bitter, he went back to bed, angry that he was not permitted to do here what he was permitted to do at home.

He couldn't bear the thought that came to him that he belonged here, that he was born here, and his mother was a dream. The thought of his mother tantalized him, and he became afraid to go beyond the ambiguous events that seemed to find their cause in her. His mother was a dream. And she—she was kind because his mother paid her to be kind. His thoughts swirled and changed in front of his eyes, approaching, departing in flaming sentences, and the image of his mother and that woman became mixed and their faces leered at him.

He awoke the next morning happily until through the haze of

sleep he realized where he was. Dressing sullenly he walked about this room trying to explain to himself this lump in his mind that he could not melt. Angrily he walked down the stairs.

He ate breakfast with the spring inside of him tightening. He knew he could say nothing, do nothing. He could not even think or stop from thinking. Things happened without his having any control over them. The frustration, the bitterness of an experience he could not fathom, still held him. His hate flowered from his anger, frustrated by all the conventions his mother had taught him. For the first time, he began to doubt her word.

The landlady coming down the stairs interrupted him. She held his suitcase out to him with a smile, and he took it shuddering with aversion. She had touched the clothes he wore next to his skin, and the thought became unbearable to him.

The taxi was standing at the curb as they came out. He waited for her to say something. Instead she embraced him and he shuddered again. He knew she would feel the movement and with a rapid twist he disentangled himself from her arms, the emotion coming to his throat and no farther. Tears sprang to his eyes, he pushed her again, opened the door of the taxi . . . Go away! he suddenly shouted. Go away!

EUDORA WELTY:

IDA M'TOY

FOR ONE human being to point out another as "unforgettable"
seems a trifle condescending, and in the ideal world we would
all keep well aware of each other, but there are nevertheless a
few persons one meets who are as inescapable of notice as sky-
rockets, it may be because like skyrockets they are radiant with
their own substance and shower it about regardlessly. Ida M'Toy,
an old Negro woman, for a long time a midwife in my little
Mississippi town and for another long time a dealer in second-
hand clothes in the same place, has been a skyrocket as far back
as most people remember. Or, rather, she is a kind of meteor (for
she is not ephemeral, only sudden and startling). Her ways seem
on a path of their own without regard to any course of ours and
of a somewhat wider circuit; she will probably leave a glow behind and return in the far future on some other lap of her career-
ing through all our duller and steadier bodies. She herself deals
with the rest of us in this mighty and spacious way, calling in
allegories and the elements, so it is owing to her nature that I may
speak a little grandly.

The slave traders of England and New England, when they
went capturing, took away the most royal of Africans along
with their own slaves, and I have not much doubt that Ida has
come down from a race of tall black queens. I wish I might have
seen her when she was young. She has sharp clever features,
light-filled black eyes, arched nostrils, and fine thin mobile lips,
and her hair, gray now, springs like a wild kind of diadem from
the widow's peak over her forehead. Her voice is indescribable
but it is a constant part of her presence and is filled with invoca-

tion. She never speaks lightly of any person or thing, but she flings out her arm and points at something and begins, "O, precious, I'm telling you to look at that—*look* at it!" and then she invokes about it, and tolerates no interruptions. I have heard long chants and utterances on the origin and history and destination of the smallest thing, any article or object her eye lights on; a bit of candle stuck on the mantelpiece will set her off, as if its little fire had ignited her whole mind. She invokes what she wishes to invoke and she has in all ways something of the seer about her. She wields a control over great numbers of her race by this power, which has an integrity that I believe nothing could break, and which sets her up, aloof and triumphant, above the rest. She is inspired and they are not. Maybe off by themselves they could be inspired, but nobody else could be inspired in the same room with Ida, it would be too crowded.

Ida is not a poor old woman, she is a rich old woman. She accepts it that she is held in envy as well as respect, but it is only another kind of tribute as far as she is concerned, and she is not at all prouder of being rich or of having been married in the home of a white lady, "in her bay window," than she is of being very wise. She expects to be gaped at, but she is not vain.

Ida's life has been divided in two (it is, in many ways, eloquent of duality); but there is a thread that runs from one part into the other, and to trace this connection between delivering the child and clothing the man is an interesting speculation. Moreover, it has some excuse, for Ida herself helps it along by a wild and curious kind of talk that sashays from one part to the other and sounds to some of her customers like "ranting and raving." It is my belief that if Ida had not been a midwife she would not be the same kind of second-hand clothes dealer she is. Midwifery set her off, it gave her a hand in the mysteries, and she will never let go that flying hold merely because she is engaged in something else. An ex-alchemist would run a second-hand clothes business with extra touches—a reminiscence of glitter would cling to the garments he sold, and it is the same with Ida. So it is well when you meet her to think what she was once.

Ida's memory goes back to her beginnings, when she was, she

says, the first practical nurse in Jackson at the age of twenty-one, and she makes the past sound very dark and far back. She thanks God, she says, that today Capitol Street is not just three planks to walk on and is the prettiest place on earth, but that "people white and black is too high and don't they know Ida seen them when they carried a little tin coal-oil lamp that wasn't any bigger than their little fingers?" Ida speaks of herself in the third person and in indirect discourse often and especially when she says something good of herself or something of herself long ago. She will intone, "Ida say that she was good to the poor white people as she was to the rich, as she made a bargain to nurse a poor white lady in obstetrical case for a peck of peas. Ida said no, she couldn't see her suffer, and therefore a peck of blackeyed peas would be sufficient." She wants all she says to be listened to with the whole attention, and declares she does wish it were all written down. "Let her keep it straight, darling, if she remember Ida's true words, the angels will know it and be waiting around the throne for her." But Ida's true words are many and strange. When she talks about the old days it is almost like a story of combat against evil. "Ida fitted a duel from twenty-one to fifty-six, and then they operated on her right side and she was never able to stoop down to the floor again. She was never like those young devils, that pace around in those white shoes and those white clothes and up and down the streets of an evening while their patient is calling for a drink of water down poor parched throat—though I wore those white shoes and those white clothes. Only, my heart was in another direction."

Ida said, "I was nursing ever since there was a big road in Jackson. There was only nine doctors, and they were the best in all the world, all nine, right here in Jackson, but they were weak in finance. There wasn't nary hospital nowhere—there wasn't nary brick in Jackson, not one brick, no brick walk, no brick store, no brick nothing-else. There wasn't no Old Ladies' Home at the end of the street, there wasn't no stopping place but the country. Town was as black as tar come night, and praise God they finally put some gas in bottles on the corners.

There wasn't no such thing in the world as a nice buggy. Never heard tell of a cotton mattress, but tore up shucks and see the bed, so high, and the hay pillow stand up so beautiful! Now they got all this electric light and other electricity. Can't do nothing without the clickety-click. And bless God they fly just like buzzards up in the air, but Ida don't intend to ride till she ride to Glory."

In those early days when Jackson seems to have been a Slough of Despond with pestilence sticking out its head in the nights as black as tar, Ida was not only a midwife, she nursed all diseases. "It was the yellow fever first, and the next after that was the worst pox that there ever was in this world—it would kill you then, in my girl-days, six or seven a day. They had to stretch a rope across the road to keep the poor sick ones apart and many's the day I've et at the rope and carried the food back to the ones suffering." Ida remembers epidemics as major combats in which she was a kind of giant-killer. She nursed through influenza "six at a blow, until the doctor told me if I didn't quit nursing by sixes I would drop dead in the room." She says the doctors wrote her a recommendation as long as where she will show you up her arm, saying that when they called, it never was too cold and it never was too hot for Ida to go, and that the whole town would bow and say Amen, from the Jews on. "Bless my patients," she says, "nary one ever did die under my nursing, though plenty were sick enough to die. But laugh here," she directs. "My husband stayed sick on me twenty-one years and cost me one thousand whole dollars, but you can't nurse the heart to do no good, and in the night he fallen asleep and left me a widow, and I am a widow still."

When Ida found she could no longer stoop to the floor she stopped being a midwife and began selling clothes. She was successful at once in that too, for there is a natural flowering-ground for the second-hand clothes business in the small American community where the richest people are only a little richer than the poor people and the poorest have ways to save pride and not starve or go naked. In Jackson the most respectable matron, if she would like a little extra cash to buy a new camellia bush or take the excursion to New Orleans, can run over to Ida's with her husband's other suit and Ida will sell it to a customer as a bargain at $5 and collect 25% for herself, and everybody except the husband ("Right off my back! Perfectly good suit!") will be satisfied.

It could be a grubby enough little business in actual fact, but Ida is not a grubby person, and in her handling it has become an affair of imagination and, to my notion, an expression of a whole attitude of life as integrated as an art or a philosophy.

Ida's store is her house, a white-painted little house with a porch across the front, a picket-fence around, and the dooryard planted to capacity in big flowers. Inside, it is a phantasmagoria of garments. Every room except the kitchen is hung with dresses or suits (the sexes are segregated) three and four times around the walls, for the turnover is large and unpredictable, though not always rapid—people have to save up or wait for cotton-money. She has assumed all the ceremonies of Business and employs its practices and its terms to a point within sight of madness. She puts on a show of logic and executive order before which the customer is supposed to quail; sometimes I think her customers take on worth with her merely as witnesses of the miracles of her workings, though that is unfair. Her house turns year by year into a better labyrinth, more inescapable, and she delights in its complication of aisles and curtains and its mystery of closed doors with little signs on ruled paper, "Nobody can come in here." Some day some little colored girl is going to get lost in Ida's house. The richer she gets, the more "departments" she builds and adds on to the house, and each one is named for the color of its walls, the pink department, or the blue. Even now her side yard is filled with miscellaneous doors, glass panes, planks, and little stacks of bricks that she is accumulating for a new green department she says she will build in 1943.

Her cupboards and drawers are a progressive series of hiding places, which is her interpretation of the filing system. She hides trinkets of mysterious importance or bits of paper filled with abbreviated information; she does not hide money, however, and she tells how much she has on hand ($660.60 is the latest figure), and her life insurance policy is nailed up on the wall over the mantel. Everybody knows her to be an old woman living with only a small grandchild to guard her in a house full of cash money, and yet she has not been murdered. She never will be. I have wondered what Ida would do if she saw a burglar coming after her money. I am convinced that she has no axe or gun ready for him, but a flow of words will be unstoppered that will put the fear of God in him for life; and I think the would-be burglars have the same suspicion, and will continue to keep away, not wanting so much fear of God as that.

She keeps as strict and full a ledger of transaction as the Book of Judgment, and in as enthusiastic and exalted a spirit of accuracy as an angel book-keeper should have. The only trouble is, it is almost impossible to find in it what she is looking for—but perhaps there will be confusion on Doomsday too. The book, a great black one, which she now has little William, her grandson, to hold for her while she consults it, (and he will kneel under it like a little mural figure) covers a period of 26 years, concerns hundreds of people, "white and black," and innumerable transactions, all noted down in a strange code full of flourishes, for Ida properly considers all she does confidential. "You could find anything in the world in this book," she says reverently, then slamming it shut in your face, "if you turn enough pages and go in the right direction. Nothing in here is wrong," she says. Loose slips are always flying out of the ledger like notes in the Sybil's book, and she sets William flying to chase them and get them inside again.

She writes her own descriptions of the garments brought to her to sell, and a lady giving over her finest white dress of last summer must not be surprised, if she looks over Ida's shoulder, to see her pen the words, "Rally Day, $2.00" or note down her best spring straw hat as "Tom Boy, 75c." The customer might be right, but Ida does not ever ask the customer. After a moment of concentration Ida goes and hangs the object for sale on the wall in the room of her choice, and a tag is pinned to the sleeve, saying simply, "Mrs. So-and-So." Accuracy is a passion with Ida, and so is her belief in her own conscience, and I do not know what it must have cost her to pin a tag on one poor sagging dress that has hung there year in, year out, saying "Don't know who this is."

She bears respect to clothes in the same degree as she bears it to the people from whose backs they come; she treats them like these people, until indeed it seems that dignity is in them, shapeless and even ridiculous as they have seemed at first; she gives them the space on the wall and the room in the house that correspond to the honor in which she holds the human beings, and she even speaks in the proper tone of voice when she is in the room with them. They hang at human height from the hangers on the walls, the brighter and more important ones in front and on top. With the most serene impartiality she makes up her mind about client and clothes, and she has been known to say, "For God's sake take it back. Wouldn't a man white or black wear that suit out of here."

There is a magnificence in Ida's business, an extent and an influence at which she hints without ceasing, that undoubtedly inspire the poorest or idlest customer with almost an anxiety to buy. It is almost like an appeasement, and the one that goes off with nothing must feel mean, foolish, and naked indeed, naked to scorn. "I clothe them," she says, "from Jackson to Vicksburg, Meridian to Jackson, Big Black to 'Azoo, Memphis to New Orleans—Clinton! Bolton! Edwards! Bovina! Pocahontas! Flora! Bentonia! 'Azoo City! Everywhere. There ain't nobody hasn't come to Ida, or sooner or later will come."

If no one else had thought of the second-hand clothes business, Ida would have originated it, for she did originate it as far as she is concerned; and likewise I am forced to believe that if there had never been any midwives in the world Ida would have invented midwifery, so ingenious and delicate-handed and wise she is, and sure of her natural right to take charge. She loves transformation and bringing things about, she simply cannot resist it. The Negro midwives of this state have a kind of organization these days and lesser powers, they do certain things in certain book-specified ways, and all memorize and sing at meetings a song about "First we put—Drops in their eyes," but in

Ida's day a midwife was a lone person, invested with the whole charge of life; she had to draw upon her own resources and imagination. Ida's constant gestures today still involve a dramatic out-thrust of the right hand, and let any prominent names be mentioned (and she mentions them) and she will fling out her palm and cry into the conversation, "Born in this hand!" "Four hundred little white babies,—or more," she says. "My God, I was bringing them all the time. I got 'em everywhere—doctors, lawyers, school teachers, and preachers, married ladies." She has been in the clothes business for twenty-six years, but she was a midwife for thirty-five.

She herself has been married, twice, and by her first husband she had one son, "the only one I ever did have and I want his name written down: Julius Knight." Her mother (before she died) and her brothers live out in the country, and only one little grandson has lived with her for a long time. Her husband, Braddie M'Toy, whom she called Toy, is remembered collecting and delivering clothes in a wagon when he was young, and was to be seen always on some street if not another, moving very slowly on account of his heart.

Now without Toy, Ida uses a telephone down the road and a kind of de luxe grapevine service to rouse up her clients and customers. Anybody who is asked to by Ida feels a duty to phone any stranger for her and "tell them for God's sake to come get their money and bring the change." Strange Negroes call people at dawn, giving news of a sale, white ladies call unknown white ladies, notes on small rolls or scraps of paper folded like doctors' "powders" are conscientiously delivered, and the whole town contrives in her own spirit of emergency to keep Ida's messages on their way. Ida takes 25% of the sales price and if she sells your dress for a dollar you have to take her a quarter when you go, or come back another time, for she will not make change for anybody. She will not violate her system of book-keeping any more than she would violate her code of ethics or her belief in God—down to the smallest thing all is absolute in Ida's sight.

Whether it is due to a savage ancestry or a philosophical turn of mind, Ida finds all Ornament a wonderful and appropriate thing, the proper materializing of the rejoicing or sorrowing soul. I believe she holds Ornament next to birth and somehow kin to it. She despises a drab color and welcomes bright clothes with a queenly and triumphant smile, as if she acknowledges the bold brave heart that chose that. Inferior color means inferior spirit, and an inferior person should not hope to get or spend more than four-bits for an outfit. She dearly loves a dress that is at once identifiable as either rich mourning or "rally-day"—the symbolic and celebrating kind appeal to her inevitably over the warm or the serviceable, and she will ask and (by oratory) get the finest prices for rather useless but splendid garments. "Girl, you buy this spangle-dress," she says to a customer, and the girl buys it and puts it on and shines. Ida's scale of prices would make a graph showing precisely the rise from her condemnation of the subdued and nondescript to her acclaim of the bright and glorious. Her customers, poverty-bound little cooks and maids and cotton-choppers, go away feeling that they have turned into queens. Ida has put second-hand clothes on their backs and, with all the abrupt bullying of a busy fairy, wrapped them in some glowing raiment of illusion, set them in a whirl of bedazzlement; and they skitter out with shining eyes and empty hands, with every hoarded penny spent. Ida has put them in inner spangles and she has taken an actual warm moist fifty-cent piece out of their palms, and in that world both items exchanged are precious above price, fifty cents being as miraculous as glory. With something second-hand, worn, yet finer than could ever be bought new, she brings to them a perfection in her own eyes and in theirs. She dresses them up and turns them with a little ceremonial jerk towards the mirror, and a magic must hang over the green cracked glass, for (I have seen it happen a hundred times) the glances that go into its surface begin to shine with a pride that could only be a kind of enchantment. It is nice on Saturdays to pass in front of Ida's house on the edge of town and see the customers emerge. With some little flash of scarf, some extra glitter of trimming for which they have paid dearly, dressed like some visions in Ida's speculations on the world, glorious or menial as befits their birth, merit, and willingness, but all rampant and somehow fulfilled by this last touch of costume as though they have been tapped by a spirit when Ida's thimble rapped them, they float dizzily down the steps and through the flowers out the gate; and you could not help thinking of the phrase "going out into the world," as if Ida had just birthed them anew.

I used to think she must be, a little, the cross between a transcendentalist and a witch, with the happiness and kind of self-wonder that this combination must enjoy. They say that all things we write could be; and sometimes in amazement I wonder if a tiny spark of the wonderful Philosopher of Clothes, Diogenes Teufelsdröckh, could be flashing for an instant, and somewhat barbarically, in the wild and enthusiastic spirit of this old black woman. Her life like his is proudly emblematic—she herself being the first to see her place in the world. It is she literally who clothes her entire world, as far and wide as she knows—a hard-worked midwife grown old, with a memory like a mill turning through it all the lives that were born in her hand or have passed through her door.

When she stalks about, alternately clapping her hand over her forehead and flinging out her palm and muttering "Born in this hand!" as she is likely to do when some lady of the old days comes bringing a dress to sell, you cannot help believing that she sees them all, her children and her customers, in the double way, naked and clothed, young and then old, with love and with contempt, with open arms or with a push to bar the door. She is moody now, if she has not always been, and sees her customers as a procession of sweet supplicant spirits that she has birthed, who have returned to her side, and again sometimes as a bunch of scarecrows or even changelings, that she wishes were well gone out of sight. "They would steal from their own mother," she says, and while she is pinning up some purchase in a newspaper and the customer is still counting out the pennies, she will shout in a deep voice to the grandchild that flutters around like a little blackbird, "Hold the door, William."

I have never caught Ida doing anything except selling clothes or holding forth on her meditations, but she has a fine garden. "If you want to carry me something I really like," she will say, bringing up the subject first, "carry me dallion potatoes (dahlia bulbs) *first*, and old newspapers second." Ida has the green finger from her mother, and she says, "You're never going to see any flowers prettier than these right here." She adores giving flowers away; under your protest she will cut every one in the garden, every red and white rose on the trellis, which is a wooden sunset with painted rays, the blossoms with little two-inch stems the way a child cuts them, and distribute them among all present and those passing in the road. She is full of all the wild humors and extravagances of the godlike toward this entire town and its environs. Sometimes, owing to her superior wisdom, she is a little malign, but much oftener she will become excruciatingly tender, holding, as if in some responsibility toward all the little ones of the world, the entire population to her great black cameoed breast. Then she will begin to call people "It." "It's all hot and tired, it is, coming so far to see Ida. Ah, take these beautiful flowers Ida grew with her own hand, *that's* what it would like. Put 'em in its bedroom," and she presses forward all the flowers she has cut and then, not content, a bouquet dripping from a vase, one of a kind of everything, all into your arms.

She loves music too, and in her house she has one room, also hung with clothes, called the music room. "I got all the music in the world in here," she used to say, jabbing a finger at a silent radio and an old gramophone shut up tight, "but what's the use of letting those contrivances run when you can make your own music?" And ignoring the humble customers waiting she would fling down at the old pump-organ in the corner and tear into a frenzy of chords. "I make my own!" she would shout into the turmoil. She would send for little William, with a voice like a little bird's, and he knew how to sing with her, though he would give out. "Bass, William!" she would shout, and in his tiny treble he sang bass, bravely.

When Ida speaks of her mother it is in a strange kind of pity, a tender amazement. She says she knew when her mother was going to die, and with her deep feeling for events and commemorations, she gave her a fine big party. Ida would no more shrink from doing anything the grand way than she would shrink from other demands upon her greatness. "Hush now," she told me, "don't say a word while I tell you this. All that day long I was cooking dinner between niggers. I had: four turkeys, four hens, four geese, four hams, red cake, white cake, chocolate cake, caramel cake, every color cake known. The table reached from the front door to the ice box. I had all the lights burning up electricity, and all the flowers cut. I had the plates changed seven times, and three waiters from the hotel. I'd got Mama a partner. Mama was eighty years old and I got her another old lady eighty years old to march with. I had everybody come. All her children—one son, the big shot, came all the way from Detroit, riding in a train, to be at Mama's grand dinner. We had somebody play 'Silent Night' and march music to follow later. And there was Mama: look at Mama! Mama loved powder. Mama had on a little old-fashioned hat, but she wouldn't take it off—had nice hair, too. Mama did all right for the march, she marched all right, and sat down on time at the right place at the head of the table, but she wouldn't take off her hat. So the waiters, they served the chicken soup first, and Mama says, 'Where my coffee? Bring on turnip and cornbread. Didn't you make a blackberry pie?' I said, 'Mama, you don't eat coffee first.' But she said, 'Where my coffee? Bring on turnip and cornbread. Didn't you make a blackberry pie? What's the matter with you?' Everything was so fine, you know. It took her two big sons, one on each side, to quiet her, that's the way Mama acted!" And Ida ended the story laughing and crying. It was plain that there was one person who had no recognition of Ida's grandeur and high place in the world, and who had never yielded at all to the glamour as others did. It was a cruelty for Ida, but perhaps all vision has lived in the house with cruelty.

Nowadays, she is carried to such heights of business and power, and its paraphernalia crowds her so, that she is overcome with herself, and suddenly gives way to the magnitude of it all. A kind of chaos comes over her. Now and then she falls down in a trance and stays "dead as that chair for three days." White doctors love her and by a little struggle take care of her. Ida bears with them. "They took my appendix," she will say. "Well, they took my teeth." She says she has a paralyzed heel, though it is hard to see how she can tell—perhaps like Achilles she feels that her end is coming by entering that way. "The doctor told me I got to rest until 1945," she declares, with a lifted hand warding you off. "Rest! Rest! Rest! I must rest." If a step is heard on the front porch she instantly cries warning from within the house, "Don't set your heels down! When you speak to me, whisper!" When a lady that was a stranger came to see her, Ida appeared, but said in haste, "Don't tell me your name, for I'm resting my mind. The doctors don't want me to have any more people in my head than I got already." Now on Saturdays if a dusty battered car full of customers from across the cotton-fields draws up, one by one all the shades in the house are yanked down. Ida wishes to see no one, she wishes to sell nothing.

Perhaps the truth is that she has expended herself to excess and now suffers with a corresponding emptiness that she does not want anyone to see. She can show you the track of the pain it gives her: her finger crosses her two breasts. She is as hard to see as a queen.

And I think she lives today the way she would rather be living, directly in symbols. People are their vestures now. Memories, the great memories of births and marriages and deaths, are nearly the same as the pieces of jewelry ("$147.65 worth") she has bought on anniversary days and wears on her person. "That's Mama's death," she says—a silver watch on a silver chain. She holds out for your admiration the yellow hands that she asserts most of this country was born in, on which now seven signet rings flash. "Don't go to church any longer," she says—"or need to go. I just sit at home and enjoy my fingers."

RICHARD WRIGHT:

THE MAN WHO LIVED UNDERGROUND

Two Excerpts from a Novel

H E HEADED toward the opening that would allow him to crawl to his dirt room and a sense of quiet expectancy suffused his entire being; the sensations of his body were given over without reservation to the elaborate emotional game he was playing with himself. When he reached the opening he pushed the sack in and climbed in himself. It was arduous work; first, he had to stretch out his arms full length, push the sack; then, clutching the pipe above him, he would draw himself forward. He finally reached the end of the passageway and gave the sack a hard shove and heard it hit the dirt floor beyond. When he struck the ground, it was with difficulty that he kept on his feet. For a long time he did not stir, then he shook his head and wiped sweat from his brow with his sleeve. He struck a match and contemplated his loot; the match died and he worked in darkness. Seeing with his fingers, he emptied the sack and set each item neatly on the earth floor.

He lit another one of his few remaining matches and bent over the tool box and took out the bulb, the socket, and the wire; he discovered to his elation that there was a double socket on one end of the wire. He crammed the stuff into his pocket as the match flickered out. He hoisted himself again upon the rusty pipes upon which he had lain and watched the men and women singing their hymns, and peered through a slit; the church was dim and empty. Somewhere in the wall that separated him from that church were live electric wires. But where? He lowered himself to the ground. It must be . . . Yes, he had got lost in an opening that led out of this dirt room and now he would go into that opening again and dig into a wall until he encountered an electric wire. As fast as the darkness would permit, he groped his way into the opening and tapped the brick wall with the butt of the screw-driver, listening vainly for hollow sounds. I'll just have to take a chance and dig, he said.

He found the wall to be of a much newer brick than the ones he had broken into before. He tried for an hour to dislodge a brick, but with no success. He struck a match and was terribly disappointed to find that he had dug a depth of only an inch! Ain't no use in fooling with this, he said with a profound sigh. He wondered what move he could make now; he raised his eyes and looked upward by the flickering light of a match, then lowered his eyes, only to glance up again, startled at what he had seen. Directly above his head was a wealth of electric wiring running along the entire length of the low ceiling. I'll be damned, he said, snickering.

He went back to the tool box and found an old, dull knife and returned to the black passageway. Seeing with his fingers, he proceeded to separate the two strands of wire and cut away the insulation. It was slow work and once or twice he received a slight shock. He scraped the wiring clean and finally managed to join the two ends of each wire. He took the bulb from his pocket and screwed it in; the illumination was so sudden that it blinded him and he shut his lids involuntarily to kill the stinging pain in his eyeballs. He turned off the light by loosening the bulb. Well, I got that much done, he thought jubilantly.

With the bulb and socket in hand, he walked back to the dirt room and placed the bulb on the floor and screwed it in tightly; the light cast a strange gleam on the bleak clay walls. The room was like an abandoned cave. Accustomed now to the glow, he plugged one end of the wire that dangled from the radio into the light socket and bent down and switched on a button and almost at once he caught the harsh sound of static, but there were no words or music. How come it don't work? he asked himself.

He toyed with the many little dials of the radio and wondered if he had damaged the mechanism in any way. Perhaps it needed grounding. He rummaged in the tool box and found another length of wire, which he fastened to the ground of the radio; then he tied the opposite end to one of the rusty pipes over his head. Rising and growing distinct, a soft, slow strain of music emerged and entranced him with its measured sound. He brought the tool box and placed it against the wall and sat. He was deliriously happy. He rummaged again in the tool box and found a half-gallon can of glue; he opened it and smelt a sharp odor. He set the can down and explored the rest of the tool box at leisure; there were nails, tacks, bolts, screws, and a hundred and one other little minor gadgets, some rusty and some new.

Then he remembered suddenly that he had not even looked at the money. He sat again upon the tool box and picked up a batch of green bills and weighed it in his palm. He broke the seal on the wad and held one of the bills up to the light and studied it closely. *The United States of America will pay to the bearer on demand one hundred dollars,* he read in slow speech; and then: *This note is legal tender for all debts public and private . . .* He broke into a slow, musing laugh. He felt that he was reading of the petty doings of a race of people who lived in some far-off planet. He turned the bill over and saw a beautiful white building with slender, soaring columns and wide, curving steps leading up to an imposing entrance. He had no impulse to count the money; it was what it stood for—all the manifold currents of life swirling above ground—that captivated him. Next he opened up the rolls of coins and let them slide from their paper wrappings to the ground; the gleaming pennies and nickels and dimes piled high in front of him, a bright mound of shimmering silver and copper. He toyed with a few of the coins and sifted them through his fingers, listening to their tinkle as they struck the conical pile.

He got the typewriter and pulled it forward and took a sheet of paper and inserted it into the machine and typed: *itwasalonghotday . . .* He looked at it and was determined to type the sentence without making any mistakes. But how did one make capital letters? He tried one way and another until he discovered how to lock the machine. Now he could not make anything but capital letters! He experimented further and luckily found how to lock the machine for capital letters and then shift it back to an adjustment for lower case. Next he learned how to make spaces. Then he wrote correctly and carefully: *It was a long hot day*. The sheet was dirty and he took it out of the machine and inserted another sheet and retyped the sentence in neat, black characters without making a single error. Just why he picked that particular sentence, he did not know; it was merely the ritual of performing the thing. Holding the white sheet with the single sentence printed across its middle, he looked around, his neck stiff, his eyes hard, and he spoke to some imaginary person:

"Yes, I'll have the contracts ready tomorrow."

He laughed. That's just the way they talk, he said to himself in a voice devoid of all envy. He grew weary of the game and pushed the machine aside. Yeah, I'll make me another cigarette. He rolled tobacco in brown wrapping paper and when he lit the clumsy cigarette he thought for a moment that he had set his stubby beard afire. He held the damp wad of tobacco far out from him until the flame died. When he sucked the smoke into his lungs it burned. I'll find some cigarettes before I get through with this, he told himself. Just what he meant when he said "through with this" did not occur to him. The future was not a reality; the future was the present, an everlasting present.

He gazed about restlessly at the clay walls and then his eyes fell upon the can of glue and quick as lightning a mischievous idea bloomed in him, filling him again with nervous eagerness. He leaped up and opened the can of glue and set it upon the tool box; then he broke open one of the wads of bills. I'm going to have me some wallpaper, he said with a luxurious, sensual laugh. He took the strip of toweling which he had used to tie the sack and balled it into a swab and dipped it into the can and dabbed glue onto an area of the wall about a foot square; then he pasted one green bill neatly by the side of another green bill. He stepped back and cocked his head. Jesus! That's funny . . . ! He bent to his knees and slapped his thighs and guffawed. He had triumphed over the world above ground.

He finally controlled his laughter and swabbed all four of the dirt walls with glue and pasted them with green bills; when he finished he stood in the center of the room and marvelled at the strange effect—the walls seemed ablaze with an indescribable yellow-green fire. He decided that this room would be his den, his main hideout. Between him and the world that had rejected him would stand this mocking symbol of his victory over the world; these green bills would remind him hourly that he was no longer subject to the code of the world. He had not stolen this money; he had simply taken it, just as a man would pick up firewood in a forest. And that was how the world above ground seemed to him, a wild forest filled with death, stalked by blind animals.

The walls of money finally palled on him and he grew sleepy, but there was no fun using a tool box for a pillow. One impulse in him urged him to start exploring again in the sewers, and another told him to lie down and take a nap. The impulse to wander prevailed and he rose and clicked off the light and radio and went to the opening and climbed through and stood once more in the glassy water, watching the checkered pattern wrought by the light falling from the manhole cover. He tramped forward with the rod and passed the street intersection where he had gone to get the money and went on past other passageways that led off to left and right, but for some reason he did not want to inspect them. He sloshed for almost an hour and suddenly, when he put his right foot forward at a street intersection, he fell backward and shot down violently into the grey water. In a spasm of terror his right hand clutched the rod and he felt the streaking water tugging at his body. The current reached his neck and for a moment he was stationary; his chest heaved and it was some time before he realized what had happened to him. He had dropped into a down-curve and had saved himself only because the rod had caught on either side of the hole. He took quick stock of his plight; if he moved clumsily he might be sucked under after all. He grasped the rod with both hands and slowly worked himself over to one side of the down-curve and grabbed hold of a concrete edge. He heaved a deep sigh and pulled himself up and stood again in the sweeping water; he peered about, thankful he had missed death.

How long he slept he did not know, but he slept more profoundly than men sleep from physiological fatigue. During the entire time not one portion of his body moved and his flesh was icy to the touch; the palms of his hands, however, were sweaty. The church singing stopped and in the silence and darkness that followed he really did not exist as a personality; his emotional state had reached a high point in its tensity and had suspended. As though for purposes of renewal, he had for a time gone back into the insensible world out of which life had originally sprung, and, before he could live again, hope or plan again, a regrouping of his faculties into a new personality structure would be necessary. It was an organic pause, such as one takes in breathing. During the past turbulent hours he had endured experiences which were like sucking his lungs full of air; but now, having drained the life-fostering oxygen from the air, he was expelling the residue of poison, leaving the tiny air sacs deflated, ready to be refilled.

He groaned and a drool of spittle trickled down from a corner of his mouth. With effort he rolled over on his back and belched and swallowed and sighed. Reluctantly, he propped up one knee and dragged the bottom of his left foot over the ground; he allowed his leg to remain in this position as though to ease some muscular strain. Then, while still sleeping, he pulled himself to a sitting posture. Yeah, he whispered vaguely. He lifted his right hand and rubbed it nervously over his face; he blinked his eyes several times and sneezed. He was fully awake now. He sought to recapture and understand the storm of passion that had laid him low, but his mind refused to function. Rising, he lurched unsteadily with a lean, taut hunger in his body and groped for the electric bulb and twisted it and the bright light pained his eyes. He blinked and looked about the floor; yes, there was the metal box of rings, the glass jar full of diamonds, the bloody

meat cleaver, the radio, the tool chest, and the walls plastered
with green bills glowing in the yellow light. He laughed when
he saw the pile of copper and silver coins glittering beside him.
He had forgotten these things and quiet amazement crept into
him as he saw them again. They seemed to stand for events that
had happened in another life. The old tensity which had driven
him to seek out so many experiences was now gone and he
seemed to be in the grip of forces stemming not from his body,
but from without, from this yellow light, these shimmering coins,
these walls of green fire, this bloody blade of steel; and he felt
that the true identity of these forces would slowly reveal themselves, not only to him but also to others. Once or twice he
made an effort to take hold of himself, to shake off this weird
feeling, to go back to his former state, for he was afraid of this
strange land; but the task of eluding these new forces was difficult and he shrugged his shoulders in surrender.

He felt in his pocket for a cigarette and was astonished when
he pulled forth a fistful of ticking golden watches that dangled
by gleaming chains. Idly he stared at them, then he began to
wind them up; he did not even attempt to set any of the watches
at a certain hour, for there was no time for him now. After
winding them carefully his eyes strayed over the green-papered
walls and a slow, mocking smile broke over his lips. He was as
sorry for himself as he looked at that money as he had been for
the man he had seen stealing it; his memory was merged with
the lives of others and he no longer appreciated the mood of
high deviltry that had bubbled in him when he had decorated
the walls. But, since he had the watches in his possession, he had
to dispose of them in some way. He held the watches and heard
their awful ticking and he hated them; these watches were
measuring time, making men tense and taut with the sense of
passing hours, telling tales of death, crowning time the king of
consciousness.

He turned to the tool box and took out a handful of nails
and a hammer and he drove the nails into the papered walls
and hung the watches upon them, letting them swing down by
their glittering chains, ticking busily against the background of

green bills with the lemon sheen of the electric bulb shining dully upon the metal watch casings, converting discs of yellow into blobs of liquid. Hardly had he hung up the last watch than the idea upon which he had been working extended itself; he took more nails from the tool box and went around the walls and drove them through the green paper and then took the box of rings and went from nail to nail and hung up the gold bands. The white and blue diamonds sparkled with quiet and brittle laughter, as though enjoying a hilarious secret. The room had a bizarre and ghostly aspect; the yellow light tinged the green money to a fiery cast and, against this blazing backdrop, the gold of the rings and watches, and the blue-white laughter of the diamonds leaped burningly to life. People sure can do some funny things, he said to himself.

He was suddenly conscious of the gun sagging at his hip and he drew it from the holster and held it in his hand. Never in his life had he fired a gun. He had seen men fire guns in movies, but somehow his life had never led him to contact with firearms. A desire to feel the sensation others felt in firing a gun came over him. But perhaps someone might hear him? If they did, they would not be able to tell where the shot had come from. Not in their wildest imagination would they say: *Look under the streets and find out who shot that gun!* He lifted the gun and pointed it at the green-papered wall and tightened his finger on the trigger and there was a deafening report and it seemed that the entire underground had caved in upon his eardrums and in the same instant there flashed in front of his eyes an orange-blue spurt of flame that died quickly but lingered on and he did not know, so vivid did the image remain, if the flame still existed or not. Then he smelt the acrid odor of burnt powder; he felt it filling his lungs. Abruptly his fingers loosened and the gun dropped to the ground. He felt that if he had held the gun in his hand a moment longer, feeling its cold slick metal against his feverish palms, he would have been embracing death in its most meaningless and stupid form.

The intensity of his emotions ebbed and he picked up the gun and hung it upon a nail in the wall; then he hung up the cartridge belt. For a long time he watched the liquid sheen of the yellow turn purple upon the blue surface of the gun barrel. The gun had a personality which he resented; he turned his back upon it and saw the jar of diamonds and at once he had another idea. He lifted the jar and turned it bottom upwards and the entire contents dumped upon the ground and he stared at the little white pellets. Like a child deeply engrossed in a game, he picked up the diamonds one by one and peeled the tissue paper from them and laid them in a neat pile in the dirt at his feet. He wiped his sweaty hands dry on his trousers and lit a cigarette and commenced playing another secret game with himself. He was a rich man who lived in the world above ground, one of those important men who walked through the obscene sunshine, and he was strolling through a beautiful park of a summer morning, smiling, nodding to his neighbors, sucking his after-breakfast cigar. Many times he crossed the dirt floor, avoiding the diamonds with his feet, but gauging his footsteps so that his shoes, damp with sewer lime, would strike the diamonds at some undetermined moment squarely but accidentally. After five minutes of sauntering, his right foot smashed into the neat heap and the diamonds lay scattered in all directions, glinting at him with a million tiny chuckles of icy laughter. Oh, shucks, he mumbled in mock regret, intrigued by the damage he had wrought. He continued walking, ignoring the brittle fire of the diamonds. He felt that he had locked deep within the recesses of his heart a glorious triumph.

Later he paused and flung the diamonds more evenly over the dirt floor; they showered sparks, collaborating with him, enjoying his game, revelling in its rebellious richness. Then he went over the entire area of the room, trampled the diamonds just deep enough into the dry earth for them to be faintly visible and cast their wavering glitter, as though they were set delicately in the prongs of a thousand rings. He stepped back and contemplated the effect he had wrought: a baleful, icy glare bathed the room. He sat on the tool box, lit a cigarette, mused, frowned, and shook his head.

II
POETRY

C. E. AUFDERHEIDE:

POEM FOR TRAITORS

Wherever traitor turned, his blood he found
Spattered on wall, pooled on floor
According to whatever escapade
Was there where he became aware

How much had been betrayed
Those monuments arose, odd pokes
Toward Heaven's own, own blood
The acts 'come memory as jokes

Declared then with the optics of recall
Of schism of the radical and tame
His heart, that powerful drab, that dull
Because of both his death, anterior, and name

BEER WITH A STRANGER

The belated claptrap which confines us here
Untimely nuisance, occipital, remote
Jerks churchbell, a verberation beer
Sends amber circles, sounds the note

Is time and not time's product
To be not judged by eager overall
Nor passive guild actor but the act
Which lifts the bottle, able ale

A scapegoat drop, a drizzle fooldom
Shocks us to complete, to terminus
But no motion makes us anyway to come
Or go; we drink the end of us

Locked, stock! And barreled over
Into an afterwards which swelled
To trillionths of the belly of the brewer
The tined and golden age down-swilled

TEXT TODAY FOR MILTON

" . . . . . no, no, I feel
The link of nature draw me: Flesh of Flesh
Bone of my bone thou art, and from thy state
Mine never shall be parted, bliss or woe."

Book IX, *Paradise Lost*

More than ever which is more than most
The seeking goes until the end is lost
The bliss begins and what is natural
Is eligible, and finally, too tall

And thus the woe demands its state of mind
A kindness lacking any other kind
Part and parcel as the saying goes
No end to this, the cumulative woes

Flesh pressed to flesh expecting (droll)
The likely soul pressed hard to likely soul
But these! So distant that the running mouse
Of mind is lost and locked in the soul's house

JOHN BERRYMAN:

THE SPINNING HEART

The fireflies and the stars our only light,
We rock, watching between the roses night
If we could see the roses. We cannot.
Where do the fireflies go by day, what eat?
What categories shall we use tonight?
The day was an exasperating day,
The day in history must hang its head
For the foul letters many women got,
Appointments missed, men dishevelled and sad
Before their mirrors trying to be proud.
But now, we say, the sweetness of the night
Will hide our imperfections from our sight,
For nothing can be angry or astray,
No man unpopular, lonely, or beset,
Where half a yellow moon hangs from a cloud.

Spinning however and balled up in space
All hearts, desires, pewter, and honeysuckle,
What can be known of the individual face?
To the continual drum-beat of the blood
Mesh sea and mountain recollection, flame,
Motives in the corridor, touch by night,
Violent touch and violence in rooms;
How shall we reconcile in any light
This blow and the relations that it wrecked?
The nineteen pressures on the single act
Freeze it at last into its season, place,

Until the flood and disorder of Spring.
To Easterfield that famous bore, defining
Space tied into a sailor's reef, our praise:
He too is useful, he is part of this,
Inimitable, tangible and human,
And Theo's disappointment has a place,
An item in that metamorphosis
The horrible coquetry of aging women.
Our superstitions barnacle our eyes
To the tide, the coming good; or has it come?—
Insufficient upon the beaches of the world
To drown that complex and that bestial drum.
Triumphant animal, upon the rest
Bearing down hard, brooding, come to announce
The causes and directions of all this
Biting and breeding: how will all your sons
Discover what you, assisted or alone,
Staring and sweating for seventy years,
Could never discover, the thing itself?
                              Your fears,
Fidelity, and dandelions grown
As big as elephants, your morning lust
Can neither name nor control. No time for shame,
Whippoorwill calling, excrement falling, time
Rushes like a madman forward. Nothing can be known.

MARIUS BEWLEY:

CITIES

Cities are not destroyed without a warning.
Somewhere a hand is lifted or a voice is raised
To start a fear. And sometimes Angels come
In kindness, or prophecies are read at morning
In the flight and song of birds, or scorning
Stripes some prophet strikes a tyrant dumb,
While all the nervous city holds its breath,
Half believing for a moment in his word of death.

For us there were rumors of a monstrous Birth:
Men whispered in the squares, but none had seen
The tangled foetus bristling with strange limbs.
The old men shook their heads beside the hearth
Knowing that something evil was spawned upon the earth,
And where, in white basilicas the lustrous seraphim
Had burned, now Fear composed of disjunct organs
Was worshipped in occult liturgies and jargons.

Christmas was left uncelebrated in that year;
A few remembered, but churches were not filled.
The uneasy bishop intoning Midnight Mass
Looked down the faces in the nave as though the Fear
Hideous and tortured might be lurking there.
And so for all his prayers it came to pass
That they remembering in the winter wild
The Heaven Born prayed to the Monstrous Child.

How a foetus sprang from a city's cornerstone
To drag at night across Palladian deserted squares
May be but legend that followed after fire and blood,
But we who haunt those ruined markets to atone
For years that happened when we were blood and bone
Remember less their steel and biting soldierhood
Than Fear that hid behind the doors and undercover
Of arcades where at night the perverts came to hover.

Women on the roof tops, dreading the scarlet streets,
Flapped the gaunt grey pinions of their tangled hair,
And shrieked sad songs in a Night of Knives
Of round towers toppling into metaphysical conceits,
The breaking up of people, statutes, and ancestral seats.
Only the stones and something else survives
Out of that crucible of fire and hate
Deeper than victory and dearer than defeat.

Old ghosts rising from cities buried undersea
Or in the lava flow think now of all they learned,
Of posthumous cruel wisdom that arrived too late:
But to learn such fear beyond impenitence and know
The spectre of perishing identity is such a woe
They only speak of levies or the melting down of plate.
Do not weep for us, we were already dead
Before the swords and cities put us into bed.

Here among the ruins where shepherds doze in shade,
The white bones that hid beneath my darkness,
Warming in the sun, recall the fear of blotted streets
And sirens that warned the city of a raid,
To leave us fearing, and of fear itself afraid.
Now is the season when the ewe lamb suckles at the teat,
And here among the toppled columns, untroubled by my bones,
Damon is rolling Phyllis among the stocks and stones.

JOHN MALCOLM BRINNIN:

VISITING CARD FOR EMILY

No chronicle, melody, alarm of strings
Informed our accident of meeting here,
Nor ploughed the atmosphere
As if an almanac had so defined
This day, this town, this wind;
Up from the Cape, a lemon morning swings
With acid light for things
Fir-pointed and oblique,
Stains the Berkshires, spreads on woods to seek
Some quiet entrance to the western state
And leave us Emily for intimate.

Hail this acre for a new world's myth,
A gayer dust than all New England's quarry;
Hail this sanctuary:
Our interstellar hostess here resigned
Her transience with the blind
To lift upon materials of death
Imperial monolith,
In echoing chambers made
Of gems and bones her private balustrade,
Or carved on quietude a spear, a wing;
This acre's measure is a learned thing.

Among the candelabra, high-branched, cold,
This baroque jail of her fine agony,
Silver, mahogany,

"Visiting Card for Emily," from *The Garden Is Political*. By permission
of The Macmillan Company.

Old silence, evident of her, presides;
Its armored air recedes
To such mementoes as the mind recalled
Nor hands may ever hold;
To such remembrance as
That of Donne, of Blake, and Shelley is.
To this degree is her distinction weighed
Who took the whitest elements to wed.

This hour was life for us, who must retreat
And force our visions on the flashing east
Where now no sign is passed
That does not speak memorials to her,
Nor arrowing vistas where
She is not ultimate; quick daisies fret
No casual field, nor shut
Their buttons on a hill
But she is imminent and super-real.
How coolly now the failing sun awards
Sweet praise for Emily, her book of words.

HARRY BROWN:

PREPARATION FOR A MYSTERY

All of the characters in this mystery are present.
They are somewhere in the house or about the grounds,
The Colonel commenting on a fine cock pheasant,
Or praising the solemn voices of the hounds,

While his hard, Episcopalian daughters stride
Around like their brothers who were never born,
And his delicate, worldly sister poses at ease beside
A bust by Houdon which bears a peruke, once worn.

Upstairs and downstairs the servants perform their duties
As the sibilant butler listens behind closed doors.
The older housemaids speak of dead family beauties
Whose feet once moved on these carpets and these floors.

And the thin-lipped lawyer is warning the profligate ward,
As storms and darkness obscure the sullen sun,
That his hot life-span, quickly moving toward
Desire's nadir, will too soon be done.

And crouched at intervals along the marsh
Are the invalid killer, and the doctor with his knife,
And the fatal nurse, and the keeper with his harsh
Manacles and his search for the mad wife.

Toward midnight move the shadowed hands of the clock,
But none of the restless family has gone to bed.
This female hears a great key turn in a lock,
Lightning presents for that one the outline of a head.

"Preparation for a Mystery," from *The Violent*. By permission of New Directions.

"What do you hear?" says the Master. "Nothing," says the aunt.
"A nervous horse in the stables," says a daughter.
"I am listening, listening," says the ward. "I can't
Hear anything." Butler: "Beg pardon, a noise of water."

Then suddenly a gaunt chair moves by itself,
And the piano, with no one near it, begins to play,
And a volume of Cyril Tourneur falls from the shelf.
And second housemaid screams and faints dead away.

The enormous threats of thunder shake the stairs,
The chandeliers go dead, and by her stove
The vociferous cook takes instantly to prayers
Calling on all the saints to show her love.

Quietly from the marsh moves the murderous quartet,
The invalid with his warped feet dragging the mud,
The doctor with his scalpel and glass pipette,
And the fatal nurse with her attitude toward blood,

And behind them the keeper with his troubled face
Surveys the mass of the house, and is prepared
To engage the terrors that before him pace,
And to hold his manacles ready and unimpaired.

Too, standing beside the family crypt, a form
That is never seen, yet arrives for each disaster,
Stands as a sentinel to warn the worm
To expect some cold repast, perhaps the Master.

And the pale form beats its wings. A scream is heard
That echoes through the wood and within the Hall.
Among the dark trees flutters a black-winged bird,
Along the marsh there is no sound at all.

But the house is full of whispers. *It is time.*
Beneath the butler's body matchlight shows a stain.
From the cellars of the past the terrible stories climb—
Something is scratching at the window pane.

HARVEY BUCHANAN:

AND DO YOU DIE SOLDIER,
DO YOU DIE?

My war I fight each hour with my mind
Soft among warriors' lips with the sky
Quite tight like the big top. I will not lie
Beneath your knees, my eyes searching and blind
Again, I will not hate the gaudy day
That comes with every ripping morning sun
With every O quick knife and hoofed fun
Down through ten thousand hairs dry with decay.

And if I walk with the clowns and the dead
Beating my drum boom before a closed door
Or crawl about a whirling fun-house floor

I think of you stinking in your soft bed
Your bride, your pride, the lovely girlie wed
Now tight behind your staggering bugle corps.

EDWIN G. BURROWS:

THE BULL

> *¡Oh blanco muro de España!*
> *¡Oh negro toro de pena!*

Lament has washed arenas with its rain
and evening sleeves are raised to catch the air.
Somewhere the toreadors are going home
with stained elaborate mantles on their shoulders;
somewhere fiesta pains the afternoon
and ears with flowers hear a pale guitar;
somewhere a dancer and a roving boy
lie folded in the gold and ardent fields.

But here lament pleads in the stillest hour:
a moon goes bumping up the charred arcades
and jackals bray. I do not want to see
the limping cricket puzzled at his echo
and night infringe with amber eyes the willow.
Deaf ears shall trace instead a clashing ring
where bellowing companies are drenched with lust
and one lone bull breathes hunger in his corner.

When creaking wheels go nagging toward the borders
and guards allow the sunset poor to pass,
when over the belly of hills tomorrow's children
crawl on their ragged hands and streams condense
their pinched abandoned prayers, the bull remains.
Oh have you seen the flank that knocks at night

or kissed the horn? His eyes are dreaded hammers
that anvil in their stalls the sword of Spain!

How many times the hissing stars remind
the edgeless headless banisters of houses
feet will not wrestle here with gravity
nor hands release the doorknobs to their latches!
Few will rebuild the thumbed utensils, few
double the moons that tagged our young decease,
or clattering through the vestibules of poems
set up the elder statues out of rain.

Across the docks of foreign states a handful
of the bewildered land like old and rival gulls,
storing against the hostile city-halls
and club-strong law their sacks of souvenirs,
unwelcome without medals, hooted to slums,
where lurk the native million alien eyes.
Shackled with mangy freedom in their cells
they hear their nimble orphans clanking home.

Sparrows at eaves indulge their city senses
and separate clocks yield twin-like grinning hours.
Tenses are two: the coming and the going.
Love answers to the price of rum and taxis.
But rhythms do not shape the rootless want
nor rifted lips employ the untongued dream.
In all the reeling ghettos west of Spain
the refugees are listening for his hooves.

His bellow will wilt the cough of planes, his roar
sting ruin from the choked and gnashing hosts
and iron will unwrap its ash, and steel
beam upwards like a pharos to the hills.
The children are lost, the leaders of the people trampled,
but in the empty seed-head leaps a wonder

and these immaculate walls of women groan
with loud and unpremeditated love.

Accumulated griefs are shouldered out,
the hands of sand are juggling copper tunes,
and the women smile their first and fearless smile
remembering in the wastes of Guernica,
when the wounded wept and the unhurt wept and the young
stared at the wreathing stars like ancient priests
concluding worlds beyond the outmost night,
how the lone bull calmed and curled them to his power.

Ponderously he traded for his features
thighs of the Grecian, muscle of the Goth,
till midmoon swayed with the grave delirium
and each neat girl was mastered in his image.
Today the ravished half-dead pamper their hate,
armored with all the consciousness and pride
that were his gifts, and know beneath their pulses
the armies of Andalusia pitch their camps.

Give us this day a meaning more than words,
a cause for carnage other than rightful wars,
for we have grown the crib and beat the doors,
stand elegant to the excusers with our proof.
The bull will lead the newborn into the towns,
the puppet sentries gored, the yachtsmen gutted;
beware the black bull in his metaphor
for marching dreams will challenge you with men.

HUBERT CREEKMORE:

MUSIC IN THE REC HUT

The pen stops in a phrase of a letter home,
The magazine drops in the sailor's lap,
Its romance defeated. Talk and jokes become

Dissolved by inner moods, as music wraps
The men in shining cords that wind
Back overseas, like hungry roots to sap

The strength of distant earth. It is behind
Their eyes the music lives, the frieze
Of Tin-Pan tunes evolving scores designed

More human than all symphonies. The keys
Fling out from the upright cataracts
Of memory in every nimble piece.

Boogie-woogie, rhumba and waltz attack
The forfeit past, and rout out nights
Of Negro piano in a dim cafe, and shacks

For barbecue across America, sights
Of lonely childhood, dancing, kiss
Of lips in tree-spread dark, the wife who died

Last week, good times and good friends. For this
Is not the song of radio,
Whose texture conjures merchandise, whose voice

Is advertising. Here the song is no
Barren orchestration of guile,
But is woven with the tones that flow

From each man into it: how the bile
Of sorrow burned them, alchemy
Of love and laughter gilded the body's vial.

Through gray smoke clouds the men stare. Each eye
Entreats the curving walls to part
On the giant swirl of scorpio in the sky,

And the sting of night and starlight in every heart.

E. E. CUMMINGS:

THREE POEMS

I

it was a goodly co
which paid to make man free
(for man is enslaved by a dread dizziz
and the sooner it's over the sooner to biz
don't ask me what it's pliz)

then up rose bishop budge from kew
a anglican was who
(with a rag and a bone and a hank of hair)'d
he picked up a thousand pounds or two
and he smote the monster merde

then up rose pride and up rose pelf
and ghibelline and guelph
and ladios and laddios
(on radios and raddios)
did save man from himself

ye duskiest despot's goldenest gal
did wring that dragon's tail
(for men must loaf and women must lay)
and she gave him a desdemonial
that took his breath away

all history oped her teeming womb
said demon for to doom
yea (fresh complexions being oke

"it was a goodly co," from *One Times One*, published by Henry Holt & Company. Copyright, 1944, by E. E. Cummings.

with him) one william shakespeare broke
the silence of the tomb

then up rose mr lipshits pres
(who always nothing says)
and he kisséd the general menedjerr
and they smokéd a robert burns cigerr
to the god of things like they err

II

Hello is what a mirror says
it is a maid says Who
and (hearing not a which) replies
in haste I must be you

no sunbeam ever lies

Bang is the meaning of a gun
it is a man means No
and (seeing something yes) will grin
with pain You so&so

true wars are never won

III

o by the by
has anybody seen
little you-i
who stood on a green
hill and threw
his wish at blue

"Hello is what a mirror says," and "o by the by," from *One Times One*,
published by Henry Holt & Company. Copyright, 1944, by E. E. Cummings.

with a swoop and a dart
out flew his wish
(it dived like a fish
but it climbed like a dream)
throbbing like a heart
singing like a flame

blue took it my
far beyond far
and high beyond high
bluer took it your
but bluest took it our
away beyond where

what a wonderful thing
is the end of a string
(murmurs little you-i
as the hill becomes nil)
and will somebody tell
me why people let go

DAVID CORNEL DE JONG:

BENNEBROEK, HOLLAND . . .

We came by train, horizontal, yet upinthesky
it seemed, uplifted from the meadows. We
to see the Dutch being clean and plain-
minded, but instead it rained: a grievous rain.

A statue stood in a park, jabbing the rain.
A statesman it said, with a deed he did.
But we were sad, and rubbed our knees
hearing bells just edged enough with pain
to make us think of Clara, when one spring,
when we were young and she sat on a swing
and we pushed, and she was cute—but we no good
thinking thoughts like that about a kid so good.

It rained as if Adeste Fidelis were being sung
by Schumann-Heink on a red-seal record while
the lights are low. It rained. And listening long
I remembered how it was when little Grandma
told me that the clouds were the white souls of
the dear departed, washed clean by God . . .
"Hear that bell? It makes you long for home."

We went back by train, but our feet were wet.
The Dutch were domestic and private, but the rain
was anybody's name. There was a war on, and
a dread of scolding anything besides the bitter rain.

DENIS DEVLIN:

ANNAPOLIS

"No, we can't get a license for liquor, being too near the church,"
Said the waiter. The church looked friends enough
On its humble, grassy hillock. So I said, "Excuse me,
I must have a drink." And I rambled on down West Street.
On my right, at the Raw Bar, a truckdriver drinking milk
And a Norwegian second-mate glared at their faces
In the mirror. We floated on heat
Like paper-boats boys prod in the bathroom.

The white-linen cadets walked with girls who had family,
It was the feast-day of the Republic and the girls
In long dresses made a drawing-room of the streets,
They were like sweet-william and buttercups,
Like petunia and sweet-pea and silver moss,
The sparse maturity and haute couture
Going in slightly opposite directions.
As I said to the truckdriver, "They are children."
He flashed a sigh and said, "Indeed they are."

Imperceptibly darkness plucked its petals,
You hear the colored people's viola laughter
And starlight one never looks up to
Blurs the woollen trees,
And the houses with no comment to make. A delicate drunk
Weaves his glass limbs together up the street.

The charm of the little capital,
Red-brick, with huge civic-spirited trees,

"Annapolis," from *Lough Derg and Other Poems*. By permission of Reynal & Hitchcock, Inc.

Is yet as intimate as if arteried with fern;
I hold my breath for the expected
According to the mechanics of fairyland.

Allow an alas! It is not Hans Andersen, the monuments
Of power impose as in any Riga. Cadets conduct
Camera-fans to the Governor's Residence,
To the Capitol and the Revolutionary General
Leading ghosts on his enthusiastic stone horse.

In the porches, loud-bellied citizens swat flies after dinner,
The band blows open the gates of the Academy,
Here a young girl walks to the dance
Her shoulders falling like a cadenza.

GEORGE P. ELLIOTT:

PASTURE WITH A BARN AND TREES SEEN FROM A SHIPYARD

Mud-flats, the homeward rhythms of a buoy,
Girls turning cartwheels on the hill, remind me
That now my oldest friends make me uneasy;
And seven horses which I couldn't harness,
That what I do is turned to deathly uses.

If I could modulate this steady beauty
To my inconstant purpose, it would make
Geometry of tilting, hostile orbits,
Prophesy comets, find the polar stars—
If not improve, legitimate my cosmos.

My seeming, my cover for the hard to touch—
Freedom to love, the way I judge, hopes, passions—
Betrays without spies the agonies that rule
A planet; exile, war, imprisonment,
Certainty of nothing but long forced migrations.

The things I do are made of iron, will rust,
Be out of date or sink in fifty years.
The things I write are scarcely read, green pauses,
Are by-way like those pastures, not to be found
In blue prints for what men schedule to survive.

Still, like the aimless movers in this scene,
I will be sorry to have ceased to live,
For maybe some who turn from iron noise
Will find my verse a welcome bell. My hopes
Must be deciduous like that apple tree.

ROBERT FITZGERALD:

COBB WOULD HAVE CAUGHT IT

In sunburnt parks where Sundays lie,
Or the wide wastes beyond the cities,
Teams in grey deploy the sunlight.

Talk it up, boys, a little practice.

Coming in stubby and fast, the baseman
Gathers a grounder in fat green grass,
Picks it stinging and clipped as wit
Into the leather: a swinging step
Wings it deadeye down to first.
Smack. Oh, attaboy, attyoldboy.

Catcher reverses his cap, pulls down
Sweaty casque, and squats in the dust;
Pitcher rubs new ball on his pants;
Chewing, puts a jet behind him;
Nods past batter, taking his time.
Batter settles, tugs at his cap.
A spinning ball: step and swing to it,
Caught like a cheek before it ducks
By shivery hickory: socko, baby:
Cleats dig into dust. Outfielder
On his way, looking over shoulder,
Makes it a triple. A long peg home.

Innings and afternoons. Fly lost in sunset.
Throwing arm gone bad. There's your old ball game.
Cool reek of the field. Reek of companions.

"Cobb Would Have Caught It," from *A Wreath for the Sea*. By permission of New Directions.

JEAN GARRIGUE:

THEME AND VARIATIONS

Dear love, if we're a continent, then we,
All strong, deserve its honors too:
Its health and insolence and quaint
Up-building walks, its trees torn down
And wild leaf smell rank as brook beds
And the elve home of owls:
Dear love, if we who meet are continents
Then we have music: bitter exodus of flutes
And sovereign basses and the cello's comment,
Then have we music dancing on the needle time,
Whose metrics make an heaven in the mind;
Then have we seasons, trumpeted and strong,
Tongue blessing and the coddler of the eye,
Spool of milkweed, eggs of youngest robins,
The pitted strawberry and the furry snow:
Then have we skies of all countries and folk
Then be us countries, weather, bells and rock
Then be us bird bone (hollow like a flute)
O oxygen of rose and synthesis
Of root, hate, love and jealousy,
And lechery that fills each sense with revelation.
Then be us each to each
O bubble of the breath of sleep,
O god-borne wing caused by our smiles' meet,
Field, rock and unfelled forest where
Laughing we chide and sleeping bite
And eating dance all hallows of the night
And curry Love who clothes us there
In moon spray and berry, ties us to tides
And laps us, dew and day, to fairs of such a continent
We are in one another's sight.

"Theme and Variations," from *Five Young American Poets, 1944.* By permission of New Directions.

BREWSTER GHISELIN:

ON THE DISAPPEARANCE OF GOD AMONG THE MACKEREL

FOR CARL GUSTAV JUNG

A thousand shuttles of green light through the seaweb thrown
Swerve to the pepper of chum bowled about us, flash
To the bowstring leap of the line and thump the boards of the
boat:
Motion without emotion, flexible metal, eyes without thought.

Except where the black shark lags rolling like a long log
They crosswhip all the waters with flashy feeding, around him
An electric field. But when he is hooked aboard, his gone
Presence widens over the ocean. And they dazzle like a mad loom.

RATTLER, ALERT

Slowly he sways that head that cannot hear,
Two-jeweled cone of horn the yellow of rust,
Pooled on the current of his listening fear.
His length is on the tympanum of earth,
And by his tendril tongue's tasting the air
He sips, perhaps, a secret of his race
Or feels for the known vibrations, heat, or trace
Of smoother satin than the hillwind's thrust
Through grass: the aspirate of my half-held breath,
The crushing of my weight upon the dust,
My foamless heart, the bloodleap at my wrist.

YVAN GOLL:

JOHN LANDLESS CLEANSED BY THE VOID

TRANSLATED BY CLARK MILLS

Under the circular moon a bath
Of chlorine waters my distress
At springs of phosphorus I drink
The spell of total nothingness

A sleeper in the asbestos town
I wander the oblivious halls
The openings of terrible doors
Watch where the dreaming lover falls

My steps are numb and without weight
Amidst the blackened bitter salt
Of night: bereft of recollection
I march against the heavenly vault

And stumble past the fallen columns
That once held up the roof of time
A moment more my spinal column
Towers over the dead stone and lime

In mines of silence you might have
Hidden the cry of cries and kept
The key that opens fears and trances
But you leaned back instead and slept

Go! Go! You never will deserve
A radiant morning free from doubt
Crucified by the commonplace
Your poor heart rots your blood goes out

John without Land: what if you are!
And without Baal and Grail and love and friend
You are but hair glands viscera
Without beginning without end

Crow perched upon my spine: my friend
With beak that living flesh must feel
Cleanse every shadow from my bones
Be more ferocious than bare steel

Oh take away what I contain
Like ore my subterranean dreams
That through my frozen loins may pass
Impenetrable cold in streams

And take my wild and futile dance
And what I know of hours and men
And my intolerable luck
To have been and not to have been

And may my sorry skeleton
More bare than when it first was mine
Be haunted only by the storm
And by the sun male and divine

HORACE GREGORY:

THE BREATHING DIAL

Time burns
   within the bronze-
Green dial,
   is the sun's
Hand quickening
Day-Spring in June
To midnight's deep December:

Always the slender
Pointing shadow within the flame
The face of time
That warns, This is the hour
You shall remember
And shall hear
Your own lips saying,
   "As in this light we stand,
All lesser fires perish:
   nor wind, nor storm
Scatter its heat
Within the sleepless heart!"

The flame-crossed dial
Stirs
In chapels of the secret-
Flowering breast
   where choiring voices join
Serpent and vine,
   laurel and hemlock

And field-scented clover,
And as the song dies
A child's face leans over
The river-mirrored, trembling asphodel.

The vision vanishes as the dial stirs
And quiet enters
                beneath the branches
Of that fragrant fiery tree
Whose veins shed light
Through circling hemispheres
Bearing their fruit in heaven
As in each heart.
             This is the place
Where all loves meet:
The naked pulse beat
Where the altars rise,
              the blood-crowned sacrifice
Seen in the glances,
              in the stilled
Amber-lighted faces
Of boys at prayer,
Of girls at their devotions
              who read their destiny
In one another's eyes.

See in the fire that lives
Upon an open hearth
             the reflected hour
Of a flaming dial:
            There the renewal
Of sun and earth that burns away
Birth-mark and stain,
Gray lips and winnowed hair,
The wild, dark, aged, distracted eye
Seen in a glass

That says,
        "The sin was not my sin;
I am not guilty.
                Where, where
Is that young face I used to wear?
Is it the shadow of a cloud
That has already passed across the sky?
Where shall I turn?
Are my limbs ashes
To be lost forever
Among the fragments of a broken urn?"

Beyond the cries of age and loss
Know grace that falls
In sunlit air,
Spirit and body joined,
Life within light:
                Even behind
The murmuring darkness of a locked
Vine-covered iron door
The vision breathes, glows in the image
Of a child's hand raised through night,
The index finger pointed to a star.

As the flame rises to flood tides of noon
(Midsummer's hour
Of encircling gold within gold
Flowing
Between the shadows of tall trees
Field lawn and flower
Brimmed with radiance that memory cannot hold)
No hand can stay its motion,
                        it is gone
Until tomorrow wakes another sun.

Know that time lives only
As the heart stirs,
Waking the spirit between the silences,

Between the rumors of air-riding, sea-driven wars,
Between the fallen moments, hours, years
Of a blind century that walks in blood,
Its voices heard
In sleep, in the dreaded silence
Of the unblessed dead
That is broken only by the sight of tears.

Even as the voices of the dead are stilled,
So a single voice wakes light among the living:
Thou breathing dial!
                    (The flush-tinted rose
Concealed within the heart
Opens the darkest hill,
                    the deepest valley
To the first sight of dawn.)

Even as we wait,
                    the pale-starred Easter morning
Resumes the course of years,
Of seasons run,
Even in the stillness of an empty street,
Doors closed, the shutters drawn,
The voice is heard,

"*Lumen me regit*—look where I stand,
Vos umbra where the body enters earth,
Falls, rises beyond death in moon-lit waters
Following the tide that journeys toward the sun.
I am the light
                    is the first cry at birth."

KENNETH O. HANSON:

THE GEOMETRY OF HEROES

                              Odysseus
was the brother of improvidence, he
saw the day's red
                         rheumy eyes rise
felt the salt breeze
                         knew another shore
lay on the beach alone
                         among anemones
brine covered before Nausikaa

was the brother of improvidence
                              knight errant
in a hard land where the syntax of an afternoon
demands Quixotic deeds
                         & craft
more devious than Odysseus'

O wise wanderer the faithless
pompous daring grave
                         impetuous courteous
kind & utterly vacuous Odysseus
Janus-fused with Munchausen
the delegation forms
                         to offer the reward
of a grateful people
                         for services rendered
you are the brief proprietor of a bar

trading
        on a fiction & free lunch

this much for the mind as wide as a movie screen
whose shadows of experience shown
                            in Technicolor
are translations for the inarticulate

the mind is wide enough
                  for all deception
is itself deceived

the shape of truth is round
                      as an arena
or the sound of an old coin falling
                           through sea water

Remember those borne on the shoulders
of hypocrites
              & the hero bound by brief attention
whose strong image is a boot on
                        the cobbled street
of the mind striking fire (& is this fire
less real
        than cobblestones or sharp desire)
consider which is shadow
                  & which source
which image & which hero, tales
                    events remarks
rewards of a grateful people

Answers to problems long since solved
                        escape me

This is the familiar story
a sudden sorcery of wit in chromic language
used
        to hide the guilty knowledge: other guts

have ached with this same rot
now in distinguished company
                        among the broken myths
you walk & still preserve the fiction

The hero
            cries a desecration on the heads
of seamen never chronicled in Ithaca
                                    well
cry a desecration now you're home
you were a fool
                to leave the Sirens' song
if it was the song you say

still the question
                    is not one of belief or disbelief
truth or untruth
                    & the problem has been
defined whose answer is not hurried
if the shape of truth
                        is round
as an afternoon arena or a coin
where was it forgotten
                        in what place does it remain

This recapitulation of the dream
                            unsubtle signs
of relief, assignation by one mistaken
                                    seems
superfluous grotesque
                        these thoughts on a deathless theme
threads from a threadbare sleeve
                                meditation
on an old tax token mean
acidulous protest
                    provide the implications

of the act & of the hero

              here Odysseus.

What then is absolute but imprecations
one who curses the cut of his trousers

                        seldom
if ever knows that motley's rare wear for the fool

                Odysseus
was the brother of improvidence

                    & scarcely hears
the ancient one at the upright piano
by the brass spittoon

           who plays for beer
             . . . O melancholy Baby . .
one for whom

        Clotho is become
an ordinary seamstress

           whoring on the side
life has gone

      to blue neon & jades

The shape of truth is round

perhaps I shouldn't ask

         but where
is your Penelope tonight

           why do you trade your tall tales
beautiful with someone's weaving

         for this
& whatever became of Telemachus

              Odysseus
borne by hypocrites assumes the endless debt
of inquisition

       the reverse of the coin demands

a detail finer counterfeit more sure
                              & the
purple epithet of liar
is for him
              who forged the world to his desire
who is at your elbow, owns a bar
                              & cannot be closed
like a door
              or the pages of a book.

MEASURE THE GRAVITY,
MEASURE THE WIT,
EYE THE SILENT WHISTLE

              B. Franklin endlessly encroaches
        on the metaphor that sings
        falsetto apt incongruous things

        the mind with stiff formality
        of unknown dogs approaches
        sudden silence
                        finds
        that days revolve like red
        wheels on a circus wagon

        the vague indecent misanthrope
        that hates through avenues of fear
        tells time by cracked chronology of hope
        a theme intriguing
                              insincere
        as payment for the pain
        of seven fat years in one lean

              our feet impatient for
        no place in particular
                              accept

the formulae of doubletalk
the terror
          of simplicity & error
we walk
          without bread in his cadence
down the foreign streets of now

Ben Franklin's ancient regimen is our disease
hard are his arteries

NAT HERZ:

A STUDY IN POSSESSION,
or THEY WERE HERS ANYWAY

She yearns for white houses to hide in her breasts,
For streets to fit in the folds of her thighs.
Towers delight her. She is maddened by stairs.

She leans on the low brown wall and weeps
For the town. The gardens would harm her,
She would splash in the flesh colored fountains.

She fears the tigers that slink through the wheat,
That bats that hang and sleep in the trees.

She would flee down the road that bends to town.
She would slip with the light into the tiger's eyes,
And hide in the wet folds of their brains.

She would float to the trees and caress
The sharp black claws of the bats.
She would shut their eyes and hide them in her armpits.

Behold, the gardens rest for her
The fountains await her.

ROBERT HORAN:

SONNET

Announced to me by trumpets and by tears,
by tempests in the silk, by paper wars,
how calendars of death in distant years
will well up in our eyes and wall our stars.
In ferns and forests, as the ghost appears
wrapped in his flags or swinging from his shores,
muffled with careful cloth, we stop our ears,
sing in our sleep to silence all his sores.

Pinned to our wrists, like butterflies to glass,
the alphabets of age, the wheels of grief.
A grain of salt, a nail, a lip, a leaf
reminds us that they melt and move through grass.

Announced to me by all they left to keep,
how soon they shall assassinate my sleep.

JEREMY INGALLS:

CONCERNING EVIL

Ponderous and operative head,
Epitome of man made flaw in nature,
Nascent will, anatomy
Of single will asserted, no dire creature
Further search for, no terror
More to dread.

Devils once were men of prince-like fame,
Hierarchy of gentlemen decayed. Far bolder
The later satrapy,
Sons of Iago, called the honest soldier,
Who, in his generation clever,
Hides his name.

Liars' generation, whoreson wiles
Seductively beguile us, fouled in murder.
And who the hangman's tree
Will risk for this endeavor,
To slay the worm, Othello's master?
Iago smiles.

MILTON KAPLAN:

POGROM

Listened: in the dusk he listened, head upturning;
hound uprearing in his skull, he listened:
heard nothing and still he listened; heard the stillness
before the rain: sensed that: then heard the patter,
the dry trickle of feet as they came running:
heard his name: called back, hound pacing through
his brain: running; found himself running,
flecking his lips with quick darts of his tongue:
yelling: heard himself yelling, holding his throat
and yelling: running faster: hound running faster,
suddenly baying, and still running: calling:
What's up? he shouted: heard himself shout,
and held his throat: *What's up?* heard curses, low
and guttural: eyes straining in the darkness:
felt the shape of men around him; felt
them brush against him; felt them lumber past him:
heard someone sobbing in his ear in time
with running feet: the hound still baying madly,
whirling madly around his skull, whirling:
running: found himself running, wheezing: pressed
his lips between his teeth: saw lights and flowed
into the baying mob, the hound now hurtling
against the door with whimpering cries: heard curses,
yet pressed his lips between his teeth, feeling
the hound hurtling against his skull, splintering
the door: pressed forward: strained forward, holding his throat
and then the door burst open; out streaked
the hound, jaws slavering: *Kill them!* he shrieked;
Kill them!

394

WELDON KEES:

THREE POEMS

I

As water from a dwindling reservoir
Uncovers mossy stones, new banks of silt,
So every minute that I spend with you reveals
New flaws, new features, new intangibles.
We have been sitting here for hours—
"I spent that summer in Madrid,
The winter on the coast of France—
The Millotsons were there, and Farnsworth.

My work has perished with the rest
Of Europe, gone, all gone. We will not see the end."

You said good-bye, and your perfume
Lingered for hours. At first it seemed
Like summer dying there, then rank and sharp.

And yet I did not air the room.

II

Among Victorian beadwork and the smell of plush,
The owls, stuffed and marvelously sinister,
Glare from dark corners, waiting for the night.
High up, the moose's passive eyes explore
Candles, unlit, within cut-glass. A door
Is opened, and you enter with a look
You might have saved for Pliny or the Pope.

The furniture has shrunk now thirty years
Have passed (with talent thinning out, and words
Gone dead), and mouths of friends in photographs
Display their hopeful and outmoded smiles.
You counted on at least a sputter of nostalgia,
However fretful. That was a mistake. Even the moose
Regards you with a tired, uncomprehending stare.

III

Signboards commemorate their restingplace,
The graveless of another century;
Came and were conquered; now their bones
Are dust where idiot highways run.

Land in their eyes, unquiet ancestors
(On fences yellow signs clang in the wind)
Unstirred by suns drying the brown weeds
Above them now in parched and caking land.

But when they speak of you, they feel the need
Of voices polished and revised by history,
The martial tone, words framed in capitals.

It is good to be deaf in a deafening time
With the sky gone colorless, while the dead
Thunder breaks, but only in the mind.

A. M. KLEIN:

PAWNSHOP

I

May none be called to visit this grim house,
all cupboards, and each cupboard skeleton'd
with ghost of gambler, spook of shiftless souse,
with rattling relict of the over-dunned!
Disaster haunts it. Scandals, once-renowned,
speak from its chattels. In its darkness glow
the minds of the poor who stalk its rooms at night.
One should have razed it to the salted ground
antitheses ago,
and put its spectres long ago to flight!

II

Near waterfront, a stone's throw from the slums,
it lifts, above its wreckage, three gold buoys;
yet to its reefage tattoo'd flotsam comes
dropping the snared bags of exotic toys.
Also those stranded on their own dear shores,
the evicted tenant, the genteel with false name,
the girl in trouble, the no-good sons and heirs,
waver, and pause before its brass-bound doors,
look right and left, in shame,
enter, and price, and ticket their despairs.

III

So, for a coloured cardboard, wave out of sight
the dear, the engraved, the boasted inventory:
the family plate hocked for the widow's mite;
the birthday gifts; the cups of victory;
the unpensioned tools; the vase picked up in Crete;
the hero's medal; ring, endowing bride;
camera; watch; lens; crushed accordion:—
O votives of penultimate defeat,
weighed, measured, counted, eyed
by the estimating clerk, himself in pawn.

IV

Whose lombard schemes, whose plotting kapital
thrusts from this lintel its three burnished bombs
set for a time, which ticks for almost all
whether from fertile suburbs or parched slums?
The architect is rusted from his plaque.
Was his name Adam? Was his trade a smith
who thought a mansion to erect of wealth
that houses now the bankrupt bricabrac,
his pleasure-dome made myth
his let-do hospitality made stealth?

V

This is our era's state-fair parthenon,
the pyramid of a pharaonic time,
our little cathedral, our platonic cave,
our childhoods' house that Jack built. Synonym
of all building, our house, it owns us; even
when free from it, our dialectic grave.
Shall one not curse it, therefore, as the cause,
type, and exemplar of our social guilt?
Our own gomorrah house,
the sodom that merely to look at makes one salt?

ANKEY LARRABEE:

PROTHALAMIUM

Ophelia's idiot smile reflects
The fishes' faces.
As they wreathe about her brows
In the dark river spaces.

The darting minnow glitters now
On azure breast.
A ring of weed upon her hand
The bride's at rest.

SONG OF A CHANGELING

Child, befriend the cockatrice,
Search him through the midnight grove—
Gaze unharmed, with deadly bliss
Deep into his eyes of love.

Follow him, and do his will,
Scaled familiar let him be,
Whose feather-lidded stare can still
All mortal curiosity.

You alone can bear the light
Of his pale, unpitying glance,
Find therein your cold delight,
Bed with lizard circumstance.

JOSEPHINE MILES:

PIKE

What was that they heard past the peal
Of the booth's bells and the squeal
Round the turned edges of the wide red sucker?
Past the turn of the game wheel,
The surf of ocean.

Here's your hot ham, folks, tells
To the peal of the booth's bells,
To the round red face round the red sucker,
The driven voice that spells
Ham to the ocean.

What was that the licker heard
That her tongue slow on the third
Round tasted there more of salt than strawberry sucker,
Marking without a word
The lick of ocean?

Here's the turn of the wheel, folks, cries
To the wheel's fall and rise,
To the fall of dimes and the face of the all day sucker,
The driven voice to the rise
And fall of ocean.

PROGRAM

Martin on every block
Is in luck,
Here's time for belt buckling.
What music says so?

> The stained glass organ raining down
> Its pelts over noon town?
> Maybe.

> The tooter at the bridge, puffer at the bay,
> Bird in the marsh at pay day?
> Maybe.

> The tyke balloon bargains, staying away from the pins,
> They promise, till the waft begins?
> Maybe so.

> The coming together at the goal line which means to press
> The full tide roar of a major success?
> Maybe yes.

> The natural sounds of far out foreigners,
> Brook water, wave washes, wind whishes and such stirs?
> Yes again.

These airs in the block, what they carry amazes,
To each his own traces.
Does one single one ever hear all these musics?
Maybe. Maybe so.

CLARK MILLS:

Poems from *THE CIRCUS*

The Approach

    The two dim, witless fellows near the highway
stared open-mouthed as we walked past them on our hands,
    and watched our somersaults with eyes unblinking
and hair uncombed and arms as limp as rubber-bands.

    And when we asked them for the sleeping wood
and where the hills of music huddled in the night
    and if at evening we might hope to find
the slow unwinding stream of sensual delight,

    those rocks alive said, Haw, spun on one foot,
and grinned at us and shrugged, and stared at one another
    and looked us up and down, and in slow motion
clomped back into the hinterland, brother and brother.

The Prisoner

    Slave to his milieu, the chained chameleon
mimics a brooch, and from lapel and bosom
observes the beasts and the absurdities.
Keen on his cardboard as an open jack-knife,
docile amidst the ranks of his pied fellows,
all afternoon he waited to be sold;

    and now in shadow of balloon and platform
he sees the world and cannot speak his terror
but plays his role: that of a jewel, living.

    "The Approach" and "The Prisoner." By permission of The Press of James A. Decker.

The Stilt-Walker

in his fine coat of cinnamon and chocolate fur
stands with his two eyes in his belvedere
beneath a pair of horns of peach-down fuzz.

Beautiful when he wanders, with vast knees
unsteady as an adolescent's, or, as tall
as a brown legend from the looking-glass,

bends down from heaven, and down, and stares
deep into the darkness of your provinces
with no sound, and as if to kiss or whisper.

The Three Rings

In the first ring the rites of blood proceed.
The faultless knife and the crusading bullet
plunge to their mark with perfect aim and speed,
and the shout rises, This is life, oh kill it!
In the third ring the thoughtless lovers lie
clean as the great beasts in their lack of shame:
Call me mirage, they cry. Say which is I.
Answer what I do not ask. Speak my name.

And solitary in the central ring
a blindfold figure, victim as well as judge,
stands vertical upon his razor-edge
and waits for his applause or the blind Thing.
The sphere of his perception flash and hover
till his performance and the world are over.

"The Stilt-Walker" and "The Three Rings." By permission of The Press
of James A. Decker.

INVOCATION III

We seek the absolute hallucination;
the sourceless voice; the fellowship of apparitions.
And voyage towards the virgin meadows of the sea
where, in the sea-light of our wake
and the white light of constellations, lucid
above our mast, the shore-lights and the buoys
fade and are lost.

              Seek strength for recollection, strength
to lift the burden of our years of wandering;
the burden of the blaze of cities in the mind
and rooms and cries and evenings and conflagrations
gone down in shipwreck with far countries and far epochs;
the burden of the faces
that have no country but their species, and no home
except their home of horror and oblivion.

Unloosed amidst the cold white nebulae of the unsounded spirit,
deep in the longing of the blood that laps the bone
and in the jungles of communal living
we shall keep watch, and question

              —till fire falls
and like dead stones that burst with leaves and water
we too are kindled to delight and insight. For in this
we are consoled, and are absolved, and rise
vertical from chaos.

NICHOLAS MOORE:

SUNNY WEATHER IN SUSSEX

Beside these windows illness looks its best,
Seeing the view, the subterranean green,
Hillocky hills, horizon-crying clouds,
A chocolate landscape for a chocolate mind,
A stone landscape for a stone mind. The smoothness
Of hills illuminates the winter sun,
Cottage and car cry country in the weather.

As if the invalid sees sunny things!
He sees a sun revolve upon a carpet,
A purple sun upon a yellow rug.
The weather misty, all the hills like rocks
Pointing their proud peaks to a rolling sky,
The meadows grey, the houses grey, the calves
Mooing grey moos across the grey evening.

The hills are dry. The windowpanes are wet.
The sun is a marine, a lucent blue.
The hedges growl like foxes at the ducks,
The caterpillars crawl upon your thumb,
Your voice is changed to a thin whistle, to
A country lullaby. Illness performs,
For its distractions, metamorphoses.

The shapes of time, the shapes, the country shapes.
It is the time of country. It is weather
Of illness, winter weather, lemon sun
Striking a delicateness across the fields,

The amber calves, the hillocks green among
The mud. All this for winter. All this
For a landscape of the mind, chocolate

For chocolate, stone for stone, the shapes
Moveable and eternal. Or we might
Sketch in the seven seas and the four winds,
And have our mermaids and our bearded priests
To worship sun and cold and wind and weather.
We might, we might. We might be possible.
We might as well have the lemon sun for winter.

THE MIND IS, THE MIND HAS

Waters and weapons, the face free, the trace
Of a beloved scenery, the palm
Of the hand turned, turned towards that
Which is the imaginary tree, the imaginary map.
The map has our designs upon it. Here
A mossy bungalow. There bole of a tree,
The handsome oak, the tall poplar. The mind

Teaches as much. Red flamingos,
Even dodos with long faces and legs
Short and stubby, weird paraphernalia,
Have their existence in that.
That effluence of mind. The mind is flat,
But draws its circles, draws its rigmarole.
We see the sea. We see the sands we see.

And what of weapons? On the imaginary
Island have we composed a tower of doubt,
Long snouts stuck from the windows in defence.
What do we fear? The panther is not here.
Across the map, our mapped love, our mapped faces
We read of love's designs. We follow lines
From here to there. The imagination is that.

ROSALIE MOORE:

JOURNEYS TOWARD CENTER

I. The Lovers

> For these happiness lies
> In their drugged dark
> And flat pans of eyes.
>
> Through the window by legerdemain
> Come coffins of sun.
>
> Afterwards, they remember as irrelevant
> The dusty boards, the pear skin.
>
> And still the love that they looked for lies
> On the lion side of a furnace.
>   Later they go
> With pennies across their eyes—
> Searching, as rubbing hands over bones;
> Seeking in faces the frank skull.
>
> In a leaf-rustle sleep they speak,
> And long after, are still;
> They see as graves do,
> They glitter like old logs.

II. The Prophets

> The bell rain—blowing across the barrows.
> The flowers hold against it their small bowls,
> And the hills keep blowing.

Out on the air, at a place where the raindrops cross
In a manner of stars and streets:

                           in back of this,
The man with the letter A for a mouth;
He speaks.
Remember his whipping face.

Many who stand in back of wire or water,
Whose mouths are marble moving,
Whose hands—
Heavy with sea.

And the rain changes its hills;
The water is filling the flowers up like roofs.

III. The Birds

The birds—their trumpet wings.
There is no man but has heard them in his time,
Their shadows a fall of stones.

By house, by hedge, he is thinking his one-time birds,
Dreaming their jungle of wind.
By dark he hopes to hear their heavy hinges;
And he goes to the door,
And looks at the few corn stars.

What fish-striking bird dives here,
And into what skull's eyes?

Remember, as in the mirror-turning autumn,
The marsh eyes and moss body of love.

HOWARD MOSS:

SUMMER MANOEUVRES

Articulation is a summer thing
And through the living mouth of that July,
The street distilled with laughter thinned to death,
The hand that held, the sign that was a word
Were banners hung to meet a subtle doom.

And when the vulgar generals in their time
With all their savage gifts of slaughter came
To mar a century already scarred,
Who was to leave the bathing beach's pall
And chat with Death a moment in the hall?

Who was to leave the candy-striped umbrella,
The breathing suburbs and the pulsing park;
Or summer with its sandy wind and water?
Through all the days and evenings we could saunter
And none of us was fearful of the dark.

A madrigal of gulls above the town
Was never planes arranged with gunman's skill,
Nor we in our precisions of escape;
No choice of action but the latest gown
Where Death already hung his dangerous cape.

JOHN NERBER:

MERCATOR

My Darling when you think of me
Think of me homeward, though I sail due west:
  Think embers once again will burn
Behind these blue and restless eyes, as coals
  Locked in your distance from a ship
          are set
To whiten blindly yet must live, I live
  Under your temperate breeze to flame
         again
In all my noon-day and expanding heat
  Beneath the level of eternal spring.

As a plant nourished by the laden air
Turns to its sun, so will my heart
  Turn to the pacific of your everyday
That from America reveals its light
  Reminding me of home, and aching, yet
         must smile
At eyes that homesick give another scene
  More real than jungle, as though
         the carpet
Of our common wish had come to bring me home,
  And I could see it swiftly through
         the trees.

Believe, in the image of my course,
The map turns roundly, will bring me back:
  Though ten years land me lost

They land me found upon your waiting banks
  Where green grapes ripen sweetly
      on the vine
I lay my starved and foundling mouth among,
  And famished, ease within your atlas
      glance
My hunger at your board, and sleep—
      will sleep
  Boxed in the native compass of your bed.

JOHN FREDERICK NIMS:

POEM FOR YOUR EYE, DANTE

I

Finger in breviary and banker's smile,
The bishop after dinner dotes on god;
E la sua volontate è nostra pace
Ponders. Forgets: the man pierced hell to say it.

The peace in fire and Florence learned
Is not the lollipop light of a six-year eye;
No barnyard heat, all life a cidery yawn;
Nor peace of ward, asylum, convent plot
Where stray the sweet Ophelias of the lord.

The Florentine's is fury and wild will:
The boy in the midnight special round the bend
Who sees a headlight on the single track
Swelling and near—his heart flies up away;
The pilot cabined in a whining dive
Watching the world grow large and photo-clear,
The meadow rocking up, the drunken barn,
The farmer pale and running, this is peace—
Quiet of queer midocean where the jaws
Of luminous lamprey, long as subways, hunt;
Quiet of stars, fire-engines reeling red
And shocking the lonely highways of the sky,
Whose influence felt a hundred hours away
Darkens all schedule of the sponsored air.

"Poem for Your Eye, Dante," from *Five Young American Poets, 1944.*
By permission of New Directions.

Tensity made perpetual is peace:
The night express head-onward, brakes in vain,
The cockpit treetop-high and screaming down,
Dante, is our desire.
Fata morgana, moment-without-end,
Candles in every heart a high chalet.

II

The scholar in a Negro house of fame
Caught in thy delicate peril, marijuana;
The child-of-mary girl, ashamed of self
And yearning for the beaten flesh of Christ;
Cop virtuous in blue, and cocktail babe
Sobbing a rosary in her room alone;
The good man with his what-the-hell and beer;
Lothario shivering in the shame of dawn;
The wassailer, the watcher, and the waif
Are torrents to one sea and cannot stop.

Their fever is a halo bright on all
As bonfires are, that aureole the bum,
Tonic the tallow scholar, gild the poor,
Lie on the broken forehead like a rose.
In saddle-shoes and woollen, sweet with soap
Wander the college girls, kicking the leaves,
Scuffing the rubber relics of bought love,
Their bright hair flaunted like a cinema queen.

Green pity, father, pity for those who know
In church or tavern the peripheral lust;
Their compass regulate and star uncloud.
Or drowned in a shoreward ripple the white arm
That might have swum midocean; cut the tongue
That might have sung forever across the hill;
Sweet Babylon broken now that never shall rise.

HEY SPINOZA!

Bishop, mayor, and quarter-back,
Doctor, lawyer, merchant, quack—
What are your credentials, mac?

"Never mind. The code is sin,
Virtue, love. And now begin."
Wait—whose blueprint am I in?

Eat, think, labor, love, and sleep.
Five little hitlers my soul keep.
In the bonds I cuss and weep.

Honest Abe, who swore to see
Rastus and Jemima free,
Take a thoughtful look at me.

Love is shiny clockwork. Lo!
Gin and starlight make it go.
That's what every young man should know.

Though the heroes die for Spain
(Gesture of the lovely brain)
Human bondage will remain.

Hormones in their witches' cup
Stir a Great Emotion up.
Heroes sniff it like a pup.

Gland and psyche, bright as steel,
Clang and trap us. No appeal:
We in Prison Ego reel.

THE GENUINE ELLIS

> The soul too is dragged by the body into the
> region of the changeable, wanders and is con-
> fused; the world spins round her, and she is
> like a drunkard when she touches change.
>
> —Plato

One thought is all the burden of our learning:
What is and what is not.
For this
The kindergarten shines at first communion
And the slugged goon is shot.
The broker yachts the Florida wave. Slum-fevered
The lungs of lovers rot.

Local Boy, Nine, Swims Lake. Hits Fortieth Homer.
Wins All-American Rate.
Condescends to coke, revered; and lolls at many
A moonlit gate.
Desires
One girl—and a highschool teacher marries
That nextdoor date.

A Phi Beta Kappa sops head in a desperate ointment;
Is bald as a toad.
Morbid, reads stoic Plutarch, dotes on a razor;
One day
Digs at his throat.
Is alarmed at the speed of blood, swabs iodine, sobbing:
"Hell of a note!"

Encircling our Coney shore the waded oceans
Loiter and loot.
And out of sky, abrupt on a pleasant evening,
The riddled airmen chute.

"The Genuine Ellis," from *Five Young American Poets, 1944.* By permission of New Directions.

Through autumn of blood advances the lonely hunter
With brutal boot.

The dunce world, capped with day, with darkness belted,
Is to this college brought,
To learn:
Love is, or it isn't love, and what is?
Mind errs and flesh is flogged. Passion is taught
To built igloos of the icy cubes of concept,
Ergo and ought.

We, nauseaed, leap to land from the reeling scupper;
Love sun, being bred of night;
Endure
Our inky earth blocked out from a somewhere planet
How terrible-bright.
Who shall know as we, we duped, the genuine Ellis,
Island of light?

RACE RIOT

Dear city, listen: famous for tin bugs
That bred and rattled in the revelling twenties,
Beetles that gas, gin, sex, and whoopee quickened;

Dear city, shrine where that notorious tongue
Spat frenzy's gospel on the purchased air,
Hated the tragic race Jehovah cherished;

City where once the reeling legionnaires
In a dry time by thug and sourpuss haunted
Flocked for authentic brandy and right beer;

Dear city, listen: these we may forget,
But how your recent crime against the sun,
That colorist for houses of the soul?

Forget the running goons with blade and fist,
Or that rare plasm in the gutter wasted?—
Because our flesh (the messenger of love)
Wiser than any sieve to filter ill,
Wove for exotic noon a russet cover.

Dear city, listen: on the virulent reef
Our captains land in helmets bald as bone,
Hang like green foliage, burrow, rot for days
Watching the yellow death that creeps in jungles.

On isle or desert, from grey ship or train
Your help, Detroit, in guarded crate arrives.
But what can the tall soldier think, who flings
His life away for rhetoric of freedom—
What think to see your guns, your perfect planes
Crusted with outrage of American blood?

HAROLD NORSE:

FIVE VOICES

> *One way outward from all terror is*
> *to drink:*

and after the cuirasso and the gin
the task of morning, incumbent to begin;
the zinc-white fact, the gyroscopic day
requires level eyes. This is no way.

> *One way outward from dilemma is*
> *to think:*

waking at night, who have drowned in self,
estuary of decisions and fauna of contradiction,
at the flaring brink of thinking your thoughts
like heat bubbles float out of sleep, hissing as they wake.

> *One way outward from an endless cycle is*
> *to compromise:*

your hair grows sparse and still you stare
at early photographs with a helpless care;
what do they say: adjust yourself: be sure
to shift towards comfort; keep from being poor.

> *One way outward from impending failure is*
> *to grow wise:*

what more egregious comfort to the weak
than power of encompassing the shadow of death?

And this is wisdom: for not only the sanctified
but you, who take the coldness of no flesh at your side.

There is no way outward for the broken self
but dying:

and all the rest is lying, lying.
I know that these killed sophistries persist
like razor returning to the coward wrist
too bare for the flashing edge, the turgid twist.

HOWARD NUTT:

WEARY-WATER SUE

A blue-blood blonde descends the stair,
Stands liquid-like before a mirror,
Dabbles the whirlpool of her hair,
Flows to a table, somersaults
The little hearts of cork and rubber
Upon her weary-water waltz;
Then pours herself into a chair
And ripples back her wrap, like froth,
And (without splashing on the cloth)
Congeals in exquisite despair.

It's rather hard
To be so bored
And O SO tired
And SO desired.

"Weary-Water Sue," from *Special Laughter*. By permission of The Press of James A. Decker.

JOHN FRANCIS PUTNAM:

RECREATION PARK, ASHEVILLE, N. C.

The easy girls at twilight, self-contained,
Provocatively sheathed with implication,
Have resentful and appraising eyes,
And mouths that, swollen red
And exquisite with promise,
Show as latent wounds upon this evening's sanctity.
Here from the braggart streets and inconsistent
City lives, they spread their picnic litter on the grass,
Assume the languid "Screenland" pose
While a late gold is washing out upon the postcard hills.

This is the hour of the usual magic, the people's
Endowment at evening, when lights on the
Merry-go-round are a neat, grinning pattern
Of seed pearls. The hydraulic prance of the
Horses is frozen in rococo frenzy, the heads
Flourished high, but obedient: they are away to the limited wars,
And serene in the plunging, the slow lunging throng,
A red and gold sleigh for the young and the timid
Is gliding, negating centrifugal law.
From the skating pavilion the manikin throng,
Leaning on the turns, and swaying in the effortless stance
Of a dream promenade, drowns the loudspeaker music
Of love and deceit in a generous roar.
And over the hooting calliope din,
Motor boats drone on the lake.
Here the ambulent longings of victimized lives
Are fulfilled in a resolute fraud:
Enchantment, with crackerjack prizes for all.

RAINER MARIA RILKE:

ALCESTIS

TRANSLATED BY DUDLEY FITTS

And suddenly the Angel was with them, tossed
into the seething of the marriage feast
like a fresh ingredient. Drinking, they did not sense
the secret entrance of the god
who held his godhead wrapped like a wet cloak
about him,
           who was one of them, or seemed so,
passing among them. But a reveller saw
how at the table's head the youthful host
failed in mid-speech, drawn from the banquet couch
upright, with all his body mirroring
a strangeness that terribly spoke to him.
                           And then,
as though it were a turbid mixture settling,
there was silence above the precipitate
of muttered confusion and the dregs of sinking chatter
already stale with the taint of musty laughter.

Thereat they recognized the slender god
standing there, full of his errand, beyond appeal:
almost, they knew what it was,
                         yet, spoken,
it passed all knowing, not to be understood.
Admetus must die. When? This very hour.

He stripped off the shell of his terror in broken pieces
and stretched out his hand from the ruin to plead with the god:
for years, for yet a single year of youth,
for months, for weeks, for only a few days,
alas not days, for nights, for one night only,
only a night, for this night only, for this.
The god was deaf as he wept,
sobbing, helpless to hold it back, screaming
as his mother had screamed when she was bearing him.

And she came to him,
and his father came, the old man his father,
and they stood before him, ancient, powerless, used.
Weeping, he saw them as though for the first time,
and ceased, and swallowed his tears, and spoke to them:
Father,
does it mean so much to you, this last drop of life,
these dregs that stick in your throat? Then go,
pour it out. And you, old woman,
you, matron,
why are you here still? You are done with bearing.

In his grasp he held them like votive beasts: then at once
loosed them, brushed them aside,
afire with a new plan, crying *Kreôn! Kreôn!*
Only that: only the single name.
But there stood in his face the thing that he dared not speak,
the unsayable hope,
and he flushed as he turned to the young friend whom he loved
across the shuddering table.
The old ones—(thus in his face)—, they are no ransom.
Look, they are drained, worn out: they have no worth here.
But you, but you, in the wholeness of your beauty—

And suddenly he saw his friend no more.

Then he stood back. And what came was she:
smaller almost than he had ever known her,

frail and sad in her white wedding gown.
All the others are but a lane for her
through which she moves and moves—(soon to be there,
soon in his arms that open so painfully for her).
But as he waits, she speaks: not to him,
but to the god,
                and the god listens to her,
and all are hearing her as though it were through the god.

There can be no other than I to take his place.
None but me: for who is more done with life
than I am? What is there left for me
of all that was here? Only that I must die.
Did she not tell you, who sent you upon this errand,
that the bed within there belongs to the world below?
And so fare well.
Farewell upon farewell: no dying man
has ever said good-bye from a fuller heart.
I have gone so that all this may be solved, dissolved
in burial under this man who is my husband.
Lead me away now. I will die his death.

And as the wind veers upon the high sea
the god went to her, almost as though she were dead,
and at once he was far from her husband, to whom, in passing,
he tossed in a small sign the hundred lives of the earth.
Admetus rushed toward them, wavering,
and grasped at them as in a dream. But they moved on
to the door where her women wept,
                        and then he saw
her face turned to him once more with a smile
as bright as a hope, as bright,
almost, as a promise to come back to him,
grown strong in deep death, into the world of life.
But he knelt; and his sudden hands
covered his face from everything but her smile.

MURIEL RUKEYSER:

MORTAL GIRL

The girl being chosen stood in her naked room
singing at last alone naked and proud
now that the god had departed and his doom
guarded her door forever and the sky
would flame in trophies all night and every day.

Sang: When your white sun stood still, I put away
my garments and my crafts and you came down.
When you took me as a flame, I turned to flame;
in whiteness lay on the mist-flower river-bank
when you as a swan arrived, and cloudy in my tower
for you as a shower of gold, the lily bright in my hand
once, you as unthinkable light.

                      Make me more human,
give me the consciousness
of every natural shape, to lie here ready
for love as every power.
I wait in all my hopes,
poet beast and woman,
wait for the superhuman,
the god who invaded the gold lady,
the god who spoke to the naked princess,
the storm over the fiery wanderer.

Within me your city burning, and your desperate tree.
All that the song and the apparition gave
to seal my mouth with fire, make me mad
with song and pain and waiting, leave me free
in all my own shapes, deep in the spirit's cave,
to sing again the entrance of the god.

VIRGINIA RUSS:

ALL IS LIGHT

The angel whose torso is of rice husks, hollow,
bound by tinsel, wearing half a barber's basin of a halo,
she, benignly a-tip the tree, twig-poised like a sparrow:

Above sprays of blue lights, like Maypole streamers,
shining through water-pale white cellophane, enhancing
stripped paper with the implied dignity of glaciers

Blue-glinting the halo's blade curve, and the straw angel's unripe
    apple face,
fountain-looped tree reflecting waterfalls through the window's
    cleared space
under coffin folds of blackout curtain lacing

Sky-ily mist magnified, from room's multiple warm breathing,
    magnet to moisture on the glass,
home pudding rum englamoring:—
while across the street, the sentry,—hollow wells echoing in his
    boots,—pacing:—

Past guns pointing to stars, within Islamic crescent of cement bags
to rows of jeeps stacked like playing cards, and boxed armored
    trucks
soundless as folded accordions, at the far end of the block

He stamps one foot, then the other, to stir the clotted ink in
    his legs

up to Fort Gunnybags, down Reconnaissance-Wagon-Row to
    the railroad track:
up, sleet of the blade wind hacks at his cheek beard; down, the
    wind prods bayonet butts into his back

Collar up, saucepan helmet down; harbor patrol boats comb the
    black
water with dragnets, while a rope of light whirls a blue lasso
    around the dock
and with searching surgeon fingers prods

For lesions infected and festering with spy
pulses seaward, blinks, revolves a long blue shoreward rod
digging under piers to gouge out a saboteur

as a barnacle clinging to the underside of wharves is pried
off as the tide ebbs, and with azure daubs the brass knob of the
    sentry's
helmet, anointing his pinched shoulders, as he moves within a
    pillar

of light, like Marley's ghost; he, square-heeling the wind-wintery
pavements, succubi of the fog insinuating against his skin, within
    his coat's cloth
as he dips, clam-lipped, through the beam's bath

WALLACE STEVENS:

LANDSCAPE WITH BOAT

An anti-master-man, floribund ascetic.

He brushed away the thunder, then the clouds,
Then the colossal illusion of heaven. Yet still
The sky was blue. He wanted imperceptible air.
He wanted to see. He wanted the eye to see
And not be touched by blue. He wanted to know,
A naked man who regarded himself in the glass
Of air, who looked for the world beneath the blue,
Without blue, without any turquoise tint or phase,
Any azure under-side or after-color. Nabob
Of bones, he rejected, he denied, to arrive
At the neutral centre. The ominous element,
The single-colored, colorless, primitive.

It was not as if the truth lay where he thought,
Like a phantom, in an uncreated night.
It was easier to think it lay there. If
It was nowhere else, it was there and because
It was nowhere else, its place had to be supposed,
Itself had to be supposed, a thing supposed
In a place supposed, a thing that he reached
In a place that he reached, by rejecting what he saw
And denying what he heard. He would arrive.
He had only not to live, to walk in the dark,
To be projected by one void into
Another.

It was his nature to suppose,
To receive what others had supposed, without
Accepting. He received what he denied.
But as truth to be accepted, he supposed
A truth beyond all truths.

                         He never supposed
That he might be truth, himself, or part of it,
And that the things that he rejected, part,
And the irregular turquoise, part, the perceptible blue
Grown denser, part, the eyes so touched, so played
Upon by clouds, the ear so magnified
By thunder, parts, and all these things together,
Parts, and more things, parts. He never supposed divine
Things might not look divine, nor that if nothing
Was divine then all things were, the world itself,
And that if nothing was the truth, then all
Things were the truth, the world itself was the truth.

Had he been better able to suppose:
He might sit on a sofa on a balcony
Above the Mediterranean, emerald
Becoming emeralds. He might watch the palms
Flap green ears in the heat. He might observe
A yellow wine and follow a steamer's track
And say, "The thing I hum appears to be
The rhythm of this celestial pantomime."

THE BED OF OLD JOHN ZELLER

This structure of ideas, these ghostly sequences
Of the mind, result only in disaster. It follows,
Casual poet, that to add your own disorder to disaster

Makes more of it. It is easy to wish for another structure
Of ideas and to say as usual that there must be
Other ghostly sequences and, it would be, luminous

Sequences, thought of among spheres in the old peak of night:
This is the habit of wishing, as if one's grandfather lay
In one's heart and wished as he had always wished, unable

To sleep in that bed for its disorder, talking of ghostly
Sequences that would be sleep and ting-tang tossing, so that
He might slowly forget. It is more difficult to evade

That habit of wishing and to accept the structure
Of things as the structure of ideas. It was the structure
Of things at least that was thought of in the old peak of night.

LESS AND LESS HUMAN, O SAVAGE SPIRIT

If there must be a god in the house, must be,
Saying things in the rooms and on the stair,

Let him move as the sunlight moves on the floor,
Or moonlight, silently, as Plato's ghost

Or Aristotle's skeleton. Let him hang out
His stars on the wall. He must dwell quietly.

He must be incapable of speaking, closed,
As those are: as light, for all its motion, is;

As color, even the closest to us, is;
As shapes, though they portend us, are.

It is the human that is the alien,
The human that has no cousin in the moon.

It is the human that demands his speech
From beasts or from the incommunicable mass.

If there must be a god in the house, let him be one
That will not hear us when we speak: a coolness,

A vermilioned nothingness, any stick of the mass
Of which we are too distantly a part.

DYLAN THOMAS:

CEREMONY AFTER A FIRE RAID

I

Myselves
The grievers
Grieve
Among the street burned to tireless death
A child of a few hours
With its kneading mouth
Charred on the black breast of the grave
The mother dug, and its arms full of fires.

Begin
With singing
Sing
Darkness kindled back into beginning
When the caught tongue nodded blind,
A star was broken
Into the centuries of the child
Myselves grieve now, and miracles cannot atone.

Forgive
Us forgive
Us your death that myselves the believers
May hold it in a great flood
Till the blood shall spurt,
And the dust shall sing like a bird
As the grains blow, as your death grows, through our heart.

Crying
Your dying
Cry,
Child beyond cockcrow, by the fire-dwarfed
Street we chant the flying sea
In the body bereft.
Love is the last light spoken. Oh
Seed of sons in the loin of the black husk left.

II

I know not whether
Adam or Eve, the adorned holy bullock
Or the white ewe lamb
Or the chosen virgin
Laid in her snow
On the altar of London,
Was the first to die
In the cinder of the little skull,
O bride and bridegroom
O Adam and Eve together
Lying in the lull
Under the sad breast of the headstone
White as the skeleton
Of the garden of Eden.

I know the legend
Of Adam and Eve is never for a second
Silent in my service
Over the dead infants
Over the one
Child who was priest and servants,
Word, singers, and tongue
In the cinder of the little skull,
Who was the serpent's
Nightfall and the fruit like a sun,
Man and woman undone,

Beginning crumbled back to darkness
Bare as the nurseries
Of the garden of wilderness.

III

Into the organpipes and steeples
Of the luminous cathedrals,
Into the weathercocks' molten mouths
Rippling in twelve-winded circles,
Into the dead clock burning the hour
Over the urn of sabbaths
Over the whirling ditch of daybreak
Over the sun's hovel and the slum of fire
And the golden pavements laid in requiems,
Into the bread in a wheatfield of flames,
Into the wine burning like brandy,
The masses of the sea
The masses of the sea under
The masses of the infant-bearing sea
Erupt, fountain, and enter to utter for ever
Glory glory glory
The sundering ultimate kingdom of genesis' thunder.

W. Y. TINDALL:

FELIX CULPA

Banking the air into the bushy sun
Two loves in one another's plane remarked
The crocodile descending from his palm.
That was no forest for a simple man.

Hand in hand prospected underwoods
While their creature muscled on his path
Springing leaves around those innocents
Covering panther serpent and giraffe.

The serpent put his lips to hand in hand
Printing with his lips a smiling wound
And wound his length along the winding path.
Father (with retractors) said "It's sound"

And pointed to the cutting on the hill
Where flatcars carried barns along the rails
And from the roundhouse infants carried trains.
He could not tell their purpose or the scale

Or ask the two librarians if his key
Was suitable for Sunday and their door.
He pushed between them; but the lock was stiff
As twelve labors and another more.

THE SECTION

Pigs travel in the street
Humping the concrete
Liquefying it. Their boar
Leaping through the carriage door
Seizes a finger and the underhand.
Forgiving him (O spear the horses) fretting
Roll on (with difficulties) to the cutting.

At our usual table now
High in that sterile bowl
(Our heads of hairs touching the sterile ceiling)
We order sections of sweet fowl
And all the waiters with their knives
Whisper around the central cow
Preparing her for the cutting.

See how the white meat lies
Part on breast and part on thighs
And how her rolling eyes
Follow the sections and knives.

With her knife the victim now (and then)
Removes a section from her thigh
And vertically bisects her jaw
From nostril to rolling eye. She hands
White meat to one who seems and understands.

Forgiving her (O spear the horses) fretting
Roll on (with difficulties) from the cutting.

HENRY TREECE:

SONG FOR THE TIMES

Slow saraband of pain in all the air:
Everywhere cadence, decay of a tune, of time,
Death of the gold days and the feathered joy,
And across the purple sky and the purple hills
The long undying pattern of despair.

It has come too soon, this sorrow's psalm,
And the black cloud-wrack scowling in the West,
Where brethren moving like uprooted trees
In a Birnam of blood drop aching twigs of hands,
And from leaves in an ancient way stare round about,

At callous, undulating plains of salt,
Where night-jar leers through a broken note,
And the scarecrow dog at the end of his rope
Gnaws at the door, howls as he feels as we,
The wide, immeasurable knowledge of an end.

BYRON VAZAKAS:

THE GLORY

The basement clinic clots with men
slouched against venereal walls.
We stand in line and wait among
ciphers anxious to achieve
placement among the absent
numerals. Opposites, so often
true, invest infirmities
with joy: a medal won without
the loss of limb or mind.
The restless queue moves forward:
another arm invaded by
the needled enemy detached
from sense, detaching blood
to speak the wordless innocence
or guilt. Abstraction begins
with silence. Rain on the hot
morning streets can never help
with sounds and scents of summer;
and early sweeping in the hall
is bitterly betrayed by the
superstition of permanence.
The taxi-driver who will faint,
the flush playboy without comment,
the musician who runs away,
the poet who is so hard to kill,
are interlocked by paper forms
dehumanized in black on white

"The Glory," from *Transfigured Night*. By permission of The Macmillan Company.

that flesh and blood may quake
and the whole soul by shaken by
routine as a stick to beat
or bar to batten down the mind.
Experience is nothing here,
nor class, nor act, nor art;
the animal deferred dignity
lurks in no bone exposed
to nakedness. The mind cannot
extol its form in flesh.
The tired arms sink down;
the obscene hair, the secret
deformity pleads best,
and the world knows.

LIEBESTOD

It must have been that Tristan
    was a lonely man, one buried,
    then resurrected by forbidden
    love. Isolde was not a woman,

But what, like music, transcends
    the boundaries of form. Their
    suffering, like ours, was the
    living for it, not for here-

After, but for the martyrdom's
    acute predicament, which music's
    perfect tongue can alter. After
    they had accepted their love's

Responsibility, their motif turned
    to flesh and fire. Even their
    narrowing time, like a ticking
    clock, lent urgent richness to

The room. It was strange, now, a
    place where others lived, as
    though the furniture became its
    former occupants. But the wood-

Winds' melancholy growl still seemed
    to hesitate, as though reluctant
    to fulfill their theme's transfigured
    sensuality. The lovers merely

Waited. What remained was to be
    done by others, the envious and
    frustrated who looked on; the
    tragic lovers of what they could

Not have, or feared to take; their
    scornful fingers pointing toward
    the mirror of desire . . . Perhaps it
    was better to die like this than

To survive long years of defeat before
    surrender; and rise up on the crest
    of that great wave's turning, when
    the passionate music broke and

Spumed upon the clamorous shore . . .
    Death, yes, frustration's trap
    released, and Tristan swept into
    the ecstatic vortex of that song.

MARGUERITE YOUNG:

THE WHITE RAT

How now could body-soul's symbol be this
By love, or calculation, this white rat enraged
Caged in a theatre of emptiness,
His, a snowfall of footsteps and glittering eyes?

Nor moon, a compound of the unseen events,
Nor earth, as principle of tear or dew on flowers
Rounding, he considers now. By him are we clarified.

Who could have nurtured his body on penurious dew
Is caged, is caught like a tyrannical dragonfly
And made to actualize, O, mute actuality

In void denuded now of all but blank him
And cleaned of all but the white rat's space
And eyes like diamonds in his empty head.

Who could have walked transparent fretted on wind and waves,
Now he runs upon a branched track abstract
And is mechanical in every wintry act

And is body-soul, is the most distant hope!
Here, in this cage, Platonic double moons,
Here, in this cage, St. Augustine
Crying, O, my God, art Thou without or within?

For this rat's sensorium is his true knowledge
Nor star will shine beyond his death for him,

"The White Rat," from *Moderate Fable*. By permission of Reynal &
Hitchcock, Inc.

Nor wild rock goose be shy and wild in the dusk of foliage,
Afraid of foxes in the light of day,
Nor hoary owls like flowers skim lost in leaves.

Does God with diamond eyes look down on these
For the purposes of what intrinsic studies?

THE PROCESS

O, could clock hands be moved in either way
And process seem, as it should be simply, reversible,
Yet would we mistrust that Lazarus of octopus and sea-
Lilies evolving then toward mute infantile

O, woeful then in the sea! nor aged fox's cracked microcosm
Of the golden grapes upon the golden bough,
For there would be no retardation of that early theme
Wherein he questioned the validity of all

And when clouded leopards leap, leap and love
How woeful then, the every brightening eye
Could God and ourselves as functioning retrieve;
For all our deaths would be our first birthday,

Ourselves, and the moose, and lotus buds in that cold, dark river,
Ourselves, and the ermine whitening in the white snow
Hastening harrowed. How woeful then, the bright electric hairs
And the vacancy of every brow,

For when toward the seed ovule would recede each green tree
And yesterday would be today, for all our sakes,
Yet would we persist in elegy,
Lament each one the rosebud of his lip,

"The Process," from *Moderate Fable*. By permission of Reynal & Hitchcock, Inc.

The womb as tomb, and foetus coiled no more to flower,
And the annihilation of our strange sorrowing
When that tomorrow of a never doubted hour
Is time before the first angel falling.

How wasted then, the flesh made rounded and firm
And winging toward childhood, every snow-greaved swan
Till brief as snow in summer
Swan there's none

Nor timeless brightness ours; for carried to a just terminus
That reason seems an ever tolling bell;
And this, the loud tumult of the whirling geese,
And our mischance may yet be possible.

THE PARACHUTIST

O, there's no neutral now, no public image,
No mirroring the movement of rat or heavenly body
But only the variant effects without source,
So multiple is every witnessed lady

Who dissolves like vapor on a glass,
Who fades as fade the lilies at her breast.
Seeing, is it believing her coldly secret,
That most subjective event of the rainbow or ghost

No one can touch? Not, I think, less tangible than this
Is the boy under his snowy canopy,
Drifter to shroud cords harnessed, with orchards like white surf
And apples big as moons in memory,

"The Parachutist," from *Moderate Fable*. By permission of Reynal & Hitchcock, Inc.

No body, he! but radiation away from the larkspur, blue nettle,
No body, but radiation away from the small fox,
That bush of flame and glittering eye
Detached with him in a wintry space,

For boy of that cloud, he is imagery,
He is the forceless stars and their release
And train which crawls beneath him like a snail
And light-tipped plumes of the voyager grass,

His body, a canopy of the vast moving clouds!
And the harp strings of his heart vibrate
With that wild music of his light,
With yucca moths which shake from his grey coat

And fly like flowers. O, his own sad head mirrors,
Mirrors in infinite this waning hour,
Cosmology he drags in curve with him,
Treetops, and sparrows homeless in the air.

III

CRITICAL PROSE

ERIC BENTLEY:

THE THEORY AND PRACTICE OF SHAVIAN DRAMA

WHEN a few years ago Thomas Mann said that reality is today seen in political terms, he was quickly pounced upon by many acute critics. Yet he was not talking nonsense, and Friedrich Hebbel had applied a comparable insight to the drama almost a century earlier. Hebbel wrote:

> The new drama, if such a thing comes into being, will differ from the Shakespearian drama, which must now be definitely abandoned, in that the dramatic dialectic will be injected not only into the characters but also directly into the idea itself, so that not alone the relation of man to the idea is debated but also the validity of the idea itself.

Hebbel's words bring us to the threshold of Shavian drama.

What is Shaw's theory of the drama? What has he said on the subject? A great deal, almost everyone would be inclined to say. Yet in fact only a very small portion of Shaw's thirty odd volumes is devoted to dramatic criticism and little of that to dramatic theory. From the earliest prefaces to the preface to *Saint Joan* (1924) we find complaints of a lack of seriousness in contemporary theatre and in criticism and we find discussions of censorship and the like, but for more general judgments one must go to two chapters added in 1912 to *The Quintessence of Ibsenism*, to Shaw's Preface to *Three Plays of Brieux*, and to Archibald Henderson's inexhaustible Shaviana. From such sources one can piece together a body of dramatic theory somewhat as follows.

The nineteenth-century theatre, consisting of the rags and

"The Theory and Practice of Shavian Drama," from *The Playwright As Thinker*. By permission of Reynal & Hitchcock, Inc.

tatters of Shakespeare and the cheap new feathers of Eugène Scribe, is decadent. It presents not life but day-dream, not thought but sentiment, not experience but conventional surrogates. Two men—Ibsen and Wagner—have struggled against the tide, and their efforts have been so successful that it can be said: ". . . there is, flatly, no future now for any drama without music except the drama of thought." Receptively, Shaw was probably more moved by Wagner; as a creative artist, however, he was to follow in the footsteps of Ibsen.

For Shaw the quintessence of Ibsen was that he was pre-occupied with morality, and that morality was in Ibsen something to be discussed and worked out, not something given. Morality is not only to do right but to discover what *is* right; immorality is not only the doing of certain things, but the deception of self in refusing to see what should and should not be done. In the drama of fixed morality there is no moral questioning at all. Hence the need of much outward action. We must see the hero in many situations, facing right and facing wrong. He must be put to tests of fire and water. Such is the nature of what Shaw calls "the tomfooleries called action" or, more explicitly, "vulgar attachments, rapacities, generosities, resentments, ambitions, misunderstandings, oddities, and so forth." Once the moral problem is one of sincerity and conscience and not merely a test of one's power to live according to the moral law, outward eventfulness becomes superfluous and therefore vulgar. Shaw denounces "crimes, fights, big legacies, fires, shipwrecks, battles, and thunderbolts" as "mistakes in a play, even when they can be effectively simulated."

Since morality is not given, we do not know who is a villain and who is a hero. This fact is both true to life and dramatically interesting. The villain cannot only be—what he always was—plausible and apparently virtuous. He can actually *be* what most people do think virtuous. This too is true to life, and it is dramatically striking because it establishes between author and audience the unusual, ironic, and Shavian relationship of antagonism. It is true that most of the audience will, after a time at least, make exceptions of themselves and assume that Shaw means everybody else. But Shaw does not mean everybody else, and the irony is redoubled. We must therefore conclude that there is more to the shock-technique of Shavian drama than high spirits or even reformism. Shaw's preaching has esthetic as well as moral point, for it is the preacher who chides his audience and who must not pretend to sympathize with their faults. When Shaw proposed a drama of ideas he did not mean a drama deprived of all dramatic elements except witty conversation. He meant, in his own words, "the substitution of a forensic technique of recrimination, disillusion, and penetration through ideals to the truth, with a free use of all the rhetorical and lyrical arts of the orator, the preacher, the pleader, and the rhapsodist."

The theory of Shavian drama is, on the negative side, a defence of the drama of discussion and, on the positive side, an assault upon all other drama, for when the artist turns literary critic he always generalizes his personal positions and arraigns all the traditions with which he is not in rapport. Shaw was not averse to arraigning Shakespeare. The arraignment was partly unashamed self-advertisement, but partly also it was an attempt to establish that non-Shakespearian drama of which Hebbel had spoken, an attempt to weaken the Bardolatry which was hindering a true understanding of Shakespeare as much as it was hampering the efforts of all who tried to make a drama which would be as expressive of our time as Shakespeare had been of his. As objective evaluation Shaw's Shakespeare criticism is unimportant. As polemic, as part of his own theory, it is consistent and significant. If he has ridiculed some plays which had been thought sacrosanct, he called attention to the fascination of some plays, such as *Troilus and Cressida*, which modern critics would later claim to have "discovered"; he observed that *Hamlet* was laudably un-Shakespearian in that here was real moral doubt and questioning of conscience and inner tragedy; he was privately a great Shakespeare fan and in Shakespeare discussion resembles an atheist who in religious discussion turns out to know and relish the Bible more than the godly.

But Shaw's major critical offensive was against the pre-Ibsenite drama of the nineteenth century. The shadow of Scribe darkened the scene. Shaw fumed. He would annihilate this *infame!* If this was technique, he would annihilate technique! Hence his polemics against the "well-made play": "Your plot construction and art of preparation are only tricks of theatrical talent and shifts of moral sterility, not the weapons of dramatic genius." Or again: "The writer who practises the art of Ibsen therefore discards all the old tricks of preparation, catastrophe, dénouement . . ." Once the mode of these polemics is understood, Shaw's disparagement of dramaturgy in his own work can also be understood for the blarney that it is. Shaw boasts of using the comic tricks of the 'sixties in *Arms and the Man;* in *The Devil's Disciple* he declares he has used those of the next generation; what the critics take for brilliance and originality, he explains, consists only of the "tricks and suspenses and thrills and jests" which were "in vogue when I was a boy." How little these remarks describe the Shavian dramaturgy we shall see in a later section of this essay.

What is the gist of Shaw's case against the Shakespearian and the Scribean traditions? It is that both are Romantic. In the Shavian use of the term, Romanticism means hocus-pocus, pretentious and deceptive artifice, the substitution of flattering but unreal and foolish conventions for realities. The theory is that Zola, Ibsen, and Shaw (and perhaps one should add the later Dickens and Samuel Butler) had made it their business to destroy Romanticism by laying bare the realities. Zola made a fine beginning, says Shaw, by trying to replace Romantic or stagey logic with a correct natural history, but unfortunately he formed a Romantic attachment with morbidity. Ibsen made a monumental contribution, but unhappily retained the catastrophic ending in his plays. The natural historian of modern society knows that the real tragedy of Hedda Gablers is precisely that they do not commit suicide. Shaw gives Chekhov some credit for this insight, and emulates his method in *Heartbreak House.* Eugène Brieux he appears to regard as the most thorough-going exponent of "natural history."

This brings us to the positive side of Shaw's dramaturgy. Shaw's theory, I repeat, is not that everything in traditional drama should be scrapped except talk, and then the residue called the New Drama. "Rhetoric, irony, argument, paradox, epigram, parable," he writes, "the re-arrangement of haphazard facts into orderly and intelligent situations: these are both the oldest and the newest arts of the drama." These words include a good deal more than clever or even profound talk. Attention should be paid to the phrase "the re-arrangement of the facts into orderly and intelligent situations" and to the word "parable." The preface to Brieux contains an assertion that drama does not merely photograph nature but attempts a "presentment in parable of the conflict between man's will and his environment: in a word, of problem." This is indeed an old and new theory of drama, old as the Greeks, new as Ibsen who had characterized his leading theme as "the contradiction between effort and capacity, between will and possibility, the tragedy and at the same time comedy of the individual and of mankind."

II

Shaw's defense of a theatre of idea brought him up against both his great bugbears—commercialized art on the one hand and Art for Art's Sake on the other. His teaching is that beauty is a by-product of other activity; that the artist writes out of moral passion (in forms varying from political conviction to religious zeal), not out of love of art; that the pursuit of art for its own sake is a form of self-indulgence as bad as any other sort of sensuality. In the end, the errors of "pure" art and of commercialized art are identical: they both appeal primarily to the senses. True art, on the other hand, is not merely a matter of pleasure. It may be unpleasant. A favorite Shavian metaphor for the function of the arts is that of tooth-pulling. Even if the patient is under gas, the tooth is still pulled.

The history of esthetics affords more examples of a didactic than of a hedonist view. But Shaw's didacticism takes an unusual turn in its application to the history of the arts. If, as Shaw holds, ideas are a most important part of a work of art, and if, as he also holds, ideas go out of date, it follows that even the best works of art go out of date in some important respects and that the generally held view that great works are in all respects eternal is not shared by Shaw. In the Preface to *Three Plays for Puritans*, Shaw maintains that renewal in the arts means renewal in philosophy, not in anything artistic; that the first great artist who comes along after a renewal gives to the new philosophy full and final form; that subsequent artists, though even more gifted, can do nothing but refine upon the master without matching him. Shaw, whose essential modesty is as disarming as his pose of vanity is disconcerting, assigns to himself the role, not of the master, but of the pioneer, the role of a Marlowe rather than of a Shakespeare. "The whirligig of time will soon bring my audiences to my own point of view," he writes, "and then the next Shakespeare that comes along will turn these petty tentatives of mine into masterpieces final for their epoch."

"Final for their epoch"—even Shakespearean masterpieces are not final beyond that. No one, says Shaw, will ever write a better tragedy than *Lear* or a better opera than *Don Giovanni* or a better music-drama than *The Niblung's Ring;* but just as essential to a play as this esthetic merit is moral relevance which, if we take a naturalistic and historical view of morals, it loses, or partly loses, in time. Shaw has the courage of his historicism, consistently withstands the view that moral problems do not change, and argues therefore that for us modern literature and music form a Bible surpassing in significance the Hebrew Bible. That is Shaw's challenge to President Hutchins and St. John's College.

Such are Bernard Shaw's expressed opinions on dramatic and artistic matters. What are we to make of it? We have seen that most of his critical prose is polemic and is not therefore to be submitted to the same kind of analysis as a more objective criticism. Even when arguing for science and natural history as against Romanticism and artifice, Shaw writes in a prose that is at once artistic, artful, and artificial. He is a poet of polemics, as Einstein seems to have felt when he compared the movement of Shavian dialogue to Mozart's music. His polemics are therefore the more dangerous, for polemics are nothing but the art of skilled deception. Now a prime device of polemics is the either / or pattern, against which so much has been said in recent times, often by great polemicists. Shaw is a great polemicist in his skilled deployment of antitheses. He always forces upon his opponent an alternative which the opponent never wanted to be confronted with and sometimes did not deserve to be confronted with. Watch how he pushes not only the Scribeans but also the Shakespeareans into a corner! He condemns not merely melodramatic action but apparently all outward action as "tomfoolery." Of course the condemnation has some substance (it is the art of the polemicist to avoid untruths, and exploit half-truths) in that not much of the history of the world can be convincingly represented on the stage. Shaw knows that the stage can only show the effect of history on a few individuals and that it is much better suited to talking than to fighting and doing. That is the true half of this remark. But he loads it with a lie in order to attract attention. He feels that the weakness of the well-made play can only be revealed if all plot-construction is ridiculed. The absurdity of melodrama can only be demonstrated by debunking tragedy. Shaw cannot always resist the temptation to remove the unoffending nose with the offending wart.

We cannot, therefore, feel wholly satisfied with Shaw's contributions to dramatic theory brilliant as some of them are. The terms of the theory are too crude. Technique and plot cannot be isolated from the rest of a work of art in so facile a manner. More explanation would be needed to make the antithesis of romantic logic and natural history convincing. Shaw's criticism, which so many ·think over-explanatory, and which many assumed to be voluminous, is actually reticent to the point of evasiveness. As his pose of conceit hides a considerable shyness about himself, so his volubility is, among other things, a way of avoiding certain issues, chief among them the esthetic issues. Shaw refuses to lecture on dramaturgy on the grounds that he is a practitioner, and of course he is entirely within his rights in this. Many a creative artist would support him. The peculiar thing about Shaw is that we have the impression that he has explained everything—"I am nothing if not explanatory," he once said—but always stops short in personal and esthetic matters. Hence we can often learn more from an *obiter dictum* of Shaw's than from an extended statement. When for instance in 1934 Shaw defends one of his plays "simply as a play" we wonder what has happened to the didactic criterion. And we learn much about the art of Shaw when we read of his writing his roles for particular actors, of his own histrionic talent, of his interest in actual production. Plays, he remarks casually, can be considered as exhibitions of the art of acting. Of this conception he says: "As I write my plays it is continuously in my mind and very much to my taste."

These are valuable hints, but they remain hints and are never developed into a critical system. Shaw's critical writing is to some extent camouflage. He has himself, consciously or not, spread the notion, recently reiterated in Hesketh Pearson's biography, that he is most interesting as a person, slightly less interesting as a sage, and least interesting as a playwright. Shaw has said that art must be subordinate to other things, and his readers have applied the theory to Shaw. But the Shavian view is that the subordination of art to morals should make the artist better as an artist. To say that beauty and happiness are by-products not to be directly aimed at is to alter our method of attaining beauty and happiness; yet beauty and happiness remain the ultimate goal, even though we reach them by doing something else. And the critic is entitled to judge for himself whether beauty has been attained or not. By no amount of polemic can Shaw evade the esthetic touchstone. Not one exceptional case only, but all his plays must stand or fall as plays.

III

One or two of Shaw's generalizations about drama do help us to an understanding of his plays. One is that there are only two dramatic characters, the long-haired aesthete and the clown. The statement is naughty, for it is either too vague to be exactly applicable or too dogmatic to be true. Yet it opens the door to an understanding of Shaw's characters, at least the male characters, and the way they are contrasted. A still more pregnant remark is that the drama, though now degenerated to a rant and a situation, began as a dance and a story. Shaw has brought dance back into the drama, not directly, to be sure, but in the lively rhythm of his lines and in the musical, rather than "well-made," structure of his scenes; and, precisely by minimizing plot, he has brought back stories to the stage by way of lengthy narratives.

The well-made play, says Shaw, is built on the scheme: exposition, situation, unravelling. *A Doll's House* is built on the scheme: exposition, situation, discussion. Discussion is the crucial technical innovation which accompanies the changes in outlook which Hebbel was one of the first to be aware of. The Shavian play—everyone agrees—is a discussion play. People sit in their chairs and talk everything over. The talk is good. And that, according to many, is Shaw.

But, in the first place, Shaw's plays, though more like each other than any one is like a non-Shavian piece, are not cut to one pattern. Indeed his plays are so various, and there are at least thirty important ones, that classification is extremely difficult even on chronological lines. Yet, though Shaw's dramatic career is not so clearly periodized as, say, Ibsen's, certain groupings do suggest themselves. A major break occurred with the First World War. The plays prior to that compose a single group which in turn may be cut in half at about the turn of the century. Dividing the post-war period also in half, we have two main periods, with two subdivisions:

1892-1899	I. i.	*Plays Pleasant and Unpleasant*, and *Three Plays for Puritans*.
1901-1912	ii.	From *Man and Superman* to *Pygmalion*.
1913-1924	II. i.	From *Heartbreak House* to *Saint Joan*.
1929-1939	ii.	From *The Apple Cart* to *In Good King Charles's Golden Days*.

The plays of the 'nineties are chiefly simple inversions of current theatrical patterns, such as Victorian melodrama (*The Devil's Disciple*), the heroic play (*The Man of Destiny, Caesar and Cleopatra*), and Gilbertian comedy (*Arms and the Man, You Never Can Tell*). But from *Man and Superman* (1901-1903) on, Shaw has his own patterns. These are the years of *Getting Married* and *Misalliance*, which are the extreme instances of Shavian discussion drama, of Shaw's toughest dialectical dramas such as *Major*

Barbara and *The Doctor's Dilemma* (two of the most original and the best of Shaw's plays), and of his most controlled and delicate fantasies such as *Androcles and the Lion*. If *Fanny's First Play* and *Pygmalion* are, like the early plays, variants on conventional patterns, they are at once subtler and tougher variants than those of the 'nineties.

The play which Shaw was at work on from 1913 to 1916—*Heartbreak House*—marks a departure in technique and mood. The socialist optimism of *Major Barbara* and the Bergsonian optimism of *Man and Superman* are gone. For the current stage of civilization, Shaw finds a metaphor which was still to be with him in 1933: civilization is a ship on the rocks. From now on, most of Shaw's plays were to be fantasias or extravaganzas in which the disappointment of many liberal hopes is announced and the apartness of Shaw from the new generation is implied. Even *Back to Methuselah*, which so anxiously tries to be optimistic, is most impressive in the extravagant satire against Lloyd George and Asquith and in the pathetic tragedy of the elderly gentleman confronted with a new generation. Even *Saint Joan*, which might seem to be aloof both from the post-war generation and from Shaw, has as its theme the homelessness of genius. Among other things it is a commentary on Shaw's autobiographical remark: "I was at home only in the realm of my imagination, and at my ease only with the mighty dead."

Whether it is fair to stress, to the extent that Edmund Wilson has done, the subjective element in the later plays of Shaw, it is evident that these plays, from *Heartbreak House* to the end of the roster, do compose a separate group which we can now see as a whole. Two of them are called by Shaw Political Extravaganzas, and the name might be extended to the five plays which are a fantastic chronicle of the interim between the two world wars: *The Apple Cart, Too True to Be Good, On the Rocks, The Simpleton of the Unexpected Isles,* and *Geneva*. Are these plays inferior? From a natural tendency to say that what a famous writer does today is not up to what he did twenty years ago, and from a natural feeling that so old a man must be in his dotage, critics have on the whole damned this last cycle of Shavian plays.

To be sure, they do not have the galvanic energy of *Man and Superman* or the tough dialectic of *Major Barbara*. But they are not poor stuff. They would be enough to establish a great reputation for any new dramatist. Moreover, the Political Extravaganza is not only a new form in drama, but the form in which Shaw's genius has been most at home. Shaw's career might be regarded as a search for a form which would fully express his genius. The Political Extravaganza is such a form, though Shaw perfected it only after he had passed his prime and written his greatest plays. The Political Extravaganza is definite enough and free enough, fantastic enough and realistic enough, uproarious enough and serious enough. It is Shavian form.

IV

The freshman can see that Shaw is funny. The sophomore can see that he is serious. The junior can see that he is a man of the theatre. To graduate, however, in Shavian analysis we must discover precisely what a Shavian work consists of. I choose for more detailed consideration a play that is probably more characteristic than outstanding in the Shavian canon, a play written while Shaw was still experimenting but was drawing towards the height of his powers: *Captain Brassbound's Conversion* (1899).

Captain Brassbound is a modern version of a pirate king. He roams the seas plotting vengeance on the wicked uncle who has caused his mother's imprisonment and death. But when he has lured the wicked uncle into the Moroccan mountains and is about to hand him over to the tender mercies of a sheikh, there arrives a superior sheikh whose head will be demanded by the British government if Englishmen are kidnapped in his territories. Brassbound is handed over to the American navy, but is finally set free through the intercession of the uncle's kindly sister-in-law. Naturally, the pirate king would like to marry the lady after this, and the lady herself is not hostile; but in the end they agree to part.

This is the simple air on which Shaw plays variations. What is his method? A silent moving picture of a performance would record scene after scene of what the Germans call Kitsch and what Americans call Corn. In a Moroccan setting, all taken, Shaw informs us, from a novel by Cunningham Graham, are enacted corny scenes of pursuit and rescue, spiced with love interest. And there are other conventional ingredients of a graver sort. The plot is unfolded in resolutely Ibsenite fashion, that is, by conversation and innuendo referring to a buried crime about which we only gradually become clear. The play is subtitled: An Adventure.

But only subtitled. The main title is *Captain Brassbound's Conversion*, and of the conversion which is the subject of the play, the narrative pattern gives no inkling. At this point we hit upon Shaw's method of inversion, which in such a play as this is not the simple inversion of *Arms and the Man*. According to the pattern an Englishman and his sister-in-law are rescued by civilization from the clutches of a pirate-villian. According, however, to the interpretation imposed upon this pattern, Brassbound is the hero and protagonist. Yet—and it is such double-twists which are the making of Shavian drama—Brassbound is no hero in Douglas Fairbanks style. He is disreputable and down at heel. He is also no villian, since the person he chiefly imposes upon is himself. He has something of the manner of a Byronic sort of hero; but the Byronic hero is himself an ambivalent figure, compounded equally of strength and weakness. How are we to take Brassbound? In view of the conversion at the end, shall we say that he is a villain converted to virtue as summarily as Edmund in *King Lear?* All possible interpretations are suggested by the play itself, and the method of their suggestion is Shaw's dramatic dialetic. The primary meaning of Brassbound's character appears in the upshot. The real man has been hiding behind the mask of a villain-hero. Degenerating further and further into a shabby tourists' escort, Brassbound, true to his name, shored up the heroic purpose of vengeance against his ruins. He hoarded photographs and newspaper cuttings for purposes of mournful and vengeful contemplation. Then a woman lays bare his soul, and he is converted to realism.

Shaw's technique is not, as has been alleged, to render a serious problem palatable by a silly story. The silly story functions as an integral part of a whole. It is the basis of dozens of ironies, of which the central irony is the contrast between romance and reality, illusion and actuality, silly stories and flinty facts. This irony pervades the whole work. When, for instance, we are told a Kitsch story of crime in the West Indies, and the question is raised why a solicitor was not sent from England, the prosaic but simple explanation is that the value of the estate was less than it would have cost to make it worth a lawyer's while to leave his practice in London. When we are confronted with fighting sheikhs out of pulp fiction, we find that their actions are determined by the plain but significant fact of British imperialism. It may be recalled that Shaw had condemned the staging of fights and crimes as mistakes. This, however, does not mean that he eschews such things. He uses them, but ironically, not naively. They are always ridiculous in Shaw, and their ridiculousness has always a point.

Like the plot, the characters are given ironical meaning. Even the American captain, primarily a tool of the plot, is given a touch of significance as "a curious ethnological specimen, with all the nations of the old world at war in his veins." Every minor character enforces an irony. Hallam, the wicked uncle, is a judge and a pillar of society; conservatism shows its other face in Rankin, the defeatist missionary whose only convert in Morocco is a London slum boy named Drinkwater. Drinkwater is Brassbound on a lower level of culture. Like Brassbound he feasts upon romance—in the pages of the pulps. Brassbound's great theme is his innocent mother punished by Hallam; Drinkwater has been acquitted by Hallam when actually guilty. This contrast shows Hallam as at once ruthless and incompetent.

In this framework of fictions, the problem of romance and realism is thrashed out by violent juxtapositions and confrontations. Rudolph Valentino is, as it were, confronted with Henry Ford. There is irony within irony. If Brassbound does not support his role of villain, Hallam does not support his role of hero. The initial irony of his character is one that Ibsen had rendered familiar: the pillar of society is a scoundrel. Hallam has played a tricky game in the West Indies and Brassbound's mother was driven to her death. The law, moreover, which Hallam administers in England is interpreted by Shaw to be crude vengeance wreaked by a class of crooks masquerading as churchgoers. Yet Hallam is not a villain, for he is more victim than agent. He only does what his class does and what he has been brought up to do. He means well and is privately harmless. Far from battening on his ill-gotten gains, he is finding the West Indies estate more a liability than an asset. Brassbound for his part is no avenging angel. His interpretation of the facts is quite as incomplete and primitive as Hallam's. In fact, his standards are the same: like Hallam, he believes above all in revenge. Pillar of society and Byronic hero are equally guilty because identically guilty.

The conversion of Brassbound is effected by Lady Cicely Waynefleet. The last page of the play, in which the two agree to part, is one of the best illustrations of the achievement of Shavian comedy. It is neither glib nor ponderous, neither flippant nor sentimental. It is a taut, terse, and true ending in which the dialogue, so far from being an independent stream rippling over the stones of a plot, is fused with theme, story, and characterization. Brassbound presses Lady Cicely to marry him to the point where she is about to consent. At that point he withdraws the offer. We infer that Brassbound has found himself anew in the experience of dominating Lady Cicely. "You can do no more for me now," he says. "I have blundered somehow on the secret of command at last." When Brassbound leaves, Lady Cicely says: "How glorious! How glorious! And what an escape!" It is one of the splendid and expressive endings of comedy. It reveals that Lady Cicely herself found the escape from the real to the romantic entirely glorious. The conversion of Brassbound almost caused the apostasy of his savior. That is the ultimate irony. But since Brassbound *was* converted, he could not allow it. The title of the piece is quite inevitable, and it is the only thing in the whole play that is not ironical.

V

What then is to be said for Shavian comedy? What are its merits? What is its nature?

The dialogue of Shavian comedy has always been praised. It was praised by Max Beerbohm and G. K. Chesterton forty years ago, and it is praised by Edmund Wilson, Edgar Johnson, and Jacques Barzun today. But my point in this essay is that Shaw's talent is not merely for conversation but also for dramaturgy. In all justice it should be said that Max Beerbohm pointed this out in a retraction of his earlier view that Shaw was a writer of conversations, not plays. This view, says Beerbohm, collapses when you actually see Shaw in the theatre: "To deny that he is a dramatist merely because he chooses, for the most part, to get drama out of contrasted types of character and thought, without action, and without appeal to the emotions, seems to be both unjust and absurd."

But these words of Beerbohm's, written in 1905, have not been heeded. Bernard Shaw has sometimes been omitted from histories of the drama and more often relegated to a humble role beside Granville Barker and Arthur Pinero. Recent critics who have rediscovered the artistry of Shaw have rediscovered the prose style much more than the dramaturgy. Even Beerbohm's praise is left-handed in its assertion that Shavian drama is "without action, and without appeal to the emotions." It is curious that almost on the same page Beerbohm had spoken of the splendid emotional crisis in the second act of *Major Barbara*, and had shown himself the first critic, so far as I know, to note the vein of spirituality in Shaw. It is curious, because it shows how a critic can revert to the cliché conception of Shaw—"a giant brain and no heart," to cite one of the critics in *Fanny's First Play*—after a momentary escape from it. It has been said of Bertolt Brecht that he thinks with his heart and feels with his head. The same could be said of Shaw. His intellect and his passions are alike all that one could expect of an artist-philosopher. But there is something perpetually unexpected and astonishing about the way they mix.

The allegation that Shaw's plays are "without action" is more plausible but still wrong. Most of the plays from *Arms and the Man* to *The Millionairess* entail every bit as much action as other authors' plays and for the good reason that many of them are other authors' plots. The misapprehension comes about because

Shaw *toys* with the plots instead of gratefully accepting them for what they are, because also he has in his prefaces railed so often against the "tomfoolery of action," and because of the interpenetration of action with discussion. Look for a moment at the most actionless of Shaw's plays, *Getting Married* and *Misalliance*. Even these are not static dramas of a sort to win the approval of a Maeterlinck or a Chekhov. In both there is enough plot for an ordinary Broadway play. (It is amusing that Shaw has to be defended by such an argument.) In *Getting Married* the destiny of a fair number of characters is not merely discussed but settled, and the routine of boy-meets-girl is given a Shavian performance. In *Misalliance*, there is all the violence and tomfoolery that anyone could wish. An aviator—and this in 1910—crashes into the precincts; his passenger turns out to be a lady whom Sidney Hook would have to term at once eventful and event-making. In *Getting Married* there is a coal-dealer's wife who makes love to a bishop through the mails under the name Incognita Appassionata; in *Misalliance* there is a gunman. It is not the lack of action but the presence of intelligent dialogue which is too much for many modern directors, actors, critics, and audiences.

So much for technique. An artist who is a critic of morality and society must also submit to a moral and social criticism. What are Shaw's values? Some will point in reply to the most extended of his philosophic works, such as *Back to Methuselah*. Others will observe that Shaw has chopped and changed. Now he is a social democrat, now an anti-democratic pessimist. Now he is a Huxleyan champion of science against religion, now a metabiological champion of religion against science. He can be represented as merely a disciple of Marx, or of Shelley, or of Samuel Butler. Edmund Wilson concludes that he is just confused.

This might not—though again, it might—be a damaging criticism of a lyric poet, but it is certainly a damaging criticism of a moralist; and one cannot be quite happy about Wilson's approval of Shaw the artist when it is qualified by so strong a disapproval of Shaw the philosopher. Of course it can be maintained that Shaw's argument against the pure artist is a deceptive strategy to

trick us into believing that he is a philosopher. Even so a confused satirist is a bad satirist, and thus a bad artist.

But surely Wilson is wrong. What he finds inconsistent—for
instance, that Shaw can be at the same time a social democrat and
an admirer of Stalin—will not seem inconsistent to everyone.
Wilson says that Shaw's thinking is on three levels—the level of
everyday life, the level of politics, and the level of metaphysics—
and that the three are never integrated. To be sure, it is no answer
to retort that *all* men think on these three levels without a successful integration of the three, for Shaw as an artist-philosopher
must be expected to succeed where other men fail. The answer,
as I have tried elsewhere to demonstrate, is that Shaw's integration is not so incomplete as is supposed.[1] Here is it enough to
state that Shaw is sometimes accused of betraying beliefs which
he never held. He is often suspected of trying to be much more
systematic than he ever intended to be. Indeed he is not utterly
systematic but he is roughly consistent; his attitude to beliefs has
been, in the main, that of a pragmatist. This is perhaps what most
clearly differentiates Shaw from satirists of previous ages, such as
Chaucer with his catholic criteria or Voltaire with his deistic
criteria. It is at once Shaw's great title to originality as an artist
and his great title to represent his age.

Shaw's pragmatic adaptability is not mere opportunism. He has
often sponsored an unpopular cause which was later recognized
to be right. He has believed in what might as justifiably be called
Romanticism as the hocus-pocus of popular novelists, namely, in
the continuity of the ideal and the real, the spiritual and the physical, the theoretic and the practical. He is a Marxist in his hatred
of hypocritical ideologies, of religions which are opiates; money,
he says, is the most important thing in the world, and you are
damned without it. On the other hand, Shaw probably agrees
with Hotchkiss in *Getting Married:* "Religion is a great force; the
only real motive force in the world." The Shavian will see no final
contradiction between the two attitudes. Religion is for Shaw a

[1] *A Century of Hero Worship*, Part Three, Chapter Two.

natural fact, not a supernatural fact; just as economics is for Shaw spiritual enough to be the subject of high comedy.

The great problem of Shaw's plays—we have examined one instance in some detail—is the relation between ideals and reality, and thus the relation between idealism and realism. There is, according to Shaw, a wrong realism and a right realism, a wrong idealism and a right idealism. A wrong realism is exemplified in Undershaft, whose realistic vision supports only egoism. Idealism on the other hand may be worse. It may be the conscious mask of a realist, as it is in the propaganda of Undershaft's factory or in the gifts of Bodger the brewer to the Salvation Army. It may be self-deception, as it is in Barbara before she sees quite clearly that she is combatting liquor with a brewer's money. In either case, idealism is painted in more horrible colors by Shaw, as it had been by Ibsen and for that matter by Jesus Christ, than is Machiavellian realism. The conclusion of *Major Barbara* is that the high purpose of the idealist should be linked to the realist's sense of fact, power, and possibility. Where practical genius is found in a lofty mind Shaw approves. His Caesar is a realist with a soul, a realist who values his own life as nothing beside the high destiny of Rome. His Joan is an idealist with a head, an idealist who can see the simple facts better than the soldiers, the politicians, and the clerics put together, a visionary whose hallucinations have more validity than the philosophic ideas of the learned.

Ibsen's Brand, striving to "live the vision into deed," had said:

> Daily drudgery be one
> With star-flights beyond the sun.

Through Ibsen Romanticism came to flower in Scandinavia; through Ibsen, Shaw, and others Romanticism was renewed after a generation of anti-Romanticism. Now the doctrine of religious-materialism or materialist-religion, of idealist-realism or realistic-idealism, is one of the themes of Romanticism from Blake to Shaw. It is a leitmotiv of Shavian drama turning up in the pseudo-flippant form of his late Political Extravangazas. In *Too True to Be Good* (1929), man is described as having higher and lower centres, as in D. H. Lawrence. But Shaw is not the spokesman of lower centres; nor is he, as many assume, the spokesman of the higher centres. He attributes our troubles to the separation of higher and lower. "Since the war," says his preacher, "the lower centres have become vocal. And the effect is that of an earthquake . . . the institutions are rocking and splitting and sundering. They leave us no place to live, no certainties, no workable morality, no heaven, no hell, no commandments, and no God." Or, as the studious Sergeant in the same play puts it, in speaking of the sexual ethics of the 'twenties: "But when men and women pick one another up just for a bit of fun, they find they've picked up more than they bargained for, because men and women have a top storey as well as a ground floor; and you can't have the one without the other."

Shaw's Romanticism is a more highly developed philosophy than the Romanticism of the first generation. Philosophically one should look for its affiliations less with "mysticism" or "material-ism"—the two systems commonly associated with Shaw—than with the pragmatic pluralism of William James. The attitudes of pragmatic pluralism are part and parcel of Shaw's art as well as of his thought. Nowhere in dogmatic communist writing does one have a sense of dialectic and antithesis as keenly as in a Shavian play. Shaw's mind is well-stocked, as everyone knows, and he is famous for the number of things he can mention on one page; but all this would mean nothing if he could not marshal his facts ironically. The chief mark of Shavian prose is its use of ironic antithesis and juxtaposition. Contrary to what one expects from a propagandist, Shaw not only shows the liberal's sense of the other man's point of view. He has a sense of every conceivable point of view, and can pack all the points of view into one long sentence, which climbs by parallelisms and antitheses to a climax, and then sinks with the finality of a conqueror to a conclusion which Shaw will not allow you to evade. In its course the Shavian sentence, still more the Shavian paragraph, looks in all possible directions. For Shaw sees the world as what James called a multi-verse, and that is unusual in a satirist, who is customarily some-thing of a monomaniac.

It is a fact of curious interest that William James, who thought

Shaw "a great power as a concrete moralist," hit upon one of the essentials of Shaw, to wit, "the way be brings home to the *eyes*, as it were, the difference between 'convention' and 'conscience.' " Such a statement would often be the cue for a discussion of Shaw as puritan and protestant. But there is more to it than that. The difference between convention and conscience is certainly a moral matter, but Shaw is a *concrete* moralist, a master of parable, who has worked out for the presentation of his protestant pragmatist morality a new dramaturgy. Shaw is one of the few artists whose grasp of political, moral, and social forces is really professional; in political, moral, and social territory he is not a mere expropriator. But he is a genuine dramatist in that he brings his matter home to the eyes, which is something that neither the historian nor the sociologist, the poet nor the novelist, need do. All these bring visions before the mind's eye; none, except the dramatist, has to unfold his vision before the physical eye. Appreciators of Shaw's dialogue have explained to us what Shaw has done for the ear; those who appreciate his dramaturgy know that he addressed himself also to the eye, not indeed in giving separate attention to the eye by way of spectacle, but in fusing the elements into the one kinetic picture which is stage production (or screen production, as Shaw's movie audiences will hasten to add). William James' statement that Shaw's genius is much more important than his philosophy is true, if by it we understand that genius is a synthesizing power which obliterates barriers between thought and technique and gives evidence of both in a particular mode of presentation. The Shavian mode is drama.

R. P. BLACKMUR:

LANGUAGE AS GESTURE

IF THERE is a puzzle in my title, it is because, like Sweeney with his ladies in Eliot's *Fragment of an Agon,* "I've gotta use wᴄ rds when I talk to you." The puzzle is verbal, something we have made ourselves, and may be solved. Language is made of words, and gesture is made of motion. There is one half the puzzle. The other half is equally self-evident if only because it is an equally familiar part of the baggage of our thought. It is the same statement put the other way round. Words are made of motion, made of action or response, at whatever remove; and gesture is made of language—made of the language beneath or beyond or alongside of the language of words. When the language of words fails we resort to the language of gesture. If we stop there, we stop with the puzzle. If we go on, and say that when the language of words most succeeds it *becomes* gesture in its words, we shall have solved the verbal puzzle with which we began by discovering one approach to the central or dead-end mystery of meaningful expression in the language of the arts. We shall have made, too, I take it, an imaginative equivalent for Kenneth Burke's more nearly intellectual thesis, which I share, that the language of poetry may be regarded as symbolic action. The difference between Mr. Burke and myself is that where he is predominantly concerned with setting up methods for analyzing the actions as they are expressed in the symbol, I choose to emphasize the created or dead-end symbol. He explores the puzzle of the language in the process of becoming symbolic. I try to show in a series of varied and progressive examples how the symbol invests

467

the actions in language with poetic actuality. Mr. Burke legislates; I would judge; the executive is between us.

There is a line in *Othello* which I think makes it all plain between us, not just between Mr. Burke and myself, but between all of us. "I understand a fury in your words / But not the words." I do not propose this language as itself a gesture, but it is proposed as a fair example of the situation in which language gains the force of gesture; and indeed it leads to the memory of my own earliest experience of language as gesture. As a small boy of six or seven walking the streets of Cambridge I used often to pass little dead-end streets, each with its sign post which at its top read, say, Trowbridge Place or Irving Terrace, and underneath in letters of a different colour and on a separate board, the following mysterious legend: Private Way Dangerous Passing. The legend meant of course merely that the City of Cambridge, since it neither built nor maintained the roadbed of this place or this terrace, would not be responsible for injury to life or property sustained through its use. But to me it meant something else. It meant that there was in passing across its mouth a clear and present danger which might, and especially if it was dusk, suddenly leap out and overcome me. Thus, to say the least of it, I had the regular experience of that heightened, that excited sense of being which we find in poetry, whenever I passed one of those signs. I understood the fury in its words, but not the words. Yet I am not sure at this late and dejected day that in understanding the words I have not become indifferent to a fury of meaning that was actually there. There was a steady over-arching gesture in those words, Dangerous Passing, which because I was included within it and indeed partly created it, meant more and touched me more deeply than any merely communicative words, deprived of their native gesture, can ever do.

For gesture *is* native to language, and if you cut it out you cut roots and get a sapless and gradually a rotting if indeed not a petrifying language. (If I may quote a poem of my own in which there was some effort to make an image for standing dead timber, what in Maine we call dri-kai, "Ghostly, these gestures are beyond repair.") But gesture is not only native to language, it comes before it in a still richer sense, and must be, as it were, carried into it whenever the context is imaginative. Living in Belmont some ten years ago I used to go into Cambridge on an orange-yellow bus which made very good time the first half of the trip. If anyone were ahead of you getting on, you might jump from ten to twenty to forty or fifty miles an hour by the time you had paid your fare and found your seat. So it was for the woman I remember one very high bright noon. She got on with a friend whom I do not remember at all except that she sat directly behind me and no doubt looked over my shoulder seeing just what I saw. But the woman herself I remember very well. She was largish and of a French figure, that is with a noticeable waist and a more noticeable rear, and she had heels too high for her balance in a spurting bus. There she stood holding the chromium rail back of the driver's seat looking at her friend (and therefore at me) while the driver made her change. She fair yawed to leeward every few yards, each time knocking the great floppy hat, which women of such figure so often wear askew, against the upright post on which the coin box was set. She had much trouble getting the two fares in the box, and considerably more trouble getting herself from the box down the aisle, hauling from seat to seat by their shining handles against the momentum of the bus, lurching, as she had to, in all directions save the right one. During the whole business—and this is what I am getting at—she managed by sniffs and snorts, by smiles, by sticking her tongue out very sharp, by batting her very blue eyes about, and generally by cocking her head this way and that, she managed to express fully, and without a single word either uttered or wanted, the whole mixed, flourishing sense of her disconcertment, her discomforture, her uncertainty, together with a sense of adventure and of gaiety, all of which she wanted to share with her companion behind me, who took it I was sure, as I did myself, all smiles. Because I was within the orbit of her gestures I felt myself, as I felt her, fairly playing in life as we say that water-lights play in the sun or moon.

That is an example of the gesture that comes before language; but reflecting upon it, it seems also an example of the gesture which when it goes with language crowns it, and so animates it as to make it independent of speaker or writer; reflecting upon it, it seems that the highest use of language cannot be made without incorporating some such quality of gesture within it. How without it could the novelist make his dialogue ring? how could the poet make his cry lyric, his incongruity comic, or his perspective tragic? The great part of our knowledge of life and of nature—perhaps all our knowledge of their play and interplay—comes to us as gesture, and we are masters of the skill of that knowledge before we can ever make a rhyme or a pun, or even a simple sentence. Nor can we master language purposefully without re-mastering gesture within it. Gesture, in language, is the outward and dramatic play of inward and imaged meaning. It is that play of meaningfulness among words which cannot be defined in the formulas in the dictionary, but which is defined in their use together; gesture is that meaningfulness which is moving, in every sense of that word: what moves the words and what moves us.

Before pursuing the means of access to the mystery of gesture in the art of poetry, let us see quickly how it behaves among the other arts. For if gesture is of such structural importance in poetry as I claim for it, then the other arts should attest for it an equivalent importance; it is in such matters that there must be a substantial unity in all art; there are not two, or three, much less seven, fundamental modes of imagination, but only one. We must use example, not argument, for we wish to remind ourselves not of formulas but of insights, and we wish to get back to poetry with our sense of gesture fortified rather than obstructed.

The clearest and most familiar example of gesture in architecture is the spire on a church, for we have all seen church spires whether we go to church or not. Bad spires weigh a church down and are an affair of carpentry rather than architecture, an example of formula stifling form. A good spire is weightless, springing, an arrow aimed at the Almighty, carrying, in its gesture, the whole church with it. Though it may have been as much made out of formula as the bad spire, it differs in that the formula has somehow seized enough life to become form again;

which is one way of saying what gesture does in art—it is what happens to a form when it becomes identical with its subject. It does this, in the case of a spire, by giving the sense of movement, of aspiration, as a tree or a shrub gives the sense of process of growth, or as a beautiful room gives the effect of extending space rather than enclosing it. This sense of movement in "actually" inert mass and empty space is what we call gesture in architecture. So, too, we feel that pillars are mighty, that a bridge spans or leaps, that a dome covers us, or a crypt appals us.

In sculpture we have much the same situation as in architecture except that the effects are more specifically human in character; for in sculpture we arrest or fix in physical mass and space those human or animal movements, or those essential shapes of body or object, which, arrested, move within themselves, whether from inwards outwards or outwards inwards, so as to make a timeless gesture. Here we get the difference between gesture and act. In bad sculpture, what bores us and annoys us and makes us feel that we are bumping our heads against stones, is the sense that the athlete wants to leap or that the horse is about to canter, or whatever it is; the arrested movement wants to go on and complete itself in action. In good sculpture there is none of this, but rather that in the movement arrested, in the moving stillness, there is a gesture completed at the moment of its greatest significance. Examples in sculpture are easy, as in architecture, but less conspicuous. A good vase shows all the gesture value of roundness; a good nude by Maillol or Lehmbruck or LaChaise gives a deep gesture of the body in some moment of meaningful balance. Let us say that good sculpture has a heaviness or lightness which has nothing to do with stone or wood or the carver's trade, but which has everything to do with the gesture which illumines the medium. It is gesture that makes a stone figure a sphinx, and it is gesture that makes the great Sphinx a smile. By which I mean that there is great momentum in great repose and inexhaustible meaningfulness in any image that makes the gesture, as the sphinx does, of the momentum and the repose in man's brooding upon himself. Sculpture is man breeding shapes out of his brooding.

Painting may combine the effect of the gestures in both sculpture and architecture, since it represents the feeling of physical mass and space, but it does so at a remove. The true play of meaning in painting lies rather in what it does with texture, with light, and especially with what it does with our great, and otherwise ineluctable, visual knowledge of human character. No knowledge is so great or so skilled and no knowledge has been so variously felt as our knowledge of what, literally, we *see* in people. But in our knowledges there is none, too, in which we so fumble when we try to say what we know as in this visual knowledge, except when we use the mode of imaginative painting in the field of the portrait or of figure painting. I think, to reach for things at hand, of Rembrandt's Polish Rider, in the Frick Galleries, with all its golden gloom and the light gathering against the rider's face, or in the same galleries of Titian's young man in ermine alive in old air—both so full of that maximum human dignity, that rightness and fullness of being, of which no man, seen, can be deprived. Or again there are the portraits of El Greco, brimming, as Marianne Moore's poem says, with inner light—the portrait of the Cardinal in the Metropolitan or that of Brother Felix in the Boston Museum; haunted faces both, haunted with that spiritual life beyond dignity which the flesh cannot ever attain in fact but which is sometimes reached as a gesture of light in eyes and features. How does a painter come by such effects? Look at a society portrait, a prettified portrait, an official portrait—all faithful enough to their sitters, all too faithful, precisely—and is it not plain that their great lack, their yawning vacuity, the almost visible yawn of suppressed inattention, comes about because the painter has rendered them as the average of a long series of unresponsive moments. Nothing is left out but the vital gesture of the single, focal moment, the gesture of some particular state, some long perspective—say the lifelong heaviness of the head upon its little fulcrum—some deep inspiration of the flesh, say the desire *in weariness* for rest, or even, say, just the gaiety and radiance of the features in play with life; nothing is left out but what the great portrait painter puts in: some caught or imagined gesture of awareness that startles the features into a maximum life. The painter puts into his portraits the crossed gesture of knowledge and mystery, of the intolerably familiar and the impossibly alien, which we see in the looking-glass. That is why in great portraits we see ourselves.

In dancing we would seem to have the art that is most directly concerned with gesture, for when the gesture breaks down or does not communicate, the dance does not speak at all. Put the other way around, this means that the gesture in ballet must be built up and infused into what is otherwise "mere" movement. Gesture is what makes dancing buoyant and what makes it possible for it to end. Without gesture there cannot be a beginning or a middle or an end to a dance. Gesture is the means through which the movements of the dance complete themselves, and for these movements to become gesture they usually require ritual (as in the Mass), or music (as in the ballet) for both source and background. I think of a rehearsal of one of the ballets based on Mozart where all was dead cluttering movement until Balanchine, by his single example, brought the movements into tune with the music and so made them suddenly into gesture. Again to revert to the Mass, we have the nature of the ritual itself (consecration, sacrifice, communion) determining the scope of the gesture, and on the other hand we reflect that it is the gesture (the posture of prayer, the elevation of the host, the service of the cup and wafer) which transforms the "mere" movements into ritual. Gesture is perhaps the stable *and* moving element in ritual; it is both what is autochthonous—reborn out of the native soil of feeling— and what is autonomous—and independently controls the meaningfulness in ritual. Still again, and not actually far afield, there is Nijinski's remark that it is the costumes of a ballet that determine what the gestures shall be, as the cut of one's cloth determines one's stride; but it is in turn the gestures of the dancers that bring the costumes, or the nakedness, of the bodies to life. Dancing *delivers* gestures otherwise conceived. It is the natural wayward play of the body, controlled.

Control is the key word with regard to gesture in acting, too, and in much the same senses as in dancing; it is the purposive, conventional control of the body's movements that produces meaningful gesture. Or perhaps we should say that it is a kind

of reduction, condensation, telescoping, of free instinctive movements that transforms them into residual gestures, almost as
closely ordained as the gestures in ritual. Historically, we can
remind ourselves, what we call play-acting came out of dumb-
show, which was conventionalized mimicry—in short, mummery.
Mummery is what the actor calls on apart from his lines when
he is making appropriate gestures, and what he calls on in spite
of his lines when he is making bad gestures. Of course, as a matter
of practice we seldom get familiar enough with a particular version of even a play of Shakespeare to be able to divorce the
mummery of it from the lines, but if we could I think we should
find that mummery alone is an extraordinary resourceful and
complex art, using the full personality of the actor, rising often
through a great span of gesture. Our nearest approach is with a
good actor making the best out of bad lines, an affair which, unless we are ourselves mummers, we enjoy apologetically. I recall
once having seen Tolstoi's *Living Corpse*, a play which I had
not read, produced in German, a language I do not know, with
the lead acted by Alessandro Moissi, an actor with whose reputation I was at that time unfamiliar, and in conditions that were
hardly propitious: with a straggling handful for audience in the
great barn of the Boston Opera House. Yet the experience of the
evening proved the case far more than seeing Bernhardt or Duse
or Mantell or the Barrymores ever did. For what I saw and heard
was nothing but the mummer at his work with movement and
posture and voice; the words of the play were transparencies
used to time and to bound the acting. What the mere words were,
it seemed to me, must have been rubbish; they were so little
needed in the face of the fast conventions of voice and movement, conventions that must have been universal to western man
since I understood them so well, through which Moissi worked
from beauty to lucid beauty of created gesture. The gamut of the
actor showed as great as that of any art just because my attention
was fastened upon it by being excluded from anything else. Yet
I knew at the time that what I felt was good for training short
of complete experience; I felt the effect of supreme control without feeling all the controlling force. I missed what the lines of the

play called upon Moissi to create; but at least I learned why poor actors ruin the best plays: they have not the knowledge within them which can be called into play. How can a man understand the play of light who has not felt the sun aching in his bones? And how, similarly, can an actor understand the play of words unless they seem to rise and set within him as his own meaning? Great acting bodies forth the gestures only of great words: no more.

It is music that of all the arts does more. Like pure acting its medium may be thought of as entirely in time as time is filled with sound. It is purer than acting because all its movement is movement of sound. But its greatest purity lies in the fact that, although other arts may use some of its effects, it alone of the arts can proceed according to its own purpose without either anterior or subsequent obligation to any other art. Roger Sessions, in the essay which he contributed to *The Intent of the Artist*, says that the purpose of music is to create gestures of the human spirit, and as my argument is on this point only a lesser version of his I refer you to it for the completion and confirmation of my own. But I will say this. I do not know what constitutes the discipline of music from a composer's point of view, except that I am sure it is severe, yet I feel as a layman that the freedom which that discipline secures is the freedom of repetition, of development, of variation within or upon or around a theme to an extent which in any other major art would be not only ineffectual but boring: the freedom, in short, to play with the elements of musical meaning until they become gesture. This is no doubt why Pater said that all the arts tend to the condition of music; the condition is gesture. The rest of music is but the means for the delivery of gesture, and for the artist who rejoices at all in his work that is the most blessed circumstance possible to imagine. It is tantamount to saying that his means—his technique—may become almost the whole object of attention, both for himself and for his audience. It is not his theme, once he has it, but what happens to his theme, that counts; and what happens to it will be precisely and immitigably what he does within his means. His form and his substance will be united in process as well as at the end: united as gesture. No wonder we are happy when we sing and sing when we are sad. The other arts take us in parts, and give us roles to play with ourselves looking on; music takes us all round, gesture without remove.

So with gesture in the six arts of which poetry is surely the natural child, as it shows variously the stigmata of all six and yet makes a fiery gesture all its own. It is the gesture, I like to think, of poetic judgment, the judgment of all the gestures, all the play of meaning, which makes up full being. Poetry is the meaning of meaning, or at least the prophecy of it. "Behold, all ye that kindle a fire, that compass yourselves about with sparks: walk in the light of your fire, and in the sparks that ye have kindled." In these words of Isaiah there is a motto for poetry, a judgment of poetry, and a poetic gesture which carries the prophetic meaning of poetry. The words sound with music, make images which are visual, seem solid like sculpture and spacious like architecture, re-peat themselves like the movements in a dance, call for a kind of mummery in the voice when read, and turn upon themselves like nothing but the written word. Yet it is the fury in the words which we understand, and not the words themselves. Let them serve as text for the rest of these remarks; for with them to buoy us up we can start on as low a level as we like.

That is the level of the writer who finds himself inarticulate be-cause, as he thinks, the words in his pen are not as viable as the words in his mouth. He says in explanation of why he cannot write—at least one such writer said to me not long ago—"The trouble is I don't have the benefit of gesture in writing—or of inflection either." He is wrong; his trouble is that he has put himself in the position of the stenographer, and what he wants is what the stenographer cannot take down—on the one hand rhythm and cadence and interval, the gestures of the voice that speaks, and on the other hand the look and feel and movement of the man while speaking, whatever is necessary to render what we may call the whole gesture of the scene. What he has to do is to forget the whole theory of stenography or reporting and make the words of his pen do not only what the words of his mouth did, but also, and most of all, what they failed to do at those crucial moments when he went off into physical gesture with face and hands and vocal gesture in shifting inflections. And he must do this by making his written words sound in the inward ear of his reader, and so play upon each other by concert and opposition and pattern that they not only drag after them the gestures of life but produce a new gesture of their own. To make words play upon each other both in small units and large is one version of the whole technique of imaginative writing. Since what is being played with is meanings and congeries of meanings, what is wanted cannot be articulated in a formula, but on the other hand it cannot be articulated at all except when delivered within a form. The point is that contrary to the general view there are relatively few formulas and relatively many forms; exactly as many as there are gestures to require them; and for forms there are many rules of thumb. Let us look at a few where the means are small enough to handle.

In a sense any word or congeries of words can be pushed to the condition of gesture either by simple repetition or by a combination of repetition and varied preparation. Macbeth's "Tomorrow and tomorrow and tomorrow," or Lear's "Never never never never never," would seem good immediate examples of simple repetition metamorphosing the most familiar words into the most engulfing gesture. To emphasize what has happened in these lines, and to indicate how words sometimes get out of mere verbal meaning when they become gesture, it may be suggested that Macbeth might have said Today and today and today, and Lear said, Always always always always always, and much the same effect have transpired in either case. It is not at all the meaning the words *had* that counts, but the meaning that repetition, in a given situation, makes them take on. The repetition of the word "will" in the will sonnets, and also all the words that rhyme with will, does much the same thing; the resultant meaning has nothing to do with will, but is an obsessive gesture of Shakespeare the man himself, made out of the single iterated syllable intensified into a half-throttled cry.

A more complex and quite different type of repetition offers itself in Iago's exhortation to Roderigo to leave off thinking of suicide and take up thinking again of Desdemona. I truncate the passage somewhat for the production purposes of these remarks.

"Put money in thy purse; follow thou the wars; defeat thy favour with an usurped beard; I say, put money in thy purse. It cannot be that Desdemona should long continue her love to the Moor—put money in thy purse—nor he his to her: it was a violent commencement, and thou shalt see an answerable sequestration; put money in thy purse. These Moors are changeable in their wills:—fill thy purse with money. ·. . She must change for youth: when she is sated with his body, she will find the error of her choice: she must have change, she must: therefore put money in thy purse. If thou wilt needs damn thyself, do it a more delicate way than drowning. Make all the money thou canst: if sanctimony and a frail vow betwixt an erring barbarian and a supersubtle Venetian be not too hard for my wits and all the tribe of Hell, thou shalt enjoy her; therefore make money." . . .

Roderigo questions him. "Wilt thou be fast to my hopes, if I depend on the issue?" and Iago resumes his charge.

"Thou art sure of me: go, make money: I have told thee often, and I re-tell thee again and again, I hate the Moor: my cause is hearted; thine hath no less reason. . . . There are many events in the womb of time, which will be delivered. Traverse; go; provide thy money."

Roderigo as he makes his exit says. "I am changed: I'll go sell all my land," and looking after him Iago begins, "Thus do I ever make my fool my purse."

So we see poor Roderigo bought and sold, bought cheap and sold dear, put on change and quite sold out, half a dozen ways at once, and always in terms of the iterated and focussing phrase, "Put money in thy purse," and the changes rung upon it. Roderigo is indeed a changed man in every sense of the word, and the dark, unclean, unconscious, equivocal nature of that change is made clearer and clearer, brought to a light of its own by Iago's phrase. Unlike the simple syllabic repetitions of Lear and Macbeth, Iago's phrase could not be altered without altering the gesture; it is rather that the material that comes between the different iterations could have been altered to almost anything else providing only that they followed the same general line. As Kenneth Burke remarked, money is a neutral symbol capable of bringing meaningful action into any situation. Money is in this situation the symbol of stored evil, and by rehearsing it Shakespeare has released the gesture of the evil.

In Hamlet's best-known soliloquy there is a passage in which the repetition of two words similarly draws upon the reservoir of chthonic meaning but with a different effect upon the words themselves:

> To die: to sleep;
> No more; and by a sleep to say we end
> The heartache, and the thousand natural shocks
> That flesh is heir to, 'tis a consummation
> Devoutly to be wish'd. To die, to sleep;
> To sleep: perchance to dream; aye, there's the rub;
> For in that sleep of death what dreams may come,
> When we have shuffled off this mortal coil,
> Must give us pause.

Here it is the context that determines the meaningfulness that the words *die* and *sleep* and their variants take on in the process of becoming gesture; but once determined, that meaningfulness, that over-arching gesture, carries on through the rest of the soliloquy and beyond, into Hamlet's answer to Ophelia's query how he is: "I humbly thank you: well, well, well," which as gesture moves us to other than the literal sense. It is all the ill of doubt and trepidation before the unknown prospect which the words "to die: to sleep" release as gesture, which in turn infect the triple, mutilating repetition: "Well, well, well."

But we should put this playing upon the meanings of sleep and death over against another kind of playing, this time from *Macbeth*, on the same words, where all the repetition comes at the beginning and is only implied, in the played upon sense, through the rest of the passage.

> Methought I hear a voice cry, "Sleep no more
> Macbeth does murder sleep!" the innocent sleep,
> Sleep that knits up the ravell'd sleave of care,
> The death of each day's life, sore labour's bath,
> Balm of hurt minds, great nature's second course,
> Chief nourisher in life's feast.

Where Hamlet's play of gesture was towards condensation, a focussing of the gesture into action, a gesture invading the very plot of the play itself, in the lines from *Macbeth* the context only suggests the gesture and provides it a means to invoke an escape from the context of the action, and sets it, in its little freed world of words, to creating other gestures in the last four phrases, which themselves both play upon each other and all backwards upon sleep. Sore labour plays upon hurt minds, and great nature's second course (meaning a second round or lap in the sense of movement) plays upon the other sense of *course* in connection with life's feast, and life's feast plays directly back upon the death of each day's life: itself sleep, which has already been murdered by Macbeth. What we have here is part prayer and part imprecation, with gesture invoking its substance: the substance of what is lacking and cannot, except in the form of prayer, be had.

What these two passages do in common—and it is their most remarkable deed—is by the power of discovered or invoked gesture to transform the simple name of sleep into a rich and complex symbol. In a large way we are familiar with such metamorphoses in the titles of poems or plays or in the names of great imaginative figures, or sometimes—though very rarely—in the names of particular authors and artists. All the gestures in *Hamlet* combine to make a symbol which has become, with each fresh use, the more inexhaustible and the more complex; so much that we do not need to ask, when we say Hamlet, whether we mean the play as a whole or the figure of a man resolving the agony of doubt in gestures. So with Macbeth and Anna Karenina and Raskolnikoff and Don Quixote; and so too with Villon and Dante and Michael Angelo and Plato and Baudelaire and Poe. It is the same operation in a small way that we have been watching in the two passages about sleep: the creation of symbols. A symbol, I take it, is what we use to express meaningfulness in a permanent way which cannot be expressed in direct words or formulas of words with any completeness; a symbol is a cumulus of meaning which, once established, attracts further meanings to it until, overloaded, it collapses. The making of symbols is a steady occupation for minds at all aware, and they are especially the objects in which meaning is shared and transmitted by those who have life in common, by lovers, friends, and that version of society which we think of as fellowship. Gestures are the first steps toward the making of symbols, and those symbols which endure are the residuary legatees of the meanings earned through gesture. Returning to our passages about sleep it is only the accident that they are a little too long to be said all at once that has kept them as gestures only, just as, on the same argument, it is their brevity more than their residual possibilities that has made actual symbols out of "The rest is silence," or "Ripeness is all," or "Flesh is grass," quite independent of their original contexts in *Hamlet* and *Lear* and *Isaiah*.

Let us take next what at first appears an even smaller context of effort than the repetition of words or phrases, namely the effort to make one word act like another, or several; that is, punning. Rhyme, which is the terminal form of punning, and alliteration, which is the initial form of punning, are the commonest uses of this mode of language and are of course the most effective to the widest audience, since they deal, on the surface, entirely with the sounds of the words played on: what we know without thought and cannot know better no matter how much thought we take. That rhyme and alliteration have other uses is not questioned; I merely want to emphasize how primitive and how pervasive is the pun in poetry. It is, taken in its fullest gamut as gesture (for any achieved pun is a gesture), the only direct avenue to undifferentiated sense that the poet has; it is what objectively joins the perceptions of the different senses together, heightening them into a single sensation. Not only that, but it also—and this is our chosen nexus—produces an undifferentiated gesture of meaning; under masterly hands punning is the onomatopoeia of meaning. Which is to say that the play upon words is both the most immediate and most final congeries of signs; it is the very gesture which identifies the elements of the sound with the elements of meaning.

Let us take three examples from Shakespeare, all short. The first centers in a single word spoken by Horatio to Hamlet. He says that the ghost had appeared two nights together "In the dead vast and middle of the night." *Vast* is of course the focal word, and it should be said at once that it appears in this form only in the first Quarto. In the second Quarto and the first Folio it was *wast*, and in the second, third and fourth folios it was *waste*. My contention is (which I borrow in part from Empson in his *Seven Types of Ambiguity*) that no matter which way the word is printed the effect of all three is evident and felt, with a strong possibility of a fourth sense, that of *waist*, as well. The accident of the recorded variations in printing forces the attention upon the variety of meanings bedded down to sleep in this single syllable. Let us read the line in the middle spelling: "In the dead wast and middle of the night," and do we not have all at once in the word the sense of the vast void of the night, the stretching and useless waste of the night, and the waist or middle and generative part of the night as well? And do we not have, finally, a kind of undifferentiated meaning which is a product of all three, a gesture of meaning which can only be less defined the more deeply it is experienced?

The second example is still shorter than the first and requires almost no exposition. There is a line in *Macbeth*, when murder is all acanter in the offing, which images "in his surcease, success." So far as the sound goes the words vary only enough to permit sharp play among them, but so far as the literal meaning goes there is almost direct contradiction, yet in the gesture or play which the two make together there is a new meaningfulness that could not be produced without the play. *Success* is so to speak the cadence that falls from *and* rounds out *surcease*; and with an evil omen in it unknown to the speaker.

The third example is from one of the sonnets most nearly packed with similar play of meaning ("The expense of spirit in a waste of shame"), but from which I take only the most obvious play. Speaking of lust, the poet says it is:

> Past reason hunted, and no sooner had,
> Past reason hated.

Reading these lines, the play of meaning between *hunted* and *hated* so grows upon me that I cannot help thinking somewhere between the two, as a kind of backward consequence, of the poet as past reason *haunted* as well, for that is what the whole sonnet gives as gesture out of the focus of the phrases quoted. Surely one is haunted by what one both hunts and hates.

To bring the three examples together, can we not say that the gesture of these plays upon and within words constitutes the revelation of the *sum* or *product* of all the meanings possible within the focus of the words played upon, even though we did not know what all those meanings were? Language as gesture creates meaning as conscience creates judgment, by feeling the pang, the inner bite, of things forced together.

Here is a good place to introduce, for relief from too high a tone, a conspicuous example of the superficially frivolous intellectual onomatopoeia. It is the first two lines from Wallace Stevens' poem, "Bantams in Pine-Woods," and conceals nothing which it does not also disclose.

> Chieftain Iffucan of Azcan in caftan
> Of tan with henna hackles, halt!

I should say that this was a maximum case of alliteration and rhyme taken as pun, and pun both of sound and meaning, for the sound of the lines presses into meaning and the meaning is pressed into sound. There is a kind of close roistering in the syllables, with such yelping at the heels of meaning and such a hullabaloo of meaning in the sound, which prevents one from knowing what is going on except in such a double and darting image as drunkards delight to see. More seriously we can say that these lines are an example of words which, by being momentarily deprived of their normal meanings, tend to become gesture, just as words which temporarily go beyond their normal meanings, such as the word *geo-politics* today, also tend to become gesture. That Stevens should practice such examples, and that we should delight in them, is altogether natural. The whole movement in the arts known progressively as dadaism and surrealism was devoted, in its poetry, to releasing such gestures from language by the deliberate obliteration of the normal modes of meaning from the context. The difference between Stevens and the surrealists is that Stevens writes his words in such a way that they are able to resume their natural modes so soon as the gesture is released. So with Eliot in such lines as "I should have been a pair of ragged claws, scuttling across the floors of silent seas," and so Shakespeare's "miching mallecho," which the glossary says means mouching mischief, but which means miching mallecho just the same. The Queen was much better informed than the glossary, when she said to Hamlet with regard to the invoked ghost:

> This is the very coinage of your brain:
> This bodiless creation ecstasy
> Is very cunning in.

The poet is likely to make his purest though not his profoundest gestures when most beside himself. If words fail they must serve just the same. Transformed into gesture, they carry the load, wield the load, lighten the load, and leap beyond the load of meaning.

But in this carrying, wielding, lightening, and leaping there are abler agents than that uncovered by the resort to nonsense; abler because, once mastered, they are always reliable. I mean such formal agents as plot and metre and refrain. Plot is too large an order to discuss here, but it may be said that it is the stress and urgency of plot that determine *what* gestures are wanted and by its exigencies *when* they shall be released. Plot does in a large way pretty much the same sort of thing that metre and refrain do in the small; and if we cannot see infinity in the palm of the hand and eternity in an hour, we shall not see them at all.

Coleridge defined metre as the motion of meaning, and accepting that we must also for our present purposes turn it around and say that motion is the metre of meaning. That is, if metre as motion brings meaning to gesture, then motion as metre moors gesture to meaning. There is a mutual tying down process, in the operation of metre, a strict and precise delivery of detail in an order of movement, which, well used, gives a sense of absolute speed and absolute position otherwise unavailable to the poet. Where would "Tiger tiger burning bright / In the forest of the night" be if its wild syllables and wilder insights were not measured out in an expected, a conventionally recognizable, order? But on the other hand where would the speed of the metre be if it were not both initially and finally established by the movement to and from gesture that the words make? These are questions that could have been asked of every quotation we have dealt with, including those in prose, for there is a pattern to the rhythm of prose which has much the same function as metre in verse.

Refrain, like metre, has to do with the ordering of perceptions, and in that sense we may say that refrain is a means of emphatic ordering; but it is more than that, it modifies meaning itself by giving to gesture a conventional form. Refrain, or nearly identical repetition, gives particular form, on a general and dependable model, to gesture that might otherwise be formless. Refrain is the emphatic measure of all those gestures that have to do with the declaration of recurrence, return, rebirth and new birth, of motion in stillness and stillness in motion, of permanence in change, and change in permanence. It is the lyric gesture of recognition and the emphatic gesture of identity. The ballads are full of it and the songbooks, whether Elizabethan or cowboy or the latest collection of popular catches. I choose as free examples, Greene's "Weep not, my wanton, smile upon my knee," which upon its last recurrence identifies with the substance of the poem, and Spenser's "Sweet Thames! runne softly, till I end my Song," which makes a gesture of inclusiveness for all that mounts up to it, and Dunbar's "Timor mortis conturbat me," which in every repetition makes the gesture of focus. A more deliberate example where the refrain is used to modify the meaning backwards and forward, would be Yeats' double refrain in "Crazy Jane and the Bishop." I give together the two lines that come four lines apart: "All find safety in the tomb / The solid man and the coxcomb." Better still is the refrain in "Crazy Jane on God," for the effect of its developing action in recurrence can be briefly abstracted. The first stanza ends, "Men come, men go; *all things remain in God*," the second emphasizes the same image, and the third contrasts it. The fourth stanza reads:

> I had wild Jack for a lover;
> Though like a road
> That men pass over
> My body makes no moan
> But sings on:
> *All things remain in God*

Thus we see by the use of refrain insight become deepening gesture.

But refrain is a mere instrument or aid to order, and will flatten a poem like a burden if it is not constantly refreshed from the common resources of language itself. Let us end, then, with brief examinations of three examples, of which the first two are determined partly by the critical words themselves and partly by the order in which they occur, and of which the third makes a pretty complete use of all the devices of lyric poetry, including all those here discussed. The first is from *Hamlet*, and is found in the dialogue between Hamlet and Horatio, just before they go in for the final duel. The passage is in prose.

> *Hor.* You will lose this wager, my lord.
> *Ham.* I do not think so; since he went into France, I have been in continual practice; I shall win at the odds. But thou wouldst not think how ill all's here about my heart: but it is no matter.

"But thou wouldst not think how ill all's here about my heart." Do not these words rise from what is past and fall toward what is coming, and both rise and fall as a gesture, almost his last, out of Hamlet himself? We see how order and cadence and the ear of the poet give the actor all that he has to do except that most arduous thing, put the gesture in the words into the gesture of his mere voice and body.

The second example is from *Othello*. Othello is at swords' points with himself over Desdemona's teasing request for him to make up his quarrel with Cassio, and has just dismissed her. Looking after her he exclaims:

> Excellent wretch! Perdition catch my soul,
> But I do love thee! and when I love thee not,
> Chaos is come again.

Here in the order both of the plot and of the lines, and in the fall of the plot and of the lines, too, the word *chaos* acts to pull into the context a whole realm of being not otherwise present. Shakespeare had undoubtedly re-made this line from its earlier version of *Venus and Adonis*, where "Black chaos comes again when beauty is dead," and he had probably in both instances the Graeco-Latin sense of chaos in mind; the yawning gulf or gap, the abyss of night, the original dark, as well as the sense of disorder and formlessness; both senses were Elizabethan. We have thus the gesture of invoked prophecy made actual in the gesture of a word. The mere actor can do no more than leave it alone to act itself.

Our third example does not envisage an actor and could not use one, if even the best offered, for more than its merely immediate effects; its major effects transpire only in the inward ear. It is a poem which, using alliteration and rhyme and metre and refrain, using symbol and making symbol, playing upon its words as it runs, escapes all the mere meaning in words and reaches the pure meaningfulness of gesture. You can do with it whatever you will, for with poems of this order all things are possible. It is Yeats' "I am of Ireland."

> '*I am of Ireland,*
> *And the Holy Land of Ireland,*
> *And time runs on,*' cried she.
> '*Come out of charity,*
> *Come dance with me in Ireland.*'
>
> One man, one man alone
> In that outlandish gear,
> One solitary man
> Of all that rambled there
> Had turned his stately head.
> 'That is a long way off,
> And time runs on,' he said,
> 'And the night grows rough.'
>
> '*I am of Ireland,*
> *And the Holy Land of Ireland,*
> *And time runs on,*' cried she.
> '*Come out of charity*
> *And dance with me in Ireland.*'
>
> 'The fiddlers are all thumbs,
> Or the fiddle-string accursed,
> The drums and the kettledrums
> And the trumpets all are burst,
> And the trombone,' cried he,
> 'The trumpet and trombone,'
> And cocked a malicious eye,
> 'But time runs on, runs on.'

'I am of Ireland,
And the Holy Land of Ireland,
And time runs on,' cried she.
'Come out of charity
And dance with me in Ireland.'

With this poem as evidence I think it may be said in conclusion that we feel almost everything that deeply stirs us as if it were a gesture, the gesture of our uncreated selves. Thus as artists we would create great gestures; and if we most often fail to do so, it is because, as Shakespeare says, "The deep of night is crept upon our talk," which is a gesture that must overwhelm us even though we realize as we consent to it, that we have made it ourselves.

MARJORIE BRACE:

WORSHIPPING SOLID OBJECTS: THE PAGAN WORLD OF VIRGINIA WOOLF

VIRGINIA WOOLF: *A Haunted House*. Harcourt, Brace

IN AN essay titled "The Traveller's-Eye View" Aldous Huxley refers to some writers who "exploit the spectator's emotion": "The most uninteresting human being, seen at a little distance by a spectator with a lively fancy takes on a mysterious charm, becomes odd and exciting. One can work up a thrilling emotion about distant and unknown people—an emotion impossible to recapture after acquaintance, but which yields place to understanding." Certain authors, however, gain their effect precisely by never trying to understand. "The mysterious charm of Joseph Conrad's characters is due to the fact that he knows nothing at all about them. He sits at a distance, he watches them acting and then wonders and wonders . . . what were their motives, what they felt and thought. . . . His bewilderment is infectious; the reader is just as hopelessly puzzled and finds the characters just as wonderfully mysterious." Katherine Mansfield, on the other hand, "invents suitable lives for the fabulous creatures glimpsed at cafés—and how thrilling those fancied lives always are! . . . Her characters are seen with extraordinary brilliance and precision, as one sees a party of people in a lighted drawing-room at night, through a window, haloed with significance . . . The glimpse of the inhabitants sipping their tea is enormously exciting, but one knows nothing, when one has passed, of what they are really like." Huxley concludes by remarking that there will always be mysteries because there will always be unknown things. "But it is best to know what is knowable. To know, one must be an actor as well as a spectator. One must dine at home as well as in restaurants, must give up the game of peeping in windows to live quietly unexcitedly indoors."

I have quoted at such length from this essay because I think its theme may have further development and implication in the work of other writers. The serious writers of the twenties were very conscious of living in an age of transition, bereft of any desirable order of values; very aware of living breathlessly in motion, in time, without roots. Psychologically speaking, they had no home for quiet living. Alone and unsupported on an unfathomable journey, their personal lives were as if confined to hotel rooms. They were spectators in every sense, observing not only other people, but themselves, with that traveller's eye which perceives nothing but gesture. Emotions—and, above all, relations with others—were seen through lighted windows as dramatic postures, and so became false. To "understand" the human character became more and more impossible, not through ignorance or superficiality or love for mystery, but because on that disintegrating journey in which no fixed standard of judgment could endure, it was absolutely what was *unknowable*.

To Virginia Woolf the unknowableness of people and the impossibilities of communion were never, as to some of her contemporaries, comic or ironic or of intellectual interest, but terrifying. The devices others used for evading genuine characterization, the "scientific" analyses, the violent caricatures, the self-conscious satirical melancholy posturing, all these were repulsive to her serious and lyrical nature. That responsiveness to the truly alive which, in her literary essays, emerged in such tender appreciations of personalities from a warmer past, left her shivering but determined before the cold looming problems of her own time. Like one of the insects she loved to describe, we see her progressing erratically through her novels, feeling, as with painfully sensitive antennae along a chilly wall, for some new approach to the mystery. With each novel, the characters become more shadowy and we have in their stead, almost alarmingly real —as large as life and twice as natural—seasons, boats, oceans, leaves, furniture; the very streams of consciousness, when not a highly lyrical poetry, sound like overheard conversations or the confessions a stranger might impart on a train. And in *A Haunted House*, her collected short stories,—some of them left unrevised at her death, some, even in final form, mere sketches—there is a kind of unity the novels, for all their elaboration, never achieved: the traveller's view has perhaps never been expressed with such purity, in all its super-vividness of seeing and hearing, its rocket-like bursts of excitement, its flat returns to the hotel room of the self.

Here is a reiterated motif of human departure from the haunted "houses" of the past: "They wanted to leave this house because they wanted to change their style of furniture, so he said . . . very interesting people because one will never see them again, never know what happened next . . . we were torn asunder, as one is torn from the old lady about to pour out tea and the young man about to hit the tennis ball in the back garden of the suburban villa as one rushes past in the train. . . . Why, if one wants to compare life to anything it is being blown through the Tube at fifty miles an hour, with one's hair flying back like the tail of a race-horse." Reality is something glimpsed as one tears past, something arrested, timeless; is a flower-stalk or the old lady about to pour tea.

But the old lady lives only in a picture. She is not "understood," she has no capacity for action other than to complete a gesture, and she fades like a landscape from our sight, her living and dying of obviously less significance to a traveller than the decay of her house or garden. This world in which old ladies may be equivalent in value to the weather or snails on a rock, while unquestionably it has uncovered new areas of awareness, has also brought fresh terror to individual experience, beside which the spectator's joy is seen dwindling to a nervous, transient release. In such a story as "An Unwritten Novel" the narrator, observing a tragic face on a train, invents a withered spinster's life story to suit it, only to have the fancy exploded when the "character" is met at the station by a son. And what is the reaction? "Well, my world's done for! What do I stand on? What do I know? Who am I? Life's bare as a bone." But almost at once (still aboard the train and not back in the hotel room) the last look "flooded her anew. Mysterious figures! Who are you? Where tonight will you sleep? . . . unknown figures, you I adore; if I open my arms it's you I embrace—adorable world!"

The note of hysteria is unmistakable: the traveller's intoxicating sense of illegitimate freedom is darkened by inevitable returns to a somehow equally spurious "reality," subjective as well as objective, where, alone and looking at himself, he is compelled to dissolve his *own* capacity for action by self-mockery: "I wish I could hit upon a pleasant track' of thought, indirectly reflecting credit on myself . . . Dressing up the figure of myself in my own mind, stealthily, not openly adoring it, for if I did that I should catch myself out . . ."

Virginia Woolf is least interesting when, defending, as it were, this powerless condition, she presents as the only possible foil the stock culprit of so many novels of the period: the ignoble person who has not the grace to realize his own self-imprisonment. Such are the humanitarians in "The Man Who Loved His Kind" who, anxious to prove their own way of loving humanity to be the only right one, end up by hating everybody. Similarly, there is the girl in "The New Dress" whose costume, designed to be exotic, appears only laughably eccentric to her once she arrives at a party where she is doomed to be either snubbed or bored because—we grasp the point only too quickly—her own unreflecting egotism turns all dresses and parties drab. We have met this girl too often before. We have been informed by too many writers that we *are* that girl, that, always taking ourselves to parties, we miss the thrills of observation through a lighted window.

We do not question the Baudelarian horrors of existence so poisoned by subjectivity that even the ocean speaks "un langage connu." What we do question is the finality of the either-or implication. Is it not just this artificial pendulum-swing between human falseness and an inhuman world of "mysterious figures" that adulterates such writing with a morally dubious quality? Is it not just as untenable and even smug, to be forever appreciative of our "honesty" and thrilled with the unknown?

Virginia Woolf's work never resolved this issue, but when it was confronted, as in her story "Solid Objects," she created some of the most remarkable symbolic expressions of our time. Here is John, standing for Parliament—that is all we are told about him—who one day at the beach finds a lump of green glass so mysteriously significant that he begins hunting everywhere for similar objects for his mantel. "They were useful," Virginia Woolf tells us slyly, "for a man upon the brink of a brilliant career has any number of papers to keep in order—addresses to constituents, declarations of policy, appeals for subscriptions. . . ." Soon he finds a fragment of china so extraordinary that he misses a meeting trying to fish it from an obscure recess. "Set opposite the lump of glass it looked a creature from another world—freakish and fantastic as a harlequin. The contrast between the china so vivid and alert, and the glass so mute and contemplative, fascinated him." He begins to haunt wastelands, rubbish heaps, demolished houses, neglects everything in the search, and the day he is not elected finds him elate, for he has discovered "a most remarkable piece of iron, massy and globular, but so cold and heavy, so black and metallic, that it was evidently alien to the earth and had its origin in one of the dead stars or was itself the cinder of a moon. And yet it stood upon the same ledge with the lump of glass and the star-shaped china."

In this apparent negation of all human values, we find a partial and—in its very inadequacy—a desperate, almost noble attempt to re-invoke them on some unapproached plane. The documents, leading articles, cabinet ministers—that reality which made Virginia Woolf exclaim, "The military sound of the word is enough!"—these things had become so profoundly inimical to the interests of the other, inner reality (in turn horrified by its own isolation) that the two realities cancelled each other out. There was nothing but to establish entirely new relations as, waking from a nightmare, "one turns on the light and lies worshipping the chest of drawers, worshipping solidity, worshipping the impersonal world which is a proof of some existence other than ours. That is what one must be sure of."

An excess of moral sensibility and humaneness caused Virginia Woolf to move into an inhuman and morally irresponsible world, making her write of insects, trees, old boards and broken china as if they were inhabited in an ancient sense by gods and spirits. She was trying to shift perspective, to start all over again, by creating in the unconscious some life-giving pagan emotion which, roving through the detritus of civilization, might also move into relation with a chemical, mineral, biological, fourth-dimensional universe, and so toward a new morality.

The virtue of the spectator's view is that, tearing down houses and disrupting dead relationships, it helps this fresh start. Its defect is that no matter how great the artist's moral anxiety and sensibility, it makes quite hopeless those human relations the difficulty of which sent him on his travels at the beginning. That is why, in almost all the novelists of the transitional group, definite or memorable characters are sacrificed to the qualities of things that should be distinct from literature, such as psychology, or music or painting. But the truth of a psychological analysis, the significance in a musical theme or a picture is complete and not, as great literature is, implicit with potential action. More successfully than any prose writer of her time, Virginia Woolf was, with words, a musician and a painter. What she was not can be seen in comparison with the few who, working with her material and intention, were not dazzled by a new conception of time, but lived densely within it; who placed human beings in new relations with each other as well as with the physical world.

This is so of Proust, whose wealth of color and object is not seen through a window, for all its brilliance, but crowds upon us; through all the subtle change and mingling of his novel the great characters flower amid the trees and founder majestically among the decaying houses and documents. And if Proust introduced new meanings for time and space, Joyce entered a new moral dimension. In his utter dispersion of the elements of character and his reintegration of them in the unique figure of Bloom, Joyce suggested a possible humanization of those complex and desolating perceptions which de-populated the world of Virginia Woolf of all but ghosts and drove her toward a pagan reanimation of objects.

But it is she who seems closer to us now, and prophetic. The martial sound of reality and the clashes of malformed egos have invaded the landscape as well as the midnight room with cold ferocity. We are reminded as we read her that journeys now have grimmer purposes, that the traveller no longer stops at those marvelous way-stations, those heavenly côtes d'Azur she explored so exquisitely. The general motivation of current fiction recalls those base persons whose lack of self-knowledge she repudiated with fastidious disgust. If we cavil at her writing like a painter, how are we to endure those novelists whose work, under such an analogy, could only be compared with some curious Landseer school, populated with people like vicious or noble dogs? who do not even comprehend the questions left unanswered by a previous literary generation? To be surrounded with what is dying, and to know it, is better than to mistake death for life.

From this perspective we look back at Leopold Bloom standing as on some distant peak, the last fully human man in literature. And we cannot help, as we open Virginia Woolf's books, climbing on her train with something of her own desperate joy. Despite our completed knowledge of the life bare as a bone at the journey's end, the rushing air is so alive, so cold and salty with the sea, so warm with flowering vines; and there is also the amazing piece of iron, solid and concentrated, to hold like a talisman in our hands.

CLEANTH BROOKS:
EMPSON'S CRITICISM

A MONG those who are much interested in modern poetry, and especially in modern criticism, William Empson has already become a legend. With the legend, this paper will have very little to do, though I have profound respect for the brilliance of mind and personality which generated it. But the qualifications of the legend—or, for all I know, expansions of it—may best be left in the hands of those who knew Empson personally—who were with him in Cambridge or in China or met him when he was in this country a few years ago. This paper limits itself to his writings where there is, in truth, God's plenty —to agree with, to quarrel with, and, all in all, to marvel over.

Yet, it may be just as well to begin with a brief biographical note of my own. I read Empson's *Seven Types of Ambiguity* for the first time in 1938, though I had known of him vaguely as the brilliant pupil and disciple of I. A. Richards. But I came to my reading of him with a head full of Richards—I must have read the *Principles of Literary Criticism* through fifteen times in the early 'thirties—and after R. P. Warren and I had tried, in a couple of textbooks, to work out some analytical methods for discussing poetry. If such a background was calculated to temper somewhat the shock which a reading of the *Seven Types* earlier might have been expected to produce, yet it did dispose one to be impressed all the more by the sheer brilliance of commentary and the fecundity of critical resourcefulness which are displayed in that book.

It was most impressive, for example, to come upon an analysis of Keats' "Ode to Melancholy" *after* you had struggled with an analysis of it yourself and had become aware of some of its difficulties and some of its subtleties. It was a surprise and a delight to find that Empson had also discovered—and years earlier—that Herbert's "The Sacrifice" was his masterpiece, and that Empson had penetrated the poem and consolidated gains while you yourself were still content with tentative explorations.

I followed a reading of the *Seven Types* the next year with Empson's *English Pastoral Poetry*, and found there all the development which one would expect on the basis of the somewhat chaotic earlier book. Again there was the brilliant performance, this time fitted into a more solid framework and reflected in a more mature and powerful prose. The second book, of course, is implicit in the first; and one may go on to observe that the second implies at least a dozen further books. If I shall have less to say about the *Pastoral Poetry* here than about the *Seven Types*, it is because the *Pastoral Poetry* is the more final and leaves one little to do other than to record his admiration. The chapters on the Elizabethan double plot, on *The Beggar's Opera*, and on Lewis Carroll's Alice are superb; and even one of the weaker chapters, that on Milton, for example, is filled with insights which any critic could be proud to dilute into a book. But I take it that the readers of ACCENT need no stimulus to read Empson for themselves and require no arguments to prove his solid merit.

But the implications of Empson's achievement may bear a little comment and underlining. For it is possible that emphasis on his special approach—which Empson, by the bye, does not claim to have invented [1]—may in itself distract attention from what is finally more important in his criticism.

The key to the significance of what Empson has been doing is to be found in a statement made by Empson in his first book:

[1] In his prefatory note to the *Seven Types* Empson makes his acknowledgments to Richards and to "Mr. Robert Graves' analysis of a Shakespeare Sonnet

The expense of spirit in a waste of shame,

in *A Survey of Modernist Poetry*." And if one cares to push the method back further still, there is William Butler Yeats' Empsonian analysis of Burns' "The white moon is setting" and Coleridge's analysis of the stanza from *Venus and Adonis* to which Richards has called especial attention.

"Some readers of this chapter, I should like to believe, will have shared the excitement with which it was written, will have felt that it casts a new light on the very nature of language, and must either be all nonsense or very startling and new." The statement is not egotistical boasting; it is not the case of the infant critic's petulantly demanding either full agreement or outright rejection.

If indeed Empson's reading of poems rests upon a misconception of the nature of poetry and the nature of language, then *nonsense* is not too harsh a term. But if his criticism does involve a sound account of language and of poetry, then it certainly is the sort of thing which the literary critic ought to have been doing all the time; it is the sort of thing which the literary critic can never again neglect doing, once he has seen it; and it is certainly the sort of thing that the critic in the past, by and large, has not done.

For the significance of Empson's criticism is this: his criticism is an attempt to deal with what the poem "means" in terms of its structure *as a poem*. To sense its importance, one must recall what the critic in the past has attempted to do: either he attempted to find the goodness of the poem (and its status as poetry) in terms of its prose argument—and in terms of the "truth" of what was being said—and thus made poetry compete with philosophy or science; or else he tried to find the poetry in the charm of the decorative elements—in the metrical pattern, in the sensuous imagery, etc. Often enough, of course, he tried to combine the two, usually in some formula which amounted to defining poetry as "truth appropriately embellished."

Empson fights throughout the *Seven Types* against this crippling division by showing how poem after poem actually "works" as a complex of meanings. Metaphor becomes functional in this account—important not for its isolated sensuous beauty but as it plays a part in establishing or qualifying the total meaning of the poem; metrics in the same way becomes functional, valuable not for its absolute beauty but rather for its corroboration of the play of meaning through the poem. Connotations become vastly important, for they are now seen to be, not hints of mysterious beauty which decorate the poem, but active forces in the development of the manifold of meanings that is the poem. And the unity of the poem becomes not something relatively static, but dynamic and the product of a development, the fulfillment of a total process.

I have taken the liberty of stating this summary in my own terms (as indeed any commentator must who is forced to make his own summary); but I do not feel that it violates the essential concept of poetry toward which Empson was working in 1930 and which seems to me clearly realized in his *English Pastoral Poetry* in 1938.

Empson in 1930, of course, was hardly prepared for neat summaries. Indeed, *Seven Types of Ambiguity* is a very difficult book. Part of the difficulty is simply a matter of style. The prose is often charming or striking but it is often elliptical and involved. As a matter of fact, it reads for the most part like uncommonly good talk, but talk which, having been transcribed to the page, suffers from the lack of gesture, of inflection of the voice, of change in tone, which in the conversation would have made all clear and easy.

But the principal difficulty of the *Seven Types* springs from the fact that Empson was forced to fight a somewhat confused action against the romantic and magical conception of poetry in order to state his case at all. I say "somewhat confused," for the term "ambiguity" involves in itself a concession to the doctrine which Empson was attacking. The concept of ambiguity is derived from the point of view of prose where one logical meaning and only one is wanted. Moreover, the seven-fold classification of ambiguity partakes of the confusion, for it too involves certain concessions to the theories of poetry which Empson, wittingly and unwittingly, was committed to destroying.

To illustrate, Empson writes in his second chapter: "Ambiguities of this sort [two or more meanings all add to the single meaning of the author] may profitably be divided into those which, once understood, remain an intelligible unit in the mind; those in which the pleasure belongs to the act of working out and understanding, which must at each reading, though with less labour, be repeated; and those in which the ambiguity works best if it is never discovered. Which class any particular poem belongs to depends in part on your own mental habits and critical opinions. . . ." But this, surely, is to concede much too much. How do we know that there is an ambiguity if we never discover it? Or if some of us know (and by our knowledge have destroyed the poem's effectiveness for ourselves) must we not regard the reader who is still innocent and for whom the poem is still effective as the victim of a trick—in short, does not this view assume that poetry is a sort of hocus-pocus?

As for the second type of ambiguity mentioned above, must we not take it logically as the imperfectly apprehended version of the first—that is, if the labor of working out and understanding becomes progressively less on further readings, might not one expect that eventually it would disappear altogether? And furthermore, surely the pleasure in "working out" an intellectual problem (either poem or puzzle) does not stand on the same footing as the pleasure of total imaginative apprehension. One can understand why Empson is making the concessions: he is trying to be fair, to be reasonable, to take his reader as he finds him, to measure the poem against the various experiences which one has in reading poems, some of which are far more difficult than others. The total context of the passage makes all this abundantly clear. But the attempt to adopt the viewpoint of the imperfect reader or the "reader in progress" seems to me not to clarify but to muddle the issues.

Take another example, the following statement made in the third chapter: "One may say, then, that in ordinary careful reading this poem [Herbert's "I gave to Hope a watch of mine"] is of the third type, but when you know it sufficiently well, and have accepted it, it becomes an ambiguity of the first or (since it is verbally ingenious) of the second type." The phrase "in ordinary careful reading" insists plainly on the fact that the system of classification of ambiguities is psychological: the categories shift as we change readers or as the reader becomes a better reader; they do not describe fixed properties of the poem (that is, of the poem "properly" read by an ideal reader). Yet would not Empson's book have been, on the whole, clearer to the apprentice reader whose vagaries he strives to accommodate if Empson had adopted a rigid system of categories and let his reader adapt his shifting readings to it? Or, better still, if Empson had not bothered with categories of ambiguity at all, but had simply given us his readings of the poems with no generalizations at all except: "This can sometimes happen in poetry—look, this poem proves it"? Clearly, the categories are the product of the developing powers of Empson himself who moulded them from his own personal process of exploration.

Yet the defective framework—if it is defective—is not of any ultimate importance. The framework selected allowed Empson to write the book; it gave him an opportunity for the brilliant asides and, most important of all, for the analytical commentaries on one poem after another. To have these is the important thing: a satisfactory codification, if one is ever feasible or necessary, may well come later and at our leisure.

The attacks on Empson's work have, however, concerned themselves with other matters than his scheme of categories. Anyone who is committed to take the details of the poem as seriously as Empson is committed to take them is bound to run afoul of the textual scholars and the literary historians. They have picked him up from time to time for slips of one sort or another—he has misquoted a text or adopted a reading which textual criticism does not sanction as that of the poet. Geoffrey Tillotson in his recently issued essays has pointed out one or two such mistakes. And I notice in the Milton chapter of *English Pastoral Poetry* the curious howler that Adam and Eve's "children were the result of the fall"—an interpretation which Genesis may possibly suggest but never *Paradise Lost*, to which Empson is referring. But the slips are just that—not seriously important, and, considering Empson's tremendous range, they are astonishingly few.

The general charge leveled at Empson is far more serious. It amounts to this: that he forces upon the poem his own personal associations, idiosyncratic readings of which the poet must have been unconscious, strained analogies of which the poet was surely innocent. And this charge, if sustained, calls in question the value of his whole enterprise.

Empson is thoroughly conscious of the power of his critical instrument and that it is a power which may be misused. For example, in his *Seven Types*, after pointing out to T. S. Eliot what some passages of Shelley criticized by Eliot might be made to mean, Empson adds: "I do not say that I agree with all this [his own explication of Shelley's lines]: it seems an unwise extremity of sensibility." After treating another such passage from Shelley, he goes on to concur generally in Eliot's criticism of the passage: "I agree very heartily with what Mr. Eliot was saying at the time, and certainly these meanings [which he points out are to be found in the passage] are not so much united as hurried on top of each other, but it is, after all, a pun, almost a conceit; it seems rather a creditable thing to have happened to Shelley."

This passage, by the bye, with its praise of Shelley for having produced a pun, almost a conceit, is calculated to leave the orthodox critic fuming. He will scarcely be disposed to disentangle the left-handed compliment to Shelley from the critical principle involved; or if he does stop to disentangle it, he will probably use it to damn Empson. How does one distinguish between meanings that are merely "hurried on top of each other" and those which are "united"? And if the reader is to meet the poet half-way, how far is he to be allowed to go in providing meanings for the poem? Is this not another instance of Empson's lamentable habit of going much more than half-way? Shelley's own meanings, clearly to be discerned there in the poem, are all that either Shelley or the orthodox critic requires.

Yet the passages quoted from Empson do show that he is quite aware of the problem involved: namely, that one can make out a case for richness and complexity in almost any poem—in the poem that has not earned it as well as the poem that has; and that the mere process of spinning out a web of complexities and ambiguities is not sufficient to validate the poem. There must be a further criterion (cf. the chapter on "Good Sense" in Richards' *Coleridge on Imagination*).

Yet, to admit the fact that there must be a further criterion does not mean that the critic can abjure the responsibility of reading the poem as fully and completely as he can or that the personal associations of the critic must not be fully engaged, and more than that, even given a loose rein.

Empson certainly gives them a loose rein himself, but that is not to say that he often lets the reins fall out of his grasp. To me this seems rarely to occur. But the principle of control has to be a flexible one. It can hardly be reduced to a hard-and-fast rule. It can, however, be adumbrated, and I can see little to quarrel with in Empson's attempt to do so in the following passage: "In so far as an ambiguity sustains intricacy, delicacy, or compression of thought, or is an opportunism devoted to saying quickly what the reader already understands, it is to be respected. . . . It is not to be respected in so far as it is due to weakness or thinness of thought, obscures the matter in hand unnecessarily . . . , or, when the interest of the passage is not focussed upon it, so that it is merely an opportunism in the handling of the material, if the reader will not easily understand the ideas which are being shuffled, and will be given an impression of incoherence." In other words, if an ambiguity is functional in developing the poet's total effect, it is justified: it is not justified if it is merely "decorative," a mere witty extravagance, a sleight of hand which calls attention to itself and resists fusion with the other elements of the poem in the total effect. It is true that Empson's statement is littered with subjective criteria, that it leaves room for many divergent judgments, that it provides no "objective" criterion. But to admit this need not commit us to mere impressionism or give criticism over to a complete relativism. We shall get into the relativistic imbroglio only if we let our desire for complete objectivity in criticism triumph over our common sense.

The strength of Empson's position can be shown most convincingly by considering the alternative to which the conventional critic is committed. Even the die-hard anti-Empsonian is forced to admit that the reader must help in imaginatively re-constructing the poem; that the reader must be alive to the asso-ciations of words; that poetry is in some sense "rich" and "thick" where prose is "thin." And if the same critic urges against Emp-son that Empson is engaged in forcing meanings on the poem whereas the conventional critic is reading out of the poem merely what the poet can be proved to have put into it, one need only ask to be allowed to examine his proof. What we can *prove* that the poet put into the poem is only that which is amenable to such proof. We shall always emerge with no more than the gaunt skeleton of the poem, for the poetry itself will have been removed in the process. We shall always come out with a theme or a logical "argument" or a plot.

The usual dodge which the conventional critic uses at this point (and I use the word "dodge" deliberately) is to say that the poetic flesh which adorns the bones of the argument is by definition beyond analysis; it can be experienced emotionally, it can be appreciated, but it cannot be discussed. In brief, the poem is defined as consisting of logic and emotion, the first subject to analysis, the second only to be "felt."

The critic, if pressed to the point, will usually appeal to magic: true poetry is invested with a magic which it is unprofitable to attempt to analyze and which analysis, indeed, may desecrate. The more intelligent proponents of this theory might actually find in Empson's own words some support for their charge that he is setting out to destroy the magical effects of poetry. For example, Empson writes: "Personally I am pleased and given faith by this analysis, because it has made something which seemed to me magical into something that seems to me sensible." One can imagine the opposition's counterblast: "See! Just so. Mr. Empson denies poetry its magic, the very thing which in the past has been its glory, the very thing which I myself ask of poetry. For, as he says himself, if he admires a poem, he feels uneasy unless he (being the heir of I. A. Richards' naturalism) can explain it away with some kind of rationalistic hocus-pocus —can dismiss it with some explanation which really explains nothing and finds its real justification in making him feel that poetry is somehow scientific; that is, sensible and worth his while."

Such a retort would not be completely wide of the mark, for the phrasing of Empson's comment does reveal a kind of personal bias which, if insisted upon, would weaken the case for his kind of criticism. But one can accept the term "magic" in all the senses in which one ought to want to apply it to poetry, and still defend the vast utility of what Empson has done. "Magical," in a sense, the effects of great poetry are and always will be; that is, such effects cannot be predicted or concocted in accordance with a formula—as Empson, of course, nowhere claims. But there is magic and magic.

What the conventional critic tends to take refuge in is a kind of *black* magic: it is secret, dark, and not to be peered into. But poetry, fortunately, is a white magic, and the more closely that we look into it the better. Its "magic" has nothing to fear from the closest inspection. And on this matter Empson's own comment is very much to the point: ". . . the view . . . that poetry cannot be safely analysed seems to me to remain ignoble; and in so far as people are sure that their pleasures will not bear thinking about, I am surprised that they have the patience not to submit them to so easy a destruction."

If the implications of Empson's criticism are profound for the esthetic of poetry, they are quite as profound for literary history. (It ought to be axiomatic that you cannot change your conception of poetry without modifying to some extent your view of the poetry of the past.) Empson, though not undertaking to write literary history in either of his books, has not been able to refrain (or has wisely decided not to refrain) from comments which take him far into considerations of literary history. A constant theme in the *Seven Types* is the special nature of nineteenth-century poetry—the ways in which it was cut off from certain poetic resources and its tendency, by way of compensation, to overexploit others. The state of the language in the Elizabethan period with its fluid grammar which allowed for certain kind of subtlety and richness comes in for a great deal of attention. There is a memorable passage which speculates on the effect on the poetry of Shakespeare of such circumstances as "the shortness of individual runs . . . [which] would keep the actors from being bored with the text," the actors' "casual but detailed knowledge" of the text, their "desire for continual additions," their "capacity to see distant verbal connections," and their "well-informed interest in the minor characters of the story." This passage, it is true, is introduced to defend some of Empson's discoveries by showing that it was possible that Shakespeare intended them, "delicate cross-references" though they are. But it is nevertheless one of the most refreshing and illuminating comments on the circumstances of Elizabethan play production that I know of.

Yet Empson's comments on the details of literary history, even in the admirable *English Pastoral Poetry*, are incidental speculations and asides. Empson has not attempted to systematize them. In spite of its title, *English Pastoral Poetry* remains a collection of stimulating samplings from the ironic mode rather than a history of the English pastoral. One can well imagine, by the way, the sense of complete frustration which that book would probably induce in the well-trained American graduate student who looked into it expecting to find what he considered pastoral poetry. The Elizabethan double plot! A Shakespeare sonnet! These are not pastorals! And though such a student might admit the relevance of the chapter on Marvell's "Garden," or the chapter on *The Beggar's Opera* through deference to Swift's having called it a "Newgate pastoral," the presence of a chapter on *Alice in Wonderland* would be likely to confound him completely.

Granted his training, he has a right to be confounded. For him, unless he is an unusual student or has had training in an unusual graduate school, the pastoral is a "form" into which "material" is poured. Or to change the metaphor, it is a kind of costume which the poet assumes, like a pirate suit at a masquerade ball. The wearer may alter the details of the costume, but only within limits: he may omit the patch over the left eye or use a broad leather belt in lieu of the gaily colored sash. If one is to have a pastoral, there must be a recognizable shepherd's costume:

the graduate student wants to see the shepherd's pipe and the sheep. He expects to see these things because his work in English literature has been a study conducted in the museum—a history of this and other costumes. He looks for something external, for he has been trained from the antiquarian's point of view.

Empson's pastoral, on the other hand, is a mode, a specialization of irony, an inner thing. It is a particular way of relating certain things to other things. It is not external and it is not dead. It is very much alive, for it sees the matter from the standpoint of the practising poet. Because it is very much alive it is capable of altering drastically some of the current generalizations about the history of English poetry. For literary history waits ultimately upon criticism.

Our established habit, however, is to reverse the roles of criticism and literary history. I read recently a statement by one of our more distinguished literary historians and bibliographers. It is curious and typical. He went on to say: "There is much work on X still to be done. The **** edition, in process, will be a help—it should not be assumed to be an end; Mr. ****'s *Letters* of X will be a help. When we have used our battery of methods and tools to establish what X said and the circumstances under which he said it, we shall then need to enquire, in a beyond-graduate-school level, what was the significance of it."

Those of us whose desire to see this inquiry "in a beyond-graduate-school level" is not immoderate, may be able to moderate it a little further by reflecting that it will never come to pass anyway since such scholarship will never actually have done with the application of its "battery of methods and tools" with which it is fascinated and which is its glory and its limitation.

Meanwhile the inquiry into significances which Empson and others are carrying on does not wait upon the dawning of the scholar's millennium. Yet it will affect profoundly the work of the literary historian and ultimately of the scholar. It will affect it by altering the estimation in which various poems, plays, and novels are held; and even more importantly by opening up another dimension of literature, if not to unconscious appreciation, at least to conscious inspection and discussion.

The scholar quoted above oversimplifies the problem: he suggests that once the text is established and once "the circumstances under which" the text was promulgated are known, all will be easy. (I hope that I understand him here, but I am confident that I do not misunderstand the sentiments of his brothers in the craft.) But important as the text is—and Empson's concern with nuances gives a fresh sanction to the textual critic's concern for detail—and important as "the circumstances under which" may be in any given case turn out to be, it is more important still that we know how the words work together and the various levels of meaning which they encompass.

In a time in which the study of literature threatens to turn into sociology and in which the death of the humanities is prophesied openly, it is impossible to overestimate the significance of the kind of criticism of which Empson remains the most brilliant exponent. He is certainly not the old-fashioned man of letters who charmingly bows us into his snug study with a quotation from Lamb and afterwards bows us out with a quotation from Hazlitt. But he is certainly not, on the other hand, merely the bright young man with a bag full of psychological gadgets. He is one of our ablest critics and one of our soundest, and his work is fraught with revolutionary consequences for the teaching of all literature and for the future of literary history.

EDWIN BERRY BURGUM:

FRANZ KAFKA AND THE BANKRUPTCY OF FAITH

W E SPEAK sometimes of our own writers of the "lost generation" of the twenties. But such terms are relative. American writers were by no means so lost at that time as their contemporaries in defeated Germany, and the importance of Kafka
is that he was without question the most lost of them all. The
fact that he was born of Jewish middle class parents in Prague
when it was under Austrian domination only emphasized an
alienation and insecurity which had become typical of the
middle class generally. Culturally, moreover, Kafka was a German. He lived in Germany and wrote in the German language.
And, though his writing was mostly done before the First World
War, his attempt to escape a dominating father left him afraid
of the responsibilities of freedom in a way symbolic of the later
passage of German society from the tyranny of the Empire to
the Weimar Republic. His own deep-seated despondency, which
had not yet routed traditional obsessions of blind faith and vague
hope, lay bare the perplexities of mind and the vacillations of
conduct typical of German life generally under the Weimar
Republic. His own diseased personality symbolized the disease
at the heart of German society. The progress of his personal
deterioration paralleled the degeneration of the society that produced him. And his own life ended as abruptly and prematurely
as that of the young republic, though he died of tuberculosis
some years before Hitler set himself up as the brutal father-
symbol of the German people. Whether the work of so dis-

ordered a talent will live at all or only for a select audience may be disputable. But its historic importance can hardly be denied. Kafka's novels cut through the distracting irrelevancies of superficial realism and afford a direct participation in the degeneration of personality of the petty bourgeoisie which began under Bismarck and was completed under Hitler. They present this degeneration even more vividly to the foreign reader than *The Magic Mountain* does, because Kafka is incapable of any reasoned judgment upon his material. He takes us into the personality structure itself, remaining unconscious of its nature since he shares it, and unconscious of its concealment in ordinary men beneath the conventions of social intercourse because of his own abnormality.

This interpretation of Kafka has received curious confirmation in the kind of praise lavished upon him by the small group of his admirers that existed in Germany and repeated by its even smaller American counterpart. They have extolled him not for the reasons which I have put forward here, but for those which would have appealed alike to his own attitude and those of the Weimar Republic. They have given an almost hypnotic attention to his perverse and mystical religious faith. In that conflict which kept him morose and helpless between a belief in God he could not renounce and a skepticism he could not deny, they have condoned the skepticism out of veneration for the faith. They have not seen that this dubious faith is psychological evidence of the dissolution of the reasoning process itself. Kafka was incapable of the common sense of everyday life, so obscure and contradictory had become the springs of personal conduct in him. Like Kierkegaard, his favorite philosopher, he represents the breakdown of mysticism itself, both as a discipline and a philosophy. In the light of the great religious mystics of history, to emphasize Kafka's religious mysticism can only mean to share his own incapacity for reasoned judgment.

Only Max Brod, the wisest among his admirers and the closest to him, has suggested the possibility of a non-mystical approach to his work. Brod has published—apparently out of sheer sense of duty to the facts, since he does not relate it to his own exposition of Kafka's mysticism—considerable evidence that his personality verged upon the psychopathic. We may anticipate that sooner or later psychiatrists will discover that his novels are as rewarding an object of investigation as those of Dostoievsky. The types of abnormal personality are not as varied as in the pre-revolutionary Russian writer. But the presentation of the particular type of which Kafka was himself an example is even more rich and detailed within its limits since his books became progressively more alien from normal attitudes as his short life ran its course. But a novel is presumably something more than the book of devotions for a degenerate mysticism or a case history in psychiatry. It is also a communication to some sort of general public. I shall therefore limit my interest in the theological and psychiatric aspects of Kafka's work to their bearing upon his novels as an expression of certain patterns of living in our own era and as the satisfaction of the esthetic needs of a limited contemporary audience.

Since Kafka's last stories are almost exclusively devoted to his hallucinations, they may be used to clarify the orientation I am seeking. I take for this purpose the most extremely subjective of them all, "The Burrow." In this short story, which has a beginning but no end, the hero conceives that he is being pursued by what must be vaguely called enemies. But there is nothing vague about the defenses with which he surrounds himself. He first digs a tunnel into the earth in which he hides like a mole. He conceals the entrance with foliage, and for a time feels safe from pursuit. But it seems wise to make safety doubly sure by digging many branches to his tunnel. Thus he will be able to elude the enemy at numerous points by circling around behind him. Next, in case through some accident he should not be able to do so, he decides to make an exit at the other end. But no sooner has he completed this escape into the upper world than he realizes with dismay that he has also created another possible source of attack. Enemies may now enter at both ends and leave him caught at the middle. He becomes so frightened that he leaves his tunnel altogether. But above ground, even though he hides in the bushes, he feels unprotected on every side; he lacks the tangible comfort of both walls and darkness. So he returns, determined at least to protect his valuables (which remain as abstract as his enemies) by building a special vault for them. His labor is baffled by the sandy soil. But he manages to beat the wall firm by desperate blows of his head; and he is delighted to discover that the blood flowing from his wounds actually welds the sand into a cement. His satisfaction is immediately interrupted, however, by the faint sound of digging elsewhere. The disconcerting suspicion crosses his mind that his enemies may have turned his own plan against him, and started digging parallel tunnels so that they may break through almost anywhere at the strategic moment. Though he listens intently and in every part of his maze, he cannot define the direction of the sound. He tries to close his ears to see whether it is a figment of his imagination. But he is too excited to make a fair test. In a crisis when his enemies may fall upon him at any moment, he flings himself the more hysterically into action. His only hope is to make the maze more labyrinthine. When the story breaks off, his frenzied digging is no longer guided by a plan and is already beginning to be baffled by fatigue.

That Kafka's anxieties have passed the norm and approached the psychotic in "The Burrow" is obvious. But there are curious proofs from the story that they have not yet reached the extreme and passed out of control. The first is a bit of symbolic action which shows that they are being kept in check by the sense of security he obtained from his disease. The image of blood from the hero's head which firmly cements the walls of his storage place for his valuables reveals Kafka's attitude toward his tuberculosis. Brod has quoted him as expressing relief that it obligated his breaking his engagement which had dragged on for five years. This passage makes it clear that his later hemorrhages afforded a more active protection of his spiritual values in general. The weakness of physical prostration by taking the burden from will and consciousness expiated his sense of guilt; and at the same time by diminishing his material values as a person seemed to reduce the liability to attack from without. The progress of his bodily disease, in other words, retarded the progress of his mental disease. The second evidence is the communicability of the story as a whole. Kafka has used no eccentric imagery or autistic language, but the simplest everyday diction. A child could understand the story as readily as an adult. Perhaps its lack of overtone, its lack of the irony I have allowed to creep into my summary, is pathetic evidence of his surviving will to remain sane, of his direct reaching out to an audience he is willing to assume is receptive, is certainly not "enemies." Indeed, the suggestion in the story, weak though it is, that the sounds may be imaginary is a literal measure of the degree of sanity remaining; while the complete absence of humor testifies to the desperateness of his situation. But at the same time his capacity to write is not only an unconscious appeal for help; it is also a temporary source of security; it is the part of himself most adequately under control. And paradoxically since his obsessions have become more simple as they grow more extreme, his stylistic expression of them can give him the satisfaction of becoming more simple too. The simple casualness of the style, its frank colloquial air, is somehow not inappropriate to the abnormality of the content. A complete psychiatric investigation of Kafka would certainly shed light on that *terra incognita*, the nature of the creative talent in more normal persons.

But my problem here is rather with his audience. Presumably Kafka would not have developed as a writer and have eventually written "The Burrow" if he had not sensed a similar agony in the society around him. The presence of a Kafka cult proves that he was not mistaken. The existence of the story, as lucid as a parable from the Bible, must be taken as an alarming measure of the amount of similar anxiety in the Weimar Republic. If an investigation could be made, I think it would be discovered that a large percentage of Kafka's admirers (excluding of course many critics whose attitude must be in part one of professional interest) share his disorders of personality. In the problem of the relation of literature to its audience, therefore, I believe that Kafka is important evidence as to the meaning of "esthetic distortion," "literary idealism," the difference, in short, between life and art. In the broadest sense, psychologically, we are permitted to conclude that art brings into the open the latent tendencies of society, whatever they may be. From this point of view, the Kafka cult would not necessarily be composed of persons as abnormal as he, but rather of those who possess similar tendencies which different life experiences may be holding in check or which are in progress of formation and doubtless will be formed more rapidly as a consequence of their admiration. I cannot imagine any other readers accepting Kafka without qualification. These alone will respond to his appeal to aid him by entering the confraternity of the doomed. For the time being, for them as for him, the very lucidity of "The Burrow" may be consoling. But in the end content passes out of esthetic control, the story breaks off; art ultimately fails in its attempt to control life.

With more normal readers the reaction, I think, must be more complex. We live in a period of unusual instability, and the average reader will not wish to add through his fiction to the amount of real anxiety circumstances are forcing upon him. He will reject "The Burrow" as repulsive, and probably decide the rest of Kafka is also a waste of time. A certain few may find a sadistic enjoyment in a story which seems to present anxieties they are free from. I find my own recollection of the story alternating between a recovery of its disturbing effect upon first reading and a protective recoil into humor; to take it as funny is to alienate oneself from contamination. The future will probably take it in similar fashion as a literary curiosity, though only a minority of readers will be interested at all. When we live in a society which permits us to accept its content without a sense of personal threat, it will appear too monotonous to sustain interest. Its concern with only one character, its unvaried repetition of the same motive, will cause its rejection for esthetic reasons. But from this point of view also, Kafka retains his importance for the esthetician, since this story illustrates the wide variation of reaction the same story may arouse in different readers.

One puts aside these later defects of personality in Kafka, and turns with relief to the esthetic defects of his earliest work.

Here the shortcomings are of a sort to testify to the initial possibility of normalcy in him. As a youth, Kafka seems to have had
his share of our wholesome human desire to meet the world
on its own terms, to act and to survive, indeed, to bring, however grotesquely, order out of conflict. He was scarcely more
eccentric than the average petty bourgeois youth, anxious to
get ahead and dominate other people. As a writer also he responded to the prevalent and I believe desirable practice of
leaving whatever intellectual conclusion his novel was reaching
to be implied symbolically from the action. But, although these
are his aims in *Amerika*, he did not succeed in writing a gracious
or even a comprehensible novel. *Amerika* consists of a series of
episodes, each clear in itself, but culminating in a fragment the
incomprehensibility of which emphatically registers his inability
to solve his problem in terms of plot or symbolic meaning. Even
though the ultimate failure so graphically presented in "The
Burrow" may be latent here, and the immediate failure is evidence of his apprenticeship in his craft, most of the blame at
this time must be put, I believe, on the inadequacy of the social
background, of which Kafka was painfully conscious. The structural defects of the book are Kafka's record of the bankruptcy
of what we sometimes call "the American way.".

As though convinced of the validity of Spengler's thesis in
The Decline of the West that the European situation was hopeless, Kafka sought to embrace Spengler's opinion that the future
of European culture might lie in the United States. He goes in
imagination to the country in which bourgeois attitudes have
been least checked by aristocratic precedents, in which pragmatic philosophy has endeavored to relate the ideal to the actual
without the least sullying of its purity. In contrast to all his
later work *Amerika* presupposes an acceptance of the validity of
the objective world, with the concomitant belief that one's ideals
must be written into actuality by sweat and blood. Its hero,
Karl Rossman, is the only one among his writings to whom Kafka
gave a name. The others are unnamed or generalized into "K."
And he is the only one who is conscious of a certain security in his
physical strength. Whatever timidity he possesses may have been

due to Kafka's latent masochism, but it is also normal to the inexperience of the adolescent. And it is concealed by a conscious acceptance of aggression as normal in human relationships. In short, Karl accepts the philosophy and psychology of rugged individualism. But like Mr. Hoover or Mr. Westbrook Pegler, he fears the combined aggression of the working class, since he conceives of the individual worker as a selfish illiterate brute and his labor union as the organization of racketeering to devour society. At the same time Karl is alarmed and disgusted to find that men of wealth live in a false security. He refuses to avail himself of their friendly offers to work not merely because he has an adolescent desire to make his way by his own will, but because he cannot trust men who are so obtuse to their real dangers. The millionaire whose palatial home outside New York he visits sits chatting in his vast drawing room indifferent to the drafts that blow through it because workmen employed to build a new wing have struck, leaving walls as open to invasion as the entrance to what was later to be the burrow. This attitude may already be a neurotic one, but it has a valid objective basis if one is an industrialist who continues to believe in rugged individualism. In other words, it anticipates the psychology of fascism. It is interesting to note that Karl ceases to worry on another occasion. He has been alarmed at the riotous street meetings of a political candidate; but he calms down when informed that all these disorders mean nothing since the outcome has already been arranged by powerful interests behind the scenes. He does not inquire as to who or what they are; that they are powerful enough to dominate is sufficient for him.

Yet Kafka remains fundamentally an individualist. Stated in political terms, his dilemma was that he could not become a fascist. Not its cruelty but its apparent denial of individualism prevented. In his concluding chapter he sought a solution in which the actuality of free competition might lie at peace with the spiritual presence of cooperation. Ruthless competition clearly has bred an unsatisfactory anarchy. The problem was to find some machinery to bring the spiritual and the material together without corrupting their essentially contradictory character: to provide that competition become spiritually cooperative and that the ideal chasten the practical like a catalyst without bureaucratic loss of its own integrity. But when one examines the final story of the "Nature Theater of Oklahoma" (as when one tries to give content to "the American way"), no tangible program for action can be found. It is impossible to determine whether the mechanism is to be governmental activity or the emergence of some private organization. Whichever it is, the improvement is clearly to be made gradually; the new organization is presumably a model which either will be imitated elsewhere or will gradually and painlessly absorb the functions of other organizations into itself. The title of the new theater suggests that Kafka is giving the naturalistic basis of pragmatism a trial, that he is testing the spiritual possibilities latent in the world of actuality. But the most confident deduction one can make from this ambiguous and fragmentary allegory is that any such approach to the problem is likely to be hypocritical, whether consciously or not. To take the project in the best light, it is probably a well-intentioned hoax. Its instigators, whoever they are (for we never get to the real motivating power in Kafka) are impelled by the delusion that the material and the spiritual can be brought together. Certainly when Karl and his friends, wearied by the hazards of competition in the East, go, like the latter-day pioneers of the New Deal into the West where handbills (such as the Joads had naively accepted) promise employment to all with the initiative to come, they find nothing adequately prepared. To be sure, a dramatic spectacle is being acted at the entrance. But one has positively to fight his way beyond the captivating static beauty of this tableau into the amphitheater behind, where everything is still chaotic. Clerks take down Karl's name, though his qualifications seem uncertain. Not only does nobody know what sort of pageant will be enacted on the cluttered race course; the reader feels an uneasy suspicion that the whole venture, the very project of a theater, is being put into the terms not of life but of some fictive and therefore practically useless if not spiritually delusory allegory of life instead. He is tempted to conclude that to believe the material world can have a spiritual aspect, to imagine that competition can be in any way allied with cooperation is a fallacy. Nor does he know whether it is wisdom on the part of the many that had kept them indifferent to the handbills; or whether the few, like Karl, who have the initiative to venture, are not themselves under the enchantment of "the American way."

Now I take it that within the limited social outlook available to Kafka all this is impressively sane comment. In *Amerika* Kafka's tendencies to abnormality have only freed him from the easy fallacious rationalizations which leave more normal individuals of prosperous bourgeois family in the realm of illusion. American readers will at first sight find Kafka's picture of American life amusingly inaccurate. He is as absurdly uninformed about the surface facts as he is incapable of the surface rationalizations. He knows America only as it is presented in our tabloid newspapers, in which the contradiction between the ideal and the actual glares from every column but is denied to exist on the editorial page. At one and the same time they present our country as the haven of the down-trodden, the land of opportunity, the hope of the future; and as the battlefield of anarchic individualism, of murder and racketeering, of Anglo-Saxon dominance, and the devil's right to the hindmost. The tabloids cut through the veil of distortion which the respectability of other papers draws over this living contradiction between our ideals of democracy and their too frequent violation in our practice. There is, of course, another side to the story, but one does not get it from this quarter, in these simon-pure reflections of petty bourgeois hysteria and inconsistency, the validity of which Kafka could recognize from his foreign land.

When he turned back to the European society he knew directly, however, Kafka became convinced that his observation in *Amerika* was superficial. Men might appear to live in a state of brutal personal competition. Go deeper into their actions, and they are found to be the puppets of a hidden authority. A different kind of Nature Theater, so to speak, is actually in operation. It is only men's trust in it that is delusive. They do not realize that they are helpless under the authority of the evil that controls the material world. So now it is not their competition but their apathy that impresses Kafka: their ignorance of their own dilemma, their indifference to the difficulties of their fellow men. Kafka anticipates the picture of the "little man" that was to become established in German fiction as one of the types of the Weimar Republic, restless, impotent, insignificant. If he treats him without the usual contempt, but as a tragic figure, it is that he saw in the story of his helplessness the bankruptcy of his own optimism in *Amerika*.

In *The Trial*, the hero, "K," a clerk, trusted and expecting promotion for his fidelity, is served in his roominghouse with a warrant for an unnamed crime by two policemen. The officers themselves do not know nor care what the crime is, since their function is only to issue warrants for court appearance. Under such circumstances, the normal man, knowing himself innocent, would go about his business, confident that the mistake will readily be cleared up. K, on the contrary, in his humility and desire to cooperate with the civil authority, must drop his business, assume the preoccupied air of the guilty man, and take over the function of pushing his case through to a decision. His uncle secures the aid of an important lawyer who assures him to his surprise that all legal cases are actually settled out of court by influence or bribery. When neither works for him within a reasonable length of time, he invades the judicial offices where he makes a nuisance of himself since nobody has heard of his case. In due time he begins to grow desperate not only because his quest remains futile, but because he begins to feel that some sinister authority has been ever-watchful and is becoming annoyed at this anxiety for the speedy triumph of justice. Perhaps this intangible authority may be outraged that so insignificant a man should inflame its own guilty conscience. So K, who has been hypnotized by trust, gradually becomes hynotized by fear. Finally, two other policemen show up, take K to the edge of town, hand him a knife to slit his throat with, and when he demurs, thrust it home themselves.

The Trial has several layers of symbolic meaning, the most superficial of which I have just presented. It is an exposure of the evils of bureaucracy from the point of view of the common assumptions of democracy. Even though Kafka's experience of a decaying bureaucracy was that of the moribund Austrian Empire, it will apply equally well to the bureaucracy, struggling to be born, of the Weimar Republic. The reader takes it first of all as a trenchant satire upon the delays of justice, the red tape by which the average man may well feel himself strangled in the modern democratic state and its characteristic business corporations, and which the inefficiency of the Weimar Republic merely pushed to the extreme of a tragic burlesque. It emphasizes the sadistic self-importance of some petty officials, the callous indifference of others, until the average citizen appears to get either no attention or abuse for having expected it. But at the same time that the action clarifies this contradiction between our bureaucratic structure and our ideals of democratic equality and individualism, it does not permit us to assume that any evil capitalists are to blame. Though bureaucracy surely defeats the natural aspirations of the common man, there is no assurance that it does anybody good. The fault is in the system, in the fact that life must be organized at all on a practical level. It would perhaps be appealing to conclude that the policemen who finally kill K have been authorized to do so by Nietzsche's supermen. But made sadistic by the system, they may have been acting at their own impulse or in obedience to an authorized or unauthorized command anywhere along the line.

A second level of meaning is perceptible if we take the action as symbolic of the change in the German personality structure as a result of the functioning of bureaucracy under the Weimar Republic. The Republic, it must be remembered, arose after the collapse of an Empire which had functioned fairly efficiently within the surviving forms of feudalism. To defeat in the First World War therefore was added the insecurity caused by a graft in government less disguised and more reckless than under the Empire, accompanied by an unsettling confusion of novel ideas and policies. Faltering experiments in social reform and magniloquent pretense of progress alternated with the unexpected fall of the iron fist of police repression. But the little man with his feudal background humbly took the blame for his unhappiness upon himself, believing that only his insignificance prevented his recognizing the remote organizational wisdom that must exist at the top. Indeed, behind apparent inefficiency he felt the abject need for, and could sense the rising anger of, some new external authority that at whatever cost would remove the spiritual burden and the practical uselessness of the new freedom of the Weimar Republic. From this point of view, K's murder symbolizes the final ascendancy of fascism, with its delusive promise of a security beyond good and evil. Psychiatrically, K was waiting to be slain, going out of his way to get somebody else to remove the burden of seeking the just and the guilt of ambition and the mirage of freedom which had grown so disturbing that the security of individual annihilation drew him like a magnet, only he must, with the pathetic submission of the Bismarck tradition, receive even death as a grant from above. K's death is thus also this strange novelist's prophecy of the fictive life beyond either pride or humility of the Nazi automaton in which the human spirit has been slain. Here, I believe, the value of the novel for most readers is to be found. It affords us the most complete and subtle delineation of the petty bourgeois German temperament, in which feudal attitudes of obedience were translated into the needs of a belated capitalism under Bismarck; then were confused by the ineffectual democracy of the Weimar Republic; became suspicious of their own dawning self-reliance, and when this self-reliance seemed of no profit either to the individual or to society invited its slaughter and replacement by an even more excessive obedience and submission under Hitler than feudalism had imposed.

But it is a third level of meaning which gives Kafka's own intention in *The Trial*. He used the book to reject his toying with the possibilities of a naturalistic theology in *Amerika*, and to state his conviction that whatever is not spirit is evil. His hero's tragedy is that he repeats Kafka's error in *Amerika*, by seeking to root the spiritual in the material when he acts to promote justice. Governments and corporations, being materialistic, the powers of evil that control the practical world, are naturally aroused by the

threat of virtue. Other ordinary citizens who accept the conditions of the material world—that it knows neither good nor evil—
and act automatically without idealism or insight, are not mo-
lested. One best survives in proportion as he can live as the passive
unconscious automaton of the powers of evil, in proportion indeed as he can remain completely in the realm of fantasy as far
as our notions of democracy and progress are concerned. K made
the mistake of acting in daily life upon principles which are real
in the spiritual world but must remain a fantasy in the material.
Thus he violated the nature of the material world, aroused the
powers of evil that control it, and promoted its revenge in his
own death. The theme was fortunately such as to permit *The
Trial* to become the only one of Kafka's writings in satisfactory
esthetic form. The finality of its conclusion, moreover, is of an
order superior to that in other novels with a fatalistic philosophy
such as Thomas Hardy's. For there is no emotional ambiguity.
The horror and the relief of dying cancel into a state of tran-
quillity. The book has fulfilled its own laws of inevitability, and
we are done with it.

But though *The Trial* adequately explains the source of Kafka's
mysticism, it is concerned with only the negative aspect of it and
does not illuminate its essentially paradoxical nature. His observation of life had become so cynical that no other escape was possible than the rejection altogether of the importance of the material world. Yet he was so involved in that world that he must
reject it both verbally and emotionally in its own terms. His
mysticism had the same flavor as well as the same origin as Tertullian's despair at the corruption of the Roman Empire. He too
was forced to believe what the evidence of his senses had convinced him was absurd. Indeed his paradox was the more glaring.
In the fourth century Tertullian's axiom was less "absurd" because his era, though disillusioned, had inherited a disposition
partial to a mystical view of the world, to which his dogma gave
the assent of a man by temper skeptical. But Kafka, living in an
industrialized world which had not secured order and happiness
at the price of its loss of faith, was overtaken by a bitterness so
harsh that he could not let it rise into consciousness. He was

forced to bury it beneath the level of emotive expression, to reduce it to a matter of no importance, to grope for belief in spite of its being absurd. He was, in short, compelled to embrace a mysticism which, unlike previous types, subdued the body neither in the oriental fashion by inducing hysteria nor in western fashion by chaining it to will under the authority of abstract logic. His must be a mysticism which justified the paralysis of will and the shrinking back from sensation, by setting up a complete dichotomy between the spiritual and the material life. Against his background of scientific rationalism, to believe the absurd might be eccentric and psychopathic. But for the time being it seemed to make the facts of his experience endurable. He might escape schizophrenia by assuming it to be the normal state of the human personality.

But the absurdity of the paradox has now to be directly faced. Experience was forcing Kafka further into his labyrinth. If *The Trial* had to be written because the optimism lurking in the conclusion of *Amerika* had proved unfounded, *The Castle* had to be written because life was scarcely possible if one accepted only the approach of *The Trial*. Personal salvation demanded that the skeptical view of the world give way to its description through the eyes of faith. The materialistic aspect of man and human institutions, valid and hopeless on its level, sent Kafka hurrying into the burrow of faith. Only faith was not really an escape since somehow the spiritual existed side by side with the material, every person having only this curious relation to every other person that they alike were split into these two aspects essentially unrelated. The new explanation was only a new dilemma. If by definition of humanity itself, the flesh is unescapable, the spiritual must appear to function through the forms of the material. *The Castle*, therefore, is only Kafka's exaggeration of K's mistake in *The Trial* (from the theological point of view). The quest for God is certainly more comprehensive than the desire for human justice and the theological dilemma consequently more august. But psychologically the new situation was less difficult. One knew that the good, unlike the evil, was incapable of revenge. The very fact that one's search was to find out if it really existed to man's perception made life indeed the safer; action banished the misgiving that action might be useless. The average man doubtless did not need to pursue the castle because he was reconciled to the contradictions that life had thrust upon him. He had become resigned to a chaos he did not understand, whether he found it within himself or in the outside world. But I think Kafka was right in assuming that this was a view of the situation from the outside; or, at all events, that if it was the true situation, it could not last. Look inside any common individual and he does not have the impulse to act for the good such as led to downfall in *The Trial*. But, certainly, we may imagine Kafka arguing, if the impulse for the good is completely divorced from the practical, if it is nothing but man's quest for the disembodied perfection of God, there can be no revenge from the sources of evil. What he did not see was that he has made life ultimately useless and boresome.

It escaped him because his talent as a novelist was a distraction from the dilemmas of his mysticism. The fascination of the immediate creative task postponed his consciousness of ultimate implacable despair. It reduced the traditional dilemma of mystic communication: that mysticism posits the impossibility of communication at all. If he had lived in the middle ages, he would have repeated the thin allegorizing which was the best the medieval writer could achieve in human characterization. But the very skepticism of his age, by obligating the sort of novel in which the human personality must be first presented in all its immediate richness and inconsistency, enabled him to postpone recognition of the fact that *The Castle* was bound to remain another unfinished work. Kafka indeed sensed the inconsistencies in our personalities more keenly than most writers; for they were locked in permanent contradiction within himself. The new interest, furthermore, in the introspective novel with its apparent indifference to the external world of material values must have normalized for him the malady of his personality, by affording him an appearance of escape from the level of *The Trial*, satisfactory for the time being. He could as a novelist thus take for the spiritual, as contrasted with the materialistic, the working of our unconscious as contrasted with our ordinary habit of living on the conscious surface of experience. By abandoning the consciousness under the joint auspices of the new technique of fiction and his developing psychosis, he could delude himself into believing that the presentation of the world as transformed by his own unconscious was the world of spiritual reality. Doubtless the process was chiefly unconscious. (And the reader should be reminded that my entire argument has been a rationalizing of what was for Kafka—who can scarcely be said to reason—a solely experiential process, the symbolic meanings of which I have been verbalizing.) But the result of the process was that for the time being the hostility of the actual lost its actuality, became transformed into the cold distance of the objective world as it appears in dreams, as, to the dreamer, it is the actuality hovering on the fringe of consciousness that is the dream. In the dream for the time being appears to lie the reality, and to Kafka's satisfaction if it did not possess the full-blown perfection that faith could hardly require this side the grave, it was at least harmless and impersonal.

Kafka has only transferred his doubts into a realm where they may be handled without emotional disturbance. The locus of *The Castle* is an isolated village high in the mountains. The atmosphere is that of the feudal pre-Bismarckian world, remote and ambiguous. The castle is even higher up, most of the time hidden in the mist and storm of the mountain top, and inaccessible because of the state of the roads. But in the village also the snow cuts off easy communication and reduces clarity of vision. Winter drives people indoors so that the scene (unlike that of *The Trial*) is never populous. When one breaks through the drifts to reach the peasant's door, it is opened as though suspicion of the stranger were confused with dislike of the cold. Even within the inn, though men crouch resentfully, they are half hidden by the shadows. The author appears to have been as much affected by the cold as his characters are. For he describes all this as though himself experiencing the same partial anesthesia. We scarcely realize, so extreme has the numbness of our sense become, that we are back in the competitive world of *Amerika*. The conviction in *The Trial* of implacable doom has disappeared. But the fact that everybody works for the castle, even though the spiritual must take this inconsistently materialistic form, guarantees to men non-competitive qualities also. Kafka's theology has succeeded in enriching his presentation of men and their social relationships. They are at last in his novels full human, to the imagination of the normal reader, in that they now show what impresses us as being a realistic complexity. They are both aggressive and considerate, both selfish and unselfish. The reader follows their conversation or the description of their actions with the same lively interest in the immediate situation which is certainly the essential characteristic of life itself, and the presence of which in this novel of Kafka's is the secret of its esthetic worth. But the esthetic satisfaction of the narrative has another ingredient in that this liveliness is entirely visual and verbal. The story has the coldness of the Grecian urn, the remoteness of the silent moving picture. Whatever happens we accept without any emotional involvement of our own. If our own emotions could be aroused, the book's flavor would become ironic as we read on. For it turns out that this flash of action and conflicting motive is a chaos. Men seem to act from impulse and their attempt to understand their action only leads into a maze of speculation. By implication, *The Castle* is a parody on the introspective novel, the elusiveness of our so-called "stream of consciousness."

In this benumbed word of Kafka's, though the act is always clear, its meaning and justification remain forever doubtful, and acts, therefore, cannot have coherence, when taken together. Now that life is presented in both its spiritual and material aspects, it becomes a bedlam of concrete particularities that lead nowhere. If we go within the single act to discover its motives, the act disintegrates. But it is the same when we pass from act to act. They fail to integrate into a pattern unless the perpetual repetition of Sysiphus' toil can be so described. The reader, for instance, gets the impression that K comes to the village bearing a definite letter employing him as a land surveyor of the castle. But as the book progresses, one begins to doubt whether K received such a letter or only came with the hunch that a job was vacant or thinking he could bluff his way. Nor do the castle officials succeed in clearing away the uncertainties. Possibly a letter had been sent some years ago, but they are positive that there has not been a valid recent communication and no such official is needed. Yet K, on his side, may well feel that a higher official (if he could reach him) may be better informed; the only guarantee that the bustling official he meets really acts for the castle is his appearance of self-assurance. Even this cannot be trusted, since if one got to know him better (as K did Amalia's brother) the arrogance might only hide his own inner doubts. For Amalia's brother, though he poses as a messenger of the castle, has no assurance that he is accepted as such on the hill. He can only try, becoming in human eyes a hypocrite, in the hope that the castle may reward him for his good intention by a sign that never comes. And since his good intention is often disproved by some human frailty, he lives in perpetual doubt of his deserving the reward he seeks. All this is clear as ecclesiastical symbolism. The existence of the spiritual itself has been reduced to the suspicious dimensions of an intuition within one's own obviously insufficient ego. The individual intuition of the divine has only the verification that other equally fallible persons seem to share it. For, if there is no inspired Bible that Kafka can trust, it goes without saying that he is not aware of the possible existence of an inspired religious institution. The castle is obviously a criticism of the organizational hierarchy in the Roman Catholic Church culminating in the inaccessible recesses of the Vatican. But since Kafka begins by positing the absolute separation of spiritual and material, the book is a broader criticism also of the notion of spiritual hierarchy among men. It is primarily the Jewish-Protestant-mystical tradition that is failing him. Its belief that the inner light, the indwelling of grace, is the only assurance of the possession of divine authority is what paradoxically he can no longer either believe or disbelieve. He cannot reject it because it seems tied up in his own personality and that of other men with the restraining influence of conscience, a reversion from the cruel deed, a reaction against pride into humility. But the evidence is against it.

Equally devastating is the book's implied attack upon the pragmatic philosophy which is the ultimate lay application of this Protestant tradition. The book acknowledges the validity of the act as clearly as it makes a parody of the "will to believe." Always the act is there; what is wanting is any test of its "working." From this point of view *The Castle* comes near to being a refutation of James' *Varieties of Religious Experience*. He gets close to shattering pragmatism by bringing into the open its explicit metaphysics, and showing that it rests on the absurd foundation that, despite our inner doubts, we believe because others act as though they do, and belief, thus secured, seems to do us good. Kafka's own mysticism is, in fact, merely an emphasis upon this assumption which the pragmatist makes only to neglect. The pragmatist has been able to neglect it because he has been distracted by the exhilaration of wallowing among particularities which seem to add up to progress. But the misery and poverty of modern life, Kafka saw, have reduced the exhilaration, indeed have transformed it for most persons into despair. At this point he seems to have become aware that the pursuit through the medium of philosophy of this assumption that the good is what works (when what works is so evidently the evil) lands the thinker in the theory of the useful make-believe, the philosophy of As-If. Though inclined to the same conclusion, Kafka hesitates to accept it. He recoils altogether from formal philosophy into that variant of functioning pragmatism which is the writing of novels and that peculiarity of its theory which accepts without a protest lack of coherent pattern in both our emotional and intellectual life. Pragmatically the only certainty in *The Castle* is the efficacy of public opinion. Faith has become a superstition in a world where nothing else but public opinion would seem to work, even though it works to the disaster of the well-intentioned. For, as though to prove he had not forgotten *The Trial*, Kafka introduces one coherent episode: the fall of Amalia's family. They are socially ostracized and reduced to beggary for a number of reasons (for nothing is simple in Kafka), but essentially, I believe, because Amalia's father believed in progress, has tried to improve the fire department, and therefore had sought to relate the spiritual to the material aspects of life. His spiritual urge became corrupted into personal pride and ambition, and the revenge of the public upon his pride was the restoration of the hopeless chasm between the two facets of the human personality.

KENNETH BURKE:

MOTIVES AND MOTIFS IN THE POETRY OF MARIANNE MOORE

I N THIS essay we would characterize the substance of Miss
Moore's work as a specific poetic strategy. And we would
watch it for insights which the contemplation of it may give us
into the ways of poetic and linguistic action generally. For this
purpose we shall use both her recently published book, *What Are
Years*, and her *Selected Poems*, published in 1935 with an introduction by T. S. Eliot (and including some work reprinted from
an earlier volume, *Observations*).

On page 8 of the new book, Miss Moore writes:

> The power of the visible
> is the invisible;

and in keeping with the pattern, when recalling her former title,
Observations, we might even have been justified in reading it as
a deceptively technical synonym for "visions." One observes the
visibles—but of the corresponding invisibles, one must be visionary. And while dealing much in things that can be empirically
here, the poet reminds us that they may

> dramatize a
> meaning always missed
> by the externalist.

It is, then, a relation between external and internal, or visible
and invisible, or background and personality, that her poems
characteristically establish. Though her names for things are rep-

"Motives and Motifs in the Poetry of Marianne Moore," from *A Grammar of Motives.* By permission of Prentice-Hall, Inc.

resentative of attitudes, we could not say that the method is Symbolist. The objects exist too fully in their own right for us to treat them merely as objective words for subjects. T. S. Eliot says that her poetry "might be classified as 'descriptive' rather than 'lyrical' or 'dramatic.' " He cites an early poem that "suggests a slight influence of H. D., certainly of H. D. rather than of any other 'Imagist.' " And though asserting that "Miss Moore has no immediate poetic derivations," he seems to locate her work in the general vicinity of imagism, as when he writes:

> The aim of 'imagism,' so far as I understand it, or so far as it had any, was to introduce a peculiar concentration upon something visual, and to set in motion an expanding succession of concentric feelings. Some of Miss Moore's poems—for instance with animal or bird subjects—have a very good spread of association.

I think of William Carlos Williams. For though Williams differs much from Miss Moore in temperament and method, there is an important quality common to their modes of perception. It is what Williams has chosen to call by the trade name of "objectivist."

Symbolism, imagism, and objectivism would obviously merge into one another, since they are recipes all having the same ingredients but in different proportions. In symbolism, the subject is much stronger than the object as an organizing motive. That is, it is *what the images are symbolic of* that shapes their treatment. In imagism, there would ideally be an equality of the two motives, the subjective and objective. But in objectivism, though an object may be chosen for treatment because of its symbolic or subjective reference, once it has been chosen it is to be studied in its own right.

A man might become an electrician, for instance, because of some deep response to electricity as a symbol of power. Yet, once he had become an electrician and thus had converted his response to this subject into an objective knowledge of its laws and properties, he would thereafter treat electricity as he did, not because each of his acts as an electrician would be symbolic like his original choice of occupation, but because such acts were required by the peculiar nature of electricity. Similarly, a poet writing in an "objectivist" idiom might select his subject because of some secret reference or personal significance it has had for him; yet having selected it, he would find that its corresponding object had qualities to be featured and appraised for themselves. And he might pay so much attention to such appraisal that the treatment of the object would in effect "transcend" the motive behind its original singling-out.

Thus, the poem "Four Quartz Crystal Clocks" (in *What Are Years*) begins:

> There are four vibrators, the world's exactest clocks;
>   and these quartz time-pieces that tell
> time intervals to other clocks,
>   these worksless clocks work well;
> and all four, independently the
>   same, are there in the cool Bell
>   Laboratory time
>
> vault. Checked by a comparator with Arlington
>   they punctualize . . .   (Etc.)

I think there would be no use in looking for "symbolist" or "imagist" motives behind the reference to the fact that precisely *four* clocks are mentioned here. It is an "objectivist" observation. We read of four, not because the number corresponds, for instance, to the Horsemen of the Apocalypse, but simply because there actually are four of them in the time vault. Similarly, "cool Bell Laboratory time vault" might have outlying suggestions of something like the coolness of a tomb—but primarily one feels that the description is there for purposes of objective statement; and had the nature of the scene itself dictated it, we should be reading of a "hot Bell Laboratory time tower." Though not journalism, it is reporting.

Yet any reader of Miss Moore's verse will quickly acknowledge that this theme, which provides an "objective" opportunity for the insertion of transitions between such words as "exactest," "punctualize," "careful timing," "clear ice," "instruments of truth," and "accuracy," is quite representative of her (and thus "symbolic" in the proportions of imagism). And the secondary level of the theme (its quality as being not the theme of clocks that tell the time, but of clocks that tell the time to clocks that tell the time)—I should consider thoroughly symbolic, as signalizing a concern not merely for the withinness of motives, but for the withinness-of-withinness of motives, the motives behind motives.[1]

We can call Miss Moore "objectivist," then, only by taking away the epithet in part. For though many details in her work seem to get there purely out of her attempt to report and judge of a thing's intrinsic qualities, to make us feel its properties as accurately as possible, the fact remains that, after you have read several of her poems, you begin to discern a strict principle of selection motivating her appraisals.

In *Selected Poems*, for instance, consider the poem, "People's Surroundings," that gives us a catalogue of correspondence between various kinds of agents and the scenes related to their roles. The poet is concerned to feature, in a background, the details that are an objective portrait of the person to whose kind of action this background belongs. "A setting must not have the air of being one"—a proscription one can observe if he makes the setting the extension of those in it. Here are relationships

[1] In passing we might consider a whole series of literary ways from this point of view. Allegory would deal with correspondences on a purely dogmatic, or conceptual basis. In the article on "Vestments," for instance, in the *Encyclopaedia Britannica*, we read of various "symbolical interpretations": "(1) the *moralizing school*, the oldest, by which—as in the case of St. Jerome's treatment of the Jewish vestments—the vestments are explained as typical of the virtues proper to those who wear them; (2) the *Christological school, i. e.* that which considered the minister as the representative of Christ and his garments as typical of some aspects of Christ's person or office—*e. g.* the stole is his obedience and servitude for our sakes; (3) the *allegorical school*, which treats the priest as a warrior or champion, who puts on the amice as a helmet, the alb as a breastplate, and so on." A work constructed about the systematic use of any such theories of correspondence would, to our way of thinking, be allegorical. The symbolic would use an objective vocabulary for its suggestion of the subjective, with the subjective motive being organizationally more important than the objective one. The specific literary movement called Symbolism would exemplify this stress to a large extent, but would also gravitate towards Surrealism, which stresses the incongruous and contradictory nature of motives by the use of gargoyles as motifs. Imagism would be "personalistic," in the idealistic sense, in using scenic material as the reflection, or extension of human

among act, scene, and agent (I use the three terms central to the philosophy of drama embodied in Henry James's prefaces). And among these people who move "in their respective places," we read of

> . . . the acacia-like lady shivering at the touch of a hand,
> lost in a small collision of orchids—
> dyed quicksilver let fall
> to disappear like an obedient chameleon in fifty shades of mauve
>   and amethyst.

Here, with person and ground merged as indistinguishably as in a pointillist painting by Seurat, the items objectify a tentative mood we encounter throughout Miss Moore's verses. The lines are like a miniature impression of her work in its entirety. And when, contemplating a game of bowls, she writes, "I learn that we are precisians, not citizens of Pompeii arrested in action / as a cross-section of one's correspondence would seem to imply," she here "learns" what she is forever learning, in her contemplation of animals and natural and fabricated things, as she seeks to

characters. The "objectivist," though rooted in symbolic and imagist concerns, would move into a plane where the object, originally selected by reason of its subjective reference, is studied in its own right. (The result will be "descriptive" poetry. And it will be "scientific" in the sense that, whereas poetry is a kind of act, the descriptiveness of science is rather the *preparation* for an act, the delayed action of a Hamletic reconnaissance in search of the accurate knowledge necessary for the act. And descriptive poetry falls across the two categories in that it acts by describing the scene preparatory to an act.) Naturalism has a greater stress upon the scenic from the polemic or depreciatory point of view (its quasi-scientific quality as delayed action, or preparation for action, often being revealed in that such literature generally either calls for action in the non-esthetic field or makes one very conscious of the fact that a "solution" is needed but is not being offered). True realism is difficult for us to conceive of, after so long a stretch of monetary idealism (accentuated as surrealism) and its counterpart, technological materialism (accentuated as behaviorism and operationalism), while pragmatic philosophies stress *making* and *doing* and *getting* in a localized way that obscures the realistic stress upon the *act*. The German term, *Realpolitik*, for instance, exemplifies a crude brand of pragmatism that completely misrepresents the realistic motive. The communicative nature of art gives all art a realistic ingredient, but the esthetic philosophies which the modern artist consciously or unconsciously absorbs continually serve to obscure this ingredient rather than to cultivate it.

isolate, for her appreciation and our own, the "great amount of poetry in unconscious fastidiousness."

I think appreciation is as strong a motive in her work as it was in the work of Henry James. "The thing is to lodge somewhere at the heart of one's complexity an irrepressible *appreciation*," he says in his preface to *The Spoils of Poynton*. And: "To criticise is to appreciate, to appropriate, to take intellectual possession, to establish in fine a relation with the criticised thing and make it one's own." It is a kind of private property available to everyone—and is perhaps the closest secular equivalent to the religious motive of glorification. It is a form of gratitude. And following out its possibilities, where one might otherwise be querulous he can instead choose to be precise. This redemption or transformation of complaint is, I think, essential to the quality of perception in Miss Moore's verse. (Rather, it is an anticipation of complaint: getting there first, it takes up all the room.)

In "Spenser's Ireland" (*What Are Years*), we may glimpse somewhat how this redemption can take place. Beginning in a mood of appreciation almost studious, the poem ends

> The Irish say your trouble is their
> trouble and your
>   joy their joy? I wish
> I could believe it;
> I am troubled, I'm dissat-
>   isfied, I'm Irish.

Since it is towards this end that the poem is directed, we may assume that from this end it derives the logic of its progression.

Note the general tenor of the other observations: on family, on marriage, on independence and yielding, on the freedom of those "made captive by supreme belief." There is talk of enchantments, of transformations, of a coat "like Venus' mantle lined with stars . . . the sleeves new from disuse," of such discriminations as we get

> when large dainty
> fingers tremblingly divide the wings
> of the fly.

And there are lines naming birds, and having a verbal music most lovely in its flutter of internal rhymes:

> the guillemot
> so neat and the hen
> of the heath and the
> linnet spinet-sweet.

All these details could be thought of as contextual to the poem's ending (for, if you single out one moment of a poem, all the other moments automatically become its context). If, then, we think of the final assertion as the act, we may think of the preceding contextual material as the scene, or background, of this act (a background that somehow contains the same quality as the act, saying implicitly what the act of the final assertion says explicitly). Viewed thus we see, as the underlying structure of this "description," a poem that, if treated as a lyric, would have somewhat the following argument: "Surrounded with details appropriate to my present mood, with a background of such items as go with matters to do with family, union, independence, I, an Irish girl (while the birds are about—and sweetly) am dissatisfied."

I won't insist that I'm not wrong. But in any case, that's the way I read it. And I would discern, behind her "objectivist" study and editorializing, what are essentially the lineaments of a lyric. But where the lyrist might set about to write, "In the moonlight, by the river, on a night like this in Spain," I can think of Miss Moore's distributing these items (discreetly and discretely) among conversational observations about the quality of light in general and moonlight in particular, about rivers mighty and tiny, in mountains, across plains, and emptying into the desert or the sea, about the various qualifications that apply to the transformation from twilight to darkness, in suburbs, or over bays, etc.; and from travel books of Spain we might get some bits that, pieced together, gave us all into which, in her opinion, the given night in Spain should be "broken down."

We might try from another angle by suggesting that Miss Moore makes "because" look like "and." That is, the orthodox lyrist might say, in effect, "I am sad *because* the birds are singing thus." A translation into Miss Moore's objectivist idiom would say in effect: "There are such and such birds—*and* birds sing thus and so—*and* I am sad." The scenic material would presumably be chosen because of its quality as objective replica of the subjective (as observed moments in the scene that correspond to observing moments in the agent). But even where they had been selected because of their bearing upon the plaint, her subsequent attention to them, with appreciation as a motive, would transform the result from a purely psychologistic rhetoric (the traditional romantic device of simply using scenic terms as a vocabulary for the sympathetic naming of personal moods). And the result would be, instead, an appraisal or judgment of many things in and for themselves. They would be encouraged to disclose their traits, not simply that they might exist through the vicarage of words, but that they might reveal their properties as workmanship (workmanship being a trait in which the ethical and the esthetic are one).

What are years? That is, if we were to assemble a thesaurus of all the important qualifications of the term "years" as Miss Moore uses it, what would these qualifications be? I suppose a title is always an assertion because it is a thing—and every thing is positive. Years, we learn by her opening poem of that title, are at least a quality of observation (vision), involving the obligation of courage, of commands laid upon the self to be strong, to see deep and be glad. And years possess the quality of one

> . . . who
> accedes to mortality
> and in his imprisonment, rises
> upon himself as
> the sea in a chasm . . .

Who does this, we are told, "sees deep and is glad." Years are also, by the nature of the case, steps from something to something. And to indicate a curve of development from the earlier volume, we might recall this same theme (of the rising water) as it was treated previously. I refer to a poem, "Sojourn in the Whale," which, beginning on the theme, "Trying to open locked doors with a sword," had likewise talked of Ireland. It is ad-

dressed to "you," a "you" who has heard men say: "she will become wise and will be forced to give / in. Compelled by experience, she / will turn back; water seeks its own level." Whereat

> . . . you
> have smiled. 'Water in motion is far
> from level.' You have seen it, when obstacles happened to bar
> the path, rise automatically.

In the earlier poem, the figure was used defensively, even op-
positionally. It is a tactic not common in Miss Moore's verse; as
against the dialectician's morality of eristic, she shows a more
feminine preference for the sheer ostracizing of the enemy, re-
futing by silence—disagreement implying the respect of intimacy,
as in her poem on "Marriage," wittily appraising the "fight to
be affectionate," she quotes, "No truth can be fully known until
it has been tried by the tooth of disputation."

(When Miss Moore was editor of *The Dial*, her ideal number,
as regards the reviews and articles of criticism, would I think
have been one in which all good books got long favorable reviews, all middling books got short favorable reviews, and all
books deserving of attack were allowed to go without mention.
One can imagine how such a norm could be reached either charit-
ably, through stress upon appreciation as motive, or not so charit-
ably, by way of punishment, as when Miss Moore observes in
"Spenser's Ireland": "Denunciations do not affect the culprit; nor
blows, but it / is torture to him not to be spoken to." We need
not decide between these motives in all cases, since they can comfortably work in unison.)

In contrast with the "oppositional" context qualifying the
figure of the rising water in the earlier poem, "Sojourn in the
Whale," its later variant has a context almost exaltedly positive.
And repeating the same pattern (of affirmation in imprisonment)
in another figure, the later poem widens the connotations of the
years thus:

> . . . The very bird
> grown taller as he sings, steels
> his form straight up. Though he is captive
> his mighty singing
> says satisfaction is a lowly

thing, how pure a thing is joy.
This is mortality,
this is eternity.

The pattern appears more conversationally (*What Are Years*, p. 12) in the suggestion that it must have been a "humorous" workman who made

this greenish Waterford
glass weight with the summit curled down toward
itself as the
grass grew,

and in "The Monkey Puzzle" (*Selected Poems*) we read

its tail superimposed upon itself in a complacent half spiral,
incidentally so witty.

Still, then, trying to discover what are years (or rather, what all are years), we might also recall, in *Selected Poems*, the poem on "The Fish," where the one fish featured as representative of its tribe is observed "opening and shutting itself like / an / injured fan"—in quality not unlike "The Student" of *What Are Years* who

. . . is too reclusive for
some things to seem to touch
him, not because he
has no feeling but because he has so much.

As the poem of "The Fish" develops, we might say that the theme is transferred "from the organism to the environment"; for we next read of a chasm through which the water has driven a wedge—and injury is here too, since

All
external
marks of abuse are present on this
defiant edifice.—

And finally

Repeated
evidence has proved that it can live
on what cannot revive
its youth. The sea grows old in it.

A chasm in the sea, then, becomes rather the sea in a chasm. And this notable reversal, that takes place in the areas of the "submerged," would also seem to be an aspect of "years." Which would mean that "years" subsume the synecdochic possibilities whereby those elements that cluster together can represent one another: here the active can become passive, the environed can become the environment, the container can be interchangeable with the contained. In possessing such attributes, "years" are poetry.

We may at this point recall our beginning—the citation concerning visible and invisible. In "The Plumet Basilisk" (*Selected Poems*) we read of this particular lizard that, "king with king,"

> He leaps and meets his
> likeness in the stream.

He is (in the poem it is a quotation)

> 'the ruler of Rivers, Lakes, and Seas,
> invisible or visible'—

and as scene appropriate to the agent, this basilisk is said to live in a basilica. (Another lizard, in the same poem, is said to be "conferring wings on what it grasps, as the airplant does"; and in "The Jerboa," we are told of "this small desert rat" that it "honours the sand by assuming its colour.") Likewise

> the plumet portrays
> mythology's wish
> to be interchangeably man and fish.

What I am trying to do, in reaching out for these various associations, is to get some comprehensive glimpse of the ways in which the one pervasive quality of motivation is modified and ramified. I am trying, in necessarily tenuous material, to indicate how the avowed relation between the visible and the invisible finds variants, or sophistications, in "objectivist" appreciation; how this appreciation, in an age of much querulousness, serves rather to transcend the querulous (*Selected Poems*, p. 34: "The staff, the bag, the feigned inconsequence / of manner, best bespeak that weapon, self-protectiveness"); and how this same pattern takes form in the theme of submergence, with its inter-

changeabilities, and so in the theme of water rising on itself. At
another point the motive takes as its object the motif of the
spinster ("You have been compelled by hags to spin / gold thread
from straw," with incidental suggestions of esthetic alchemy, lines
that appear in "Sojourn in the Whale," and so link with submergence, Ireland, and the theme of spirited feminine independence, thus relating to kindred subjects in the later poem,
"Spenser's Ireland"). I have also suggested that a like quality of
imagination is to be found in the intellectual ways of one who
selects as his subject not clocks, but clocks for clocks. (To appreciate just what goes on here, one might contrast these contemplative clocks—serene in their role as the motives behind
motives—with the ominous clock-faces of Verhaeren, or in the
grotesque plays of Edmund Wilson, which no one seems to have
read but me.) From these crystal clocks, I could then advance
to another variant, as revealed in the treatment of ice and glass.
These would, I think, be animated by the same spirit. See for
instance (in *Selected Poems*) the study of the glacier as "an
octopus of ice":

> this fossil flower concise without a shiver,
> intact when it is cut,
> damned for its sacrosanct remoteness.

"Relentless accuracy is the nature of this octopus / with its capacity for fact"—which would make it a glacier with an objectivist
esthetic. And two levels of motive are figured in the splendid
concluding vista of

> . . . the hard mountain 'planed by ice and polished by the
> wind'—the white volcano with no weather side;
>
> the lightning flashing at its base,
> rain falling in the valleys, and snow falling on the peak—[2]

[2] This is cited from the poem that follows the one on "Marriage," and is
in turn followed by "Sea Unicorns and Land Unicorns." The three could
be taken together as a triptych that superbly illustrates three stages in the
development of one idea. First, we have the subtly averse poem on marriage
(done in a spirit of high comedy that portrays marital quarrelings as inter-
related somewhat like the steps of a minuet). Then comes the precise yet

We might have managed more easily by simply demarcating several themes, like naming the different ingredients that go to make up a dish. Or as with the planks that are brought together, to make a campaign platform, regardless of their fit with one another. But the relation among the themes of a genuine poetry is not of this sort. It is *substantial*—which is to say that all the branches spread from a single trunk.

I am trying to suggest that, without this initial substantiality, "objectivism" would lead not to the "feigned inconsequence of manner" that Miss Moore has mastered, but to inconsequence pure and simple. But because of this substantiality, the surfaces are derived from depth; indeed, the strict lawfulness in their choice of surfaces is depth. And the objects treated have the property not simply of things, but of volitions. They derive their poignancy as motifs from their relation to the sources of motive. And the relation between observer and observed is not that of news and reporter, but of "conversities" (her word).

In the earlier volume there is a poem, "Black Earth," wherein surprisingly the poet establishes so close an identification with her theme as not merely to "observe" it with sympathy and appreciation, but to speak for it. This is one of her rare "I" poems—

exalted contemplation of the glacier. And finally a discussion of the unicorn, a legendary solitaire:

> Thus this strange animal with its miraculous elusiveness,
> has come to be unique,
> 'impossible to take alive,'
> tamed only by a lady inoffensive like itself—
> as curiously wild and gentle.

And typically, she cites of it that, since lions and unicorns are arch enemies, and "where the one is the other cannot be missing," Sir John Hawkins deduced an abundance of lions in Florida from the presence of unicorns there.

The theme of the lightning that flashes at the base of the glacier is varied in the unicorn poem (in a reference to "the dogs / which are dismayed by the chain lightning / playing at them from its horn"). And it is varied also in a poem on the elephant (still to be discussed) that

> has looked at the electricity and at the earth-
> quake and is still
> here; . . .

and in it the elephant sometimes speaks with the challenge and confidence of an Invictus. Beginning on the theme of emergence (coupled with delight in the thought of submergence at will), there is first a celebration of the sturdy skin; then talk of power ("my back is full of the history of power"); and then: "My soul shall never be cut into / by a wooden spear." Next comes mention of the trunk, and of poise. And interwoven with the vigor of assertion, the focal theme is there likewise:

> that tree-trunk without
> roots, accustomed to shout
>   its own thoughts to itself . . .

and:

>   . . . The I of each is to
> the I of each
> a kind of fretful speech
>   which sets a limit on itself; the elephant is
>   black earth preceded by a tendril?

I think we can make a point by recalling this earlier poem when, in "Smooth Gnarled Crape Myrtle" (*What Are Years*), the theme of the elephant's trunk appears again, this time but in passing, contextual and "tangential" to the themes of birds, union, loneliness:

>   . . . 'joined in
> friendship, crowned by love.'
> An aspect may deceive; as the
> elephant's columbine-tubed trunk
> held waveringly out—
> an at will heavy thing—is
> delicate.

Surely, "an at will heavy thing" is a remarkable find. But one does not make such observation by merely looking at an elephant's trunk. There must have been much to discard. In this instance, we can know something about the omissions, quite as though we had inspected earlier drafts of the poem with their record of revisions. For though a usage in any given poem is a finished thing, and thus brilliant with surface, it becomes in effect but "work in progress" when we align it with kindred usages (emergent, fully developed, or retrospectively condensed) in other poems. And here, by referring to "Black Earth," we can find what lies behind the reference to the elephant's trunk in "Smooth Gnarled Crape Myrtle." We can know it for a fact what kind of connotations must, for the poet, have been implicit in the second, condensed usage. Hence we can appreciate the motives that enabled this trunk to be seen not merely as a *thing*, but as an *act*, representative of the assertion in "Black Earth." And by reviewing the earlier usage we can know the kind of volitional material which, implicit in the later usage, led beyond the perception of the trunk as a thing to this perception of it as an act. At such moments, I should say, out of our idealistic trammels we get a glimpse of realism in its purity. For as materialism is a stress upon the scene, idealism a stress upon the agent, mysticism a stress upon the purpose, and pragmatism a stress upon the means or agency, so realism is complete when it enables us to see in terms of the act.

Or let us look at another instance. Sensitivity in the selection of words resides in the ability, or necessity, to feel behind the given word a history—not a past history, but a future one. Within the word, collapsed into its simultaneous oneness, there is implicit a sequence, a complexity of possible narratives that could be drawn from it. If you would remember what words are in this respect, and how in the simúltaneity of a word histories are implicit, recall the old pleasantry of asking someone, "What's an accordion," whereat invariably as he explains he will start pumping a bellows.

Well, among Miss Moore's many poems enunciating aspects of her esthetic credo, or commenting on literary doctrines and methods, there is one, "To a Snail," beginning:

> If 'compression is the first grace of style,
> you have it. Contractility is a virtue
> as modesty is a virtue.

And this equating of an esthetic value with a moral one is summed up by locating the principle of style "in the curious phenomenon of your occipital horn."

In her poem on the butterfly (*What Are Years*, p. 17), the mood of tentativeness that had been compressed within the term "contractility" reveals its significant narrative equivalents. As befits the tentative, or contractile, it is a poem of jeopardy, tracing a tenuous relationship between a butterfly ("half deity half worm," "last of the elves") and a nymph ("dressed in Wedgwood blue"), with light winds (even a "zephyr") to figure the motives of passion. Were not the course of a butterfly so intrinsically akin to the "inconsequential ease" and "droverlike tenacity" of Miss Moore's own versa-tilities, one might not have much hope for a poem built about this theme (reminiscent of many musical Papillons—perhaps more than a theme, perhaps a set idiom, almost a form). Here, with the minute accuracy of sheerly "objectivist" description, there is a subtle dialectic of giving and receiving, of fascinations and releases—and interchange of delicately shaded attitudes. In this realm, things reached for will evade, but will follow the hand as it recedes.

Through the tracery of flight, there are two striking moments of stasis, each the termination of a course: one when "the butterfly's tobacco-brown unglazed / china eyes and furry countenance confront / the nymph's large eyes"—and the second when, having broken contact with the nymph's "controlled agitated glance," the "fiery tiger-horse" (at rest, but poised against the wind, "chest arching / bravely out") is motivated purely by relation to the zephyr alone. The poem concludes by observing that this "talk" between the animal and the zephyr "was as strange as my grandmother's muff."

I have called it a poem of jeopardy. (When butterfly and nymph confront each other, "It is Goya's scene of the tame magpie faced / by crouching cats.") It is also a poem of coquetry (perhaps our last poem of coquetry, quite as this butterfly was the last of the elves—coquetry now usually being understood as something that comes down like a ton of brick).[3]

[3] In the earlier volume there is an epigram-like poem, "To a Steam Roller," that I have always thought very entertaining. It excoriates this sorry, ungainly mechanism as a bungling kind of fellow that, when confronting such discriminations as are the vital purpose of Miss Moore's lines, would "crush all the particles down / into close conformity, and then walk back and forth / on them." We also read there:

The tentativeness, contractility, acquires more purely the theme of jeopardy in "Bird-Witted" (*What Are Years*), reciting the incident of the "three large fledgling mocking-birds," awaiting "their no longer larger mother," while there approaches

> the
> intellectual cautious-
> ly c r e e p ing cat.

If her animals are selected for their "fastidiousness," their fastidiousness itself is an aspect of contractility, of jeopardy. "The Pangolin" (*What Are Years*), a poem which takes us through odd nocturnal journeys to the joyous saluting of the dawn, begins: "Another armoured animal"—and of a sudden you realize that Miss Moore's recondite menagerie is almost a thesaurus of

> As for butterflies, I can hardly conceive
> of one's attending upon you, but to question
> the congruence of the complement is vain, if it exists.

Heretofore I had been content to think of this reference to a butterfly simply as a device for suggesting weight by a contrasting image of lightness. But the role of butterfly as elf conversant to nymph might also suggest the presence of such overtones as contrasting types of masculinity. (This would give us a perfect instance of what Coleridge meant by fancy, which occurs when we discern behind the contrast an element that the contrasted images share in common.)

As for the later poem, where the theme of the butterfly is fully developed, I might now try to make more clearly the point I had in mind with reference to the two moments of stasis. In the opening words ("half deity half worm" and "We all, infant and adult, have / stopped to watch the butterfly") the poem clearly suggests the possibility that it will figure two levels of motivation, a deity being in a different realm of motives than a worm, and the child's quality of perception being critically distinct from the adult's. Examining the two moments of stasis, we find here too the indications of an important difference between them. At the first stasis, elf and nymph confront each other, while "all's a-quiver with significance." But at the final stasis, the conversity is between butterfly and west wind, a directer colloquy (its greater inwardness linking it, in my opinion, with the motive-behind-motive figuration in the theme of clocks-for-clocks). At this second stage, the butterfly is called "historic metamorphoser / and saintly animal"; hence we may take it that the "deity" level of motive prevails at this second stage. The quality of the image in the closing line ("their talk was as strange as my grandmother's muff") would suggest that the deified level is equated with the quality of perception as a child. (The grandmother theme also appears in "Spenser's Ireland," where we are told that "Hindered characters . . . in Irish stories . . . all have grandmothers." Another reason for believing that the second stage of the butterfly poem protectivenesses. Thus also, the poem in which occur the lines anent visible and invisible, has as its conclusion:

> unsolicitude having swallowed up
> all giant birds but an
> alert gargantuan
> little-winged, magnificently
> speedy running-bird. This one
> remaining rebel
> is the sparrow-camel.

The tentativeness also manifests itself at times in a cult of rarity, a collector's or antiquarian interest in the present, a kind of stylistic tourism. And it may lead to a sheer word play, of graduated sort (a Laforguian delight in showing how the pedantries can be reclaimed for poetry):

> The lemur-student can see
> that the aye-aye is not
>
> an angwan-tíbo, potto, or loris.

Yet mention of the "aepyornis" may suggest the answer we might have given, were we up on such matters, to one who, pencil in hand and with the newspaper folded to make it firmer, had asked, "What's a gigantic bird, found fossil in Madagascar in nine letters?" As for her invention, "invis   ible," I can't see it.

Tonally, the "contractility" reveals itself in the great agility, even restlessness, which Miss Moore imparts to her poetry by assonance, internal rhyme, and her many variants of the run-over line. We should also note those sudden nodules of sound which are scattered throughout her verses, such quick concentrations as

is also the "motives-behind-motives" stage is offered tenuously by this tie-up with the word "hindered," since the final poem in the book, as we shall know when we come to it, does well by this word in proclaiming a morality of art.)

Another poem, "Virginia Britannia" (*What Are Years*), that seems on the surface almost exclusively descriptive (though there is passing reference to a "fritillary" that "zigzags") is found to be progressing through scenic details to a similar transcendence. At the last, against sunset, two levels are figured, while the intermediate trees "become with lost identity, part of the ground." The clouds, thus marked off, are then heralded in words suggestive of Wordworth's ode as 'to the child an intimation of / what glory is."

"rude root cudgel," "the raised device reversed," "trim trio on the tree-stem," "furled fringed frill," or tonal episodes more sustained and complex, as the lines on the birds in Ireland (already quoted), or the title, "Walking-Sticks and Paper-Weights and Water-Marks," or

> . . . the redbird
> the red-coated musketeer,
> the trumpet-flower, the cavalier,
> the parson, and the
> wild parishioner. A deer-
> track in a church-floor
> brick . .

One noticeable difference between the later selection and the earlier one is omission of poems on method. In *Selected Poems* there were a great many such. I think for instance of: "Poetry," containing her ingenious conceit, "imaginary gardens with real toads in them"; "Critics and Connoisseurs"; "The Monkeys"; "In the Days of Prismatic Colour"; "Picking and Choosing"; "When I Buy Pictures"; "Novices" (on action in language, and developed in imagery of the sea); "The Past is the Present" ("ecstasy affords / the occasion and expediency determines the form"); and one which propounds a doctrine as its title: "In This Age of Hard Trying, Nonchalance is Good and."

But though methodological pronouncements of this sort have dropped away, in the closing poem on "The Paper Nautilus," the theme does reappear. Yet in an almost startlingly deepened transformation. Here, proclaiming the poet's attachment to the poem, there are likenesses to the maternal attachment to the young. And the themes of bondage and freedom (as with one "hindered to succeed") are fiercely and flashingly merged.

DAVID DAICHES:

PROBLEMS FOR MODERN NOVELISTS

I. THE NOVEL AS SYMBOLIC COMMUNICATION

IT WOULD be a rash person who, in the face of the many and diverse shapes which the novel has assumed in modern times, would be prepared to give a simple definition of fiction which would embrace all the different varieties. The novel has been serving a great number of different functions, ethical, rhetorical, scientific, and if we attempt to find a definition which will be equally apposite to the work of Virginia Woolf and James T. Farrell, of James Branch Cabell and Sinclair Lewis, of Upton Sinclair and Julian Green, we shall find ourselves held up by the initial difficulty of finding, even in the most general sense, a literary purpose common to all these writers. The fact is that the novel, while retaining all its older functions, has become, and has been for some time, the standard way of drawing the attention of the public to any set of ideas or facts in which the author happens to be interested. It may be a fable or a report, a piece of history or a piece of rhetoric, pure speculation or pure description. The subject matter may be past or present, largely real or purely imaginary, plausible or fantastic—anything from the fantasies of Kafka to the plain chronicling of the "social realists" of the 1930's. It is still fashionable for the literary critic to begin a review of a book of verse by defining poetry: but who in our time defines fiction?

Any differences existing between the practitioners of any art are reflected in exaggerated form in the standards and judgments of the critics, and it is not therefore to be wondered at that one critic will today judge a given novel with reference to the degree with which it suggests an effective remedy for certain social ills, another will consider merely the accuracy with which the author portrays a given environment, a third will concentrate his attention on the plausibility of the action in terms of some psychological theory, a fourth will talk about the extent to which the novel reminded him of his childhood in a midwestern town, a fifth will discuss whether it is "well written," and yet a sixth will draw attention to its merits or defects by comparing it with *War and Peace*. In other words, the critics are not certain what they ought to look for in a novel.

And of course there are many things which the critic might reasonably look for in a novel. Two features, however, our academic critics have long since established as indispensable to a work of fiction, namely, plot and character. Both have been implicitly re-defined by modern novelists to include what Fielding and Jane Austen and Dickens and even Henry James would hardly have recognized as such. But they are still there. It might therefore be useful to begin a discussion of the problems facing the modern writer and critic of fiction with some examination of these traditional concepts. We shall start with character, for reasons that will become obvious as the argument proceeds.

Most novels develop their meaning through a communication to the reader of the imagined adventures (psychological and physical, occasionally only one or the other of these two kinds) of imaginary characters. These characters always function in some degree as symbols: that is, the characters insofar as they act and are acted upon are represented, through any of a variety of devices, as illuminating more than the behavior of some fortuitously chosen individual. Characters in fiction are always symbols to some extent, and their interest largely derives from this fact. The reader is interested because the character illuminates more than just himself. A character who sheds light only on himself is felt to be inadequately treated even on historical standards (for, obviously, good historical writing is not simply atomistic) and is even more inadequate by any artistic criterion. The hero of a novel is always more than what he appears to be at first sight.

The kind of symbolization employed by the novelist varies in accordance with his interest and intention. The character might be expanded into an historical symbol, illuminating a certain section of man's past, as for example in *Rob Roy;* or the symbol might be social, exemplifying certain kinds of relations between man and his fellows or man and his environment, as in *The Grapes of Wrath;* or it might be political, presenting situations determined primarily by problems of government and organization, as in the novels of Malraux; or the symbol might be psychological, as in the novels of James or Virginia Woolf, indicating phases of the relation between man and his consciousness; or it might be topographical, as in the regional novel, presenting man in the light of his local traditions. But always the characters are symbols: they represent situations which, though unique in the way they are presented, are not unique in their implications. They become, as the novel proceeds, not simply characters taking part in a given action, but characters illuminating, through their "doing and suffering," certain phases of experience.

These examples of kinds of symbolization are not, of course, meant to be exhaustive, nor is it suggested that any one character in any one novel remains in only one of these categories. A novel such as *How Green Was My Valley* combines social, psychological and topographical symbolization, and perhaps historical as well. Indeed, it may be questioned whether there can be such a thing, for the purposes of the novelist, as a *purely* historical symbol.

A novel sets up a series of symbolic characters and situations that are made convincing through appropriate machinery. One can make a distinction (more easily in theory than in practice) between the skill required to handle this machinery, which is a question of the writer's skill or *craft*, and the symbolic quality of the situations, which derive from the author's insight or *art*. So see an object or an incident or a character as a symbol demands the insight of an artist; to know how to convey your vision to your readers demands the skill of a craftsman. But of course this distinction, while helpful in theory, is constantly blurred in practice. A sense of language might suggest to a writer a certain train of images or incidents which would then take on a symbolic significance because of the sound and pattern of the words which suggested them. The insight of an artist is never independent of his sensitivity to his medium.

But what kind of machinery is the "appropriate" machinery that will enable the writer to get across effectively the symbolic nature of his characters? This is not an easy question to answer. It depends to some extent on the writer's ability to elicit a guaranteed response, on his ability to throw around the reader, as he reads, the kind of atmosphere that will make him sensitive to the kind of insight the writer is trying to communicate. In a sense, therefore, the question is not wholly an esthetic one: what might almost be called tricks of the propagandist are needed. From one point of view, all art is in its initial effects a form of persuasion.

To take some examples from novelists of the past: It is essential for Jane Austen to communicate to the reader a sense that he is sharing her placid elevation; the reader here is not one of the author's characters (as he is in the average motion picture) but shares the author's superiority to her characters. Unless this relationship is established, the proper symbolization of character and incident cannot take place. The machinery used by Jane Austen to establish it is largely the device of irony, judiciously and not too heavily employed. Sir Walter Scott's problem is very different. If his readers cannot be brought to share his warmhearted interest in history "romantically" interpreted and his feeling of satisfaction in following characters in and out of an historical situation, then they remain unable to appreciate the real meaning both of characters and action. Scott is a good example of the novelist whose lack of confidence in his own ability to communicate his symbolization leads him to introduce an "over-plot," that is, to superimpose on the real action a superficial love story, with hero and heroine who generally marry at the end. That is why, from *Waverley* on, the ostensible theme of Scott's novels is never the real theme. The story of the love of Waverley and Rose Bradwardine is the apparent but not the real story of

Waverley: the real theme is the tragic one of the Jacobite Rebellion and the lost cause of Scotland's independence. (For to Scott, as to so many 18th-century Scotsmen, the Jacobite movement meant a struggle for the old, romantic, independent Scotland.) The main theme of all Scott's better novels is essentially tragic: it is that the union with England and the material gains which resulted meant the loss of all that was romantic and picturesque in Scotland's history. That explains both Scott's conservatism in politics and his technique as a novelist. As a loyal supporter of the crown, he could not admit—scarcely even to himself—that his sympathies were with the Jacobites and the old romantic Scotland which he saw passing away so rapidly; therefore, as most of his novels are really the tragic record of this passing away, he had to give them some other meaning on the surface. His plot patterns are, consequently, almost always dual, and the true symbolization is played down so that the superficial reader will not notice that Waverley is an irrelevant character for a real understanding of the novel of that name; that the real centre of interest in *The Heart of Midlothian* is the smugglers and the old-fashioned backward-looking characters and an English queen's reactions to Scotland (a tragic necessity that Scotland's fate should be in the hands of an English queen); that the defeated rebel, Balfour of Burleigh, is the real hero of *Old Mortality;* that the love interests in *Guy Mannering* and *The Antiquary* are extraneous to the story; and that the greatest of Scott's novels is *Redgauntlet*, where for the only time he faces openly the problem that haunts him throughout his career, the problem of the fate of feudal ideals of glory in the modern world, and writes a tragedy in which the marriage of the hero and heroine represents the thinnest of all disguises. The belated little band of forlorn Jacobites in *Redgauntlet*, and the fate they meet, are (as Edwin Muir was first to see [1]) the real key to an understanding of Scott's mind and art.

Scott's problem is an example of the problems that sometimes arise in finding adequate machinery for achieving the proper symbolization of character and action in fiction. In his work, the

[1] See Edwin Muir's *Scott and Scotland.* London, 1936; p. 157 ff.

dualism in symbolization resulted from a psychological conflict within his own character. But to return to the discussion of the prerequisites for effective symbolization. The necessity for Dickens was that his readers should acquiesce in accepting some defeats as comic and others as tragic, and that this line should be kept always perfectly distinct. (When it is not kept distinct, as in his treatment of Jingle at the end of the Pickwick Papers, the result is that the symbolic meaning of the characters becomes confused.) The necessity for Thomas Love Peacock—a novelist who deserves more discussion than he generally receives—was that the reader should succumb to a mood of intellectual and physical well being: only such a mood would allow the novel to be read properly and the proper meanings to arise out of character and incident. As a final example we may cite Hardy, who is almost unique among novelists in demanding from his readers a certain acquiescence in the importance of unmotivated events: if the reader does not grant that acquiescence he can never see the novel for what it is meant to be. The opening of *The Mayor of Casterbridge* provides a very good example of how Hardy tries to predispose the reader to accept this premise. The action out of which the whole of the novel arises is the product of a freak and fortuitous mood.

All these novelists must employ machinery whose function it is to enable the reader to make the proper symbolization of character and action. Machinery is the method of necessary preliminary contact between writer and reader. Readers of Scott's novels will have noticed how often he begins by projecting before the reader's eyes two—or more—travellers who "might have been seen" wending their way across a mountain pass in the late summer of 17—. This device of referring to the hypothetical observer of real characters in a specific region and in a year which is deliberately left unspecified yet indirectly made clear to any reader who has his wits about him—this device succeeds in drawing together writer and reader into a common historical excursion; both peer into the past, and the author has the reader by the arm. Often Scott opens with an historical discussion of the state of the country in the period and then proceeds abruptly to take the reader by the arm and introduce him to the two travellers or the solitary stranger. In his earlier novels, he is just as likely to open with a laborious account of the early life and education of the nominal hero; but it was not long before he found machinery more appropriate to the kind of contact he wanted to make with his readers. No better contrast with this kind of contact could be made than by citing as our next example the methods of Sterne, whose relation to his readers is fairly uncommon among novelists. The symbolization which Sterne achieves is such that his characters and incidents become in a sense illustrations of the author's own character; the symbols are what might be called *confessional*, and have more in common with the methods of a personal essayist such as Lamb than with those of any of the novelists of his day. "Confessional symbolization"—to coin an ugly but suggestive phrase—has become less rare since Sterne's day, but still causes confusion among critics who cannot see it for what it is. A study of the opening chapters of *Tristram Shandy* and *A Sentimental Journey* will show how brilliantly Sterne manages to establish that preliminary contact with the reader that the nature of his work demands. The methods of, say, Virginia Woolf in the openings of her novels, show another way of making such contact, with a very different kind of symbolization in view. In Mrs. Woolf's novels the incidents and impressions that occur in daily life become, when properly recorded, means to the communication of subtle and transient insights into the nature of experience. Hence that sense of familiar everyday activity in association with highly rarefied speculation must be got across right away if the novel is not to fall apart (as her earliest novels in fact did, because the opening chapters were inadequate to their task). The opening chapters of *Mrs. Dalloway* and *To the Lighthouse* give a clear indication to the reader of the kind of symbols the novels are going to bring before him. Joyce, who differs from all other novelists in that the symbolic expansion of character and incidents in his work is (theoretically at least) infinite, suggests this not only by the title but by introducing the speculative and symbolizing mind of Stephen Dedalus before Bloom, the real hero, is allowed to enter.

These are random examples, introduced to show the importance of the preliminary contact made by the novelist. Without such contact the novel falls apart, however brilliantly written. The contact might be ironic, sentimental, tragic, comic, or of a kind that cannot be defined in any of these traditional terms. It provides the envelope, the frame, with reference to which the correct symbolic expansion is made by the reader. Is the character of Hamlet a symbol of the meditative man in a world of extroverts, or of the unpolitical man in a political environment, or of the man who seeks a revenge too tremendous to be achieved in any single act, or of something much more complex than any of them? The author must provide us with machinery for reading the work properly, for expanding characters and incidents into the proper symbolic meaning.

From the point of view of the writer, the most important initial problem is to find the point of preliminary contact—the thin edge of the wedge, as it were. Or, to change the metaphor, the reader must be made to fall down the rabbit-hole before the narrative which follows can take on its proper meaning for him. Indeed, *Alice in Wonderland* provides a very simple example of this sort of procedure: after Alice has fallen down the rabbit-hole, both the kind of probability the reader will accept and the kind of meaning he will see in the characters and events are determined—the book can now be read properly. The problem is at its most complex in novels like those of Franz Kafka, who deliberately refuses to admit that probability and symbolization change, and yet (as in *The Trial*) the events themselves indicate a change. It is this conflict between machinery and meaning that gives Kafka's work its strange, almost sinister quality, something that is not quite allegory and not quite reportage. It is not an easy method to imitate and is very rare in the history of fiction. For writers like Swift and Samuel Butler do not employ this deliberate paradox: they prepare the reader for the shift, by a voyage or some other kind of transition comparable to Alice's falling down the rabbit-hole.

This question of establishing preliminary contact with the reader is not one that can be discussed in a purely formal manner. It is not, that is to say, a matter simply of the relation of the parts of the work to the whole, for it concerns also the relation of the parts to the envelope which stretches from writer to reader and is partly dependent on the reader's prejudices, attitudes, and general mental situation.

Thus the problem for the novelist really becomes the problem of utilizing to the maximum the available prejudices of the reader, for the purpose of creating the proper symbolization. And this suggests that all fiction—indeed, all art—possesses a rhetorical aspect whether we like to admit it or not. Most art makes its initial appeal in some sense rhetorically: that is, the devices employed in order to ensure proper symbolization are nearly always rhetorical, persuasive, working on the reader's available preconceptions and prejudices. In employing these devices the writer must take into account the needs of special audiences.

But here an objection can immediately be raised. If this is so, why should novels written for one generation be effective for another? The answer is two-fold. In the first place, many novels —in fact, the majority—are properly appreciated only by the audience which the writer had in mind in contriving his machinery. These are the great numbers of bad novels which each generation takes to its heart but which the next generation forgets. Bad novels are often popular for the generation for which they were written for the simple reason that their authors contrive not only the methods of symbolization but the actual kind of symbolization they employ with reference to the prejudices and desires of the majority. The love stories in the pulp magazines are meant to serve as wish-fulfilments and satisfactions of desires to escape for a vast number of people whose lives are drab and uninteresting. But what about the great novels which are enjoyed with even more enthusiasm by readers of later generations? If the machinery of these novels was devised in order to utilize the prejudices of the author's contemporaries, is that machinery effective for readers of a later age? And if not, why do the books continue to be appreciated?

Let us consider once again the openings of Scott's novels. One will have to go far to find a modern critic who will defend these opening chapters: to modern eyes they seem clumsy, even naive. We appreciate Scott in spite of his clumsy techniques, not because of them. For modern readers, in fact, the writer's quasi-rhetorical attempt to establish preliminary contact does not work. We are not put into the frame of mind by Scott's introductory chapters that he expected of us. But—and this is important—the preliminary rhetorical preparations are less necessary for novelists who have established themselves in the tradition of great writers, for, taking for granted that their symbolization is effective, we actively try to "get" it—and we succeed. In other words, we read the classics more *actively* than we read contemporary works. Homer's devices to achieve proper symbolization may often be artificial and unconvincing to us, but then we do not need them, because we are actively looking for the proper symbolization, and so we find it without the helps that were necessary for an earlier audience. We are prepared to work harder in reading a classic, because we know, from the report of generations of critics, that there is something worth getting in the work. We do not trust to our first reactions in reading Lucretius or Dante; we do not surrender passively to the atmosphere which Dante created in his *Divine Comedy* so that he might be sure of the proper kind of attention from his contemporaries; knowing that whatever our initial lack of acquiescence in the machinery the writer has, nevertheless, something impressive to say, we persist until finally the meaning is adequately expanded.

This is one reason why the judging of contemporary writing is so difficult. We are much more at the mercy of the initial rhetoric with a contemporary writer than with a classic, whose worth has been proved and the rhetorical aspects of whose works we can ignore. The rhetoric of symbolization diminishes in importance as the work becomes accepted as great. Hemingway, in putting across the proper kinds of meaning in *For Whom the Bell Tolls*, has to employ devices relying on the contemporary definition of a hero and the contemporary view of what is most worth recording in human affairs; but the book could be appreciated, if the reader applied himself, without any dependence on these devices. The less rhetorical devices, such as his "epic" use of scenery and his ability to relate a sense of terrain to a sense of human destiny, will be noted by readers long after the machinery for indicating that the hero is a significant and symbolic figure has ceased to be persuasive.

Yet Hemingway commits himself to the use of rhetorical machinery to a greater extent than many of his contemporaries: in most of his novels he tries to construct a fairly substantial envelope stretching between himself and his readers, an envelope based on certain positive beliefs or at least on violent acceptances and rejections. Sometimes—as in *To Have and Have Not*—the machinery falls apart from the novel proper, and the rhetoric sticks out, appearing to have no relation to the characters and events it was meant to interpret. Steinbeck is another modern novelist who depends on a fairly substantial envelope, and the expansion of characters into symbols in *The Grapes of Wrath* is done by means of devices which arouse indignation and pity.

The antithesis of the Hemingway and Steinbeck kind of machinery is that employed by Virginia Woolf, who endeavors constantly to make the envelope that stretches between reader and writer sufficiently tenuous that it depends on the minimum of prejudice. (Joyce tries to make his depend on no prejudice at all.) Non-rhetorical fiction is rarer than most critics care to admit, and Virginia Woolf does come close to it. The more nearly fiction approaches lyric poetry, the more possible does non-rhetorical fiction become. When fable is completely replaced by vision, the non-rhetorical novel emerges—but then the novel ceases to exist as a novel. *Between the Acts* is barely fiction at all.

The problem for the novelist of today is that he has to make up his mind about this question of the "envelope": is he going to accept, with Hemingway and Steinbeck, the necessity for a more solid envelope, making his machinery more rhetorical and less lyrical—and in doing so return to the great English tradition in fiction, which is a rhetorical tradition in its main line (Fielding, Dickens, Thackeray, George Eliot, etc.)? Or is he moving towards the more tenuous envelope, in the tradition of James, Proust, and Virginia Woolf? It looks as though the phase of the tenuous envelope has been passed. A world struggling to discover values would find rhetorical machinery too heavy to handle, but a world struggling to assert values will be likely to return to it. And it would be rash to regard such a return as a melancholy omen: after all, perhaps the two greatest novels of the western world, *The Brothers Karamazov* and *War and Peace*, have been written in the rhetorical tradition.

II. PLOT, STYLE, & THE QUESTION OF VALUE

Fiction as an art form is the narration of a series of situations which are so related to each other that a significant unity of meaning is achieved; the narration, moreover, is couched in such a "style" that at each point in its progress the kind of relation between retrospect and anticipation is set up which continually and cumulatively reinforces the desired implications of the plot, so that the plot becomes symbolic as well as literal in its meaning. The novelist thus has a problem both of structure and of style: he must know both how to put a story together and how to express each of its parts. Both these aspects of the novelist's job are important in any discussion of the means that he employs in his endeavor to give the proper symbolic expansion to his characters and incidents. Such expansion is achieved not only by the way in which each incident is related to the sum total of incidents; the kind of language through which the incidents are communicated helps continually and progressively to expand the implications of the novel as it develops, until the full richness of meaning has been attained.

Obviously the novelist must be clear concerning the *kind* of symbol that he wants to make out of his characters and incidents, and the *method* that he will employ in producing it. The symbol need not be of one kind only—i.e. the novelist need not restrict the symbolic implications of characters and incidents to historical or social or psychological references only. The good historical novel, for example—and this is one thing that distinguishes a good historical novel from a good history—will have at least both historical and psychological symbolization: the situation will illuminate an historical state of affairs and the nature of man in general. In the great majority of the American novels dealing with the Civil War, the historical symbolization is more adequate than the psychological, and in a novel that is a defect: the reader gets a sense of history but no adequate or convincing sense of character. In a novel like *The Cloister and the Hearth* historical and psychological symbols are more effectively balanced. The method of achieving and of communicating these kinds of symbolization will vary with the novelist's relations to his audience—a factor which many novelists take into consideration without being fully conscious that they are doing so.

Both structure and style are important as methods of symbolization, and of the two structure is perhaps the more fundamental. This seems to be what Aristotle was getting at when he said that "plot is the first principle and as it were the soul of tragedy." It is the order of events that gives them their proper meaning. But for this to be true some agreement must exist between author and reader concerning the significance of those events in themselves. For the hero and heroine to marry after a series of vicissitudes is only a successful resolution of the plot if author and reader agree in taking marriage as a symbol of a happy ending. If the reader held the view that marriage, far from symbolizing a happy ending, is an uncertain beginning, no conclusion at all but the commencement of a hazardous experiment, the novel, however well constructed, would not be able to communicate to that reader its full meaning. For in matters of this kind Coleridge's "willing suspension of disbelief" will not work: we may all, in reading any novel, be able to bring ourselves to refrain from disbelief in the actuality of the events narrated, but belief in the actuality of events is not the same thing as agreement concerning their significance.

There is a relation between the kind of assumptions which the author expects to share with his readers and the kind of technique he employs in putting his full meaning across. The fictional techniques of Tchekhov and Dickens are very different, and so are their assumptions. Dickens's assumptions are more definite, and more ethical in their immediate implications, than those of Tchekhov: his structure is therefore more mechanical, his style more rhetorical, his envelope more solid. The private visions of Virginia Woolf and Katherine Mansfield—personal intuitions concerning the significance of what on any public standard are insignificant events—depend for their effective communication on a minimum of general assumptions, and demand therefore a technique whose lyrical sensitivity is able to make contact with those few and half-hidden intuitions which the reader shares without knowing that he does, or, alternatively, is able to persuade the reader as he reads of the validity of those personal intuitions of the author. Thus these more personal writers are both more rhetorical and less rhetorical than novelists like Dickens. They are less rhetorical in the obvious sense that they are not using certain common convictions concerning the significance or quality of events and characters and ideas in order to achieve full communication with their readers: they are more rhetorical in that, patterning their work largely in accordance with private intuitions, they must make the reader accept the validity of those intuitions while he reads. In a sense, all art is persuasion, and the more lyrical it is the more persuasive it must be. It is a great paradox, but an illuminating one, that, in a sense, music is the most rhetorical of the arts, for no differences in intellectual belief alter its effect. Music can persuade people who agree on nothing to join in a common emotion. Hitler's taste in literature is very different from that of the intellectuals he hounded from their country, but many of those he exiled and persecuted share his enthusiasm for Wagner.

At any rate, whether we accept this extension of the argument or not, it is clear that the proper organization of plot in fiction cannot be divorced from the question raised earlier, the question of the rhetorical aspect of fiction, of whether to choose the Hemingway or the Virginia Woolf tradition. In constructing his plot, therefore, the novelist must consider his "audience," real or ideal, and the beliefs of that audience, and the way in which he is going to utilize those beliefs; or, if he decides not to utilize those beliefs at all, he must work out some compensating techniques, some devices that will enable the reader to make the proper symbolic expansions as he reads without any initial agreement between writer and reader on questions of significance and value. This last task is much harder for the novelist than for the lyrical poet. In proportion as the arts become less "concrete" in content (moving from simple narrative through epic to lyric poetry and finally to music, "pure form") it becomes easier to ignore the assumptions and beliefs of your audience. Fiction depends more than any of the other arts on these assumptions. To assume (as Pater did) that art is "purer" in proportion as it moves away from dependence on these assumptions and "tends toward the condition of music," is to adopt a very arbitrary definition of art. The rhetorical aspect of fiction, which is treated by far too many critics as though it is something to be ashamed of and argued away, gives to the novel a kind of richness and profundity unique among the arts. The richness and profundity of, say, a late Beethoven quartet is as great of its kind as that of *The Brothers Karamazov*, but comparison between the two through any means except the demonstration of the utter difference between the medium employed by the one and that employed by the other can only confuse esthetic discussion. Appreciation of the *oikeia hedone*, the "peculiar pleasure"—and the peculiar medium—of each art is the first requirement of an adequate esthetic, and the eighteenth-century discussions of "parallels" between painting, music and poetry have left a permanent legacy of harm to art criticism in the same way that late nineteenth-century discussions of the relation of literature to music have confused literary theory.

As soon as a novelist decides to employ a subject matter which is obviously significant and interesting for his generation as a whole—if, say, he should write about the Second World War—he is more or less committed to the more solid envelope, to the more rhetorical devices. The temptation, in fact, for a novelist who chooses such a subject is to over-emphasize the rhetorical element in these devices, to make the symbolization too specific, so that the work becomes, not fiction employing legitimate rhetorical devices, but simply rhetoric. This is a fault that can be charged to Eric Knight's *This Above All*, which is more a persuasive discussion of contemporary Britain than a work of literary art. The problem is to give the proper significance to the events by arranging them in the proper order and patterning them in the proper way. And the "proper" significance is their significance as symbols in a novel rather than in a tract or a sermon. A symbol appropriate to fiction is more profound in its implications, is capable of much greater expansion, than a symbol appropriate to simple rhetoric or simple exposition.

But the order of events is obviously only one of the devices which the novelist uses in order to achieve proper symbolization for character and incident. The other is style, the kind of language employed in expressing the individual incident. Style provides a means of symbolizing as you move, it makes possible at each point communication with maximum implication. It is in virtue of style that a description of a walk along a city street can become more than a record of things seen and heard but an interpretation of human experience, a comment on humanity. Style is that unique use of the medium of expression which gives to the thing expressed a meaning which cannot be given in any other way. Like structure, it is a means of providing symbolic expansion of incidents: through style man's behavior becomes man's fate.

Both the proper choice of words, then, and the order and pattern of the incidents, contribute to making minimum into maximum communication, to making a neutral situation into a significant and symbolic one. (Art, indeed, can be defined as unneutral communication, where the belligerency of the artist is unnoticed until it has had its effect: but the artist is fighting to achieve meaning, not to induce action.) What is the relation of these two devices to each other, the relation of style to plot? The fact is that style is really a function of plot: it is the proper handling of the plot at any given moment. Considerations of plot refer to the arrangement of larger units of the story; considerations of style refer to smaller units. But the distinction is theoretical only; actually, they are part of the same thing, they flow into each other.

Literature, like music and unlike painting, communicates its effect in a chronological sequence, in time. And style, depending, like plot, on time, becomes a function of a plot in that by order, emphasis and vocabulary we bring out the implications of (i.e. define *and* enrich) the parts as they are being shaped, by sequence and structure, into a unity. The proper unity and the proper meaning, the proper symbolic expansion, is thus attained in virtue of the style of the writing.

One of the differences between literature and journalism is that, in the former, style is a function of the plot and in the latter it is not. By style we are able to make the time dimension our slave instead of our master, expanding each unit to its proper symbolic significance, building up, by proper retrospect and anticipation, the attitude and the atmosphere in the light of which the work has unity, and the proper unity. Through style an account of a man walking along a busy street on a summer afternoon can be presented as a profound and symbolic interpretation of experience—not through conscious ratiocination or elaboration, not through sentimentality or vagueness, not through digressions or whimsies, but through discipline merely, through proper organization, through style.

To put the matter in yet another way, we might say that style is what adds insight to recognition. This statement presupposes that literature, or at least fiction, ought to communicate to the reader both insight and recognition. That this is so will appear from reflection on the differences between literature and journalism or between purely representative photography and a portrait which is at the same time a work of art. Any work of literary art communicates a note of conviction, of authenticity, so that the reader responds not with the simple reaction of "how true" but with more complex gestures of recognition—not of literal recognition, for few of us have had our fathers murdered by our uncles like Hamlet or have spent our childhood at Combray like Proust, but none the less recognition of the situation presented as fundamentally authentic, as really belonging to human experience. But the function of art is not simple recognition: many a second rate photographer or an indifferent sketcher can produce a reasonable likeness which we will recognize as a picture of a friend or even of a type, and any competent journalist can give a description of a street which we recognize as a street we know or might have known. No, imitation, *mimesis*, is not the function of art: imitation is too easy. If imitation were the sole function of art then the best art would be the real thing—the thing imitated, and art would simply be an approximation to life. But the relation of literature to life is not that of approximation, it is that of illumination. Literature must communicate recognition *and* insight. The reader's reaction is a combination of the "how true" and the "how new." Recognition is communicated through the fundamental agreement between reader and writer about the broad nature of the subject matter, while insight is provided through the illumination given by the proper symbolic expansion, in achieving which both style and plot play their parts.

Writing which produces recognition without insight is journalism, and what produces insight without recognition is philosophy. The majority of routine novels must be classed as journalism rather than as literature, for they communicate recognition without insight (there is no symbolic expansion). The radio serial is another example of this kind of writing: most of the incidents in these stories are extremely true to life, but that is all they are. An interest in the routine daily living of a family just like one's own does not of itself argue any interest in or appreciation of literature. Another kind of inadequate literature is that which depends on the stock response, where the style is a list of clichés and has no organic relation to the plot: here we have second-hand insights presented without that uniqueness of expression necessary for their adequate communication. Much magazine fiction is of this order, and nearly all bad poetry can be explained in a similar way. A third, and not so common type of literary failure derives from improbabilities in the plot—not things which are physically improbable in real life, for these, as Aristotle pointed out, are not necessarily improbabilities for the artist, but contradictions within the work itself which remove all authenticity from the picture of life presented: here we have no recognition and so can have no insight. Occasionally a work of literature strikes us as possessing simply a false pattern—we recognize it as a lie, and no subtlety of style or organization can atone for that. This was at least one reader's reaction to Charles Morgan's *Sparkenbroke*. Fiction which is philosophy rather than art, which communicates insight through discussion or dialogue but not through the way in which we are brought to recognize reality in the work is occasionally found in modern literature; perhaps Santayana's *The Last Puritan*, or Mann's *The Beloved Returns* falls into this category. *Marius the Epicurean* represents an attempt to maintain a precarious balance between the artist's and philosopher's methods of communicating insight, and Pater's novel stands at the head of the modern tradition.

The function of fiction—and perhaps of literature in general —is by producing in the reader a combination of recognition and insight to increase human self-consciousness in a manner which provides both knowledge and pleasure. It is, in fact, a unique way of communicating a unique kind of knowledge. But it would be both puritanical and unrealistic to refuse to admit that while this may be the main function of literature, or the main function of the greatest literature, there are other legitimate if minor kinds of literature which have no other function. A writer of fiction might, for example, choose to produce pure fantasy, having for its function the continual breaking down of the reader's expectations, which results in the reader's refreshment and his discovery of new angles of approach to things. Fantasy in literature has its own laws; it is not simply irresponsible writing. And it has its own special function. It may not be the most profound kind of writing, but it has its place. Fantasy, paradoxically enough, is most likely to make its appearance either in an age where community belief is particularly stable, so that the distinction between fantasy and reality is readily appreciated by the reader, or in a transition period when community belief is so uncertain that the author falls back on fantasy as a kind of relief from the uncertain and difficult business of distinguishing between the real and the fantastic. The latter kind of fantasy is less simple than the former; it represents the abrogation of any responsibility to reality on the author's part rather than a deliberate intention to be unreal, and may appear more or less fantastic to different readers. The former kind of fantasy is a relief from reality: the latter is a relief from deciding what is reality.

If fantasy has its own function, differing from what I have discussed as the main function of literature, so has allegory. In allegory we do not get the kind of expansive symbolization that is appropriate to fiction in general; we get, on the other hand, a specific and limited symbolization with a didactic or illustrative function. Occasionally we get works in which the symbolization is both specific and universal, depending on the way in which it is read, and this is perhaps true of any allegory which survives the audience for which it was written and remains as great literature. Literature can also serve a purely rhetorical function, and a novel can be written, like *Uncle Tom's Cabin*, simply in order to persuade the reader to take up a given course of action; such works ought to be read and assessed as rhetoric, as examples of what the older critics used to call "deliberative oratory." The incidents and characters in such works are not symbols but examples: the difference between the two is very significant. A novel with a rhetorical purpose can nevertheless survive as a great novel if the examples are so treated that, while they are read by the immediate audience as examples, they survive for later audiences not as examples but as symbols.

And we must not forget that a legitimate, if minor, function of literature is simply recreation, play. English literature is particularly rich in this kind of writing: Lewis Carroll and Edward Lear represent a movement that has never been totally dead in England and which seems to emerge whenever the pomposity of the critics has proceeded beyond endurance.

Finally, writing may be just good journalism—vivid description and narration merely. Good journalism is not literature in the fullest sense, for literature is something more than lucid verbal communication; it is, as we have seen, also (in virtue of its style and organization) continuous symbolization. But the line between good journalism and genuine literature is not always easy to draw.

The distinction between the two, however, can best be seen

if we consider the distinction between art and craft. We have already defined journalism as writing which produces recognition without insight and distinguished it from literature, which produces both, simultaneously and cumulatively. Because the artist's insight is unique, it must be communicated uniquely. What we call literary craftsmanship is the means necessary for conveying a unique insight uniquely. For a writer to be an artist he must possess both insight and the skill to convey it. He must have a special kind of vision and a special kind of skill. But the vision, the insight, must be there first. Skill without vision, craftsmanship without insight, is like a telephone with no one to talk into it: it is a useful instrument but it is not serving any purpose. One is reminded of Ruskin's remark on hearing that the first transatlantic cable had been laid and that now one could speak in London and be heard simultaneously in New York. But has the speaker anything to say that is worth saying? What is the use of being able to speak in London and be heard in New York if you have nothing to speak about?

Though we can have craftsmanship without art—skill without insight—it is impossible to have art without craftsmanship. And it is impossible to tell whether the kind of insight demanded of the artist exists or not unless it is communicated through adequate craftsmanship. The matter is complicated by the fact that often the skill appears to be creating the insight, and the experienced artist may often find (at a late stage) that his creative process works best that way. The musical *étude*, which is generally composed simply as a test of craftsmanship in the composer and executive ability in the performer, often automatically becomes art. Who can tell at what point a technical exercise in the writing of a fugue may cease to be an exercise and become a work of art? Anyone who has learned to play a musical instrument will know how a "study" tends to become a "piece."

This particular problem is more acute in music because, unlike painting and literature, music does not have any representational element: the distinction between form and content ceases to exist. Yet the problem is present in some degree in the other arts as well, and is clearly illustrated today in the great number of writers who possess a high degree of skill but seem to have no insights to justify their employing their skill. The typical *New Yorker* short story provides a good example of the writer who possesses craftsmanship without insight. These stories are not works of art; they are studies, exercises, études, übungen— yet occasionally they manage to approach art through sheer competence of technique, as though insight were created by skill. What actually takes place is more a problem for the psychologist than the critic; the psychology of literary creation is a vast and complicated subject in itself, and is not really relevant to the present discussion. For the important thing to the critic is what the work is, not how the author managed to produce it.

If craftsmanship without insight produces a kind of superior journalism—something between ordinary journalism and genuine art—it might perhaps be said that a Silver Age in literature is simply an age of excellent craftsmen who are not artists, an age of skill without insight. The twenty years between the two world wars seems to have been such a period both in Europe and America. As for the problem of insight without craft—we can never know about that, for if the skill is not there to communicate the insight we can never be aware of it. It might even be maintained that the kind of insight we associate with the artist cannot exist except in conjunction with the appropriate craftsmanship, so closely are the two bound up. That this kind of insight actually derives from sensitivity to the art medium is perhaps too rash a generalization, though it does appear to do so in the case of particular writers. There appear, in fact, to be two main classes of artists, those who begin with a sensitivity to the medium and are stimulated into their vision by an excitement over the potentialities of the medium, and those who begin with their insight and then proceed to find the appropriate means of adequate communication. At least in poetry this seems to be the case (witness the difference between Keats, say, and Milton) though in actual fact neither group may work in such a simple manner. But we are deviating again into the psychology of artistic creation.

What, then, are the problems for modern novelists? The novelist ought to possess, first, an understanding of the nature of his symbolization and, second, an understanding of the method he employs to achieve that symbolization. Third, he must be aware of the way in which his methods depend on his relation to his audience. A fourth problem concerns the significance of the relation between plot and style, and a fifth is the more complicated one raised by the question of rhetoric, belief and symbolization that we have already discussed. Two further problems face the modern novelist. He must be aware of the kinds of faults that most threaten the contemporary writer, and he must have some real understanding of the nature and value of his art. The latter point is particularly important in a time when a total war is being waged for civilization, for at such a time we must prepare to justify everything we hold valuable.

RICHARD EBERHART:
EMPSON'S POETRY

"Delicate goose-step of penned scorpions"

C OINCIDENCE dictated that I should be up at Cambridge co-
terminously with Empson, hence that I should be intimately
aware of his poetic career from its inception. At twenty-one
Empson was, with Hugh Sykes-Davies, editing *Experiment,* the
livelier of the two literary magazines which mushroomed among
the undergraduates, and was also contributing to the other, *New
Venture.*

In the first number of *Experiment* appeared three of Empson's
poems: "Letter," beginning "You were amused to find you too
could fear / 'The eternal silence of the infinite spaces' " (entitled
"Letter I" in the 1935 edition of his first *Poems,* from Chatto
and Windus); the amusing, startling "Part of Mandevil's Travels"
(likewise republished in the book); and "Disillusion with Metaphysics" (later printed as "Dissatisfaction with Metaphysics" with
variations in two lines). George Reavy, J. Bronowski, E. E.
Phare, Hugh Sykes, and T. H. White were other original contributors. (Miss Phare, who was later to write one of the first
books on Hopkins, here contributed an article on Valéry and
Hopkins.)

The second number of *Experiment* contained two other Empson poems, "Camping Out," a brain-tickler which exercised
many hours of drawing-room discussion in Cambridge, and with-
held its ultimate ambiguous secrets for years, and "The Earth
Has Shrunk in the Wash." The same issue offered the prose
"Ambiguity in Shakespeare's Sonnet XVI," which began those

extraordinary microscopic and expanding views of grammatical context in poetry which were elaborated to make *Seven Types of Ambiguity*. The pupil of I. A. Richards inflamed the imagination of his master: Richards understood instantly Empson's value. Although the chief indebtedness in the association of the two Magdalene men since 1927 has been that of Empson to Richards —the prefatory note to *Seven Types* includes the author's statement that Richards "told me to write this essay"—, the master exploited the fineness of mind of the pupil, wise to see in Empson's beginning criticism a nice adjunct to and a different end from his own. And as late as 1940, he wrote an appreciation of Empson in *Furioso*. In this same second number of *Experiment* appeared my "Request for Offering." I, too, in a less direct manner, was to fall under the spell of the master; to him I owed, and owe, heady allegiance for the sensitivity he evinced in every manifestation of poetry one exhibited.

Experiment began in November, 1928, and ended in October, 1930, with its sixth number. Empson made contributions to all the remaining numbers: prose on Herbert's "The Sacrifice" and on T. S. Eliot, and five additional poems, all of which have reappeared in his later volumes of verse, some with alterations. Empson also published a good many poems at this time in *The Cambridge Review*.

The scholar may enjoy noting how Empson worked alterations as I quote first the periodical version (1928) of "Relativity," then the 1935 book version with its new title, "The World's End":

RELATIVITY

"Fly to the world's end, dear.
Plumb space through stars.
Let final chasm, topless cliffs, appear;
What tyrant there our variance debars?

Live there, your back freezing to All's Wall,
Or brinked by chasm that all chasms bounds;
There, with two times at choice, all plots forestall,
Or, no time backing you, what force surrounds?"

Alas, now hope for freedom, no bars bend;
Space is like earth, rounded, a padded cell.

Plumb the stars' depth, your lead bumps you behind;
Blind Satan's voice rattled the whole of Hell.

On air, on cushions, what's a file worth
To pierce that chasm lies so snugly curled?
Each tangent plain touches one top of earth;
Each point in one direction ends the world.

Apple of knowledge and forgetful mere
From Tantalus too differential bend;
The world's end is here.
This place's curvature precludes its end.

THE WORLD'S END

"Fly with me then to all's and the world's end
And plumb for safety down the gap of stars;
Let the last gulf or topless cliff befriend,
What tyrant there our variance debars?"

Alas, how hope for freedom, no bars bind;
Space is like earth, rounded, a padded cell;
Plumb the stars' depth, your lead bumps you behind;
Blind Satan's voice rattled the whole of Hell.

On cushioned air what is such metal worth
To pierce to the gulf that lies so snugly curled?
Each tangent plain touches one top of earth,
Each point in one direction ends the world.

Apple of knowledge and forgetful mere
From Tantalus too differential bend.
The shadow clings. The world's end is here.
This place's curvature precludes its end.

It has always seemed a pity to me that several excellent poems,
of the profusion of work Empson produced in a relatively short
time, have been omitted from his books. Three poems in particular deserve to be more available than they are in the files of
The Cambridge Review and in the anthology *Cambridge Poetry
1929*. Conditions are such that I am unable to credit *The Cambridge Review* with thanks for the liberty of quotation, but it
is hoped that the editors would have no objection to my quoting
these three poems at this time.

The first poem, "Une Brioche Pour Cerbere," employs Empson's sly wit, the first four lines reminding one in tone of "Rolling

the Lawn" with its unforgettable "Holding the Holy Roller at
the slope / (The English symbol, not the Texas Pope)":

UNE BRIOCHE POUR CERBERE

Tom nods. No senior angels see or grapple.
Tom enters Eden, nodding, the back way.
Borrows from Adam, and then eats, the Apple.
"Thank you so much for a delightful stay."

If it works, it works. Nod to the man at the door.
Nor heed what gulfs, nor how much the earth between.
If radio light, from the last sphere before
Outer dark, reflects you, you are seen.

So can the poles look in each other's eyes.
Within that charmed last vacuate of air
Who is my neighbor, and who safe from spies?
Earth sees me nod. No, nothing to declare.

Porter, report not my heart contraband.
Of you, you primitive culture, stored flame,
I scotophile, friend by short cut, had planned
To view the rites, no high priest first to tame.

My dear, my earth how offer me your halls?
Grant me your Eden, I see Eden Station,
Whence stationed gauge you whose full scale appals
And all whose porters would ask explanation?

The next poem shows a spirit of gaiety even then characteristic of the author: unbridled, but well-reined, gaiety of word-
play:

NEW WORLD BISTRES

The darkest is near dawn, we almost butter.
The churning is fixed now; we have "gone to sleep"
In body, and become a living pat;
It is then that the arm churning it aches most
And dares least pause against the ceaseless turning.
I am sure he will soon stumble upon the gift,
Maypole his membranes, Ciro be his eyes,
A secret order, assumptive, distillation;
Fitting together it will be won and seem nothing.
    Oh socketed too deep, Oh more than tears,
Than any faint unhurrying resurrection,
That ever rain, manna (the manner born,
The man born of the manor, and that bourne
Turn Cardinal Bourne. The Palace, Washing Day.

Lux and her cherub, here is a nymph handy.)
Those glacial, dried soap film, shaken packets,
That rain of hushing, elixir-centred sequins,
Falling through space, gracious, a feather swaying.
　　　Rising, triumphant, hooter, whine, mosquito,
The separator, pausing by violent movement
Stands at the even not skimming of stood cream.
Moss can be grown on tops. Gyroscopes
Holed with grim jewels set in resounding brass
Rector and tractor of earth's vertiges,
Claw, widely patented, pierce, sinking,
Armoured resentience their lead fathom line.

The third poem, in loaded gear, follows:

INSOMNIA

Satan when ultimate chaos he would fly
battered at random by hot dry wet cold
(Probably nor Probability
his view the total cauldron of a sky
Milton nor Brownian hesitance foretold)
One purposed whirlwind helpless whole hours could hold.

　　From Bottomless Pit's bottom originally
　　who durst his sail-broad vans unfold
　　thence till (God's help the rival gust came by)
　　Hell seemed as Heaven undistinguishedly high
　　Through pudding still unstirred of Anarch Old
　　had sunk yet, down for ever, by one blast controlled.

So to the baked Chaos that am I,
Potion whose cooling boat grates crystal shoaled
gears on a mixed bank allotropically
untempered patchwork to the naked eye,
one hour the snow's one pattern, and I bold,
gale knew its point all night, though nine through compass rolled.

　　Though large charged carpet units insulately
　　alone processed, each from the former's mould,
　　each further angle could new shades supply,
　　roads every earlier opposite to tie
　　in single type Hell's very warders scrolled,
　　Nine intersterile species nightmare's full Nine were foaled.

There is another early poem, never reprinted since its appearance in *Experiment* No. 4 (November, 1929), which has stuck
in my mind and calls for comment now:

UFA NIGHTMARE

Gramophony. Telephony. Photophony.
The mighty handles and persensate dials
That rule my liner multi-implicate
Ring round, Stonehenge, a wide cold concrete room.
(I run the row from A to O, and so
—To and fro; periscope, radio—
We know which way we go)
        "If we can reach the point
Before the tide, there is another style.
I shall checkmate, given the whole board;
Juggling the very tittles in the air
Shall counterblast the dreadnought machiner."
        (Scamper, scamper, scamper.
Huge elbows tumble towards chaos.
Lurch, sag, and hesitation of the dials.)
        A tiny figure, seated in the engine,
        Weevil clicking in a hollow oak,
        Pedals, parched with the fear of solitude.

Here was a remarkable poem, timely then as it still is. Its title, wickedly foreign, excused its oddity, let one wander in the dream, yet there was something scientifically precise about it. It had wit; originality in every line; very subtle music; drama; lines that strode across the years, summing up the age; and, as in most of Empson's poetry, a strange quality of hiding the meanings, hoarding its strength, elusively secreting delicacies of perception.

The first line was novel. One had not heard a poem start that way. The license, however, was not excessive: something balanced about the three terms, which you never knew whether you were pronouncing properly, a fact giving the more pleasure —you wondered whether the author calculated even on that, or whether it was merely your stupidity—, and there was the other level of meaning in the sound of "phony." Line two went off with a great swish, quite released from the first, or even a Miltonic dignity. One had the tendency in Empson to enjoy single successful lines, savoring them as they were, out of context with their grammatical relation to previous or succeeding lines; and this was one. What his "liner" was one did not yet know;

"multi-implicate" was new; "Stonehenge" was thrown up in your face. You finally derived pleasure from using this last as a verb, certainly a novel notion, but you could take it as a noun singly, giving a different and yet quite similar suggestion to "wide cold concrete room." Contrast of the static with the dynamic, ancient simplicity with modern complexity. Then the musical lilt of the next three parenthetical lines, how accurately the music controlled! I recall a vague feeling of similarity with Hart Crane here, the only place in Empson, quite evanescent, probably wrong. "We know which way we go" struck me as masterful, for I never knew in those years which way I was going—would have loved to know—but that is going out of context again.

Now supposedly the technician is speaking. Something dramatic and opulent in the first two lines. Switch to a chess image; odd, but provocative, keeping it from being too nautical. "Juggling the very tittles in the air" was a ravishing line. It was what the greatest critical insight always did: it lifted you up high into the rarefied air of exquisite contemplation. I always thought of it as what Empson as poet and critic was doing. Again that nice contrast between two lines, in the heavier consonantal values of the "counterblast." "Juggling the very tittles in the air" was delicious! Juggling them, all most delicate thought or perception would finally overcome the heavy opposing weight of world or matter, put all in order.

The scamper motif was transitional, referred back to the first line. The huge elbows tumbling toward chaos went on telling the story, commenting on machinery. "Lurch, sag, and hesitation of the dials" was another line which stuck in my head. As a single line it was magnificent. You could take it all together, or you could draw it out. The line following, "A tiny figure, seated in the engine," stuck, too, became for me universal, a universal picture of modern man. The ensuing shift to the weevil "clicking" (strange relation to mechanics) in the hollow oak (even the weevil endowed with some mechanical similarity to man) was justified in the same way the chess image had been. And then the poem ended subtly with another change of tone, stress, grammar, seemingly awkwardly, and you could take it more ways than one. The whole poem was a compact piece, in which a various new world was ready to expand in the mind, baring images not violently opposed to the world as it was.

II

In December, 1939, when he had come to America from Japan but before he had returned to England, Empson told me that he considered his early poems in the nature of experiments, trial balloons or something of the sort. He was glad his criticism had "caught on" in this country, but was not surprised that his poetry had not. He said he had written some verse in the East, but not much. I recall prophesying that it would take America a decade to discover and estimate Empson as a poet, and I was short of the mark. It may be permissible now to discuss the nature of his contribution to poetry, in his early phase, before considering his second book.

First, let it be said that during my time at Cambridge, 1927-1929, Empson was considered a startling poet by the learned. His mind had early been weighted on the mathematical and scientific side; he was rather Shelleyan in that, as he was in his exodus from Cambridge, for reasons as interesting to this century as were those of Shelley to his. Empson was brisk, quick-moving, florid. When he took the Tripos in June, 1929, they had had to give him not only a First, but a starred First, a rare distinction. No American, I understand, has ever won one.

In Cambridge everybody talked about Empson's poetry. His poems challenged the mind, seemed to defy the understanding; they amused and they enchanted; and even then they afforded a kind of parlor game, whiling away lively hours of puzzlement at many a dinner party. The shock and impact of this new kind of poetry were so considerable that people at that time had no way to measure its contemporary or its timeless value. They were amazed by it. Eliot was already enthroned. The "Oxford

Group" had not yet got fully under way. And Cambridge was buzzing with activity.

Empson had the power to shock. Old dowagers who had known Meredith (I remember one), or young girls from Girton who knew their Hopkins, or dons who talked much but did not know where they stood, were stumped, balked and rebuked by "Camping Out," which began: "And now she cleans her teeth into the lake." You could read the poem twenty times and not know what it meant! You could read it so many ways! You could argue about the grammar by the hour! And as for the meaning, did Richards himself know for sure? It was all so intellectual, so exciting, so very Cantabridgean.

This is not the place to dwell upon the course of the poet's activities. Had Richards not gone to China, where he was for one thing preparing his book on Mencius, it is questionable whether Empson would have gone to the East. The reserve of his mind was such that the *Poems*, his first volume, did not appear until 1935. This seems significant. Meanwhile, the "Auden gang" had raged on the world, the world was listening to them, there was a bewilderment of opinion as to the relative merits and demerits of each, they had their "little mag," their anthologies. The new signatures were on the wing. The excavations into sociological reality made by Auden constituted an enlargement of English poetry from its immediate past; one thought of the service of enlargement made earlier by Browning. (Or, better, one did not think of it; Browning was unmentionable.) I have said an enlargement, not a deepening. And if Oxford had seemed to produce something thought of at this time as a school, the Cambridge writers maintained their lack of group consciousness, their strict individuality and, in Empson's case, their austere meticulous distance. The Oxford writers went out to woo the world; Empson, as an epitome of Cambridge attitudes, remained aloof, in a kind of scientific maze of his own words. Let the world come to his poetry when it would. His modesty coupled with his wit might have convinced him it was not a worldshake anyway. But Empson, whatever initially caused his poetry, was typically a Cambridge writer: the passion for meticulous truth, the scientific attitudes intruding on poetry to rule out anything "romantic," the care for minute perceptions communicated in a subtle way, the daring exercise of new grammatical possibilities of English, under the aegis of a master, these made for a poetry not in the old style of the humanities, but in a new, a sharper, a keener but also perhaps a less profound mode.

Some points in favor of the early poems follow. Not only did Empson load every rift with ore; he loaded them with more than one kind of substance. The compression of his images and the conscious ambiguity of his grammar, when he exercised both, were salutary in that they insured the reader against the ragged or the loose. A poem of his would not yield its meanings immediately, but one would be well paid in time: a sign of good poetry. It was a poetry of concealed riches. Another point was in the seemingly almost perfect control of the use of language. There was no excess in these poems. If they were bizarre, they did not offend; if witty, they did not degenerate into foolishness; if elaborate, they did not invite careless attention; if puzzling, they enchanted one with the answers. They expressed a certain aristocracy of intellect, but were not aloof from fundamental propositions. They constituted a microcosm of realities.

Against Empson's early poetry charges could be leveled and were indeed applied. This poetry was not "great" because it was not "universal." There was no world-view, no philosophic, inclusive view behind the poems. It was repeatedly said that they were too purely intellectual: the compliment was turned into an adverse criticism. His look was too rarefied for human nature's daily food. On an old measuring rod of the simple, the sensuous, and the passionate, these poems could not rate high; they were not simple, they were not sensuous, and their passion was limited to the intellectual kind. Others held that the poems did not cohere; these found disorder who had not imagination enough to divine the niceties of a new order. Others held that when wit dominates to the extent it did in these poems, the sign was of a certain smallness; the great poets all had a nobility, a depth, a seriousness lacking in this work. And still others believed that a religious consciousness, traditionally based, in one mode or another, such as had given Eliot "Ash Wednesday," was necessary for the scale of importance which these poems did not touch.

For perfection of form, precision of statement, and delight of language, some of Empson's early poems will last as long as any of those of his contemporaries. Richards, who may be excused the bias of a learned teacher upon a learned pupil, thinks Empson is the best of the lot. Be that as it may. It is probable that the early poems constitute minor poetry of a high order. That in itself is very considerable achievement. Some are satisfied with a few poems of Marvell; some would be satisfied with one. Values notoriously change; a decade or two hence those now considered major may be considered minor, and vice versa. It is conceivable that a few of Empson's poems may be read ages hence.

Some single lines which impressed themselves upon me for a decade I shall quote. They became part of the fullness of one's consciousness. "How small a chink lets in how dire a foe." "Space is like earth, rounded, a padded cell." "Blind Satan's voice rattled the whole of Hell." "Each point in one direction ends a world." "Delicate goose-step of penned scorpions." "Gods cool in turn, by the sun long outlasted." "I approve, myself, dark spaces between stars." "It is the pain, it is the pain, endures." " 'Twixt devil and deep sea, man hacks his caves." "Solomon's gems, white vistas, preserved kings." "Law makes long spokes of the short stakes of men." "One daily tortures the poor Christ anew." "The laughing god born of a startling answer." "All those large dreams by which men long live well / Are magic-lanterned on the smoke of Hell." "The beam of Justice as in doubt for ever Hung like a Zeppelin over London river."

III

Before going on to consider Empson's second book, *The Gathering Storm*, we may take a poem of his from the first book, which also appeared in *New Signatures*, and work it as a good specimen of Empson's poetical powers.

THIS LAST PAIN

This last pain for the damned the Fathers found:
"They knew the bliss with which they were not crowned."
    Such, but on earth, let me foretell,
    Is all, of heaven or of hell.

Man, as the prying housemaid of the soul,
May know her happiness by eye to hole:
    He's safe; the key is lost; he knows
    Door will not open, nor hole close.

"What is conceivable can happen too,"
Said Wittgenstein, who had not dreamt of you;
    But wisely; if we worked it long
    We should forget where it was wrong:

Those thorns are crowns which, woven into knots,
Crackle under and soon boil fool's pots;
    And no man's watching, wise and long,
    Would ever stare them into song.

Thorns burn to a consistent ash, like man;
A splendid cleanser for the frying-pan:
    And those who leap from pan to fire
    Should this brave opposite admire.

All those large dreams by which men long live well
Are magic-lanterned on the smoke of hell;
    This then is real, I have implied,
    A painted, small, transparent slide.

These the inventive can hand-paint at leisure,
Or most emporia would stock our measure;
    And feasting in their dappled shade
    We should forget how they were made.

Feign then what's be a decent tact believed
And act that state is only so conceived,
    And build an edifice of form
    For house where phantoms may keep warm.

Imagine, then, by miracle, with me,
(Ambiguous gifts, as what gods give must be)
    What could not possibly be there,
    And learn a style from a despair.

Line 1. The question to be asked about this line is: do we need to know what theology is intended? Also, do we need to know about the author's private attitude to religion to determine what he may want to suggest by Fathers?

2. Supposedly they are in hell; supposedly they knew the bliss before they were damned. Paolo and Francesca?

3. "Such" refers to the bliss. Empson would be the one to dilate on his use of "but" here. If bliss occurs on earth, that is all there is to heaven and hell. "Let me foretell" rings ominously.

4. The comma could be left out after "all." Used, it emphasizes "all," makes it substantial, a universal, and affects a nuance in the rhythm of the line. The comma also throws a slight stress on the word "or," which it otherwise might not have, lending a slightly different connotation than if "heaven" and "hell" were equally stressed, with "or" merely as a link. Bliss we might have expected to have been all of heaven; now we are invited to the notion that it would be "all" of hell. He can be using both terms in a generic, and also in a "worldly" way, simultaneously. It may be illogical to suppose there could be any bliss in hell; yet this may be taken in the sense of the pleasures of worldly sin. The point of the quatrain is, however, that they had known bliss in this life; that was final, whatever would happen to them upon damnation after death.

The first quatrain is firm in tone, dignified, serious, controlled, stating the problem. The musical quality of the verse is apparent. Low-register rhyme words are employed for damnation, "found," "crowned." When he makes a dictum, the poet uses higher-register rhyme words, "foretell," "hell," as appropriate to the sense of bliss.

5-8. These four lines can be considered together, the sense running on. Recall "the damp souls of housemaids." Housemaids need not be prying, but are so posited for purposes of the comparison. We must expect here a kind of Empsonian wit available in other poems of his. The tone, therefore, is made lighter than in the first quatrain; a kind of metaphysical joke is supplied. But the meaning behind the levity is equal to that in the first quatrain; the basis is agnosticism, astringently intellectualized. Man may know the happiness of the soul as a prying housemaid might look through a keyhole. The use of "to hole" as an infinitive is a liberty taken with grammatical oddity which is characteristic of Empson: but it comes off. But, again, the words are ambiguous; if "hole" is taken as a noun, a less metaphysical, more straightforward possibility will pertain: you are getting somewhere. Maybe "the key *is* lost." This is all rather funny. At any rate, man is safe; he knows the door of the soul will not open, therefore he can go on looking through it; the keyhole will not close, so that he can go on contemplating. There is a smirk to the passage, which is both a criticism of and a satire upon bliss, a criticism and satire upon man contemplating his own soul.

9-12. Perhaps the key is not lost. Empson had watched Wittgenstein walk through the streets of Cambridge. The sentence (I have not looked it up in the *Tractatus*) is pompous. "But wisely" suggests the egocentric nature of the philosopher (or of the author); he may be looking through a keyhole, but certainly he is not looking at us. The rest of the quatrain speaks common sense, which is, however, too often forgotten in such matters as these: it doesn't do any good to ponder too long: you can see things at a glance with greater clarity than through prolonged study, sometimes.

13-16. These begin to bind together the foregoing information. Some changes were made in the grammar of lines 13, 14. You can play with the idea of the crown of thorns here. The negative statement is at least affirmative!

17-20. These four lines were added to the original version. The teacher is at the board with his pointer.

21-24. The first two lines are the most compelling of the poem. They weigh upon the memory. The rhythm recalls line 13, 14 of Shakespeare's Sonnet 129:

> All this the world well knows yet none knows well,
> To shun the heaven that leads men to (this) hell.

Empson does not go so far as this last line of Shakespeare, yet he has implied a similar attitude in the poem up to this point. The large dreams are magic-lanterned on the smoke of hell. The smoke of hell may justify the boiling pot, although not only fools go to hell. "Magic-lanterned" gives a tone of artifice to the large dreams, seen as pictures (through the keyhole?) on or in smoke which itself is shifting by nature. But magical, too.

In lines 9-16 low-register rhyme words were employed; now, as in lines 3-4, when the poet offers his dictum, higher-register rhyme sounds are used. The slide, the keyhole, the membrane through which reality is perceived seems to be called the final reality, arbiter of the knower and the known.

25-28. "Most" was substituted for "all" in line 2, a musical loss, I feel. Here the will seems to be given the initiating power; else a great prince lies in prisons he did not build. Subjectivity is not easily lost. The inventive mind can make its own pictures of heaven and hell. Agnosticism again; or at least no acceptance of orthodox dogma; and at most, skepticism. Empson, or you, or I, can feast in a Marvellian dappled shade if we like, forgetful in our own wish.

29-32. This begins the resolution of the poem. Keep up the pretense for what it is worth. There is delicate self-abnegation here, grave reticence, although they may carry a strong under-tone of recognition of the futility of the position—yet there is some pleasure in it.

33-36. Higher-register rhyme sounds are used to round off the whole proposition. It is the complete skeptic who can and must imagine miracles. The poem is so good that one wonders why it might not be enjoyed in 2044. But see Empson's note to the poem; a reader may read more into it than was intended. "The idea of the poem is that human nature can conceive divine states which it cannot attain."

IV

In 1940, five years after the first volume, appeared *The Gathering Storm*, from Faber's. We might begin with the notes. Again he has supplied these, this time in greater abundance, and in themselves they constitute occasional prose of remarkable nicety. The note to "Bacchus" is reprinted intact, with one sentence tidied up: "*Glancer:* she made eyes at both opposites at once" becomes "Glancer: she looked both ways and wanted heaven as real as earth." Indeed, the total new note to "Bacchus," which goes on for about six pages, is a mine of Empsoniana. He is as good on his own poem as he can be on any poem, approaches it with as avid a disinterest, and divulges what minutiae his critical acumen deems sufficient. He does the critic's job for him. This is bound up in the notion that "many people (like myself) prefer to read poetry mixed with prose; it gives you more to go by; the conventions of poetry have been getting far off from normal life, so that to have a prose bridge makes reading poetry seem more natural." The idea gives on to a deeper apology for his poems: "But partly they are meant to be like answers to a crossword puzzle; a sort of puzzle interest is part of the pleasure that you are meant to get from the verse, and that I get myself when I go back to it." The earlier poems seem to me to come more closely under this concept than the later ones, which are not as difficult as those, excepting that "Bacchus," now stretched out to seven stanzas, remains fascinatingly difficult. His "clotted kind of poetry" does not actually have the clots of the earlier work. Nobody could improve on his notes; one could only quibble here or there. So there is nothing to say on this score, and they are recommended to the reader entire. You could read the new poems without the notes; or you could read the notes without the poems, if only to savor the exegetical Empson mind.

The poems in the second book take in a wider range of experience (China principally); they maintain his near-genius for precision; they bear the undeniable look and stamp of his other poems, are on the whole less ambiguous, become merrier and gayer in tone, and they achieve a break-down of his style, towards the end, into what seems to be a newer style, but this is not as masterful as the old. The density of sense is the same; the poet writes with authority and charm; yet the adverse criticisms heretofore mentioned stay, and the favorable notations are given again. There has been no profound change in the nature of his thinking; this volume is a continuance of the first, rather than a new departure.

"Your Teeth Are Ivory Towers" regales us with the witty rhymes, "Ba," "Pa," and "Ha," which only Empson could achieve. He likes the three-line stanza, which he employed so successfully before. The poem is marred for me, however, by two phrases, "only the child" and "we must deliberate," which echo directly Auden in "Another Time."

"Aubade" is a telling poem. Note the plainness, the directness of it in comparison with earlier poems. He says what he says. Note also the reluctance to part with the three-line stanza, here interspersed.

"Four Legs, Two Legs, Three Legs" returns nearly to the difficulty of the early work, but is easier to comprehend than, say, "Camping Out." It seems revealing that Empson should take a "Reflection from Rochester." He would not reflect from Wordsworth (cf. the sally in "New World Bistres"). He is further revealed, dated, savored, in a "Reflection from Anita Loos."

Empson earlier dignified the villanelle form with serious import in the two excellent pieces beginning, "It is the pain, it is the pain, endures" and "Twixt devil and deep sea, man hacks his caves." We are now given another equal to these, the beautiful poem entitled "Missing Dates," beginning "Slowly the poison the whole blood stream fills." In addition to this masterful line, a second of equal single power is "The waste remains, the waste remains and kills." These add to the universality of utterance I claimed for Empson above. "The fat is in the pyre, boy, waiting for the end," from "Just a Smack at Auden," in his rollicking vein, will not soon be forgotten. The cleverness of the satirical monotony with which he builds up his rhymes on the word "end" in this poem deserves mention: a cutting and a cunning imitation and devitalization.

Nothing is more characteristic of his funds of abstruse knowledge than the matter of the liver fluke in the poem "China." "That the thing can play these tricks without having any structure at all is what is so frightening; it is like demoniacal possession."

In the last poem, "Autumn on Nan-Yueh," Empson cuts loose from compression and lets his words fly with an ease and brilliancy unparalleled in his other work, although you may think the poem is not serious enough. He writes with the sheerest pleasure, making perfect strokes ("We do not fly when we are clay. / We hope to fly when we are dust." Or "And all styles can come down to noise") with rapid energy forming the most readable verse, seemingly informal and off-hand, yet composed in a strict but stately measure recalling the eighteenth century. If this is the stylistic way out of his formerly tortured verse, we can ask for more, even if we reproach him a bit for confiding his matter to the architecture of an old verse form rather than beating out something new to him and new to us. Although one line, "Excuses, consequences, signs" sounds of Pope, "the heat-mists" of his vision drive the words into strongly original ways, and the pleasure of reading is the pleasure of reading the best kind of light verse, a heady pleasure. "I hope the gaiety of the thing comes through."

OTIS FERGUSON:

WHILE WE WERE LAUGHING

THE STATUS of film comedy in America has suffered from two
things. The first may be called Hollywood apathy. The
second and more important is the low-rating of Hollywood, the
breast-beating, the abject apology for the near and native that has
been the occupation of our intellectual classes and the stand-by of
what leaders they may have in the critics. This last attitude has
its importance as attitude, though of all the arts today the movie
is the least affected by what thinking people find to think about it.

When I got the Chair of Films in a journal seven years ago,
there were two things you could be outside of (1) a trade-critic,
whose job is to report on comparative values and box-office
chances, and (2) Gilbert Seldes, whose enthusiasms for the vulgar
arts were designedly and successfully flash. You were on the
dailies as an ex-legman or press-agent with broken wind and a
liquid yearning eye on the dramah page; or you went upper-case
on the weeklies and monthlies, seeing what played at the arty
shoebox houses and speaking sternly in tongues such as the French
(*regisseur*) to confound your readers, who felt elevated by the
experience and then sneaked off twice a week to see the feature
at Loew's.

In those days there were two names operative in American
film comedy, and you used them in constant allusion: Chaplin
and Disney. Enough authoritative and erroneous articles had been
published so that you could mention the Selig and Keystone lots
for an historical footnote. Otherwise you stayed abroad, where
in Russian films the characters spoke Russian.

I bring this up only because, getting started at that time, I was in at the birth of another institution in American movie humor and was still reading carefully to find out what a critic ought to criticize. And I can report that you could have read the critics' circle until it squared without ever having guessed that within a year of its modest opening "It Happened One Night" would have become an absolutely gilt-edged source of reference for lowbrow and highbrow alike. The film came in as another comedy—oh, quite harmless and amusing if you like that sort of thing. But it stuck so well that—with Capra now gone off the deep end apparently for good, hunting the wild platitude in Shangri-La and all that—his name is spelled in some of the biggest letters that ever went up on a marquee.

And what made him? The critics? Baby talk. The critics have given wilder raves to pictures they couldn't remember the director of to save their space-rates today. Capra had already made a few pictures, his "Lady for a Day" and "The Bitter Tea of General Yen" being clearly recalled by a small but intense following. What made him on this comedy was the public, which went back to "It Happened One Night," and went back again. They talked it up, and it kept replaying dates all year and became an outstanding example of what the trade calls word-of-mouth build-up. It made history while the historians were asleep. The pay-off was that, while it was just a picture at the beginning of the year and was only in third place in the fall when five hundred national movie reviewers were rounded up in the Film Daily poll, it swept the field of awards by Christmas.

So Capra was a genius, yet was in print; it was enough to say of any other director that he wasn't Capra. In some fonts of type it was only necessary to remark that Hollywood had a director who was *presque regisseur* and to add his name to those of Disney and Charlot (as we lovingly call him) for a perfect three-point landing.

But this sort of thing cuts two ways. A certain universal acceptance and delight will put a director's name up in lights, and reviewers just have to go down the line. But once the people who are all the time talking and writing have got a thing accepted as a topic of polite literary allusion, the bird with the big director's

name can throw the weight of his prestige around in either direction. He can make the world's best features and get away with
it. Or he can make the world's worst, and for all you can read
anywhere he is still getting away with it. And that is where the
intellectuals come in, with the sub-intellectuals on the popular
magazines and feature-sections following with their tongues hanging down like red neckties. All the talk, talk, talk gives a man a
rating. It's the simple human assumption that where there is
smoke someone must be burning.

This is where we come to the subject of film comedy in America. It is really a tradition, with the great anonymous back-log of
all the people who have worked something out, or set a standard,
or patterned a custom, that has to be in anything before it can be
a tradition. It isn't just the two or ten names you can remember
because they have been spattered all over the place in bold face.
Just ask yourself: who made "The Front Page"? "The Gilded
Lily"? "My Man Godfrey"? "The Milky Way"? "Sing and Like
It"? "The Captain Hates the Sea"? "Forsaking All Others"? "Stage
Door"? "The Shop Around the Corner"? "Stand In"? "Twen-
tieth Century"? "Design for Living"? "The Gay Divorcee"?
"Jimmie the Gent"? "Something to Sing About"? "I Met Him in
Paris"? "Swing High Swing Low"? "The Beachcomber"? "The
Thin Man"? "Desire"? "Vivacious Lady"? "Bachelor Mother"?

All right—you remember some of the titles, what the stories
were about and who played the leads. But who was responsible
for a story's being done the way you remember it? Of course
any given picture includes a range of talents and many lucky
combinations—with this story but a different cast, or treatment,
etc.; with this director but a different producer or budget, etc.
(If you try to go past who was responsible for anything *as
credited* to who was actually responsible, you will go crazy—let
it alone.) The point is that we have in the best pictures a comedy
expression that is peculiar to the films. Many men in the American
studios worked this funny thing out by hand and at great labor—
yet who of those laughing knew what men they were, or cared?

While we were laughing, were we paying attention? Do we
realize even today that there is a form in comedy as native as the

air we breathe, that it has been developed partly in writing and on the stage but finds its most individual expression in the quick shadows of the screen? I doubt it.

Like any true thing ever achieved, this form owes many debts to other things and times and places. Its kingpin, Chaplin, got his training in the music-halls of England; its more subtle directors have learned a good deal from Lubitsch and René Clair; it is endlessly dependent on what in the Western World is funny and what isn't. But it has used these many old things to make a new thing, and it has been jabbed along to much faster and funnier effects than the old stage ever achieved, *per minute*, by the original demand of films for speed and variety.

This new comedy form, without the presence of flesh-and-blood performers and in the early years without music and voices, placed a severe demand on the department of visual contrasts and upsets. There was no room for gradual development, for the labored, tedious exposition of stage shows, for the stagnant patter of vaudeville turns and minstrel endmen. Something had to be happening all the time, and it couldn't be the same thing. After the first few years, even camera and cutting tricks were old stuff unless they kept being new stuff or were used differently.

Against these challenges to the inventive mind, the men of the old Mack Sennett productions worked day and night. It is too easy to remember that the pies thrown were invariably coconut-custard and five inches deep. It is not so easy to identify such elemental confectionary with comedy as we know it today. But what they were working on was the outline of it: the fast and furious, the surprise through a new kind of motion developed in the camera eye and the cutting room. Since something had to be happening every minute, new effects were devised on location, and pioneers in the technical department kept on developing ways to make them more visible—learning that there is an angle and an instant at which the true point of any motion may be caught, figuring distances and planes and cutting possibilities toward this end. Although the main formula for early comedy, as still remembered by its ever-bawdy and succinct practitioners, was "a kick in the ass and cut to chase," the way of capturing this for the screen was vastly complicated and became not only more so but a governing factor in the business of making comedy and still getting a laugh.

Now it is ironic but provable that before Capra the one man to make best uses of the screen art as it had been developed in the old days by Keystone was René Clair, whose early sound pictures have never been surpassed for what I call the old domino play. That is, you take one incident good enough in itself to set off a laugh, and then use it to explode another, and before anybody has recovered from the first, let alone the second, you apply both to setting off a third. It goes like string-firecrackers. The first gets you off-balance, the second knocks you over altogether, and the third jumps up and down on your chest. At ninety feet of film per minute, the process only runs about twenty or thirty feet, but it always takes you the next five hundred to recover.

Here a parenthesis to say that this is no jingo piece: Clair took the best available things in film technique when he was ready to use them; it didn't matter a hole in the snow where they had been developed; it mattered everything what he was able to make out of them, which was the first truly modern film comedy. Whatever he got was in the manner of treatment, not second-hand ideas for things to treat—which, I am sorry to say, was exactly the thing got from his "A Nous la Liberté" by our beloved Charlot for the conveyor-belt sequence in "Modern Times."

The parenthesis should, in fact, be extended to French films in general, for the Frenchmen are the only producers who have approached comedy on our level. (The Russians have done some fine real-life comedy, but mostly in pictures where comedy was strictly in passing, no more than relief.) A distinction not frequently enough made is that the most French thing about most French movies is that there are Frenchmen in them. Actually, the effects are achieved by players recruited from the Parisian stage, which ranks with that of Moscow as one of the greatest theatre reservoirs ever heard of. And by those familiar with the French habit of literature. When comedy in the French manner is good it is terrific, droll, and lovely at once. But this should not blind us to the fact that what there is in it of actual screen art is something the Hollywood men have worked out and taken for granted years before—and to the fact that French pictures often seem to have been taken in somebody's cellar with a pocket kodak.

The French are droll. O.K. Making pictures in an off-hand way at something like a nickel a throw, they do not have a big and stifling mass-production business around their necks. They can dare to fool around with the more charming aspects of life as people live it. O.K.

But, to end the parenthesis, what we are talking about is the development of screen comedy as a department of art in itself, owing goodness knows what to the stage, the original burlesque idea, the vaudeville blackout, and the comic postcard—but assimilating all of them and still remaining unique.

In the jumping invention of American movie comedies there was a general drying-up after the crazy, cuff-shooting Mack Sennett days, with their near-perfection of the balanced plank, the pratfall, the pie, the teeter, the ubiquitous chase. We gradually got over into the comedy with the star in it. Whereas you could once hang a sign in front of the theater with just the word Keystone, it got to be, for years, a Buster Keaton picture, a Harold Lloyd picture, a Ham Hamilton short, a W. C. Fields short, an Our Gang short. Or it was the legitimate-stage type of drawing-room ruckus, advertised as a Wallace Reid or Douglas Fairbanks or Adolphe Menjou picture. Even the cartoons didn't keep their identity: people went to see a Mickey Mouse, knowing the guy behind it was Disney to be sure—but how long do you think the Fleischer studios have been working, and would you be able to say even today who produces Popeye and who Betty Boop and whether either or both ever had anything to do with the "Out of the Inkwell" series? Comedy in the twenties became pretty dull and copycat, I am afraid, and a thing like the Broadway stage, where it is abundantly known that nobody cares what the book is like if Ed Wynn is playing it.

The big change and new impetus came with the introduction of sound and the addition of ripping dialogue to the original bedlam of the visual gagmen. Sound was an expensive and rather horrible trick at first; but after 1930 comedy really began to take over. Sound opened up the field for the voice of Jimmy Durante, with its overtones of someone making a prison break through a set of iron bars; for such madmen as the Marx Brothers; for a list of minor and major roles you can make as long as your arm. The movies began to approach naturalism—and that seems their dedicated goal.

And as they approached naturalism, emphasis was thrown more to character, not as played by some renegade from the Broadway tradition of saying "Morning, Zeke" as though eating a pork chop, but as devised in the script and worked into some place in the overall framework. They were American characters—what else could they have been? They came from every kind of place and tried out for all kinds of parts. The old stock roles of City Slicker, Cranky Spinster, Deacon, and Uncle Tom were being chased off the set simply because they had become cartoons and cartoons don't talk. The movies had the means and the press-agent flamboyance to screen-test anything that could get out of bed and walk. They didn't have to develop a school of acting. They accumulated, from all the fields of entertainment, including real life, a gallery of natural types such as was never seen on the face of the earth.

This applies to Hollywood in general, but particularly to comedy. The majority of the people you see on any screen today were people before they were actors, and it is hard for them to forget it. Under bad direction and their own worst compulsions they are typed without mercy. But given leeway or tricked into being natural, there they stand and talk and breathe at you, the whole amazing lot of them, busboys and hotel clerks and court clerks and plug-uglies and C. Aubrey Smith, but from life.

Hollywood at its best is as near to American humor at its best as you will get, purely because Hollywood has the fabulous wealth and appeal to get everybody from anywhere, professional or not. W. C. Fields, say, is a veteran trouper, operating the perpetual shell-game by which he once undoubtedly paid the rent. They have him. Frank Albertson, say, was so recently cutting out of high school for a quick butt between classes that he couldn't possibly make a Barrymore out of the situation even if his uncle's name were Drew. They have him.

In having these people to work with, to nurse along or hold back, the director has come back into his own—at least as much as the producer will let him. He has them and he has his story: when both are right and he is right, he makes pictures that have a styling, a speed and lightness and frequency of absurd surprise that combines sight, sound, motion, and recognition into something like music. When there is such styling, with its inevitable base in the life all around, there is a good approximation of what is most typical and good in American humor, which is fast and salty, a bit sentimental and a bit frantic, tough and gay and sweet.

Of course there may not be any such thing as American humor. All I know is I keep laughing every now and then.

If you will think back to "It Happened One Night," you will remember that it wasn't the plot, which was corny, or the dialogue, which was of the sort to snap the brim of a very old hat very smartly. It was a trick of building a whole thing out of little ordinary things, all caught in the shifting eye of the camera and picked out as clearly within the cross-country bus with its ranged seats and mission through the night as over the countryside and in the cabins later; and all joined to make a pattern of life as we all know it, with the unfailing tough surface and the grace beneath that we at least hope to find. It had the direction of a man who had a special talent for the mixed absurdity and loveliness of little things. But, more important, it had a man with the whole range of a medium at his back—a medium that had long studied and finally developed a way to bring up the constant and perfectly focused detail until it became the main thing by sheer force of numbers and their light progression; and common people and common things became real, and eloquent.

Though the movies had already produced fast, nifty pieces like "The Front Page" and "Design for Living," 1934 was a calendar year for American pictures in more ways than that "It Happened One Night" introduced it. Three or four months later we had "The Thin Man," which kept romance on a modified scale and added crime-detection and had people laughing and holding their breaths until the time more than two years later when it was called in to make way for the sequel. "Twentieth Century" came about the same time and managed some ripping comedy before it got down to the shrill and rather made-up business of the original stage play. And toward the end of the year, the Astaire-Rogers "Gay Divorcee" just about rounded everything out, with music, dancing, and a balance of high-frequency comedy that hasn't been equalled by anything in the class since, or before.

It wasn't that something new had been given the world, but merely that the movies had arrived at a new ease and maturity in form, a form that became most distinguishable in that it had tempered all effects from wipe-dissolves to Clark Gable into a steady line of clear motion. The funny character with or without the funny pants, the funny incidents, the gag and the breakaway and the wash-tub full of cake-dough, were assimilated into the progression of a main effect—namely, the whole story and the whole show. Since understatement had become possible through the new fluidity of camera eye and cutting scissors, the thumps and mugging of unrelated clowning were out. To a master of this new art, it was possible for the first time in any art to make the sentiment and absurdity of life as natural on a black-and-white screen as getting up from a good breakfast in a sunny room, kissing your wife a hurried bye-dear-back-at-six, and discovering it was your mother-in-law or somebody with a mustache like her.

With "My Man Godfrey" in the middle of 1936, the discovery of the word screwball by those who had to have some words to say helped build the thesis of an absolutely new style in comedy. Actually a movie released two and a half years before was not only consistently funnier but more screwball as well—only nobody knows what it is. The film, "Sing and Like It," hangs very near the main entrance of the Ferguson gallery. And a half year before that they got out another prominent Ferguson acquisition called "The Milky Way," which was just as fine and crazy as anything that had ever been called by a new name for pure dumb lack of knowing the venerable branch of the family it honored.

In the five years or so since, there have been a thousand tries and dismal misses. But there have been "The Captain Hates the

Sea," "Stage Door," "Bachelor Mother," "Ninotchka," etc. Comedy may get something new and better some day, but it hasn't yet; and when it is good in its tradition, it is still tops so far as we know. The argument isn't, of course, that, once you have such a tradition of speed, relevance, and gayety, you can just go out and knock off laughs as with a cookie cutter. It is rather that this tradition is forever there as a means to production for use and for laughter. The form is ready to hand and a ferryboat to glory for the man who has the talent to find it out and use it. It is complex, but it may be made as bright and warm as sunshine; and among all the things men can do, it is a thing inimitable.

STORY-TELLER'S WORKSHOP

A GOOD story is the easiest thing to read there is, and the damnedest thing to write; and while there are many writers who can take a day off now and then and do a story, there are very few story-writers. Erskine Caldwell is one of these rare birds. He is certainly more famous for the endless *Tobacco Road* companies, and he has got known recently for his work in fitting out Margaret Bourke-White photographs with a running text. But he is still a story-writer essentially, and that is a thing essentially different from anything else.

This is not an essay on How the Short Story Is Born, Its Care and Feeding. That sort of thing is best left to those spirits doomed not to learn the first fact: that nobody in the world knows "how" to write a story. Through talent and trial and error some arrive at a state of grace where they *can* write a story or make a song or tell a joke; the rest had better let it alone, for it is not a game with rules or a carpentry with lumber and T-squares. Part of it is a gift for yarning—though this is sometimes part of the equipment of the novelist or the columnist as well. And if you *did* take one of the more classic efforts of the local liar (cracker-barrel or fo'c'sl) and write it all down, every word, you'd find (1) that in length it ran all to hell beyond space limitations, and (2) that the magic had just slipped out of it.

Anybody who can write can begin a story (how many trunks are there which were never used for traveling?); and a lot of people can keep things happening well enough, with characters, dialogue, and exciting situations or backgrounds. But the end of a good story is not just where you stop, and that is where the trunks gather around as if for feeding time. The end has to be a completion, implicit from the beginning but not anticipated; everything must have happened by then, and by then everything that has happened must be clear and just and inevitable. Anyone who has been a professional reader (*i. e.*, has been forced after every reading to sign himself as yes, no, or maybe) will know how many good things will not stand up under the retrospective light of the end page, which can be either a fine illumination over the whole or a harsh glare which reveals trickery and shallow water with artificial fireworks over it.

It is no such device as the smash curtain-line. It can be an ending in a statement of fact, or it can trail off. It is nothing in itself but the same measure of success as the completion of an inscribed circle: the compass may have swung smoothly as you followed it, and may have made some proud, ambitious arcs, but if at the end it misses its starting point or has to cheat and jiggle, then you know that something has been set wrong or that the hand has been shaky from the start. A story must be self-contained and self-containing as nothing else in writing is outside of lyric poetry, and its end must be there from the beginning and all through— the logical completion of the writer's appointed round and his point of reference about what to put in, what discard, how deep to go and how fast. The hell of the thing is that there is no invention like the radio beam for it; however bright you are yourself, you must proceed toward it by blind navigation, and still proceed with authority and decision.

Of course there are writers who master the difficult art of the exact circle and are able to repeat time and again for large sums of money because the circle has nothing inside, because the whole thing to them is in making it come out slick and even. We needn't go into that—or be so very superior about it, either, for while they don't make literature, neither do they need to make a career of fierce appreciation for it out of their own writing incompetence. Then also there is the lucky-strike type of writer, the fellow with an experience or two so ready-made from life that a story writes itself. He will appear as, say, one out of the two hundred new geniuses turned up by Story, Inc., and O'Brien, Ltd., every year, and forgotten by the next. These people aren't quite the story-writers we are talking of.

Erskine Caldwell is a tale-teller, possessing the natural gift with the long work-out of a writer's discipline over it. I don't know how many hundred stories he has started or finished. His recent collection, *Jackpot*, contains seventy-five, many of them reprinted several times before. Many are only fair and some are duds, but name any hero in story-writing of whom you would not have to say the same. The point is that he has developed so fine a writer's eye for just the advance and the tension and the right fall of the thing for which he had a natural talent in the first place, that he can take a situation he has known and imagined, put people in it, and go on with the work as surely as the master builder of the Baltimore Clippers, without needing to tinker or wrench or worry if it will float.

Caldwell has in writing that peculiar and deceptive American drawl; he just seems to be talking and looking the other way and spitting on the hot stove, and all the time things are happening. Some of his best stories when he is in his best vein stand with those which do not resemble the writing of any other country in the world, nor are excelled anywhere—"The Spotted Horses," for example, or "Benny and the Bird Dogs." And here, as elsewhere, he is into a story before you know it—as simple as getting up in the morning. Take the first three paragraphs from one of the corkers, "Handsome Brown and the Aggravating Goats":

"If it's not one thing your Pa's done," Ma said, looking all helpless and worn, "it's something else. I declare, sometimes I think I'll never have a minute's peace as long as I live."

She walked up and down in the back yard wringing her hands, trying to think of something to do.

The goats that Pa and our Negro houseboy, Handsome Brown, had brought home from our farm in the country were standing on top of the house chewing and looking down at us. The big billy goat had long white chin whiskers that made him look like Mr. Carter who lived across the street.

It is all there in a sudden picture, the place and the characters and the problem, not a word to spare and every word exactly fitted. And the story is ready to go.

It is the speaking voice always, but deceptive because its easy flow covers a most shrewd mixture of economy and selection, because everything is there as it should be, with no words between, showing natural and vivid.

In the main, Caldwell has worked on three levels: love, humor, and the tragic under-dog. Often he travels from one to the other in the same piece, as he did in one of the funniest and strangest books I ever read, *God's Little Acre;* often he calls in the mystic symbol to help him out (also *God's Little Acre*). But his best vein, his most assured, is the broad vein of regional humor, the whopper complete with characters and the smell of home cooking. I will stack "Handsome Brown and the Aggravating Goats" and "The Night My Old Man Came Home" up against any man's yarn, and there are a lot of others you won't read merely once: "Country Full of Swedes," "The Grass Fire" (these are New England, which he does as well and salty as the South), "Hamrick's Polar Bear," "A Small Day."

With love as with humor he is more successful when he is more robust, though there is a deal of sensitive writing in the boy-and-girl passages through his work. With tragedy, the inhumanity of man, the crushed lives of poor whites, Negroes, the floating unemployed, Caldwell is less the complete story-teller. His purpose is admirable, his sincerity is not to be questioned, his facts are straight. It is all true, and a shame on the face of the earth, that a poor or a colored man hasn't a chance against the arrogance and pitiless squeeze of men in boots. But in the stories it never quite measures up; there is the effect of violence and large passion, but there is not the actual living thing, the solid-inevitable that marks all great writing on great themes. To take three in a row: "Slow Death," "A Knife to Cut the Cornbread With," and "Daughter." In these pieces, the more brutal ones Caldwell has been more and more concerned with in recent years, the story moves and the people talk; but the thing, the miracle of life in fiction, doesn't happen. Some of it is just a little laid on—or trick; some of it is simply too brief for the long measure implied; some of it is simply put together out of an open letter of protest to the *New Masses*. But you may not think so, and you will want to have *Jackpot* contain all the stories anyway.

There ought to be some Caldwell in your library, either *Jackpot* or some smaller collection, if you have a proper appreciation of the short story in American literature and the things from life it brings us. Caldwell is one of the good men writing, and bound someday to have a place in the courses of the professors who irk him so. They may not know a good thing when they see it because it is a new thing; but their literary history has always been a growth of new things which lay familiar on the tongue into the standard things people would not forget because of their being also true and beautiful and craftsmanwise and nice to have around.

WALLACE FOWLIE:

ELIOT AND TCHELITCHEW

I. FOUR QUARTETS

SINCE the time of the medieval poems on the Holy Grail legend
and the Divine Comedy, the major works of literature have
dealt more exclusively with the tragedy of love than with the
quest for love. But in his *Four Quartets* Mr. Eliot has composed
a poem unlike the work of his contemporary peers, in that his
unnamed hero (who is, of course, on one level of interpretation
the poet himself) is the quester, a modern Parsifal traversing the
dangers and the dryness of the world in his search for the grail
castle. In accordance with the modern tradition, the hero of *Four
Quartets* is a diminished personality comparable to the clown of
the painters and Prufrock of Eliot's earlier poem. Like Emily
Dickinson, he is saying throughout the pages, "I'm nobody! Who
are you?" and like Rilke in *Das Lied der Waise*, "Ich bin niemand
und werde auch niemand sein." He is the undeveloped and the
undifferentiated one, the clown who performs best before a public of children, as uncharacterized and as unportrayed as the hero
in *Une Saison en Enfer*.

Burnt Norton, first of the *Quartets*, is the poem of the rose
garden. It is the first world of the children, not the world we
actually lived in, but the mythic world constructed by our child's
imagination, the perfect rose garden of the fairy stories and the
great legends of the children of men. *Burnt Norton* evokes the
gardens of the medieval romances as well as "tous les paysages
possibles" of Rimbaud. The child's moment is the exhausting of
time and age: the moment when one is all characters, all sexes, all

ages—the prodigiously unreal moment when we bear most of reality. Everything is unseen and unheard in childhood. And yet it is the moment when we see and hear the most, when we see the blooms of the rose garden we never entered and hear the birds that sing there.

The second quartet, *East Coker*, is the poem of growing old. It represents therefore an opposing movement to *Burnt Norton*, which described the static moment of childhood in which we grow wondrously. *East Coker* is the literal growth and decay, the cycle of the family and of human ugliness. After the first quartet with its strong theme relating the triumph of imagination, the second quartet resounds with the eternally imminent danger of emotion. After leaving the world's garden of our childhood, we enter the earth's hospital of our maturity.

The last two quartets are religious interpretations of the first two: *The Dry Salvages*, the third quartet, interprets *East Coker*, the second, and *Little Gidding*, the fourth, interprets *Burnt Norton*, the first. The real world and its principle of growth and change are first interpreted, in *The Dry Salvages*, by the image of the sea, symbol of timelessness, and the symbol of the bone on the beach, image of man's fate in time. The strange drama of human flesh becomes comprehensible to Eliot only in terms of the "calamitous annunciation" of man's fall and that other Annunciation of the Redeemer's birth. The destructive element of time and the wasting of human flesh are offset by the prayer of the Lady on the promontory and the doctrine of the Incarnation. The timeless explains the timed, as the spirit explains the body, as the sea explains the river, as the Annunciation explains the Incarnation.

In the final quartet, *Little Gidding*, the springtime of *Burnt Norton* has become midwinter spring and the rose garden has become a secluded chapel. The roseate imagined world of the child has become England in the early 1940's darkened by the menaces and the knowledge of war. To the doctrines of the Annunciation and the Incarnation succeeds the doctrine on Love: the descent of the Holy Spirit in the form of Pentacostal fires. The language of the dead is superior to the language of the living. It is tongued with fire and communicates to the timed from the timeless. From the Heraclitean sentences on the death of air and earth, and of water and fire, to the allusions concerning air warden patrols in England,—from the Pentacostal fire to the flickering tongues of the Messerschmitts, a tremendous span in time is effaced.

The evolution of Mr. Eliot's work parallels the cycle of the *Divine Comedy*. *The Waste Land*, with its persistent theme of dryness and sterility, its interrupted dramatic episodes on frustration, its nightmarish and static quality, is the *Inferno* where the modern world is seized by its own guilt and transfixed by its own conscience. In this first major poem by Eliot, time is held within itself as though it could never be redeemed. The movements in it, as in Dante's *Inferno*, are not progressive, they are endless repetitions, and their visions are the dry landscapes already seen. *Ash Wednesday* marks the transition from the first period of Eliot's poetry to the most recent volume, as *Purgatory* involves on the one hand the total understanding and memory of sin, and on the other hand the promise that with sin's acknowledgment and repentance the end of its realm will be reached. *Four Quartets* are not in any literal sense a poem on Paradise, but they bring the spirit of man, the modern man who has made the absolute turning of *Ash Wednesday*, to the very frontier of the third realm where the suffering of indifference and ignorance (*The Waste Land*) and the suffering of spiritual knowledge (*Ash Wednesday*) are converted into the suffering of love (*Four Quartets*).

II. CHILDREN IN THE TREE

The rose bush and the yew tree are constantly recurring symbols in Mr. Eliot's work, used to designate time and eternity. The leaves of the shrubbery, mentioned in the opening lines of *Four Quartets*, and the apple tree growing in the same garden, referred to in the final lines of the work, form a major theme in the elaborate musical construction. The tree moves in its leaves as the entire sky seems to move in the drift of its stars, but one is the movement of time, exhausting itself and recommencing, and the other is the movement of eternity, absolute in itself, conquered and conquering. As in Mallarmé's remarkable sonnet, *M'Introduire dans ton histoire* (drawn upon heavily by Mr. Eliot in *Burnt Norton*, part II), there is a strong relation in *Four Quartets* between the human timed drama taking place on the earth, "un gazon de territoire" and the timeless omnipresent Divine Love flashed across the heavens like the permanent sun.

Perhaps more than a relation between the cycle of human life: its birth, fulfilment, and death—and the never exhausted, never changing energy of Divine Love—there exists an intersecting or a collision when, on one level, the bread becomes the Real Presence, and on another level, when man, while remaining held in time, transcends it in his sudden apprehension of Love, and when, on still another level, God or His spirit of timelessness and excessive Love, enters a body He created for His own reception. This drama of collision which permits man to comprehend, bear, and transcend the great principle of flux in which he lives, is the drama of *Four Quartets*. The hero is the quester, the searcher for that moment in time which is timeless and always, the visionary of all the possible landscapes, the prototype of Parsifal whose vision of the grail is the prepared and explicit moment of his salvation. And like Parsifal, the quester in *Four Quartets* relies upon the children in the tree for direction.

The purity of the children's voices can be apprehended only by the pure in heart. Verlaine, in his sonnet on *Parsifal*, breaks off the narration of grail ceremonial at the precise moment of elevation, as in the mass, and with his fourteenth line, "Et ô ces voix d'enfants chantant dans la coupole" (used in *The Waste Land*), translates the moment of religious ecstasy by evoking the purity of boys' voices. In the Holy Grail legend, Parsifal is guided to the grail castle by the voices of children in the tree (as Siegfried followed the voice of a bird), and in these new poems by T. S. Eliot, the poet is guided by the voices of children and birds hidden in the shrubbery and rose bushes of a child's garden (*Burnt Norton*) to the secluded chapel of his mature faith (*Little Gidding*).

The symbol of the tree is all-important, whether it be the rose, testifying to carnal love in the child's first sexual experience and hence to the principle of change and decay, or whether it be the yew tree, which like the grail castle and the Anglican shrine of Little Gidding, testifies to the permanency of Divine Love. In the medieval tradition the tree can easily be explained on the four levels of interpretation: first, as the literal tree in the setting of Eliot's rose garden; second, as the allegorical tree of the Crucifixion from the top of which the Voice speaks and directs; third, as the tropological tree whose life cycle is the moral divisioning of time; and fourth, as the anagogical tree when, suddenly, at the end of the final poem, it is called the apple tree and alludes, as does the spitting out of the apple seed in *Ash Wednesday*, to the spiritual drama of man's fall and redemption. As the tree in the First Garden was the gauge or barometer of man's obedience and love, so the tree in Eliot's poems is the symbol of time and eternity which are the two aspects of man's personal drama.

At the beginning of *Burnt Norton*, we read that "the leaves were full of children" and at the end of *Little Gidding* we read that "the children in the apple tree" were "not known, because not looked for." The tree of Eden is at the source of the world, and the children who inhabit it are those beings possessed by that immediate kind of love which is innocency, by the deep intuition which accompanies original love and permits a breathless lucidity concerning the purpose and the actions of man. The children in the Parsifal story know the way to the grail castle because they are pure, and the children in Eliot's poems are still waiting for the modern quester to recover sufficient innocency to ask for the way. In Pavel Tchelitchew's painting *Cache-Cache*, completed in 1942 and now exhibited in the Museum of Modern Art in New York, the same subject reappears invested with a dramatic anguish which illumines the entire theme of the children in the tree.

Childhood is that period when man's mission of fidelity is easy and natural to accomplish. And since the tree of knowledge is the eternalized symbol of God's fidelity to man, there exists an intimate relation between the child and the tree. The child understands the tree without needing to understand the knowledge of the tree. As the vegetable and the mineral do not dissimulate any one of the elements of which they are composed, so the child has no need of hiding its life which is one with that of the tree. Tchelitchew's genius has fused the faces of hundreds of children with the leaves and the flowers. *Cache-Cache* is a vast painting of metamorphosis and symbolism, comparable in its complexity to *Ulysses* and *Finnegans Wake*. Two opposing principles are at work everywhere on the canvas: first, the process by which nature imitates the coarseness or at least the terror of man in the resemblance between the tree (its trunk, roots, and branches) and the bones and nails of some monstrous hand; and second, the process by which the children, who represent the human species, are being transformed into the tree and therefore into a non-human species. The tree and the child are both being transformed simultaneously and to the same degree, and they are both undergoing a simultaneous torture and liberation.

As in the dawns of the earliest days of the world, the children in *Cache-Cache* are rushing toward one another, blindly, the same blood in their veins animating them, the same desperate love and fate joining them. Liturgical colors mark the children's encirclement of the seasons. A testicle and a foetus indicate, at the bottom of the tree, the male and female origin of life, and, at the top, wheat and an apple symbolize the apex and fruition of life. The figure of the little girl in the center of the picture, pressing her face against the trunk and counting out the seconds in the game of *Hide and Seek*, is the hero, a kind of Hamlet gone child. She and the small boy to her right appear to be fornicating with the tree rather than with themselves in their sprawled attitude which is an effort to lose themselves in nature. Tchelitchew's children in the tree, Parsifal lost in the dry places of the world, Hamlet in his father's castle, and the poet Eliot in his memory of the rose garden and in the reality of Little Gidding are all seeking to identify themselves. But self-identification and self-annihilation are regions extraordinarily close one to the other. As there is no interval between day and night, there is no intermediary hope or risk between the hope of salvation and the risk of destruction.

Thus, in the children, meet the two worlds of hope and fear, of knowledge and ignorance, of success and failure. A little girl in *Cache-Cache* is blindfolded, but no more so than Hamlet, and the children in the poem are unknown because unseen. Tchelit-chew and Eliot have both composed works which are simultaneously a cycle and a drama. Their memory of pure childhood provides the cycle, and their memory of the agonized search for the world in childhood and the subsequent desperate search for the child in adulthood provide the drama. Both the poet and the painter have been guided by the children, and in each case the artist is depicted against the background of the awful lucidity of children. The inner landscapes of the children, which are their dream and their horror, are recast by the artist who, alone in the society of men, remains the child in his power of metamorphosis and symbolism.

RUTH HERSCHBERGER:

"POISED BETWEEN THE TWO ALARMS . . ."

ROBERT PENN WARREN: *Selected Poems 1923-1943.*
Harcourt, Brace.

THIS is a volume of collected poems by one of the best of living poets. Its first and longest section is of recent poems, the small and later section comprised of early poems. One could make many fanciful descriptive beginnings about the subject, content, and effect of these works. To the eye and ear of future centuries, the entire realm of modern poetry will possibly be known as the dream period, or—Dylan Thomas's poems—the underwater era in poetry. And Robert Penn Warren's poems are chiefly of this dream tradition. The toxic or beguiling subconscious, the huge avenues of terror, the scintillating anxieties which Freud uncovered are represented here, more or less consciously. A previous volume of Warren's poetry, *Eleven Poems on the Same Theme*, is included; these poems draw at least one of their dominant motifs from the impingement of the Past upon the present, the Past conceived in a Freudian way as persisting throughout one's lifetime, the years serving merely to fructify the fears we acquired as children.

> The *then*, the *now:* each cenotaph
> Of the other.

Cenotaph: a monument where no one is buried. This is the experience within the poems: elusive, terrible, but satisfying once one realizes the tomb is real, but that there is nothing within but shadows and half-imagined terrors. We are shown this slowly, with magnificent metaphor and knit meter, sometimes with a shock of unveiling, always with a profound wisdom of poetry and its richness. For an excellent poetry should enrich its content, though that content be terror and "emptiness." This is what Warren's poetry emphatically does.

Can we ever judge poems apart from what they say? Even the notion of "richly done," so wonderfully adverbial and seemingly referring to the poem-in-itself, has behind it a demand that poetic terror be animated by a metaphor of viable, animate things, that the life presented, even in a cenotaph, be full of "tidal lust," "protruding eye," "jaguar breath," and a "twinge of distress" which one, yes, can feel. These poems, vital with regret and rude with their knowledge of crime, will inevitably be judged against the experience of their readers; but since fear and anxiety are native to us all, they should resound assuredly. In pursuing our hypothesis on the content of the poems, one might say that beyond the presence of vigor and passionate mindfulness, what is lacking here is any overflowing, any exuberance. The overflow is one of rancor, an obsessive gaiety when gay, a hunted exuberance; never sustaining an easy, humored, or pastoral mood.

It is this tautness, this tense alertness toward life, that makes all of us marvel at Warren's prosody. The wakeful-dream that penetrates the poems conveys itself to the meter as well. He lulls us with assonance, prods us with commas; his prosody is not for the indolent. The commas wonderfully studded ("Or are we dead, that we, unmanned, / Are vacant, and . . ."), the assonance and rhyme ("The amber light laved them, and us; / Or light then so untremulous") are enough to vanquish one with their strength and relaxed-tension, unless one is in a lively and capable mood.

All power to the Elizabethan richness and vigor of this poetry. It is good to hear boldly the "cold heart heaves like a toad," and to realize, sagely, of a hero—

> It is your custom to recline,
> Clutching between the forefinger and thumb
> Honor, for death shy valentine.

This is new knowledge of the profoundest sort, exciting and perpetual. Warren's themes are loaded with the heightened mood of the Elizabethans, but chiefly of the post-Elizabethans, of John Webster, for instance, whose "friendless bodies of unburied men" reminds of the Warren theme, the half-live, half-dead past that persists and galls us all, the buried crime that refuses to stay buried.

> Of what is 't fools make such vain keeping?
> Sin their conception, their birth weeping,
> Their life a general mist of error,
> Their death a hideous storm of terror.

No lack of poetic genius here! Webster deserves his eminence. As does Robert Penn Warren, who sees

> All our debate is voiceless here,
> As all our rage, the rage of stone;
> If hope is hopeless, then fearless fear,
> And history is thus undone.

Magnificent, but with terror always present, all loveliness with its mildewed edge. Rose-buds and oaks may have their place in this poetry of The Terror, but we are swiftly dispossessed of any tendency to lean on their virtues. "All the flowers of the spring," says Webster, "Meet to perfume our burying." And Warren, too, has known flowers: "She blinks and croaks, like a toad or a Norn, in the horrible light, / And rattles her crutch, which may put forth a small bloom, perhaps white." The "wind-heaved gull . . . But question, not replies," the "green-lipped pool, / Or where moving waters sang / And algae swayed beneath, / But thirsting and accurst— / Tongue black between the teeth / Whence no sweet spittle sprang—."

Why has the best of modern poetry adhered to a sombre and decaying view of existence? We have had a sad life, it is true, but there is an ideology that almost accidentally nurtured and is nurturing this outlook. Modern science, with all the cockiness of youth, took some delight in tearing apart the Faiths of the latter generation. Both God and Hope became mere metaphors, mere psycho-physiological expectations on the part of our helpless chemic frames. No one seemed to notice that Hume, way back in the 1700's, had shown that science, too, was built on probability and expectation, and that its imposing Cause and Effect were no more than figures of speech based on past actualities, and anticipating—rather fearfully—a future recurrence. The poets should then and there have insisted that metaphor and its evaluations were in the same class of reliability as science, and that poetry should not be ridiculed for the complex ambiguity of its subject matter. But the poets didn't fight back; they rushed frightened to the world of "things," and the moment they got there they erroneously saw their job as identical with that of the scientist or teacher. They believed they must pass judgment with extreme care, or the ethical balance of their generation might snap in two. They became moralists, and lesser poets, for their moralism was cautious, unimaginative, and *down-to-earth*, as the bourgeois call it. Keats is an exception, for his devotion to the Bards of Passion and of Mirth drove him on to a more daring combination of images than his stodgier brethren, Shelley and Wordsworth.

The poets felt their poems were accountable to science, and had to be built of nicely distinguishable blocks which could be knocked down and laid out for Scientific Inspection now and then. It was the ebullient Coleridge who had to take off so much time to give verbal justification for his poems. Wordsworth's congenial brooks and moralisms left him plenty of time for an effortless poesy. It is an accusation against the century that Wordsworth and his attitudes found such a comfortable berth within it, and Coleridge such a difficult one. But as things stood, poetry was on the defensive, and metaphor was justifiable only in terms of "simplicity" and "soundness." Freud truly saved us from this, and though heirs of War and Depression, the modern poet ought to feel more grateful for the break that psychoanalysis gave him.

Science banned metaphor because it was equivocal, but Freud brought it back with his scientific justification of Ambivalence. Yet with Freud as the Muse, a sombre (and patriarchal) attitude toward life arose. The price of this reinstatement of poetry was that the poet must forever act the neurotic; only neurotics could turn to poetry and conceive any anxious evocative figure of speech. All serious poets, grateful to Freud for their liberation from a weak Tennysonian prison, gladly donned madman's rags or withdrew to a Childhood of deliverance. Affirmations returned, but they had to be of a special hue. Poetry went underground, so to speak. Its affirmations had to be buried ones, its glimpses of the upper world had to be through the shimmering distortion of water, its rejection of the present was carried out on strict Freudian grounds, and its "infantilisms" callously or tenderly exhibited. The poetry of Rilke, Eliot, Auden, Warren demonstrates the gamut and the vitality of this strange rebirth.

There are two modern poets strikingly different from this tradition: Whitman (c. 1855) and Hopkins (c. 1875). Whitman was an early bird, and resided in the rebellious country of Brooklyn; we can understand how he dared his pioneer exuberance. Hopkins was a rich being who escaped from the deadly Victorian moralism of the English countryside by joining the Jesuits. Within this continent faith, and when not morally occupied with translating Shakespeare's lyrics into more pietistic Latin, Hopkins wrote impudent English verse. "Wert thou my enemy, O thou my friend," he writes to the divine Providence, "How wouldst thou worse, I wonder, than thou dost / Defeat, thwart me?" Though the Church may claim him now, for all the world wants genius in its footnotes, the Institution that knew him did not particularly approve, nor did it adopt the patronizing tolerance of his "eccentricities" so common now. Hopkins' poetry was as much inhibited by his loyalty to God as it was inspired by it. Not only did metaphor suggest sensory pleasures and a Scotist particularity, there was also his guilty sense of affinity with the heretic Whitman. "I always knew in my heart," Hopkins wrote, "Walt Whitman's mind to be more like my own than any other man's living. As he is a very great scoundrel this is not a pleasant confession." And Hopkins endeavored to infect his poems with "a more Miltonic plainness and severity." Such radiant failure as his should encourage us all. How much more bacchic, in fact, are the fragments of "St. Winefred's Well" by Gerard Hopkins, S. J., than the dull paganism of Robert Bridges' "Feast of Bacchus."

The main point of this digression is to note that Robert Penn

Warren's poetry is far from this world of Whitman's "Children of Adam" and Hopkins' praise of "All things counter, original, spare, strange"; Warren is well within the twentieth-century dream-milieu, haunted by the Past, Freudian or otherwise, and with no future or present to speak of. And while there is no consistency of exuberance in Whitman and Hopkins in the sense that either of them struck a static pollyanna attitude toward life (consider "Out of the rolling ocean, the crowd," or "No worst, there is none"), there is, I believe, a consistent *denial* of exuberance in much of Warren's work. From my point of view, this is a criticism; others may defend it as the only attitude possible today.

One feels no sharp line between Warren's early and late poems. The early poems in some ways show more sharply the underlying themes of his poetry, for here already are "the blind and nameless bones," "the dry essential of tomorrow," the invocation to "keep the sweet sterility of stone," the "blind tides," "the bitter tendons of the stone," "the shuddering and sweat of stone." In fact, one of the earliest poems, "For a Self-Possessed Friend," outlines the very characteristics which Warren himself tended to leave behind in his poetry. What he indicts his friend for is an unwillingness to praise anything: "But you, my friend . . . you do not praise at all, / Or praising, stop and seem to cast your eye / Toward some commensurate cold finality. . . ." The speaker in the poem admits that he himself too often praises the worthless or the imperfect, but says, "It is an arrogance to save your breath," refusing to grant any praise at all. Among the things over-praised by the speaker and others, we find listed:

> We praise the word, forget the deed;
> Praise furred gold leaves in April, not the seed
> Tissued of delicate blind agony.

I think it is fair to say that Warren's later poems find increasingly fewer things worthy of praise. To say that they praise the "sweet sterility of bone" is a left-handed comment, inasmuch as few persons would refer "praise" to the de-animation and rejection of life. We can admittedly refer *truth* to this, however.

Contrast is the marrow of poetry, and furred gold leaves with no knowledge of decay, blind agony, or their equivalent would be dull indeed. But at some moments in Warren's poetry one feels it is the blind agony that needs a contrast. This is one of those delicate "relative" matters, strictly bound to personal preference. The Elizabethans may have talked "Gather ye rosebuds while ye may" a great deal, but in the short time given them to gather, they enjoyed the live scent of the flowers. It was Webster who every moment saw the skull beneath the skin, and who probably felt that no sensitive poet should see anything else. For it is not that a defender of Terror asks the privilege of omitting the rosebuds and the furred gold leaves from his own poems; he more often (in esthetic judgments) denies any "truth" to the buds and leaves in other writers. The poet has as strong tendencies to regiment as anyone else. At any rate, my regret for the lack of exuberance in Warren's poetry, while admittedly preferential, is nonetheless an esthetic criticism of lack of contrast, and not a denial of the truth of the Terror, nor a moral jibe at "morbidity," nor a wish to speak for other readers.

Warren's chief concepts are hinted at in the frequent use of arrogant, bitter, lean, bone, terror, innocence, stone, Time, and so on. The curious inclusion of innocence can but equivocally be explained. "Time is innocence," but one can "Weary of innocence and the husks of Time."

> For the beginning is death and the end may be life,
> For the beginning was definition and the end may be definition,
> And our innocence needs, perhaps, new definition. . . .

The new definition, one gleans, will be "frail as the clasped dream beneath the blanket's wool," a mocking attainment. In general, the escape from terror and past guilt (once indicated as "fault not our own") is into stone, "lapped in the arrogant chastity of our desire," "voiceless," for "purity was wordless." While summer has hopes and gold leaves, it is winter for Warren that has knowledge: "Summer's wishes, winter's wisdom." This, I believe, is a fair statement of Warren's predominant theme, the vulgar buzzard-nature of this life countered not by a voluptuous escape into death, but by a new "definition," a "secret," somewhat cerebral in conception, or by conversion into bone and stone. The poet stands "poised between the two alarms / Of summer's lusts and winter's harms," where "weakness has become our strength, / And strength, confused, can but reject / Its object . . ." It is hard not to react somewhat morally, even politically, to the pervasive notion that a "confused" strength must invariably reject its object, suspend judgment, one presumes, and that it is satisfied to call its weakness strength. But one resists.

The most recent poem, "The Ballad of Billie Potts," is excellently done. Its dramatic construction has a very curious emotional factor: drama typically has a sympathetic character, a person who is put-upon undeservedly and whose virtues we are happy to suppose our own, through their honest goodness or fine sensibility. In order to "care," we must feel an identification. The Ballad begins with Big Billie Potts and his wife; Big Billie may be a rat and a murderer, but there is something boisterous and clever about him; he "could smell the nest where the egg was laid . . . in the land between the rivers." The author seems benevolent up to the point of Little Billie's introduction. Even aside from the "piss and vinegar" in Little Billie, he is disgustingly stupid and insensitive. Strong malice enters the account here. And along with the presence of this ugly mortal, Little Billie, there is an iterated chorus-effect, the emotions of you and you and the author, finely and sensitively written, produced in parentheses now and then, which forces us relentlessly to identify ourselves with the disgusting Billie! The neurotic conflict this sets up in the reader is certain to behold. The sensitive reflections of the chorus (or commentator) are immediately paralleled by similar but repellent emotions in Little Billie. For example, when we in the chorus are hypnotically hearing "There is always another country and always another place," we are brought up against the fact that Little Billie is at that moment going west . . . The self-laceration, not to say self-degradation, this identification promotes in the reader is, I think, a powerful certainty. And again one must decide whether this helps or hinders the impact of the tale. It is a considerable feat to persuade us to *feel for* Little Billie at the same time that he repels us.

Even if April gets only a small showing, and autumn a big one, the imagery in these *Selected Poems* is strong and effective. Even if the birds going south have as little escape from winter's cruel wisdom as the rest of us, the conception is brave and the image fine:

> The grackles, yellow-beaked, beak-southward, fly
> To the ruined ricelands south, leaving empty our sky.

And what more melodious horror could one find than "Slack dugs by the dry thorn torn"; what more impressive view of death:

> . . . a womb more tender than her own
> That builds not tissue or the little bone,
> But dissolves them to itself in weariness.

Or wryer humor:

> When in the midnight's pause I mark
> The breath beside me in the dark,
> And know that breath's a clock, and know
> That breath's the clock that's never slow,
> *Timor mortis conturbat me.*

I have surely exaggerated the "morbidity" of Warren's themes; there is more tenderness and human insight than has been indicated. The scattered quotations remain the best witness to the warmth and vitality of these *Selected Poems;* for the book as a whole sustains this impression of richness and deep sensibility.

F. O. MATTHIESSEN:

"THAT TRUE AND HUMAN
WORLD . . ."

KATHERINE ANNE PORTER: *The Leaning Tower
and Other Stories.* Harcourt, Brace.

Mɪss ᴘᴏʀᴛᴇʀ's high reputation among nearly all schools of
critics may now have reached the point where it is doing
her a disservice. She is bracketed as "a writer's writer," which
she certainly is, so far as that phrase implies that almost any
other craftsman can learn important things from her about the
handling of both language and structure. But the common
reader has too frequently been led to believe that "style" is
something esoteric, something to be relished apart from what it
conveys, and that Miss Porter's relatively slim production must
mean that she has not much to say. This misconception has also
been nourished unwittingly by her admirers who like her quality
so much that they want more and keep urging her to write a
novel. But Miss Porter herself, when introducing the work of
Eudora Welty, saw that for the master of the short story the
novel may simply be the next trap ahead. The assumed superiority
of the longer form is a product of our American supposition that
bigger must be better, and has blown up many a lyric poet into
an abortive epic bard, as well as the content adequate for a decent
novel into a limp trilogy.

What we tend to forget is that in such a characteristically
French form as the novelette, in the story of twenty to forty
thousand words, we have also an American tradition. The kind

of intensification that Melville gained in *Benito Cereno* and *Billy Budd*, and that James, working so differently, accomplished in *Pandora*, *The Coxon Fund*, *The Bench of Desolation* and a dozen others, would seem to have much to offer to our period whose syntheses are often so precarious that they may be lost through extension. Miss Porter has set her special signature on this form, as Hemingway has on the contemporary practice of the short story. Not that she hasn't worked brilliantly in short stories as well, but sometimes hers can seem too fragmentary, as, for instance, do the first half dozen pieces in this new volume in comparison with the more integrated structure of *Old Mortality*, which dealt with the same descendants of Kentucky against a Louisiana and Texas background.

Yet these very stories can demonstrate the searching originality of her content. She may seem to be dealing with the stock material of the local colorists, with older Southern manners and customs as they persisted down into this century. Yet you quickly realize, in "The Old Order" and "The Last Leaf," that the human relationships are being examined with a new depth and honesty, that the sentimental view of the devoted old slave living on serenely with her former mistress is punctured once for all by such a quiet observation as that Nannie thrived on "a species of kindness not so indulgent, maybe, as that given to the puppies."

Such discoveries of the living intricacy in any relationship are Miss Porter's most recurrent resource. A passage at the end of "The Grave," the last of this group, gives a very explicit clue as to how she comes into possession of her material. This passage records how Miranda, by a chance of seemingly irrelevant association, is suddenly struck with the full violence of an episode long buried in her childhood, by her first knowledge of the mystery of birth as it had come to her through seeing a pregnant rabbit that her brother had shot and was skinning. This passage, too long to quote here, reveals Miss Porter's understanding of how much enters into any mature experience, of how deeply bathed in imaginative richness any event must be if it is to become a fluid and viable symbol.

The frequence with which violence lies at the heart of her

discoveries helps to explain a main source of strength in her delicate prose. "The Circus," the best short story here, conveys the naked agony with which Miranda, too young to grasp the conventions, reacts to the dangers and brutalities of the show. What the others can take in the comic spirit presses upon her a first initiation into the pity and terror of life. Violence in modern fiction has been so often a substitute for understanding that Miss Porter's ability to use it to reveal ethical values is another of her particular distinctions, as she showed especially in *Noon Wine*. In "The Downward Path to Wisdom," one of the three longer stories in this collection, her control seems far less sure, since the brutalities which are poured down upon the helpless child by his elders are not sufficiently motivated to make a coherent pattern. Violence seems to have been manipulated almost for its own sake.

Still another of Miss Porter's distinctions has been her refutation of the local colorists and other narrow regionalists by her extraordinary ability to portray a whole series of different environments. It may only be our anticipation of so much variety from her that causes a story like "A Day's Work" to seem for the first time a repetition of material handled more freshly in "The Cracked Looking-Glass." In comparison with that earlier story, which was a sustained miracle of Irish feeling and rhythm, both the situation and characters here may seem slightly expected. But when we turn to the longest story, to the novelette which gives title to the volume, we have again the rare combination of virtuosity with moral penetration.

Here Miss Porter uses a controlling symbol in the way that James often did, since the leaning tower not only is a souvenir of the Berlin landlady's long past happiness in Italy, but also becomes a compelling image for the tottering balance of the German world in the year before Hitler's rise to power. Many bestselling accounts have now been written of that time, and yet it seems doubtful whether any of them will preserve its form and pressure longer than Miss Porter's presentation of it through the consciousness of a young American painter. The reason for her success may be suggested by a comment James once made when noting that Turgenieff's *Memoirs of a Sportsman*, dealing with the question of serfdom, had appeared in the very same year as *Uncle Tom's Cabin*: "No single episode pleads conclusively against the 'peculiar institution' of Russia; the lesson is the cumulative testimony of a multitude of fine touches—in an after-sense of sadness that sets wise readers thinking . . . It offers a capital example of moral meaning giving a sense to form and form giving relief to moral meaning."

Some of Miss Porter's "fine touches" consist in her recurrent stress on the city's poverty, through Charles Upton's gradual realization of the difference from the depression he had left behind at home, where everybody took it for granted that things would improve, whereas in Berlin "the sufferers seemed to know that they had no cause for hope." No journalist or social historian analyzing the collapse of the republic has come closer to the central cause. And concerning the interpenetration of form and moral meaning, a comparison with Christopher Isherwood's *Good-Bye to Berlin* is instructive. Isherwood looked back to the same kind of student and boarding house life, and he dealt more explicitly with some of the manifestations of social decay. But his characters seem self-consciously worked up from a Freudian hand-book, or they exist to shock like the figures in a cinema thriller. They have none of the deep authenticity that springs from Miss Porter's humility and tenderness before life. She has been able to apprehend many kinds of Germans, ranging from the lumpish solemn mathematician who "loves study and quiet" to the young aristocrat whose new cheek-wound brings out in his expression a mixture of "amazing arrogance, pleasure, inexpressible vanity and self-satisfaction." Miss Porter does not slight the bestial brutalities in this hard city. No more, however, does she indulge in easy propaganda. When Charles Upton remarks lightly that Americans are sentimental and "like just everybody," the young mathematician stares at him earnestly and says: "I do not think you really like anybody, you Americans. You are indifferent to everybody and so it is easy for you to be gay, to be careless, to seem friendly. You are really cold-hearted indifferent people."

As a result of weaving back and forth through contradictions and incongruities, from one flickering center of human conviction to another, Miss Porter has done again what she did in *Pale Horse, Pale Rider*. She has created the atmosphere of a haunting moment of crisis. In that earlier novelette she gave us the end of the last war as it was felt in America through the crazy fever of the flu epidemic. Here, as she brings her group of students close together for a moment of New Year's Eve conviviality, what reverberates through their every speech and gesture is a premonition of disaster. In writing of Miss Welty, Miss Porter warned the artist against political beliefs, but here we can see that her remark was not the reactionary one that such a remark generally is. For she has penetrated into the economic and social sicknesses that brought on Fascism, but she has also held to her knowledge that the realm of the creator of fiction must be broader and more resilient than theories or opinions, that it can be nothing less than "that true and human world of which the artist is a living part."

HENRY MILLER:

LET US BE CONTENT WITH THREE LITTLE NEW-BORN ELEPHANTS

LAUTRÉAMONT: *Maldoror*, translated by Guy Wernham. New Directions.

EVERYTHING was working towards its destiny: the trees, the plants, the sharks. All—except the Creator!" Thus sings Lautréamont in the third canto wherein the Omnipotent is made to assume the role of He Who Gets Slapped. But that was all long ago, as Isidore himself says, only to add quickly: "but I think he knows where I am now." (I wonder.) And then, in one of the most revelatory passages of the entire work, he continues: "He avoids my place and we both live like two neighboring monarchs who are aware of one another's respective powers, cannot overcome one another, and are weary of the useless battles of the past."

Like two neighboring monarchs! Or, The Ego and his Own . . .

Maldoror deals almost exclusively with God the Omnipotent One. God in man, man in God, and the Devil take the hindmost. But always God. This is important to stress, because should it become overnight a best seller (due to those by-products so hungrily sought after by Anglo-Saxons, viz., lust, cruelty, vice, hate, vindictiveness, rage, violence, despair, ennui, rape, etc.), God may be forgotten and only the ferocious little Isidore Ducasse, alias the Comte de Lautréamont, remembered. God had a hand in the creation of this book, as he did in the creation of

A Season in Hell, Flowers of Evil and other so-called disturbing works, which are disturbing only because we are loath to recognize the shadow as well as the majesty of the Almighty. It is most important to emphasize this because, unless the miracle happens or Chance be defeated, some obscure and innocent printer will, like Etienne Dolet, take the rap and go to the gibbet.

Almost seventy-five years after the appearance of this infamous work (which, incidentally, failed to establish a precedent for the *Hundred and Twenty Days*) an eminent American lawyer, elated over the decision rendered by Judge Woolsey (James Joyce vs. America), raves publicly in a Foreword to a cheap edition of *Ulysses*, about the body-blow then (1933—year of forgotten miracles) delivered the censors. "The necessity," says he, "for hypocrisy and circumlocution in literature has been eliminated. Writers need no longer seek refuge in euphemisms. They may now describe basic human functions without fear of the law." This is precisely what the young Isidore did. He asked no quarter and he gave none. His predecessor was Jonathan Swift and his chief executor was the Marquis de Sade who spent most of his life in jail. Isidore escaped with a whole skin by dying young. In time he came to be for André Breton and his group what Rimbaud was for Claudel and the unknown galaxy to follow.

Baudelaire was a rain of frogs, Rimbaud a nova (which still blazes), and Lautréamont a black messenger heralding the death of illusion and the nightmare of impotence to follow. Had there been only these three sinister luminaries in the whole of the nineteenth century that century would have claim to being one of the most illustrious in all literature. But there were others—Blake, Nietzsche, Whitman, Kierkegaard, Dostoievski, to cite just a few. In the middle of this amazing century a border line was crossed, and there will be no returning. Almost every European nation, and even America, contributed to this putsch: it was the century of great gangsters in every walk of life, in every realm, including the celestial.

The three great bandits were Baudelaire, Rimbaud and Lautréamont. And now they have become sanctified. Now we see that they were angels in disguise. Seventy-five years behind time, like a derailed train which finds its own way, even through Pontine marshes, cemeteries and the crooked deals of financiers, Lautréamont arrives in America. (He arrived at least once before, if I am not mistaken, but passed unnoticed. Just as Breton moves along Third Avenue, New York, looking into junk shop windows, entirely unnoticed.)

"I go on existing, like basalt! In the middle as in the beginning of life, angels resemble themselves: how long it has been since I ceased to resemble myself!" Thus he laments in the fourth canto, which opens: "It is a man or a stone or a tree about to begin the fourth canto." *It is*. It is like nothing ever before invented, not even the Fourth Eclogue of Vergil. But so indeed are the other cantos. They do not even resemble one another: they are angel-lamps. Sometimes they "bellow like vast flocks of buffaloes from the pampas." Or they spout sperm, like the sperm whale. Or they impersonate themselves, like "The Hair" which the Creator left behind in the brothel, to his great embarrassment. To get the true flavor of them one has to visualize this young Montevidean (who "probably died of some respectable bourgeois disease induced by his unhealthy and Bohemian habits of life") pounding the piano as he composed them. They are French only in the language chosen. There is something Aztec, something Patagonian, in all of them. Something too of Tierra del Fuego, which lies buried like a dislocated toe in the chill waters that wrap it round. And perhaps too something of Easter Island. Not perhaps—*certainly*, most certainly.

What I wonder is not how the Anglo-Saxon will take this book, but how the Oriental will. Tamerlane could not have inspired in his own people the feelings he awakened in the peoples he slaughtered. Similarly, Ramakrishna has become for the Westerner a sort of "monster" of ecstasy. Lautréamont, following his own example exclusively, took the European gong (which had been sounding its own death knell for centuries) and literally kicked the gong around. This does not make him in the least like Cab Calloway, nor Minnie the Moocher. It makes him more and more like Lautréamont, which (to us) is insufferable.

It might be called a new Bible, written from a new Sinai, expressly for "the boa of absent morality and the monstrous snail of idiocy." The mysterious brothers are implicated, as well as the neighboring monarchs—*and the angel-lamp*. Nor can we ignore his first cruel love, the shark, with all her fins. Marvelous. Marvelous throughout, and not like the ink spots—just here and there. Pluto rising, God and man sealed in one death. Enter now the janissaries of Satan and his camelot the machine. Enter the weird birds and beasts from North America. Enter Broken Blossom and Broken Brow, followed in strict sequence by that movie which we are still making, called "The Slaughter of the Innocents."

Rimbaud was doomed at birth—he hadn't the ghost of a chance. Yet no one had noticed, prior to his coming, that the sun was burned out. *Now*, do you hear it plainly?—piteous moans smothered in sea wrack. Frabjous caterwauls, since the snails (shorn of their temples) are out in force. Oh yes, there will be more delightful little works of fantasy—that man all in black, Lewis Carroll, for instance—but the horse has been definitely disembowelled. Look no more for drunken boats, or Armageddons where dragon and eagle fight it out. Don't look for doubt's duck with the vermilion lips, because we are all out of that flavor.

Suddenly, as if a volcano had erupted under the floor of a boudoir, just when France is about to receive her first mortal blow, comes a burst of passion black as pitch. Passion, I say, and not luke-warm piss from a printer's soiled bladder. All personal feuds have passion, even if the feud is only with the Creator. Isidore had one feud, one passion. He was alone. But *alone*, mind you, and that in a world where even to take a walk, as one French genius put it laconically, costs money. There was no sadder world than the world of the nineteenth century—for those who had wings. What does one do in such periods? One takes wing. One flees. One sails aloft with the albatross. But whither? *That* we are just beginning to discover. *Wing it first*, that's the moral of the nineteenth century. And leave the world of snails and boas to sink like a diseased cork.

It is the habit of critics to deal with style and such things. There is no style here to talk about. It was out of style even before it was written. Understand, please, that we are dealing with a Bedouin in a button factory. We have, if you insist, the ode, the litany, the apostrophe, the invective, the jeremiad, the bromide, the round dance, the refrain, the revolver shot, the death and the resurrection, the apocrypha, the curse and the maul, together with the vocabulary of a diamond cutter pickled in Malmsey—all in full glory like a six-masted schooner. There is also the foam on the beer, even the louse, if you are itchy. You will learn nothing from analyzing these ingredients and scaffoldings. Someone crucified himself: that's all that matters. And he had an evil name, worse than it sounds. (But it always rings like a tocsin, no matter what the language!) You will also find tenderness in these cantos, and abysmal humility. And if you have never travelled to the nadir, then here is the opportunity.

When Isidore took himself to Paris the whole world was rolling down hill. A veritable toboggan slide, but taking place in the Unconscious, as we imagine. A right jolly *dégringolade* it was. So jolly that some, like Wordsworth, Tennyson and other infatuates, were sticking their toes through Heaven's bangled tambourine. Then began a series of the most unethical assassinations, now taking on the proportions of a pogrom. (We're still at the threshold . . . livelier things are in store, don't fret.) When the split could no longer be concealed a fusion took place, a piece of expert welding, and dream and reality—like two boxers in the arena—shook hands. The man who had sawed the two realms apart folded up like a jack-knife. It was as if he had sawed the Virgin Mary in two on a busy street, fired a revolver to summon the police, waited calmly for the next bus, and then at some unpredicted *carrefour* transferred to a vehicle more to his liking. Ordinarily, were such a man apprehended, he would be put in a strait-jacket. Not Isidore. He lives beyond apprehension. He writes those advertisements in the sky which when read backwards always spell Maldoror. A golden roar of pure spite, malice, vituperation. In it is the roar of gold—pure gold, not gleet-gold. And in it too is pure evil, not the counterfeit of spinsters and clericals. (How little genuine evil is in the world! And how much gold! And what do all these black crucifixes mean?)

"NOW WE ARE IN THE MIDST OF REALITY, INSOFAR AS THE TARAN-
TULA IS CONCERNED."

The style, the effect, the intent, everything about this black
bible is monstrous. So is the image of Kali. So is mathematics, if
only you would think about it. So are the good deeds of little
men. So are the legends of heroes. And so finally and inevitably
is the Creator, seen from here below. Otherwise would it not
be too simple, like a beautiful dream, say, that had turned sour?
And why not monsters now and then, in a world packed with
fools and angels? In the evil tongue of Maldoror—"I shall advise
them to **** *** ***** of crime, since *another* has already
done it." Not the language of the court, to be sure, but then
we are not dealing with a charlatan.

So, in the middle of the nineteenth century, just when the
Minnesingers seemed to have a clear field, a time bomb went off.
It was like a most horrendous ****. It splattered too. And that
is how almost a century later—how swift is progress!—we have
a beautiful mauve edition of an infernal machine which, in ex-
ploding the caul, blew up the embryo as well. That is why we
all resemble one another so disgustingly, even when we are not
beautiful and maimed. That is why we are so many BB bullets
hitting the same target and always the bull's eye. The bull doesn't
even blink. Nobody blinks or winks. It's a shambles, with the
bull's eye remaining wide open, staring ceaselessly and remorse-
lessly. What happened never occurred, because it was a bad
dream. It hangs like a flitch of bacon and rots. It points the azi-
muth. In the end it will make that most delightful of all mathematical figures, the asymptote. And there approximately you
have it in a nut-shell.

ARTHUR MIZENER:

IDEAS IN AUDEN

W. H. AUDEN: *For the Time Being*. Random House.

IT IS customary, in writing about Auden, to discuss either the failure of his poems to convey any sense of final conviction about the attitudes to which they are most obviously committed or their dazzling and suspicious technical facility. This custom seems to me both unbalanced and ungrateful. Not that there is not some support for it, but that after the worst has been said Auden remains, if not the wisest, surely the most intelligent poet writing in English today and, if not above an occasional ad lib, the most honestly skilful. Under these circumstances I think we would do better to devote the bulk of our attention to elucidation rather than to grumbling about Auden's occasional shortcomings.

In the present book he is dealing with two closely connected problems, the problem of the relation of the artist's imagination to reality and the problem of reality's relation to actuality:

> Art opens the fishiest eye
> To the Flesh and the Devil who heat
> The Chamber of Temptation
> Where heroes roar and die.
> We are wet with sympathy now;
> Thanks for the evening; but how
> Shall we satisfy when we meet,
> Between Shall-I and I-Will,
> The lion's mouth whose hunger
> No metaphors can fill?

In "The Sea and the Mirror" the emphasis is on the former problem and in "For the Time Being" on the latter. Neither poem

is a closely integrated whole; the first is called "a commentary"
and the second an "oratorio." Each is a loosely connected series
of lyrics having to do with a subject suggested to Auden more
by an anterior interest of his own than by either *The Tempest*
or Christmas.

There are two passages in the notes to the "New Year Letter"
which are of considerable importance here, especially for an
understanding of "The Sea and the Mirror." The first is a quotation from Kierkegaard's *Journals* on pp. 84-5 and the second a
note of Auden's own on p. 129. Here are a few sentences from
each.

"In order really to be a great genius, a man must be an exception . . .
There is a definite point in which he suffers; it is impossible for him to
run with the herd. Perhaps his dementia has nothing whatsoever to do
with his real genius, but it is the pain by which he is nailed out in isolation
—and he must be isolated if he is to be great; and no man can freely isolate
himself; he must be compelled if it is to be a serious matter."

Any idea has two practical purposes, to justify our satisfaction, and to
suggest a way to relieve our wants. As justification, an idea is a pure reflection of our material life and cannot re-enter history as an effective agent
because it does not want to.

In "The Sea and the Mirror" Prospero is presented as the
great poet who is giving up his magic because it is self-justifying
and enchanting:

> When I woke into my life, a sobbing dwarf
> Whom giants served only as they pleased, I was not what I seemed;
>   Beyond their busy backs I made a magic
> To ride away from a father's imperfect justice,
>   Take vengeance on the Romans for their grammar, . . .
> Now, Ariel, I am that I am, your late and lonely master,
>   Who knows now what magic is;—the power to enchant
> That comes from disillusion.

Caliban is the poet's quotidian self, the person who, when the
audience at the end of the play cries for the author, steps from
the wings to address them. His voice is the voice of the James
prefaces to the New York Edition:

If now, having dismissed your hired impersonators with verdicts ranging
from the laudatory orchid to the disgusted and disgusting egg, you ask

and, of course, notwithstanding the conscious fact of his irrevocable absence, you instinctively *do* ask for our so good, so great, so dead author . . .

Like the James of the prefaces, he speaks to the audience about poetry, the poet as poet, and the poet as man; as in the case of James, it is the elaborate convention of speech that allows Auden to say so much as he does. It is typical of the ingenious muddlement which results from Auden's free handling of Shakespeare's play that he should manage to make Caliban speak for both poet and audience, Prospero, Ariel, and Caliban for poet and man, and then, to top it all off, to have Caliban deliver "a message from our late author." Your feeling that at any given moment you do not certainly know how many worlds of discourse you are in is equalled only by your conviction that Auden does.

Most of the other important characters of Shakespeare's play are presented as people who have been "soundly hunted / By their own devils into their human selves." All, except Antonio, have been awakened from their self-admiring dreams.

> But we have only to sit still and give no orders
>   To make you offer us your echo and your mirror;
> We have only to believe you, then you dare not lie;
>   To ask for nothing, and at once from your calm eyes,
> With their lucid proof of apprehension and disorder,
>   All we are not stares back at what we are,

as Prospero says to Ariel. The wonderful variety of ideas and techniques with which these personages are presented has to be seen at first hand to be appreciated.

It might be said, from the dramatic point of view, that Auden's characters are, like Congreve's, too uniformly witty, the would-be wits speaking with a brilliance hardly less than that of the wits. On the whole, however, this is not a very serious consideration as long as the reader does not mistake Auden's poem for a dramatically unified whole and remembers that he is "presenting" rather than "representing" these characters. It might also be said that occasionally the operation of his figures, as Coleridge said of Cowley's, "consists in the excitement of surprise by the juxtaposition and *apparent* reconciliation of widely different or incompatible things . . . and is therefore a species of *wit*, a pure work of the *will*." But this is comparatively rare considering how many widely different things Auden has undertaken to reconcile here.

The most serious limitation on the ideas of the poem seems to me the insistence with which Auden still clings to the genetic fallacy. It is not so much that from the point of view of the writer the whole psychological explanation he offers for the poet's activity may not be true, as that his preoccupation with it tends to make him take too lightly the product of the poet's activity, not, perhaps, excluding his own. The genesis of a poem is far from being the measure of its value, or even the most entertaining thing about it. The account of Shakespeare's career in the song on page ten, for example, is, for all its cleverness, trivial to the point of irrelevance. The idea even looms discomfortingly in Ariel's beautiful song to Caliban.

The lyrics in "For the Time Being" are held together by an almost uniformly brilliant narrator. Auden is really developing here, in terms of the story of Christ's birth, an idea which has been in his poetry from the start:

> I mean
> That the world of space where events reoccur is still there,
> Only now it's no longer real; the real one is nowhere
> Where time never moves and nothing can ever happen.

This idea is clearly developed in XVII of *Poems*, which goes back at least as far as the Faber *Poems* of 1930; and it has recurred regularly ever since. This is our true existence, but

> Since Adam, being free to choose,
> Chose to imagine he was free
> To choose his own necessity,
> Lost in his freedom, Man pursues
> The shadow of his images

(compare the fifth sonnet in "The Quest"). To the frustration, the deception, and the despair of living altogether in the world of space and the difficulty of living in the real one Auden directs the attention of his speakers. The attitudes toward this subject which he invents for them are always beautifully realized. The opening chorus, for example, sets forth the despair of the world before the birth of Christ in a marvelous variation on the stanza form of Momus' famous song in the *Secular Masque*. Joseph is given a combination of folk ballad, popular song, and pure Auden in which to express a dilemma no less truly tragic for being popularly and rightly thought comic:

> The bar was gay, the lighting well-designed,
> And I was sitting down to wait
>   My own true Love:
> A voice I'd heard before, I think,
> Cried: 'This is on the House. I drink
>   To him
> Who does not know it is too late';
>   When I asked for the time
> Everyone was very kind.

>   CHORUS (off)
>   Mary may be pure,
>   But, Joseph, are you sure?
>   How is one to tell?
>   Suppose, for instance . . . Well . . .

The shepherds are Auden's poor with their "sufferings to which they are fairly accustomed"; and Herod is the liberal trying to establish the Rational Life:

Things are beginning to take shape. It is a long time since anyone stole the park benches or murdered the swans. There are children in this province who have never seen a louse, shopkeepers who have never handled counterfeit coin, women of forty who have never hidden in a ditch except for fun. Yes, in twenty years I have managed to do a little.

Now he is confronted by the irrational:

Naturally this cannot be allowed to happen. Civilization must be saved even if this means sending for the military, as I suppose it does. How dreary . . . O dear, why couldn't this wretched infant be born somewhere else? Why can't people be sensible? I don't want to be horrid.

I do not suppose Auden will ever be an epic or dramatic or perfect poet. He has very little gift for characterization and is much more uniformly successful in providing "a distinct gratification from each component *part*" than in producing "such delight from the *whole*, as is compatible with" this gratification.

But if his powers are not unlimited, if his conception of his subject is occasionally more clever than just, if he is, in Coleridge's sense, sometimes merely witty, this seems to me a small price to pay for the general intelligence and seriousness of his verse and the almost incredible ease with which he handles a great variety of styles and forms.

PAUL ROSENFELD:

FLORINE STETTHEIMER

A SHOW recently on the walls of the Museum of Modern Art
in New York included a brilliant American canvas, clear
in tone, bright in mood, elegantly decorative, breathing personal distinction. Its title is "Family Portrait." Four finely dressed
women are represented, a mother and her daughters, on what
appears to be a brightly lit terrace. The pretty, intensely blue-
eyed little old lady is playing solitaire with a miniature deck of
cards. One daughter in velvet romantic painting-togs gracefully
stands with a palette in hand; another sits, half-reflectively adream
over an open book. The third poses, hostess-like at some social
affair. Behind in the blue of dusk New York floats in the shapes
of Radio City, the Chrysler Tower, the Bartholdi statue.

Four names are inscribed on the canvas. They are "Mother,"
"Carrie," "Ettie," and "Florine." The family represented here
was that of the painter, the late little-known Florine Stettheimer.
The sinuous figure in the velvet togs is herself. When she died
a few months ago, Henry McBride, the New York *Sun's* veteran
art critic, wrote that she "had passed as unremarked by the general public as did the poet Emily Dickinson in the 1880's."
Prophetically he added: "But when a few years shall have put
the event in perspective, it will be found by the new group of
connoisseurs that Miss Stettheimer's place among the artists is
just as distinct and just as secure as Emily Dickinson's is among
the poets."

She was an offshoot of Victorian American-Jewish society;
of its most genteel, its banking circles. She had been taken abroad
for her education, placed in continental boarding-schools. She

had stately, numerous uncles and aunts, and boy-cousins the objects of teen-age romantic friendships. For her education she was taken abroad, placed in a continental day-school. Her family atmosphere as one afterward felt it was densely feminine: all mother, sisters, aunts. She did not have close women-friends.

To the general public Florine Stettheimer was known mainly through the performance of *Four Saints in Three Acts*, the ironic little opera by Virgil Thomson. She was conspicuously one of the mainstays of the piece, as the author of its glistening cellophane stage-designs. In 1916 she had a one-man show of her paintings at Knoedler's, but later rarely priced a picture for sale. But she exhibited at the Carnegie International; in the Art Institutes or Museums of Chicago and Philadelphia; at Wanamaker's, the Whitney Museum and many other places; and sometime was a member of the American Society of Painters, Sculptors and Gravers.

In her home and her fantastically ornate studio in the Beaux Arts Building, for years with her unmarried sisters she maintained a salon: inevitably, like her paintings, it will figure in all accounts of the modern art movement in New York. It was a genuine gathering-place of its sort; not one of those which, in the wit's words, "set out to be salons and succeed only in becoming restaurants." "The celebrities in the world of art and literature" periodically appeared there. God knows, on many occasions they formed notable collections of freaks. But one also met Henry Mencken, Sherwood Anderson, Georgia O'Keeffe. Artists indeed voluntarily went there and not at all merely because of the individualities of the trio of women and their tasteful hospitality. They went for the reason that they felt themselves at home with the Stetts—so the trio was affectionately called—and the Stetts seemed to feel themselves entirely at home in their company. Art was an indispensable component of the modern, open, intellectual life of the place. The sisters felt it as a living issue. Sincerely they lived it. Nor was Florine the only "creator" among them. Another of the sisters was the author of a couple of distinguished novels, *Philosophy* and *Love Days of Susanna Moore*, under the pseudonym Henrie Waste. The third, who presided at table, amused herself with the arrangement of a palatial doll-house designed and executed by herself in every detail with unending patience and great ingenuity and skill. Its "art gallery" contained a miniature replica of "Nude Descending a Staircase," made for it by Duchamp himself, and an oval Venus carved from a fragment of alabaster by Lachaise. It is now a possession of the Museum of the City of New York.

At Florine Stettheimer's home and at her studio one also made the acquaintance of many pieces of her work. They also hung on the walls or were brought out and shown to privileged guests. There, were certain of her fanciful family-portraits—say, the touching full-length of the severe, ignorant Irish nurse who reared the painter, her brother and sisters, masterfully erect beside a prie-Dieu, surrounded by the cherubically-winged heads of her nurselings. Or the playful picture of "Henrie Waste," her cheeks aflame under dream-bewildered eyes, sailing on a crimson wishing carpet through the night beneath a blazing Christmas tree. There one also saw some of the slyly humorous autobiographic canvases narrative in the naive manner of the medieval draftsmen; presenting separate events or successions of them simultaneously within the limits of single designs. Also certain of the witty social satires: "Cathedrals of Broadway," for instance, the spoofing apotheosis of the giant Broadway movie houses, all domes, columns, beds of light with the vulgarly handsome face of Mayor "Jimmie" Walker on the silverscreen; or the rosy, elfish "Atlantic City Beauty-Contest." And sitting before these pictures probably more than one musing art-lover reached the conclusion that the painter was one of the most talented and individual artists of her sex that have appeared in English-speaking lands.

This is not quite to say that these art-lovers may be thought to have reached conclusions like Henry McBride's recent one; found themselves prepared to promise Florine Stettheimer's work a place in art comparable to Emily Dickinson's in poetry. Her body of work and the dazzling New Englander's doubtless have traits in common: the frequent ebullience of mood, the quaintly

personal lyricism. Only: from Emily Dickinson there flowed
lyrics as great as any written in America and the greatest uttered
by any woman in the English tongue. Extraordinarily this spinster possessed the gift of imagination, the power to move the
soul in us. Florine Stettheimer's gift was slighter. It was eminently
for fancy, for charming or whimsical images or combinations of
them; for daintiness of workmanship and fantasy. Her canvases
beguile and quicken us.

Take "Family Portrait," the brightly colored terrace-scene
lately in the Museum of Modern Art. Every detail in it, every
one of the minor forms cunningly assembled in the structure,
surprises and diverts the eye and mind. The shapes nearly all are
dainty in proportion, slightly bizarre, lacy or scalloped. Some
resemble those of birds. Others resemble those of shells or objects
intended for embellishment: passementerie, say, or the mould-
ings and the tassels and the fringes of the furniture and the
draperies in elegant periods, the Louis XVth, the Art Nouveau.
Meanwhile the total form rivals the theatre, the opera, even the
circus. Its center is composed of three fantastic floral shapes—
one silver, one scarlet, one rose, draped with pale-green streamers
—that hang startlingly, lavishly, a trifle incredible before us, as
though just sprung up at the wave of a conjurer's wand. Or like
fantastic sky-rockets or balloons suddenly and silently let aloft.
Inevitably the lavish shapes and their ascension give us the illusion of assisting at some fabulous party or scene from a baroque
opera with magic effects.

Simultaneously the picture entertains with its urbane irony.
There is a piquant ambiguity or doubleness in its mood and
meaning. At first it appears full of a lyricism of the life of complete self-sufficience, estheticism, independence. The four figures
seem entirely engrossed in, satisfied by, an existence of amuse-
ments and refinements, beautiful decorations, art, literature; while
at the top of the scene the effigy of Liberty with skirts strictly
to her ankles triumphantly flaunts her torch. There is more than
a suggestion of spiritual attainment in the floating flowers. Gradually, possibly because of the ghostliness of certain of the shapes
and the ornamental quality of many of them, we receive a sense

of elegant waste, a feeling that this life of independence and estheticism is illusory, a bauble, a bubble. The two meanings together face us.

Finally: the conception before us is as manifestly and unmistakably feminine as is a boudoir; frail, delicate, ornate. Perhaps it is not quite characteristic of the run of women. We feel something slightly anaemic, a trifle blasé in the spirit and style—in retreat as it were from everything primordial and earthfast. If there is springtime in this little world, we feel, it is exclusively "springtime among the saffron satins." Still the personality addressing us is gracious, tender, animated, loyal; nor are we assailed by any selfish utilization of feminine charm such as we associate with some recent French women painters—Marie Laurencin, for example. We meet no affectation here; only truthfulness to a feminine temperament which happens to be uncommon. Love of immediate kin, in pale green streamers, scatters itself upon the canvas. But love of kin also directs itself from out the canvas onto us.

"Family Portrait" may well be Florine Stettheimer's museum-piece: it nonetheless typifies her performance, her over-a-hundred canvases mainly now in storage. Fantasies, decorations, witty sometimes mordant ironies, all are marvelous: like faery operas, lighted Christmas trees, the snowstorms in the little glass paperweights which used to lie on writing-tables. All are self-revelations of the uncommon temperament whose play they are; revelations of the dream it secretly bears about. In the past this temperament provided the living ornaments of small exclusive societies, delicate as it is, lightly ironic, finely discriminative in matters of taste. But only its masculine counterpart would seem to have found expression through art, in that of the painters of the *fêtes galantes* in France; of Charles Demuth, Florine Stettheimer's ally, in America. Now in her paintings it tells the world something of what it is searching for: some circumstance where everything possesses a delicacy, a daintiness, an ethereality "present in the world in no satisfying measure, or not at all"; and lends something of that very charm, the grace, the ethereality not to any small closed society, but the world.

DELMORE SCHWARTZ:

THE CRITICISM
OF EDMUND WILSON [1]

READERS of Edmund Wilson's latest collection of essays ought
to go back to his novel, *I Thought of Daisy* (1929). The
view of the artist and of the genesis of literary works which
has become a method for Wilson in *The Wound and the Bow*
is stated there in terms of personal experience. It is not perfectly clear that *I Thought of Daisy* is a novel—its success depends too much upon two long meditations on the hero's part,
and not on any dramatic action—but, in any case, it is a good
book, better now, perhaps, than when published, for it can be
seen as defining a period (as a photograph gains new qualities
with the passage of time), but chiefly because it makes clear
Wilson's basic attitudes as an author.

The Wound and the Bow rests upon the thesis that the artist
is strong and weak at the same time; his great virtue as an artist
inseparable from his weakness; his weakness perhaps (Wilson is
not too clear on this point) the cause or one of the causes of
his strength; or, to use Wilson's sentence, the artist is "the victim
of a malodorous disease which renders him abhorrent to society
and periodically degrades him and makes him helpless; but is
also the master of a superhuman art which everybody has to
respect and which the normal man finds he needs."

Just this conception of the artist disturbs the unnamed hero
of *I Thought of Daisy*. Of this unnamed "I," one gets a most
touching image in the course of the novel. He is a modest and
humble young man who wants to write verse and to know the

[1] This is the first part of a longer study of Edmund Wilson.

interesting intellectual and artistic people in the New York of the twenties. But this is not the right way to state his complex attitude, for it seems at times that what he wants most of all is to know life, to break out of his own personal isolation and limitation into life at its best; and life at its best he takes to be the literary life in the best sense of the phrase. He does not draw a sharp distinction between literary people and literary works. He admires the literary people of his acquaintance— among them, the famous poetess and the famous novelist—and is willing to stand for a great deal from them. But they often disgust him: there is a gap between the nobility of their writing, and the stupidity, viciousness, weakness, and self-absorption of their lives. What good is literature, after all, he asks himself, if it must arise from such lives? This question is inspired by a disagreeable, utterly pointless Greenwich Village drinking party, but it leads the hero to a feeling of doubt about the worth of literature and the literary life in which he turns on Dostoyevsky and Sophocles (both cited in *The Wound and the Bow*) and rejects them also because their great works seem to have been generated by lives which are equally offensive. In the end, this emotion is transcended by a new attitude on the part of the hero, an attitude of critical and reasonable acceptance of the people he knows. He accepts them as inextricable mixtures of good and evil. How this attitude is arrived at in the novel is not relevant right now; the point here is the way in which the resolution of shifting attitudes in *I Thought of Daisy* can be seen as the keynote of all of Wilson's writing. Some of the hero's concluding thoughts might well serve as quotations for the title pages of the critic's later books:

So, by the way of literature itself, I should break through into the real world. . . . On that very day when she [the famous poetess] had filled my imagination with the splendor of her genius and her beauty, when she had seemed to me a goddess or a muse—on that day, her own mind had been haunted by visions of imbecility and deformity.

These phrases and thoughts echo through *Axel's Castle*, the critical work which established Wilson. Amid a careful, reflective, judicious analysis of Yeats, Joyce, Proust, and Valéry, one can hear again and again the reproaches of the unnamed hero of *I Thought of Daisy*. Valéry, for instance, is reproached for his condemnation of Anatole France on an occasion—his election to the French Academy to take France's seat—when the customary thing was to compose an eulogy. This is, says Wilson, pretentiousness and snobbery; and one feels that the reproach is directed not against literary taste or opinion, but against *a person*. It is as a person, too, that Proust seems to be reproached as engaged in "self-coddling, chronic complaining, over-cultivated sensibility"—Wilson quotes a French critic's remark that there was much of the spoiled child in Proust. And yet Wilson says also that these elements were important factors in the making of Proust's great work. And the whole movement of which *Axel's Castle* is a proposed history is accused of "over-cultivated sensibility" and of not being at the center of life, even as Joyce is scolded, in passing, because he did not make the reading of his work easier for the common reader by providing introductions. As a history, *Axel's Castle* suffers from the virtue of being addressed—how deliberately one does not know—to an audience which is vague in extent, but is certainly constituted for the most part of readers who would like to be helped to read the difficult new authors. The essays are good introductions for such readers (*Axel's Castle* ran first as a serial in the *New Republic*); but for the reader who has mastered Proust and Joyce, there is little which he really needs. To define the point further, the book is not the kind of criticism which helps to germinate new writing; it is not a book for writers. The definition of Symbolism intended to unify the book is so general and so loose that it permits the inclusion of authors who are really apart from Symbolism, such as Yeats. "To intimate things rather than to state them plainly was thus one of the primary aims of the symbolists," to compete with the suggestiveness of music, "to communicate unique personal feelings by a complicated association of ideas represented by a medley of metaphors"—this is the closest Wilson can come to a *literary* definition, although he is excellent on the social and intellectual background of Symbolism.

Actually Symbolism was a prolonged cultivation of the power

of language for its own sake which eventuated in an emphasis upon the connotative usages of language to an exclusion, which varied from author to author, of the denotative usages. The purest and completest example is Mallarmé. Wilson knows very well and paints with sure strokes the isolation of the artist from the rest of society which brought about the desire and the need to cultivate language in this way. He knows the life in back of the work. But when it becomes a point of describing the technical working, the craftsmanship and the unique forms, which are an essential part of Symbolism, and the authors who were greatly influenced by the Symbolists, Wilson is impatient and hurried. He is not actually interested in the formal working which delivers the subject-matter to the reader (as the rhyme-scheme of a limerick delivers its wit). It is for him the wrapping-paper which covers the gift; it is necessary to spend some time taking off the wrapping-paper and undoing the difficult knots of the cord tied about it, but the main thing is the gift inside, the subject-matter, which always turns out to be an intimate life: in *Ulysses*, we "possess Dublin seen, smelt, heard, and felt, brooded over, imagined, and remembered." So, by way of literature, one can break through into the real world. It is life that matters; books are a way of getting into life; we forget the formal character of the book as we forget the door through which we came into the house. *Axel's Castle* concludes by suggesting that, important as the authors in question are, and unique and valuable though their discoveries may be in the future, literature must return to wholesome objectivity—not, however, without remembering and using the discoveries of these authors.

Axel's Castle appeared in 1931, two years after *I Thought of Daisy*. By this time, life had broken in on every private life, however isolated and limited. The social decade of American literature had begun, showing itself first in the intellectual uneasiness of the neo-humanist controversy, and then, as the depression continued, in the explicit affirmations and denials of the importance of social consciousness and class allegiances in literature.

The effect upon Wilson was profound; and partly because he

had already felt, before the depression and before almost any other author of his generation, the relevance of social criticism, and the intimate relationship between the individual and the society which gave him life and kept him alive. Most authors of the twenties had been able to express their criticism and rejection of our business civilization merely in some version of the attitudes made popular and colorful by H. L. Mencken. The phrase, "the civilized minority," expresses and virtually exhausts the insight which these authors depended upon. The curious resemblances one can find between H. L. Mencken and Edna St. Vincent Millay, so far as their leading attitudes and sentiments go, sum up the period. Wilson admired both these authors —in later years, he seems unable to forget to be loyal to these admirations, as if loyalty were actually relevant, as if it were once more friendship and not literature that was in question— but in going from an editorship of *Vanity Fair* to the literary editorship of the *New Republic*, the development of his interests, before the depression, is clear. It is clear too in his admiration of John Dos Passos, the one important author of the twenties who really depended upon an explicit social consciousness.

Thus Wilson was prepared for the thirties, and the three books he wrote after *Axel's Castle* are a direct and a strong product of the impress of the depression upon him. *The American Jitters, Travels in Two Democracies,* and *To the Finland Station* are all efforts inspired by an interest in the depression and in socialism. The first two works are on the surface merely superior notebooks; but the sensibility and the honesty of the traveller are so great that these works are far more than journalism. Both contain chapters which, with hardly a change, might have been part of *I Thought of Daisy.* The last chapter of *The American Jitters* presents "The Case of the Author": after declaring his rejection of American capitalism and the life it made possible, and after affirming his acceptance of Marxism as a correct analysis of society and of the necessity of socialism, Wilson goes on to apply the Marxist formula to himself:

My family have on both sides belonged for several generations to what used to be called the learned professions. . . . My father's and uncles'

generation were obviously alienated by their old-fashioned education from
the world of the great American money-making period. . . . My father,
for example, was a lawyer in New Jersey and at one time Attorney-General
of the state; but his love of independence and his distrust of big business
were so great that he stuck all his life to his miscellaneous local practice and resisted all temptations to become a corporation lawyer in a state
governed by corporations. He even refused to invest in the corporations.
. . . One of the results of this [family background] has been that I have
grown up in modern prosperous America with a slightly outside point of
view, due not merely to the professional tradition in the family . . . but
also to the fact that my family have never really departed very far from
the old American life of the countryside and the provincial cities. . . . It
began to dawn on me that the best people were usually satisfied with a
very thin grade of culture, that when you tried to go into the adventures
of creation or the exploration of the causes of things they didn't follow
or approve of you. . . . My life had seemed to me both false and dull.
. . . I have tried at one time or another all the attitudes with which
thoughtful Americans have attempted to reconcile themselves to the
brokers' world . . . they were all ways of compromising with the broker.

These sentences point to a depth of feeling and attitude on
Wilson's part which is not stated in theory but which is made
perfectly clear in its applications and concrete instances. The
right phrase is difficult to find: "fundamental scrupulousness"
will have to do, and it will do very well if it reminds the reader
of the heroes of Henry James. This sense of a fundamental scrupulousness, a living remnant perhaps of Christianity, operates in
the hero of *I Thought of Daisy* when he resents the excesses
and weaknesses of literary people, even though he is much more
appalled by the business civilization against which they are re-
belling. He is thinking of the dignified and self-contained *person*
of "the old American life" when he is dismayed by the anger
and hatred in Dante, the weakness and viciousness in the life of
Dostoyevsky, the savagery and madness in the life of Sophocles,
or when he reproves Valéry for priggishness and Proust for
coddling himself, or when he speaks of "rather childish" rages
of Greek heroes, actual and imaginary.

The picture can be rounded out, perhaps too patly, if we
move ahead to the moment in *Travels in Two Democracies* when
the traveller, disappointed and dismayed by the squalor, drabness, and narrowness of the brave new world of Soviet Russia,
turns with immense pleasure to the poetry of Elinor Wylie, a

pure although dead product of "the old American life": "I had never before felt so vividly the rarity and value of people who could do something fine very well."

Travels in Two Democracies continues the excellent reporting, the clear, sensitive descriptive prose, of *The American Jitters*. One remarkable chapter, "The Old Stone House," describes a place where "the old American life" was lived; and the book concludes, after the traveller's fundamental goodness has been shocked any number of times in America and the Soviet Union, with an almost lyrical return to the individual who determines his own existence with strength of character—"accuracy of insight," "courage of judgment" independent of "obsolete authorities," "invisible forces," and "all the names in all the books."

This disillusion and return corresponds not only to the disillusion with the literary life in *I Thought of Daisy*, but also and more importantly with a breaking of the spell of Marxism, a spell which had never been complete. It apparently halted and modified the writing of Wilson's next and most ambitious book, *To the Finland Station*. The same thing happened in the writing of John Dos Passos's *U. S. A.*, in between the second and third novels. Both instances are interesting examples of life breaking in on the author.

To the Finland Station is an important work in itself, apart from its connection with, and the light it sheds upon, all of Wilson's writing. What is relevant here is the continued and indeed the augmented interest in persons. Although he is writing about men who made or wrote history, it is to personal traits that he returns again and again, dwelling, for example, upon Karl Marx's family life (and with especial love upon the Sunday picnics of the Marx family), Lenin's asceticism, and Trotsky's pride of intellect. This process of mind sometimes arrives at absurdity, as when Wilson suggests that Bakunin's politics had their real origin in the conspirational games he played with his sister when he was a boy; and it keeps the book from complete success by suggesting that the failure of the Russian Revolution was a failure of Trotsky and Lenin as persons; or perhaps one should say the embodiment of their personal defects in political and social policies. Or again, Marx's personal traits and failings are suggested as causes of the inadequacy of Marxism. On the other hand, the book justifies itself precisely because it contains so many good portraits of persons. The same excellence of portraiture is to be found in *The Triple Thinkers*, which was published before *To the Finland Station*. The essays on A. E. Housman and Paul Elmer More are actually concerned with these two men as inadequate human beings, and again we are presented with—and gratified by—the reproofs Wilson administers to them. It is perhaps because Housman and More are in so many ways inferior to Valéry and Proust as authors that the personal emphasis and judgment seem just and worth bringing to the forefront of attention. Elsewhere in the book is an essay on Flaubert's politics, in which, by the additional device of quoting from two letters of Flaubert, the novelist is used as a figure of the proper attitude of the artist toward the social problems and the social claims of his time, and towards life as a whole. And then there is what is perhaps Wilson's best essay, on Pushkin, in which the feats of introduction which marked *Axel's Castle* are repeated, but this time with an author not otherwise available to most readers, and with more concern with *placing* his literary quality, an act performed by citing Byron and Keats.

In the same essay, Wilson resumes the habit of breaking through to the subject-matter: he provides the reader with an interesting synopsis of the plot of *Evgeni Onegin*. This is mentioned particularly because in another essay of this book, "Is Verse a Dying Technique?", it is just this conception of the relationship of form to subject-matter and just this habit of wanting to get as quickly as possible to the subject-matter in itself that leads Wilson to suppose that versification is finished, at least for the modern author. This is far from being the first time that Wilson has felt this is to be true. In an essay published in 1926, Wilson reviewed American writing and in passing spoke of Marianne Moore, asking whether or not it was actually possible to consider her verse poetry. In *Axel's Castle*, Wilson makes the point that Joyce is really a poet. But in this essay of *The*

Triple Thinkers, Wilson is prepared to go much further and to suppose the devices of versification are no longer necessary to the ambitious modern author.

Wilson's reasons are mixed. One reason is the fact that William Butler Yeats and Edna St. Vincent Millay, taken together and providing a common denominator, appear to serve Wilson as a touchstone for what verse, as verse, ought to be, so that as a consequence he views with much suspicion such a poet as Auden, who seems to be using too many of the devices of prose and whose verse-writing seems to sound too much like prose. But a more important and less limited reason is the fact, which Wilson cites at length, that the major literary works of the last one hundred years have been in prose and not in verse. But most of all, I think, Wilson is prepared to regard versification as a dying technique because the formal character of the work is for him merely the wrapping of the package. It does not seem to be necessary to the representation of the subject-matter, which is what we really want.

This is not the place to discuss his view at length. So far as this essay goes, it should be enough to point out that what we really want is the formal character of the literary work penetrating, illuminating, and uniting with the subject-matter. Moreover, the major prose authors who, for Wilson, have succeeded the major poets not only learned a great deal from versification as a technique, but in their prose works reveal a dependence upon rhythm and metaphor which would be impossible without a thriving school of versifiers and body of versification: Baudelaire and Hugo influenced Flaubert, just as the poets of the nineties and the early Yeats influenced Joyce. But it is Wilson's attitude toward literary technique which I want to underline once more, in this instance.[2]

[2] *The Boys in the Back Room* represents another aspect of the same fundamental attitude toward literature. In this small book, published in 1941 by the Colt Press, Wilson writes of authors who, apart from Steinbeck and Saroyan, are what circulating libraries call "good rentals." His remarks are as usual penetrating, and what he has to say about Steinbeck is especially revealing; but it is perfectly clear that what makes these authors interesting to Wilson is the fact that they are significant products of Hollywood and

The Wound and the Bow represents the next, the latest, and one should think the last step in Wilson's interest in the author as a person and in the literary work as a means of getting to know the person. About two-thirds of the book is devoted to Dickens and to Kipling; the rest is made up of fairly short essays on Casanova, Edith Wharton, Hemingway, *Finnegans Wake*, and the *Philoctetes* of Sophocles. In each author some weakness, pain, or sorrow—such as blindness in Joyce, a nervous breakdown in Edith Wharton, childhood unhappiness and marital difficulty in Dickens and Kipling, old age and cruel sons for Sophocles—seems to Wilson to be one of the prime factors in the creation of the literary work. I say *one* of the prime factors, although at times Wilson writes as if it were *the* prime factor; indeed, he goes so far as to say of one of Dickens' novels that it cannot be understood without reference to his personal life—so that there is the inevitable suggestion that perhaps all of these authors were mistaken in their method: what they should have done first of all, even if they did nothing else, was to provide a full *dossier* of their childhood and their married life. This is to press Wilson's view to an absurd extreme, of course; but the suggestion is there, and it renews itself whenever the personal connection is forced, or over-burdened, as an explanation of the genesis and the *interest* of the work.

In the long essay on Dickens, it is quite evident that Wilson has not forgotten all that he learned from Marxism. There is an effort throughout to see the social aspect as well as the purely personal aspect of the trauma which is to mean so much in the writing of Dickens. The six-month period spent by Dickens at the age of twelve in a blacking bottle factory is seen as a fall in the social scale as well as a shocking episode in the life of a boy who is in despair because he has been taken out of school. But the union of Freud and Marx is incomplete, and the Freudian em-

California. Hollywood and California and life are what make him pay so much serious attention to such authors, of whose lack of literary distinction he is aware. The boys in the back room have always been very interesting to one intent on breaking into the real world, and this may also be why Wilson has long been fascinated by Hemingway.

phasis wins out. Thus in writing of the very poor books which Edith Wharton produced during the last twelve years of her life, Wilson suggests, although without conviction, that it is mainly the fading of the shock of the nervous breakdown which made her begin to write—this fading of the trauma together with a lack of a professional sense of authorship—which explains the poor writing. Yet there is a much better explanation in the work itself, and particularly in the shift in subject-matter. We can see how Mrs. Wharton lost most of her fine power every time she abandoned her genuine subject-matter, the conflict between a rising plutocracy and the morality of the old merchant society of her forbears; and we can see how she made a perfect recovery each time she went back to this subject-matter by returning to the periods in which it was best located, first in *The Age of Innocence*, which Wilson underestimates, and the four small novels about *Old New York*, and later in her last and unfinished book, *The Buccaneers*.

The same thing is true of what Wilson has to say, in general, of Kipling: the personal situation is emphasized to the extreme where one almost forgets, critic and reader both, that a much simpler and much more persuasive explanation of Kipling's decline is to be found in the difficulty of maintaining and nourishing the view of the British Empire which inspired him to write at the very start. I do not want to press forward the claims of social criticism beyond a certain point. The difficulty in *The Wound and the Bow* is the converse of this, the over-emphasis of the personal event, and the personal situation. And even if the Freudian analysis is taken as a primary explanation, it is clear that Wilson does not want to adopt it with any degree of fullness. Thus Dickens' childhood exile in the blacking factory, which was to become so important, brought about a renewal of nervous fits Dickens had known in earlier childhood. But of course, for the true and thoroughgoing Freudian, the important thing is the cause of these nervous fits in earlier childhood and not their recurrence at the age of twelve, a very late date in the psyche from the Freudian standpoint.

Yet one of Wilson's virtues as an author has always been to

avoid giving himself to any systematic view of life, to see how life is more than any systematic view of it, but at the same time to see how systematic views are useful instruments. This *roundedness* of feeling and interest was apparent in the books Wilson wrote in the thirties, when Marxism was uppermost in his mind, and it is clear in *The Wound and the Bow*, too. If the long essays on Dickens and Kipling press an amateur Freudianism too far, they nevertheless contain much else, and they carry forward the old concern with authors as human beings: Kipling is reproached for snobbery and for excessive anger, as Housman and More were condemned for like faults. If we try to take these factors as causes of the work, we are bound to be dissatisfied; there is too much complication in the genesis of any literary work, despite the *Philoctetes*.[3] But if we see this interest in the

[3] It is interesting and pleasant to have a critic in America feel the need to refer to Sophocles. But not only does the *Philoctetes* suggest a number of other interpretations quite different from the one Wilson gives it, but we cannot help thinking of the many other classical stories, from Orpheus to Oedipus, which express aspects of the creative life. Thus, the poet can be viewed in these legends as depending upon a great exaltation, a kind of madness, and ecstasy; or he can be regarded as one who goes down into Hell to regain from death or oblivion that which he loves; or he can be seen as the man who kills his father and marries his mother and whose crime must be revealed and expiated in order that sickness may depart from the city. The latter interpretation is the richest, for it contains the strict Freudian view and yet emphasizes the necessity of revelation, discovery, and knowledge.

Each of these stories is illuminating. There seems to be no reason to insist on one to the exclusion of the others. Various authors seem to be moved to write for a variety of reasons. But there is one thing they have in common, however different they may be, a *mastery of language;* if Wilson were able to show that such a mastery was always traumatic in origin, there might be more reason to emphasize as he does the necessary union of strength and weakness in the creative artist.

Or, to examine Wilson's view in reverse, a number of women in Edith Wharton's time must have suffered from a nervous breakdown consequent upon an unsuccessful marriage. The difference between them and Mrs. Wharton, so far as literary criticism is concerned, is in Mrs. Wharton's literary powers. No doubt such an event as a nervous breakdown had something to do with her becoming an author, but the all-important factor is precisely the grasp of literary devices and forms which Wilson, despite his sensitivity to it, is always brushing aside in his actual scrutiny of his authors. I do not mean to say that a gift for literary expression is itself a

human being in the context of such books as *I Thought of Daisy*
and *Travels in Two Democracies*, if we remember the tone and
lucidity of Wilson's prose throughout, then it is easy to understand and to accept not only the thoughts and observations in this
new work, but the whole body of Wilson's writing.

Is it not true, I mean to say, that literary history and literary
criticism have always been merely pretexts for Wilson? For we
do not get from his ostensibly critical essays the strict formal
analysis, which is one kind of traditional literary criticism; we do
not get the reformation, correction, and extension of taste, which
is another important kind; nor do we get the propagation of the
leading ideas of an age, which is a third kind and which also tends
to forget the literary work as such. Coleridge, Matthew Arnold,
and T. S. Eliot illustrate in different aspects of their work each
of these kinds, for good or for evil as the case may be, and we
can see how Coleridge's criticism helped to bring about the
poetry of Wordsworth, how Arnold created the consciousness
of neo-humanism, and how Eliot reformed taste. But if we look
for literary judgment in Wilson, we find a singular weakness and
lack of critical pioneering. There is a curious tenderness for such
authors as Thornton Wilder, Edna St. Vincent Millay, the later
Van Wyck Brooks, Max Eastman, and Henry Miller, an author
who merely turns Céline upside-down with a stale optimism. On
the other hand, there is an equally curious indifference or aversion
to such authors as Gide, Kafka, Thomas Mann, Rilke, Wallace

simple and irreducible fact; it obviously springs from a complex of conditions; but it is the gift for expression and the expression as such which
separates authors from other human beings, whether they suffer from childhood unhappiness, marital failure, psychological disorders, or are beautifully normal. A further possibility is that the unhappiness and disorder
of creative lives is the *effect* and not the cause of creative effort, which
does, after all, tend to make a human being more sensitive, more easily
disturbed, and, last but not least, less able to make a living and be a
devoted husband and friend.

To return to the *Philoctetes*, it is clear in the story itself that Philoctetes
not only has his matchless bow (it is given him by Heracles) before he
suffers his wound, but the wound is in no way connected with the power
of the bow. One might contract wounds as a result of having and using a
bow, but it seems much less likely that one would gain a bow as a result
of being wounded.

Stevens (who really extends the Symbolist movement as much as any of the authors discussed in *Axel's Castle*), and Céline. Thus, Wilson speaks in the same sentence of Proust and Dorothy Parker, and compares Max Eastman favorably with Gide. And there are like defects, as I have tried to point out, in Wilson as a literary historian.

The whole of Wilson's work actually represents something else and something just as important as literary history and literary criticism. Once we have seen both history and criticism as a device or pretext or convenient form, we can see how Wilson has provided a history of the American of "fundamental scrupulousness," who has come from "the old American life," and has borne this feeling about life throughout the America of his time, Princeton, the first World War, the Greenwich Village and the New York of the twenties, the social ferment and the moral disillusion of the thirties. The actuality of this experience is to be found nowhere else in the writing of our time. It is as if we were provided, to vary an earlier reference, with a history of one of the sons of a hero of Henry James; but this character has not only gone to Europe to bring back the art treasures of the Old World in *Axel's Castle*—he has had his moral experience in the Soviet Union, rather than in the Italy of Milly Theale, or the France of Lambert Strether, who also wanted to break into the real world. Another resemblance is to *The Education of Henry Adams*, for in Wilson we have another and later and more difficult education under circumstances which Adams foresaw but did not live to experience. It is an education without conclusion, but fruitful and illuminating as an experience: the Soviet Union, for example, is grasped as something lived through by one kind of American.

The actuality of the experience, the education, and the American background is rendered by the lucidity and the sensitivity of the prose style. Wilson's prose is above all a *friendly* and a *reasonable* prose; the phrase, "Isn't it true," recurs at crucial moments to express the reasonableness, the judiciousness, and the "fundamental scrupulousness" of attitude. It is because this attitude and this tone are genuine and native that we can accept the characteristic act of taking hold of the literary work in order to find the human being, break into the real world, and know life concretely and fully. The attitude can be seen perhaps most explicitly in a passage from *Axel's Castle*.

It is at the death of Bergotte that Proust's narrator, in what is perhaps the noblest passage of the book, affirms the reality of those obligations, culminating in the obligation of the writer to do his work as it ought to be done, which seem to be derived from some other world, 'based on goodness, scrupulousness, sacrifice,' so little sanction can we recognize them as having in the uncertain and selfish world of humanity—those 'laws which we have obeyed because we have carried their precepts within us without knowing who inscribed them there—those laws to which we are brought by every profound exercise of the intelligence, and which are invisible only—and are they really?—to fools.'

HARRY SLOCHOWER:

TANGENTIAL CONCLUSIONS OF THE JOSEPH STORY

*T*he *Beloved Returns* and *The Transposed Heads*, which followed *Joseph in Egypt*, seemed at first glance to have no
connection with Mann's Joseph myth. The first was characterized
as a tribute to Goethe, and the Hindu legend as a "finger exercise" in the rest period made necessary by the exacting labors on
the Joseph story

Now the conception and execution of these novels fall into the
time when Mann continued to work and deliberate on Joseph's
final stage. This circumstance recalls the fact that Goethe interspersed his work on *Faust* with other projects, all of which reveal
in some way Goethe's preoccupation with the "main business" of
Faust. Sounded for similar clues, Mann's novels also appear as
ruminations on his "main business," as convergences from distant
peripheries toward the center of the Joseph story.

GOETHE—THE HISTORICAL ANALOGY

The story of Joseph, following his descent into the Pharaoh's
prison, is to take an ascending curve. But where was Mann to find
the source for such inspirational direction? He himself was an
exile, and all signs of this time (1938-40) pointed to the continued
triumph of fascism. With the historical present holding the spirit
imprisoned, what was the artist to draw on for Joseph's elevation
from the prison-pit?

The Goethe novel we interpret as a backward look to history
for a prototype and approximation of the Joseph personality. The

subject of Goethe offered Mann a historical analogy to himself
and to his theme. More than any other historical figure Goethe
has been Mann's own prototype. Moreover, Goethe himself once
planned a drama dealing with Joseph. And just as Mann has
tended to identify himself with the great German, so in *The Beloved Returns* Goethe is likened to Joseph, endowed with "blessings of heaven above, blessings of the deep that lieth under."
While "waiting" for Joseph's visions to take form Mann invokes
the past for a nineteenth-century foreshadowing. Goethe, by
whom Mann himself has been nourished, is resurrected to serve as
the "nourisher" of Joseph's future. Mann's regression in *The Beloved Returns* is an invocation to the Mothers of History to give
up the son.

Mann shows Goethe at the period of his fullest maturity. He is
sixty-seven (approximately Mann's own age at the time the novel
was written), at work on the second part of *Faust* and ready to
close the circle by reintegrating his beginnings in the higher phase.
To his followers he is a kind of God-Father, androgynous and
complete ("womb and seed"), combining opposites in an all-
embracing irony. He is pictured as embodying a divine disinter-
estedness, "at once absolute love and absolute nihilism and indifference." Goethe appears here as an absolute, but his public
perfection as artist has been gained at the cost of deep private
tragedy.

Goethe has attained absolute stature by disallowing himself
living participation in events and people. Beneath his Olympian
serenity, Mann discloses the searing pain of the human being who
has sacrificed his body to art and spirit. Goethe did love, but he
never allowed himself to "live out" his love, to marry and have
a family. He flirted and kissed, but no children come from kisses.
"The making of children," Goethe muses, "is no affair of
poetry's." Consummation he achieved only in his art. Here again
Mann treats sex-fulfillment as an obstruction to the creative stress.
Renunciation of the physical increases the tension and thereby
spurs man on to *symbolic* fulfillment through artistic and spiritual
refraction. This, Mann shows, was the case with Goethe. His
fusion of nature and art, of physics and ideality, of "kisses" and

"children" was largely in the symbolic sphere. He was averse to wedlock in order to enjoy the perpetual honeymoon of poetic ecstasy. He refused to "settle down," in order to allow his spirit to be eternally transformed. The result is a majestic portrait, admired and worshipped by the many who are pilgrims to his seat at Weimar. But these see only the mask of the spirit, not the terrible aloneness of the man. Goethe did marry, but Christiane Vulpius never ventured to address the great man with the familiar "thou." He did have a son, but August is shown as a weak echo of his father, an imitator who coarsens, sensualizes and stratifies his qualities. Goethe had a large following, but the Riemers and the Meyers are servants who fawn and bow. In short, Goethe's life failed of the interaction which his work effected. His progeny is more in the character of Thomas Buddenbrook who denies his son, of the faded Peeperkorn, of the eunuch Potiphar, than of Joseph, destined to become a father of a family and father to the people of Egypt.

Lotte—the Lotte whom Goethe wooed as a youth—is the representation of the nature element which Goethe renounced. Where he chose "kisses" and the parody of life through art, Lotte chose to give up the lover Goethe for the husband Kestner, to live in orderly bourgeois wedlock and become a mother of many children. Her simple nature preferred the stability of organized, sober living to the might-have-been which Goethe's adventurous genius held out to her.

However, this is no simple repetition of the Tonio Kroeger theme in which the artist is deprived of the blond and blue-eyed ones. Mann's work has taken him through the magic values of enchantment which enriched the personalities of Gustav Aschenbach and Hans Castorp. If art suffers from deprivation of nature, the later, in becoming conscious, feels the lack of art. If Goethe has missed a wife and marriage, Lotte has missed the honeymoon with the lover. And so, after forty-four years since the days of Werther, she undertakes a pilgrimage to Weimar in a somewhat childlike attempt to recapture the poetic past. In a final mythical setting, in a talk carried on amid the shadows of Goethe's rolling carriage, they reveal to each other their reciprocal incompleteness. Goethe speaks of the hidden agony behind his dignity, of his body-sacrifice that the light might burn: "I am the drunken butterfly that falls to the flame—figure of the eternal sacrifice, body transmuted into soul, and life to spirit." As in *Royal Highness*, renunciation remains the poet's pact with the Muse and life the forbidden garden. The final words, "Peace to your old age," are Lotte's, whispered to him who can now look forward only to the last Antaean compensation, to death, the ultimate transformation of nature into the flame. But the words may as well have been addressed to Lotte, who has also come to feel the need of "the other." The dream-nature of this scene suggests an identification of the two characters with these spoken words applying to either and to both.[1]

The Beloved Returns thus questions the possibility of complete fusion between the spiritual and the physical. Goethe was the genius who, like his Faust, left no offspring. Lotte was nature who produced many children that remained unknown. It is the story of unfulfillment seen from the distinct perspectives of art and nature. It presents the either-or between the genius and the simple people, between the aristocratic individual and the folk, between honeymoon and wedlock. However, now when they are at the end of the holy season of renewal and rejuvenescence, they may hope that in the final "flight into the flame," the sublimation of their individual existence may yet mean their union in the "All-in-One."

The First World Nurse—The Original Analogy

In *The Beloved Returns* Mann goes to specific history for aid in establishing the Joseph coordinates. *The Transposed Heads* regresses to the prehistoric. It is an even purer myth than that of Joseph, for it stands outside historical time altogether. Mann's Hindu legend is an approach to the Joseph problem from absolute beginnings unencrusted by historical contingencies. It takes place in the land which gave birth to the mother-tongue from

---

[1] Mann's word "sie," of course, may mean "she"; but in the context it may also refer to Goethe's "Stimme."

which our Indo-European speech developed. It is the land which, according to legendary tradition, was the site of Paradise. Mann is in quest of the first enactment of the human drama, repeated in more involved forms in later ages. Here perhaps may be found the original formula in simple, naked outline, before it became obscured by moralistic canons and guilt associations brought by Western religions and civilizations. In this early pattern there is as yet a minimum of "false" consciousness and no fear of punishment in an after-life. For these people know of only one world, the world of Sansara or Appearance. The realm to which the departed go they call Nirvana or Nothing.

As a "plain" summary of human relations, *The Transposed Heads* encompasses the entire gamut of man's way, beginning with his state in paradise, the innocent plane of unity and peace, through his awakening to consciousness, passion and knowledge which split the original oneness and bring divisiveness and war, to the final reintegration by "flight into the flame." In this necessary process, man is fated ever to strive for unification, ever succeeding to a limited extent and always feeling the insufficiency of both satedness and want. What distinguishes this story of Mann's is that, for the first time, the tragic surd is treated from the vantage point of high comedy, viewed as part of nature's way and accepted with cheerful sympathy (*"heiteres Mitleid"*).

In this tale Mann transposes the problem of "head" and "body," of genius and organization, of art and business, into an elementary plot involving a woman's desire for simultaneous enjoyment of a lover and a husband. Sita is married to Schridamann with the wise head but unimpressive body. Her marriage only awakens her to the knowledge of lust, and in the arms of her husband Sita longs for the lover, for Schridamann's friend Nanda, the youth with the coarser head and the manlier body. When the heads of the two friends are transposed, Sita is happy—she now possesses the lover's body as well as the husband's head. In the Hindu legend this rearrangement makes for their common happiness. Thomas Mann's account diverges from this happy ending. There is bliss at first, but even this "at first" is questionable, and the author suggests that what transpires later makes itself felt from the very beginning. The acquired lover-body becomes the husband-body, and the distant husband-body takes on the qualities of the longed-for lover. Having what she had desired, Sita now desires what she has not.

Possessing the husband-head on the friend-body, she yearned for the friend-head on the husband-body. And just as certainly would she feel pity and sympathy for the husband-head on the friend-body, nor would she find any peace and satisfaction, the distant husband would ever be the friend whom she loves.

As the mores forbid their all living together, the three agree that their desire for unification can be fulfilled only in their common death.

Together Schridamann and Nanda combine the wisdom and practicality which Joseph's personality embodies. In the opening paradisiacal setting they are united in friendship, each finding it inconceivable to live without the other. Their first stage is an innocent male union. They "intrigued each other," by virtue of being perfect complements to each other. This peaceful state is upset by the appearance of the beautiful girl. Sita is the "Snake" emerging from the waters, bringing to them the fruit from the tree of knowledge and sin, the Eros element arousing them from the quietude of their existence to a Maya-longing which becomes a longing for absolute beauty and happiness that can be stilled only by death. Through her the two become divided, differentiated, awakened to the particularity of their sex-beings. She is the "Fall," making for individuation and estrangement. But this is only her lower phases of "customary" sensuousness. (This aspect is also suggested by Mann's play on her name: "Sitte," "sittsam," "sitzen.") She is also the liberator from appearance, leading out "beyond the darkness of confusion to knowledge and truth." She is Earth Spirit in the dual role of awakening matter to consciousness (the Nanda-evolution) and conversely of materializing the spiritual (the Schridamann development). She is the "furrow" through which the two men find their common road, the "All-Mother" and "All-Nourisher" of both the simple and the complex, who find the meaning of life and death through her. In the attempt to bind to herself the wisdom of Schridamann and the immediacy of Nanda, in her desire for both husband and lover, Sita reenacts Jacob's dual wooing of Leah and Rachel, Mut's effort to hold Joseph while wedded to Potiphar and Lotte's craving for both her good Kestner and the romantic friend. (Mann subtly "modernizes" Sita's error in putting the heads back. Her error is the truth of her subconscious will.) Sita is, finally, a foreshadowing of Joseph's attempt to wed his prophetic gifts to the practical business of politics and government. Mut and Lotte failed. Even Jacob soon lost his beloved Rachel. To be sure, the world's goal is "union between spirit and beauty, a bliss no longer divided but whole and consummate." But the story of Sita, Mann tells us, is an "illustration of the failures and false starts attending the effort to reach the goal." The dream visions when translated into the actual, become grounded and limited. Hence, "makeshifts, renunciations and resignation are the common lot." Mann's story of the "original" failure is a preview of the later Joseph when the enthusiasm of his lyrical beginnings is stabilized and regulated.

Still, the isolation and difference which Mann's characters suffer constitute a value. For,

difference makes for comparisons, comparisons give rise to uneasiness, uneasiness to wonderment, wonderment tends to admiration; and finally admiration turns to a yearning for mutual exchange and unity.

Ultimately this spells tragedy. Yet by *knowing* that all peace, harmony and silence are illusions, that man has the power to arouse desire but not to sate it, he can raise himself above the tragic, can even smile at his fate in cheerful sympathy. In *The Beloved Returns* Goethe muses on the high value of the light touch:[2]

The depths must laugh! Profundity must smile. . . . All seriousness springs from death and its reverence for it. But dread of death is despair of the idea—is the stream of life run dry.

Never before has Mann treated a tragic subject with the same equanimity and aloofness. There is a sort of debunking of the

[2] The reference to this novel is relevant also since Goethe is shown here as planning a similar theme of transposed heads.

tragic through common-sense humor when Nanda calls Schridamann's longing for death after he sees Sita simple "lovesickness,"
and when the Goddess treats the whole episode in a rough, matter-of-fact manner as something entirely normal. At the end this
light touch is carried out by the three characters in the non-
tragic way in which they decide to die together. What makes all
this possible is that the head has now assumed undisputed leader-
ship as the all-important factor in establishing human identity. In
the end, "the head decides the value of the body."

The tale has a concrete issue as well. It is the son, the common
fruit of the three parents. He is called "*Sammlung*." The German
term has the double meaning of "collection" and "concentration."
Samadhi is nearsighted, and we are led to imagine that this handi-
cap will restrain him from looking as far afield as his parents did.
It may also lead him to concentrate on those goals which lie
within man's limited periphery.

T. WEISS:

GERARD MANLEY HOPKINS:
REALIST ON PARNASSUS

GERARD MANLEY HOPKINS has several times been impeached for inaugurating prepossession with literary rather than human ends; rather than employing his pen for forthright expression, he has spent himself on expression itself. He, some maintain, reflects the romantic retreat from life into the ivory tower of art, on the one hand, and of religion, on the other. But his life, I will attempt to show, proves not only the ruthlessness of art in its exposure of the basic inacceptability for him of religion, but also the common incompatibility today between art and religion. An art as piercing and rigorously honest as Hopkins' could allow him little contentment with what became for him increasingly evasion.

Within himself Hopkins encompassed both belief and its merciless turning upon itself. His life, accordingly, epitomizes the career of the last hundred years. Because of this religious doubt, in our day poets have clung more and more to the immediate, for its own sake. A visible god, some tell us, is necessary for the welling up of hymns, poised and passionate, such as antiquity enjoyed; Hopkins, however, yearning for the hymn, had only the words, not the vision to support this yearning. I agree that this hymnic urge was a constant pressure within him. But I maintain that in his earlier days he knew such a visibility of wonder. For him the spiritual world experienced no dichotomy from the earthly one. The imputation that his poetry lacks profundity of content, inscape if you will, fails the obvious truth of his early poetry. He saw profundity everywhere. Inscapes were as casual as birds upon a twig and as radiantly sure. In the beginning of his faith, as in the Eden beginning, the world *was* inscape—the content of God. So all Hopkins needed to do to be supremely spiritual was copy God's handiwork, bring it to others less aware. Adam-wise, he went about his rapturous business of naming his world and trimming the wanton growths from his senses' precisions. No distance distracted his senses from his world; they were a crystalline one.

Hopkins, though he would have probably stoutly denied it, was intrigued not so much by "the fruit of experience, but experience itself." According to him:

All the world is full of inscape and chance left free to act falls into an order as well as purpose: looking out of my window I caught it in the random clods and broken heaps of snow made by the cast of a broom. The same of the path trenched by footsteps in ankle deep snow across the fields.

How closely this approaches the climax of Pater's "Conclusion" I need not say. Also like Pater, one of his teachers, Hopkins lamented the plethora of unappreciated beauty. For beauty, he believed, is "the virtue of inscape" or the floruit, the maturity, of an object's form and being. Talking of the hay stacked in a barn, he says:

I thought how sadly beauty of inscape was unknown and buried away from simple people and yet how near at hand it was if they had eyes to see it and it could be called out everywhere again.

But Hopkins' inscape enjoyed wider scope than Pater's beauty-quest.

It is not that inscape does not govern the behaviour of things in slack and decay as one can see even in the pining of the skin in the old and even in a skeleton but that horror prepossesses the mind.

The withering flower, the rotting body have a ripeness of their own and approach realization of the metaphor peculiar to this condition of being. Ripeness is all.

As his *Notebooks* tell us, Hopkins early put himself to the sweet duty of direct observation. Largely relieved, at least in his younger years, of the basic spiritual problems, he could give himself to objective worship. We need to believe and to articulate our belief chiefly when we need or desire something; the Edenites, the pure pagans, and Hopkins for a moment were free of the need. Indeed, so thingful and moraless are his observations, they strike one almost as purely pagan: sight is sufficiency. Examples drawn from his *Notebooks* readily illustrate his well-nigh unparalleled acuteness and delicacy of perception. His is the terrible crystal of clarity.

Sometimes I hear the Cuckoo with wonderful clear and plump and fluty notes; it is when the hollow of a rising ground conceives them and palms them up and throws them out, like blowing into a big humming ewer.

Or:

July 22—Very hot, though the wind, which was south, dappled very sweetly on one's face and when I came out I seemed to put it on like a gown as a man puts on the shadow he walks into and hoods or hats himself with the shelter of a roof, a penthouse, or a copse of trees, I mean it rippled and fluttered like light linen, one could feel the folds and braids of it—and indeed a floating flag is like wind visible and what weeds are in a current; it gives it thew and fires it and bloods it in.

Or:

At the end of the month hard frosts wonderful downpour of leaf: when the morning sun began to melt the frost they fell at one touch and in a few minutes a whole tree was flung of them; they lay mashing and papering the ground at the foot. Then the tree seems to be looking down on its cast self as blue sky on snow after a long fall, its losing, its doing.

Or his study of clouds, a patient delight suggesting that he wrote as though inside things, looking out: he is their instress or inscape. Many of these for sheer strength of description, the force of simple concrete words, are superb imagist poems, almost bewildering in their brilliant plenitude of detail. By his faithfulness to fact, Hopkins proves himself a scientist or profound scholar of observation and little the mystic. Yet in his degree of perception he surpasses most men and reaches a perspicuity and a passion of detachment that might "save" all of us. One critic has suggested, "Nowhere in his work does he draw on an experience . . . beyond the range of any thoughtful and sensitive Catholic who meditates on his Faith." In fact, he does not draw on an experience beyond the range of any thoughtful and sensitive man. Hopkins' treatment, however, his experience of intensity and imagination, is something to challenge anyone.

Thus those impatient of his exacting have sometimes dubbed him a great stutterer; but his is the stutter of ecstasy, the overflow of fervor and embrace when words buckle and fuse. The voice of passion is not loose and by its speed not clear. To a certain extent, therefore, Hopkins resembles his own portrait of Browning:

. . . Browning has, I think, many frigidities. Any untruth to nature, to human nature, is frigid. Now he has got . . . a way of talking . . . with the air and spirit of a man bouncing up from the table with his mouth full of bread and cheese and saying that he meant to stand no blasted nonsense . . . The effect of this style is a frigid bluster.

We may wonder whether Hopkins' later conduct was not somewhat antithetical to human nature. (As he himself admitted, congratulating Bridges on his engagement: "A single life is a difficult, not altogether a natural life.") Much of Hopkins' poetry also seems to bounce up, not with a mouthful of bread and cheese, but with a mouthful of praise and rapture where syllables in their rush trip over each other. So he seeks to convey his hurlyburly of soar by suppressing unstressed syllables. Rockily eruptive and monosyllabic, in his search for the rugged and fierce, his weaker poems are the real sputterers; they try, by manipulation mainly, to reach his best poems, and so degenerate into self-caricature. But Hopkins is difficult because he is direct—a directness that means detachment or anonymity. Once his idiom is understood, in his resolute responsibility to his craft, clarity is constant. At first reading one is immediately struck by new atmosphere, new earth, and new heaven. Hopkins may not construct a new world as Blake or Milton sought to do; he did not need to: it was there before him in overwhelming abundance and before us in every phrase he wrote, almost to be taken for granted.

Here we return to Hopkins' early seity with the earth. The seeming conflict between earth and spirit met with new intensity in the romantic period. Professor Fairchild's *The Romantic Quest* formally discusses this problem under the terms of Transcenden- .

talism and Descendentalism; they embody the Dr. Jekyll-Mr. Hyde elements in human nature. I would attach this modification: Dr. Jekyll is not superior to or separable from Mr. Hyde, and vice versa. These two personalities, two expressions of one individual, are indispensable in the composition of the complete human being. Today, with the tendency of the artistic as well as the political and social world toward anti-intellectualism, the Mr. Hyde personality has gradually superseded Dr. Jekyll as the desideratum of human conduct. Mr. Hyde is the intuitive, primitive, spontaneous person. This attitude is probably what Hopkins meant when he wrote to Coventry Patmore of the "tykishness" necessary to all artists. Hopkins, however, displayed in much of his life no leaning toward one to the other's exclusion.

Professor Fairchild has remarked of Transcendentalism and Descendentalism: "In romanticism, the two extremes . . . are combined and often reconciled." But he believes that for any large length of time such an alliance is virtually impossible. He designates Wordsworth "the exemplar of that phase of romanticism in which the descendental and transcendental elements are about evenly balanced." Yet even in Wordsworth, Professor Fairchild owns, the reconciliation at best is very shortlived and almost always a strain. Sometime earlier he recognizes a possible solution in Catholicism—a solution Hopkins promptly accepted. Huysmans cited Barbey d'Aurevilly's review of *A Rebours:* ". . . after such a book, it only remains for the author to choose between the muzzle of a pistol and the foot of the cross." And Huysmans answered, "The choice has been made." For a time Hopkins merged beauty and holiness. Catholicism provided him with a firm base which contributed to his temporary calm.

Though hardly a decadent in ambition, Hopkins more than participated in the decadents' almost excessive sensitivity and their paradoxical delight in the stronger pagan parts of nature. And Hopkins was wise and objective enough to appreciate the value of decadence. He answers a letter from Bridges:

'The first touch of decadence destroys all merit whatever': this is a hard saying. What, all technical merit—as chiaroscuro, anatomical knowledge, expression, feeling, colour, drama. It is plainly too true. And come to that, the age of Raphael and Michelangelo was in a decadence and its excellence is technical. Everything after Giotto is decadent in form, though advancing in execution. Go to.

But though appreciative of decadence, Hopkins in his immediacy of treatment resembles the naif or primitive. This is the fresh and eager spirit of the child and the childlike spirit Wordsworth celebrated in his Intimations Ode. "Growing up," losing his vividness of impression, Wordsworth dwindled as a poet. But even more, Hopkins here approaches what Baudelaire somewhere set forth as the paragon for artists: the child's firm, crisp comprehension of reality concomitant with the mature artist's articulation and control of it. Hopkins, despite the circumstances of his life, retained longer than most this impression-innocence. This naked naïveté was by no means delicate to the point of fragility; if anything was sturdy about Hopkins it was his vision. After he mastered his medium, he never lapsed into the sybaritism of sheer sensation. He represents something like the opposite of *ex forte dulcedo*—more accurately, strength out of sensation and sensitivity. Such mastery must persuade us of the presence of remarkable energy. Only such unjaded power could win through to such luminance of form. Michelangelo believed the forms already exist, buried in the rock, waiting impatiently for their deliverer. But it takes the might of a giant to knock off their stony trammels and release them into the beauty of expression, to strike the right spring of inspiration in the heart of the rock.

In truth, much of Hopkins' innocence amounts to omniscience —freedom from the fold upon fold of artificiality blinding and binding the senses of "modern" man: such innocence also involves the "tykishness" I earlier mentioned, a trait Hopkins deemed an essential. He explained it to Patmore in this wise:

As there is something of the 'Old Adam' in all but the holiest men and in them at least enough to make them understand it in others so there is an old Adam of barbarism, boyishness, wildness, rawness, rankness, the disreputable, the unrefined in the refined and educated. It is that I mean by tykishness . . .

This "something of the 'Old Adam' " seems a most singular quality for a Jesuit.

That this quality of tykishness originally grained Hopkins' character no one can gainsay. It would have fed his conviction that "There lives the dearest freshness deep down things" and prompted his desire, "O let them be left, wildness and wet: / Long live the weeds and the wilderness yet." The whole world— even that which most of us might consider its debris and filth— he saw as essential. In light of his oneness with objects, the first thing that strikes the reader is the "freshness fuming," the extreme yet natural novelty of Hopkins' world. His ecstasy in earth drove him into terms of foam and fume and flame, but terms accurate and mightily held.

And his grip on the earth also rarely deserted him. Accordingly, he quickly recognized, with misgivings, a kinship in Whitman with his gusto for all degrees of the earth. So too we remember Hopkins' insistence that "Common sense is never out of place anywhere, neither on Parnassus nor on Tabor nor on the Mount where our Lord preached." We remember Hopkins' response to a metaphor by Dixon: "Angels are the very cheapest things in literature." In a similar rational vein Hopkins defined "inspiration," which he believed ascribable to physical causes generally, "as good health or state of the air, or prosaic as it is, length of time after a meal." More, he appreciated the importance of critical concentration upon one's initial creativeness. A most painstaking craftsman, only so could he attain many of the seemingly carelessly cast-off results, the impetuous music that insists we run while we read. As he confessed to Bridges, ". . . I have of myself made verse so laborious." He knew how fruitless out-of-hand frenzy is. His work at best, therefore, shared the superb, almost irritating tension present in the greatest art, that which sets the mind and heart on edge. He took advantage of the gifts of intellect, so much so some critics have concluded that his poetry suffers from "overdiscipline." Such conclusions still harbor the romantic superstition that poetry to be "creative," "original," and the work of genius must be spontaneous—that is, must spring full-panoplied from the head (more accurately, the heart) with little rime and less reason. These critics do not seem to recognize that the critical and technical faculty often lames the creative faculty, not because there is too much of the former, but because there is not enough. Probably such uncritical critical attitude is part and parcel of the anti-intellectualism rampant in our world. And after all, Hopkins' critical acumen to the contrary notwithstanding, his poetry was at heart, even technically, instinctive. Hopkins' theories tagged his practice; for his rhythms were inherent in his nature. Coventry Patmore, myopic to much of Hopkins' mastery, accused him of truckling to his theories. In a letter to Bridges, Patmore relayed Hopkins' answer: "He assures me that 'his thoughts involuntary moved' in such numbers, and that he did not write them from preconceived theories."

Nor did Hopkins in his hardheadedness wish to reduce nature to man's image or desire. Rather he reveled in its variety and strange wildness. Things "barbarous in beauty" delighted him immeasurably. Spiritually fastidious, rich in the control of conviction, he could luxuriate in the world's plenty, further token of God's graciousness. "Hurrahing in Harvest" was the mood that claimed his first years of Catholicism; "brute beauty" was his ambition. But traveler in reality that he was, he little indulged in a rapture of fantasy. His eyes were in his head.

His importance to us, other than as a metrical influence, is still intensely controverted. Yet memories of Hopkins jut from almost all our younger poets. A rollcall of those influenced would be equivalent nearly to a rollcall of those writing. But many critics still demur as to the extent of his influence; these would limit it to technicalities. If they were correct, his influence would indeed be regrettable. They fail to see how immensely Hopkins' metrics partook of his total sensibility. The reasons for his hold, I suggest, revert to his intimacy with the world as it is—a quality that endears the later work of Yeats to us. Not a few of Hopkins' traits wield a general appeal. With his abiding love for nature in all its myriad behaviors, and with his sensitivity to it achieving a pitch tantamount to a second sense, he writes so magnificently of the visible that the invisible begins to appear. His work should be the finest corrective for poetry the last fifty-odd English years have produced. He denounced the flabbiness and turgidity of much of the romantics. His commitment to sprung rhythm—a rhythm which promised him, he believed, the freedom and directness of expression Wordsworth aspired to—amounted to a declaration of independence and, accordingly, implied constant personal vigilance: the greater the freedom of form the more severe the demands on the individual poet.

But Hopkins has proved himself a prominent citizen of our poetic times in many other ways. Repelled by the excessive limpidities of the Swinburneans, eager to sinew his verse, and attracted to the more turbulent moods of nature, he turned to the hardiness of Anglo-Saxon, a language which has appealed to not a few of the leading poets of our time. In addition, he objurgated the custom of garnishing poems with archaisms. Artificiality he generally abjured: ". . . inversions . . . I do avoid them because they weaken and because they destroy the earnestness or in-earnestness of the utterance." Criticizing Swinburne, he proposes: ". . . a perfect style must be of its age." Even as a poet absorbs the past, he must saturate his work in the rich dyes of his day.

Furthermore, even as Hopkins' artistry best displays itself in his ability to give us poetically transmuted the texture of his delights and his agonies, the fibers that formed his personality— every inch of Hopkins is behind and in his art; so concurrently he wins us with his child and workingman poems. With great love he dwelt on the beauty of manhood. As "Felix Randal" and "Harry Ploughman" testify, he especially joyed in the robustness of the laborer. In his fundamental democracy Hopkins equally felt the strength of the workers' misery. In a letter to Dixon he avows:

My Liverpool and Glasgow experience laid upon my mind a conviction, a truly crushing conviction, of the misery of town life to the poor and more than to the poor, of the misery of the poor in general, of the degradation even of our race, of the hollowness of the century's civilisation: it made even life a burden to me to have daily thrust upon me the things I saw.

This conviction, growing always more tenacious, became one of the taproots of his eventual overwhelming despondency. Need I indicate his similarity here to Pound, Eliot, and all the other Waste-Landers?

But Hopkins' most explicit statement occurs in one of his early letters to Bridges, his "red letter" as Hopkins later named it.

I remember that you never relished 'the intelligent artisan.' I must tell you I am always thinking of the Communist future . . . I am afraid some great revolution is not far off. Horrible to say, in a manner I am a Communist. Their ideal bating some things is nobler than that professed by any secular statesman I know of . . . Besides it is just.—I do not mean the means of getting it are. But it is a dreadful thing for the greatest and most necessary part of a very rich nation to live a hard life without dignity, knowledge, comforts, delights or hopes in the midst of plenty—which plenty they make. They profess that they do not care what they wreck and burn. This is a dreadful look out but what has the old civilisation done for them? As it at present stands in England it is itself in great measure founded on wrecking. But they got none of the spoils, they came in for nothing but harm from it then and thereafter. England has grown hugely wealthy but this wealth has not reached the working classes; I expect it has made their condition worse. Besides this iniquitous order the old civilisation embodies another order mostly old and what is now in direct entail from the old, the old religion, learning, law, art, etc. . . . But as the working classes have not been educated they know next to nothing of all this and cannot be expected to care if they destroy it. The more I look the more black and deservedly black the future looks, so I will write no more.

In the face of the above confession it is little to be wondered the young revolutionary poets held Hopkins dear. For many of them Communism seemed Christianity made flesh. No one would attempt to impugn the fact that Hopkins' utterances stemmed from humanitarian sentiment. But few compassionate churchmen, it seems to me, particularly in Hopkins' day, would confess, ". . . in a manner I am a Communist." Furthermore, how did the great number of Communists begin if not as humanitarians?

Nor did Hopkins ever abandon (could not) his own jealous personality. As he tasted himself above all else in the beginning, so he did unfailingly to the end—but with what difference! "Bitter would have me taste: my taste was me." How could such a powerful individualism, reminiscent in its strength and in its counter-hunger for humility also of Milton's, how could it yield to the anonymity the Jesuit order exacted—the very thing his individualism by its strength yearned for? For Hopkins continues the struggle of modern man, perhaps first summarized in Milton: the desire for something greater than oneself to believe in—

whether religion or the state in our time or, for small people, the conventions of their society—and be disciplined by, and the counter-realization of the demands of the ego and the discipline within. *Lycidas* voices Milton's debate between fame and hedonism; Hopkins' life expresses his wrestling between religion and fame. Perhaps fame in God was not enough. Clearly it was Hopkins' death to hide his truculent talents; they burned through his side. We have learned from his letters of his numerous flirtations with publishing. Probably as much as his fear of outraging his order, his fear of rejection—after several abortive attempts at print—decided him. He shrank from rejection because he craved recognition.

From another point of view, the later, tormented Hopkins must appeal to our poets. Isolated in a faith which the world was hostile to, or worse, increasingly indifferent to and unaffected by, he knew the anguish the more sensitive must experience in our always more crassly materialistic world. For Hopkins' realism was relentless. Rather than cushioning him, his religion in its failure to cope with the pressing problems of his time became more and more suspect. The very integrity that had compelled him to conversion refused to allow him to fail bringing his daily world to bear in test on his belief.

At first sight we would assume that men of, say, Eliot's temperament would especially be drawn to Hopkins. For a few years at least Hopkins enjoyed the full faith Eliot has been seeking. Indeed, it is surprising the ghostly side of Hopkins has not lured Eliot more openly. Perhaps, with his admirable instinct, Eliot has sensed how little of the ghostly side there is to Hopkins! The order of their dilemmas, however, is antipodal. Failing to solve his conflict, Eliot has turned to religion as his *pis aller;* Hopkins, contrariwise, went to religion at once and only gradually discovered himself falling into the abyss, widening steadily, between religion and actuality. For Eliot art and religion are not to be confused; for Hopkins, engaged in, they cannot help being confused. Avoid this delinquent music and listen to God's word. For literature is a worldly occupation; in it one does not serve God. Uneasily his religious applications close his poems; nor was he sure that these "morals" should be there. His sermons, we recall, were models of poetic failure rather than of religious success. But in spite of reasons for affinity, Eliot has shied away from Hopkins. In his *After Strange Gods* Eliot writes:

His accent . . . is quite different, I am sure, from the correct one. To be converted, in any case, while it is sufficient for entertaining the hope of individual salvation, is not going to do for a man as a writer, what his ancestry and his country for some generations have failed to do.

Why Eliot should hope for more "entertainment" I do not know. He does seem to suggest, however, that one is converted not for one's salvation's sake, but for one's situation as a writer. With his insistent realism, most intent in his writing, Hopkins soon learned how inadequate religion was for him. Eliot here seems to realize it, but he persists in forgetting it.

But the fear of the flesh and the temptations of the appetites that Hopkins, and Eliot too, must have known to an overwhelming degree, and the suppression of these, eventually took their toll. Denied, starved, Hopkins' senses waned. Religion and the earth no longer synonymous for him, in his last years he could not accept the realizations living, with ever more urgent cogency, thrust upon him. Certainly he could no longer reconcile them to his life, religion. This and the ways of acceptance had broken him for the nakedness his realizations required. Bent to the yoke of the cross some twenty years, he could no longer either drop or carry it. His very appreciation that one must live widely in one's day and his touching envy of Shakespeare's profound and vast knowledge of the ways of the world, plus religion's refusal to free him to the infinite delights of this world—these crushed him. His love of literature, and life reflected there, superseded his love of religion. But though the drayhorse once knew youthful full-pastured freedoms, harnessed many years, how shall it finally break away save in death?

Physically too, aside from their fasting and the gnawing of doubt, his senses suffered. As Hopkins put it in a letter to Dixon:

. . . insight is more sensitive, in fact is more perfect, earlier in life than later and especially toward elementary impressions: I remember that crimsons and pure blues seemed to me spiritual and heavenly sights fit to draw tears once; now I can just see what I once saw, but can hardly dwell on it and should not care to do so.

Once more I recall Wordsworth and Coleridge, those who also momentarily balanced Transcendentalism and Descendentalism. Directly Hopkins' sentiments above echo those of Coleridge's *Dejection*. As Coleridge says of natural beauties:

> I see them all so excellently fair,
> I see, not feel, how beautiful they are!

And what sharper correspondence of despondency than that between Coleridge's

> All Nature seems at work. Slugs leave their lair—
> . . . .
> And I, the while, the sole unbusy thing,
> Nor honey make, nor pair, nor build, nor sing

and Hopkins'

> See, banks and brakes
> Now leavèd how thick! lacèd they are again
> With fretty chervil, look, and fresh wind shakes
> Them; buds build—but not I build; no, but strain,
> Time's eunuch, and not breed one work that wakes.

Both were bereft of "the fine delight that fathers thought." If we can conjecture with some feeling of security that the opium of speculation unstrung Coleridge, surely we can with similar security suggest that the charges of religion put a resembling strain upon Hopkins. Like Coleridge, nobly honest in admission, Hopkins could not deny the testimony of his senses and the insistence of his conscience.

Though Wordsworth accompanied them in their plight, he followed an easier course. At his highest he was already finished. Even his best poems are mainly memories. Exhausting these, with comparatively little questioning, he succumbed more and more to orthodoxy and the conventional. But Hopkins, with a much more alert and merciless integrity, racked himself on the realization of the distance between his beliefs and the world as he experienced it. The ever-widening gap tore him apart. The very oneness he first knew now taught him a fierce feeling of separateness, aloneness. Desperately and futilely, we see, he endeavored to subdue his understanding to what he had believed and would still believe. Relentlessly his frustrations revenged themselves and harvested his rich despair. When he had succeeded finally in domesticating his senses, he found that God as the mystics claimed Him still did not come to him; nor did he longer joy in God's world. With the one he lost the other. With spirit and earth identical for him, as his first poems were joyous, so his last had to be agonized. In the first the vigors of spirit approved the earth; in the last the weight of the world compromised and crushed the spirit, one thoroughly weakened by an ascesis which in its fanaticism can also be lust.

Though he took what seemed the definitive step towards total acceptance and mysticism, he did not go with it; he could not. And he knew; so he was broken between his wish and his doubt, and his fear of his doubt. As I proposed earlier, his is the drama of modern man, ripped between two opposing positions, between past and future, superstition and knowledge, skepticism and learning. Others after him have suffered kindred fate. A Yeats with his resolute spurning of science as a dehumanizer; a Lawrence with his fitful flirting with psychology and then his denunciation of it for diluting the blood; and Eliot with his velleities for the past's permanence. The theme smacks of anti-intellectualism still. Hopkins could not turn his intellect away. Starting with religion, he saw it synonymous with the material world—as it is at its best, whether Plato or Christ. We, it seems, must work in reverse. Somehow returning from the straddle and the pull, we may at least envision the most basic Platonic ideal, the identity of earth and spirit. As long as they resent each other in us, we shall have neither, nor certainly peace from either.

CONTRIBUTORS

SIDNEY ALEXANDER. Recently released from the Army Air Forces, where he served as a radio operator and an editor. *The Man on the Queue* (poems, 1941). (Reprint of "The White Boat": *Best American Short Stories 1944.*)

C. E. AUFDERHEIDE. Educated at Midwestern universities. Employed by Technicolor in Hollywood. First published writing: *Accent*, Spring 1944.

PAUL BARTLETT. Has lived chiefly in Mexico during the past five years. Co-editor, with his wife Elizabeth Winters, of *Workshop*, a literary annual. Contributor to the *Kenyon Review*, *Mexican Life*, and other magazines.

DORIS BENARDETE. Instructor of English at Brooklyn College. First published story: *Accent*, Summer 1941. In progress: a novel, *Adder's Fork*.

ERIC BENTLEY. A British critic. In the English department at Minnesota. An advisory editor of the *Kenyon Review*. *A Century of Hero-Worship* (1944); *The Playwright as Thinker* (1946); a translation of Brecht's play, *The Private Life of the Master Race*.

JOHN BERRYMAN. Has taught at Harvard and Princeton. Contributor to *Five Young American Poets*, 1st series (1940). Winner of the *Kenyon Review* story prize, 1945. In progress: a critical edition of *King Lear*.

MARIUS BEWLEY. Educated at Cambridge. Associated with the New York gallery, Art of This Century. A contributing editor of *View*. First published poetry: *Accent*, Winter 1945.

R. P. BLACKMUR. On the staff of the Institute for Advanced Study at Princeton. Two books of critical essays: *The Double Agent* (1935) and *The Expense of Greatness* (1940). Poetry: *From Jordan's Delight* (1937) and *The Second World* (1942). In progress: a study of Henry Adams.

CHRISTOPHER BLOOM. The pen-name of a young California writer, a graduate of the University of California. Author of several recently completed manuscripts including a play, a novel, and a collection of poems.

KAY BOYLE. Has lived in Europe since 1922 except during the war years. Among her best-known publications: *Plagued by the Nightingale* (novel, 1931), *The White Horses of Vienna* (short stories, 1936), *A Glad Day* (poems, 1938).

ERNEST BRACE. Teaches woodworking at the School for American Craftsmen at Hanover, N. H. Articles on modern painting in the *Magazine of Art;* stories in *New Masses, Story,* the *American Caravan,* and the O'Brien and O. Henry yearbooks. Novels: *Commencement* (1924) and *Buried Stream* (1946).

MARJORIE BRACE (Mrs. Ernest Brace). Has been a reviewer for the literary supplements of the *Herald-Tribune* and the *Post* and for *New Masses.* Stories, poems, and essays in several literary quarterlies.

JOHN MALCOLM BRINNIN. Born in Nova Scotia. Educated at Michigan and Harvard. In the English department at Vassar. Poetry: *The Garden Is Political* (1942), *The Lincoln Lyrics* (1942), *No Arch, No Triumph* (1945).

CLEANTH BROOKS. Professor of English at Louisiana State and now at Chicago. Co-editor of the *Southern Review* and an advisory editor of the *Kenyon Review.* Author of *Modern Poetry and the Tradition* (1939) and collaborator on several analytical anthologies.

HARRY BROWN. Has done editorial work for the *New Yorker, Yank,* and his own poetry magazine, *Vice Versa.* Poetry: *The End of a Decade* (1940), *The Poem of Bunker Hill* (1941), *The Violent* (1943). Other recent writing: a play, film dialogue, the novel *A Walk in the Sun* (1944), and a war book, *Artie Greengroin, Pfc.* (1945).

HARVEY BUCHANAN. Now in France doing relief and reconstruction work with the American Friends Service Committee. To return to Yale for graduate work in the fall of 1946. First published work: *Accent,* Winter 1944.

EDWIN BERRY BURGUM. Teaches English at New York University. Editor of *Science and Society* and of the anthology, *The New Criticism* (1930). In progress: a book of critical essays.

KENNETH BURKE. Lives in Andover, N. J. Among his critical and philosophical volumes: *Counter-Statement* (1931), *Permanence and Change* (1935), *Attitudes Toward History* (1937), *The Philosophy of Literary Form* (1941), *A Grammar of Motives* (1945).

EDWIN G. BURROWS. Has returned to Ann Arbor after three years in the Navy. Hopwood Award winner, 1940. First published work: *Accent,* Spring 1941. Soon to appear: a book of poems.

WALTER VAN TILBURG CLARK. Lives in Rye, N. Y. Well-known for his novels—*The Ox-Bow Incident* (1940) and *The City of Trembling Leaves* (1945)—and for his short stories, as yet uncollected. (Reprints of "The Indian Well": *Great Tales of the American West* and the German-Austrian magazine *Neue Auslese*.)

HUBERT CREEKMORE. A Mississippi poet, living in New York since his release from the Navy. On the staff of New Directions. Poetry: *Personal Sun* (1940) and *The Stone Ants* (1943). Novel: *A Stranger and Afraid* (1946).

E. E. CUMMINGS. Lives in New York. Ten books of poetry—including *Collected Poems* (1938) and *One Times One* (1944). Several prose volumes, notably *The Enormous Room* (1922) and *Eimi* (1933).

DAVID DAICHES. A Scotsman, whose recent years have been spent in the English department at Chicago and in the British Embassy in Washington. Among his critical works: *The Novel and the Modern World* (1939), *Poetry and the Modern World* (1940), *Virginia Woolf* (1942).

DAVID CORNEL DE JONG. Born in Holland. Lives in Providence. Author of half a dozen novels, a book of poems, *Across the Board* (1943), and an autobiography, *With a Dutch Accent* (1944).

DENIS DEVLIN. First Secretary of the Irish Legation in Washington. *Poems* (Dublin, 1932), *Intercessions* (London, 1937), *Lough Derg and Other Poems* (New York, 1946).

RICHARD EBERHART. An American poet, educated at Cambridge and often published in England. Recently released from the Navy. Co-editor, with Selden Rodman, of the anthology, *War and the Poet*. Poetry: *A Bravery of Earth* (1930), *Reading the Spirit* (1937), *Song and Idea* (1942), *Poems, New and Selected* (1944).

GEORGE P. ELLIOTT. Lives in Berkeley. Graduate study at California; wartime employment as shipfitter and labor-management consultant in the Kaiser Richmond Shipyards. Now working on a novel and reporting part-time for a labor paper. Contributor to *Poetry* and *Circle*.

JAMES T. FARRELL. Author of the *Studs Lonigan* trilogy and other fiction. Most recent publications: *The League of Frightened Philistines* (criticism, 1945) and *Bernard Clare* (novel, 1946).

OTIS FERGUSON. Was killed in naval action early in the war. Articles on jazz, films, and books—chiefly in the *New Republic*.

BEN FIELD. A native New Yorker. Spends most of his time as farmhand and factory worker in various parts of the country. Short story collection: *The Cock's Funeral* (1937). Novels: *The Open Leaf* (1943), *Peter Tomkins* (1946).

DUDLEY FITTS. Teaches at Phillips Academy. *Poems* (1937). Translations from Greek drama, from the Palatine Anthology, from contemporary Latin-American poetry.

ROBERT FITZGERALD. Was an editor of *Time* till he joined the Navy. Married to the novelist Eleanor Green. *Poems* (1935); *A Wreath for the Sea* (1944); translations (in collaboration with Dudley Fitts) of *Alcestis* and *Antigone*.

WALLACE FOWLIE. In the Romance Language department at Yale. Several books of poetry and criticism in French and English, the best known being *Clowns and Angels* (a study of modern French writers, 1943) and *Rimbaud* (1946).

JEAN GARRIGUE. A Midwesterner, educated at Chicago and Iowa. Now lives in New York. Contributor to *Five Young American Poets*, 3rd series (1944). Winner of the *Kenyon Review* story prize, 1944.

BREWSTER GHISELIN. Professor of English at Utah. A painter; a writer of fiction, poetry, and criticism for many literary magazines; an editor of *Rocky Mountain Review*. *Against the Circle* (poems, 1946).

YVAN GOLL. A French poet now living in New York. Best known for the *Jean sans terre* series (Paris, 1936, 1938, 1939), selections from which have appeared in translation in many countries—including America (1944). Editor of *Hemispheres*.

HORACE GREGORY. Teaches at Sarah Lawrence. Three books of poems in the 1930's; a collected edition in 1941. Criticism: *Pilgrim of the Apocalypse* (on Lawrence, 1933), *The Shield of Achilles* (1944), *A History of American Poetry, 1900-1940* (in collaboration with his wife, Marya Zaturenska; 1946).

JAMES HANLEY. Lives in Llanfechain, North Wales. Many volumes of fiction, most familiar to American readers being *The Furys* (1935) and *Stoker Bush* (1936).

KENNETH O. HANSON. Has left Army service at Fort Douglas, Utah, and is living in Seattle. Contributor to *Rocky Mountain Review, Circle, Interim*. First published poetry: *Accent*, Summer 1944.

RUTH HERSCHBERGER. Educated at Chicago. Living in New York; poetry editor of the *Humanist*. Verse and criticism in the *New Republic*, the *Chimera, Partisan Review*, the *Kenyon Review*.

NAT HERZ. Educated at Iowa. Has lived off and on in Germany; has worked for *Life*. Living on a cooperative farm in the Berkshires. Contributor to *American Prefaces*.

ROBERT HORAN. Lives in Mt. Kisco, N. Y. Poetry in the *Yale Review*, *Furioso*, the *Kenyon Review*, the *Chimera*. In progress: a novel and an opera libretto (commissioned by Koussevitsky, for Samuel Barber).

JEREMY INGALLS. Is working in Chinese language and literature, on a scholarship established by the Chinese government for graduate study at the University of Chicago. *The Metaphysical Sword* (1941 prize of the Yale Series of Younger Poets) and *Tahl* (narrative poem, 1945).

JOHN JAMIESON. Has been in the Library Branch of the Special Services Division, stationed principally in Texas. Now lives in New York.

JACK JONES. Lives in Jackson Heights. Has attended Swarthmore. First published writing: *Accent*, Winter 1944. (Reprints of "The Mugging": *Modern Digest* and *Spearhead*.)

MILTON KAPLAN. Lives in New York. Has done graduate study, at Columbia, on poetry in radio. Contributor to *Poetry*, *Harper's Bazaar*, *Common Ground*.

WELDON KEES. Lives in New York. Contributor of stories, poems, and reviews to various periodicals and to *New Directions*. *The Last Man* (poetry, 1943).

A. M. KLEIN. A lawyer in Montreal and one of Canada's leading poets. *Hath Not a Jew* (1940), *The Hitleriad* (1944), *Poems* (1945).

JULES LAFORGUE. 1860-1887. One of the most important influences, among late 19th-century French writers, upon contemporary poetry and prose.

ANKEY LARRABEE. Has studied at Bennington and Columbia. First published criticism and poetry: *Accent*, Winter 1943 and Spring 1944, respectively.

HARRY LEVIN. A member of the English department at Harvard. *James Joyce* (1941); *Toward Stendhal* (1945; part of the forthcoming study of French realism, *The Gates of Horn*).

MEYER LIBEN. Lives in New York. Contributor to *New Directions*, *Twice a Year*, *Poetry*. (Reprint of "The Caller": *The Best American Short Stories 1946*.)

AGNES MACDONALD. Lives in St. Paul. Educated at Minnesota and Columbia. First published story: *Accent*, Summer 1945.

VENARD McLAUGHLIN. Lives in Peoria. Educated at Iowa State. Has practised law. Publishes extensively—among juveniles and pulps as well as literary magazines.

684 CONTRIBUTORS

ROGER MARTIN DU GARD. Best known for *Les Thibault* (1922-1940). Nobel Prize for literature, 1937. ("Confidence Africaine" was published as a separate book in Paris, 1931.)

F. O. MATTHIESSEN. Professor of history and literature at Harvard. Most important critical writing: *The Achievement of T. S. Eliot* (1935), *American Renaissance* (1941), *Henry James, the Major Phase* (1944).

JOSEPHINE MILES. A member of the English department at California. Poetry: *Lines at Intersection* (1939), *Poems on Several Occasions* (1941), *Local Measures* (1946). Criticism: *The Vocabulary of Poetry* (1946).

HENRY MILLER. Lives in Big Sur, Calif. No American editions as yet of *Tropic of Cancer* and *Tropic of Capricorn*. Several later works available through New Directions, including *The Cosmological Eye* (1939) and *The Air-Conditioned Nightmare* (1945).

CLARK MILLS. Was, until entering service, a member of the Romance Language faculty at Cornell. Poetry: *The Migrants* (1941), *A Suite for France* (1941), *Five Young American Poets*, 2nd Series (1941), *The Circus* (1943). Translator of Mallarmé, Breton, Goll, Rimbaud and other French poets.

ARTHUR MIZENER. Professor of English at Carleton College. Poetry and criticism in the *Sewanee Review*, the *Southern Review*, *Partisan Review*, and other magazines.

NICHOLAS MOORE. Lives in Cambridge, England. Editor of *New Poetry* and of several anthologies. Author of four books of poetry and a critique of Henry Miller. No American editions as yet.

ROSALIE MOORE. Is one of the Lawrence Hart group of poets in Berkeley. Winner of the Albert Bender Award in Literature for 1943.

HOWARD MOSS. Was educated at Wisconsin and is teaching at Vassar. Contributor to *Foreground*, *Poetry*, etc. First published work: *Accent*, Spring 1941.

GILBERT NEIMAN. Has lived mainly in Colorado and California in recent years. Translator of Garcia Lorca's *Blood Wedding*. Contributor to *Rocky Mountain Review*, *New Directions*. A long novel *There Is a Tyrant in Every Country*, to appear late in 1947.

JOHN NERBER. Lives in Bloomfield, Conn. Attended Kenyon College. Contributor to *Poetry*, the *New Mexico Quarterly Review*, the *Kenyon Review*. A book of poems, *Landfall*, accepted for publication.

JOHN FREDERICK NIMS. Left the Notre Dame English faculty for the University of Toronto in 1945. Winner of *Poetry* awards in 1942 and 1943; contributor to *Five Young American Poets*, 3rd Series (1944). A book of poems, *An Iron Pastoral*, soon to appear.

HAROLD NORSE. Lives in New York. Poetry reviewer for *Tomorrow* and other magazines. Poems in *Circle, Interim, Poetry.*

HOWARD NUTT. Is an industrial draftsman and lives in Peoria. Contributor to the *New Caravan*, the *Yale Review*, the *New Republic*, *Poetry*. Poetry: *Special Laughter* (1940).

ROSEMARY PARIS. Lives in Northfield, Minn. Married to Arthur Mizener. Contributor to *Cross-Section*.

KATHERINE ANNE PORTER. Lives in Santa Monica. Books of stories: *Flowering Judas* (1930, 1935), *Pale Horse, Pale Rider* (1939), *The Leaning Tower* (1944). In progress: a novel, *No Safe Harbor*.

RICHARD POSNER. Educated at Syracuse University. Lives in New York and works on the editorial staff of *Free World*. First published story: *Accent*, Winter 1945.

J. F. POWERS. Has lived in Chicago and St. Paul in recent years. First published story: *Accent*, Winter 1943. (Reprints of "Lions, Harts, Leaping Does": *O. Henry Memorial Award Prize Stories of 1944, The Best American Short Stories 1944*, and *Our Father's House*.)

JOHN FRANCIS PUTNAM. Has lived in France, Hollywood, Key West and, recently, near New York City. First published work: *Accent*, Spring 1945.

RAINER MARIA RILKE. 1875-1926. The greatest of 20th-century German poets. Available to American readers in the translations of M. D. Herter Norton and others.

PAUL ROSENFELD. Until his death in 1946, one of our leading critics of music, painting, and literature for twenty-five years. Among his books: *Port of New York* (1924), *Men Seen* (1925), *Discoveries of a Music Critic* (1936).

MURIEL RUKEYSER. Is living in San Francisco. Poetry: *Theory of Flight* (1935 prize of the Yale Series of Younger Poets), *U. S. 1* (1938), *A Turning Wind* (1939), *Beast in View* (1944). Biography: *Willard Gibbs* (1942).

VIRGINIA RUSS. A native San Franciscan. A professional dancer and choreographer; a member of Lawrence Hart's group of poets; author of *Salt and Seeds: Legends of San Francisco* (1941).

DELMORE SCHWARTZ. Teaches at Harvard and is an editor of *Partisan Review*. *In Dreams Begin Responsibilities* (a story, a verse play, and poems; 1938), *Shenandoah* (verse play, 1941), *Genesis* (narrative poem, 1943). In progress: *The Imitation of Life and Other Problems of Literary Criticism.*

KATHARINE SHATTUCK. Teaches at Westminster College. Contributor to *American Prefaces, Poetry, Rocky Mountain Review.* (Reprint of "The Beast": *Mid-Country.*)

IRWIN SHAW. Recently discharged from the Army after three years' service in Egypt and England. *Bury the Dead* (1936) and other plays. Story collections: *Sailor Off the Bremen* (1939) and *Welcome to the City* (1942). (Reprints of "The Veterans Reflect": *The Best American Short Stories 1944* and *American Writing: 1944.*)

HARRY SLOCHOWER. Professor of German at Brooklyn College. Critical works: *Richard Dehmel* (Leipzig, 1928), *Three Ways of Modern Man* (1937), *Thomas Mann's Joseph Story* (1938), *No Voice Is Wholly Lost* (1945).

WALLACE STEVENS. Lives in Hartford. Poetry: *Harmonium* (1923), *Ideas of Order* (1935), *The Man with the Blue Guitar* (1937), *Parts of a World* (1942), *Notes Toward a Supreme Fiction* (1942), *Esthétique du mal* (1945).

RICHARD SULLIVAN. On the faculty at Notre Dame. Novels: *Summer After Summer* (1942), *The Dark Continent* (1943), *Idella May* (in progress). (Reprints of "The Women": *Out of the Midwest* and *The Best American Short Stories 1943.*)

HYMAN SWETZOFF. Lives in Boston. Poems, short stories, art commentary in various magazines. Translator of Cocteau's *Le Grand Ecart* and Redon's *A Soi-même.*

DYLAN THOMAS. A Welsh poet. American publications: *The World I Breathe* (poems and stories, 1939), *Portrait of the Artist as a Young Dog* (1940). *New Poems* (1943).

W. Y. TINDALL. Professor of English at Columbia. Poetry in *Quarterly Review of Literature, Rocky Mountain Review. John Bunyan, Mechanick Preacher* (1934); *D. H. Lawrence and Susan His Cow* (1940). In progress: a book on 20th-century British writers.

HENRY TREECE. A young British writer. Editor of *Herbert Read, an Introduction to His Work* (London, 1944). Three books of poetry published in England, and *Collected Poems* (New York, 1946).

BYRON VAZAKAS. Lives in Reading. Contributor to *Partisan Review*, the *Briarcliff Quarterly, Arizona Quarterly. Transfigured Night* (poems, 1946).

T. WEISS. In the English department at Yale. Editor of *Quarterly Review of Literature* and of *Selections from the Note-Books of Gerard Manley Hopkins* (1945).

EUDORA WELTY. Lives in Jackson, Miss. *A Curtain of Green* (stories, 1941), *The Robber Bridegroom* (fairy tale, 1942), *The Wide Net* (stories, 1943), *Delta Wedding* (novel, 1946).

RICHARD WRIGHT. Lives in New York. *Uncle Tom's Children* (stories, 1938), *Native Son* (novel, 1940), *Twelve Million Black Voices* (folk history, 1941), *Black Boy* (autobiography, 1945). (A fuller version of the novelette, "The Man Who Lived Underground," appeared in *Cross-Section.*)

MARGUERITE YOUNG. Has done graduate study at Chicago and Iowa and is now living in New York. Poetry: *Prismatic Ground* (1937) and *Moderate Fable* (1944). A fable-history of the New Harmony community: *Angel in the Forest* (1945). In progress: a novel, *The Worm in the Wheat.*